COMING OF AGE IN PHILOSOPHY

COMING OF AGE IN PHILOSOPHY

edited by

ROGER EASTMAN, Reedley College

Canfield Press · San Francisco
A Department of Harper & Row, Publishers, Inc.
New York · Evanston · London

COMING OF AGE IN PHILOSOPHY
Copyright © 1973 by Roger Eastman

International Standard Book Number: 0–06–382594–5

Library of Congress Catalog Card Number: 72–10903

76   6

credits——————————————————————————————

PROLOGUE

James Agee, "Knoxville: Summer 1915." Reprinted from A *Death in the Family* by James Agee. Copyright © 1957 by James Agee Trust. First published in *The Partisan Review*. Reprinted by permission of the publisher, Grosset & Dunlap, Inc.

CHAPTER ONE

Eugene Ionesco, "Fragments of a Journal." From *Fragments of a Journal* by Eugene Ionesco. Reprinted by permission of Grove Press, Inc. Copyright © 1968 by Faber and Faber.
Blaise Pascal, "Pensées." From the book *Pensées* by Blaise Pascal. Translated by W. F. Trotter. Published 1958 by E. P. Dutton & Co., Inc., in a paper edition and used with their permission.
Ira Wolfert, "Of Stars and Man." From "Of Stars and Man" by Ira Wolfert, *The Reader's Digest*, May 1970. Copyright 1970 by The Reader's Digest Association, Inc.

(*credits continued on p. 607*)

preface

Philosophy is much more than a "relevant" subject: it is unavoidably a dimension of our existence, an aspect of all our thoughts and actions. Students, consequently, come to their first course in philosophy already enmeshed in philosophical questions and theories, and that course ought to be the most fascinating and valuable in any curriculum.

Unfortunately, what the introductory course ought to be and what it is are sometimes different matters. It is a notoriously difficult course to do well. The academic discipline of philosophy is a formidable field: the questions are complex and the terminology confusing. For all too many students the subject becomes a meaningless maze, just another one of those many courses to be gotten "out of the way" during their requirement-laden lower-division days. Most of us who have tried to teach the course have learned how quickly students can be turned off, and how dreadful a course can be when its students are not interested. Perhaps it is the remarkable potentialities of the course that make its disappointments especially painful.

The present textbook, then, makes a concentrated effort to present topics and readings which will stimulate and enlarge students' involvement in philosophy. Without their involvement, there is nothing. The chapter topics are many and varied; they have been selected on the basis of both their appeal to students and their philosophical significance. The readings have been drawn from diverse sources. For example, there are short stories by Kafka and Hemingway, excerpts from Ionesco's Fragments of a Journal, and a portion of Tolstoy's My Confession. Psychologists R. D. Laing and Abraham Maslow are included, and there are selections by the theologian Michael Novak and the historian Carl Becker. Throughout the text are philosophers from Plato to Sartre; there are Christians and mystics, Marx and Marcuse. Philosophy, after all, is that which lies at the heart of all serious reflection upon human existence; it is not merely a specialty among other specialties.

A fellowship from the National Endowment for the Humanities gave me precious time to read and think. Colleagues at Reedley College answered every plea for assistance. Jacob Needleman accepted the burden of a very large and unwieldy manuscript and offered suggestions when they mattered most. Ted Ricks, Canfield Press editor, brought it all together.

Roger Eastman, 1973

For Jeannie,
Carolyn, and Jennifer

contents

PROLOGUE

Knoxville: Summer 1915   2   JAMES AGEE

chapter one: THE ENIGMA OF BEING

Introduction	8	
Fragments of a Journal	10	EUGENE IONESCO
Pensées	17	BLAISE PASCAL
Of Stars and Man	21	IRA WOLFERT
Hymn to Creation	22	from the RIG VEDA
The Creation of the World	23	KARL JASPERS
The Mystery of Existence	29	MILTON K. MUNITZ
This Dream of Time	36	THOMAS WOLFE
Further Reading	39	

chapter two: THE EXAMINED LIFE

Introduction	42	
A Yaqui Man of Knowledge	44	CARLOS CASTANEDA
The Wayfarer	49	STEPHEN CRANE
My Confession	50	LEO TOLSTOY
The Unknown Citizen	60	W. H. AUDEN
The Freak of the Universe	61	ERICH FROMM
Yoga and Self-Knowledge	62	P. D. OUSPENSKY
On the Improvement of the Understanding	73	BENEDICT DE SPINOZA
The Meaning of Life	77	RICHARD TAYLOR
Further Reading	85	

chapter three: ON THE NATURE OF PHILOSOPHY

Introduction	88	
The Apology	90	PLATO
The Study of Philosophy	105	EPICURUS
The Art of Living	106	EPICTETUS
Critical Thought	113	C. D. BROAD
What Is Philosophy?	120	JOSÉ ORTEGA Y GASSET
Philosophy Means Liberty	124	HENRI-FREDERIC AMIEL
Further Reading	125	

chapter four: ALIENATION & THE DEATH OF MEANING

Introduction	128	
The Bucket Rider	130	FRANZ KAFKA
A Clean, Well-Lighted Place	133	ERNEST HEMINGWAY
The Hollow People	137	ROLLO MAY
"Normal" Alienation	145	R. D. LAING
Alienated Labour	148	KARL MARX
Anguish, Forlornness, and Despair	159	JEAN-PAUL SARTRE
The Experience of Nothingness	167	MICHAEL NOVAK
Further Reading	176	

chapter five: VALUES: DEFINING THE GOOD LIFE

Introduction	178	
George F. Babbitt	180	SINCLAIR LEWIS
Aunt Arie	187	THE FOXFIRE BOOK
The Valuing Process in the Mature Person	191	CARL R. ROGERS
The Ethics	203	ARISTOTLE
The Good Will	209	IMMANUEL KANT
Utilitarianism	216	JOHN STUART MILL
Further Reading	222	

chapter six: THE ELUSIVE GROUND OF MORALITY

Introduction	224	
In Dreams Begin Responsibilities	226	DELMORE SCHWARTZ
The Nature of Moral Theory	233	JOHN DEWEY
Confession Overheard in a Subway	240	KENNETH FEARING
A Righteous Cockroach	242	DON MARQUIS
Ethical Relativity	243	W. T. STACE
Gyges' Ring	250	PLATO
Why Should We Be Moral?	252	KURT BAIER ✓
Further Reading	262	

chapter seven: THE PROBLEM OF EVIL

Introduction	266	
Letters from the Earth	268	MARK TWAIN
✗ *A Plague Death*	275	ALBERT CAMUS
The Best of All Possible Worlds	281	GOTTFRIED WILHELM LEIBNIZ
Evil and Omnipotence	287	J. L. MACKIE
The Problem of Evil	299	JOHN HICK
Further Reading	305	

chapter eight: RELIGIOUS VISIONS

Introduction	308	
The Search for Truth	310	NICOLAS BERDYAEV
Taoism	317	HUSTON SMITH
Mysticism	333	WILLIAM JAMES
A Free Man's Worship	344	BERTRAND RUSSELL
The God Above God	351	PAUL TILLICH
Further Reading	355	

You are the world
The meaning of Life
The Hollow People

chapter nine: RELIGION: MOVING ON

Introduction	358	
The Living God of Nowhere and Nothing	360	NELS F. S. FERRÉ
Zen Center	369	JACOB NEEDLEMAN
Peak-Experiences	380	ABRAHAM H. MASLOW
Meditations on the Jesus Movement	386	PETER MARIN
Rain and the Rhinoceros	394	THOMAS MERTON
Further Reading	401	

chapter ten: THE DEBATE OVER DETERMINISM

Introduction	404	
Appointment in Samarra	406	W. SOMERSET MAUGHAM
A Game of Catch	407	RICHARD WILBUR
Computers and the Brain	411	DEAN E. WOOLDRIDGE
What's a Man?	417	R. BUCKMINSTER FULLER
The Dilemma of Determinism	418	WILLIAM JAMES
The Free-Will Controversy	426	LEDGER WOOD
Further Reading	437	

chapter eleven: FACT OR FICTION, DREAM OR REALITY?

Introduction	440	
In a Grove	442	RYŪNOSUKE AKUTAGAWA
What Are Historical Facts?	450	CARL L. BECKER
How Do I Know I Am Not Now Dreaming?	457	JEROME A. SHAFFER
Meditations I and II	460	RENÉ DESCARTES
Skeptical Doubts	472	DAVID HUME
Eyes of Flesh, Eyes of Fire	484	THEODORE ROSZAK
Further Reading	490	

chapter twelve: IDENTITY AND FREEDOM

Introduction	494	
Freedom and Learning	496	PAUL GOODMAN
The Crisis in Woman's Identity	502	BETTY FRIEDAN
Black and White Freedom	511	LERONE BENNETT
The New Forms of Control	521	HERBERT MARCUSE
The Coming American Revolution	533	CHARLES A. REICH
You Are the World	544	JIDDU KRISHNAMURTI
Further Reading	553	

chapter thirteen: GRAVEYARD REFLECTIONS

Introduction	556	
Notes on Dying	558	WARREN BEATH
Death Is Nothing to Us	563	EPICURUS
Death, Be Not Proud	564	JOHN DONNE
Dirge Without Music	565	EDNA ST. VINCENT MILLAY
There Is No Cure for Death	566	A BUDDHIST PARABLE
Phaedo	568	PLATO
The Crisis Called Death	578	CORLISS LAMONT
Is Life After Death Possible?	581	C. J. DUCASSE
Further Reading	591	

EPILOGUE

The Grand Inquisitor	594	FYODOR DOSTOYEVSKY
Further Reading	606	

There is a sense in which no one needs an introduction to philosophy: no one is really a stranger to it. Philosophy is an activity we are all engaged in for most of our lives. Our philosophizing begins in childhood with our wondering about ourselves and the world we discover around us, and thereafter we wonder and question to the end of our days. It is to the philosophizing of other men, particularly the unusually perceptive men of the past and present, that we may require an introduction. With their ideas to test and invigorate our own, we are less likely to succumb to philosophical provincialism. But no matter how tremendously helpful the philosophers may be, they cannot do our philosophizing for us—no more than someone else can do our loving for us. In the last analysis, philosophy is an intensely personal affair: its questions we must experience, and our answers must be our own.

For each of us, it all begins in some place like "Knoxville: Summer 1915."

The writings of James Agee (1910–1955) take surprisingly varied forms. There is a book of poetry (Permit Me Voyage), journalism, and screen plays ("The African Queen"). Agee lavished painstaking care upon all of his work. He spent three years on Let Us Now Praise Famous Men, *a study of tenant farmers in the South. On his way to submit the manuscript to his publishers, Agee suddenly realized how a section might be improved. He returned to his home and the book was not published until two years later. Such intense work, coupled with chronic insomnia and drink, led to a heart attack and death at the age of forty-five. Virtually completed at the time of his death was the heart-breaking* A Death in the Family, *an autobiographical novel for which Agee was awarded the Pulitzer Prize in 1958.*

"Knoxville: Summer 1915," written years earlier, was added by editors to A Death in the Family *as an introductory statement. In a scene rich with the hauntingly familiar sights and sounds of a family summer, a young boy asks one of those questions that are basic to philosophy.*

We are talking now of summer evenings in Knoxville, Tennessee in the time that I lived there so successfully disguised to myself as a child. It was a little bit mixed sort of block, fairly solidly lower middle class, with one or two juts apiece on either side of that. The houses corresponded: middle-sized grace-fully fretted wood houses built in the late nineties and early nineteen hundreds, with small front and side and more spacious back yards, and trees in the yards, and porches. These were softwooded trees, poplars, tulip trees, cottonwoods. There were fences around one or two of the houses, but mainly the yards ran into each other with only now and then a low hedge that wasn't doing very well. There were few good friends among the grown people, and they were not poor enough for the other sort of intimate acquaintance, but everyone nodded and spoke, and even might talk short times, trivially, and at the two extremes of the general or the particular, and ordinarily nextdoor neighbors talked quite a bit when they happened to run into each other, and never paid calls. The men were mostly small business-men, one or two very modestly executives, one or two worked with their hands, most of them clerical, and most of them between thirty and forty-five.

But it is of these evenings, I speak.

Supper was at six and was over by half past. There was still daylight, shining softly and with a tarnish, like the lining of a shell; and the carbon lamps lifted at the corners were on in the light, and the locusts were started, and the fire flies were out, and a few frogs were flopping in the dewy grass, by the time the fathers and the children came out. The children ran out first hell bent and yelling those names by which they were known; then the fathers sank out leisurely in crossed suspenders, their collars removed and their necks looking tall and shy. The mothers stayed back in the kitchen washing and drying, putting things away, recrossing their traceless footsteps like the lifetime journeys of bees, measuring out the dry cocoa for breakfast. When they came out they had taken off their aprons and their skirts were dampened and they sat in rockers on their porches quietly.

It is not of the games children played in the evening that I want to speak now, it is of a contemporaneous atmosphere that has little to do with them: that of the fathers of families, each in his space of lawn, his shirt fishlike pale in the unnatural light and his face nearly anonymous, hosing their lawns. The hoses were attached at spigots that stood out of the brick founda-tions of the houses. The nozzles were variously set but usually so there was a long sweet stream of spray, the nozzle wet in the hand, the water trickling the right forearm and the peeled-back cuff, and the water whishing out a long loose and low-curved cone, and so gentle a sound. First an insane noise of violence in the nozzle, then the still irregular sound of adjustment, then the smoothing into steadiness and a pitch as accurately tuned to the size and style of stream as any violin. So many qualities of sound out of one hose: so many choral differences out of those several hoses that were in earshot. Out of any one hose, the almost dead silence of the release, and the short still arch of the separate big drops, silent as a held breath, and the only noise the flattering noise on leaves and the slapped grass at the fall of each big drop. That, and the intense hiss with the intense stream; that, and that same intensity not growing less but growing more quiet and delicate with the turn of the nozzle, up to that extreme tender whisper when the water was just a wide bell of film. Chiefly, though, the hoses were set much alike, in a compro-mise between distance and tenderness of spray (and quite surely a sense of art behind this compromise, and a quiet deep joy, too real to recognize itself), and the sounds therefore were pitched much alike; pointed by the snorting start of a new hose; decorated by some man playful with the nozzle; left empty, like God by the sparrow's fall, when any single one of them desists: and all, though near alike, of various pitch; and in this unison. These sweet pale streamings in the light lift out their pallors and their voices all together, mothers hushing their children, the hushing unnaturally prolonged, the men gentle and silent and each snail-like withdrawn into the quietude of what he singly is doing, the urination of huge children stood loosely mili-tary against an invisible wall, and gentle happy and peaceful, tasting the mean goodness of their living like the last of their suppers in their mouths; while the locusts carry on this noise of hoses on their much higher and sharper key. The noise of the locust is dry, and it seems not to be rasped or

3

vibrated but urged from him as if through a small orifice by breath that can never give out. Also there is never one locust but an illusion of at least a thousand. The noise of each locust is pitched in some classic locust range out of which none of them varies more than two full tones: and yet you seem to hear each locust discrete from all the rest, and there is a long, slow pulse in their noise, like the scarcely defined arch of a long and high set bridge. They are all around in every tree, so that the noise seems to come from nowhere and everywhere at once, from the whole shell heaven, shivering in your flesh and teasing your eardrums, the boldest of all the sounds of night. And yet it is habitual to summer nights, and is of the great order of noises, like the noises of the sea and of the blood her precocious grandchild, which you realize you are hearing only when you catch yourself listening. Meantime from low in the dark, just outside the swaying horizons of the hoses, conveying always grass in the damp of dew and its strong green-black smear of smell, the regular yet spaced noises of the crickets, each a sweet cold silver noise threenoted, like the slipping each time of three matched links of a small chain.

But the men by now, one by one, have silenced their hoses and drained and coiled them. Now only two, and now only one, is left, and you see only ghostlike shirt with the sleeve garters, and sober mystery of his mild face like the lifted face of large cattle enquiring of your presence in a pitchdark pool of meadow; and now he too is gone; and it has become that time of evening when people sit on their porches, rocking gently and talking gently and watching the street and the standing up into their sphere of possession of the trees, of birds hung havens, hangars. People go by; things go by. A horse, drawing a buggy, breaking his hollow iron music on the asphalt; a loud auto; a quiet auto; people in pairs, not in a hurry, scuffling, switching their weight of aestival body, talking casually, the taste hovering over them of vanilla, strawberry, pasteboard and starched milk, the image upon them of lovers and horsemen, squared with clowns in hueless amber. A street car raising its iron moan; stopping, belling and starting; stertorous; rousing and raising again its iron increasing moan and swimming its gold windows and straw seats on past and past and past, the bleak spark crackling and cursing above it like a small malignant spirit set to dog its tracks; the iron whine rises on rising speed; still risen, faints; halts; the faint stinging bell; rises again, still fainter; fainting, lifting, lifts, faints forgone: forgotten. Now is the night one blue dew.

> Now is the night one blue dew, my father has drained, he has coiled the hose.
> Low on the length of lawns, a frailing of fire who breathes.
> Content, silver, like peeps of light, each cricket makes his comment over and over in the drowned grass.

4

A cold toad thumpily flounders.

Within the edges of damp shadows of side yards are hovering children nearly sick with joy of fear, who watch the unguarding of a telephone pole.

Around white carbon corner lamps bugs of all sizes are lifted elliptic, solar systems. Big hardshells bruise themselves, assailant: he is fallen on his back, legs squiggling.

Parents on porches: rock and rock: From damp strings morning glories: hang their ancient faces.

The dry and exalted noise of the locusts from all the air at once enchants my eardrums.

On the rough wet grass of the back yard my father and mother have spread quilts. We all lie there, my mother, my father, my uncle, my aunt, and I too am lying there. First we were sitting up, then one of us lay down, and then we all lay down, on our stomachs, or on our sides, or on our backs, and they have kept on talking. They are not talking much, and the talk is quiet, of nothing in particular, of nothing at all in particular, of nothing at all. The stars are wide and alive, they seem each like a smile of great sweetness, and they seem very near. All my people are larger bodies than mine, quiet, with voices gentle and meaningless like the voices of sleeping birds. One is an artist, he is living at home. One is a musician, she is living at home. One is my mother who is good to me. One is my father who is good to me. By some chance, here they are, all on this earth; on the grass, in a summer evening, among the sounds of the night. May God bless my people, my uncle, my aunt, my mother, my good father, oh, remember them kindly in their time of trouble; and in the hour of their taking away.

After a little I am taken in and put to bed. Sleep, soft smiling, draws me unto her: and those receive me, who quietly treat me, as one familiar and well beloved in that home: but will not, oh, will not, not now, not ever; but will not ever tell me who I am.

FURTHER READING

Irwin Edman wrote of his first encounters with philosophy in "Intimations of Philosophy in Early Childhood," in his very popular *Philosopher's Holiday* (1941).

Pär Lagerkvist's short story "Father and I," in *The Eternal Smile and Other Stories* (1954), relates a stunning incident of philosophical importance in the life of a boy.

chapter one

THE ENIGMA OF BEING

1

The problems of philosophy must be felt as well as understood. The questions raised cannot really be appreciated—perhaps they cannot even be properly understood—if they are met only on an abstract level. And many of the feelings involved in the philosophic enterprise are anything but agreeable. The calmness and serenity traditionally associated with philosophers may still be among the qualities of mind sought for, but the quest itself is better characterized as a turbulent one. The student of philosophy is one who has felt the "wonder" that is the beginning of philosophical seriousness, and he lives in a perplexed and uneasy state. Philosophy is an endeavor undertaken out of necessity.

These matters are epitomized in the issues grouped here as "The Enigma of Being." The starting point is a unique experience:

> If one has never felt it oneself, no amount of explanation will convince. If one has felt it, one will never forget, however much one may try. It may come upon you when you have been asleep, withdrawn from the world; you wake up in the middle of the night and feel a kind of astonishment at being there, which gives way to a fear and horror at the mere fact of being there. It is then that you catch yourself by yourself, just for a moment, against the background of a kind of nothingness all around you, and with a gnawing sense of your powerlessness, your utter helplessness in the face of this astonishing fact that you are there at all. Usually, we avoid this experience as much as possible, because it is so shattering and painful.[1]

Eugene Ionesco and Blaise Pascal, in the reading selections which follow, clearly express such a mixture of astonishment and anxiety. Ionesco, in fact, has been led to despair; he has come to believe his questions to be unanswerable. Still, he is haunted by "that ultimate why" and cannot set it aside. "What is this world?" he asks. "What is it that's all around me? Who am I? . . . I have been asking myself these questions from the beginning."

[1] Edward Conze, *Buddhism* (New York: Harper Torchbooks, 1959), p. 23.

8

Pascal, on the other hand, believed that he had found answers; his professions of Christian faith fill many of the pages of his Pensées. *But Pascal also reveals the degree to which he is aware of the problematic nature of existence. Both he and Ionesco speak of the terror that can come.*

Karl Jaspers deals specifically with one of the most ancient and basic of questions—the creation of the world. As with all philosophical issues, its complexities are manifold and its implications profound. As Jaspers explains, the discussion of the creation of the world involves epistemological questions; that is, questions about the nature of human knowledge.

Milton K. Munitz raises the ultimate question: Why is there a world at all? Why is there something rather than nothing? So puzzling is the question that it is debated whether it is a legitimate, meaningful question. Munitz reviews three different attitudes that prevail regarding the question of the world. In later pages in The Mystery of Existence, *Munitz takes his stand with the third of the positions he outlines in the pages presented here. It is a meaningful philosophical question, but one which cannot be resolved.*

The problems of philosophy, by definition, are those perennial problems that have defied definitive answers. The wisest of men have disagreed over them. "In philosophizing," Karl Jaspers has written, "everyone is referred to himself. There are no human guides analogous to the priesthood. . . . There are no sacred writings. . . ."

9

eugene ionesco　　　FRAGMENTS OF A JOURNAL

Eugene Ionesco (1912–　　) was born in Rumania, but has lived and worked principally in France. Acclaimed as one of the great playwrights of this century and now a member of the French Academy, he is the author of such plays as The Chairs, The Lesson, The Bald Soprano, The Rhinoceros, *and* Exit the King. *Also of note are his short stories and his essays about the function of the writer and of the theater. "A writer," he has written, "is neither a saint nor a sage, neither a prophet nor a doctor. His work is an architecture of interrogations. The questions raised are his own, but since each of us is at the same time everyone else, his questioning is also everyone else's. The questions raised are the very problems of creation. . . ." Graphically illustrating these lines are the following passages from his* Fragments of a Journal *(1968).*

I was born quite a long time ago.

A very long time, and yet a very short time ago. I haven't yet succeeded in understanding what has happened to me. I have very little time left to understand what I have not yet understood, and I scarcely think I shall manage to do so. I have not managed to accept existence and to accept myself. I can see nothing beyond the beings and things that surround me and that seem to me enigmas, more or less. I can never, or seldom, or with great difficulty, get on with other people, because I cannot get on with myself either. The forms of satisfaction I have sought, and found, to fill my life, its emptiness, its nostalgia, have sometimes succeeded, but how inadequately, in disguising the malaise of existence. They once distracted me, but can no longer do so. Pain, grief, failure have always seemed to me truer than success or pleasure. I have always tried to live, but I have passed life by. I think that is what most men feel. To forget oneself one must not only forget one's own death, but forget that those one loves will die and that the world will come to an end. The thought of the end fills me with anguish and fury. I have never been really happy except when drunk. Unfortunately alcohol destroys memory and I have only retained blurred recollections of my moments of euphoria. Life is unhappiness. That does not prevent me from preferring life to death, existence to non-existence, because I am not sure of being once I have ceased to exist. Existence being the only mode of being I know, I cling to this existence, for I cannot, alas, imagine any mode of being apart from existence.

I am limited and alienated, others are limited and alienated, and all forms of action, of revolution, of literature are only ways of forgetting alienation for a moment, not remedies for alienation. The end of it all can only be an even more lucid, hence more desperate, awakening.

I cannot help laughing bitterly when I see all around me believing they believe, and being engulfed.

A vast weariness overwhelms me: presumably psychological in origin, with no apparent cause, but the cause of which I know: the certain, or almost certain, knowledge that all is vanity.

I have written a whole set of plays, a lot of books to show what everybody knows and to confirm to myself what I have always known: the strangeness of the universe, the banality of ordinary life shot through by horror, etc. This implies that I became adult very young. Not on every plane.

.   .   .   .

If I tell these private thoughts of mine, it is because I know they are not mine alone, and that practically everyone is trying to say the same things and that the writer is only a man who says out loud what other people think or whisper. Even if I thought that what I am confessing is not a universal confession but the expression of an individual experience, I should confess it all the same in the hope of being cured or of finding relief. But I have no such hope, we have no such hope; we share a common distress. Then, why? What good can it do? It's because, in spite of everything, we cannot but become aware, become more acutely aware of a certain reality, the reality of the unhappiness of existing, the fact that the human condition is beyond bearing: a useless awareness, which cannot but be, and which finds expression, such is literature.

Ever since I was fifteen, that's to say from that moment when I lost all that was left me of my childhood, from the moment when I ceased to be aware of the present and knew only the past hurrying into the future, that's to say into the abyss, ever since I became fully conscious of time I have felt old and I have wanted to live. I have run after life as though to catch time, and I've tried to live. I have run after life so much that it has always escaped me, I have run, I have never been late and never too early, and yet I have never caught up with it: it's as though I had run alongside of it.

What is life? I may be asked. For me, life is not Time; it is not this state of existence, for ever escaping us, slipping between our fingers and vanishing like a ghost as soon as you try to grasp it. For me it is, it must be, the present, presentness, plenitude. I have run after life so much that I have lost it.

11

I am at the age when you grow ten years older in one year, when an hour is only a few minutes long and you cannot even note the passing quarters. And yet I still run after life in the hope of catching it at the last minute, as one jumps on to the steps of the last carriage of a moving train.

I remember the quarter of an hour break at my primary school. A quarter of an hour! what a long, busy space of time; enough to think of one game, play it, end it, start another. . . .

Of course, even before I was fifteen, I had had this sense of time passing. Thursdays and Sundays went by; I mean that I knew they were going by. Discovering time means being aware of its passage, believing and indeed being sure that tomorrow will come, waiting for something, expecting something.

I had always been told that the days followed one another, that the seasons came to an end. Of course, this was what they told me and I was bound to believe what grown-up people and the schoolmaster asserted. I had been told it, granted. But 'next year' was only a word; and even if I believed that this 'next year' would one day come, it seemed so far away that it wasn't worth thinking about; the time in between was as long as eternity; so it was just as if it was never going to come. You made no plans, you could make none, since it was so far ahead, so very far ahead. . . . In any case, though to-morrow was going to come, though the seasons would end and then return, it was they that would go and come back, while I should stay in the same place. The sun and the stars moved around me, who stood still at the centre of everything. The earth and its colours and its fields and its snow and rain all moved around me. I don't know at what point it was that I must have taken a sort of step. How did it happen? From that moment onward I became aware of the past. I ought not to have stirred, I was swept into the dance, caught up in the whirling movement of things. Being in Time means running after the present. You run after things, you run with things, you flow away.

. . . .

A finite universe is unimaginable, inconceivable. An infinite universe is unimaginable, inconceivable. Doubtless the universe is neither finite nor infinite, since the finite and the infinite are only man's ways of thinking about it; in any case, that finiteness and infiniteness should only be ways of thinking and speaking is also something inconceivable, unimaginable. We cannot take a single step beyond our own impotence; outside those walls I feel sick and giddy. If the wall is no longer there, the gulf opens at my feet and I am seized with dizziness.

I wonder how I can still be excited, or at any rate preoccupied, by economic, social and political problems since I know: (1) that we are going to die, (2) that revolution saves us neither from life nor from death, (3) that I cannot imagine a finite universe, an infinite universe, nor yet a universe that is neither finite nor infinite.

We are in life in order to die. Death is the aim of existence, that seems to be a commonplace truth. Sometimes, in a trite expression, the banality may vanish and truth appear, reappear, newborn. I am living through one of those moments when it seems to me that I am discovering for the first time that the only aim of existence is death. There's nothing we can do. There's nothing we can do. There's nothing we can do. But what sort of a puppet-like condition is this, what right have they to make a fool of me?

I still feel surprised, sometimes, that I'm no longer twelve years old.

On reading *Phaedo*, it's only towards the end of the dialogue that I realize what a fine mess we are in. Socrates has not managed to convince me that the soul is immortal and that he is going to live in a better world. You get the impression that Socrates' disciples are not convinced either, since they weep; otherwise, why should they weep? When evening comes and Socrates takes the poison, when his feet grow cold and then his stomach, when at last he dies, I am seized with terror and boundless unhappiness. The description of the death of Socrates is so convincing, far more convincing than his arguments for immortality. In any case, the arguments vanish in an instant; we forget them at once, but the image of Socrates dead is graven in my memory; all men are mortal, Socrates is a man, therefore Socrates is mortal. I lay awake last night thinking about this. For a long time I had not felt such lucid, vivid, glacial anguish. A fear of nothingness. How can I describe it? I clutched my breast to make sure that I was still there; then I suddenly had the sensation that the black nothingness had already begun to devour me and that I had lost my feet, my legs, my thighs; I was merely a torso, being consumed by the icy fire of nothingness. I put on the light. How good it is to be alive. I felt a surge of fondness for life, which seemed to me something miraculous, a luminous fairy tale springing out of the darkness. We kill one another because we know that we shall all be killed. It's out of hatred for death that we kill each other. Socrates' death, so peaceful and serene, seems to me quite improbable, and yet it is possible. But how?

It's impossible to understand anything about it. All those who fancy they do are fools. It's only when I say that everything is incomprehensible that I come as close as possible to understanding the only thing it is given to us to understand.

Nothing is mightier than our *why*, nothing stands above it, because in the end there is a *why* to which no answer is possible. In fact, from *why* to *why*, from one step to the next, you get to the end of things. And it is only by travelling from one *why* to the next, as far as the *why* that is unanswerable,

13

that man attains the level of the creative principle, facing the infinite, equal to the infinite maybe. So long as he can answer the *why* he gets lost, he loses his way among things. 'Why this?' I answer, 'because that,' and from one explanation to the next I reach the point where no explanation is satisfying, from one explanation to the next I reach zero, the absolute, where truth and falsehood are equivalent, become equal to one another, are identified with one another, cancel each other out in face of the absolute *nothing*. And so we can understand how all action, all choice, all history is justified, at the end of time, by a final cancelling-out. The *why* goes beyond everything. Nothing goes beyond the *why*, not even the *nothing*, because the *nothing* is not the explanation; when silence confronts us, the question to which there is no answer rings out in the silence. That ultimate *why*, that great *why* is like a light that blots out everything, but a blinding light; nothing more can be made out, there is nothing more to make out.

. . . .

I read a page of Plato's great work. I can no longer understand anything, because behind the words on the page, which have their own heavenly brightness, to be sure, there shines an even brighter, an enormous, dazzling *why* that blots out everything, cancels out, destroys all meaning. All individual intelligence. When one has understood, one stops, satisfied with what one has understood. *I do not understand*. Understanding is far too little. To have understood is to be fixed, immobilized. It's as though one wanted to stop on one step in the middle of a staircase, or with one foot in the void and the other on the endless stair. But a mere *why*, a new *why* can set one off again, can unpetrify what was petrified and everything starts flowing afresh. How can one 'understand'? One cannot.

(When I shall no longer exist, God will say: 'I do a lot of things that everybody understands. There's nobody left not to understand them.')

It's to Death, above all, that I say 'Why?' with such terror. Death alone can, and will, close my mouth.

. . . .

I am in it too, I am a man, and I have to accept the unacceptable: I don't want to make war, and I make war; I want to know, and I know nothing. If in the end I come to love this state of existence into which I have been plunged, I suffer because it is taken from me. I have certain powers, and they fail, I grow old and I don't want to grow old, I die and I don't want to die. This is the incredible thing: to love a life that has been thrust upon me and that is snatched away from me just when I have accepted it. There are old men of eighty who are happy to be alive: there are young men of twenty on whom the years weigh heavy. For thousands and thousands of years the same questions have been asked thousands of times, so often that it has become absurd to ask them again, they are worn out before we can find the slightest fragment of an answer. Men are beginning to know a little bit of the universe, the earth has been photographed from the moon, we know the laws of physics and the chemical constitution of the cosmos; we still have only a few faint gleams to light up the profound darkness of our psyche; we can see through flesh, we can disintegrate matter, of course, we can foresee the movements of the stars, of course, of course, and so many other things, of course, of course. Science is not knowledge, rhetoric and philosophy are nothing but words, sets of words, strings of words, but words are not speech. When we have learnt everything, or if we could learn everything, we should still know nothing. What sets it all in motion? What is the life behind things? The universe appears to me as merely a storehouse of objects in disorderly, or perhaps in orderly array, mobile objects flung into the immensity of space, but who flung them, and what is that which I call space, which appears to me as space? But even if I know what governs their trajectory, if I know the rules of the movement of things and how things are organized and how certain mutations, transformations, gestations take place, even if I know all that, I shall only have learnt how to get along after a fashion in the enormous gaol, the oppressive prison in which I am held. What a farce, what a snare, what a booby-trap. We were born cheated. For if we are not to know, if there is nothing to know, why do we have this longing to know?

. . . .

It is natural that things should appear, or be manifest, because they are. Essence is a perfectly sufficient and satisfactory explanation for existence. If a thing is, it must also logically exist. What I cannot succeed in understanding is this: How can anything be? Why something is? It would be more 'natural,' if I may use the word, for nothing to be. For the whole thing not to be. For nothing ever to have been. Of course it is inconceivable that nothing should be, that there should be nothing. I try to conceive the inconceivable: I suddenly picture a kind of solid whole, compact and absurdly full. Not to be, that there should be no being, is impossible and absurd; to be is equally absurd, though 'possible.' Why is there what there is, why does what is there appear as it does, why isn't there something different, why are things as they are? Everything is there, all the time, and it's exhausting.

. . . .

Any way will do. In any case, all the ways are known, they have been analysed and explained: we have them there in front of us, on a tray, like cakes. One can either live for oneself, in freedom, since one man is as good as another and I've as much right as anyone else to take advantage of life; with all the risks this implies, of course, for if one has the right to abandon other people, one finds it hard to accept their abandonment of oneself; or else one can renounce oneself, live only for others, devote one's life to the happiness of others; or else one can be wholly indifferent, expecting nothing from others, expecting nothing from oneself and living in a sort of sage neutrality; or else one can live quite casually, taking what comes and asking oneself no questions of any sort; or else, if one finds existence intolerable, one can commit suicide. All these methods are valid. You only have to choose one of them, a single one, and follow it through to the end. I myself choose them all, but since I cannot follow them all at once I adopt one at a time, only for a couple of minutes of course, then I change my mind and choose another, then I choose the third and so forth. This leaves me in a state of confusion. Fortunately, or unfortunately, I'm a man of letters and I chatter about it all as if I were in a café or a brasserie.

. . . .

What a flood of images, words, characters, symbolic figures, signs, all at the same time and meaning more or less the same thing, though never exactly the same, a chaotic jumble of messages that I may perhaps end by understanding but which tells me no more about the fundamental problem: what is this world? What is it that's all around me? Who am I? Is there an 'I' and if there is an 'I' where am I going? What am I doing, what am I doing here, what am I to do? I have been asking myself these questions from the beginning, I have always been at the foot of the wall, I have always been in front of a locked door. There is no key. I am waiting for the answer whereas I ought to provide it myself, to invent it. I keep waiting for a miracle which does not come. Presumably there is nothing to understand. But one's got to have a reason, to find a reason. Or else to lose one's reason.

. . . .

I am told, in a dream: 'You can only find the key to the riddles, you can only get the answer to all your questions through a dream. You must dream that dream.' So, in my dream, I fall asleep, and I dream, in my dream, that I'm having that absolute, revealing dream. I wake up, in my dream. I remember, in my dream, the dream of a dream, and now 'I know,' and an immense, serene joy possesses me. When I wake up, really wake up, I clearly remember having dreamed that I dreamed, I remember having dreamed that I dreamed the revealing dream, but I remember nothing at all about its content, and once again the dream that explains everything, that dream of absolute truth, has eluded me.

16

At the age of eleven Blaise Pascal (1623–1662) performed experiments with sound and wrote a "treatise" on the results. At sixteen he had attracted the notice of the philosopher Descartes, and at nineteen he had designed and constructed the first real calculating machine. One of the geniuses of his age, Pascal went on to make lasting contributions to mathematics and the sciences. A religious experience of great intensity came upon Pascal when he was thirty; he immediately wrote an account of it (the "Memorial") which he always carried with him. It was found after his death sewn into the lining of his coat.

His Pensées ("Thoughts"), from which the following selections are taken, concern his philosophical and religious reflections. The portions presented here form a classic statement of man's paradoxical position in a vast and mystifying universe.

---

72. Returning to himself, let man consider what he is in comparison with all existence; let him regard himself as lost in this remote corner of nature; and from the little cell in which he finds himself lodged, I mean the universe, let him estimate at their true value the earth, kingdoms, cities, and himself. What is a man in the Infinite?

But to show him another prodigy equally astonishing, let him examine the most delicate things he knows. Let a mite be given him, with its minute body and parts incomparably more minute, limbs with their joints, veins in the limbs, blood in the veins, humours in the blood, drops in the humours, vapours in the drops. Dividing these last things again, let him exhaust his powers of conception, and let the last object at which he can arrive be now that of our discourse. Perhaps he will think that here is the smallest point in nature. It will let him see therein a new abyss. I will paint for him not only the visible universe, but all that he can conceive of nature's immensity in the womb of this abridged atom. Let him see therein an infinity of universes, each of which has its firmament, its planets, its earth, in the same proportion as in the visible world; in each earth animals, and in the last mites, in which he will find again all that the first had, finding still in these others the same thing without end and without cessation. Let him lose himself in wonders as amazing in their littleness as the others in their vastness. For who will not be astounded at the fact that our body, which a little while ago was imperceptible in the universe, itself imperceptible in the bosom of the whole, is now a colossus, a world, or rather a whole, in respect of the nothingness which we cannot reach? He who regards himself in this light will be afraid of himself, and observing himself sustained in the body given him

17

by nature between those two abysses of the Infinite and Nothing, will tremble at the sight of these marvels; and I think that, as his curiosity changes into admiration, he will be more disposed to contemplate them in silence than to examine them with presumption.

For in fact what is man in nature? A Nothing in comparison with the Infinite, an All in comparison with the Nothing, a mean between nothing and everything. Since he is infinitely removed from comprehending the extremes, the end of things and their beginning are hopelessly hidden from him in an impenetrable secret; he is equally incapable of seeing the Nothing from which he was made, and the Infinite in which he is swallowed up.

What will he do then, but perceive the appearance of the middle of things, in an eternal despair of knowing either their beginning or their end. All things proceed from the Nothing, and are borne towards the Infinite. Who will follow these marvellous processes? The Author of these wonders understands them. None other can do so. . . .

Let us then take our compass; we are something, and we are not everything. The nature of our existence hides from us the knowledge of first beginnings which are born of the Nothing; and the littleness of our being conceals from us the sight of the Infinite.

Our intellect holds the same position in the world of thought as our body occupies in the expanse of nature.

Limited as we are in every way, this state which holds the mean between two extremes is present in all our impotence. Our senses perceive no extreme. Too much sound deafens us; too much light dazzles us; too great distance or proximity hinders our view. . . .

This is our true state; this is what makes us incapable of certain knowledge and of absolute ignorance. We sail within a vast sphere, ever drifting in uncertainty, driven from end to end. When we think to attach ourselves to any point and to fasten to it, it wavers and leaves us; and if we follow it, it eludes our grasp, slips past us, and vanishes for ever. Nothing stays for us. This is our natural condition, and yet most contrary to our inclination; we burn with desire to find solid ground and an ultimate sure foundation whereon to build a tower reaching to the Infinite. But our whole groundwork cracks, and the earth opens to abysses. . . .

Who would not think, seeing us compose all things of mind and body, but that this mixture would be quite intelligible to us? Yet it is the very thing we least understand. Man is to himself the most wonderful object in nature; for he cannot conceive what the body is, still less what the mind is, and least of all how a body should be united to a mind. This is the consummation of his difficulties, and yet it is his very being. . . .

83. *We must thus begin the chapter on the deceptive powers.* Man is only a subject full of error, natural and ineffaceable, without grace. Nothing shows him the truth. Everything deceives him. These two sources of truth, reason and the senses, besides being both wanting in sincerity, deceive each other in turn. The senses mislead the reason with false appearances, and receive from reason in their turn the same trickery which they apply to her; reason has her revenge. The passions of the soul trouble the senses, and make false impressions upon them. They rival each other in falsehood and deception. . . .

205. When I consider the short duration of my life, swallowed up in the eternity before and after, the little space which I fill, and even can see, engulfed in the infinite immensity of spaces of which I am ignorant, and which know me not, I am frightened, and am astonished at being here rather than there; for there is no reason why here rather than there, why now rather than then. Who has put me here? By whose order and direction have this place and time been allotted to me? . . .

206. The eternal silence of these infinite spaces frightens me.

347. Man is but a reed, the most feeble thing in nature; but he is a thinking reed. The entire universe need not arm itself to crush him. A vapour, a drop of water suffices to kill him. But, if the universe were to crush him, man would still be more noble than that which killed him, because he knows that he dies and the advantage which the universe has over him; the universe knows nothing of this.

All our dignity consists, then, in thought. By it we must elevate ourselves, and not by space and time which we cannot fill. Let us endeavour, then, to think well; this is the principle of morality.

434. . . . What then shall man do in this state? Shall he doubt everything? Shall he doubt whether he is awake, whether he is being pinched, or whether he is being burned? Shall he doubt whether he doubts? Shall he doubt whether he exists? We cannot go so far as that; and I lay it down as a fact that there never has been a real complete sceptic. Nature sustains our feeble reason, and prevents it raving to this extent.

Shall he then say, on the contrary, that he certainly possesses truth—he who, when pressed ever so little, can show no title to it, and is forced to let go his hold?

What a chimera then is man! What a novelty! What a monster, what a chaos, what a contradiction, what a prodigy! Judge of all things, imbecile worm of the earth; depositary of truth, a sink of uncertainty and error; the pride and refuse of the universe!

Who will unravel this tangle? Nature confutes the sceptics, and reason confutes the dogmatists. What then will you become, O men! who try to find out by your natural reason what is your true condition? You cannot avoid one of these sects, nor adhere to one of them.

Know then, proud man, what a paradox you are to yourself. Humble yourself, weak reason; be silent, foolish nature; learn that man infinitely transcends man, and learn from your Master your true condition, of which you are ignorant. . . .

692. When I see the blindness and the wretchedness of man, when I regard the whole silent universe, and man without light, left to himself, and, as it were, lost in this corner of the universe, without knowing who has put him there, what he has come to do, what will become of him at death, and incapable of all knowledge, I become terrified, like a man who should be carried in his sleep to a dreadful desert island, and should awake without knowing where he is, and without means of escape. And thereupon I wonder how people in a condition so wretched do not fall into despair.

ira wolfert   OF STARS AND MAN

It is impossible to do more than suggest the incredible immensity of the universe. We are able to follow the descriptions of those reaches of space for only a moment or two, and then our minds stagger. "The eternal silence of these infinite spaces frightens me," said Pascal. From the perspective of the most distant stars, what is man? Our physical dimensions, of course, have no logical bearing upon the question of our significance, but they are hardly comforting. How reassuring it must have been for those men prior to the time of Copernicus to have believed the earth to be the center of the universe! The following is an excerpt from an article which appeared in The Reader's Digest *(May 1970).*

. . . Consider how inconceivably huge is the stage on which creation unfolds. A quick trip out into the universe at the speed of light—186,000 miles a second—will help set the scene. In a mere 1⅓ seconds, traveling at that speed, we pass the moon. In five hours we're out of the solar system. But it's four years later before we approach the nearest star.

Going on through the Milky Way—the family or "galaxy" of stars to which our solar system belongs—we pass a star only every five years on the average, despite traveling at more than 11 million miles a minute. Yet there are 100 billion stars in our galaxy. It would take 80,000 years to go from one end of it to the other. Once out of it, space is really empty. For the next galaxy, Andromeda, is two million years away!

But even after Andromeda we're not really out in the wide open spaces yet. The galaxies come in groups. Some groups have as few as three galaxies. Our own galaxy is one of a cluster of about 17 which astronomers call, without cracking a smile, the Local Group. The largest group, Hercules (it would take us 300 million years to reach it), contains more than 10,000 galaxies, each containing billions of stars. In all, there are at least ten billion galaxies in the known universe.

Estimates of the age of this Hindu hymn vary widely. Frederic Spiegelberg holds it to be perhaps 4000 years old. Karl Jaspers, in the essay which follows the hymn, places the figure closer to 3000 years. It is the 129th hymn of the 10th book of the Rig Veda, *a collection of the most ancient of the sacred scriptures of Hinduism.*

Then there was neither being nor non-being:
There was no air, nor firmament beyond it.
Was there a stirring? Where? Beneath what cover?
Was there a great abyss of unplumbed water?

There was no death nor anything immortal;
Nor any sign dividing day from night.
That One Thing, in the stillness, breathed quiescent;
No second thing existed whatsoever.

Darkness was hidden in a deeper darkness;
This All was as a sea without dimensions;
The void still held unformed what was potential,
Until the power of Warmth produced the sole One.

Then, in that One, Desire stirred into being,
Desire that was the earliest seed of Spirit.
(The sages probing in their hearts with wisdom
Discovered being's kinship in non-being.

Stretching their line across the void, they pondered;
Was aught above it, or was aught below it?)
Bestowers of the seed were there; and powers;
Free energy below; above, swift action.

Who truly knows, and who can here declare it?
Whence It was born, and how this world was fashioned?
The gods came later than the earth's creation:
Who knows then out of what the world has issued?

Whether he made the world or did not make it,
He knows whence this creation came, he only
Who in the highest heaven guards and watches;
He knows indeed, but then, perhaps, *he* knows not!

karl jaspers   THE CREATION OF THE WORLD

Born in Germany in 1883, Karl Jaspers' earliest professional training was in medicine. He later specialized in psychotherapy and held a professorship in the psychiatric clinic at the University of Heidelberg. In 1937 he was dismissed from his position by the Nazis, partly because of his Jewish wife, and partly due to his outspoken criticism of the Nazis. In Heidelberg in 1945 he and his wife were scheduled for a concentration camp, but the city was liberated just two weeks prior to the date set for their deportation. After the war Jaspers served as president of the University of Heidelberg and then moved to the University of Basel, Switzerland, where he was a professor of philosophy until his death in 1969. One of the most respected philosophers of the twentieth century, his works include Psychopathology, The Future of Mankind, The Perennial Scope of Philosophy, The Way to Wisdom, Man in the Modern Age, *and* The Great Philosophers. *The following essay is from a collection of his papers entitled* Philosophy and the World (1963).

In a hymn of the Rig Veda, a thousand years before Christ, the Hindu poet asks how the world came to be. What was before? Not being, he says, nor non-being; not air, not sky, not death, not immortality. . . . Only the One breathed. There was nothing else. This was the source of the world. . . . But, the poet asks at once, who really knows the source? The gods, he says, do not reach that far. Who can tell whether the world is created or un-created? And the answer: he alone knows, the One, the all-seeing—or does he not know, either?

The poet inquires even beyond the gods. He comes to the last, the ultimate One whom he calls the surveyor and master of all. To ask whether even this One may not know seems skeptical to the point of blasphemy. But is it? If the question about "before" has been raised in earnest, if the eye has glimpsed the mystery, there is no longer any statement that would fit the all-encompassing, the infinite. Thought pauses inquiringly. It comes to a halt before Being. Being is not to be touched by supposed knowledge, nor by the mere expectation that it might be knowable at all, in the form we call knowledge. The question, "Or does he not know either?" shrouds the in-effability of the essence, the fact that fundamental, objectless cognition not only transcends all definite knowledge but defies knowledge.

This was experienced three thousand years ago. Have we made any progress? Do we know more about how the world came to be? Many an-swers have been given since. Let us consider them.

There are the age-old cosmogonies (theories about the origin of the world). It is envisioned either as gestation, by sexual duplication and union, or as evolution from the primal egg, or from the sea; then as production by a Maker constructing the world like the builder who puts up an edifice; finally as the growth of consciousness out of unconsciousness, of duality out of unity, of conceivability out of the inconceivable, as the egress of force and name from invisibility and inaudibility, as the process of opposition and reunion. In all these, the origin of the world is conceived along the lines of events in the world, of living, material, intellectual, logical processes.

All these concepts, up to the most sublime, have one thing in common: their proponents seem to know what happened. They operate with forces, gods, substances, categories, whose own source is not further inquired into. The mystery stressed by the Vedic poet has been lost in the idea of knowing all about it. The inquiry does not halt before the mystery; instead, it ceases thoughtlessly in the answer.

Beyond all these mythical cosmogonies, a more truthful answer seems to lie in the concept of creation from nothingness. This creation is unimaginable, not to be visualized by an analogy in the world. It is not even a temporal process any more, since time itself has only been created along with everything else. The creation of the world is exempted from temporality, which is part of the world.

There are two historic instances of this idea:

First, the Biblical idea of the Creation. God made the world out of nothing, not by any of the ways we use, along the lines of events in the world, to illustrate something which transcends all of the world. But even this idea, once conceived, will not put a stop to our thinking. Whence, we go on to ask, is God? Could this, too, be nothing? Like the Vedic poet, Kant confronted the mystery: "It is an inescapable thought, but an unbearable one as well, that what we imagine as supreme among all possible beings should say to itself, as it were: 'I am from eternity to eternity; beside myself there is nothing but what I willed to be—yet whence am I?'"

The other instance is the Hindu idea that the world is no self-based reality but *maya*, magic. It is reality for our existence, to be sure, but along with this existence it is the concealment of reality in a mirage. The creation of the world is a flash of this non-being in the seductive guise of being. And yet, whence the spell? Who casts it? Again the source defies inquiry. Here, too, the end is the abyss before the dizzying question.

Countering all questions about the origin of the world is a very different answer: that the question is wrongly put. The world is eternal, is unborn, is not derived from anything else—the world itself is everything.

This answer, too, has been given in great historic forms.

In China it is a matter of course, beyond question. The Chinese world has

24

existed forever, is forever the same in the rhythm of life and the courses of the stars. It is directed by the order of *tao*, the quietly supreme but non-violent force. Deviations will disturb this order for a moment, but it is never destroyed and always restored.

In India and in the West, many thinkers have thought in terms of the beginning and the end of the world. But if worlds begin and end, the being of *the* world is still eternal; a world is born and will perish, but a new beginning will follow upon its end. In this view the world is eternal as a process of perpetual recurrence of the worlds in world cycles.

Of many examples, we cite the words of Heraclitus: "This world has not been created either by God nor by any of mankind; it was and is and will be everlasting fire, self-kindled and self-extinguished."

In such ideas from China, India, and the West, the world itself is seen as divine, as God; gods come to be in the worlds, in the cycle of worlds, and themselves are subject to change.

The quoted answers to the question about the origin of the world were either a mere game of finding words for the mystery, or they turned into a false knowledge in which the mystery was lost, or they cut off the question by stating that the world is eternal.

But has modern physics not unveiled the mystery by means of cogent cognition?

We hear the physicists relate the story of the universe. A primal explosion set off the process which now, in the centrifugal motion of the astral nebulae, shows itself to the astronomer as a still constantly expanding universe. When we hear this, along with the actual scientific findings, we stand in amazement before a now largely known cosmos, thinking, perhaps, that at last we know whence it came. Where measurements and mathematics reign, modern man is inclined to submit.

For all the accuracy of the various discoveries, however, we are on the wrong track if we go on to make statements about the world as a whole, its source, and its total content. Wherever deductions exceed the realm of possible experience and the results will not be subject to experience, either, we are about to delude ourselves. Constructions of mathematical possibilities are as speculative and deceptive as the old, conceptual ones of metaphysics, and equally tempting.

The facts are what counts, and they are not easy to grasp. First, as Kant realized, the world in its entirety cannot become an object. We are in the world, and we never face it as a whole. If we attempt to grasp it as a whole, we get into antinomies—that is to say, into contradictions whose thesis and antithesis seem equally demonstrable to abstract thought, and equally insoluble to experience.

And secondly, the world does not consist only of the astronomical universe cogently known by mathematical abstractions in so far as it can be measured and verified. In this sort of knowledge, the universe is necessarily conceived as lifeless. That there is life, and that we are human beings, and that consciousness appears and becomes capable of knowing all this to an unpredictable extent—for these facts our present, purely mathematical view of the world provides no better explanation than our past mechanical one of the playing atoms. What we can know of the universe does not tell us how we come to think, and thus to know.

The result, in brief, is this: the world as a whole can never be an object for us; we always remain within it. But in the awareness of our freedom, which is incomprehensible in terms of the world, we transcend the incomplete world we can know.

For the man who can see this, whose thinking about the world has touched these boundaries, the world comes, so to speak, into a state of suspension.

The idea of God's creation of the world will be a symbol, then, not a matter of knowledge. It is in the abyss revealed by the idea of Creation that we, along with all our mundane knowledge and activities, are engulfed and sheltered at the same time.

Yet there is truth to the idea only if its symbolic character is maintained. Being a symbol, the idea does not lie on the level of our mundane knowledge. Thinking it through will serve, rather, to illuminate the absence of knowledge from it—about as follows:

The creation of the world is not a process in the world. Before there was a world, there was no time, no space, no matter—but we, with all our concepts conditioned by the being of the world, cannot help thinking that there was a time before, that there was something before. We can, however, realize that we are so conditioned. The symbol serves to support and to reassure us by the very fact of consciously uttering paradoxes. We say, "God created time"—but the word "created" describes a temporal process, contradicting the meaning of the sentence. We say, "God made the world out of nothing" —and we operate with the word "nothing" as if it were something, again contradicting the meaning of the sentence.

What is conceived in the symbolic idea of Creation is not a process we might observe, not even as a figment of our imagination. What it means cannot be adequately meant by us, for it transcends our faculties of imagining and thinking.

Yet this symbolic idea is vitally important to the consciousness of our own essence. The two basic concepts, eternity of the world or createdness of the world—these two embattled symbols return wholly different answers to the question after our own source. If the world is eternal, it is from the world that man has come into the world; he is its product. But if the world was created, man himself was directly created by God. Bodily, in the physical and psychological functions of the body, he is a product of the world, but in his essence he is outside the world, now as before.

It is as though we had been created as the world has been, but not by way of the world. As animated bodies we are a part of Creation, but our freedom comes directly from God. Thus, while being in the world, we are also from elsewhere. We find ourselves in the world, and yet we are not of this world alone.

We do not, however, know this in the sense in which the science of psychology enables us to know ourselves in our aspects. In other words, we do not know it.

If we could grasp where we come from, we would cease to be human. We can only touch the frontiers in the consciousness of our humanity, which consists in being imperfect and imperfectible. We live in time—that is to say, we are never finished; we are only searching and striving. We never know what eternity is, nor what is eternal in us and in our doings, but it comes to be present in ciphers, in parables, in reflections—for example, in the cipher of the idea of Creation.

The idea of Creation stirs us by the very fact that it does not permit us to know. It points to depths in which, at the same time, it hides our origin. If we knew how we came to be, if we shared in the knowledge of our creation as if we had been there, our humanity would stop moving in time. Any knowledge of the process of creation, how it was, how it took place, would be perfect knowledge. Knowing what we are, we would no longer need to become so. Once the "before" is fully, completely clear, there is no more need for an "afterwards" to clarify it. We would no longer be living in the possibilities of our situation; we would command a view of it, would have control over it, and would thus have terminated it. Everything would be manifest. Knowing our beginnings, we would be at the end of our humanity. By our way of knowing we would have come to another, a presently inconceivable sense of being and capacity of thought, which would make us different creatures. We would no longer be human.

But since we are human—that is to say: en route to realization, only to find out there what we really are—the condition in which we find ourselves seems to pose the following challenges:

Not vainly to make the world as a whole an object of knowledge—as though to take it in hand, so to speak—but to keep exploring it *ad infinitum*;

not to interpret the world on grounds of a supposed total knowledge, but to make our way in it with knowledge as our orientation;

to comprehend, from the utmost possible knowledge, how little we know;

to acquiesce in our historic realization here and now;

to become aware of the boundaries, by being constantly alive to them, shunning tranquillity, and refusing to be definitely satisfied with any concept of the world;

and, by the very means of realizing ourselves, to come to relate to Transcendence.

For this is part of our essence: instead of understanding ourselves in mundane terms, there is in us somethoing that can set itself against all mundane things. If we are in the world from elsewhere, our mission in the world transcends the world.

In all our human possibilities it remains essential to illuminate, not to conceal, the mystery that a world exists, and that we are in it.

Since the times of the Vedic poet we have made vast strides in our knowledge of the world. We know much more clearly what we do not know. But in the crucial point we are not a step farther.

For our human communion in the depths of ignorance, it is inspiring to meet the ancient bard—as well as thinkers from all ages—in one encompassing mystery.

To fulfill this mystery with the spirit of the language of our reality—this is what makes our historic life. But its unveiling would either be the delusion of a pseudo-knowledge, causing us to neglect what we can do, or it would be truth—and then it would mean our transformation into other beings than we humans are.

milton k. munitz   # THE MYSTERY OF EXISTENCE

Milton K. Munitz (1913–   ) was born in New York City and received his Ph.D. from Columbia University. Prior to World War II he was an instructor at the City College of New York. After the war he moved to New York University, becoming Professor of Philosophy in 1958. Professor Munitz has received Guggenheim and Fulbright fellowships and is the author of The Moral Philosophy of Santayana, *and* Space, Time, and Relativity. *He edited* Theories of the Universe *and* A Modern Introduction to Ethics. *The selection which follows is from* The Mystery of Existence: An Essay in Philosophical Cosmology *(1965).*

STATEMENT OF THE PROBLEM

Philosophy, or the love of wisdom, as Aristotle noted long ago, begins in wonder. "At first," he says, "men wondered about the more obvious problems that demanded explanation; gradually their inquiries spread farther afield, and they asked questions upon such larger topics as changes in the sun and moon and stars, and the origin of the world."[1]

Let us consider this last-mentioned topic, "the origin of the world." What kind of question does it raise? When the pre-Socratics asked this question—and it was their speculations that, apparently, Aristotle had in mind—they understood this to mean: "How did the world get to be the way it is at the present time? Through what processes of transformation and growth did it pass before it emerged as the ordered structure it is found to be now?" The entire subsequent history of science, including the recent development of scientific cosmology, may be thought of as continuing to ask (with some modifications, and along with a variety of other questions) roughly the same type of question initiated by the pre-Socratics. There has been, of course, a notable advance in the quality of the answers to which we, in our own day, can now turn. It would be naive to expect that the type of wonderment represented by scientific curiosity will someday find total satisfaction in the answers provided by a finished and perfected science. Nevertheless, there cannot be any doubt of the enormous progress already made since the days of the pre-Socratics, or of the likely progress yet to come.

Meanwhile, there is another side to human wonderment, not considered by Aristotle, that finds expression in a different kind of question from that which he listed under the heading "the origin of the world" (as he understood this phrase). While one may continue to use even this same terminology to formulate this new question, it would no longer have the meaning

[1] Aristotle, *Metaphysics*, translated by J. Warrington, Everyman Library (London and New York, 1956), Book A, chapter 2.

previously mentioned. For, it would now be roughly equivalent to what is meant by speaking of "the mystery of existence." For those who are provoked by the mystery of existence, and so display another dimension of human wonderment, the root question is *why there should be a world at all*. To ask this latter type of question is not to ask a scientific question. If we are caught in the toils of this question, no amount of scientific explanation of how the world underwent various stages of development, on a cosmological or on a more restricted level, will serve, in any way, to allay the difficulty summed up by asking why there should even be a world in existence, whatever its stages of development or its patterns and qualities. It is with this side, or form, of human wonderment that the present book is concerned.

In asking the question I have labelled "the mystery of existence," we are at once struck by the differences from the type of question that the pre-Socratics first asked. Why is it that the scientific type of question is readily understandable, whereas it is by no means the case all would agree, in asking the type of question about the mystery of existence, we are asking something that is even meaningful? Why is it that whereas we can note steady progress in the development of our scientific understanding of the world, those who dwell on the mystery of existence are confined to reiterating the question, and cannot either claim any progress in its past study, or encourage us to believe that the prospects for answering it are likely to be better in the future, than they were when men first asked this question?

We are prompted, by these reflections, to ask whether the question about the mystery of existence illustrates what is sometimes the case with other "perennial" problems of philosophy. May it not be that the asking of this question derives, at bottom, from certain confusions of thought, or from some radical misuse of language? Since the discussion of the mystery of existence does not depend on any settlement of an issue of fact, in the way ordinary scientific questions are commonly thought to be so dependent, should we not regard the mystery of existence as an intellectual knot into which we get ourselves in asking a meaningless, because unanswerable, question? We could then treat the mystery, not as a genuine intellectual problem, but as a puzzlement that needs disentangling through the patient analysis of language. If successful in such analysis, we should then find that the mental cramp will have disappeared—the question will have dissolved, and will no longer bother us.

In opposition to the foregoing suggestion, however, we need to consider the possible merits of another line of approach. Should we not say that while, admittedly, we are not dealing with a soluble problem, neither are we expressing something that is intellectually spurious and in need of being dissolved? May it not be that the mystery of existence is entirely genuine, that it is a *sui generis* question, and is neither a soluble scientific problem nor a dissoluble puzzle? Perhaps, then, the only way of dealing with it is to recognize it as an ineradicable feature of the human response to the world, and to understand it for what it is, rather than to seek to remove it, or to reduce it to something else? Instead of saying that the question expressing the mystery of existence is faulty or eliminable, because not a genuine problem, should we not declare that not all meaningful questions need be reducible to those that are answerable? Would not a more fruitful treatment of the question expressing the mystery of existence be found by undertaking a comparison of those respects in which it is similar to, and different from, other types of questions raised by the human mind? And might it not be found, through such an analysis, that it occupies a legitimate place in the manifold of the mind's question-raising propensities?

There is still another line of thought worth pursuing. We might ask whether the question "Why is there a world at all?" is indeed a universal question, the germs of which are to be found in all men, and, therefore, present to human consciousness in some degree, or form, throughout history, or whether, on the contrary, it is characteristic of only a very special and limited intellectual tradition in our own culture. Why is it that the Greeks, generally speaking, did not raise the question? May it not be that the question expressing the mystery of existence is linked with the creation myth of The Book of Genesis, and its subsequent elaboration by theology? Would, then, the mystery of existence be likely to occur to anyone not influenced by the entire body of doctrine of Hebraic-Christian theism, at the core of which is the belief in a creation *ex nihilo*? Should we not, therefore, treat the question "Why is there a world at all?" as an echo, ostensibly independent of the Hebraic-Christian tradition, as in fact originating primarily in that tradition?

On the other hand, if we say that the question expressing the mystery of existence is intimately related to the tradition of Hebraic-Christian theism, are we not overlooking, thereby, still another possibility? Should we not say, rather, that what is being expressed by the sense of the mystery of existence is independent of both the Greek and the Hebraic traditions? Why need we vacillate, or be under tension, between choosing either a "Greek" way of looking at the world, as something to be understood in itself, or a "Hebraic" way of looking at the world, as something made by a Power that transcends it? Both modes of thought are trying, each in its own way, to satisfy the human drive for rationality and intelligibility. Both operate with some form of a Principle of Sufficient Reason. Might we not say, instead, that the mystery of existence consists precisely in the fact that we do not know, nor do we have any reliable way of finding out, *whether* there is a reason for the existence of the world? If, however, we link a more acceptable treatment of the mystery of existence to a rejection of the presupposition that the demand for rationality *must* be satisfied by the very existence of the world, does this have any genuine philosophic merit? How could this view be developed, and by what arguments could it be supported?

As a final proposal, we need to consider whether use of the phrase "the mystery of existence" serves merely to express an emotional response to the awesome magnitude of the world. People seem to vary in their capacity to make their response; some are more prone to it than others. In this case, are we not obliged to say that the phrase "the mystery of existence" does not have a genuine cognitive content at all?

These are some of the questions that need to be explored in any consideration of the theme summed up by the use of the phrase "the mystery of existence." As with other concepts that have philosophical interest, the essential task posed by the use of this phrase is primarily one of clarification. Such clarification can have, broadly speaking, two different types of outcome. In one, the concept, however meaningful it may appear at first glance, or by dint of repeated though uncritical usage, shows itself to be weak and indefensible. The concept and the position it sums up, therefore, presumably can be replaced by more adequate ones. Now, if this is the outcome of analysis, the process of philosophic discussion will have performed a valuable therapeutic service of exorcism. On the other hand, if the idea is at bottom sound and useful, analysis will have succeeded in giving us a firmer grip and deeper understanding of its conceptual ramifications and involvements. In the latter case, the concept in question can now be used with greater confidence and sophistication. In either case, the gain is indisputable. Thus, with respect to the present theme, we need to ask: Does the phrase "the mystery of existence" cloak a changeling, or does it, when clarified and disentangled, point to something that has a legitimate place in our efforts at arriving at a sound philosophy?

CONTEMPORARY VIEWPOINTS

In current philosophy, those who consider the question "Why is there a world at all?" (or variants of this, such as "Why is there something, rather than nothing?") belong, generally speaking, to one or another of three groups.

(1) Some reject, outright, both the question and any attempt to find an "answer" to it, on the ground that the very asking of the question is itself a mistake and philosophically vacuous. Within this group are to be found those who appeal to some form of positivist or empiricist philosophy, as well as many who would be called "pragmatists" or "naturalists."

In an age such as ours, when science provides the unexcelled and acknowledged standard for achieving intellectual and technical control over Nature, it is readily understandable that many persons should hold the view that any reference to mystery smacks of obscurantism. Talk about "the mystery of existence," it is held, either tends to denigrate the powers of reason to exploit the sources of intelligibility *in* the world, or else it invites a non-rational and, therefore, irresponsible leap *beyond* the world. For those conscious of the former of these dangers, acknowledgement of mystery marks the abandonment of confidence in man's rational capacities, and a surrender of the belief in the world as an intelligible domain awaiting men's endless explorative probings. Representative of this viewpoint is the claim made by Moritz Schlick that "in principle there are no limits to our knowledge. The boundaries which must be acknowledged are of an empirical nature and therefore never ultimate; they can be pushed back further and further; there is no unfathomable mystery in the world."[2]

Those conscious of the other form of danger bound up with talk of "mystery" are of the opinion that this way of thinking induces an irresistible drive to transcend the world, and to account for the world's character and existence by reference to a God whose nature cannot be established or known in any genuinely rational way. Since this outcome represents a breakdown of thought, the source of this breakdown must be traced to the asking of a faulty and illegitimate question. This latter viewpoint has been summed up as follows:

> That anything exists at all seems a problem, in itself puzzling. There might have been nothing. Why should there be anything? There must always have been moods when people thought like this and wondered, when they stared at the mere fact of existence, as at a mystery requiring an explanation. If you think of the fact of existence itself as a mystery, then you will soon find yourself looking for an explanation of the universe outside of the universe itself; in other words, you will look for a transcendental explanation—for something beyond all existence which explains why anything at all exists. Immanuel Kant gave reasons why it must be a mistake to look for something beyond, which would explain the fact of existence.[3]

Not only the positivist or the neo-Kantian, but various other groups of contemporary thinkers, as well, would tend to reject the theme of "the mystery of existence" as a fruitful one for philosophy. The question is one that most naturalists, linguistic analysts, or empirically oriented thinkers have shunned. Insofar as they are at all concerned with ontological questions, these philosophers undertake to clarify such basic concepts as "time," "individual," "cause," "mind," and the like. But they do not find anything puzzling in the very existence of the world.

(2) Needless to say, there are many who remain unconvinced by the

[2] M. Schlick, "Meaning and Verification," *The Philosophical Review*, 45 (1936), p. 352.
[3] S. Hampshire, "Metaphysical Systems" in *The Nature of Metaphysics*, edited by D. F. Pears (London, 1957), p. 23.

arguments of the positivist, neo-Kantian, naturalist, empiricist, or linguistic analyst. There have been several recent philosophic attempts at reviving the question classically posed by Leibniz in the form "Why is there something, rather than nothing?"[4] Those who find the question important and intriguing will be found to belong, for the most part, to one or another of two groups in contemporary thought.

One group comprises various types of theists, who use the concept of the mystery of existence as a stepping-stone to God. Belief in God serves to answer the question, or solve the mystery of the existence of the world. Jacques Maritain expresses the neo-Thomist strand of this position as follows:

> The Supreme "mystery" is the supernatural mystery which is the object of faith and theology. It is concerned with the Godhead Itself, the interior life of God, to which our intellect cannot rise by its unaided natural powers. But philosophy and science also are concerned with mystery, another mystery, the mystery of nature and the mystery of being. A philosophy unaware of mystery would not be a philosophy.[5]

The other group of writers who find the theme of the mystery of existence central, includes various "atheistic existentialists." Prominent among these is Heidegger. For these philosophers, the very asking of the question is an important step in the search for metaphysical wisdom. Unfortunately, Heidegger's own treatment (as the chief example of this approach) takes the form of a reiterated insistence that this question is first in rank for us "because it is the most far-reaching, second, because it is the deepest, and finally because it is the most fundamental of all questions."[6] Absent from his discussion, however, is any clear analysis of what the question means. It is the need for such analysis, nevertheless, that must be met if the question is to be taken seriously.

(3) There are some philosophers, finally, who are uncommitted with respect to this question, though largely dissatisfied with the treatment given by the first two groups of writers. Within this category are to be found some who take their point of departure from the outlook and use of techniques associated with contemporary linguistic philosophy. J. J. C. Smart belongs to this group, and speaks for many, I suspect, when he writes:

> That anything should exist at all does seem to me a matter for the deepest awe. But whether other people feel this sort of awe, and whether they or

[4] G. Leibniz, *Principles of Nature and Grace*, 7.

[5] J. Maritain, *A Preface to Metaphysics* (New York, 1958), p. 5.

[6] M. Heidegger, *An Introduction to Metaphysics*, translated by R. Mannheim (New Haven, 1959), p. 2.

I ought to is another question. I think we ought to. If so, the question arises: If 'Why should anything exist at all?' cannot be interpreted after the manner of the cosmological argument, that is, as an absurd request for the nonsensical postulation of a logically necessary being, what sort of question is it? What sort of question is this question, 'Why should anything exist at all?' All I can say is, that I do not yet know.[7]

[7] J. J. C. Smart, "The Existence of God" in A. Flew and A. McIntyre (editors), *New Essays in Philosophical Theology* (London, 1955), p. 46.

Thomas Wolfe (1900–1938) filled crateboxes with his manuscripts, and from those millions of words editors extracted the series of immense novels that made him famous: Look Homeward, Angel, You Can't Go Home Again, The Web and the Rock, *and* The Hills Beyond. *All of his work was strongly autobiographical. Wolfe seemingly attempted to record in his vivid, poetical prose everything that he had ever seen or felt. The following is an excerpt from* Of Time and The River *(1935).*

For a moment as the gouty old rake had spoken of the boy's dead brother, the boy had felt within him a sense of warmth: a wakening of dead time, a stir of grateful affection for the gross old man as if there might have been in this bloated carcass some trace of understanding for the dead boy of whom he spoke—an understanding faint and groping as a dog who bays the moon might have of the sidereal universe, and yet genuine and recognizable.

And for a moment present time fades out and the boy sits there staring blindly out at the dark earth that strokes forever past the train, and now he has the watch out and feels it in his hands. . . . And suddenly Ben is standing there before his vision, smoking, and scowls down through the window of the office at the boy.

He jerks his head in a peremptory gesture: the boy, obedient to his brother's command, enters the office and stands there waiting at the counter. Ben steps down from the platform in the window, puts the earphones on a table and walks over to the place where the boy is standing. For a moment, scowling fiercely, he stands there looking at the boy across the counter. The scowl deepens, he makes a sudden threatening gesture of his hard white hand as if to strike the boy, but instead he reaches across the counter quickly, seizes the boy by the shoulders, pulls him closer, and with rough but skillful fingers tugs, pulls and jerks the frayed string of neck-tie which the boy is wearing into a more orderly and presentable shape.

The boy starts to go.

"Wait!" says Ben, quietly, in a deliberately off-hand kind of tone. He opens a drawer below the counter, takes out a small square package, and scowling irritably, and without looking at the boy, he thrusts it at him. "Here's something for you," he says, and walks away.

"What is it?" The boy takes the package and examines it with a queer numb sense of expectancy and growing joy.

"Why don't you open it and see?" Ben says, his back still turned, and scowling down into a paper on the desk.

"Open it?" the boy says, staring at him stupidly.

"Yes, open it, fool!" Ben snarls. "It's not going to bite you!"

While the boy fumbles with the cords that tie the package, Ben prowls over toward the counter with his curious, loping, pigeon-toed stride, leans on it with his elbows and, scowling, begins to look up and down the want-ad columns, while blue, pungent smoke coils slowly from his nostrils. By this time, the boy has taken off the outer wrapping of the package, and is holding a small case, beautifully heavy, of sumptuous blue velvet, in his hands.

"Well, did you look at it?" Ben says, still scowling up and down the want-ads of the paper, without looking at the boy.

The boy finds the spring and presses it, the top opens, inside upon its rich cushion of white satin is a gold watch, and a fine gold chain. It is a miracle of design, almost as thin and delicate as a wafer. The boy stares at it with bulging eyes and in a moment stammers:

"It's—it's a watch!"

"Does it look like an alarm clock?" Ben jeers quietly, as he turns a page and begins to scowl up and down the advertisements of another column.

"It's—for me?" the boy says thickly, slowly, as he stares at it.

"No," Ben says, "it's for Napoleon Bonaparte, of course! . . . You little idiot! Don't you know what day this is? Have I got to do all the thinking for you? Don't you ever use your head for anything except a hat-rack? . . . "Well," he goes on quietly in a moment, still looking at his paper, "what do you think of it? . . . There's a spring in the back that opens up," he goes on casually. "Why don't you look at it?"

The boy turns the watch over, feels the smooth golden surface of that shining wafer, finds the spring, and opens it. The back of the watch springs out, upon the inner surface is engraved, in delicate small words, this inscription:

"To Eugene Gant
Presented To Him On His Twelfth Birthday
By His Brother
B. H. Gant
October 3, 1912"

"Well," Ben says quietly in a moment. "Did you read what it says?"

"I'd just like to say—" the boy begins in a thick, strange voice, staring blindly down at the still open watch.

"Oh, for God's sake!" Ben says, lifting his scowling head in the direction of his unknown demon, and jerking his head derisively towards the boy. "Listen to this, won't you? . . . Now, for God's sake, try to take good care of it and don't abuse it!" he says quickly and irritably. "You've got to look after a watch the same as anything else. Old man Enderby"—this is the name of the jeweller from whom he has bought the watch—"told me that a watch like that was good for fifty years, if you take care of it. . . . You know," he goes on quietly, insultingly "you're not supposed to drive nails with it or use it for a hammer. You know that, don't you?" he says, and for the first time turns and looks quietly at the boy. "Do you know what a watch is for?"

"Yes."

"What is it for?"

"To keep time with," says the boy.

Ben says nothing for a moment, but looks at him.

"Yes," he says quietly at length, with all the bitter weariness of a fathomless resignation and despair, the infinite revulsion, scorn, disgust which life has caused in him. "That's it. That's what it's for. To keep time with." The weary irony in his voice has deepened to a note of passionate despair. "And I hope to God you keep it better than the rest of us! Better than Mama or the old man—better than me! God help you if you don't! . . . Now go on home," he says quietly in a moment, "before I kill you."

"To keep time with!"

What is this dream of time, this strange and bitter miracle of living? Is it the wind that drives the leaves down bare paths fleeing? Is it the storm-wild flight of furious days, the storm-swift passing of the million faces, all lost, forgotten, vanished as a dream? Is it the wind that howls above the earth, is it the wind that drives all things before its lash, is it the wind that drives all men like dead ghosts fleeing? Is it the one red leaf that strains there on the bough and that forever will be fleeing? All things are lost and broken in the wind: the dry leaves scamper down the path before us, in their swift-winged dance of death the dead souls flee along before us driven with rusty scuffle before the fury of the demented wind. And October has come again, has come again.

What is this strange and bitter miracle of life? Is it to feel, when furious day is done, the evening hush, the sorrow of lost, fading light, far sounds and broken cries, and footsteps, voices, music, and all lost—and something murmurous, immense and mighty in the air?

And we have walked the pavements of a little town and known the passages of barren night, and heard the wheel, the whistle and the tolling bell, and lain in the darkness waiting, giving to silence the huge prayer of our intolerable desire. And we have heard the sorrowful silence of the river in October—and what is there to say? October has come again, has come again, and this world, this life, this time are stranger than a dream.

May it not be that some day from this dream of time, this chronicle of smoke, this strange and bitter miracle of life in which we are the moving and phantasmal figures, we shall wake? Knowing our father's voice upon the porch again, the flowers, the grapevines, the low rich moons of waning August, and the tolling bell—and instantly to know we live, that we have dreamed and have awakened, and find then in our hands some object, like this real and palpable, some gift out of the lost land and the unknown world as token that it was no dream—that we have really been there? And there is no more to say.

For now October has come back again, the strange and lonely month comes back again, and you will not return.

Up on the mountain, down in the valley, deep, deep, in the hill, Ben— cold, cold, cold.

"To keep time with!"

And suddenly the scene, the shapes, the voices of the men about him swam back into their focus, and he could hear the rhythmed pounding of the wheels below him, and in his palm the frail-numbered visage of the watch stared blank and plain at him its legend. It was one minute after twelve o'clock, Sunday morning, October the third, 1920, and he was hurtling across Virginia, and this world, this life, this time were stranger than a dream.

FURTHER READING

George Gamow, *The Creation of the Universe* (rev. ed., 1961). The champion of the "Big Bang" hypothesis discusses that controversy and related topics.

Sir Arthur Eddington's Gifford Lectures of 1927 were published as *The Nature of the Physical World* (1928). See Chapter 8, "Man's Place in the Universe."

Fred Hoyle is an eminent and controversial Cambridge University astronomer. His *Man in the Universe* (1966) briefly presents his philosophical reflections on the cosmos.

Few philosophers are as readable and worthwhile as William James: see Chapter 3, "The Problem of Being," in *Some Problems of Philosophy* (1911).

Sir James Jeans, *The Mysterious Universe* (1930). The last chapter of this short volume contains Jeans' often-quoted speculation that "the universe begins to look more like a great thought than like a great machine."

Arthur Koestler's *The Sleepwalkers* (1958) makes fascinating reading of the history of cosmology from the Babylonians to the modern age.

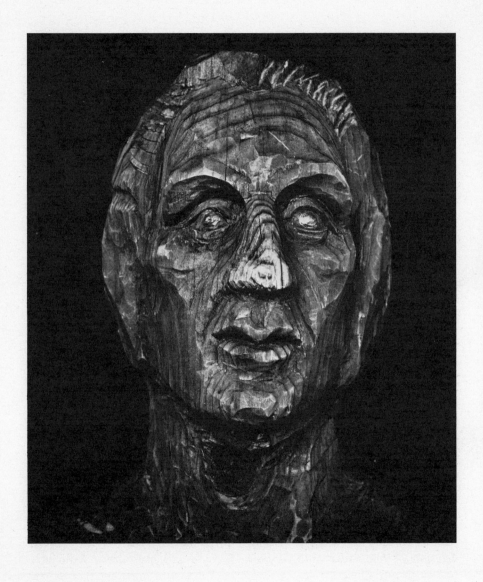

chapter two

THE EXAMINED LIFE

2

An ancient ideal of philosophy is that of the examined life. It was Socrates who expressed it in its most memorable form, stating that the unexamined life was not worth living. Embedded in this ideal is the conviction that wisdom and happiness are intimately related. This theme recurs repeatedly in the history of philosophy: if we are to achieve happiness, intelligence must be brought to bear upon our lives. We cannot possibly get what we want unless we know what we want; we cannot know what we want unless we know who we are.

The task, however, is exceedingly difficult. It requires a prodigious and courageous effort over a lifetime. Our ignorance is massive and stubborn, and our lethargy notorious. We prefer to do easier things, and we unceasingly deceive ourselves about the value of what we are doing. The evidence of human folly is the bulk of the history of mankind, and today we need only look at a daily newspaper to see the stupidities of which men are capable. Substitutes for the examined life are plentiful and cheap. The opportunities for an inauthentic existence, for error and failure, seem limitless. Abraham Maslow was once asked what percentage of people achieve "self-actualization." "I'd say only a fraction of one per cent," he replied.

It is on the difficulties of the examined life that the reading selections of this chapter open. "The enemies a man encounters on the path of learning . . . are truly formidable," says the old Yaqui Indian described by Carlos Castaneda, and don Juan's portrayal of those "enemies" seems drawn from long experience. Leo Tolstoy illustrates the matter further: born into wealth and gifted with genius and boundless energy, he was concerned even in the diaries of his boyhood with understanding himself. In his early twenties, inspired by Benjamin Franklin, he kept a "Franklin Journal" devoted exclusively to self-surveillance and self-criticism. In spite of such persistent efforts, there is "My Confession," a report of what Tolstoy felt were years of failure. Written when he was nearing fifty, Tolstoy spoke of his "former delusion of happiness" and of how "I could not attribute a reasonable motive to any single act in my whole life." Years of apparent success had turned to dust in his mouth.

42

> *The source of philosophy is to be sought in won-*
> *der, in doubt, in a sense of forsakenness. In any case,*
> *it begins with an inner upheaval.*
>
> karl jaspers

P. D. Ouspensky's essay on Yoga presents an Asian conception of the ex-amined life—one which has been practiced and refined over the ages. The severity of the way of the Yogis is all but unimaginable to most of us, but it suggests the seemingly unlimited potentialities of man. Benedict de Spinoza's "On the Improvement of the Understanding" is no less impressive. In these pages, composed when he was a young man, Spinoza reviewed the values deemed worthy of pursuit by the mass of men, and then proceeded to reject them all. Spinoza proposed another end, a "true good." The document was a blueprint for a lifetime, and Spinoza followed it with single-minded dedi-cation until his days had ended.

We undertake to examine our lives in the hope that we can render them "meaningful," a term discussed by Richard Taylor. What does it mean to have "meaning" in life? The endless, repetitive labor of Sisyphus in the famous myth is the image of meaninglessness, and Taylor uses it to point to a possible understanding of what the meaningful may be.

In 1960 Carlos Castaneda was a UCLA graduate student in anthropology doing field work in Arizona on the medicinal plants used by Indians. He met don Juan, a white-haired Yaqui Indian in his seventies. Don Juan, he learned, was a "sorcerer, medicine man, curer"—or, in his own more formal terms, a "man of knowledge." Over a five-year period Castaneda spent a great deal of time with don Juan as his apprentice. But then, unnerved by his experiences which included the use of certain hallucinatory drugs, he withdrew from the apprenticeship and published The Teachings of Don Juan (1968), *from which the following selection is taken. Later, Castaneda returned to don Juan for a "second cycle" of apprenticeship, which is described in* A Separate Reality (1971).

SATURDAY, APRIL 8, 1962

In our conversations, don Juan consistently used or referred to the phrase "man of knowledge," but never explained what he meant by it. I asked him about it.

"A man of knowledge is one who has followed truthfully the hardships of learning," he said. "A man who has, without rushing or without faltering, gone as far as he can in unraveling the secrets of power and knowledge."

"Can anyone be a man of knowledge?"

"No, not anyone."

"Then what must a man do to become a man of knowledge?"

"He must challenge and defeat his four natural enemies."

"Will he be a man of knowledge after defeating these four enemies?"

"Yes. A man can call himself a man of knowledge only if he is capable of defeating all four of them."

"Then, can *anybody* who defeats these enemies be a man of knowledge?"

"Anybody who defeats them becomes a man of knowledge."

"But are there any special requirements a man must fulfill before fighting with these enemies?"

"No. Anyone can try to become a man of knowledge; very few men actually succeed, but that is only natural. The enemies a man encounters on the path of learning to become a man of knowledge are truly formidable; most men succumb to them."

"What kind of enemies are they, don Juan?"

He refused to talk about the enemies. He said it would be a long time before the subject would make any sense to me. I tried to keep the topic alive and asked him if he thought *I* could become a man of knowledge. He said no man could possibly tell that for sure. But I insisted on knowing if there were any clues he could use to determine whether or not I had a chance of becoming a man of knowledge. He said it would depend on my battle against the four enemies—whether I could defeat them or would be defeated by them—but it was impossible to foretell the outcome of that fight.

I asked him if he could use witchcraft or divination to see the outcome of the battle. He flatly stated that the results of the struggle could not be foreseen by any means, because becoming a man of knowledge was a temporary thing. When I asked him to explain this point, he replied:

"To be a man of knowledge has no permanence. One is never a man of knowledge, not really. Rather, one becomes a man of knowledge for a very brief instant, after defeating the four natural enemies."

"You must tell me, don Juan, what kind of enemies they are."

He did not answer. I insisted again, but he dropped the subject and started to talk about something else.

SUNDAY, APRIL 15, 1962

As I was getting ready to leave, I decided to ask him once more about the enemies of a man of knowledge. I argued that I could not return for some time, and it would be a good idea to write down what he had to say and then think about it while I was away.

He hesitated for a while, but then began to talk.

"When a man starts to learn, he is never clear about his objectives. His purpose is faulty; his intent is vague. He hopes for rewards that will never materialize, for he knows nothing of the hardships of learning.

"He slowly begins to learn—bit by bit at first, then in big chunks. And his thoughts soon clash. What he learns is never what he pictured, or imagined, and so he begins to be afraid. Learning is never what one expects. Every step of learning is a new task, and the fear the man is experiencing begins to mount mercilessly, unyielding. His purpose becomes a battlefield.

"And thus he has stumbled upon the first of his natural enemies: Fear! A terrible enemy—treacherous, and difficult to overcome. It remains concealed at every turn of the way, prowling, waiting. And if the man, terrified in its presence, runs away, his enemy will have put an end to his quest."

"What will happen to the man if he runs away in fear?"

"Nothing happens to him except that he will never learn. He will never become a man of knowledge. He will perhaps be a bully, or a harmless, scared man; at any rate, he will be a defeated man. His first enemy will have put an end to his cravings."

"And what can he do to overcome fear?"

"The answer is very simple. He must not run away. He must defy his fear, and in spite of it he must take the next step in learning, and the next, and the next. He must be fully afraid, and yet he must not stop. That is the rule! And a moment will come when his first enemy retreats. The man begins to feel sure of himself. His intent becomes stronger. Learning is no longer a terrifying task.

"When this joyful moment comes, the man can say without hesitation that he has defeated his first natural enemy."

"Does it happen at once, don Juan, or little by little?"

"It happens little by little, and yet the fear is vanquished suddenly and fast."

"But won't the man be afraid again if something new happens to him?"

"No. Once a man has vanquished fear, he is free from it for the rest of his life because, instead of fear, he has acquired clarity—a clarity of mind which erases fear. By then a man knows his desires; he knows how to satisfy those desires. He can anticipate the new steps of learning, and a sharp clarity surrounds everything. The man feels that nothing is concealed.

"And thus he has encountered his second enemy: Clarity! That clarity of mind, which is so hard to obtain, dispels fear, but also blinds.

"It forces the man never to doubt himself. It gives him the assurance he can do anything he pleases, for he sees clearly into everything. And he is courageous because he is clear, and he stops at nothing because he is clear. But all that is a mistake; it is like something incomplete. If the man yields to this make-believe power, he has succumbed to his second enemy and will fumble with learning. He will rush when he should be patient, or he will be patient when he should rush. And he will fumble with learning until he winds up incapable of learning anything more."

"What becomes of a man who is defeated in that way, don Juan? Does he die as a result?"

"No, he doesn't die. His second enemy has just stopped him cold from trying to become a man of knowledge; instead, the man may turn into a buoyant warrior, or a clown. Yet the clarity for which he has paid so dearly will never change to darkness and fear again. He will be clear as long as he lives, but he will no longer learn, or yearn for, anything."

"But what does he have to do to avoid being defeated?"

"He must do what he did with fear: he must defy his clarity and use it only to see, and wait patiently and measure carefully before taking new steps; he must think, above all, that his clarity is almost a mistake. And a moment will come when he will understand that his clarity was only a point before his eyes. And thus he will have overcome his second enemy, and will arrive at a position where nothing can harm him anymore. This will not be a mistake. It will not be only a point before his eyes. It will be true power.

46

"He will know at this point that the power he has been pursuing for so long is finally his. He can do with it whatever he pleases. His ally is at his command. His wish is the rule. He sees all that is around him. But he has also come across his third enemy: <u>Power</u>!

"Power is the strongest of all enemies. And naturally the easiest thing to do is to give in; after all, the man is truly invincible. He commands; he begins by taking calculated risks, and ends in making rules, because he is a master.

"A man at this stage hardly notices his third enemy closing in on him. And suddenly, without knowing, he will certainly have lost the battle. His enemy will have turned him into a cruel, capricious man."

"Will he lose his power?"

"No, he will never lose his clarity or his power."

"What then will distinguish him from a man of knowledge?"

"A man who is defeated by power dies without really knowing how to handle it. Power is only a burden upon his fate. Such a man has no command over himself, and cannot tell when or how to use his power."

"Is the defeat by any of these enemies a final defeat?"

"Of course it is final. Once one of these enemies overpowers a man there is nothing he can do."

"Is it possible, for instance, that the man who is defeated by power may see his error and mend his ways?"

"No. Once a man gives in he is through."

"But what if he is temporarily blinded by power, and then refuses it?"

"That means his battle is still on. That means he is still trying to become a man of knowledge. A man is defeated only when he no longer tries, and abandons himself."

"But then, don Juan, it is possible that a man may abandon himself to fear for years, but finally conquer it."

"No, that is not true. If he gives in to fear he will never conquer it, because he will shy away from learning and never try again. But if he tries to learn for years in the midst of his fear, he will eventually conquer it because he will never have really abandoned himself to it."

"How can he defeat his third enemy, don Juan?"

"He has to defy it, deliberately. He has to come to realize the power he has seemingly conquered is in reality never his. He must keep himself in line at all times, handling carefully and faithfully all that he has learned. If he can see that clarity and power, without his control over himself, are worse than mistakes, he will reach a point where everything is held in check. He will <u>know then when and how to use his power</u>. And thus he will have defeated his third enemy.

"The man will be, by then, at the end of his journey of learning, and almost without warning he will come upon the last of his enemies: <u>Old</u>

age! This enemy is the cruelest of all, the one he won't be able to defeat completely, but only fight away.

"This is the time when a man has no more fears, no more impatient clarity of mind—a time when all his power is in check, but also the time when he has an unyielding desire to rest. If he gives in totally to his desire to lie down and forget, if he soothes himself in tiredness, he will have lost his last round, and his enemy will cut him down into a feeble old creature. His desire to retreat will overrule all his clarity, his power, and his knowledge.

"But if the man sloughs off his tiredness, and lives his fate through, he can then be called a man of knowledge, if only for the brief moment when he succeeds in fighting off his last, invincible enemy. That moment of clarity, power, and knowledge is enough."

Stephen Crane (1871–1900) wrote Maggie: A Girl of the Streets *when he was twenty-one and followed it two years later with his memorable* The Red Badge of Courage. *He was also a journalist and poet, and among his short stories are the often reprinted "The Open Boat" and "The Blue Hotel." The son of a minister and a college dropout, Crane was inclined toward love affairs, adventures, and disasters. Although he died at the age of twenty-eight, of tuberculosis and yellow fever, there are twelve volumes in* The Collected Works of Stephen Crane.

The wayfarer,
Perceiving the pathway to truth,
Was struck with astonishment.
It was thickly grown with weeds.
"Ha," he said,
"I see that none has passed here
In a long time."
Later he saw that each weed
Was a singular knife.
"Well," he mumbled at last,
"Doubtless there are other roads."

leo tolstoy   MY CONFESSION

Leo Tolstoy (1828–1910) did nothing in moderation. Not untypical is this entry from his diary: "I'm firmly resolved to dedicate my life to the service of my neighbors. For the last time I tell myself: 'If three days pass without my having done anything of service to people, I will kill myself.' " Tolstoy, however, was capable of breaking his resolutions as fervently as he made them. Passionate and brilliant, he threw himself into a wide variety of activities and causes. His interpretation of Christianity led him to think that wealth was a hindrance to the religious life, and his family had to fight his efforts to give away his possessions. In his last years, determined to practice his beliefs, he set out on various occasions dressed as a peasant and without money. It was on such an excursion, at the age of eighty-two, that he died in the house of a railroad station master.

Few lives are as well documented as Tolstoy's. For most of his life he kept remarkably candid diaries and journals. "My Confession," probably written in 1879, is an account of the great moral and spiritual crisis that arose in the middle of his life. That same crisis appeared only thinly disguised as fiction in the better known "Notes of a Madman" and in the frequently anthologized "The Death of Ivan Ilyich." While he was writing "My Confession," his wife recorded in her diary, "His eyes are fixed in a strange gaze, he scarcely talks, he has quite left this world and is absolutely incapable of thinking about everyday matters."

II. At some future time I may relate the story of my life, and dwell in detail on the pathetic and instructive incidents of my youth. I think that many and many have had the same experiences as I did. I desired with all my soul to be good; but I was young, I had passions, and I was alone, wholly alone, in my search after goodness. Every time I tried to express the longings of my heart to be morally good, I was met with contempt and ridicule, but as soon as I gave way to low passions, I was praised and encouraged.

Ambition, love of power, love of gain, lechery, pride, anger, vengeance, were held in high esteem.

As I gave way to these passions, I became like my elders, and I felt that they were satisfied with me. A kind-hearted aunt of mine, a really good woman with whom I lived, used to say to me that there was one thing above all others which she wished for me—an intrigue with a married woman: "*Rien ne forme un jeune homme, comme une liaison avec une femme comme il faut.*"[1] Another of her wishes for my happiness was that I should become an adjutant, and, if possible, to the Emperor; the greatest piece of good fortune of all she thought would be that I should find a very wealthy bride, who would bring me as her dowry as many slaves as could be.

[1] "Nothing shapes a young man more than a relationship with a real woman."

I cannot now recall those years without a painful feeling of horror and loathing.

I put men to death in war, I fought duels to slay others, I lost at cards, wasted my substance wrung from the sweat of peasants, punished the latter cruelly, rioted with loose women, and deceived men. Lying, robbery, adultery of all kinds, drunkenness, violence, murder. . . . There was not one crime which I did not commit, and yet I was not the less considered by my equals a comparatively moral man.

Such was my life during ten years. . . .

I grew disgusted with mankind and with myself, and I understood that this belief was a delusion. The strangest thing in all this was that, though I soon saw the falseness of this belief and renounced it, I did not renounce the rank given me by these men,—the rank of artist, poet, teacher. I was simple enough to imagine that I was a poet and artist, and could teach all men without knowing what I was teaching. But so I did.

By my companionship with these men I had gained a new vice,—a pride developed to a morbid extreme, and an insane self-confidence in teaching men what I myself did not know.

When I now think over that time, and remember my own state of mind and that of these men (a state of mind common enough among thousands still), it seems to me pitiful, terrible, and ridiculous; it excites the feelings which overcome us as we pass through a madhouse. . . .

It is now clear to me that between ourselves and the inhabitants of a madhouse there was no difference: at the time I only vaguely suspected this, and, like all madmen, thought all were mad except myself.

III. I lived in this senseless manner another six years, up to the time of my marriage. During this time I went abroad. My life in Europe, and my acquaintance with many eminent and learned foreigners, confirmed my belief in the doctrine of general perfectibility, as I found the same theory prevailed among them. This belief took the form which is common among most of the cultivated men of our day. This belief was expressed in the words "progress." It then appeared to me this word had a real meaning. I did not as yet understand that, tormented like every other man by the question, "How was I to live better?" when I answered that I must live for progress, I was only repeating the answer of a man carried away in a boat by the waves and the wind, who to the one important question for him, "Where are we to steer?" should answer, "We are being carried somewhere."

I did not see this then; only at rare intervals my feelings, and not my reason, were roused against the common superstition of our age, which leads men to ignore their own ignorance of life.

Thus, during my stay in Paris, the sight of a public execution revealed to me the weakness of my superstitious belief in progress. When I saw the head divided from the body, and heard the sound with which they fell separately into the box, I understood, not with my reason, but with my whole being, that no theory of the wisdom of all established things, nor of progress, could justify such an act; and that if all the men in the world from the day of creation, by whatever theory, had found this thing necessary, I knew it was not necessary, it was a bad thing, and that therefore I must judge of what was right and necessary, not by what men said and did, not by progress, but what I felt to be true in my heart.

Another instance of the insufficiency of this superstition of progress as a rule for life was the death of my brother. He fell ill while still young, suffered much during a whole year, and died in great pain. He was a man of good abilities, of a kind heart, and of a serious temper, but he died without understanding why he had lived, and still less what his death meant for him. No theories could give an answer to these questions, either to him or to me, during the whole period of his long and painful lingering.

But these occasions for doubt were few and far between; on the whole, I continued to live in the profession of the faith of progress. "Everything develops, and I myself am developing; and why this is so will one day be apparent," was the formula I was obliged to adopt. . . .

I believed that I had found a solution abroad, and, armed with all the essence of wisdom, I returned to Russia, the same year in which the peasants were freed from serfdom; and, accepting the office of arbitrator, I began to teach the uneducated people in the schools, and the educated classes in the journal which I began to publish. Things seemed to be going on well, but I felt that my mind was not in a normal state and that a change was near. I might even then, perhaps, have come to that state of despair to which I was brought fifteen years later, if it had not been for a new experience in life which promised me safety—family life.

For a year I was occupied with arbitration, with the schools, and with my newspaper, and got so involved that I was harassed to death; the struggle over the arbitration was so hard for me, my activity in the schools was so dubious to me, my shuffling in the newspaper became so repugnant to me, consisting as it did in forever the same thing,—in the desire to teach all people and to hide the fact that I did not know how or what to teach,—that I fell ill, more with mental than physical sickness, gave up everything, and started for the steppes to the Bashkirs to breathe a fresher air, to drink kumiss, and live an animal life.

After I returned I married. The new circumstances of a happy family life completely led me away from the search after the meaning of life as a whole. My life was concentrated at this time in my family, my wife and children, and consequently in the care for increasing the means of life. The effort to effect my own individual perfection, already replaced by the striving after general progress, was again changed into an effort to secure the particular happiness of my family.

In this way fifteen years passed.

Notwithstanding that during these fifteen years I looked upon the craft of authorship as a very trifling thing, I continued all the time to write. I had experienced the seductions of authorship, the temptations of an enormous pecuniary reward and of great applause for valueless work, and gave myself up to it as a means of improving my material position, and of stifling in my soul all questions regarding my own life and life in general. In my writings I taught what for me was the only truth,—that the object of life should be our highest happiness and that of our family.

Thus I lived; but, five years ago, a strange state of mind began to grow upon me: I had moments of perplexity, of a stoppage, as it were, of life, as if I did not know how I was to live, what I was to do, and I began to wander, and was a victim to low spirits. But this passed, and I continued to live as before. Later, these periods of perplexity began to return more and more frequently, and invariably took the same form. These stoppages of life always presented themselves to me with the same questions: "Why?" and "What after?"

At first it seemed to me that these were aimless, unmeaning questions; it seemed to me that all they asked about was well known, and that if at any time when I wished to find answers to them I could do so without much trouble—that just at that time I could not be bothered with this, but whenever I should stop to think them over I should find an answer. But these questions presented themselves to my mind with ever increasing frequency, demanding an answer with still greater and greater persistence, and like dots grouped themselves into one black spot.

It was with me as it happens in the case of every mortal internal ailment— at first appear the insignificant symptoms of indisposition, disregarded by the patient; then these symptoms are repeated more and more frequently, till they merge in uninterrupted suffering. The sufferings increase, and the patient, before he has time to look around, is confronted with the fact that what he took for a mere indisposition has become more important to him than anything else on earth, that it is death!

This is exactly what happened to me. I became aware that this was not a chance indisposition, but something very serious, and that if all these questions continued to recur, I should have to find an answer to them. And I tried to answer them. The questions seemed so foolish, so simple, so childish; but no sooner had I taken hold of them and attempted to decide them than I was convinced, first, that they were neither childish nor silly, but were concerned with the deepest problems of life; and, in the second place, that I could not decide them—could not decide them, however I put my mind upon them.

Before occupying myself with my Samara estate, with the education of my son, with the writing of books, I was bound to know why I did these things. As long as I do not know the reason "why" I cannot do anything, I cannot live. While thinking about the management of my household and estate, which in these days occupied much of my time, suddenly this question came into my head:—

"Well and good, I have now six thousand desyatins in the government of Samara, and three hundred horses—what then?"

I was perfectly disconcerted, and knew not what to think. Another time, dwelling on the thought of how I should educate my children, I asked myself, "Why?" Again, when considering by what means the well-being of the people might best be promoted, I suddenly exclaimed, "But what concern have I with it?" When I thought of the fame which my works were gaining me, I said to myself:—

"Well, what if I should be more famous than Gogol, Pushkin, Shakespear, Molière—than all the writers of the world—well, and what then?". . . .

I could find no reply. Such questions will not wait: they demand an immediate answer; without one it is impossible to live; but answer there was none.

I felt that the ground on which I stood was crumbling, that there was nothing for me to stand on, that what I had been living for was nothing, that I had no reason for living.

IV. My life had come to a stop. I was able to breathe, to eat, to drink, to sleep, and I could not help breathing, eating, drinking, sleeping; but there was no real life in me because I had not a single desire, the fulfilment of which I could feel to be reasonable. If I wished for anything, I knew beforehand that, were I to satisfy the wish, or were I not to satisfy it, nothing would come of it. Had a fairy appeared and offered me all I desired, I should not have known what to say. If I had, in moments of excitement, I will not say wishes, but the habits of former wishes, at calmer moments I knew that it was a delusion, that I really wished for nothing. I could not even wish to know the truth, because I guessed in what it consisted.

The truth was, that life was meaningless. Every day of life, every step in it, brought me, as it were, nearer the precipice, and I saw clearly that before me there was nothing but ruin. And to stop was impossible; to go back was impossible; and it was impossible to shut my eyes so as not to see that there was nothing before me but suffering and actual death, absolute annihilation.

Thus I, a healthy and a happy man, was brought to feel that I could live no longer,—some irresistible force was dragging me onward to escape from life. I do not mean that I wanted to kill myself.

The force that drew me away from life was stronger, fuller, and more universal than any wish; it was a force like that of my previous attachment to life, only in a contrary direction. With all my force I struggled away from life. The idea of suicide came as naturally to me as formerly that of bettering my life. This thought was so attractive to me that I was compelled to practise upon myself a species of self-deception in order to avoid carrying it out too hastily. I was unwilling to act hastily, only because I wanted to employ all my powers in clearing away the confusion of my thoughts; if I should not clear them away, I could at any time kill myself. And here was I, a man fortunately situated, hiding away a cord, to avoid being tempted to hang myself by it to the transom between the closets of my room, where I undressed alone every evening; and I ceased to go hunting with a gun because it offered too easy a way of getting rid of life. I knew not what I wanted; I was afraid of life; I struggled to get away from it, and yet there *was* something I hoped for from it.

Such was the condition I had to come to, at a time when all the circumstances of my life were preeminently happy ones, and when I had not reached my fiftieth year. I had a good, loving, and beloved wife, good children, and a large estate, which, without much trouble on my part, was growing and increasing; I was more than ever respected by my friends and acquaintances; I was praised by strangers, and could lay claim to having made my name famous without much self-deception. Moreover, I was not mad or in an unhealthy mental state; on the contrary, I enjoyed a mental and physical strength which I have seldom found in men of my class and pursuits; I could keep up with a peasant in mowing, and could continue mental labor for eight or ten hours at a stretch, without any evil consequences. And in this state of things it came to this—that I could not live, and as I feared death I was obliged to employ ruses against myself so as not to put an end to my life.

The mental state in which I then was seemed to me summed up in the following: My life was a foolish and wicked joke played on me by some one. Notwithstanding the fact that I did not recognize a "Some one," who may have created me, this conclusion that some one had wickedly and foolishly made a joke of me in bringing me into the world seemed to me the most natural of all conclusions.

I could not help reasoning that *there*, somewhere, is some one who is now diverting himself at my expense, as he watches me, as after from thirty to forty years of a life of study and development, of mental and bodily growth, with all my powers matured and having reached that summit of life from which it is seen in its completeness, I stand like a fool on this height, understanding clearly that there is nothing in life, that there never was anything, and never will be. To him it must seem ridiculous.

But whether there is, or is not, such a being, in either case it did not help me. I could not attribute a reasonable motive to any single act in my whole life. I was only astonished that I could not have realized this at the very beginning. All this had so long been known to me! Illness and death would come (indeed, they had come), if not to-day, then to-morrow, to those whom I loved, to myself, and nothing remains but stench and worms. All my acts, whatever I did, would sooner or later be forgotten, and I myself be nowhere. Why, then, busy one's self with anything? How could men fail to see this, and live? How wonderful this is! It is possible to live only as long as life intoxicates us; as soon as we are sober again we see that it is all a delusion, and a stupid delusion! In this, indeed, there is nothing either ludicrous or amusing; it is only cruel and stupid!

There is an old Eastern fable about a traveler in the steppes who is attacked by a furious wild beast. To save himself the traveler gets into a waterless well; but at the bottom of it he sees a dragon with its jaws wide open to devour him. The unhappy man dares not get out for fear of the wild beast, and dares not descend for fear of the dragon, so he catches hold of the branch of a wild plant growing in a crevice of the well. His arms grow tired, and he feels that he must soon perish, death awaiting him on either side, but he still holds on; and he sees two mice, one black and one white, gradually making their way round the stem of the wild plant on which he is hanging, nibbling it through. The plant will soon give way and break off, and he will fall into the jaws of the dragon. The traveler sees this, and knows that he must inevitably perish; but, while still hanging, he looks around him, and, finding some drops of honey on the leaves of the wild plant, he stretches out his tongue and licks them.

Thus do I cling to the branch of life, knowing that the dragon of death inevitably awaits me, ready to tear me to pieces, and I cannot understand why such tortures have fallen to my lot. I also strive to suck the honey which once comforted me, but this honey no longer rejoices me, while the white mouse and the black, day and night, gnaw through the branch to which I cling. I see the dragon plainly, and the honey is no longer sweet. I see the dragon, from which there is no escape, and the mice, and I cannot turn my eyes away from them. It is no fable, but a living, undeniable truth, to be understood of all men.

The former delusion of happiness in life which hid from me the horror of the dragon no longer deceives me. However I may reason with myself that I cannot understand the meaning of life, that I must live without thinking, I cannot do this, because I have done so too long already. Now I cannot help seeing the days and nights hurrying by and bringing me nearer to death. I can see but this, because this alone is true—all the rest is a lie. The two drops of honey, which more than anything else drew my eyes away from the cruel truth, my love for my family and for my writings, to which latter I gave the name of art, were no longer sweet to me.

"My family," I said to myself; "but a family—a wife and children—are also human beings, and subject to the same conditions as I myself; they must either be living in a lie, or they must see the terrible truth. Why should they live? Why should I love them, care for them, bring them up, and watch over them? To bring them to the despair which fills myself, or to make dolts of them? As I love them, I cannot conceal from them the truth—every step they take in knowledge leads them to it, and that truth is death."

"Art, poetry?". . . .

Under the influence of success, and flattered by praise, I had long been persuading myself that this was a work which must be done notwithstanding the approach of death, which would destroy everything—my writings, and the memory of them; but I soon saw that this was only another delusion, I saw clearly that art is only the ornament and charm of life. Life having lost its charm for me, how could I make others see a charm in it? While I was not living my own life, but one that was external to me was bearing me away on its billows, while I believed that life had a meaning, though I could not say what it was, the reflections of life of every kind in poetry and art gave me delight; it was pleasant to me to look at life in the mirror of art; but when I tried to discover the meaning of life, when I felt the necessity of living myself, the mirror became either unnecessary, superfluous, and ridiculous, or painful. I could no longer take comfort from what I saw in the mirror— that my position was stupid and desperate.

It was a genuine cause of rejoicing when in the depths of my soul I believed that my life had a meaning. Then this play of lights, the comic, the tragic, the pathetic, the beautiful, and the terrible in life, amused me. But when I knew that life was meaningless and terrible, the play in the mirror could no longer entertain me. No sweetness could be sweet to me when I saw the dragon, and the mice nibbling away my support.

Nor was that all. Had I simply come to know that life has no meaning, I might have quietly accepted it, I might have known that was my allotted portion. But I could not rest calmly on this. Had I been like a man living in a forest, out of which he knows that there is no issue, I could have lived on; but I was like a man lost in a forest, and who, terrified by the thought that he is lost, rushes about trying to find a way out, and, though he knows each step leads him still farther astray, cannot help rushing about.

It was this that was terrible! And to get free from this horror, I was ready to kill myself. I felt a horror of what awaited me; I knew that this horror was more horrible than the position itself, but I could not patiently await the end. However persuasive the argument might be that all the same a blood-vessel in the heart would be ruptured or something would burst and all be over, still I could not patiently await the end. The horror of the darkness was too great to bear, and I longed to free myself from it as speedily as possible by a rope or a pistol ball. This was the feeling that, above all, drew me to think of suicide.

V. "But it is possible that I have overlooked something, that I have failed to understand something," I asked myself; "may it not be that this state of despair is common among men?"

And in every branch of human knowledge I sought an explanation of the questions that tormented me; I sought that explanation painfully and long, not out of mere curiosity; I did not seek it indolently, but painfully, obstinately, day and night; I sought it as a perishing man seeks safety, and I found nothing.

I sought it in all branches of knowledge, and not only did I fail, but, moreover, I convinced myself that all those who had searched like myself had likewise found nothing; and not only had found nothing, but had come, as I had, to the despairing conviction, that the only absolute knowledge man can possess is this,—that life is without meaning.

I sought in all directions, and thanks to a life spent in study, and also to my connections with the learned world, the most accomplished scholars in all the various branches of knowledge were accessible to me, and they did not refuse to open to me all the sources of knowledge both in books and through personal intercourse. I knew all that learning could answer to the question, "What is life?"

It was long before I could believe that human learning had no clear answer to this question. For a long time it seemed to me, as I listened to the gravity and seriousness of tone wherewith Science affirmed its positions on matters unconnected with the problem of life, that I must have misunderstood something. For a long time I was timid in the presence in learning, and I fancied that the insufficiency of the answers which I received was not its fault, but was owing to my own gross ignorance; but this thing was not a joke or pastime with me, but the business of my life, and I was at last forced, willy-nilly, to the conclusion that these questions of mine were the only legitimate questions underlying all knowledge, and that it was not I that was in fault in putting them, but science in pretending to have an answer to them.

The question, which in my fiftieth year had brought me to the notion of suicide, was the simplest of all questions, lying in the soul of every man, from the undeveloped child to wisest sage; a question without which, as I had myself experienced, life was impossible. That question was as follows:—

"What will come from what I am doing now, and may do to-morrow? what will come from my whole life?"

Otherwise expressed, the question will be this:—

"Why should I live? why should I wish for anything? why should I do anything?"

Again, in other words, it is:—

"Is there any meaning in my life which will not be destroyed by the inevitable death awaiting me?"

w. h. auden   THE UNKNOWN CITIZEN

*Wystan Hugh Auden (1907–   ), born in England and Oxford-educated,
came to the United States in 1939 and became an American citizen in 1946.
His earlier work expressed a concern for political and social problems (he drove
an ambulance for the Spanish Loyalists during the Civil War), while his later
work turned more frequently to religious and philosophical themes. Among his
many honors are the King's Gold Medal, the Award of Merit from the American
Academy of Arts and Letters, and, in 1947, the Pulitzer Prize for* The Age of
Anxiety.

(To JS/07/M/378 This Marble Monument Is Erected by the State)

He was found by the Bureau of Statistics to be
One against whom there was no official complaint,
And all the reports on his conduct agree
That, in the modern sense of an old-fashioned word, he was a saint,
For in everything he did he served the Greater Community.
Except for the War till the day he retired
He worked in a factory and never got fired,
But satisfied his employers, Fudge Motors Inc.
Yet he wasn't a scab or odd in his views,
For his Union reports that he paid his dues,
(Our report on his Union shows it was sound)
And our Social Psychology workers found
That he was popular with his mates and liked a drink.
The Press are convinced that he bought a paper every day
And that his reactions to advertisements were normal in every way.
Policies taken out in his name prove that he was fully insured,
And his Health-card shows he was once in hospital but left it cured.
Both Producers Research and High-Grade Living declare
He was fully sensible to the advantages of the Installment Plan
And had everything necessary to Modern Man,
A phonograph, a radio, a car and a frigidaire.
Our researchers into Public Opinion are content
That he held the proper opinions for the time of year;
When there was peace, he was for peace; when there was war, he went.
He was married and added five children to the population,
Which our Eugenist says was the right number for a parent of his
    generation,
And our teachers report that he never interfered with their education.
Was he free? Was he happy? The question is absurd:
Had anything been wrong, we certainly should have heard.

Erich Fromm (1900–   ) studied sociology in preparation for his psycho-analytic training; he received his doctorate from Heidelberg in 1922. He fled his native Germany and Hitler in the 1930's and has since taught at a number of major universities. A prolific and immensely popular writer with a wide range of interests, he is the author of Escape from Freedom, The Art of Loving, The Sane Society, Psychology and Religion, May Man Prevail?, Beyond the Chains of Illusion, The Heart of Man, The Forgotten Language, *and* Sigmund Freud's Mission. *The following excerpt is from* Man for Himself (1947).

Self-awareness, reason, and imagination have disrupted the "harmony" which characterizes animal existence. Their emergence has made man into an anomaly, into the freak of the universe. He is part of nature, subject to her physical laws and unable to change them, yet he transcends the rest of nature. He is set apart while being a part; he is homeless, yet chained to the home he shares with all creatures. Cast into this world at an accidental place and time, he is forced out of it, again accidentally. Being aware of himself, he realizes his powerlessness and the limitations of his existence. He visualizes his own end: death. Never is he free from the dichotomy of his existence: he cannot rid himself of his mind, even if he should want to; he cannot rid himself of his body as long as he is alive—and his body makes him want to be alive.

Reason, man's blessing, is also his curse; it forces him to cope everlastingly with the task of solving an insoluble dichotomy. Human existence is different in this respect from that of all other organisms; it is in a state of constant and unavoidable disequilibrium. Man's life cannot "be lived" by repeating the pattern of his species; *he* must live. Man is the only animal that can be *bored,* that can be *discontented,* that can feel evicted from paradise. Man is the only animal for whom his own existence is a problem which he has to solve and from which he cannot escape. He cannot go back to the pre-human state of harmony with nature; he must proceed to develop his reason until he becomes the master of nature, and of himself.

p. d. ouspensky   YOGA AND SELF-KNOWLEDGE

Peter Demianovitch Ouspensky (1878–1947) was born in Moscow but left Russia at the time of the Revolution. He went to England in 1921, where he lived out his life writing and teaching. His education had been acquired from varied Eastern sources; as a matter of principle, he took no examinations and held no degrees. A decisive influence on him was his years of study under the Russian mystic Gurdjieff. Ouspensky is the author of Tertium Organum: The Third Canon of Thought, In Search of the Miraculous: Fragments of an Unknown Learning, *and* The Psychology of Man's Possible Evolution. *"Yoga and Self-Knowledge" is from* A New Model of the Universe (1931).

THE MYSTERY OF THE EAST

For the West the East has always been the land of mystery and enigmas. About India in particular many legends and fantastic tales have existed and still exist, chiefly about the mysterious knowledge of Indian sages, philosophers, fakirs and saints.

Indeed many facts have long since shown that apart from the knowledge contained in the ancient books of India, in its holy scriptures, legends, songs, poems and myths, there exists certain other knowledge which cannot be drawn from books and which is not revealed openly, but traces of which are quite clearly seen.

It is impossible to deny that the philosophy and the religions of India contain inexhaustible sources of thought. And European philosophy has made and is making wide use of these sources, but strangely enough it can never take from them what is most important and most essential in them.

This fact has been realised by many Europeans who have studied the religious and philosophical teachings of the East. They have felt that they receive from the books not all that the Indians know, and this feeling has strengthened the idea that besides the knowledge contained in books there exists another, a secret, knowledge, concealed from the "uninitiated," or that besides the known books there are others, kept hidden, containing the "secret teaching."

A great deal of energy and time has been spent on the search for this secret doctrine of the East. And there is good ground for believing that in fact there exist not only one, but many doctrines unknown to the West, which grow from one general root.

But apart from *doctrines,* known and unknown, there exist also a number of systems of self-discipline which are known under the name of *Yoga.*

The word Yoga can be translated by the word *unity* or *union* or *subjugation;* in the first meaning it corresponds to the word "harnessing," from the Sanskrit word *yug,* to which correspond the English word *yoke* and the Russian *eego.*

One of the meanings of the word "Yoga" is "right action."

To follow Yoga means to subjugate to the control of one or another system of Yoga thought, feeling, internal and external movements, etc., that is, the functions, most of which ordinarily work without control.

"Yogis," is the name given to those who live and act according to "Yoga." These are men who pass or have passed through a certain school and live according to rules that are known only to themselves and are incomprehensible to the uninitiated, and according to knowledge which infinitely increases their powers as compared with the powers of ordinary men.

There are many tales and beliefs about "Yogis"; sometimes they are said to be mystics leading a life of contemplation, indifferent to food and clothing; at other times, to be men possessing miraculous powers, able to see and hear at a distance, men whom wild beasts and the forces of nature obey. These powers and capacities are acquired by methods and exercises which constitute the secret of Yoga and which enable Yogis to understand people and to act rightly and expediently in all circumstances and on all occasions in life.

Yogis have nothing in common with "fakirs," that is, with men who endeavour to subjugate the physical body to the will by the way of suffering, and who are very often ignorant fanatics torturing themselves in order to attain heavenly beatitude or conjurors who for money perform "miracles," which are based upon skill, patience and the accustoming of the body to assume incredible postures or to exercise its functions in an abnormal way.

These conjurors and fakirs often call themselves Yogis, but a true Yogi can always be recognised, for he can never have the fanaticism and frenzied sectarianism of fakirs; he will display nothing for payment, and above all he will possess knowledge surpassing the knowledge of ordinary men.

"The science of Yogis," that is, the methods used by Yogis for the development in themselves of extraordinary powers and capacities, comes from remote antiquity. Thousands of years ago the sages of ancient India knew that the powers of man in all the spheres and provinces of his activity can be greatly increased by means of right training and by accustoming man to control his body, mind, attention, will, emotions and desires.

In connection with this the study of man in ancient India was on a level quite inconceivable to us. This can only be explained by the fact that the philosophical schools existing at that time were directly connected with esoteric schools.

Man was considered not as a completed entity, but as containing in himself a multitude of latent powers. The idea was that in ordinary life and in ordinary man these powers are dormant but can be awakened and developed by means of a certain mode of life, by certain exercises, by certain work upon oneself. This is what is called Yoga. An acquaintance with the ideas of Yoga enables man first to know himself better, to understand his latent capacities and inclinations, to find out and determine the direction in which they ought to be developed; and second, to awaken his latent capacities and learn how to use them in all paths of life.

"The science of Yogis," or, to put it more correctly, the cycle of the sciences of Yogis, consists in descriptions of these methods, adapted to men of different types and different activities in life, and also in the exposition of the theories connected with these methods.

Each of the "sciences" composing Yoga falls into two parts: the theoretical part and the practical part.

The theoretical part aims at setting forth the fundamental principles and general outline of the given subject as a complete and connected whole, without descending into unnecessary details.

The practical part teaches the methods and ways of the best training for the desired activity, the methods and means of development of latent powers and capacities.

It is necessary to mention here that even the theoretical part can never really be learned from books. Books can at best serve as synopses only for the purpose of repetition and for remembering, while the study of the ideas of Yoga requires direct oral tuition and explanation.

As regards the practical part, very little of it can be expounded in writing. Consequently even if there are books containing attempts at an exposition of the practical methods of Yoga, they cannot possibly serve as a manual for practical and independent work.

In general, in speaking about Yoga it is necessary to point out that the relationship between its practical and theoretical parts is analogous to the relationship between practical and theoretical sides in art. There exists a theory of painting, but the study of the theory of painting does not enable one to paint pictures. There exists a theory of music, but the study of the theory of music will not enable one to play any musical instrument.

In the practice of art as in the practice of Yoga there is something which does not exist and cannot exist in the theory. Practice is not built up according to theory. Theory is derived from practice.

The sciences of Yoga in India were for a long time kept secret, and these methods, which increase the power of man in an almost miraculous way, were the privilege of special schools or the secret of ascetics and hermits who had completely renounced the world. In Indian temples (or in connection with them) there were schools where the pupils, *Chelas*, who had traversed a long path of tests and preparatory education, were initiated into the science of the Yogis by special teachers, *Gurus*. Europeans were unable to obtain any information about Yoga, and what was usually related by travellers concerning this question bore a purely fantastic character.

The first correct information about Yoga began to appear only in the second half of the 19th century, though many methods of Yogis were known in mystical societies much earlier.

But though Europeans had borrowed a great deal from the Yogis, they were nevertheless unable to understand and realise all the significance of the "sciences of Yogis" taken as a whole.

In reality *Yoga is the key to all the ancient wisdom of the East.*

The ancient books of India cannot be comprehensible to Western scientists. That is because all these books were written by *Yogis*, that is, by men possessing not merely a developed intellect, but powers and capacities infinitely surpassing the powers and capacities of an ordinary man.

The powers which Yoga gives are not limited to the strengthening of the capacity of understanding. Yoga increases the creative capacity of man in all the spheres and domains of life, gives him the possibility of *direct* penetration into the mysteries of nature, discloses to him the secrets of eternity and the enigmas of existence.

At the same time Yoga increases the powers of man, first, for the struggle with life, that is, with all the physical conditions in which man is born and which are all hostile to him; second, for the struggle with Nature, who always wishes to use man for her own ends; and third, for the struggle with the illusions of his own consciousness, which being dependent on his limited psychic apparatus, creates an enormous number of mirages and delusions. Yoga helps man to struggle against the deception of words, shows him clearly that a thought expressed in words cannot be true, that there can be no truth in words, that at best they can only hint at truth, reveal it for a moment and then hide it. Yoga teaches the way to find the hidden truth concealed in things, in the actions of men, in the writings of great sages of all times and peoples.

Yoga falls into five divisions:

1. Raja-Yoga or the Yoga of the development of consciousness.
2. Jnana-Yoga (Gnyana or Gnana-Yoga), the Yoga of knowledge.
3. Karma-Yoga or the Yoga of right actions.
4. Hatha-Yoga, the Yoga of power over the body.

5. Bhakti-Yoga, the Yoga of right religious action.

The five Yogas are five paths leading to the same goal: to perfection, to the transition to higher levels of knowledge and life.

The divisions of the five Yogas depends on the division of types of man, his capacities, preparation, and so on. One man can begin with contemplation, with the study of his own "I." Another needs the objective study of nature. A third must first of all understand the rules of conduct in ordinary life. For a fourth before anything else it is necessary to acquire control over the physical body. For a fifth it is necessary to "learn to pray," to understand his religious feelings and to learn how to govern them.

Yoga teaches the way to do rightly everything that man does. Only by studying Yoga can man see how wrongly he has acted on all occasions in his life; how much of his strength he has spent quite uselessly, attaining only the poorest results with an enormous expenditure of energy.

Yoga teaches man the principles of the right economy of forces. It teaches him to be able to do whatever he does, consciously, *when this is necessary*. This immeasurably increases man's powers and improves the results of his work.

The study of Yoga first of all shows man how greatly he has been mistaken about himself.

Man becomes convinced that he is far weaker and much more insignificant than he has considered himself to be, and at the same time that he can become stronger and more powerful than the strongest and most powerful man he can imagine.

He sees not only what he is, but what he may become. His conception of life, of man's place, rôle and purpose in life, undergoes a complete change. He loses the feeling of separateness, and the feeling of the senseless and chaotic nature of life. He begins to understand his aim and to see that his pursuit of this aim brings him into contact with other people going in the same direction.

Yoga does not seek, as its primary object, to guide man. Yoga only increases his powers in any of the directions of his activity. But at the same time, in using the powers given by Yoga man can follow one direction only. Should he change this direction, Yoga itself will turn against him, will stop him, will deprive him of all powers, and may possibly even destroy him altogether. Yoga carries enormous power, but this power can be used only in a certain direction. This is a law which becomes clear to any one who studies Yoga.

In everything it touches Yoga teaches man to discriminate between the real and the false, and this capacity for proper discrimination helps man to find hidden truths where hitherto he had seen or supposed nothing hidden.

When a man studying Yoga takes up certain books which he thought he knew quite well, to his profound astonishment he suddenly finds in them an infinite amount that is new. Some hidden depth seems to be revealed to him in these books, and with surprise and awe he feels this depth and understands that until now he has seen nothing but the surface.

Such an effect is produced by many books belonging to the holy scriptures of India. There is no necessity for these books to be kept hidden. They may be accessiblle to all and yet hidden from all except those who know how to read them. And such hidden books exist in all countries and among all peoples. One of the most occult books, the New Testament, is the most widely known. But of all books this is the one people least know how to read, the one they most distort in their understanding of it.

Yoga teaches how to search for truth and how to find truth in everything. It teaches that there is nothing that could not serve as a starting point for the finding of truth.

Yoga is not accessible all at once in its entirety. It has many degrees of varying difficulty. This is the first thing to be realised by anyone who wishes to study Yoga.

The limits of Yoga cannot be seen all at once or from a distance at the beginning of the way. For the man who studies Yoga new horizons open before him as he continues on his way. Each new step shows him something new ahead, something that he has not seen and could not have seen before. But a man cannot see very far ahead. And at the beginning of the study of Yoga he cannot know all that this study will give. Yoga is an entirely new way, and on entering upon it it is impossible to know where it will lead.

To put it in another way, Yoga cannot be defined as one can define what medicine is, what chemistry is, what mathematics is. In order to define what Yoga is, study and *knowledge* of Yoga are necessary.

Yoga is a closed door. Anyone may knock if he wishes to enter. But until he has entered he cannot know what he will find behind this door.

A man who enters the path of Yoga with the aim of reaching its summits must give himself up entirely to Yoga, give to Yoga all his time and all his energy, all his thoughts, feelings and motives. He must endeavour to harmonise himself, to achieve an inner unity, *to create in himself a permanent "I,"* to protect himself from continual strivings, moods and desires, which sway him now in one direction, now in another. He must compel all his powers to serve one aim. Yoga demands all this, but it also helps to attain it by showing the means and methods by which it can be reached. For every kind of activity there are special conditions which are favourable to it and which Yoga helps to define.

The study of Yoga is impossible in the scattered condition of thoughts, desires and feelings amidst which an ordinary man lives. Yoga demands the whole of man, the whole of his time, all his energy, all his thoughts, all his feelings, the whole of his life. Only Karma-Yoga allows man to remain in the conditions of his ordinary life. All the other Yogas demand immediate and complete withdrawal from life, *even if only for a certain time*. The study of Yogas, with the exception of Karma-Yoga, is impossible in life circumstances. Equally impossible is the study of Yoga without a teacher, without his constant and incessant watch over the pupil.

A man who hopes to know Yoga by reading a few books will be greatly disappointed. In a book, in written exposition, it is impossible to transmit to a man any practical knowledge—everything depends on the work of the teacher upon him and on his own work upon himself.

The common aim of all the forms of Yoga is the changing of man, the broadening of his consciousness. At the basis of all the Yogas there lies one principle, which is that man as he is born and lives in an uncompleted and imperfect being, but one who can be altered and brought to the development possible to him by means of suitable instruction and training.

From the point of view of the principles of Yoga man is simply material upon which it is possible and necessary to work.

This refers first of all to man's inner world, to his consciousness, his psychic apparatus, his mental capacities, his knowledge, which according to the teachings of Yogis can be completely changed, freed from all the usual limitations and strengthened to a degree surpassing all imagination. As a result, man acquires new possibilities of knowing the truth and new powers for surmounting obstacles on his way, no matter whence these obstacles arise. Further, it refers to the physical body of man, which is studied and gradually subjected to the control of mind and consciousness, even in those of its functions of which man is not usually aware in himself at all.

The opening up of higher consciousness is the aim of all the Yogas.

Following the way of Yoga a man must reach the state of samadhi, that is, of ecstasy or enlightenment, in which alone truth can be understood. . . .

RAJA-YOGA

Raja-Yoga is the Yoga of the education of consciousness. The man who studies Raja-Yoga practically, acquires consciousness of his "I." At the same time he acquires extraordinary inner powers, control over himself and the capacity to influence other people.

Raja-Yoga in relation to the psychic world of man, to his self-consciousness, has the same meaning as Hatha-Yoga has in relation to the physical world. Hatha-Yoga is the Yoga of the overcoming of the body, the acquiring of control over the body and its functions; Raja-Yoga is the Yoga of the overcoming of the illusory and erroneous self-consciousness of man and of the acquiring of control over consciousness.

Raja-Yoga teaches man that which constitutes the basis of the philosophy of the whole world—*knowledge of himself*.

Just as Hatha-Yoga regards the physical body as imperfect but capable of being changed for the better, so Raja-Yoga regards the psychic apparatus of man as being far from ideal, but capable of being set right and improved.

The task of Raja-Yoga is the "placing of consciousness," which is completely analogous to the "placing of the voice" in singing. Ordinary Western thought does not in the least realise the necessity of "placing the consciousness," finds in general that ordinary consciousness is quite sufficient, and that man can have nothing else.

Raja-Yoga establishes that consciousness, like a powerful voice, requires proper "placing," which would multiply its power and quality tenfold, increase its efficiency, make it "sound better," reproduce better, reconstruct the interrelation of ideas, embrace more at one time.

The first assertion of Raja-Yoga is that man does not know himself at all, has a completely false, distorted idea of himself.

This lack of understanding of himself is man's chief difficulty on his way, the chief cause of his weakness. If we imagine a man who does not know his body, does not know the parts of his body, their number and relative position, does not know that he has two arms, two legs, one head and so on, it will give an exact illustration of our position in relation to our psychic world.

From the point of view of Raja-Yoga man's psychic apparatus is a system of darkened and crooked lenses through which his consciousness looks upon the world and upon itself, receiving a picture which in no way corresponds to the reality. The chief defect of the psychic apparatus is that it makes man accept as separate that which it shows as separate. A man who believes in his his psychic apparatus is a man who believes in the field of view of the binoculars through which he looks, in the full conviction that what enters the field of view of his binoculars at that moment exists separately from that which does not enter it.

The new self-knowledge is attained in Raja-Yoga through a study of the principles of man's psychic world and through a long series of exercises of the consciousness.

A study of the principles of psychic life shows man the four states of consciousness possible for him, which in the usual Indian psychology are called:
deep sleep,
sleep with dreams,
waking state,
Turiya or the state of enlightenment.

(In esoteric teachings these states of consciousness are defined somewhat

69

differently, but they remain four and their mutual relations remain near to the above.)

After this follows the study of psychic functions, thinking, feeling, sensing and so on, both separately and in their relation to each other; the study of dreams, the study of semi-conscious and unconscious psychic processes, the study of illusions and self-deceptions, the study of various forms of self-hypnosis and self-suggestion, *with the object of freeing oneself from them.*

One of the first practical tasks set before a man who begins to study Raja-Yoga is the attainment of the ability to stop thoughts, the capacity *not to think,* that is, entirely to stop the mind at will, to give a complete rest to the psychic apparatus.

This ability to stop thought is regarded as a necessary condition for awakening certain powers and possibilities latent within man, and as a necessary condition for subordinating the unconscious psychic processes to the will. Only when a man has created in himself this capacity for stopping the flow of his thoughts can he approach the possibility of hearing the thoughts of other people, and all the voices which incessantly speak in nature, the voices of various "small lives," which are component parts of himself, and the voices of "big lives," of which he is a component part. Only when he has acquired the capacity to create a passive state of his mind can a man hope to hear the *voice of the silence,* which alone can reveal to him the truths and secrets hidden from him.

Moreover (and this is the first thing that is attained), in learning to stop thinking at will man acquires the power of reducing the useless expenditure of psychic energy consumed in unnecessary thinking. Unnecessary thinking is one of the chief evils of our inner life. How often it happens that some thought gets into our mind, and the mind, having no power to throw it out, turns the thought over and over endlessly, just as a stream turns a stone over and over in its bed.

This happens especially when a man is agitated or annoyed or hurt, is afraid of something, is suspicious of something, and so on. And people do not realise what an enormous amount of energy is spent on this unnecessary turning over in the mind of the same thoughts, of the same words. People do not realise that a man, without noticing it, may repeat many thousand times in the course of an hour or two some silly sentence or fragment of verse, which has stuck in his mind without any reason.

When the "disciple" has learned *not to think,* he is taught to *think*—to think of what he wants to think of, and not of anything that comes into his head. This is a method of concentration. Complete concentration of mind on one subject and the capacity for not thinking of anything else at the same time, the capacity for not being drawn aside by accidental associations, give a man enormous powers. He can then force himself not only to think, but also not to feel, not to hear, not to see anything happening around him; he can avoid having the sensation of any kind of physical discomfort, either of heat or of cold or of suffering; he is able by a single effort to make himself insensible to any pain, even the most terrible. This explains one of the theories that Hatha-Yoga becomes easy after Raja-Yoga.

The next step, the third, is meditation. The man who has studied concentration is taught to use it, that is, to meditate, to enter deeply into a given question, to examine its different sides one after another, to find in it correlations and analogies with everything he knows, everything he has thought or heard before. Right meditation discloses to man an infinite amount that is new to him in things which he previously thought were known to him. It shows him depths about which it has never occurred to him to think and, above all, it brings him nearer the "new consciousness," flashes of which, like lightning, begin to illuminate his meditations, revealing to him for a moment infinitely remote horizons.

The next step—the fourth—is contemplation. Man is taught, having placed before himself one or another question, to enter into it as deeply as possible *without thinking*; or even without putting any question before himself, to enter deeply into an idea, a mental picture, landscape, phenomenon of nature, sound, number.

A man who has learned to contemplate awakens the higher faculties of his soul, lays himself open to influences which come from the higher spheres of the life of the world and, as it were, communes with the deepest mysteries of the universe.

At the same time Raja-Yoga makes man's "I" the object of concentration, meditation and contemplation. Having taught man to economise his mental powers and direct them at will, Raja-Yoga requires him to direct them upon self-knowledge, knowledge of his real "I."

The altering of man's self-consciousness and of his "self-feeling" is the principal aim of Raja-Yoga. Its object is to make man really feel and become conscious of the heights and depths in himself, by which he comes into contact with eternity and infinity, that is, to make man feel that he is not a mortal, temporary and finite speck of dust in the infinite universe, but an immortal, eternal and infinite quantity equal to the whole universe, a drop in the ocean of the spirit, but a drop which may contain the whole ocean. The broadening of the "I" according to the methods of Raja-Yoga is precisely this bringing together of the self-consciousness of man with the self-consciousness of the world, the transferring of the focus of self-consciousness from a small separate unit into infinity. Raja-Yoga broadens man's "I" and reconstructs his view of himself and his feeling of himself. . . .

The study of Raja-Yoga is impossible without the constant and direct guidance of a teacher. Before the pupil begins to study himself he is studied by the teacher, who determines the way he must follow, that is, the sequence of exercises he must do, since the exercises can never be the same for different men.

The aim of Raja-Yoga is to bring man nearer to higher consciousness, proving to him the possibility of a new state of consciousness, similar to awakening after sleep. As long as a man does not know the taste and sensation of this awakening, as long as his mind is still asleep, Raja-Yoga aims at making the idea of awakening understandable to him by telling him of the people who have awakened, teaching him to recognize the fruits of their thought and activity, which are entirely different from the results of the activity of ordinary people.

benedict de spinoza   ON THE IMPROVEMENT
OF THE UNDERSTANDING

*Benedict de Spinoza (1632–1677) was born in Amsterdam of a Jewish family.
His education led him to unorthodox ideas and he was excommunicated at the
age of twenty-four. He lived a deliberately quiet, scholarly life, grinding lenses
to acquire the means for his few needs. Offered a professorship at Heidelberg,
Spinoza rejected it, concerned that his freedom would be restricted.* His Treatise
of Theology and Politics *included an analysis of the Bible that has warranted
his being called the father of Higher Criticism. He spent twelve years on his
greatest work, the* Ethics, *one of the classics of philosophy. Dying of tuberculosis
at the age of only forty-four, he left the manuscript of the* Ethics *in a drawer
with instructions that his name was not to appear on it; he felt its truths were
self-evident and needed no name attached to them. In short, Spinoza lived
exactly as he proposed in the early and unfinished essay "On the Improvement
of the Understanding."*

After experience had taught me that all the usual surroundings of social life
are vain and futile; seeing that none of the objects of my fears contained in
themselves anything either good or bad, except in so far as the mind is affected by them, I finally resolved to inquire whether there might be some
real good having power to communicate itself, which would affect the mind
singly, to the exclusion of all else: whether, in fact, there might be anything
of which the discovery and attainment would enable me to enjoy continuous, supreme, and unending happiness. I say "I *finally* resolved," for at first
sight it seemed unwise willingly to lose hold on what was sure for the sake
of something then uncertain. I could see the benefits which are acquired
through fame and riches, and that I should be obliged to abandon the
quest of such objects, if I seriously devoted myself to the search for something different and new. I perceived that if true happiness chanced to be
placed in the former I should necessarily miss it; while if, on the other hand,
it were not so placed, and I gave them my whole attention, I should equally
fail.

I therefore debated whether it would not be possible to arrive at the new
principle, or at any rate at a certainty concerning its existence, without
changing the conduct and usual plan of my life; with this end in view I
made many efforts, but in vain. For the ordinary surroundings of life which
are esteemed by men (as their actions testify) to be the highest good, may
be classed under the three heads—Riches, Fame, and the Pleasures of Sense:
with these three the mind is so absorbed that it has little power to reflect

73

on any different good. By sensual pleasure the mind is enthralled to the extent of quiescence, as if the supreme good were actually attained, so that it is quite incapable of thinking of any other object; when such pleasure has been gratified it is followed by extreme melancholy, whereby the mind, though not enthralled, is disturbed and dulled.

The pursuit of honours and riches is likewise very absorbing, especially if such objects be sought simply for their own sake, inasmuch as they are then supposed to constitute the highest good. In the case of fame the mind is still more absorbed, for fame is conceived as always good for its own sake, and as the ultimate end to which all actions are directed. Further, the attainment of riches and fame is not followed as in the case of sensual pleasures by repentance, but, the more we acquire, the greater is our delight, and, consequently, the more are we incited to increase both the one and the other; on the other hand, if our hopes happen to be frustrated we are plunged into the deepest sadness. Fame has the further drawback that it compels its votaries to order their lives according to the opinions of their fellow-men, shunning what they usually shun, and seeking what they usually seek.

When I saw that all these ordinary objects of desire would be obstacles in the way of a search for something different and new—nay, that they were so opposed thereto, that either they or it would have to be abandoned, I was forced to inquire which would prove the most useful to me: for, as I say, I seemed to be willingly losing hold on a sure good for the sake of something uncertain. However, after I had reflected on the matter, I came in the first place to the conclusion that by abandoning the ordinary objects of pursuit, and betaking myself to a new quest, I should be leaving a good, uncertain by reason of its own nature, as may be gathered from what has been said, for the sake of a good not uncertain in its nature (for I sought for a fixed good), but only in the possibility of its attainment.

Further reflection convinced me, that if I could really get to the root of the matter I should be leaving certain evils for a certain good. I thus perceived that I was in a state of great peril, and I compelled myself to seek with all my strength for a remedy, however uncertain it might be; as a sick man struggling with a deadly disease, when he sees that death will surely be upon him unless a remedy be found, is compelled to seek such a remedy with all his strength, inasmuch as his whole hope lies therein. All the objects pursued by the multitude not only bring no remedy that tends to preserve our being, but even act as hindrances, causing the death not seldom of those who possess them, and always of those who are possessed by them. There are many examples of men who have suffered persecution even to death for the sake of their riches, and of men who in pursuit of wealth have exposed themselves to so many dangers, that they have paid away their life

74

as a penalty for their folly. Examples are no less numerous of men, who have endured the utmost wretchedness for the sake of gaining or preserving their reputation. Lastly, there are innumerable cases of men, who have hastened their death through over-indulgence in sensual pleasure. All these evils seem to have arisen from the fact, that happiness or unhappiness is made wholly to depend on the quality of the object which we love. When a thing is not loved, no quarrels will arise concerning it—no sadness will be felt if it perishes—no envy if it is possessed by another—no fear, no hatred, in short no disturbances of the mind. All these arise from the love of what is perishable, such as the objects already mentioned. But love towards a thing eternal and infinite feeds the mind wholly with joy, and is itself unmingled with any sadness, wherefore it is greatly to be desired and sought for with all our strength. Yet it was not at random that I used the words, "If I could go to the root of the matter," for, though what I have urged was perfectly clear to my mind, I could not forthwith lay aside all love of riches, sensual enjoyment, and fame. One thing was evident, namely, that while my mind was employed with these thoughts it turned away from its former objects of desire, and seriously considered the search for a new principle; this state of things was a great comfort to me, for I perceived that the evils were not such as to resist all remedies. Although these intervals were at first rare, and of very short duration, yet afterwards, as the true good became more and more discernible to me, they became more frequent and more lasting; especially after I had recognized that the acquisition of wealth, sensual pleasure, or fame, is only a hindrance, so long as they are sought as ends not as means; if they be sought as means, they will be under restraint, and, far from being hindrances, will further not a little the end for which they are sought, as I will show in due time.

I will here only briefly state what I mean by true good, and also what is the nature of the highest good. In order that this may be rightly understood, we must bear in mind that the terms good and evil are only applied relatively, so that the same thing may be called both good and bad, according to the relations in view, in the same way as it may be called perfect or imperfect. Nothing regarded in its own nature can be called perfect or imperfect; especially when we are aware that all things which come to pass, come to pass according to the eternal order and fixed laws of nature. However, human weakness cannot attain to this order in its own thoughts, but meanwhile man conceives a human character much more stable than his own, and sees that there is no reason why he should not himself acquire such a character. Thus he is led to seek for means which will bring him to this pitch of perfection, and calls everything which will serve as such means a true good. The chief good is that he should arrive, together with other individuals if possible, at the possession of the aforesaid character. What that character is we shall show in due time, namely, that it is the knowledge of the union existing between the mind and the whole of nature. This, then, is the end for which I strive, to attain to such a character myself, and to endeavour that many should attain to it with me. In other words, it is part of my happiness to lend a helping hand, that many others may understand even as I do, so that their understanding and desire may entirely agree with my own. In order to bring this about, it is necessary to understand as much of nature as will enable us to attain to the aforesaid character, and also to form a social order such as is most conducive to the attainment of this character by the greatest number with the least difficulty and danger. We must seek the assistance of Moral Philosophy and the Theory of Education; further, as health is no insignificant means for attaining our end, we must also include the whole science of Medicine, and, as many difficult things are by contrivance rendered easy, and we can in this way gain much time and convenience, the science of Mechanics must in no way be despised. But, before all things, a means must be devised for improving the understanding and purifying it, as far as may be at the outset, so that it may apprehend things without error, and in the best possible way.

Thus it is apparent to everyone that I wish to direct all sciences to one end and aim, so that we may attain to the supreme human perfection which we have named; and, therefore, whatsoever in the sciences does not serve to promote our object will have to be rejected as useless. To sum up the matter in a word, all our actions and thoughts must be directed to this one end. Yet, as it is necessary that while we are endeavouring to attain our purpose, and bring the understanding into the right path, we should carry on our life, we are compelled first of all to lay down certain rules of life as provisionally good, to wit the following:—

I. To speak in a manner intelligible to the multitude, and to comply with every general custom that does not hinder the attainment of our purpose. For we can gain from the multitude no small advantages, provided that we strive to accommodate ourselves to its understanding as far as possible: moreover, we shall in this way gain a friendly audience for the reception of the truth.

II. To indulge ourselves with pleasures only in so far as they are necessary for preserving health.

III. Lastly, to endeavour to obtain only sufficient money or other commodities to enable us to preserve our life and health, and to follow such general customs as are consistent with our purpose.

richard taylor THE MEANING OF LIFE

Richard Taylor (1919–   ) received his B.A. in zoology, but his Ph.D. from Brown University is in philosophy. The author of Metaphysics *and the editor of* The Will to Live, *he was the William H. P. Faunce Professor of Philosophy at Brown University and became, more recently, a professor of philosophy at the University of Rochester. "The Meaning of Life" is from* Good and Evil: A New Direction *(1970). In the opening pages Taylor writes, "There will come a day for each of us to die, and on that day, if we have failed, we shall have failed irrevocably. This simple truth, so obvious, needs to be driven home. It is easy to make a mess of the whole thing, to end up with nothing, with no life that was really much worth living."*

The question whether life has any meaning is difficult to interpret, and the more one concentrates his critical faculty on it the more it seems to elude him, or to evaporate as any intelligible question. One wants to turn it aside, as a source of embarrassment, as something that, if it cannot be abolished, should at least be decently covered. And yet I think any reflective person recognizes that the question it raises is important, and that it ought to have a significant answer.

If the idea of meaningfulness is difficult to grasp in this context, so that we are unsure what sort of thing would amount to answering the question, the idea of meaninglessness is perhaps less so. If, then, we can bring before our minds a clear image of meaningless existence, then perhaps we can take a step toward coping with our original question by seeing to what extent our lives, as we actually find them, resemble that image, and draw such lessons as we are able to from the comparison.

MEANINGLESS EXISTENCE

A perfect image of meaninglessness, of the kind we are seeking, is found in the ancient myth of Sisyphus. Sisyphus, it will be remembered, betrayed divine secrets to mortals, and for this he was condemned by the gods to roll a stone to the top of a hill, the stone then immediately to roll back down, again to be pushed to the top by Sisyphus, to roll down once more, and so on again and again, *forever*. Now in this we have the picture of meaningless, pointless toil, of a meaningless existence that is absolutely *never* redeemed. It is not even redeemed by a death that, if it were to accomplish nothing more, would at least bring this idiotic cycle to a close. If we were invited to imagine Sisyphus struggling for awhile and accomplishing

77

nothing, perhaps eventually falling from exhaustion, so that we might suppose him then eventually turning to something having some sort of promise, then the meaninglessness of that chapter of his life would not be so stark. It would be a dark and dreadful dream, from which he eventually awakens to sunlight and reality. But he does not awaken, for there is nothing for him to awaken to. His repetitive toil is his life and reality, and it goes on forever, and it is without any meaning whatever. Nothing ever comes of what he is doing, except simply, more of the same. Not by one step, nor by a thousand, nor by ten thousand does he even expiate by the smallest token the sin against the gods that led him into this fate. Nothing comes of it, nothing at all.

This ancient myth has always enchanted men, for countless meanings can be read into it. Some of the ancients apparently thought it symbolized the perpetual rising and setting of the sun, and others the repetitious crashing of the waves upon the shore. Probably the commonest interpretation is that it symbolizes man's eternal struggle and unquenchable spirit, his determination always to try once more in the face of overwhelming discouragement. This interpretation is further supported by that version of the myth according to which Sisyphus was commanded to roll the stone *over* the hill, so that it would finally roll down the other side, but was never quite able to make it.

I am not concerned with rendering or defending any interpretation of this myth, however. I have cited it only for the one element it does unmistakably contain, namely, that of a repetitious, cyclic activity that never comes to anything. We could contrive other images of this that would serve just as well, and no myth-makers are needed to supply the materials of it. Thus, we can imagine two persons transporting a stone—or even a precious gem, it does not matter—back and forth, relay style. One carries it to a near or distant point where it is received by the other; it is returned to its starting point, there to be recovered by the first, and the process is repeated over and over. Except in this relay nothing counts as winning, and nothing brings the contest to any close, each step only leads to a repetition of itself. Or we can imagine two groups of prisoners, one of them engaged in digging a prodigious hole in the ground that is no sooner finished than it is filled in again by the other group, the latter then digging a new hole that is at once filled in by the first group, and so on and on endlessly.

Now what stands out in all such pictures as oppressive and dejecting is not that the beings who enact these roles suffer any torture or pain, for it need not be assumed that they do. Nor is it that their labors are great, for they are no greater than the labors commonly undertaken by most men most of the time. According to the original myth, the stone is so large that Sisyphus never quite gets it to the top and must groan under every step, so that his enormous labor is all for nought. But this is not what appalls. It is not that his great struggle comes to nothing, but that his existence itself is without meaning. Even if we suppose, for example, that the stone is but a pebble that can be carried effortlessly, or that the holes dug by the prisoners are but small ones, not the slightest meaning is introduced into their lives. The stone that Sisyphus moves to the top of the hill, whether we think of it as large or small, still rolls back every time, and the process is repeated forever. Nothing comes of it, and the work is simply pointless. That is the element of the myth that I wish to capture.

Again, it is not the fact that the labors of Sisyphus continue forever that deprives them of meaning. It is, rather, the implication of this: that they come to nothing. The image would not be changed by our supposing him to push a different stone up every time, each to roll down again. But if we supposed that these stones, instead of rolling back to their places as if they had never been moved, were assembled at the top of the hill and there incorporated, say, in a beautiful and enduring temple, then the aspect of meaninglessness would disappear. His labors would then have a point, something would come of them all, and although one could perhaps still say it was not worth it, one could not say that the life of Sisyphus was devoid of meaning altogether. Meaningfulness would at least have made an appearance, and we could see what it was.

That point will need remembering. But in the meantime, let us note another way in which the image of meaninglessness can be altered by making only a very slight change. Let us suppose that the gods, while condemning Sisyphus to the fate just described, at the same time, as an afterthought, waxed perversely merciful by implanting in him a strange and irrational impulse; namely, a compulsive impulse to roll stones. We may if we like, to make this more graphic, suppose they accomplish this by implanting in him some substance that has this effect on his character and drives. I call this perverse, because from our point of view there is clearly no reason why anyone should have a persistent and insatiable desire to do something so pointless as that. Nevertheless, suppose that is Sisyphus' condition. He has but one obsession, which is to roll stones, and it is an obsession that is only for the moment appeased by his rolling them—he no sooner gets a stone rolled to the top of the hill than he is restless to roll up another.

Now it can be seen why this little afterthought of the gods, which I called perverse, was also in fact merciful. For they have by this device managed to give Sisyphus precisely what he wants—by making him want precisely what they inflict on him. However it may appear to us, Sisyphus' fate now does not appear to him as a condemnation, but the very reverse. His one desire in life is to roll stones, and he is absolutely guaranteed its endless fulfillment. Where otherwise he might profoundly have wished surcease, and even welcomed the quiet of death to release him from endless boredom and meaninglessness, his life is now filled with mission and meaning, and he seems to himself to have been given an entry to heaven. Nor need he even fear death, for the gods have promised him an endless opportunity to indulge his single purpose, without concern or frustration. He will be able to roll stones *forever*.

What we need to mark most carefully at this point is that the picture with which we began has not really been changed in the least by adding this supposition. Exactly the same things happen as before. The only change is in Sisyphus' view of them. The picture before was the image of meaningless activity and existence. It was created precisely to be an image of that. It has not lost that meaninglessness, it has now gained not the least shred of meaningfulness. The stones still roll back as before, each phase of Sisyphus' life still exactly resembles all the others, the task is never completed, nothing comes of it, no temple ever begins to rise, and all this cycle of the same pointless thing over and over goes on forever in this picture as in the other. The *only* thing that has happened is this: Sisyphus has been reconciled to it, and indeed more, he has been led to embrace it. Not, however, by reason or persuasion, but by nothing more rational than the potency of a new substance in his veins.

THE MEANINGLESSNESS OF LIFE

I believe the foregoing provides a fairly clear content to the idea of meaninglessness and, through it, some hint of what meaningfulness, in this sense, might be. Meaninglessness is essentially endless pointlessness, and meaningfulness is therefore the opposite. Activity, and even long, drawnout and repetitive activity, has a meaning if it has some significant culmination, some more or less lasting end that can be considered to have been the direction and purpose of the activity. But the descriptions so far also provide something else; namely, the suggestion of how an existence that is objectively meaningless, in this sense, can nevertheless acquire a meaning for him whose existence it is.

Now let us ask: Which of these pictures does life in fact resemble? And let us not begin with our own lives, for here both our prejudices and wishes are great, but with the life in general that we share with the rest of creation. We shall find, I think, that it all has a certain pattern, and that this pattern is by now easily recognized.

We can begin anywhere, only saving human existence for our last consideration. We can, for example, begin with any animal. It does not matter where we begin, because the result is going to be exactly the same.

Thus, for example, there are caves in New Zealand, deep and dark, whose floors are quiet pools and whose walls and ceilings are covered with soft light. As one gazes in wonder in the stillness of these caves it seems that the Creator has reproduced there in microcosm the heavens themselves, until one scarcely remembers the enclosing presence of the walls. As one looks more closely, however, the scene is explained. Each dot of light identifies an ugly worm, whose luminous tail is meant to attract insects from the surrounding darkness. As from time to time one of these insects draws near it becomes entangled in a sticky thread lowered by the worm, and is eaten. This goes on month after month, the blind worm lying there in the barren stillness waiting to entrap an occasional bit of nourishment that will only sustain it to another bit of nourishment until. . . . Until what? What great thing awaits all this long and repetitious effort and makes it worthwhile? Really nothing. The larva just transforms itself finally to a tiny winged adult that lacks even mouth parts to feed and lives only a day or two. These adults, as soon as they have mated and laid eggs, are themselves caught in the threads and are devoured by the cannibalist worms, often without having ventured into the day, the only point to their existence having now been fulfilled. This has been going on for millions of years, and to no end other than that the same meaningless cycle may continue for another millions of years.

All living things present essentially the same spectacle. The larva of a certain cicada burrows in the darkness of the earth for seventeen years, through season after season, to emerge finally into the daylight for a brief flight, lay its eggs, and die—this all to repeat itself during the next seventeen years, and so on to eternity. We have already noted, in another connection, the struggles of fish, made only that others may do the same after them and that this cycle, having no other point than itself, may never cease. Some birds span an entire side of the globe each year and then return, only to insure that others may follow the same incredibly long path again and again. One is led to wonder what the point of it all is, with what great triumph this ceaseless effort, repeating itself through millions of years, might finally culminate, and why it should go on and on for so long, accomplishing nothing, getting nowhere. But then one realizes that there is no point to it at all, that it really culminates in nothing, that each of these cycles, so filled with toil, is to be followed only by more of the same. The point of any living thing's life is, evidently, nothing but life itself.

This life of the world thus presents itself to our eyes as a vast machine, feeding on itself, running on and on forever to nothing. And we are part of that life. To be sure, we are not just the same, but the differences are not so great as we like to think; many are merely invented, and none really cancels the kind of meaninglessness that we found in Sisyphus and that we find all around, wherever anything lives. We are conscious of our activity. Our goals, whether in any significant sense we choose them or not, are things of which we are at least partly aware and can therefore in some sense appraise. More significantly, perhaps, men have a history, as other animals do not, such that each generation does not precisely resemble all those before. Still, if we can in imagination disengage our wills from our lives and disregard the deep interest each man has in his own existence, we shall find that they do not so little resemble the existence of Sisyphus. We toil after goals, most of them—indeed every single one of them—of transitory significance and, having gained one of them, we immediately set forth for the next, as if that one had never been, with this next one being essentially more of the same. Look at a busy street any day, and observe the throng going hither and thither. To what? Some office or shop, where the same things will be done today as were done yesterday, and are done now so they may be repeated tomorrow. And if we think that, unlike Sisyphus, these labors do have a point, that they culminate in something lasting and, independently of our own deep interests in them, very worthwhile, then we simply have not considered the thing closely enough. Most such effort is directed only to the establishment and perpetuation of home and family; that is, to the begetting of others who will follow in our steps to do more of the same. Each man's life thus resembles one of Sisyphus' climbs to the summit of his hill, and each day of it one of his steps; the difference is that whereas Sisyphus himself returns to push the stone up again, we leave this to our children. We at one point imagined that the labors of Sisyphus finally culminated in the creation of a temple, but for this to make any difference it had to be a temple that would at least endure, adding beauty to the world for the remainder of time. Our achievements, even though they are often beautiful, are mostly bubbles; and those that do last, like the sand-swept pyramids, soon become mere curiosities while around them the rest of mankind continues its perpetual toting of rocks, only to see them roll down. Nations are built upon the bones of their founders and pioneers, but only to decay and crumble before long, their rubble then becoming the foundation for others directed to exactly the same fate. The picture of Sisyphus is the picture of existence of the individual man, great or unknown, of nations, of the race of men, and of the very life of the world.

On a country road one sometimes comes upon the ruined hulks of a house and once extensive buildings, all in collapse and spread over with weeds. A curious eye can in imagination reconstruct from what is left a once warm and thriving life, filled with purpose. There was the hearth, where a family once talked, sang, and made plans; there were the rooms, where people loved, and babes were born to a rejoicing mother; there are the musty remains of a sofa, infested with bugs, once bought at a dear price to enhance an ever-growing comfort, beauty, and warmth. Every small piece of

82

junk fills the mind with what once, not long ago, was utterly real, with children's voices, plans made, and enterprises embarked upon. That is how these stones of Sisyphus were rolled up, and that is how they became incorporated into a beautiful temple, and that temple is what now lies before you. Meanwhile other buildings, institutions, nations, and civilizations spring up all around, only to share the same fate before long. And if the question "What for?" is now asked, the answer is clear: so that just this may go on forever.

The two pictures—of Sisyphus and of our own lives, if we look at them from a distance—are in outline the same and convey to the mind the same image. It is not surprising, then, that men invent ways of denying it, their religious proclaiming a heaven that does not crumble, their hymnals and prayer books declaring a significance to life of which our eyes provide no hint whatever.[1] Even our philosophies portray some permanent and lasting good at which all may aim, from the changeless forms invented by Plato to the beatific vision of St. Thomas and the ideals of permanence contrived by the moderns. When these fail to convince, then earthly ideals such as universal justice and brotherhood are conjured up to take their places and give meaning to man's seemingly endless pilgrimage, some final state that will be ushered in when the last obstacle is removed and the last stone pushed to the hilltop. No one believes, of course, that any such state will be final, or even wants it to be in case it means that human existence would then cease to be a struggle; but in the meantime such ideas serve a very real need.

THE MEANING OF LIFE

We noted that Sisyphus' existence would have meaning if there were some point to his labors, if his efforts ever culminated in something that was not just an occasion for fresh labors of the same kind. But that is precisely the meaning it lacks. And human existence resembles his in that respect. Men do achieve things—they scale their towers and raise their stones to their hilltops—but every such accomplishment fades, providing only an occasion for renewed labors of the same kind.

But here we need to note something else that has been mentioned, but its significance not explored, and that is the state of mind and feeling with which such labors are undertaken. We noted that if Sisyphus had a keen

[1] A popular Christian hymn, sung often at funerals and typical of many hymns, expresses this thought:

> Swift to its close ebbs out life's little day;
> Earth's joys grow dim, its glories pass away;
> Change and decay in all around I see;
> O thou who changest not, abide with me.

and unappeasable desire to be doing just what he found himself doing, then, although his life would in no way be changed, it would nevertheless have a meaning for him. It would be an irrational one, no doubt, because the desire itself would be only the product of the substance in his veins, and not any that reason could discover, but a meaning nevertheless.

And would it not, in fact, be a meaning incomparably better than the other? For let us examine again the first kind of meaning it could have. Let us suppose that, without having any interest in rolling stones, as such, and finding this, in fact, a galling toil, Sisyphus did nevertheless have a deep interest in raising a temple, one that would be beautiful and lasting. And let us suppose he succeeded in this, that after ages of dreadful toil, all directed at this final result, he did at last complete his temple, such that now he could say his work was done, and he could rest and forever enjoy the result. Now what? What picture now presents itself to our minds? It is precisely the picture of infinite boredom! Of Sisyphus doing nothing ever again, but contemplating what he has already wrought and can no longer add anything to, and contemplating it for an eternity! Now in this picture we have a meaning for Sisyphus' existence, a point for his prodigious labor, because we have put it there; yet, at the same time, that which is really worthwhile seems to have slipped away entirely. Where before we were presented with the nightmare of eternal and pointless activity, we are now confronted with the hell of its eternal absence.

Our second picture, then, wherein we imagined Sisyphus to have had inflicted on him the irrational desire to be doing just what he found himself doing, should not have been dismissed so abruptly. The meaning that picture lacked was no meaning that he or anyone could crave, and the strange meaning it had was perhaps just what we were seeking.

At this point, then, we can reintroduce what has been until now, it is hoped, resolutely pushed aside in an effort to view our lives and human existence with objectivity; namely, our own wills, our deep interest in what we find ourselves doing. If we do this we find that our lives do indeed still resemble that of Sisyphus, but that the meaningfulness they thus lack is precisely the meaningfulness of infinite boredom. At the same time, the strange meaningfulness they possess is that of the inner compulsion to be doing just what we were put here to do, and to go on doing it forever. This is the nearest we may hope to get to heaven, but the redeeming side of that fact is that we do thereby avoid a genuine hell.

If the builders of a great and flourishing ancient civilization could somehow return now to see archaeologists unearthing the trivial remnants of what they had once accomplished with such effort—see the fragments of pots and vases, a few broken statues, and such tokens of another age and greatness—they could indeed ask themselves what the point of it all was, if this is all it finally came to. Yet, it did not seem so to them then, for it was just the building, and not what was finally built, that gave their life meaning. Similarly, if the builders of the ruined home and farm that I described a short while ago could be brought back to see what is left, they would have the same feelings. What we construct in our imaginations as we look over these decayed and rusting pieces would reconstruct itself in their very memories, and certainly with unspeakable sadness. The piece of a sled at our feet would revive in them a warm Christmas. And what rich memories would there be in the broken crib? And the weed-covered remains of a fence would reproduce the scene of a great herd of livestock, so laboriously built up over so many years. What was it all worth, if this is the final result? Yet, again, it did not seem so to them through those many years of struggle and toil, and they did not imagine they were building a Gibraltar. The things to which they bent their backs day after day, realizing one by one their ephemeral plans, were precisely the things in which their wills were deeply involved, precisely the things in which their interests lay, and there was no need then to ask questions. There is no more need of them now—the day was sufficient to itself, and so was the life.

This is surely the way to look at all of life—at one's own life, and each day and moment it contains; of the life of a nation; of the species; of the life of the world; and of everything that breathes. Even the glow worms I described, whose cycles of existence over the millions of years seem so pointless when looked at by us, will seem entirely different to us if we can somehow try to view their existence from within. Their endless activity, which gets nowhere, is just what it is their will to pursue. This is its whole justification and meaning. Nor would it be any salvation to the birds who span the globe every year, back and forth, to have a home made for them in a cage with plenty of food and protection, so that they would not have to migrate any more. It would be their condemnation, for it is the doing that counts for them, and not what they hope to win by it. Flying these prodigious distances, never ending, is what it is in their veins to do, exactly as it was in Sisyphus' veins to roll stones, without end, after the gods had waxed merciful and implanted this in him.

A human being no sooner draws his first breath than he responds to the will that is in him to live. He no more asks whether it will be worthwhile, or whether anything of significance will come of it, than the worms and the birds. The point of his living is simply to be living, in the manner that it is his nature to be living. He goes through his life building his castles, each of these beginning to fade into time as the next is begun; yet, it would be no salvation to rest from all this. It would be a condemnation, and one that would in no way be redeemed were he able to gaze upon the things he has done, even if these were beautiful and absolutely permanent, as they never are. What counts is that one should be able to begin a new task, a new castle, a new bubble. It counts only because it is there to be done and he has the will to do it. The same will be the life of his children, and of theirs; and if the philosopher is apt to see in this a pattern similar to the unending cycles of the existence of Sisyphus, and to despair, then it is indeed because the meaning and point he is seeking is not there—but mercifully so. The meaning of life is from within us, it is not bestowed from without, and it far exceeds in both its beauty and permanence any heaven of which men have ever dreamed or yearned for.

FURTHER READING

For introductory purposes, autobiographical materials are endlessly fascinating, and in them we often catch startling glimpses of ourselves. Thomas Wolfe's long exploration of his life in his novels has already been mentioned. W. Somerset Maugham's *Of Human Bondage* (1915) is largely autobiographical and takes strongly philosophical turns in many chapters. Samuel Butler's *The Way of All Flesh* (1903) is a modern classic. F. Scott Fitzgerald wrote revealingly of personal disintegration in the notebooks, letters, and other materials collected in *The Crack-Up* (edited by Edmund Wilson, 1945).

Fyodor Dostoyevsky, *The Brothers Karamazov* (1880). Philosophical fiction at its finest: the great Russian novelist always dealt with matters of life and death.

Rollo May's popular *Man's Search for Himself* (1953) offers the background of a distinguished psychotherapist on the topic of contemporary man's manifold confusions about himself.

A negative example—an unexamined life—is studied in Arthur Miller's *Death of a Salesman* (1949). Willy Loman was a man who, in his son Biff's words, "never knew who he was," and the consequences were tragic. In the same vein, see the short stories "Walter T. Carriman" by John O'Hara (in *Selected Short Stories of John O'Hara*, 1956) and "The Enormous Radio" by John Cheever (in *The Enormous Radio and Other Stories*, 1953).

John Wisdom, "The Meanings of the Questions of Life," in *Paradox and Discovery* (1965). The Cambridge University philosopher discusses the meaning of the *question* about the meaning of life.

chapter three

__ON THE NATURE OF PHILOSOPHY

3

It is frequently a source of embarrassment to those who work in philosophy to be asked to define "philosophy." It is not an easy question to answer; it has itself achieved the status of being termed a problem in philosophy.

> What subject matter is peculiar to philosophy, what questions about it are philosophical, what method is appropriate to the solving of them, . . . what philosophy contributes to the life of man—all these are genuinely philosophical questions. They belong to a branch of inquiry which, although it is seldom explicitly included in lists of the philosophical disciplines, is unquestionably one of them. This discipline is the philosophy of philosophy.[1]

It should not be surprising that there is little agreement among philosophers about the nature of philosophy. Philosophers do their own thinking about everything, including philosophy, and are, if anything, delighted by their disagreements. Still, there are other reasons for there not being any single "definition" of philosophy. It is a subject that moves along a broad front, and its concerns are multiple and varied. As climates of opinion have changed over the centuries, emphases among its interests have sometimes shifted, and not all philosophers are equally interested in the different divisions of the field.

But to speak of philosophy as a "subject" or a "field" is somewhat misleading. Philosophy is not merely a fixed body of knowledge or a given set of problems; it is the activity of philosophizing. The meaning of the activity must be defined largely in terms of what it does to the man engaged in it. Usually, he learns to look critically at the assumptions upon which his life has rested, and he discovers or creates the values that he believes will give significance to his existence. Inevitably, in this process of self-examination and reflection upon the ends of life, he changes.

What philosophy meant to Socrates may be seen in "The Apology," which has long been considered one of the most impressive of all statements about

[1] C. J. Ducasse, *Philosophy as a Science* (New York: Oskar Piest, 1941), p. vii.

88

> *Philosophy subverts man's satisfaction with himself, exposes custom as a questionable dream, and offers not so much solutions as a different life.*
>
> walter kaufmann

philosophy. Because Socrates so completely embodied the spirit and pursuit of philosophy, his explanation of his life and activities is at the same time an explanation of philosophy. Philosophy, for Socrates, was the quest for wisdom, but to be wise meant to be good. At bottom there was that ethical concern, and the force and depth of that concern was immense:

It was Socrates who, so far as can be seen, created the conception of the *soul*. . . . For more than two thousand years it has been the standing assumption of the civilized European man that he has a *soul*, something which is the seat of his normal waking intelligence and moral character, and that, since this *soul* is either identical with himself or at any rate the most important thing about him, his supreme business in life is to make the most of it and do the best for it.[2]

In the hands of Epictetus, philosophy takes on a more "practical" flavor. It becomes the means whereby one may cope with an unpredictable, and sometimes dangerous, world. By distinguishing sharply between those matters over which one has no control (toward which one ought be indifferent) and those which one can govern (one's own attitudes and actions), the followers of Epictetus sought for a state of security through rational self-discipline.

The essays by C. D. Broad and José Ortega y Gasset represent two schools of thought which have become sharply defined in the twentieth century. The most fervent followers of each are now pained by the very existence of the other. Broad's description of philosophy as "critical thought" stresses the analytic function of philosophy, in which there is reflected a scientific attitude of mind. There is in this movement the belief that much of the speculative thought of the past and present—especially in metaphysics—is hopelessly beyond the reach of proof or disproof. In contrast, Ortega y Gasset has proclaimed the philosopher "a specialist in universes." Philosophy for him is much more than science: the philosopher seeks integrated knowledge, a vision of the wholeness of things.

[2] A. E. Taylor, *Socrates* (New York: Doubleday Anchor Books, 1956), pp. 132–133.

89

Plato (427–347 B.C.) was of the wealthy, aristocratic class in Athens. He was a young poet twenty years of age when he met Socrates, who was then already over sixty. Plato became one of those many youths who followed Socrates, first in the streets and public places of Athens, and later in spirit to the end of their lives. Plato developed and had aspirations to put into practice theories about the governance of society, but they were never realized. In the middle of his life, he founded the Academy (hence our term "academic"), the first of the famous schools of Athens. The brilliance and magnitude of his philosophical achievements are most succinctly suggested by Whitehead's often-quoted remark that "western philosophy is a series of footnotes to Plato."

Socrates (469–399 B.C.) is one of the truly unique men of history. Karl Jaspers, in fact, ranks him with Buddha, Confucius, and Jesus. By profession a stone-cutter, Socrates married and had children, and he served with distinction as a soldier. Socrates himself wrote nothing; most of what we know of him comes to us through the Dialogues of Plato, one of the most illuminating of which is "The Apology."

SCENE.—THE COURT OF JUSTICE

Socrates. I cannot tell what impression my accusers have made upon you, Athenians: for my own part, I know that they nearly made me forget who I was, so plausible were they; and yet they have scarcely uttered one single word of truth. But of all their many falsehoods, the one which astonished me most, was when they said that I was a clever speaker, and that you must be careful not to let me mislead you. I thought that it was most impudent of them not to be ashamed to talk in that way; for as soon as I open my mouth the lie will be exposed, and I shall prove that I am not a clever speaker in any way at all: unless, indeed, by a clever speaker they mean a man who speaks the truth. If that is their meaning, I agree with them that I am a much greater orator than they. My accusers, then I repeat, have said little or nothing that is true; but from me you shall hear the whole truth. Certainly you will not hear an elaborate speech, Athenians, drest up, like theirs, with words and phrases. I will say to you what I have to say, without preparation, and in the words which come first, for I believe that my cause is just; so let none of you expect anything else. Indeed, my friends, it would hardly be seemly for me, at my age, to come before you like a young man with his specious falsehoods. But there is one thing, Athenians, which I do most earnestly beg and entreat of you. Do not be surprised and do not interrupt, if in my defence I speak in the same way that I am accustomed to speak in the market-place, at the tables of the money-changers, where many of you have heard me, and elsewhere. The truth is this. I am more than seventy years old, and this is the first time that I have ever come before a Court of Law; so your manner of speech here is quite strange to me. . . .

I have to defend myself, Athenians, first against the old false charges of my old accusers, and then against the later ones of my present accusers. For many men have been accusing me to you, and for very many years, who have not uttered a word of truth: and I fear them more than I fear Anytus and his companions, formidable as they are. But, my friends, those others are still more formidable; for they got hold of most of you when you were children, and they have been more persistent in accusing me with lies, and in trying to persuade you that there is one Socrates, a wise man, who speculates about the heavens, and who examines into all things that are beneath the earth, and who can "make the worse appear the better reason." These men, Athenians, who spread abroad this report, are the accusers whom I fear; for their hearers think that persons who pursue such inquiries never believe in the gods. And then they are many, and their attacks have been going on for a long time: and they spoke to you when you were at the age most readily to believe them: for you were all young, and many of you were children: and there was no one to answer them when they attacked me. And the most unreasonable thing of all is that commonly I do not even know their names: I cannot tell you who they are, except in the case of the comic poets. But all the rest who have been trying to prejudice you against me, from motives of spite and jealousy, and sometimes, it may be, from conviction, are the enemies whom it is hardest to meet. For I cannot call any one of them forward in Court, to cross-examine him: I have, as it were, simply to fight with shadows in my defence, and to put questions which there is no one to answer.

. . . .

Let us begin again, then, and see what is the charge which has given rise to the prejudice against me, which was what Meletus relied on when he drew his indictment. What is the calumny which my enemies have been spreading about me? I must assume that they are formally accusing me, and read their indictment. It would run somewhat in this fashion: "Socrates is an evil-doer, who meddles with inquiries into things beneath the earth, and in heaven, and who 'makes the worse appear the better reason,' and who teaches others these same things." . . .

But, the fact is, that not one of these stories is true; and if you have heard that I undertake to educate men, and exact money from them for so doing, that is not true either; though I think that it would be a fine thing to be able to educate men. . . .

. . . .

Perhaps some of you may reply: But, Socrates, what is this pursuit of yours? Whence come these calumnies against you? You must have been engaged in some pursuit out of the common. All these stories and reports of you would never have gone about, if you had not been in some way different from other men. So tell us what your pursuits are, that we may not give our verdict in the dark. I think that that is a fair question, and I will try to explain to you what it is that has raised these calumnies against me, and given me this name. Listen, then: some of you perhaps will think that I am jesting; but I assure you that I will tell you the whole truth. I have gained this name, Athenians, simply by reason of a certain wisdom. But by what kind of wisdom? It is by just that wisdom which is, I believe, possible to men. In that, it may be, I am really wise. . . . You remember Chærephon. From youth upwards he was my comrade; and he went into exile with the people, and with the people he returned. And you remember, too, Chærephon's character; how vehement he was in carrying through whatever he took in hand. Once he went to Delphi and ventured to put this question to the oracle—I entreat you again, my friends, not to cry out—he asked if there was any man who was wiser than I: and the priestess answered that there was no man. Chærephon himself is dead, but his brother here will confirm what I say.

Now see why I tell you this. I am going to explain to you the origin of my unpopularity. When I heard of the oracle I began to reflect: What can God mean by this dark saying? I know very well that I am not wise, even in the smallest degree. Then what can he mean by saying that I am the wisest of men? It cannot be that he is speaking falsely, for he is a god and cannot lie. And for a long time I was at a loss to understand his meaning: then, very reluctantly, I turned to seek for it in this manner. I went to a man who was reputed to be wise, thinking that there, if anywhere, I should prove the answer wrong, and meaning to point out to the oracle its mistake, and to say, "You said that I was the wisest of men, but this man is wiser than I am." So I examined the man—I need not tell you his name, he was a politician—but this was the result, Athenians. When I conversed with him I came to see that, though a great many persons, and most of all he himself, thought that he was wise, yet he was not wise. And then I tried to prove to him that he was not wise, though he fancied that he was: and by so doing I made him, and many of the bystanders, my enemies. So when I went away, I thought to myself, "I am wiser than this man: neither of us probably knows anything that is really good, but he thinks that he has knowledge, when he has not, while I, having no knowledge, do not think that I have. I seem, at any rate, to be a little wiser than he is on this point: I do not think that I know what I do not know." Next I went to another man who was reputed to be still wiser than the last, with exactly the same result. And there again I made him, and many other men, my enemies.

Then I went on to one man after another, seeing that I was making enemies every day, which caused me much unhappiness and anxiety: still I thought that I must set God's command above everything. So I had to go to every man who seemed to possess any knowledge, and search for the meaning of the oracle: and, Athenians, I must tell you the truth; verily, by the dog of Egypt, this was the result of the search which I made at God's bidding. I found that the men, whose reputation for wisdom stood highest, were nearly the most lacking in it; while others, who were looked down on as common people, were much better fitted to learn.

. . . .

By reason of this examination, Athenians, I have made many enemies of a very fierce and bitter kind, who have spread abroad a great number of calumnies about me, and people say that I am "a wise man." For the by-standers always think that I am wise myself in any matter wherein I convict another man of ignorance. But, my friends, I believe that only God is really wise: and that by this oracle he meant that men's wisdom is worth little or nothing. I do not think that he meant that Socrates was wise. He only made use of my name, and took me as an example, as though he would say to men, "He among you is the wisest, who, like Socrates, knows that in very truth his wisdom is worth nothing at all." And therefore I still go about testing and examining every man whom I think wise, whether he be a citizen or a stranger, as God has commanded me; and whenever I find that he is not wise, I point out to him on the part of God that he is not wise. And I am so busy in this pursuit that I have never had leisure to take any part worth mentioning in public matters, or to look after my private affairs. I am in very great poverty by reason of my service to God.

And besides this, the young men who follow me about, who are the sons of wealthy persons and have a great deal of spare time, take a natural pleasure in hearing men cross-examined: and they often imitate me among themselves: then they try their hands at cross-examining other people. And, I imagine, they find a great abundance of men who think that they know a great deal, when in fact they know little or nothing. And then the persons who are cross-examined, get angry with me instead of with themselves, and say that Socrates is an abominable fellow who corrupts young men. And when they are asked, "Why, what does he do? what does he teach?" they do not know what to say; but, not to seem at a loss, they repeat the stock charges against all philosophers, and allege that he investigates things in the air and under the earth, and that he teaches people to disbelieve in the gods, and "to make the worse appear the better reason." For, I fancy, they would not like to confess the truth, which is that they are shown up as ignorant pretenders to knowledge that they do not possess. And so they have been filling your ears with their bitter calumnies for a long time, for they are zealous and numerous and bitter against me; and they are well disciplined and plausible in speech. On these grounds Meletus and Anytus and Lycon have attacked me.

. . . .

[*Socrates takes up the charges of his "present accusers." He cross-examines Meletus and refutes his accusations.*] But in truth, Athenians, I do not think that I need say very much to prove that I have not committed the crime for which Meletus is prosecuting me. What I have said is enough to prove that. But, I repeat, it is certainly true, as I have already told you, that I have incurred much unpopularity and made many enemies. And that is what will cause my condemnation, if I am condemned; not Meletus, nor Anytus either, but the prejudice and suspicion of the multitude. They have been the destruction of many good men before me, and I think that they will be so again. There is no fear that I shall be their last victim.

Perhaps some one will say: "Are you not ashamed, Socrates, of following pursuits which are very likely now to cause your death?" I should answer him with justice, and say: My friend, if you think that a man of any worth at all ought to reckon the chances of life and death when he acts, or that he ought to think of anything but whether he is acting rightly or wrongly, and as a good or a bad man would act, you are greviously mistaken. . . . Wherever a man's post is, whether he has chosen it of his own will, or whether he has been placed at it by his commander, there it is his duty to remain and face the danger, without thinking of death, or of any other thing, except dishonor.

When the generals whom you chose to command me, Athenians, placed me at my post at Potidæa, and at Amphipolis, and at Delium, I remained where they placed me, and ran the risk of death, like other men: and it would be very strange conduct on my part if I were to desert my post now from fear of death or of any other thing, when God has commanded me, as I am persuaded that he has done, to spend my life in searching for wisdom, and in examining myself and others. That would indeed be a very strange thing: and then certainly I might with justice be brought to trial for not believing in the gods: for I should be disobeying the oracle, and fearing death, and thinking myself wise, when I was not wise. For to fear death, my friends, is only to think ourselves wise, without being wise: for it is to think that we know what we do not know. For anything that men can tell, death may be the greatest good that can happen to them: but they fear it as if they knew quite well that it was the greatest of evils. And what is this but that shameful ignorance of thinking that we know what we do not know? In this matter too, my friends, perhaps I am different from the mass of mankind: and if I were to claim to be at all wiser than others, it would be because I do not think that I have any clear knowledge about the other world, when, in fact, I have none. But I do know very well that it is evil and base to do wrong, and to disobey my superior, whether he be man or god. And I will never do what I know to be evil, and shrink in fear from what, for all that I can tell, may be a good. And so, even if you acquit me now, and do not listen to Anytus' argument that, if I am to be acquitted, I ought never to have been brought to trial at all; and that, as it is, you are bound to put me to death, because, as he said, if I escape, all your children will forthwith be utterly corrupted by practising what Socrates teaches; if you were therefore to say to me, "Socrates, this time we will not listen to Anytus: we will let you go; but on this condition, that you cease from carrying on this search of yours, and from philosophy; if you are found following those pursuits again, you shall die": I say, if you offered to let me go on these terms, I should reply:—Athenians, I hold you in the highest regard and love; but I will obey God rather than you: and as long as I have breath and strength I will not cease from philosophy, and from exhorting you, and declaring the truth to every one of you whom I meet, saying, as I am wont: "My excellent friend, you are a citizen of Athens, a city which is very great and very famous for wisdom and power of mind; are you not ashamed of caring so much for the making of money, and for reputation, and for honor? Will you not think or care about wisdom and truth, and the perfection of your soul?" And if he disputes my words, and says that he does care about these things, I shall not forthwith release him and go away: I shall question him and cross-examine him and test him: and if I think that he has not virtue, though he says that he has, I shall reproach him for setting the lower value on the most important things, and a higher value on those that are of less account. This I shall do to every one whom I meet, young or old, citizen or stranger: but more especially to the citizens, for they are more nearly akin to me. For, know well, God has commanded me to do so. And I think that no better piece of fortune has ever befallen you in Athens than my service to God. For I spend my whole life in going about and persuading you all to give your first and chiefest care to the perfection of your souls, and not till you have done that to think of your bodies, or your wealth; and telling you that virtue does not come from wealth, but that wealth, and every other good thing which men have, whether in public, or in private, comes from virtue. If then I corrupt the youth by this teaching, the mischief is great: but if any man says that I teach anything else, he speaks falsely.

And therefore, Athenians, I say, either listen to Anytus, or do not listen to him: either acquit me, or do not acquit me: but be sure that I shall not alter my way of life; no, not if I have to die for it many times.

Do not interrupt me, Athenians. Remember the request which I made to you, and listen to my words. I think that it will profit you to hear them. I am going to say something more to you, at which you may be inclined to cry out: but do not do that. Be sure that if you put me to death, who am what I have told you that I am, you will do yourselves more harm than me. Meletus and Anytus can do me no harm: that is impossible: for I am sure that God will not allow a good man to be injured by a bad one. They may indeed kill me, or drive me into exile, or deprive me of my civil rights; and perhaps Meletus and others think those things great evils. But I do not think so: I think that it is a much greater evil to do what he is doing now, and to try to put a man to death unjustly. And now, Athenians, I am not arguing in my own defence at all, as you might expect me to do: I am trying to persuade you not to sin against God, by condemning me, and rejecting his gift to you. For if you put me to death, you will not easily find another man to fill my place. God has sent me to attack the city, as if it were a great and noble horse, to use a quaint simile, which was rather sluggish from its size, and which needed to be aroused by a gadfly: and I think that I am the gadfly that God has sent to the city to attack it; for I never cease from settling upon you, as it were, at every point, and rousing, and exhorting, and reproaching each man of you all day long. You will not easily find any one else, my friends, to fill my place: and if you take my advice, you will spare my life. You are vexed, as drowsy persons are, when they are awakened, and of course, if you listened to Anytus, you could easily kill me with a single blow, and then sleep on undisturbed for the rest of your lives, unless God were to care for you enough to send another man to arouse you. And you may easily see that it is God who has given me to your city: a mere human impulse would never have led me to neglect all my own interests, or to endure seeing my private affairs neglected now for so many years, while it made me busy myself unceasingly in your interests, and go to each man of you by himself, like a father, or an elder brother, trying to persuade him to care for virtue. There would have been a reason for it, if I had gained any advantage by this conduct, or if I had been paid for my exhortations; but you see yourselves that my accusers, though they accuse me of everything else without blushing, have not had the effrontery to say that I ever either exacted or demanded payment. They could bring no evidence of that. And I think that I have sufficient evidence of the truth of what I say in my poverty.

Perhaps it may seem strange to you that, though I am so busy in going about in private with my counsel, yet I do not venture to come forward in the assembly, and take part in the public councils. You have often heard me speak of my reason for this, and in many places: it is that I have a certain divine sign from God, which is the divinity that Meletus has caricatured in his indictment. I have had it from childhood: it is a kind of voice, which whenever I hear it, always turns me back from something which I was going to do, but never urges me to act. It is this which forbids me to take part in politics. And I think that it does well to forbid me. For, Athenians, it is quite certain that if I had attempted to take part in politics, I should have perished at once and long ago, without doing any good either to you or to myself. And do not be vexed with me for telling the truth. There is no man who will preserve his life for long, either in Athens or elsewhere, if he firmly opposes the wishes of the people, and tries to prevent the commission of much injustice and illegality in the State. He who would really fight for injustice, must do so as a private man, not in public, if he means to preserve his life, even for a short time.

I will prove to you that this is so by very strong evidence, not by mere words, but by what you value highly, actions. Listen then to what has happened to me, that you may know that there is no man who could make me consent to do wrong from the fear of death; but that I would perish at once rather than give way. What I am going to tell you may be a commonplace in the Courts of Law; nevertheless it is true. The only office that I ever held in the State, Athenians, was that of Senator. When you wished to try the ten generals, who did not rescue their men after the battle of Arginusæ, in a body, which was illegal, as you all came to think afterwards, the tribe Antiochis, to which I belong, held the presidency. On that occasion I alone of all the presidents opposed your illegal action, and gave my vote against you. The speakers were ready to suspend me and arrest me; and you were clamoring against me, and crying out to me to submit. But I thought that I ought to face the danger out in the cause of law and justice, rather than join with you in your unjust proposal, from fear of imprisonment or death. That was before the destruction of the democracy. When the oligarchy came, the Thirty sent for me, with four others, to the Council-Chamber, and ordered us to bring over Leon the Salaminian from Salamis, that they might put him to death. They were in the habit of frequently giving similar orders to many others, wishing to implicate as many men as possible in their crimes. But then I again proved, not by mere words, but by my actions, that, if I may use a vulgar expression, I do not care a straw for death; but that I do care very much indeed about not doing anything against the laws of God or man. That government with all its power did not terrify me into doing anything wrong; but when we left the Council-Chamber, the other four went over to Salamis, and brought Leon across to Athens; and I went away home: and if the rule of the Thirty had not been destroyed soon afterwards, I should very likely have been put to death for what I did then. Many of you will be my witnesses in this matter.

Now do you think that I should have remained alive all these years, if I had taken part in public affairs, and had always maintained the cause of justice like an honest man, and had held it a paramount duty, as it is, to do so? Certainly not, Athenians, nor any other man either.

. . . .

Well, my friends, this, together it may be with other things of the same nature, is pretty much what I have to say in my defence. There may be some one among you who will be vexed when he remembers how, even in a less important trial than this, he prayed and entreated the judges to acquit him with many tears, and brought forward his children and many of his friends and relatives in Court, in order to appeal to your feelings; and then finds that I shall do none of these things, though I am in what he would think the supreme danger. Perhaps he will harden himself against me when he notices this: it may make him angry, and he may give his vote in anger. If it is so with any of you—I do not suppose that it is, but in case it should be so—I think that I should answer him reasonably if I said: "My friend, I have kinsmen too, for, in the words of Homer, 'I am not born of stocks and stones,' but of woman"; and so, Athenians, I have kinsmen, and I have three sons, one of them a lad, and the other two still children. Yet I will not bring any of them forward before you, and implore you to acquit me. And why will I do none of these things? It is not from arrogance, Athenians, nor because I hold you cheap: whether or no I can face death bravely is another question: but for my own credit, and for your credit, and for the credit of our city, I do not think it well, at my age, and with my name, to do anything of that kind. Rightly or wrongly, men have made up their minds that in some way Socrates is different from the mass of mankind. And it will be a shameful thing if those of you who are thought to excel in wisdom, or in bravery, or in any other virtue, are going to act in this fashion. I have often seen men with a reputation behaving in a strange way at their trial, as if they thought it a terrible fate to be killed, and as though they expected to live for ever, if you did not put them to death. Such men seem to me to bring discredit on the city: for any stranger would suppose that the best and most eminent Athenians, who are selected by their fellow-citizens to hold office, and for other honors, are no better than women. Those of you, Athenians, who have any reputation at all, ought not to do these things: and you ought not to allow us to do them: you should show that you will be much more merciless to men who make the city ridiculous by these pitiful pieces of acting, than to men who remain quiet.

But apart from the question of credit, my friends, I do not think that it is right to entreat the judge to acquit us, or to escape condemnation in that way. It is our duty to convince his mind by reason. He does not sit to give away justice to his friends, but to pronounce judgment: and he has sworn not to favor any man whom he would like to favor, but to decide questions according to law. And therefore we ought not to teach you to forswear yourselves; and you ought not to allow yourselves to be taught, for then neither you nor we would be acting righteously. Therefore, Athenians, do not require me to do these things, for I believe them to be neither good nor just nor holy; and, more especially do not ask me to do them today, when Meletus is prosecuting me for impiety. For were I to be successful, and to prevail on you by my prayers to break your oaths, I should be clearly teaching you to believe that there are no gods; and I should be simply accusing myself by my defence of not believing in them. But, Athenians, that is very far from the truth. I do believe in the gods as no one of my accusers believes in them: and to you and to God I commit my cause to be decided as is best for you and for me. [*He is found guilty by 281 votes to 220.*]

I am not vexed at the verdict which you have given, Athenians, for many reasons. I expected that you would find me guilty; and I am not so much surprised at that, as at the numbers of the votes. I, certainly, never thought that the majority against me would have been so narrow. But now it seems that if only thirty votes had changed sides, I should have escaped. So I think that I have escaped Meletus, as it is: and not only have I escaped him; for it is perfectly clear that if Anytus and Lycon had not come forward to accuse me too, he would not have obtained the fifth part of the votes, and would have had to pay a fine of a thousand drachmæ.

So he proposes death as the penalty. Be it so. And what counter-penalty shall I propose to you, Athenians? What I deserve, of course, must I not? What then do I deserve to pay or to suffer for having determined not to spend my life in ease? I neglected the things which most men value, such as wealth, and family interests, and military commands, and popular oratory, and all the political appointments, and clubs, and factions, that there are in Athens; for I thought that I was really too conscientious a man to preserve my life if I engage in these matters. So I did not go where I should have done no good either to you or to myself. I went instead to each one of you by himself, to do him, as I say, the greatest of services, and strove to persuade him not to think of his affairs, until he had thought of himself, and tried to make himself as perfect and wise as possible; nor to think of the affairs of Athens, until he had thought of Athens herself; and in all cases to bestow his thoughts on things in the same manner. Then what do I deserve for such a life? Something good, Athenians, if I am really to propose what I deserve; and something good which it would be suitable to me to receive. Then what is a suitable reward to be given to a poor benefactor, who requires leisure to exhort you? There is no reward, Athenians, so suitable for him as a public maintenance in the Prytaneum. It is a much more suitable reward for him than for any of you who has won a victory at the Olympic games with his horse or his chariots. Such a man only makes you seem happy, but I make you really happy: and he is not in want, and I am. So if I am to propose the penalty which I really deserve, I propose this, a public maintenance in the Prytaneum.

Perhaps you think me stubborn and arrogant in what I am saying now, as in what I said about the entreaties and tears. It is not so, Athenians; it is rather that I am convinced that I never wronged any man intentionally, though I cannot persuade you of that, for we have conversed together only a little time. If there were a law at Athens, as there is elsewhere, not to finish a trial of life and death in a single day, I think that I could have convinced you of it: but now it is not easy in so short a time to clear myself of the gross calumnies of my enemies. But when I am convinced that I have never wronged any man, I shall certainly not wrong myself, or admit that I deserve to suffer any evil, or propose any evil for myself as a penalty. Why should I? Lest I should suffer the penalty which Meletus proposes, when I say that I do not know whether it is a good or an evil? Shall I choose instead of it something which I know to be an evil, and propose that as a penalty? Shall I propose imprisonment? And why should I pass the rest of my days in prison, the slave of successive officials? Or shall I propose a fine, with imprisonment until it is paid? I have told you why I will not do that. I should have to remain in prison for I have no money to pay a fine with. Shall I then propose exile? Perhaps you would agree to that. Life would indeed be very dear to me, if I were unreasonable enough to expect that strangers would cheerfully tolerate my discussions and reasonings, when you who are my fellow-citizens cannot endure them, and have found them so burdensome and odious to you, that you are seeking now to be released from them. No, indeed, Athenians, that is not likely. A fine life I should lead for an old man, if I were to withdraw from Athens, and pass the rest of my days in wandering from city to city, and continually being expelled. For I know very well that the young men will listen to me, wherever I go, as they do here; and if I drive them away, they will persuade their elders to expel me: and if I do not drive them away, their fathers and kinsmen will expel me for their sakes.

Perhaps some one will say, "Why cannot you withdraw from Athens, Socrates, and hold your peace?" It is the most difficult thing in the world to make you understand why I cannot do that. If I say that I cannot hold my peace, because that would be to disobey God, you will think that I am not in earnest and will not believe me. And if I tell you that no better thing can happen to a man than to converse every day about virtue and the other matters about which you have heard me conversing and examining myself and others, and that an unexamined life is not worth living, then you will believe me still less. But that is the truth, my friends, though it is not easy to convince you of it. And, what is more, I am not accustomed to think that I deserve any punishment. If I had been rich, I would have proposed as large a fine as I could pay: that would have done me no harm. But I am not rich enough to pay a fine, unless you are willing to fix it at a sum within my means. Perhaps I could pay you a mina: so I propose that. Plato here, Athenians, and Crito, and Critobulus, and Apollodorus bid me propose thirty minæ, and they will be sureties for me. So I propose thirty minæ. They will be sufficient sureties to you for the money. [*He is condemned to death.*]

You have not gained very much time, Athenians, and, as the price of it, you will have an evil name from all who wish to revile the city, and they will cast in your teeth that you put Socrates, a wise man, to death. For they will certainly call me wise, whether I am wise or not, when they want to reproach you. If you would have waited for a little while, your wishes would have been fulfilled in the course of nature; for you see that I am an old man, far advanced in years, and near to death. I am speaking not to all of you, only to those who have voted for my death. And now I am speaking to them still. Perhaps, my friends, you think that I have been defeated because I was wanting in the arguments by which I could have persuaded you to acquit me, if, that is, I had thought it right to do or to say anything to escape punishment. It is not so. I have been defeated because I was wanting, not in arguments, but in overboldness and effrontery: because I would not plead before you as you would have liked to hear me plead, or appeal to you with weeping and wailing, or say and do many other things, which I maintain are unworthy of me, but which you have been accustomed to from other men. But when I was defending myself, I thought that I ought not to do anything unmanly because of the danger which I ran, and I have not changed my mind now. I would very much rather defend myself as I did, and die, than as you would have had me do, and live. Both in a law suit, and in war, there are some things which neither I nor any other man may do in order to escape from death. In battle a man often sees that he may at least escape from death by throwing down his arms and falling on his knees before the pursuer to beg for his life. And there are many other ways of avoiding death in every danger, if a man will not scruple to say and to do anything. But, my friends, I think that it is a much harder thing to escape from wickedness than from death; for wickedness is swifter than death. And now I, who am old and slow, have been overtaken by the slower pursuer: and my accusers, who are clever and swift, have been overtaken by the swifter pursuer, which is wickedness. And now I shall go hence, sentenced by you to death; and they will go hence, sentenced by truth to receive the penalty of wickedness and evil. And I abide by this award as well as they. Perhaps it was right for these things to be so: and I think that they are fairly measured.

And now I wish to prophesy to you, Athenians who have condemned me. For I am going to die, and that is the time when men have most prophetic power. And I prophesy to you who have sentenced me to death, that a far severer punishment than you have inflicted on me, will surely overtake you as soon as I am dead. You have done this thing, thinking that you will be relieved from having to give an account of your lives. But I say that the result will be very different from that. There will be more men who will call you to account, whom I have held back, and whom you did not see. And they will be harder masters to you than I have been, for they will be younger, and you will be more angry with them. For if you think that you will restrain men from reproaching you for your evil lives by putting them to death, you are very much mistaken. That way of escape is hardly possible, and it is not a good one. It is much better, and much easier, not to silence reproaches, but to make yourselves as perfect as you can. This is my parting prophecy to you who have condemned me.

With you who have acquitted me I should like to converse touching this thing that has come to pass, while the authorities are busy, and before I go to the place where I have to die. So, I pray you, remain with me until I go hence: there is no reason why we should not converse with each other while it is possible. I wish to explain to you, as my friends, the meaning of what has befallen me. A wonderful thing has happened to me, judges—for you I am right in calling judges. The prophetic sign, which I am wont to receive from the divine voice, has been constantly with me all through my life till now, opposing me in quite small matters if I were not going to act rightly. And now you yourselves see what has happened to me; a thing which might be thought, and which is sometimes actually reckoned, the supreme evil. But the sign of God did not withstand me when I was leaving my house in the morning, nor when I was coming up hither to the Court, nor at any point in my speech, when I was going to say anything: though at other times it has often stopped me in the very act of speaking. But now, in this matter, it has never once withstood me, either in my words or my actions. I will tell you what I believe to be the reason of that. This thing that has come upon me must be a good: and those of us who think that death is an evil must needs be mistaken. I have a clear proof that that is so; for my accustomed sign would certainly have opposed me, if I had not been going to fare well.

And if we reflect in another way we shall see that we may well hope that death is a good. For the state of death is one of two things: either the dead man wholly ceases to be, and loses all sensation; or, according to the common belief, it is a change and a migration of the soul unto another place.

And if death is the absence of all sensation, and like the sleep of one whose slumbers are unbroken by any dreams, it will be a wonderful gain. For if a man had to select that night in which he slept so soundly that he did not even see any dreams, and had to compare with it all the other nights and days of his life, and then had to say how many days and nights in his life he had spent better and more pleasantly than this night, I think that a private person, nay, even the great King [of Persia] himself, would find them easy to count, compared with the others. If that is the nature of death, I for one count it a gain. For then it appears that eternity is nothing more than a single night. But if death is a journey to another place, and the common belief be true, that there are all who have died, what good could be greater than this, my judges? Would a journey not be worth taking, at the end of which, in the other world, we should be released from the self-styled judges who are here, and should find the true judges, who are said to sit in judgment below, such as Minos, and Rhadamanthus, and Æacus, and Triptolemus, and the other demi-gods who were just in their lives? Or what would you not give to converse with Orpheus and Musæus and Hesiod and Homer? I am willing to die many times, if this be true. And for my own part I should have a wonderful interest in meeting there Palamedes, and Ajax the son of Telamon, and the other men of old who have died through an unjust judgment, and in comparing my experiences with theirs. That I think would be no small pleasure. And, above all, I could spend my time in examining those who are there, as I examine men here, and in finding out which of them is wise, and which of them thinks himself wise, when he is not wise. What would we not give, my judges, to be able to examine the leader of the great expedition against Troy, or Odysseus, or Sisyphus, or countless other men and women whom we could name? It would be an infinite happiness to converse with them, and to live with them, and to examine them. Assuredly there they do not put men to death for doing that. For besides the other ways in which they are happier than we are, they are immortal, at least if the common belief be true.

And you too, judges, must face death with a good courage, and believe this as a truth, that no evil can happen to a good man, either in life, or after death. His fortunes are not neglected by the gods; and what has come to me today has not come by chance. I am persuaded that it was better for me to die now, and to be released from trouble: and that was the reason why the sign never turned me back. And so I am hardly angry with my accusers, or with those who have condemned me to die. Yet it was not with this mind that they accused me and condemned me, but meaning to do me an injury. So far I may find fault with them.

Yet I have one request to make of them. When my sons grow up, visit them with punishment, my friends, and vex them in the same way that I have vexed you, if they seem to you to care for riches, or for any other thing, before virtue: and if they think that they are something, when they are nothing at all, reproach them, as I have reproached you, for not caring for what they should, and for thinking that they are great men when in fact they are worthless. And if you will do this, I myself and my sons will have received our deserts at your hands.

But now the time has come, and we must go hence; I to die, and you to live. Whether life or death is better is known to God, and to God only.

Epicurus (c. 341–270 B.C.) was the founder and leader of a school in his home in Athens. A generous, gentle, and kindly man who suffered poor health most of his life, he was widely respected, even adorated, by his students and friends. Over the ages the term "epicurean" has taken on meanings not advocated by Epicurus, who urged a restrained and prudent hedonism, stressing pleasure as the "absence of pain." Epicurus himself lived a simple life, dying at the age of seventy-two. The following brief selection is the opening paragraph of his "Letter to Menoeceus."

Let no one when young delay to study philosophy, nor when he is old grow weary of his study. For no one can come too early or too late to secure the health of his soul. And the man who says that the age for philosophy has either not yet come or has gone by is like the man who says that the age for happiness is not yet come to him, or has passed away. Wherefore both when young and old a man must study philosophy, that as he grows old he may be young in blessings through the grateful recollection of what has been, and that in youth he may be old as well, since he will know no fear of what is to come. We must then meditate on the things that make our happiness, seeing that when that is with us we have all, but when it is absent we do all to win it.

Epictetus (c. 50–130) was a Greek slave to a Roman officer. His master's death meant freedom and he became a teacher of the Stoic philosophy. His own hardships as a slave provided him with insight into the manner in which the general difficulties of life might be met, and he was a popular teacher. He joins the long list of philosophers who through the ages have been deemed subversive, as he was forced to leave Rome by order of the emperor Domitian, who banned all philosophers (and astrologers) from the city in the year 89. The writings of Epictetus have been lost, but the Roman historian Arian was one of his students and apparently took almost stenographic notes. The Discourses is the major work; of an original eight volumes, four exist today. The Encheiridion ("Manual") is a summary of his doctrines.

---

from THE DISCOURSES

When a man was consulting him how he should persuade his brother to cease being angry with him, Epictetus replied, Philosophy does not propose to secure for a man any external thing. If it did . . . philosophy would be allowing something which is not within its province. For as the carpenter's material is wood, and that of the statuary is copper, so the matter of the art of living is each man's life. What then is my brother's? That again belongs to his own art; but with respect to yours, it is one of the external things, like a piece of land, like health, like reputation. But philosophy promises none of these. In every circumstance I will maintain, she says, the governing part conformable to nature. Whose governing part? His in whom I am, she says.

How then shall my brother cease to be angry with me? Bring him to me and I will tell him. But I have nothing to say to you about his anger.

When the man, who was consulting him, said, I seek to know this, How, even if my brother is not reconciled to me, shall I maintain myself in a state conformable to nature? Nothing great, said Epictetus, is produced suddenly, since not even the grape or the fig is. If you say to me now that you want a fig, I will answer to you that it requires time: let it flower first, then put forth fruit, and then ripen. Is then the fruit of a fig-tree not perfect suddenly and in one hour, and would you possess the fruit of a man's mind in so short a time and so easily? Do not expect it, even if I tell you. . . .

Observe, this is the beginning of philosophy, a perception of the disagreement of men with one another, and an inquiry into the cause of the disagreement, and a condemnation and distrust of that which only "seems," and a certain investigation of that which "seems" whether it "seems" rightly, and a discovery of some rule . . . as we have discovered a balance in the determination of weights, and a carpenter's rule . . . in the case of straight and crooked things. This is the beginning of philosophy. Must we say that all things are right which seem so to all? And how is it possible that contradictions can be right? Not all then, but all which seem to us to be right. How more to you than those which seem right to the Syrians? why more than what seem right to the Egyptians? why more than what seems right to me or to any other man? Not at all more. What then "seems" to every man is not sufficient for determining what "is"; for neither in the case of weights or measures are we satisfied with the bare appearance, but in each case we have discovered a certain rule. In this matter then is there no rule superior to what "seems?" And how is it possible that the most necessary things among men should have no sign . . . , and be incapable of being discovered? There is then some rule. . . .

. . . And to philosophize is this, to examine and confirm the rules; and then to use them when they are known is the act of a wise and good man. . . .

What is the first business of him who philosophizes? To throw away self-conceit. For it is impossible for a man to begin to learn that which he thinks that he knows. . . .

Does a philosopher invite people to hear him? As the sun himself draws men to him, or as food does, does not the philosopher also draw to him those who will receive benefit? What physician invites a man to be treated by him? Indeed I now hear that even the physicians in Rome do invite patients, but when I lived there, the physicians were invited. I invite you to come and hear that things are in a bad way for you, and that you are taking care of everything except that of which you ought to take care, and that you are ignorant of the good and the bad and are unfortunate and unhappy. A fine kind of invitation: and yet if the words of the philosopher do not produce this effect on you, he is dead, and so is the speaker. Rufus was used to say: If you have leisure to praise me, I am speaking to no purpose. Accordingly he used to speak in such a way that every one of us who were sitting there supposed that some one had accused him before Rufus: he so touched on what was doing, he so placed before the eyes every man's faults.

The philosopher's school, ye men, is a surgery: you ought not to go out of it with pleasure, but with pain. For you are not in sound health when you enter.

from THE ENCHEIRIDION

I. Of things some are in our power, and others are not. In our power are opinion, movement toward a thing, desire, aversion (turning from a thing);

and in a word, whatever are our own acts: not in our power are the body, property, reputation, offices (magisterial power), and in a word, whatever are not our own acts. And the things in our power are by nature free, not subject to restraint nor hindrance: but the things not in our power are weak, slavish, subject to restraint, in the power of others. Remember then that if you think the things which are by nature slavish to be free, and the things which are in the power of others to be your own, you will be hindered, you will lament, you will be disturbed, you will blame both gods and men: but if you think that only which is your own to be your own, and if you think that what is another's, as it really is, belongs to another, no man will ever compel you, no man will hinder you, you will never blame any man, you will accuse no man, you will do nothing involuntarily (against your will), no man will harm you, you will have no enemy, for you will not suffer any harm.

If then you desire (aim at) such great things, remember that you must not (attempt to) lay hold of them with a small effort; but you must leave alone some things entirely, and postpone others for the present. But if you wish for these things also (such great things), and power (office) and wealth, perhaps you will not gain even these very things (power and wealth) because you aim also at those former things (such great things): certainly you will fail in those things through which alone happiness and freedom are secured. Straightway then practice saying to every harsh appearance, You are an appearance, and in no manner what you appear to be. Then examine it by the rules which you possess, and by this first and chiefly, whether it relates to the things which are in our power or to the things which are not in our power: and if it relates to anything which is not in our power, be ready to say, that it does not concern you.

V. Men are disturbed not by the things which happen, but by the opinions about the things: for example, death is nothing terrible, for if it were, it would have seemed so to Socrates; for the opinion about death, that it is terrible, is the terrible thing. When then we are impeded or disturbed or grieved, let us never blame others, but ourselves, that is, our opinions. It is the act of an ill-instructed man to blame others for his own bad condition; it is the act of one who has begun to be instructed, to lay the blame on himself; and of one whose instruction is completed, neither to blame another, nor himself.

VIII. Seek not that the things which happen should happen as you wish; but wish the things which happen to be as they are, and you will have a tranquil flow of life.

IX. Disease is an impediment to the body, but not to the will, unless the will itself chooses. Lameness is an impediment to the leg, but not to the will. And add this reflection on the occasion of everything that happens; for you will find it an impediment to something else, but not to yourself.

XIV. If you would have your children and your wife and your friends to live forever, you are silly; for you would have the things which are not in your power to be in your power, and the things which belong to others to be yours. So if you would have your slave to be free from faults, you are a fool; for you would have badness not to be badness, but something else. But if you wish not to fail in your desires, you are able to do that. Practice then this which you are able to do. He is the master of every man who has the power over the things, which another person wishes or does not wish, the power to confer them on him or to take them away. Whoever then wishes to be free, let him neither wish for anything nor avoid anything which depends on others: if he does not observe this rule, he must be a slave.

XV. Remember that in life you ought to behave as at a banquet. Suppose that something is carried round and is opposite to you. Stretch out your hand and take a portion with decency. Suppose that it passes by you. Do not detain it. Suppose that it is not yet come to you. Do not send your desire forward to it, but wait till it is opposite to you. Do so with respect to children, so with respect to a wife, so with respect to magisterial offices, so with respect to wealth, and you will be some time a worthy partner of the banquets of the gods. But if you take none of the things which are set before you, and even despise them, then you will be not only a fellow-banqueter with the gods, but also a partner with them in power. For by acting thus Diogenes and Heracleitus and those like them were deservedly divine, and were so called.

XIX. You can be invincible, if you enter into no contest in which it is not in your power to conquer. Take care then when you observe a man honored before others or possessed of great power or highly esteemed for any reason, not to suppose him happy, and be not carried away by the appearance. For if the nature of the good is in our power, neither envy nor jealousy will have a place in us. But you yourself will not wish to be a general or senator or consul, but a free man: and there is only one way to this, to despise (care not for) the things which are not in our power.

XX. Remember that it is not he who reviles you or strikes you, who insults you, but it is your opinion about these things as being insulting. When then a man irritates you, you must know that it is your own opinion which has irritated you. Therefore especially try not to be carried away by the appearance. For if you once gain time and delay, you will more easily master yourself.

XXI. Let death and exile and every other thing which appears dreadful be daily before your eyes; but most of all death: and you will never think of anything mean nor will you desire anything extravagantly.

XXII. If you desire philosophy, prepare yourself from the beginning to be ridiculed, to expect that many will sneer at you, and say, He has all at once returned to us as a philosopher; and whence does he get this supercilious look for us? Do you not show a supercilious look; but hold on to the things which seem to you best as one appointed by God to this station. And remember that if you abide in the same principles, these men who first ridiculed will afterward admire you: but if you shall have been overpowered by them, you will bring on yourself double ridicule.

XXIII. If it should ever happen to you to be turned to externals in order to please some person, you must know that you have lost your purpose in life. Be satisfied then in everything with being a philosopher; and if you wish to seem also to any person to be a philosopher, appear so to yourself, and you will be able to do this.

XXVI. We may learn the wish (will) of nature from the things in which we do not differ from one another; for instance, when your neighbor's slave has broken his cup, or anything else, we are ready to say forthwith, that it is one of the things which happen. You must know then that when your cup also is broken, you ought to think as you did when your neighbor's cup was broken. Transfer this reflection to greater things also. Is another man's child or wife dead? There is no one who would not say, this is an event incident to man. But when a man's own child or wife is dead, forthwith he calls out, Wo to me, how wretched I am. But we ought to remember how we feel when we hear that it has happened to others.

XXIX. In every act observe the things which come first, and those which follow it; and so proceed to the act. If you do not, at first you will approach it with alacrity, without having thought of the things which will follow; but afterward, when certain base (ugly) things have shown themselves, you will be ashamed. A man wishes to conquer at the Olympic games. I also wish indeed, for it is a fine thing. But observe both the things which come first, and the things which follow; and then begin the act. You must do everything according to rule, eat according to strict orders, abstain from delicacies, exercise yourself as you are bid at appointed times, in heat, in cold, you must not drink cold water, nor wine as you choose; in a word, you must deliver yourself up to the exercise master as you do to the physician, and then proceed to the contest. And sometimes you will strain the hand, put the ankle out of joint, swallow much dust, sometimes be flogged, and after all this be defeated. When you have considered all this, if you still choose, go to the contest: if you do not, you will behave like children, who at one time play as wrestlers, another time as flute players, again as gladiators, then as trumpeters, then as tragic actors: so you also will be at one time an athlete, at another a gladiator, then a rhetorician, then a philosopher, but with your whole soul you will be nothing at all; but like an ape you imitate everything that you see, and one thing after another pleases you. For you have not undertaken anything with consideration, nor have you surveyed it well; but carelessly and with cold desire. Thus some who have seen a philosopher and having heard one speak, as Euphrates speaks,—and who can speak as he does?—they wish to be philosophers themselves also. My man, first of all consider what kind of thing it is: and then examine your own nature, if you are able to sustain the character. Do you wish to be a pentathlete or a wrestler? Look at your arms, your thighs, examine your loins. For different men are formed by nature for different things. Do you think that if you do these things, you can eat in the same manner, drink in the same manner, and in the same manner loathe certain things? You must pass sleepless nights, endure toil, go away from your kinsmen, be despised by a slave, in everything have the inferior part, in honor, in office, in the courts of justice, in every little matter. Consider these things, if you would exchange for them, freedom from passions, liberty, tranquillity. If not, take care that, like little children, you be not now a philosopher, then a servant of the publicani, then a rhetorician, then a procurator (manager) for Cæsar. These things are not consistent. You must be one man, either good or bad. You must either cultivate your own ruling faculty, or external things; you must either exercise your skill on internal things or on external things; that is you must either maintain the position of a philosopher or that of a common person.

XXXV. When you have decided that a thing ought to be done and are doing it, never avoid being seen doing it, though the many shall form an unfavorable opinion about it. For if it is not right to do it, avoid doing the thing; but if it is right, why are you afraid of those who shall find fault wrongly?

XLI. It is a mark of a mean capacity to spend much time on the things which concern the body, such as much exercise, much eating, much drinking, much easing of the body, much copulation. But these things should be done as subordinate things: and let all your care be directed to the mind.

XLII. When any person treats you ill or speaks ill of you, remember that he does this or says this because he thinks that it is his duty. It is not possible then for him to follow that which seems right to you, but that which seems right to himself. Accordingly if he is wrong in his opinion, he is the person who is hurt, for he is the person who has been deceived; for if a man shall suppose the true conjunction to be false, it is not the conjunction which is hindered, but the man who has been deceived about it. If you proceed then from these opinions, you will be mild in temper to him who reviles you: for say on each occasion, It seemed so to him.

XLIV. These reasonings do not cohere: I am richer than you, therefore I am better than you; I am more eloquent than you, therefore I am better than you. On the contrary these rather cohere, I am richer than you, therefore my possessions are greater than yours: I am more eloquent than you, therefore my speech is superior to yours. But you are neither possession nor speech.

XLVI. On no occasion call yourself a philosopher, and do not speak much among the uninstructed about theorems (philosophical rules, precepts): but do that which follows from them. For example at a banquet do not say how a man ought to eat, but eat as you ought to eat. For remember that in this way Socrates also altogether avoided ostentation: persons used to come to him and ask to be recommended by him to philosophers, and he used to take them to philosophers: so easily did he submit to being overlooked. Accordingly if any conversation should arise among uninstructed persons about any theorem, generally be silent; for there is great danger that you will immediately vomit up what you have not digested. And when a man shall say to you, that you know nothing, and you are not vexed, then be sure that you have begun the work (of philosophy). For even sheep do not vomit up their grass and show to the shepherds how much they have eaten; but when they have internally digested the pasture, they produce externally wool and milk. Do you also show not your theorems to the uninstructed, but show the acts which come from their digestion.

XLVIII. The condition and characteristic of an uninstructed person is this: he never expects from himself profit (advantage) nor harm, but from externals. The condition and characteristic of a philosopher is this: he expects all advantage and all harm from himself. The signs (marks) of one who is making progress are these: he censures no man, he praises no man, he blames no man, he accuses no man, he says nothing about himself as if he were somebody or knew something; when he is impeded at all or hindered, he blames himself: if a man praises him, he ridicules the praiser to himself: if a man censures him, he makes no defense: he goes about like weak persons, being careful not to move any of the things which are placed, before they are firmly fixed: he removes all desire from himself, and he transfers aversion to those things only of the things within our power which are contrary to nature: he employs a moderate movement toward everything: whether he is considered foolish or ignorant, he cares not: and in a word he watches himself as if he were an enemy and lying in ambush.

LI. The first and most necessary place (part) in philosophy is the use of theorems (precepts), for instance, that we must not lie: the second part is that of demonstrations, for instance, How is it proved that we ought not to lie: the third is that which is confirmatory of these two and explanatory, for example, How is this a demonstration? For what is demonstration, what is consequence, what is contradiction, what is truth, what is falsehood? The third part (topic) is necessary on account of the second, and the second on account of the first; but the most necessary and that on which we ought to rest is the first. But we do the contrary. For we spend our time on the third topic, and all our earnestness is about it: but we entirely neglect the first. Therefore we lie; but the demonstration that we ought not to lie we have ready to hand.

c. d. broad   CRITICAL THOUGHT

Charlie Dunbar Broad (1887–   ) was born in London and educated at Cambridge. He was a fellow at Trinity College, Cambridge for most of his teaching career; he lived there in rooms occupied two centuries earlier by Isaac Newton. Following his retirement from Cambridge, Broad was a visiting professor at the University of Michigan and at UCLA in 1953–1954. One of the most influential philosophers of this century, Professor Broad is a Fellow of the British Academy, and he has been president of the British Society for Psychical Research. He is the author of Perception, Physics, and Reality, The Mind and Its Place in Nature, Ethics and the History of Philosophy, Religion, Philosophy, and Psychical Research, *and* Lectures on Psychical Research. *The following selection is from* Scientific Thought *(1923).*

I shall devote this introductory chapter to stating what I think philosophy is about, and why the other sciences are important to it and it is important to the other sciences. A very large number of scientists will begin such a book as this with the strong conviction that philosophy is mainly moonshine, and with the gravest doubts as to whether it has anything of the slightest importance to tell them. I do not think that this view of philosophy is true, or I should not waste my time and cheat my students by trying to teach it. But I do think that such a view is highly plausible, and that the proceedings of many philosophers have given the general public some excuse for its unfavourable opinion of philosophy. I shall therefore begin by stating the case against philosophy as strongly as I can, and shall then try to show that, in spite of all objections, it really is a definite science with a distinct subject-matter. I shall try to show that it really does advance and that it is related to the special sciences in such a way that the cooperation of philosophers and scientists is of the utmost benefit to the studies of both.

I think that an intelligent scientist would put his case against philosophy somewhat as follows. He would say: "Philosophers discuss such subjects as the existence of God, the immortality of the soul, and the freedom of the will. They spin out of their minds fanciful theories, which can neither be supported nor refuted by experiment. No two philosophers agree, and no progress is made. Philosophers are still discussing with great heat the same questions that they discussed in Greece thousands of years ago. What a poor show does this make when compared with mathematics or any of the natural sciences! Here there is continual steady progress; the discoveries of one age are accepted by the next, and become the basis for further advances in knowledge. There is controversy indeed, but it is fruitful controversy which advances the science and ends in definite agreement; it is not the aimless wandering in a circle to which philosophy is condemned. Does this not very strongly suggest that philosophy is either a mere playing with words, or that, if it has a genuine subject-matter, this is beyond the reach of human intelligence?"

Our scientist might still further strengthen his case by reflecting on the past history of philosophy and on the method by which it is commonly taught to students. He will remind us that most of the present sciences started by being mixed up with philosophy, that so long as they kept this connexion they remained misty and vague, and that as soon as their fundamental principles began to be discovered they cut their disreputable associate, wedded the experimental method, and settled down to the steady production of a strapping family of established truths. Mechanics is a case in point. So long as it was mixed up with philosophy it made no progress; when the true laws of motion were discovered by the experiments and reasoning of Galileo it ceased to be a part of philosophy and began to develop into a separate science. Does this not suggest that the subject-matter of philosophy is just that ever-diminishing fragment of the universe in which the scientist has not yet discovered laws, and where we have therefore to put up with guesses? Are not such guesses the best that philosophy has to offer; and will they not be swept aside as soon as some man of genius, like Galileo or Dalton or Faraday, sets the subject on the sure path of science?

Should our scientist talk to students of philosophy and ask what happens at their lectures, his objections will most likely be strengthened. The answer may take the classical form: "He tells us what everyone knows in language that no one can understand." But, even if the answer be not so unfavourable as this, it is not unlikely to take the form: "We hear about the views of Plato and Kant and Berkeley on such subjects as the reality of the external world and the immortality of the soul." Now the scientist will at once contrast this with the method of teaching in his own subject, and will be inclined to say, if *e.g.* he be a chemist: "We learn what *are* the laws of chemical combination and the structure of the Benzene nucleus, we do not worry our heads as to what exactly Dalton thought or Kekule said. If philosophers really know anything about the reality of the external world why do they not say straightforwardly that it is real or unreal, and prove it? The fact that they apparently prefer to discuss the divergent views of a collection of eminent 'backnumbers' on the question strongly suggests that they know that there is no means of answering it, and that nothing better than groundless opinions can be offered."

I have put these objections as strongly as I can, and I now propose to see just how much there is in them. First, as to the alleged unprogressive character of philosophy. This is, I think, an illusion; but it is a very natural one. Let us take the question of the reality of the external world as an example. Common-sense says that chairs and tables exist independently of whether anyone happens to perceive them or not. We study Berkeley and find him claiming to prove that such things can only exist so long as they are perceived by someone. Later on we read some modern realist, like Alexander, and we are told that Berkeley was wrong, and that chairs and tables can and do exist unperceived. We seem merely to have got back to where we started from, and to have wasted our time. But this is not really so, for two reasons. (i) What we believe at the end of the process and what we believed at the beginning are by no means the same, although we express the two beliefs by the same form of words. The original belief of common-sense was vague, crude and unanalysed. Berkeley's arguments have forced us to recognise a number of distinctions and to define much more clearly what we mean by the statement that chairs and tables exist unperceived. What we find is that the original crude belief of common-sense consisted of a number of different beliefs, mixed up with each other. Some of these may be true and others false. Berkeley's arguments really do refute or throw grave doubt on some of them, but they leave others standing. Now it may be that those which are left are enough to constitute a belief in the independent reality of external objects. If so this final belief in the reality of the external world is much clearer and subtler than the *verbally* similar belief with which we began. It has been purified of irrelevant factors, and is no longer a vague mass of different beliefs mixed up with each other.

(ii) Not only will our final belief differ in content from our original one, it will also differ in certainty. Our original belief was merely instinctive, and was at the mercy of any sceptical critic who chose to cast doubts on it. Berkeley has played this part. Our final belief is that part or that modification of our original one that has managed to survive his criticisms. This does not of course *prove* that it is true; there may be other objections to it. But, at any rate, a belief that has stood the criticisms of an acute and subtle thinker, like Berkeley, is much more likely to be true than a merely instinctive belief which has never been criticised by ourselves or anyone else. Thus the process which at first sight seemed to be merely circular has not really been so. And it has certainly not been useless; for it has enabled us to replace a vague belief by a clear and analysed one, and a merely instinctive belief by one that has passed through the fire of criticism.

The above example will suggest to us a part at least of what philosophy is really about. Common-sense constantly makes use of a number of concepts, in terms of which it interprets its experience. It talks of *things* of various kinds; it says that they have *places* and *dates*, that they *change*, and that changes in one *cause* changes in others, and so on. Thus it makes constant use of such concepts or categories as thinghood, space, time, change, cause, etc. Science takes over these concepts from common-sense with but slight modification, and uses them in its work. Now we can and do *use* concepts without having any very clear idea of their meaning or their mutual relations. I do not of course suggest that to the ordinary man the words *substance, cause, change,* etc., are mere meaningless noises, like *Jabberwock* or *Snark*. It is clear that we mean something, and something different in each case, by such words. If we did not we could not use them consistently, and it is obvious that on the whole we do consistently apply and withhold such names. But it is possible to apply concepts more or less successfully when one has only a very confused idea as to their meaning. No man confuses place with date, and for practical purposes any two men agree as a rule in the places that they assign to a given object. Nevertheless, if you ask them what exactly they mean by *place* and *date*, they will be puzzled to tell you.

Now the most fundamental task of philosophy is to take the concepts that we daily use in common life and science, to analyse them, and thus to determine their precise meanings and their mutual relations. Evidently this is an important duty. In the first place, clear and accurate knowledge of anything is an advance on a mere hazy general familiarity with it. Moreover, in the absence of clear knowledge of the meanings and relations of the concepts that we use, we are certain sooner or later to apply them wrongly or to meet with exceptional cases where we are puzzled as to how to apply them at all. For instance, we all agree pretty well as to the place of a certain pin which we are looking at. But suppose we go on to ask: "Where is the image of that pin in a certain mirror; and is it in this place (whatever it may be) in precisely the sense in which the pin itself is in *its* place?" We shall find the question a very puzzling one, and there will be no hope of answering it until we have carefully analysed what we mean by *being in a place*.

Again, this task of clearing up the meanings and determining the relations of fundamental concepts is not performed to any extent by any other science. Chemistry *uses* the notion of substance, geometry that of space, and mechanics that of motion. But they assume that you already know what is meant by *substance* and *space* and *motion*. So you do in a vague way; and it is not their business to enter, more than is necessary for their own special purposes, into the meaning and relations of these concepts as such. Of course the special sciences do in some measure clear up the meanings of the concepts that they use. A chemist, with his distinction between elements and compounds and his laws of combination, has a clearer idea of substance than an ordinary layman. But the special sciences only discuss the meanings of their concepts so far as this is needful for their own special purposes. Such discussion is incidental to them, whilst it is of the essence of philosophy, which deals with such questions for their own sake. Whenever a scientist begins to discuss the concepts of his science in this thorough and disinterested way we begin to say that he is studying, not so much Chemistry or Physics, as the *philosophy* of Chemistry or Physics. It will therefore perhaps be agreed that, in the above sense of philosophy, there is both room and need for such a study, and that there is no special reason to fear that it will be beyond the compass of human faculties.

At this point a criticism may be made which had better be met at once. It may be said: "By our own admission the task of philosophy is purely verbal; it consists entirely of discussions about the meanings of words." This criticism is of course absolutely wide of the mark. When we say that philosophy tries to clear up the meanings of concepts we do not mean that it is simply concerned to substitute some long phrase for some familiar word. Any analysis, when once it has been made, is naturally *expressed* in words; but so too is any other discovery. When Cantor gave his definition of Continuity, the final result of his work was expressed by saying that you can substitute for the word "continuous" such and such a verbal phrase. But the essential part of the work was to find out exactly what properties are present in objects when we predicate continuity of them, and what properties are absent when we refuse to predicate continuity. This was evidently not a question of words but of things and their properties.

Philosophy has another and closely connected task. We not only make continual use of vague and unanalysed concepts. We have also a number of uncriticised beliefs, which we constantly assume in ordinary life and in the sciences. We constantly assume, *e.g.*, that every event has a cause, that nature obeys uniform laws, that we live in a world of objects whose existence and behaviour are independent of our knowledge of them, and so on. Now science takes over those beliefs without criticism from common-sense, and simply works with them. We know by experience, however, that beliefs which are very strongly held may be mere prejudices. Negroes find it very hard to believe that water can become solid, because they have always lived in a warm climate. Is it not possible that we believe that nature as a whole will always act uniformly simply because the part of nature in which the human race has lived has happened to act so up to the present? All such beliefs then, however deeply rooted, call for criticism. The first duty of philosophy is to state them clearly; and this can only be done when we have analysed and defined the concepts that they involve. Until you know exactly what you mean by *change* and *cause* you cannot know what is meant by the statement that *every change has a cause*. And not much weight can be attached to a person's most passionate beliefs if he does not know what precisely he is passionately believing. The next duty of philosophy is to test such beliefs; and this can only be done by resolutely and honestly exposing them to every objection that one can think of oneself or find in the writings of others. We ought only to go on believing a proposition if, at the end of

117

this process, we still find it impossible to doubt it. Even then of course it may not be true, but we have at least done our best.

These two branches of philosophy—the analysis and definition of our fundamental concepts, and the clear statement and resolute criticism of our fundamental beliefs—I call *critical philosophy*. It is obviously a necessary and a possible task, and it is not performed by any other science. The other sciences *use* the concepts and *assume* the beliefs; critical philosophy tries to analyse the former and to criticise the latter. Thus, so long as science and critical philosophy keep to their own spheres, there is no possibility of conflict between them, since their subject-matter is quite different. Philosophy claims to analyse the general concepts of substance and cause, *e.g.*, it does not claim to tell us about particular substances, like gold, or about particular laws of causation, as that *aqua regia* dissolves gold. Chemistry, on the other hand tells us a great deal about the various kinds of substances in the world, and how changes in one cause changes in another. But it does not profess to analyse the general concepts of substance or causation, or to consider what right we have to assume that every event has a cause.

It should now be clear why the method of philosophy is so different from that of the natural sciences. Experiments are not made, because they would be utterly useless. If you want to find out how one substance behaves in the presence of another you naturally put the two together, vary the conditions, and note the results. But no experiment will clear up your ideas as to the meaning of *cause* in general or of *substance* in general. Again, all conclusions from experiments rest on some of those very assumptions which it is the business of philosophy to state clearly and to criticise. The experimenter assumes that nature obeys uniform laws, and that similar results will follow always and everywhere from sufficiently similar conditions. This is one of the assumptions that philosophy wants to consider critically. The method of philosophy thus resembles that of pure mathematics, at least in the respect that neither has any use for experiment.

There is, however, a very important difference. In pure mathematics we start either from axioms which no one questions, or from premises which are quite explicitly assumed merely as hypotheses; and our main interest is to deduce remote consequences. Now most of the tacit assumptions of ordinary life and of natural science claim to be true and not merely to be hypotheses, and at the same time they are found to be neither clear nor self-evident when critically reflected upon. Most mathematical axioms are very simple and clear, whilst most other propositions which men strongly believe are highly complex and confused. Philosophy is mainly concerned, not with remote conclusions, but with the analysis and appraisement of the original premises. For this purpose analytical power and a certain kind of insight are necessary, and the mathematical method is not of much use.

Now there is another kind of philosophy; and, as this is more exciting, it is what laymen generally understand by the name. This is what I call *speculative philosophy*. It has a different object, is pursued by a different method, and leads to results of a different degree of certainty from critical philosophy. Its object is to take over the results of the various sciences, to add to them the results of religious and ethical experiences of mankind, and then to reflect upon the whole. The hope is that, by this means, we may be able to reach some general conclusions as to the nature of the Universe, and as to our position and prospects in it. . . .

josé ortega y gasset   WHAT IS PHILOSOPHY?

José Ortega y Gasset (1883–1955) received his Ph.D. from the Central University of Madrid. In 1910 he became Professor of Metaphysics at the Central University of Madrid, remaining in that position until his departure from Spain at the outbreak of the Civil War in 1936. After a long exile in France, Argentina, and Portugal, he returned to Madrid, leaving only to take part with Albert Schweitzer in the Goethe Festival in Aspen, Colorado in 1949. A prolific writer, he was the author of Meditations on Quixote, Man and Crisis, The Dehumanization of Art, History as a System, The Mission of the University, *and* The Origin of Philosophy. The Revolt of the Masses *was perhaps his most notable book. The following selection is from* What Is Philosophy? *(1928).*

One might begin by defining philosophy as knowledge of the Universe. But this definition, while accurate enough, allows the very thing that is specific to escape from us, namely the peculiar dramatic quality and the tone of intellectual heroism peculiar to philosophy and only philosophy. In effect, that definition seems to balance the one we were giving for physics when we said that it is knowledge of matter. But the fact is that the philosopher does not set himself in front of his object—the Universe—as does the physicist in front of his object, which is matter. The physicist begins by defining the profile, the outline of matter, and only then does he start working in an attempt to understand its internal structure. The mathematician defines number and extension by a similar process. Thus all the individual sciences begin by marking off for themselves a bit of the Universe, by limiting their problem, which, once limited, ceases in part to be a problem. Or to put it another way, the physicist and the mathematician know in advance the extent of their object and its essential attributes; therefore they begin not with the problem, but with something which they give or take as already known.

But the Universe on whose investigation the philosopher sets out, audacious as an Argonaut—no one knows what this is. *Universe* is an enormous and monolithic word which, like a vague and vast gesture, conceals this concept—everything that is—rather than stating it. Everything that is—for the moment, that is the Universe. That, note it well, nothing more than that, for when we think the concept, "everything there is," we do not know what that "everything there is" may be; the only thing we think is a negative concept, namely the negation of that which would only be a part, a piece, a fragment. *So the philosopher, in contradistinction to every other scientist, sets sail for the unknown as such.* The more or less known is a part, a

120

portion, a splinter of the Universe. The philosopher sets himself in front of his object in an attitude which is different from that of any other expert; the philosopher does not know what his object is, of it he knows only this—first, that it is no one of the other objects; second, that it is an integral object, the authentic whole, that which leaves nothing outside, and by the same token, the only one which is sufficient unto itself. No other one of the objects which are known or suspected possesses this condition. Therefore the Universe is that which basically we do not know, that of which we are absolutely ignorant insofar as its positive content is concerned.

Swinging around this subject on an earlier spiral, we could say that to the other sciences their object is given, but the object of philosophy is precisely that which cannot be given; because it is the whole, and because it is not given, it must in a very special sense be that which is sought for, perennially sought for. There is nothing strange in the fact that the very science whose object must at the start be sought for, the science that is problematical even as to its object and its subject matter, should have a life less tranquil than the others, and should not at first sight enjoy what Kant called *der sichere Gang*.[1] Philosophy, which is pure theoretic heroism, will never have this sure, peaceful and bourgeois stage. Like its object, philosophy will consist in being the universal and absolute science which is sought for. This Aristotle, the first master of our discipline, calls it philosophy, the science which is sought for—. . .

Where, one asks, does this appetite for the Universe, for the wholeness of the world, which is the root of philosophy, come from? To put it simply, that appetite, seeming peculiar to philosophy, is in fact the native and spontaneous attitude of the live mind. In the very act of living we sense, clearly or cloudily, a world about us which we assume to be complete. It is the man of science, the mathematician, the scientist, who cuts down through that integral aspect of our living world, who isolates a piece of it and out of this makes his own particular question. If knowledge of the Universe, if philosophy, does not yield truths of the same type as "scientific truth," so much the worse for scientific truth.

"Scientific truth is characterized by its exactness and the rigorous quality of its assumptions. But experimental science wins these admirable qualities at the cost of maintaining itself on a plane of secondary problems and leaving the decisive and ultimate questions intact. Out of this renunciation it makes its essential virtue, and for this, if for nothing else, it deserves applause. But experimental science is only a meager portion of the mind and the organism. Where it stops, man does not stop. If the physicist stays the hand with which he delineates things at the point where his methods end, the human

[1] "the steady gait"

121

being who stands behind every physicist prolongs the line and carries it on to the end, just as our eye, seeing a portion of a broken arch, automatically completes the missing airy curve. . . .

. . . How can we live deaf to the last, dramatic questions? Where does the world come from, whither is it going? What is the definitive power in the cosmos? What is the essential meaning of life? Confined to a zone of intermediate and secondary themes, we cannot breathe. We need a complete perspective, with foreground and background, not a maimed and partial landscape, not a horizon from which the lure of the great distances has been cut away. Lacking a set of cardinal points, our footsteps would lack direction. To assert that no manner of resolving the ultimate questions has yet been discovered is no valid excuse for a lack of sensitiveness toward them. All the more reason for feeling in the depths of our being their pressure and their hurt! Whose hunger has ever been stilled by knowing that he will not be able to eat? Insoluble though they be, those questions will continue to rise, pathetic, on the clouded vault of the night, blinking at us like the twinkle of a star. As Heine put it, the stars are the night's thoughts, restless and golden. North and South help to orient us despite their not being accessible cities reached simply by buying a railroad ticket.

"What I mean by this is that we are given no escape from the ultimate questions. Whether we like it or not, they live, in one fashion or another, within us. 'Scientific truth' is exact, but it is incomplete and penultimate; it is of necessity embedded in another kind of truth, complete and ultimate, although inexact, which could be called 'myth.' Scientific truth floats, then, in mythology, and science itself, as a whole, is a myth, the admirable European myth." . . .

. . . We insist that the physicist, and by the same token the mathematician, the historian, the artist, the politician—on seeing the limits of his craft, shall pull back within himself. Then he finds that he himself is not solely a physicist, but that physics is only one among an innumerable series of things which he does in his man's life. At the bottom of his being, in his deepest stratum, the physicist turns out to be a man, he is a human life. And this human life is inevitably and constantly submitting itself to an integrated world, to the Universe. Before being a physicist, he is a man, and being a man, he is preoccupied with the Universe, that is to say, he philosophizes, well or poorly, spontaneously or with a care for technique, in a fashion which may be barbarous or may be cultivated. Ours will not be the road that leads over and beyond physics; on the contrary, it will draw back from physics to basic life and find the root of philosophy here. The result will not be metaphysical but ante-physical. It is born out of life itself, and as we will see clearly, life cannot avoid philosophizing, no matter in how elemental a form. Therefore

122

the first reply to our question, "what is philosophy?" may be phrased thus —"Philosophy is—a thing which is inevitable." . . .

Philosophy is knowledge of the Universe, or of whatever there is. We have already seen that for the philosopher this implied the need to set for himself an absolute problem, that is to say, he cannot take as his point of departure the earlier beliefs, and cannot accept anything as known in advance. The known is what is no longer a problem. Well then, that which is known outside of, apart from or previous to philosophy, is known from a point of view which is partial and not universal, is knowing on an inferior level which is no help on the heights where philosophic knowledge moves *a nativitate*.[2] Seen from philosophic heights, all other knowing has about it a touch of the ingenuous and the relatively false, that is to say, it again becomes problematical. Hence Nicolas of Cusa called the sciences *docta ignorantia*.[3]

This position of the philosopher, which accompanies his extreme intellectual heroism and would be so uncomfortable if it did not bear with it his inevitable vocation, imposes on his thought what I call the imperative of *autonomy*. This means renouncing the right to lean on anything prior to the philosophy which he may be creating, and pledging himself not to start from supposed truths. Philosophy is a science without suppositions. I understand by this a system of truths which has been constructed without admitting as groundwork any truth that is given as proven outside of that system. So there is no philosophic admission which the philosopher does not have to forge with his own means. Philosophy is an intellectual law unto itself, it is self-contained. This I call the principle of autonomy—and this links us directly to the whole critical past of philosophy; it brings us back to the great mover and shaker of modern thought and qualifies us as the latest grandsons of Descartes. But have no faith in the tenderness of grandsons. Tomorrow we are going to cast up accounts with our grandfathers. The philosopher begins by purging his spirit of received beliefs, by converting that spirit into a desert isle devoid of truths, and then, a recluse on this island, he condemns himself to a methodic procedure in the Robinson Crusoe tradition. Such was the meaning of the methodical doubt which places Descartes forever on the doorstep of philosophic knowledge. Its meaning was not simply the doubting of all that stirs doubt within us—every intelligent man does this continually—but it consists in doubting even that which in fact is not doubted, but in principle could be doubtful. This instrumental and technical doubt, which is philosophy's scalpel, has a radius of action far broader than man's habitual suspicion, in that leaving behind it that which is doubtful, it moves toward that which can be doubted.

[2] "from birth"
[3] "learned ignorance"

henri-frederic amiel   PHILOSOPHY MEANS LIBERTY

Henri-Frederic Amiel (1821–1881) was born in Geneva, and he lived and worked there most of his life. He showed early promise as a scholar. At the age of twenty he published an article in Geneva's leading literary journal, and at twenty-eight he was Professor of Aesthetics and French Literature at the Academy of Geneva, later becoming Professor of Moral Philosophy. But Amiel's retiring personality and introspective habits of thought led him to an increasingly solitary and "unproductive" existence. He was a conscientious but undistinguished teacher. After his death, there came to light his private journal, which ran to 17,000 pages of manuscript. Amiel had said of it, "What a prodigious waste of time, of thought, of strength!" The world has thought otherwise.

Philosophy means the complete liberty of the mind, and therefore independence of all social, political, or religious prejudice. It is to begin with neither Christian nor pagan, neither monarchical nor democratic, neither socialist nor individualist; it is critical and impartial; it loves one thing only —truth. If it disturbs the ready-made opinions of the Church or the State—or the historical medium—in which the philosopher happens to have been born, so much the worse, but there is no help for it. . . .

Philosophy means, first, doubt; and afterwards the consciousness of what knowledge means, the consciousness of uncertainty and of ignorance, the consciousness of limit, shade, degree, possibility. The ordinary man doubts nothing and suspects nothing. The philosopher is more cautious, but he is thereby unfitted for action, because, although he sees the goal less dimly than others, he sees his own weakness too clearly, and has no illusions as to his chances of reaching it.

The philosopher is like a man fasting in the midst of universal intoxication. He alone perceives the illusion of which all creatures are the willing playthings; he is less duped than his neighbour by his own nature. He judges more sanely, he sees things as they are. It is in this that his liberty consists—in the ability to see clearly and soberly, in the power of mental record. Philosophy has for its foundation critical lucidity. The end and climax of it would be the intuition of the universal law, of the first principle and the final aim of the universe. Not to be deceived is its first desire: to understand, its second. Emancipation from error is the condition of real knowledge. The philosopher is a sceptic seeking a plausible hypothesis, which may explain to him the whole of his experiences. When he imagines that he has found such a key to life he offers it to, but does not force it on, his fellow-men.

Translated by Mrs. Humphry Ward

FURTHER READING

Textbooks in philosophy are unusually difficult to write, but John Herman Randall and Justus Buchler succeeded admirably in their *Philosophy: An Introduction* (1942). A more recent success is Jerome A Shaffer's *Reality, Knowledge, and Value* (1971), which is clear, interest-provoking and brief (126 pages).

Three excellent essays are Moritz Schlick's "The Future of Philosophy," Bertrand Russell's "The Value of Philosophy," and Alfred North Whitehead's "The Aim of Philosophy." All appear in *Basic Problems of Philosophy*, edited by Daniel J. Bronstein, *et al.* (3rd ed., 1964), an anthology which is itself to be recommended to those prepared for what is sometimes rigorous reading.

Another valuable anthology is Paul Edwards and Arthur Pap's *A Modern Introduction to Philosophy* (rev. ed., 1965). Here, too, a number of the readings require close attention.

Abraham Kaplan's *New World of Philosophy* (1961) presents nine lucid and concise introductory "lectures" on systems of thought ranging from pragmatism and existentialism to Indian philosophy and Zen.

What Is Philosophy? (1965), edited by Henry W. Johnstone, Jr., is a collection of ten contemporary essays which deal specifically with the question of the nature of philosophy.

The central function of philosophy in education is eloquently stated in *Philosophy in American Education* (1945), by Brand Blanshard, C. J. Ducasse, Charles W. Hendel, Arthur E. Murphy, and Max C. Otto.

ALIENATION & THE DEATH OF MEANING

4

This has been a century in which certainties of the past have been overwhelmed by the crises and disasters of the present. It would seem that nothing has gone quite right. The progress of technology has not made men more content; some suspect that the glittering gadgetry may in fact be part of the problem. The so-called comforts and conveniences of modern life are often of superficial value, and the price we pay for them is high.

There have also been the unmitigated catastrophes of our times: we have had murderous wars, there is considerable ecological ruin, hunger and poverty exists around the world, political and racial tensions persist everywhere, and an ominous lawlessness is growing.

But these issues are only the tip of the iceberg. In the lives of individual men there has been a parallel devastation. This is the "wasteland," the world of the alienated, and these themes have dominated the thoughts of serious writers for decades. One such writer, typical of a thousand others, is F. Scott Fitzgerald. During the 1920s, he wrote, "a widespread neurosis began to be evident, faintly signalled, like the nervous beating of the feet, by the popularity of cross-word puzzles." His contemporaries began to "disappear into the dark maw of violence":

> A classmate killed his wife and himself on Long Island, another tumbled "accidently" from a skyscraper in Philadelphia, another purposely from a skyscraper in New York. One was killed in a speak-easy in Chicago; another was beaten to death in a speak-easy in New York and crawled home to the Princeton Club to die; still another had his skull crushed by a maniac's axe in an insane asylum where he was confined. These are not catastrophes that I went out of my way to look for—these were my friends; moreover, these things happened not during the depression but during the boom.[1]

The weight of such testimony and commentary has produced an overworked lexicon of despair. Man is said to experience a great emptiness, apathy, anxiety, and nothingness; he lives displaced and detached in a dehumanized world in which there has been a collapse of values. While the

[1] Arthur Mizener (ed.), The Fitzgerald Reader (New York: Charles Scribner's Sons, 1963), p. 329.

terms may be trite, the reality of the situation is not. Franz Kafka and Ernest Hemingway have captured some of this emptiness in their fiction.

Kafka's "The Bucket Rider" presents an eerie image of the age: that of a man freezing to death. He is in a city but very much alone; he doesn't require much but even that is unavailable. The sky above is "pitiless" and the words "lost forever" end the story. Equally despairing is Hemingway's "A Clean, Well-Lighted Place." Confronted by a pervading nothingness ("It was all a nothing and a man was a nothing too"), one must guard carefully what little dignity it is possible to maintain.

Psychotherapists such as Rollo May and R. D. Laing are able to speak from a unique perspective. May finds his clients a revealing "barometer" to what is happening in society at large, and in them he discerns a sense of individual powerlessness which results in their conformity, boredom, and other symptoms. Laing's charge is more encompassing: his concern is with what we consider normal. He points out that "normal men have killed perhaps 100,000,000 of their fellow normal men in the last fifty years," and that seems to say it all.

The alienating potentialities of one's work were explored well over a hundred years ago by Karl Marx in "Alienated Labor." When man works merely for money, under conditions established by others, he is prey to estrangement from himself and, subsequently, from others. In a capitalist society, Marx argues, such alienation is inevitable; men are divorced both from the means of production and the product of their labor.

Jean-Paul Sartre assigns existential significance to man's experiences of "Anguish, Forlornness, and Despair." Such experiences are consequences of man's freedom, and they are to be confronted and accepted.

Michael Novak, in a preface to his recent book The Experience of Nothingness, writes that "the form of the question as it arises today is: Granted that I have the experience of nothingness, what shall I do with it?" In the following chapter, taken from that book, he traces that experience as it has appeared in America and Europe, and finds it to consist essentially of the radical and terrifying questioning of everything. And that, I would add, is a very philosophical state of affairs.

franz kafka   # THE BUCKET RIDER

The name of Franz Kafka has virtually come to represent all that is tortured and anxiety-ridden in modern life. His writings are studies in frustration and horror in which the real and the nightmarish are hopelessly mixed together. The reports of Kafka's life suggest that he was superbly prepared to write about a world which defies reason and sensibility. Born in Prague in 1883, Kafka had endless difficulties with his father and his health, marriage engagements were made and broken, and although he frequently worked to the point of exhaustion, his writing seldom pleased him. Very little was published during his lifetime. He died in 1924 at the age of forty-one, having requested that his unpublished manuscripts be destroyed. His writings include the novels The Trial, The Castle, *and* Amerika; *and the well-known short stories "Metamorphosis" and "A Hunger Artist." Some of his diaries and letters have also been published. The following excerpt is from* The Penal Colony.

Coal all spent; the bucket empty; the shovel useless; the stove breathing out cold; the room freezing; the leaves outside the window rigid, covered with rime; the sky a silver shield against anyone who looks for help from it. I must have coal; I cannot freeze to death; behind me is the pitiless stove, before me the pitiless sky, so I must ride out between them and on my journey seek aid from the coal-dealer. But he has already grown deaf to ordinary appeals; I must prove irrefutably to him that I have not a single grain of coal left, and that he means to me the very sun in the firmament. I must approach like a beggar who, with the death-rattle already in his throat, insists on dying on the doorstep, and to whom the grand people's cook accordingly decides to give the dregs of the coffee-pot; just so must the coal-dealer, filled with rage, but acknowledging the command, "Thou shalt not kill," fling a shovelful of coal into my bucket.

My mode of arrival must decide the matter; so I ride off on the bucket. Seated on the bucket, my hands on the handle, the simplest kind of bridle, I propel myself with difficulty down the stairs; but once down below my bucket ascends, superbly, superbly; camels humbly squatting on the ground do not rise with more dignity, shaking themselves under the sticks of their drivers. Through the hard frozen streets we go at a regular canter; often I am upraised as high as the first story of a house; never do I sink as low as the house doors. And at last I float at an extraordinary height above the vaulted cellar of the dealer, whom I see far below crouching over his table, where he is writing; he has opened the door to let out the excessive heat.

"Coal-dealer!" I cry in a voice burned hollow by the frost and muffled in the cloud made by my breath, "please, coal-dealer, give me a little coal. My bucket is so light that I can ride on it. Be kind. When I can I'll pay you."

The dealer puts his hand to his ear. "Do I hear rightly?" He throws the question over his shoulder to his wife. "Do I hear rightly? A customer?"

"I hear nothing," says his wife, breathing in and out peacefully while she knits on, her back pleasantly warmed by the heat.

"Oh, yes, you must hear," I cry. "It's me, an old customer; faithful and true; only without means at the moment."

"Wife," says the dealer, "it's some one, it must be; my ears can't have deceived me so much as that; it must be an old, a very old customer, that can move me so deeply."

"What ails you, man?" says his wife, ceasing from her work for a moment and pressing her knitting to her bosom. "It's nobody, the street is empty, all our customers are provided for; we could close down the shop for several days and take a rest."

"But I'm sitting up here on the bucket," I cry, and unfeeling frozen tears dim my eyes, "please look up here, just once; you'll see me directly; I beg you, just a shovelful; and if you give me more it'll make me so happy that I won't know what to do. All the other customers are provided for. Oh, if I could only hear the coal clattering into the bucket!"

"I'm coming," says the coal-dealer, and on his short legs he makes to climb the steps of the cellar, but his wife is already beside him, holds him back by the arm and says: "You stay here; seeing you persist in your fancies I'll go myself. Think of the bad fit of coughing you had during the night. But for a piece of business, even if it's one you've only fancied in your head, you're prepared to forget your wife and child and sacrifice your lungs. I'll go."

"Then be sure to tell him all the kinds of coal we have in stock; I'll shout out the prices after you."

"Right," says his wife, climbing up to the street. Naturally she sees me at once. "Frau Coal-dealer," I cry, "my humblest greetings; just one shovelful of coal; here in my bucket; I'll carry it home myself. One shovelful of the worst you have. I'll pay you in full for it, of course, but not just now, not just now." What a knell-like sound the words "not just now" have, and how bewilderingly they mingle with the evening chimes that fall from the church steeple nearby!

"Well, what does he want?" shouts the dealer. "Nothing," his wife shouts back, "there's nothing here; I see nothing, I hear nothing; only six striking, and now we must shut up the shop. The cold is terrible; tomorrow we'll likely have lots to do again."

She sees nothing and hears nothing; but all the same she loosens her apron-strings and waves her apron to waft me away. She succeeds, unluckily. My bucket has all the virtues of a good steed except powers of resistance, which it has not; it is too light; a woman's apron can make it fly through the air.

"You bad woman!" I shout back, while she, turning into the shop, half-contemptuous, half-reassured, flourishes her fist in the air. "You bad woman! I begged you for a shovelful of the worst coal and you would not give me it." And with that I ascend into the regions of the ice mountains and am lost forever.

Translated by Willa and Edwin Muir

ernest hemingway   A CLEAN, WELL-
                                                LIGHTED PLACE

Ernest Hemingway (1898–1961) was only eighteen when he was badly wounded and decorated on the Italian front during World War I. His fame as a writer also came early. In the 1920s he wrote In Our Time, The Sun Also Rises, *and* A Farewell to Arms. *There followed the stuff of the Hemingway "legend": deep-sea fishing, big-game hunting in Africa, and the bullfights in Spain. He was a war correspondent in Spain during the Civil War, and* For Whom the Bell Tolls *is a product of that period. During World War II, again as a war correspondent, he stayed close to the front lines in Europe, when he was not patrolling the Caribbean for German submarines in his own fishing boat. In 1954 he was awarded the Nobel Prize for literature. Troubled and ill, he took his own life in 1961. Of his later works,* The Old Man and the Sea *was notable, but citing only the novels is an injustice; Hemingway was also a master of the short story. "A Clean, Well-Lighted Place" was written in 1933.*

It was late and every one had left the café except an old man who sat in the shadow the leaves of the tree made against the electric light. In the day time the street was dusty, but at night the dew settled the dust and the old man liked to sit late because he was deaf and now at night it was quiet and he felt the difference. The two waiters inside the café knew that the old man was a little drunk, and while he was a good client they knew that if he became too drunk he would leave without paying, so they kept watch on him.

"Last week he tried to commit suicide," one waiter said.

"Why?"

"He was in despair."

"What about?"

"Nothing."

"How do you know it was nothing?"

"He has plenty of money."

They sat together at a table that was close against the wall near the door of the café and looked at the terrace where the tables were all empty except where the old man sat in the shadow of the leaves of the tree that moved slightly in the wind. A girl and a soldier went by in the street. The street light shone on the brass number on his collar. The girl wore no head covering and hurried beside him.

"The guard will pick him up," one waiter said.

"What does it matter if he gets what he's after?"

"He had better get off the street now. The guard will get him. They went by five minutes ago."

The old man sitting in the shadow rapped on his saucer with his glass. The younger waiter went over to him.

"What do you want?"

The old man looked at him. "Another brandy," he said.

"You'll be drunk," the waiter said. The old man looked at him. The waiter went away.

"He'll stay all night," he said to his colleague. "I'm sleepy now. I never get into bed before three o'clock. He should have killed himself last week."

The waiter took the brandy bottle and another saucer from the counter inside the café and marched out to the old man's table. He put down the saucer and poured the glass full of brandy.

"You should have killed yourself last week," he said to the deaf man. The old man motioned with his finger. "A little more," he said. The waiter poured on into the glass so that the brandy slopped over and ran down the stem into the top saucer of the pile. "Thank you," the old man said. The waiter took the bottle back inside the café. He sat down at the table with his colleague again.

"He's drunk now," he said.

"He's drunk every night."

"What did he want to kill himself for?"

"How should I know."

"How did he do it?"

"He hung himself with a rope."

"Who cut him down?"

"His niece."

"Why did they do it?"

"Fear for his soul."

"How much money has he got?"

"He's got plenty."

"He must be eighty years old."

"Anyway I should say he was eighty."

"I wish he would go home. I never get to bed before three o'clock. What kind of hour is that to go to bed?"

"He stays up because he likes it."

"He's lonely. I'm not lonely. I have a wife waiting in bed for me."

"He had a wife once too."

"A wife would be no good to him now."

"You can't tell. He might be better with a wife."

"His niece looks after him."

"I know. You said she cut him down."

"I wouldn't want to be that old. An old man is a nasty thing."

"Not always. This old man is clean. He drinks without spilling. Even now, drunk. Look at him."

"I don't want to look at him. I wish he would go home. He has no regard for those who must work."

The old man looked from his glass across the square, then over at the waiters.

"Another brandy," he said, pointing to his glass. The waiter who was in a hurry came over.

"Finished," he said, speaking with that omission of syntax stupid people employ when talking to drunken people or foreigners. "No more tonight. Close now."

"Another," said the old man.

"No. Finished." The waiter wiped the edge of the table with a towel and shook his head.

The old man stood up, slowly counted the saucers, took a leather coin purse from his pocket and paid for the drinks, leaving half a peseta tip.

The waiter watched him go down the street, a very old man walking unsteadily but with dignity.

"Why didn't you let him stay and drink?" the unhurried waiter asked. They were putting up the shutters. "It is not half-past two."

"I want to go home to bed."

"What is an hour?"

"More to me than to him."

"An hour is the same."

"You talk like an old man yourself. He can buy a bottle and drink at home."

"It's not the same."

"No, it is not," agreed the waiter with a wife. He did not wish to be unjust. He was only in a hurry.

"And you? You have no fear of going home before your usual hour?"

"Are you trying to insult me?"

"No, hombre, only to make a joke."

"No," the waiter who was in a hurry said, rising from pulling down the metal shutters. "I have confidence. I am all confidence."

"You have youth, confidence, and a job," the older waiter said. "You have everything."

"And what do you lack?"

"Everything but work."

"You have everything I have."

"No. I have never had confidence and I am not young."

"Come on. Stop talking nonsense and lock up."

"I am of those who like to stay late at the café," the older waiter said. "With all those who do not want to go to bed. With all those who need a light for the night."

"I want to go home and into bed."

"We are of two different kinds," the older waiter said. He was now dressed to go home. "It is not only a question of youth and confidence although those things are very beautiful. Each night I am reluctant to close up because there may be some one who needs the café."

"Hombre, there are bodegas open all night long."

"You do not understand. This is a clean and pleasant café. It is well lighted. The light is very good and also, now, there are shadows of the leaves."

"Good night," said the younger waiter.

"Good night," the other said. Turning off the electric light he continued the conversation with himself. It is the light of course but it is necessary that the place be clean and pleasant. You do not want music. Certainly you do not want music. Nor can you stand before a bar with dignity although that is all that is provided for these hours. What did he fear? It was not fear or dread. It was a nothing that he knew too well. It was all a nothing and a man was nothing too. It was only that and light was all it needed and a certain cleanness and order. Some lived in it and never felt it but he knew it all was nada y pues nada y pues nada. Our nada who art in nada, nada be thy name thy kingdom nada thy will be nada in nada as it is in nada. Give us this nada our daily nada and nada us our nada as we nada our nadas and nada us not into nada but deliver us from nada; pues nada. Hail nothing full of nothing, nothing is with thee. He smiled and stood before a bar with a shining steam pressure coffee machine.

"What's yours?" asked the barman.

"Nada."

"Otro loco mas," said the barman and turned away.

"A little cup," said the waiter.

The barman poured it for him.

"The light is very bright and pleasant but the bar is unpolished," the waiter said.

The barman looked at him but did not answer. It was too late at night for conversation.

"You want another copita?" the barman asked.

"No, thank you," said the waiter and went out. He disliked bars and bodegas. A clean, well-lighted café was a very different thing. Now, without thinking further, he would go home to his room. He would lie in the bed and finally, with daylight, he would go to sleep. After all, he said to himself, it is probably only insomnia. Many must have it.

136

Rollo May (1909–   ) was born in Ohio and raised in Michigan. His editorship of a radical student publication resulted in his leaving Michigan State for Oberlin College, where he received his first degree. He lived in Europe for a few years, beginning there his psychotherapeutic studies under Alfred Adler, and then returned to the U. S. for a degree from Union Theological Seminary. In 1949 he was graduated summa cum laude from Columbia University with a Ph.D. in clinical psychology. After a serious bout with tuberculosis, he began to publish those volumes that attracted both scholarly and widespread popular attention. In addition to being on the faculty of the William Alanson White Institute of Psychiatry, Psychoanalysis and Psychology, May has lectured at many universities and is a practicing psychotherapist. His books include The Meaning of Anxiety, The Art of Counseling, Psychology and the Human Dilemma, *and* Love and Will. *He edited* Existence: A New Dimension in Psychiatry and Psychology *and* Symbolism in Religion and Literature. *"The Hollow People" is from* Man's Search for Himself *(1953).*

It may sound surprising when I say, on the basis of my own clinical practice as well as that of my psychological and psychiatric colleagues, that the chief problem of people in the middle decade of the twentieth century is *emptiness.* By that I mean not only that many people do not know what they want; they often do not have any clear idea of what they feel. When they talk about lack of autonomy, or lament their inability to make decisions —difficulties which are present in all decades—it soon becomes evident that their underlying problem is that they have no definite experience of their own desires or wants. Thus they feel swayed this way and that, with painful feelings of powerlessness, because they feel vacuous, empty. The complaint which leads them to come for help may be, for example, that their love relationships always break up or that they cannot go through with marriage plans or are dissatisfied with the marriage partner. But they do not talk long before they make it clear that they expect the marriage partner, real or hoped-for, to fill some lack, some vacancy within themselves; and they are anxious and angry because he or she doesn't.

They generally can talk fluently about what they *should* want—to complete their college degrees successfully, to get a job, to fall in love and marry and raise a family—but it is soon evident, even to them, that they are describing what others, parents, professors, employers, expect of them rather than what they themselves want. Two decades ago such external goals could be taken seriously; but now the person realizes, even as he talks, that actually his parents and society do not make all these requirements of him. In theory at least, his parents have told him time and again that they give him freedom to make decisions for himself. And furthermore the person realizes himself that it will not help him to pursue such external goals. But that only makes his problem the more difficult, since he has so little conviction or sense of the reality of his own goals. As one person put it, "I'm just a collection of mirrors, reflecting what everyone else expects of me."

In previous decades, if a person who came for psychological help did not know what he wanted or felt, it generally could be assumed that he wanted something quite definite, such as some sexual gratification, but he dared not admit this to himself. As Freud made clear, the desire was there; the chief thing necessary was to clear up the repressions, bring the desire into consciousness, and eventually help the patient to become able to gratify his desire in accord with reality. But in our day sexual taboos are much weaker; the Kinsey report made that clear if anyone still doubted it. Opportunities for sexual gratification can be found without too much trouble by persons who do not have pronounced other problems. The sexual problems people bring today for therapy, furthermore, are rarely struggles against social prohibitions as such, but much more often are deficiencies within themselves, such as the lack of potency or the lack of capacity to have strong feelings in responding to the sexual partner. In other words, the most common problem now is not social taboos on sexual activity or guilt feeling about sex in itself, but the fact that sex for so many people is an empty, mechanical and vacuous experience.

A dream of a young woman illustrates the dilemma of the "mirror" person. She was quite emancipated sexually, but she wanted to get married and could not choose between two possible men. One man was the steady, middle-class type, of whom her well-to-do family would have approved; but the other shared more of her artistic and Bohemian interests. In the course of her painful bouts of indecision, during which she could not make up her mind as to what kind of person she really was and what kind of life she wished to lead, she dreamt that a large group of people took a vote on which of the two men she should marry. During the dream she felt relieved —this was certainly a convenient solution! The only trouble was when she awoke she couldn't remember which way the vote had gone.

Many people could say out of their own inner experience the prophetic words T. S. Eliot wrote in 1925:

> We are the hollow men
> We are the stuffed men
> Leaning together
> Headpiece filled with straw. Alas!

>Shape without form, shade without colour,
>Paralyzed force, gesture without motion; . . .*

Perhaps some readers are conjecturing that this emptiness, this inability to know what one feels or wants, is due to the fact that we live in a time of uncertainty—a time of war, military draft, economic change, with a future of insecurity facing us no matter how we look at it. So no wonder one doesn't know what to plan and feels futile! But this conclusion is too superficial. As we shall show later, the problems go much deeper than these occasions which cue them off. Furthermore, war, economic upheaval and social change are really symptoms of the same underlying condition in our society, of which the psychological problems we are discussing are also symptoms.

Other readers may be raising another question: "It may be true that people who come for psychological help feel empty and hollow, but aren't those *neurotic* problems, and not necessarily true for the majority of people?" To be sure, we would answer, the persons who get to the consulting rooms of psychotherapists and psychoanalysts are not a cross-section of the population. By and large they are the ones for whom the conventional pretenses and defenses of the society no longer work. Very often they are the more sensitive and gifted members of the society; they need to get help, broadly speaking, because they are less successful at rationalizing than the "well-adjusted" citizen who is able for the time being to cover up his underlying conflicts. Certainly the patients who came to Freud in the 1890's and the first decade of this century with the sexual symptoms he described were not representative of their Victorian culture: most people around them went on living under the customary taboos and rationalizations of Victorianism, believing that sex was repugnant and should be covered up as much as possible. But after the First World War, in the 1920's, those sexual problems became overt and epidemic. Almost every sophisticated person in Europe and America then experienced the same conflicts between sexual urges and social taboos which the few had been struggling with a decade or two earlier. No matter how highly one thinks of Freud, one would not be naive enough to suggest that he in his writings caused this development; he merely predicted it. Thus a relatively small number of people—those who come for psychotherapeutic help in the process of their struggle for inner integration—provide a very revealing and significant barometer of the conflicts and tensions under the psychological surface of the society. This barometer should be taken seriously, for it is one of the best indexes of the disruptions and problems which have not yet, but may soon, break out widely in the society.

Furthermore, it is not only in the consulting rooms of psychologists and

* "The Hollow Men," in *Collected Poems* (New York: Harcourt, Brace and Co., 1934), p. 101.

psychoanalysts that we observe the problem of modern man's inner emptiness. There is much sociological data to indicate that the "hollowness" is already cropping out in many different ways in our society. David Riesman, in his excellent book, *The Lonely Crowd*, which came to my attention just as I was writing these chapters, finds the same emptiness in his fascinating analysis of the present American character. Before World War I, says Riesman, the typical American individual was "inner-directed." He had taken over the standards he was taught, was moralistic in the late Victorian sense, and had strong motives and ambitions, derived from the outside though they were. He lived as though he were given stability by an inner gyroscope. This was the type which fits the early psychoanalytic description of the emotionally repressed person who is directed by a strong super-ego.

But the present typical American character, Riesman goes on to say, is "outer-directed." He seeks not to be outstanding but to "fit in"; he lives as though he were directed by a radar set fastened to his head perpetually telling him what other people expect of him. This radar type gets his motives and directions from others; like the man who described himself as a set of mirrors, he is able to respond but not to choose; he has no effective center of motivation of his own.

We do not mean—nor does Riesman—to imply an admiration for the inner-directed individuals of the late Victorian period. Such persons gained their strength by internalizing external rules, by compartmentalizing will power and intellect and by repressing their feelings. This type was well suited for business success, for, like the nineteenth-century railroad tycoons and the captains of industry, they could manipulate people in the same way as coal cars or the stock market. The gyroscope is an excellent symbol for them since it stands for a completely mechanical center of stability. William Randolph Hearst was an example of this type: he amassed great power and wealth, but he was so anxious underneath this appearance of strength, particularly with regard to dying, that he would never allow anyone to use the word "death" in his presence. The gyroscope men often had disastrous influences on their children because of their rigidity, dogmatism, and inability to learn and to change. In my judgment the attitudes and behavior of these men are examples of how certain attitudes in a society tend to crystallize rigidly just before they collapse. It is easy to see how a period of emptiness would have to follow the breakdown of the period of the "iron men"; take out the gyroscope, and they are hollow.

So we shed no tears for the demise of the gyroscope man. One might place on his tombstone the epitaph, "Like the dinosaur, he had power without the ability to change, strength without the capacity to learn." The chief value in our understanding these last representatives of the nineteenth century is that we shall then be less likely to be seduced by their pseudo "inner strength." If we clearly see that their gyroscope method of gaining psychological power was unsound and eventually self-defeating, and their inner direction a moralistic substitute for integrity rather than integrity itself, we shall be the more convinced of the necessity of finding a new center of strength within ourselves.

Actually, our society has not yet found something to take the place of the gyroscope man's rigid rules. Riesman points out that the "outer-directed" people in our time generally are characterized by attitudes of *passivity* and *apathy*. The young people of today have by and large given up the driving ambition to excel, to be at the top; or if they do have such ambition, they regard it as a fault and are often apologetic for such a hangover from their fathers' mores. They want to be accepted by their peers even to the extent of being inconspicuous and absorbed in the group. This sociological picture is very similar in its broad lines to the picture we get in psychological work with individuals.

A decade or two ago, the emptiness which was beginning to be experienced on a fairly broad scale by the middle classes could be laughed at as the sickness of the suburbs. The clearest picture of the empty life is the suburban man, who gets up at the same hour every weekday morning, takes the same train to work in the city, performs the same task in the office, lunches at the same place, leaves the same tip for the waitress each day, comes home on the same train each night, has 2.3 children, cultivates a little garden, spends a two-week vacation at the shore every summer which he does not enjoy, goes to church every Christmas and Easter, and moves through a routine, mechanical existence year after year until he finally retires at sixty-five and very soon thereafter dies of heart failure, possibly brought on by repressed hostility. I have always had the secret suspicion, however, that he dies of boredom.

But there are indications in the present decade that emptiness and boredom have become much more serious states for many people. Not long ago, a very curious incident was reported in the New York papers. A bus driver in the Bronx simply drove away in his empty bus one day and was picked up by the police several days later in Florida. He explained that, having gotten tired of driving the same route every day, he had decided to go away on a trip. While he was being brought back it was clear from the papers that the bus company was having a hard time deciding whether or how he should be punished. By the time he arrived in the Bronx, he was a "cause célèbre," and a crowd of people who apparently had never personally known the errant bus driver were on hand to welcome him. When it was announced that the company had decided not to turn him over for legal punishment but to give him his job back again if he would promise to make no more jaunts, there was literal as well as figurative cheering in the Bronx.

Why should these solid citizens of the Bronx, living in a metropolitan section which is almost synonymous with middle-class urban conventionality, make a hero out of a man who according to their standards was an auto thief, and worse yet, failed to appear at his regular time for work? Was it not that this driver who got bored to death with simply making his appointed rounds, going around the same blocks and stopping at the same corners day after day, typified some similar emptiness and futility in these middle-class people, and that his gesture, ineffectual as it was, represented some deep but repressed need in the solid citizens of the Bronx? On a small scale this reminds us of the fact that the upper middle classes in bourgeois France several decades ago, as Paul Tillich has remarked, were able to endure the stultifying and mechanical routine of their commercial and industrial activities only by virtue of the presence of centers of Bohemianism at their elbows. People who live as "hollow men" can endure the monotony only by an occasional blow-off—or at least by identifying with someone else's blow-off.

In some circles emptiness is even made a goal to be sought after, under the guise of being "adaptable." Nowhere is this illustrated more arrestingly than in an article in *Life* Magazine entitled "The Wife Problem."* Summarizing a series of researches which first appeared in *Fortune* about the role of the wives of corporation executives, this article points out that whether or not the husband is promoted depends a great deal on whether his wife fits the "pattern." Time was when only the minister's wife was looked over by the trustees of the church before her husband was hired; now the wife of the corporation executive is screened, covertly or overtly, by most companies like the steel or wool or any other commodity the company uses. She must be highly gregarious, not intellectual or conspicuous, and she must have very "sensitive antennae" (again that radar set!) so that she can be forever adapting.

The "good wife is good by *not* doing things—by *not* complaining when her husband works late, by *not* fussing when a transfer is coming up; by *not* engaging in any controversial activity." Thus her success depends not on how she actively uses her powers, but on her knowing when and how to be passive. But the rule that transcends all others, says *Life*, is "*Don't be too good*. Keeping up with the Joneses is still important. But where in pushier and more primitive times it implied going substantially ahead of the Joneses, today keeping up means just that: keeping up. One can move ahead, yes—but slightly, and the timing must be exquisite." In the end the company conditions almost everything the wife does—from the companions she is permitted to have down to the car she drives and what and how much she drinks and reads. To be sure, in return for this indenture the modern corporation "takes care of" its members in the form of giving them

* January 7, 1952.

142

added security, insurance, planned vacations, and so on. *Life* remarks that the "Company" has become like "Big Brother"—the symbol for the dictator—in Orwell's novel, *1984*.

The editors of *Fortune* confess that they find these results "a little frightening. Conformity, it would appear, is being elevated into something akin to a religion. . . . Perhaps Americans will arrive at an ant society, not through fiat of a dictator, but through unbridled desire to get along with one another. . . ."

While one might laugh at the meaningless boredom of people a decade or two ago, the emptiness has for many now moved from the state of boredom to a state of futility and despair which holds promise of dangers. The widespread drug addiction among high-school students in New York City has been quite accurately related to the fact that great numbers of these adolescents have very little to look forward to except the army and unsettled economic conditions, and are without positive, constructive goals. The human being cannot live in a condition of emptiness for very long: if he is not growing *toward* something, he does not merely stagnate; the pent-up potentialities turn into morbidity and despair, and eventually into destructive activities.

What is the psychological origin of this experience of emptiness? The *feeling* of emptiness or vacuity which we have observed sociologically and individually should not be taken to mean that people *are* empty, or without emotional potentiality. A human being is not empty in a static sense, as though he were a storage battery which needs charging. The experience of emptiness, rather, generally comes from people's feeling that they are *powerless* to do anything effective about their lives or the world they live in. Inner vacuousness is the long-term, accumulated result of a person's particular conviction toward himself, namely his conviction that he cannot act as an entity in directing his own life, or change other people's attitudes toward him, or effectually influence the world around him. Thus he gets the deep sense of despair and futility which so many people in our day have. And soon, since what he wants and what he feels can make no real difference, he gives up wanting and feeling. Apathy and lack of feeling are also defenses against anxiety. When a person continually faces dangers he is powerless to overcome, his final line of defense is at last to avoid even feeling the dangers.

Sensitive students of our time have seen these developments coming. Erich Fromm has pointed out that people today no longer live under the authority of church or moral laws, but under "anonymous authorities" like public opinion. The authority is the public itself, but this public is merely a collection of many individuals each with his radar set adjusted to finding out what the others expect of him. The corporation executive, in the *Life* article, is at the top because he—and his wife—have been successful in "adjusting to" public opinion. The public is thus made up of all the Toms, Marys, Dicks and Harrys who are slaves to the authority of public opinion! Riesman makes the very relevant point that the public is therefore afraid of a ghost, a bogeyman, a chimera. It is an anonymous authority with a capital "A" when the authority is a composite of ourselves, but ourselves without any individual centers. We are in the long run afraid of our own collective emptiness.

And we have good reason, as do the editors of *Fortune*, to be frightened by this situation of conformity and individual emptiness. We need only remind ourselves that the ethical and emotional emptiness in European society two and three decades ago was an open invitation to fascist dictatorships to step in and fill the vacuum.

The great danger of this situation of vacuity and powerlessness is that it leads sooner or later to painful anxiety and despair, and ultimately, if it is not corrected, to futility and the blocking off of the most precious qualities of the human being. Its end results are the dwarfing and impoverishment of persons psychologically, or else surrender to some destructive authoritarianism.

*Unconventional and controversial, Ronald David Laing (1927–   ) by 1971
attracted that level of popular interest which called forth a* Life *article (October
8, 1971). In the style of that magazine, the pictorial essay was entitled "Philosopher of Madness" and featured Laing doing Yoga exercises and crouching
reflectively in a tree. Born in Glasgow, he studied medicine at Glasgow University, served for two years in the British Army, and was for a time a physician
at the Glasgow Royal mental hospital. After teaching at Glasgow University in
the Department of Psychological Medicine, he worked at the Tavistock Institute
of Human Relations in London. His research has centered in the area of schizo-
phrenia and the family, and he has been Director of the Langham Clinic and
Chairman of the Philadelphia Association. Among his writings are* The Divided
Self, The Self and Others, The Families of Schizophrenics, The Politics of the
Family, *and* Knots. *The essay which follows is from* The Politics of Experience
(1967).

The relevance of Freud to our time is largely his insight and, to a very
considerable extent, his *demonstration* that the *ordinary* person is a
shriveled, desiccated fragment of what a person can be.

As adults, we have forgotten most of our childhood, not only its contents
but its flavor; as men of the world, we hardly know of the existence of the
inner world: we barely remember our dreams, and make little sense of them
when we do; as for our bodies, we retain just sufficient proprioceptive
sensations to coordinate our movements and to ensure the minimal requirements for biosocial survival—to register fatigue, signals for food, sex, defeca-
tion, sleep; beyond that, little or nothing. Our capacity to think, except in the
service of what we are dangerously deluded in supposing is our self-interest
and in conformity with common sense, is pitifully limited: our capacity even
to see, hear, touch, taste and smell is so shrouded in veils of mystification
that an intensive discipline of unlearning is necessary for *anyone* before one
can begin to experience the world afresh, with innocence, truth and love.

And immediate experience of, in contrast to belief or faith in, a spiritual
realm of demons, spirits, Powers, Dominions, Principalities, Seraphim and
Cherubim, the Light, is even more remote. As domains of experience become more alien to us, we need greater and greater openmindedness even
to conceive of their existence.

Many of us do not know, or even believe, that every night we enter zones
of reality in which we forget our waking life as regularly as we forget our
dreams when we awake. Not all psychologists know of fantasy as a modality

of experience, and the, as it were, contrapuntal interweaving of different experiential modes. Many who are aware of fantasy believe that fantasy is the farthest that experience goes under "normal" circumstances. Beyond that are simply "pathological" zones of hallucinations, phantasmagoric mirages, delusions.

This state of affairs represents an almost unbelievable devastation of our experience. Then there is empty chatter about maturity, love, joy, peace.

This is itself a consequence of and further occasion for the divorce of our experience, such as is left of it, from our behavior.

What we call "normal" is a product of repression, denial, splitting, projection, introjection and other forms of destructive action on experience (see below). It is radically estranged from the structure of being.

The more one sees this, the more senseless it is to continue with generalized descriptions of supposedly specifically schizoid, schizophrenic, hysterical "mechanisms."

There are forms of alienation that are relatively strange to statistically "normal" forms of alienation. The "normally" alienated person, by reason of the fact that he acts more or less like everyone else, is taken to be sane. Other forms of alienation that are out of step with the prevailing state of alienation are those that are labeled by the "normal" majority as bad or mad.

The condition of alienation, of being asleep, of being unconscious, of being out of one's mind, is the condition of the normal man.

Society highly values its normal man. It educates children to lose themselves and to become absurd, and thus to be normal.

Normal men have killed perhaps 100,000,000 of their fellow normal men in the last fifty years.

Our behavior is a function of our experience. We act according to the way we see things.

If our experience is destroyed, our behavior will be destructive.

If our experience is destroyed, we have lost our own selves.

How much human *behavior*, whether the interactions between persons themselves or between groups and groups, is intelligible in terms of human *experience*? Either our inter-human behavior is unintelligible, in that we are simply the passive vehicles of inhuman processes whose ends are as obscure as they are at present outside our control, or our own behavior towards each other is a function of our own experience and our own intentions, however alienated we are from them. In the latter case, we must take final responsibility for what we make of what we are made of.

We will find no intelligibility in behavior if we see it as an inessential phase in an essentially inhuman process. We have had accounts of men as animals, men as machines, men as biochemical complexes with certain ways

146

of their own, but there remains the greatest difficulty in achieving a human understanding of man in human terms.

Men at all times have been subject, as they believed or experienced, to forces from the stars, from the gods, or to forces that now blow through society itself, appearing as the stars once did to determine human fate.

Men have, however, always been weighed down not only by their sense of subordination to fate and chance, to ordained external necessities or contingencies, but by a sense that their very own thoughts and feelings, in their most intimate interstices, are the outcome, the resultant, of processes which they undergo.

A man can estrange himself from himself by mystifying himself and others. He can also have what he does stolen from him by the agency of others.

If we are stripped of experience, we are stripped of our deeds; and if our deeds are, so to speak, taken out of our hands like toys from the hands of children, we are bereft of our humanity. We cannot be deceived. Men can and do destroy the humanity of other men, and the condition of this possibility is that we are interdependent. We are not self-contained monads producing no effects on each other except our reflections. We are both acted upon, changed for good or ill, by other men; and we are agents who act upon others to affect them in different ways. Each of us is the other to the others. Man is a patient-agent, agent-patient, interexperiencing and interacting with his fellows.

It is quite certain that unless we can regulate our behavior much more satisfactorily than at present, then we are going to exterminate ourselves. But as we experience the world, so we act, and this principle holds even when action conceals rather than discloses our experience.

We are not able even to *think* adequately about the behavior that is at the annihilating edge. But what we think is less than what we know; what we know is less than what we love; what we love is so much less than what there is. And to that precise extent we are so much less than what we are.

Yet if nothing else, each time a new baby is born there is a possibility of reprieve. Each child is a new being, a potential prophet, a new spiritual prince, a new spark of light precipitated into the outer darkness. Who are we to decide that it is hopeless?

147

Karl Marx (1818–1883) *was born in Germany of prosperous Jewish parents who had recently been converted to Christianity. During the decade of the 1840's, Marx married the lovely daughter of a Prussian aristocrat, began his lifelong friendship and collaboration with Friedrich Engels, and engaged in the journalistic and political activities which brought authorities down upon him in Cologne, Paris, and Brussels. The* Communist Manifesto *("A specter is haunting Europe—the specter of Communism") was a product of this period. Withdrawing to England, Marx and his family lived in abject poverty in a London slum. Reading and writing for years in the British Museum, he sacrificed everything ("my health, my happiness, and my family") to his studies. Only the first volume of his greatest work,* Das Kapital, *had been published at the time of his death; Engels, working with Marx's notes, finished the remaining two volumes. "Alienated Labour" is from the* Economic and Philosophical Manuscripts (1844) *written during Marx's earlier years in Europe.*

XXII.   We have begun from the presuppositions of political economy. We have accepted its terminology and its laws. We presupposed private property; the separation of labour, capital and land, as also of wages, profit and rent; the division of labour; competition; the concept of exchange value, etc. From political economy itself, in its own words, we have shown that the worker sinks to the level of a commodity, and to a most miserable commodity; that the misery of the worker increases with the power and volume of his production; that the necessary result of competition is the accumulation of capital in a few hands, and thus a restoration of monopoly in a more terrible form; and finally that the distinction between capitalist and landlord, and between agricultural labourer and industrial worker, must disappear, and the whole of society divide into the two classes of property *owners* and *propertyless* workers.

Political economy begins with the fact of private property; it does not explain it. It conceives the *material* process of private property, as this occurs in reality, in general and abstract formulas which then serve it as laws. It does not *comprehend* these laws; that is, it does not show how they arise out of the nature of private property. Political economy provides no explanation of the basis for the distinction of labour from capital, of capital from land. When, for example, the relation of wages to profits is defined, this is explained in terms of the interests of capitalists; in other words, what should be explained is assumed. Similarly, competition is referred to at every point and is explained in terms of external conditions. Political economy tells us nothing about the extent to which these external and apparently accidental conditions are simply the expression of a necessary development. We have seen how exchange itself seems an accidental fact. The only motive forces which political economy recognizes are *avarice* and the *war between the avaricious, competition.*

Just because political economy fails to understand the interconnexions within this movement it was possible to oppose the doctrine of competition to that of monopoly, the doctrine of freedom of the crafts to that of the guilds, the doctrine of the division of landed property to that of the great estates; for competition, freedom of crafts, and the division of landed property were conceived only as accidental consequences brought about by will and force, rather than as necessary, inevitable and natural consequences of monopoly, the guild system and feudal property.

Thus we have now to grasp the real connexion between this whole system of alienation—private property, acquisitiveness, the separation of labour, capital and land, exchange and competition, value and the devaluation of man, monopoly and competition—and the system of *money.*

Let us not begin our explanation as does the economist, from a legendary primordial condition. Such a primordial condition does not explain anything; it merely removes the question into a grey and nebulous distance. It asserts as a fact or event what it should deduce, namely, the necessary relation between two things; for example, between the division of labour and exchange. In the same way theology explains the origin of evil by the fall of man; that is, it asserts as a historical fact what it should explain.

We shall begin from a *contemporary* economic fact. The worker becomes poorer the more wealth he produces and the more his production increases in power and extent. The worker becomes an ever cheaper commodity the more goods he creates. The *devaluation* of the human world increases in direct relation with the *increase in value* of the world of things. Labour does not only create goods; it also produces itself and the worker as a *commodity*, and indeed in the same proportion as it produces goods.

This fact simply implies that the object produced by labour, its product, now stands opposed to it as an *alien being*, as a *power independent* of the producer. The product of labour is labour which has been embodied in an object and turned into a physical thing; this product is an *objectification* of labour. The performance of work is at the same time its objectification. The performance of work appears in the sphere of political economy as a *vitiation* of the worker, objectification as a *loss* and as *servitude to the object*, and appropriation as *alienation*.

So much does the performance of work appear as vitiation that the worker is vitiated to the point of starvation. So much does objectification appear as loss of the object that the worker is deprived of the most essential things not only of life but also of work. Labour itself becomes an object which he can acquire only by the greatest effort and with unpredictable interruptions. So much does the appropriation of the object appear as alienation that the more objects the worker produces the fewer he can possess and the more he falls under the domination of his product, of capital.

All these consequences follow from the fact that the worker is related to the *product of his labour* as to an *alien* object. For it is clear on this presupposition that the more the worker expends himself in work the more powerful becomes the world of objects which he creates in face of himself, the poorer he becomes in his inner life, and the less he belongs to himself. It is just the same as in religion. The more of himself man attributes to God the less he has left in himself. The worker puts his life into the object, and his life then belongs no longer to himself but to the object. The greater his activity, therefore, the less he possesses. What is embodied in the product of his labour is no longer his own. The greater this product is, therefore, the more he is diminished. The *alienation* of the worker in his product means not only that his labour becomes an object, assumes an *external* existence, but that it exists independently, *outside himself,* and alien to him, and that it stands opposed to him as an autonomous power. The life which he has given to the object sets itself against him as an alien and hostile force.

XXIII. Let us now examine more closely the phenomenon of *objectification; the worker's production and the *alienation* and *loss* of the object it produces, which is involved in it. The worker can create nothing without *nature,* without the *sensuous external world.* The latter is the material in which his labour is realized, in which it is active, out of which and through which it produces things.

But just as nature affords the *means of existence* of labour, in the sense that labour cannot *live* without objects upon which it can be exercised, so also it provides the *means of existence* in a narrower sense; namely the means of physical existence for the *worker* himself. Thus, the more the worker *appropriates* the external world of sensuous nature by his labour the more he deprives himself of *means of existence,* in two respects: first, that the sensuous external world becomes progressively less an object belonging to his labour or a means of existence of his labour, and secondly, that it becomes progressively less a means of existence in the direct sense, a means for the physical subsistence of the worker.

In both respects, therefore, the worker becomes a slave of the object; first, in that he receives an *object of work,* i.e. receives *work,* and secondly, in that he receives *means of subsistence.* Thus the object enables him to exist, first as a *worker* and secondly, as a *physical subject.* The culmination of this enslavement is that he can only maintain himself as a *physical subject* so far as he is a *worker,* and that it is only as a *physical subject* that he is a worker.

×(The alienation of the worker in his object is expressed as follows in the laws of political economy: the more the worker produces the less he has to consume; the more value he creates the more worthless he becomes; the more refined his product the more crude and misshapen the worker; the more civilized the product the more barbarous the worker; the more powerful the work the more feeble the worker; the more the work manifests intelligence the more the worker declines in intelligence and becomes a slave of nature.)

Political economy conceals the alienation in the nature of labour in so far as it does not examine the direct relationship between the worker (work) and production. Labour certainly produces marvels for the rich but it produces privation for the worker. It produces palaces, but hovels for the worker. It produces beauty, but deformity for the worker. It replaces labour by machinery, but it casts some of the workers back into a barbarous kind of work and turns the others into machines. It produces intelligence, but also stupidity and cretinism for the workers.

The direct relationship of labour to its products is the relationship of the worker to the objects of his production. The relationship of property owners to the objects of production and to production itself is merely a consequence of this first relationship and confirms it. We shall consider this second aspect later.

Thus, when we ask what is the important relationship of labour, we are concerned with the relationship of the *worker* to production.

So far we have considered the alienation of the worker only from one aspect; namely, *his relationship with the products of his labour.* However, alienation appears not merely in the result but also in the *process of production,* within *productive activity* itself. How could the worker stand in an alien relationship to the product of his activity if he did not alienate himself in the act of production itself? The product is indeed only the *résumé* of activity, of production. Consequently, if the product of labour is alienation, production itself must be active alienation—the alienation of activity and the activity of alienation. The alienation of the object of labour merely summarizes the alienation in the work activity itself.

What constitutes the alienation of labour? First, that the work is *external* to the worker, that it is not part of his nature; and that, consequently, he does not fulfil himself in his work but denies himself, has a feeling of misery rather than well-being, does not develop freely his mental and physical energies, but is physically exhausted and mentally debased. The worker, therefore, feels himself at home only during his leisure time, whereas at work he feels homeless. His work is not voluntary but imposed, *forced labour.* It is not the satisfaction of a need, but only a *means* for satisfying other needs. Its alien character is clearly shown by the fact that as soon as there is no physical or other compulsion it is avoided like the plague. External labour, labour in which man alienates himself, is a labour of self-sacrifice, of mortification. Finally, the external character of work for the worker is shown by the fact that it is not his own work but work for someone else, that in work he does not belong to himself but to another person.

Just as in religion the spontaneous activity of human fantasy, of the human brain and heart, reacts independently as an alien activity of gods or devils upon the individual, so the activity of the worker is not his own spontaneous activity. It is another's activity and a loss of his own spontaneity.

We arrive at the result that man (the worker) feels himself to be freely active only in his animal functions—eating, drinking and procreating, or at most also in his dwelling and in personal adornment—while in his human functions he is reduced to an animal. The animal becomes human and the human becomes animal.

Eating, drinking and procreating are of course also genuine human functions. But abstractly considered, apart from the environment of human activities, and turned into final and sole ends, they are animal functions.

We have now considered the act of alienation of practical human activity, labour, from two aspects: (1) the relationship of the worker to the *product of labour* as an alien object which dominates him. This relationship is at the same time the relationship to the sensuous external world, to natural objects, as an alien and hostile world; (2) the relationship of labour to the *act of production* within *labour*. This is the relationship of the worker to his own activity as something alien and not belonging to him, activity as suffering (passivity), strength as powerlessness, creation as emasculation, the *personal* physical and mental energy of the worker, his personal life (for what is life but activity?), as an activity which is directed against himself, independent of him and not belonging to him. This is *self-alienation* as against the above-mentioned alienation of the *thing*.

XXIV. We have now to infer a third characteristic of *alienated labour* from the two we have considered.

Man is a species-being not only in the sense that he makes the community (his own as well as those of other things) his object both practically and theoretically, but also (and this is simply another expression for the same thing) in the sense that he treats himself as the present, living species, as a *universal* and consequently free being.

Species-life, for man as for animals, has its physical basis in the fact that man (like animals) lives from inorganic nature, and since man is more universal than an animal so the range of inorganic nature from which he lives is more universal. Plants, animals, minerals, air, light, etc. constitute, from the theoretical aspect, a part of human consciousness as objects of natural science and art; they are man's spiritual inorganic nature, his intellectual

152

means of life, which he must first prepare for enjoyment and perpetuation. So also, from the practical aspect, they form a part of human life and activity. In practice man lives only from these natural products, whether in the form of food, heating, clothing, housing, etc. The universality of man appears in practice in the universality which makes the whole of nature into his inorganic body: (1) as a direct means of life; and equally (2) as the material object and instrument of his life activity. Nature is the inorganic body of man; that is to say nature, excluding the human body itself. To say that man *lives* from nature means that nature is his *body* with which he must remain in a continuous interchange in order not to die. The statement that the physical and mental life of man, and nature, are interdependent means simply that nature is interdependent with itself, for man is a part of nature.

Since alienated labour: (1) alienates nature from man; and (2) alienates man from himself, from his own active function, his life activity; so it alienates him from the species. It makes *species-life* into a means of individual life. In the first place it alienates species-life and individual life, and secondly, it turns the latter, as an abstraction, into the purpose of the former, also in its abstract and alienated form.

For labour, *life activity, productive life,* now appear to man only as *means* for the satisfaction of a need, the need to maintain his physical existence. Productive life is, however, species-life. It is life creating life. In the type of life activity resides the whole character of a species, its species-character; and free, conscious activity is the species-character of human beings. Life itself appears only as a *means of life.*

The animal is one with its life activity. It does not distinguish the activity from itself. It is *its activity.* But man makes his life activity itself an object of his will and consciousness. He has a conscious life activity. It is not a determination with which he is completely identified. Conscious life activity distinguishes man from the life activity of animals. Only for this reason is he a species-being. Or rather, he is only a self-conscious being, i.e. his own life is an object for him, because he is a species-being. Only for this reason is his activity free activity. Alienated labour reverses the relationship, in that man because he is a self-conscious being makes his life activity, his *being,* only a means for his *existence.*

The practical construction of an *objective world,* the *manipulation* of inorganic nature, is the confirmation of man as a conscious species-being, i.e. a being who treats the species as his own being or himself as a species-being. Of course, animals also produce. They construct nests, dwellings, as in the case of bees, beavers, ants, etc. But they only produce what is strictly necessary for themselves or their young. They produce only in a single direction, while man produces universally. They produce only under the compulsion of direct physical needs, while man produces when he is free from physical need and only truly produces in freedom from such need. Animals produce only themselves, while man reproduces the whole of nature. The products of animal production belong directly to their physical bodies, while man is free in face of his product. Animals construct only in accordance with the standards and needs of the species to which they belong, while man knows how to produce in accordance with the standards of every species and knows how to apply the appropriate standard to the object. Thus man constructs also in accordance with the laws of beauty.

It is just in his work upon the objective world that man really proves himself as a *species-being*. This production is his active species-life. By means of it nature appears as *his* work and his reality. The object of labour is, therefore, the *objectification of man's species-life*; for he no longer reproduces himself merely intellectually, as in consciousness, but actively and in a real sense, and he sees his own reflection in a world which he has constructed. While, therefore, alienated labour takes away the object of production from man, it also takes away his *species-life*, his real objectivity as a species-being, and changes his advantage over animals into a disadvantage in so far as his inorganic body, nature, is taken from him.

Just as alienated labour transforms free and self-directed activity into a means, so it transforms the species-life of man into a means of physical existence.

Consciousness, which man has from his species, is transformed through alienation so that species-life becomes only a means for him. (3) Thus alienated labour turns the *species-life of man,* and also nature as his mental species-property, into an *alien* being and into a *means* for his *individual existence*. It alienates from man his own body, external nature, his mental life and his *human* life. (4) A direct consequence of the alienation of man from the product of his labour, from his life activity and from his species-life, is that *man* is *alienated* from other *men.* When man confronts himself he also confronts *other* men. What is true of man's relationship to his work, to the product of his work and to himself, is also true of his relationship to other men, to their labour and to the objects of their labour.

In general, the statement that man is alienated from his species-life means that each man is alienated from others, and that each of the others is likewise alienated from human life.

Human alienation, and above all the relation of man to himself, is first realized and expressed in the relationship between each man and other men. Thus in the relationship of alienated labour every man regards other men according to the standards and relationships in which he finds himself placed as a worker.

XXV. We began with an economic fact, the alienation of the worker

154

and his production. We have expressed this fact in the conceptual terms as *alienated labour,* and in analysing the concept we have merely analysed an economic fact.

Let us now examine further how this concept of alienated labour must express and reveal itself in reality. If the product of labour is alien to me and confronts me as an alien power, to whom does it belong? If my own activity does not belong to me but is an alien, forced activity, to whom does it belong? To a being *other* than myself. And who is this being? The *gods*? It is apparent in the earliest stages of advanced production, e.g. temple building, etc. in Egypt, India, Mexico, and in the service rendered to gods, that the product belonged to the gods. But the gods alone were never the lords of labour. And no more was *nature.* What a contradiction it would be if the more man subjugates nature by his labour, and the more the marvels of the gods are rendered superfluous by the marvels of industry, the more he should abstain from his joy in producing and his enjoyment of the product for love of these powers.

The *alien* being to whom labour and the product of labour belong, to whose service labour is devoted, and to whose enjoyment the product of labour goes, can only be *man* himself. If the product of labour does not belong to the worker, but confronts him as an alien power, this can only be because it belongs to *a man other than the worker*. If his activity is a torment to him it must be a source of *enjoyment* and pleasure to another. Not the gods, nor nature, but only man himself can be this alien power over men.

Consider the earlier statement that the relation of man to himself is first *realized, objectified,* through his relation to other men. If he is related to the product of his labour, his objectified labour, as to an *alien*, hostile, powerful and independent object, he is related in such a way that another alien, hostile, powerful and independent man is the lord of this object. If he is related to his own activity as to unfree activity, then he is related to it as activity in the service, and under the domination, coercion and yoke, of another man.

Every self-alienation of man, from himself and from nature, appears in the relation which he postulates between other men and himself and nature. Thus religious self-alienation is necessarily exemplified in the relation between laity and priest, or, since it is here a question of the spiritual world, between the laity and a mediator. In the real world of practice this self-alienation can only be expressed in the real, practical relation of man to his fellow men. The medium through which alienation occurs is itself a *practical* one. Through alienated labour, therefore, man not only produces his relation to the object and to the process of production as to alien and hostile men; he also produces the relation of other men to his production and his product, and the relation between himself and other men. Just as he creates his own production as a vitiation, a punishment, and his own product as a loss, as a product which does not belong to him, so he creates the domination of the non-producer over production and its product. As he alienates his own activity, so he bestows upon the stranger an activity which is not his own.

We have so far considered this relation only from the side of the worker, and later on we shall consider it also from the side of the non-worker.

Thus, through alienated labour the worker creates the relation of another man, who does not work and is outside the work process, to this labour. The relation of the worker to work also produces the relation of the capitalist (or whatever one likes to call the lord of labour) to work. *Private property* is, therefore, the product, the necessary result, of *alienated labour*, of the external relation of the worker to nature and to himself.

Private property is thus derived from the analysis of the concept of *alienated labour*; that is, alienated man, alienated labour, alienatel life, and estranged man.

We have, of course, derived the concept of *alienated labour* (*alienated life*) from political economy, from an analysis of the *movement of private property*. But the analysis of this concept shows that although private property appears to be the basis and cause of alienated labour, it is rather a consequence of the latter, just as the gods are *fundamentally* not the cause but the product of confusions of human reason. At a later stage, however, there is a reciprocal influence.

Only in the final stage of the development of private property is its secret revealed, namely, that it is on one hand the *product* of alienated labour, and on the other hand the *means* by which labour is alienated, *the realization of this alienation*.

This elucidation throws light upon several unresolved controversies—

1. Political economy begins with labour as the real soul of production and then goes on to attribute nothing to labour and everything to private property. Proudhon, faced by this contradiction, has decided in favour of labour against private property. We perceive, however, that this apparent contradiction is the contradiction of *alienated labour* with itself and that political economy has merely formulated the laws of alienated labour.

   We also observe, therefore, that *wages* and *private property* are identical, for wages, like the product or object of labour, labour itself remunerated, are only a necessary consequence of the alienation of labour. In the wage system labour appears not as an end in itself but as the servant of wages.

   An enforced *increase in wages* (disregarding the other difficulties, and especially that such an anomaly could only be maintained by force) would be nothing more than a *better remuneration of slaves,* and would not restore, either to the worker or to the work, their human significance and worth.

Even the *equality of incomes* which Proudhon demands would only change the relation of the present-day worker to his work into a relation of all men to work. Society would then be conceived as an abstract capitalist.

2. From the relation of alienated labour to private property it also follows that the emancipation of society from private property, from servitude, takes the political form of the *emancipation of the workers*; not in the sense that only the latter's emancipation is involved, but because this emancipation includes the emancipation of humanity as a whole. For all human servitude is involved in the relation of the worker to production, and all the types of servitude are only modifications or consequences of this relation.

As we have discovered the concept of *private property* by an *analysis* of the concept of *alienated labour,* so with the aid of these two factors we can evolve all the *categories* of political economy, and in every category, e.g. trade, competition, capital, money, we shall discover only a particular and developed expression of these fundamental elements.

However before considering this structure let us attempt to solve two problems.

1. To determine the general nature of *private property* as it has resulted from alienated labour, in its relation to *genuine human and social property.*

2. We have taken as a fact and analysed the *alienation of labour.* How does it happen, we may ask, that *man alienates his labour?* How is this alienation founded in the nature of human development? We have already done much to solve the problem in so far as we have *transformed* the question concerning the *origin of private property* into a question about the relation between *alienated labour* and the process of development of mankind. For in speaking of private property one believes oneself to be dealing with something external to mankind. But in speaking of labour one deals directly with mankind itself. This new formulation of the problem already contains its solution.

We have resolved alienated labour into two parts, which mutually determine each other, or rather, which constitute two different expressions of one and the same relation. *Appropriation* appears as *alienation* and *alienation* as *appropriation,* alienation as genuine acceptance in the community.

We have considered one aspect, *alienated* labour, in its bearing upon the *worker* himself, i.e. *the relation of alienated labour to itself.* And we have found as the necessary consequence of this relation the *property relation* of the *non-worker* to the *worker* and to labour. *Private property* as the material, summarized expression of alienated labour includes both relations; *the relation of the worker to labour, to the product of his labour and to the non-worker,* and the relation of the *non-worker to the worker and to the product of the latter's labour.*

We have already seen that in relation to the worker, who *appropriates* nature by his labour, appropriation appears as alienation, self-activity as activity for another and of another, living as the sacrifice of life, and production of the object as loss of the object to an alien power, an alien man. Let us now consider the relation of this *alien* man to the worker, to labour, and to the object of labour.

It should be noted first that every thing which appears to the worker as an *activity of alienation,* appears to the non-worker as a *condition of alienation.* Secondly, the *real, practical* attitude (as a state of mind) of the worker in production and to the product appears to the non-worker who confronts him as a *theoretical* attitude.

XXVII. Thirdly, the non-worker does everything against the worker which the latter does against himself, but he does not do against himself what he does against the worker.

Let us examine these three relationships more closely. (*The manuscript breaks off unfinished at this point.*)

jean-paul sartre ANGUISH, FORLORNNESS, AND
DESPAIR

*Due to his literary and philosophical works, and his great talent for vivid and
dramatic language, Jean-Paul Sartre (1905–   ) is easily the most widely read
of the existentialists. Born and educated in France, he studied under, and was
strongly influenced by, the philosophers Husserl and Heidegger in Germany.
Sartre achieved early acclaim with his novel* Nausea, *published just prior to
World War II. Captured by the Germans, held prisoner for nine months, and
later active in the French Resistance, Sartre came out of the war years with his
ideas reinforced by intense personal experience. His thinking found striking expression in plays ("No Exit," "The Flies," "The Condemned of Altona"),
short stories ("The Wall," "The Room"), and novels* (The Age of Reason,
The Reprieve, Troubled Sleep). *In 1964 he was awarded the Nobel Prize for
literature, which he declined to accept. His lengthy and difficult* Being and
Nothingness *could attract only a specialized audience, but works such as* Existentialism and the Human Emotions (1945), *from which the following selection is
taken, were popular and had a great deal to do with the rise of an existentialist
"cult" in the years following World War II.*

First, what is meant by anguish? The existentialists say at once that man is
anguish. What that means is this: the man who involves himself and who
realizes that he is not only the person he chooses to be, but also a law-
maker who is, at the same time, choosing all mankind as well as himself, cannot help escape the feeling of his total and deep responsibility. Of course,
there are many people who are not anxious; but we claim that they are hiding
their anxiety, that they are fleeing from it. Certainly, many people believe
that when they do something, they themselves are the only ones involved,
and when someone says to them, "What if everyone acted that way?" they
shrug their shoulders and answer, "Everyone doesn't act that way." But
really, one should always ask himself, "What would happen if everybody
looked at things that way?" There is no escaping this disturbing thought except by a kind of double-dealing. A man who lies and makes excuses for
himself by saying "not everybody does that," is someone with an uneasy conscience, because the act of lying implies that a universal value is conferred
upon the lie.

Anguish is evident even when it conceals itself. This is the anguish that
Kierkegaard called the anguish of Abraham. You know the story: an angel
has ordered Abraham to sacrifice his son; if it really were an angel who has
come and said, "You are Abraham, you shall sacrifice your son," everything

would be all right. But everyone might first wonder, "Is it really an angel, and am I really Abraham? What proof do I have?"

There was a madwoman who had hallucinations; someone used to speak to her on the telephone and give her orders. Her doctor asked her, "Who is it who talks to you?" She answered, "He says it's God." What proof did she really have that it was God? If an angel comes to me, what proof is there that it's an angel? And if I hear voices, what proof is there that they come from heaven and not from hell, or from the subconscious, or a pathological condition? What proves that they are addressed to me? What proof is there that I have been appointed to impose my choice and my conception of man on humanity? I'll never find any proof or sign to convince me of that. If a voice addresses me, it is always for me to decide that this is the angel's voice; if I consider that such an act is a good one, it is I who will choose to say that it is good rather than bad.

Now, I'm not being singled out as an Abraham, and yet at every moment I'm obliged to perform exemplary acts. For every man, everything happens as if all mankind had its eyes fixed on him and were guiding itself by what he does. And every man ought to say to himself, "Am I really the kind of man who has the right to act in such a way that humanity might guide itself by my actions?" And if he does not say that to himself, he is masking his anguish.

There is no question here of the kind of anguish which would lead to quietism, to inaction. It is a matter of a simple sort of anguish that anybody who has had responsibilities is familiar with. For example, when a military officer takes the responsibility for an attack and sends a certain number of men to death, he chooses to do so, and in the main he alone makes the choice. Doubtless, orders come from above, but they are too broad; he interprets them, and on this interpretation depend the lives of ten or fourteen or twenty men. In making a decision he cannot help having a certain anguish. All leaders know this anguish. That doesn't keep them from acting; on the contrary, it is the very condition of their action. For it implies that they envisage a number of possibilities, and when they choose one, they realize that it has value only because it is chosen. We shall see that this kind of anguish, which is the kind that existentialism describes, is explained, in addition, by a direct responsibility to the other men whom it involves. It is not a curtain separating us from action, but is part of action itself.

When we speak of forlornness, a term Heidegger was fond of, we mean only that God does not exist and that we have to face all the consequences of this. The existentialist is strongly opposed to a certain kind of secular ethics which would like to abolish God with the least possible expense. About 1880, some French teachers tried to set up a secular ethics which went something like this: God is a useless and costly hypothesis; we are discarding it; but, meanwhile, in order for there to be an ethics, a society, a civilization, it is essential that certain values be taken seriously and that they be considered as having an *a priori* existence. It must be obligatory, *a priori*, to be honest, not to lie, not to beat your wife, to have children, etc., etc. So we're going to try a little device which will make it possible to show that values exist all the same, inscribed in a heaven of ideas, though otherwise God does not exist. In other words—and this, I believe, is the tendency of everything called reformism in France—nothing will be changed if God does not exist. We shall find ourselves with the same norms of honesty, progress, and humanism, and we shall have made of God an outdated hypothesis which will peacefully die off by itself.

The existentialist, on the contrary, thinks it very distressing that God does not exist, because all possibility of finding values in a heaven of ideas disappears along with Him; there can no longer be an *a priori* Good, since there is no infinite and perfect consciousness to think it. Nowhere is it written that the Good exists, that we must be honest, that we must not lie; because the fact is we are on a plane where there are only men. Dostoievsky said, "If God didn't exist, everything would be possible." That is the very starting point of existentialism. Indeed, everything is permissible if God does not exist, and as a result man is forlorn, because neither within him nor without does he find anything to cling to. He can't start making excuses for himself.

If existence really does precede essence, there is no explaining things away by reference to a fixed and given human nature. In other words, there is no determinism, man is free, man is freedom. On the other hand, if God does not exist, we find no values or commands to turn to which legitimize our conduct. So, in the bright realm of values, we have no excuse behind us, nor justification before us. We are alone, with no excuses.

That is the idea I shall try to convey when I say that man is condemned to be free. Condemned, because he did not create himself, yet, in other respects is free; because, once thrown into the world, he is responsible for everything he does. The existentialist does not believe in the power of passion. He will never agree that a sweeping passion is a ravaging torrent which fatally leads a man to certain acts and is therefore an excuse. He thinks that man is responsible for his passion.

The existentialist does not think that man is going to help himself by finding in the world some omen by which to orient himself. Because he thinks that man will interpret the omen to suit himself. Therefore, he thinks that man, with no support and no aid, is condemned every moment to invent man. Ponge, in a very fine article, has said, "Man is the future of man." That's exactly it. But if it is taken to mean that this future is recorded in heaven, that God sees it, then it is false, because it would really no longer be a future. If it is taken to mean that, whatever a man may be, there is a future to be forged, a virgin future before him, then this remark is sound. But then we are forlorn.

To give you an example which will enable you to understand forlornness better, I shall cite the case of one of my students who came to see me under the following circumstances: his father was on bad terms with his mother, and, moreover, was inclined to be a collaborationist; his older brother had been killed in the German offensive of 1940, and the young man, with somewhat immature but generous feelings, wanted to avenge him. His mother lived alone with him, very much upset by the half-treason of her husband and the death of her older son; the boy was her only consolation.

The boy was faced with the choice of leaving for England and joining the Free French forces—that is, leaving his mother behind—or remaining with his mother and helping her to carry on. He was fully aware that the woman lived only for him and that his going off—and perhaps his death—would plunge her into despair. He was also aware that every act that he did for his mother's sake was a sure thing, in the sense that it was helping her to carry on, whereas every effort he made toward going off and fighting was an uncertain move which might run aground and prove completely useless; for example, on his way to England he might, while passing through Spain, be detained indefinitely in a Spanish camp; he might reach England or Algiers and be stuck in an office at a desk job. As a result, he was faced with two very different kinds of action: one, concrete, immediate, but concerning only one individual; the other concerned an incomparably vaster group, a national collectivity, but for that very reason was dubious, and might be interrupted en route. And, at the same time, he was wavering between two kinds of ethics. On the one hand, an ethics of sympathy, of personal devotion; on the other, a broader ethics, but one whose efficacy was more dubious. He had to choose between the two.

Who could help him choose? Christian doctrine? No. Christian doctrine says, "Be charitable, love your neighbor, take the more rugged path, etc., etc." But which is the more rugged path? Whom should he love as a brother? The fighting man or his mother? Which does the greater good, the vague act of fighting in a group, or the concrete one of helping a particular human being to go on living? Who can decide *a priori*? Nobody. No book of ethics can tell him. The Kantian ethics says, "Never treat any person as a means, but as an end." Very well, if I stay with my mother, I'll treat her as an end and not as a means; but by virtue of this very fact, I'm running the risk of treating the people around me who are fighting, as means; and, conversely, if I go to join those who are fighting, I'll be treating them as an end, and, by doing that, I run the risk of treating my mother as a means.

If values are vague, and if they are always too broad for the concrete and specific case that we are considering, the only thing left for us is to trust our instincts. That's what this young man tried to do; and when I saw him, he said, "In the end, feeling is what counts. I ought to choose whichever pushes me in one direction. If I feel that I love my mother enough to sacrifice everything else for her—my desire for vengeance, for action, for adventure—then I'll stay with her. If, on the contrary, I feel that my love for my mother isn't enough. I'll leave."

But how is the value of a feeling determined? What gives his feeling for his mother value? Precisely the fact that he remained with her. I may say that I like so-and-so well enough to sacrifice a certain amount of money for him, but I may say so only if I've done it. I may say "I love my mother well enough to remain with her" if I have remained with her. The only way to determine the value of this affection is, precisely, to perform an act which confirms and defines it. But, since I require this affection to justify my act, I find myself caught in a vicious circle.

On the other hand, Gide has well said that a mock feeling and a true feeling are almost indistinguishable; to decide that I love my mother and will remain with her, or to remain with her by putting on an act, amount somewhat to the same thing. In other words, the feeling is formed by the acts one performs; so, I cannot refer to it in order to act upon it. Which means that I can neither seek within myself the true condition which will impel me to act, nor apply to a system of ethics for concepts which will permit me to act. You will say, "At least, he did go to a teacher for advice." But if you seek advice from a priest, for example, you have chosen this priest; you already knew, more or less, just about what advice he was going to give you. In other words, choosing your adviser is involving yourself. The proof of this is that if you are a Christian, you will say, "Consult a priest." But some priests are collaborating, some are just marking time, some are resisting. Which to choose? If the young man chooses a priest who is resisting or collaborating, he has already decided on the kind of advice he's going to get. Therefore, in coming to see me he knew the answer I was going to give him, and I had only one answer to give: "You're free, choose, that is, invent." No general ethics can show you what is to be done; there are no omens in the world. The Catholics will reply, "But there are." Granted—but, in any case, I myself choose the meaning they have.

When I was a prisoner, I knew a rather remarkable young man who was a Jesuit. He had entered the Jesuit order in the following way: he had had a number of very bad breaks; in childhood, his father died, leaving him in poverty, and he was a scholarship student at a religious institution where he was constantly made to feel that he was being kept out of charity; then, he failed to get any of the honors and distinctions that children like; later on, at about eighteen, he bungled a love affair; finally, at twenty-two, he failed in military training, a childish enough matter, but it was the last straw.

163

This young fellow might well have felt that he had botched everything. It was a sign of something, but of what? He might have taken refuge in bitterness or despair. But he very wisely looked upon all this as a sign that he was not made for secular triumphs, and that only the triumphs of religion, holiness, and faith were open to him. He saw the hand of God in all this, and so he entered the order. Who can help seeing that he alone decided what the sign meant?

Some other interpretation might have been drawn from this series of setbacks; for example, that he might have done better to turn carpenter or revolutionist. Therefore, he is fully responsible for the interpretation. Forlornness implies that we ourselves choose our being. Forlornness and anguish go together.

As for despair, the term has a very simple meaning. It means that we shall confine ourselves to reckoning only with what depends upon our will, or on the ensemble of probabilities which make our action possible. When we want something, we always have to reckon with probabilities. I may be counting on the arrival of a friend. The friend is coming by rail or streetcar; this supposes that the train will arrive on schedule, or that the streetcar will not jump the track. I am left in the realm of possibility; but possibilities are to be reckoned with only to the point where my action comports with the ensemble of these possibilities, and no further. The moment the possibilities I am considering are not rigorously involved by my action, I ought to disengage myself from them, because no God, no scheme, can adapt the world and its possibilities to my will. When Descartes said, "Conquer yourself rather than the world," he meant essentially the same thing.

The Marxists to whom I have spoken reply, "You can rely on the support of others in your action, which obviously has certain limits because you're not going to live forever. That means: rely on both what others are doing elsewhere to help you, in China, in Russia, and what they will do later on, after your death, to carry on the action and lead it to its fulfillment, which will be the revolution. You even *have* to rely upon that, otherwise you're immoral." I reply at once that I will always rely on fellow-fighters insofar as these comrades are involved with me in a common struggle, in the unity of a party or a group in which I can more or less make my weight felt; that is, one whose ranks I am in as a fighter and whose movements I am aware of at every moment. In such a situation, relying on the unity and will of the party is exactly like counting on the fact that the train will arrive on time or that the car won't jump the track. But, given that man is free and that there is no human nature for me to depend on, I cannot count on men whom I do not know by relying on human goodness or man's concern for the good of society. I don't know what will become of the Russian revolution; I may make an example of it to the extent that at the present time it is apparent that the proletariat plays a part in Russia that it plays in no other nation. But I can't swear that this will inevitably lead to a triumph of the proletariat. I've got to limit myself to what I see.

Given that men are free and that tomorrow they will freely decide what man will be, I cannot be sure that, after my death, fellow-fighters will carry on my work to bring it to its maximum perfection. Tomorrow, after my death, some men may decide to set up Fascism, and the others may be cowardly and muddled enough to let them do it. Fascism will then be the human reality, so much the worse for us.

Actually, things will be as man will have decided they are to be. Does that mean that I should abandon myself to quietism? No. First, I should involve myself; then, act on the old saw, "Nothing ventured, nothing gained." Nor does it mean that I shouldn't belong to a party, but rather that I shall have no illusions and shall do what I can. For example, suppose I ask myself, "Will socialization, as such, ever come about?" I know nothing about it. All I know is that I'm going to do everything in my power to bring it about. Beyond that, I can't count on anything. Quietism is the attitude of people who say, "Let others do what I can't do." The doctrine I am presenting is the very opposite of quietism, since it declares, "There is no reality except in action." Moreover, it goes further, since it adds, "Man is nothing else than his plan; he exists only to the extent that he fulfills himself; he is therefore nothing else than the ensemble of his acts, nothing else than his life."

According to this, we can understand why our doctrine horrifies certain people. Because often the only way they can bear their wretchedness is to think, "Circumstances have been against me. What I've been and done doesn't show my true worth. To be sure, I've had no great love, no great friendship, but that's because I haven't met a man or woman who was worthy. The books I've written haven't been very good because I haven't had the proper leisure. I haven't had children to devote myself to because I didn't find a man with whom I could have spent my life. So there remains within me, unused and quite viable, a host of propensities, inclinations, possibilities, that one wouldn't guess from the mere series of things I've done."

Now, for the existentialist there is really no love other than one which manifests itself in a person's being in love. There is no genius other than one which is expressed in works of art; the genius of Proust is the sum of Proust's works; the genius of Racine is his series of tragedies. Outside of that, there is nothing. Why say that Racine could have written another tragedy, when he didn't write it? A man is involved in life, leaves his impress on it, and outside of that there is nothing. To be sure, this may seem a harsh thought to someone whose life hasn't been a success. But, on the other hand, it prompts people to understand that reality alone is what counts, that dreams, expectations, and hopes warrant no more than to define a man as a disappointed dream, as miscarried hopes, as vain expectations. In other words, to define him negatively and not positively. However, when we say, "You are nothing else than your life," that does not imply that the artist will be judged solely on the basis of his works of art; a thousand other things will contribute toward summing him up. What we mean is that a man is nothing else than a series of undertakings, that he is the sum, the organization, the ensemble of the relationships which make up these undertakings.

When all is said and done, what we are accused of, at bottom, is not our pessimism, but an optimistic toughness. If people throw up to us our works of fiction in which we write about people who are soft, weak, cowardly, and sometimes even downright bad, it's not because these people are soft, weak, cowardly, or bad; because if we were to say, as Zola did, that they are that way because of heredity, the workings of environment, society, because of biological or psychological determinism, people would be reassured. They would say, "Well, that's what we're like, no one can do anything about it." But when the existentialist writes about a coward, he says that this coward is responsible for his cowardice. He's not like that because he has a cowardly heart or lung or brain; he's not like that on account of his physiological make-up; but he's like that because he has made himself a coward by his acts. There's no such thing as a cowardly constitution; there are nervous constitutions; there is poor blood, as the common people say, or strong constitutions. But the man whose blood is poor is not a coward on that account, for what makes cowardice is the act of renouncing or yielding. A constitution is not an act; the coward is defined on the basis of the acts he performs. People feel, in a vague sort of way, that this coward we're talking about is guilty of being a coward, and the thought frightens them. What people would like is that a coward or a hero be born that way. . . .

michael novak   THE EXPERIENCE
                                              OF NOTHINGNESS

*Michael Novak (1933–   ) studied in Rome and at the Catholic University
of America and Harvard. He has taught at Stanford University, where he was
honored as an outstanding undergraduate teacher, and at the State University
of New York in Old Westbury. He is the author of* The Open Church, A New
Generation: American and Catholic, The Tiber Was Silver *(a novel),* Belief
and Unbelief: A Philosophy of Self-Knowledge, A Time to Build, *and* Theology
for Radical Politics. *With Robert McAfee Brown and Abraham Heschel he co-
authored* Vietnam: A Crisis of Conscience. *His most recent work is* The Experience of Nothingness (1970), *from which the following selection has been
taken.*

THE EXPERIENCE OF AMERICA

"The experience of nothingness" is an experience, not a concept. It can be
pointed to, described, built up indirectly, but not defined. Meursault's experience in *The Stranger*, Tolstoy's *The Death of Ivan Illich*, Kafka's
"Metamorphosis," Sartre's *The Age of Reason*, and Saul Bellow's *The Dangling Man* are among its literary expressions. The experience of nothingness,
however, arises in original forms today. The literature of preceding generations comforts us that we are not alone, but it does not precisely define our
state of soul.

Today, for the young, consciousness is shaped by the fluidity of percepts.
Undifferentiated time is the medium of consciousness, like a sea on which
and in which images float. The shaper of an alert, intelligent consciousness
is no longer a corpus of writings ("literature") nor the pursuit of a rigorous,
analytical line of argument ("the sciences"). Many good students, of good
will, who really want to read and to learn about the past, find it very difficult to concentrate. The new shaper of alert, discerning consciousness is
the camera. The images on a screen are not sequential; time is dissolved,
turned upon itself, defeated. The present gains at the expense of past and
future. The attention of the camera zooms in, pulls back, superimposes, cuts
away suddenly, races, slows, flashes back, flicks ahead, juxtaposes, repeats,
spins. A turn of the wrist at the channel indicator alters reality. For those
introduced to consciousness by such a teacher, the world is fluid. The percepts are too many and too rich to order, except by certain rhythms of emotion.

Roland Barthes describes in *Writing Degree Zero* the gradual collapse after 1850 of the canonical "literature" of the European aristocracy and bourgeoisie. The language of the poor, the prostitutes, and the beggars entered the consciousness of writers; the pretensions of the classical and bourgeois traditions to universality were shattered. The use by middle class historians and novelists of the narrative past tense ("The marchioness went out at five o'clock") and of the third person ("he") had masked an ordered worldview, a definiteness, a position in the cosmos, safely observed. Such a universe could easily be shaped by stories: beginning, middle, end. Madness, chaos, and profound diversity were neatly kept outside. After the revolution of 1848, the writer began to feel uneasy in the literary tradition; that tidy image had been shattered. He listened for a voice of his own, listened, finally, for the neutral, clear, amoral voice achieved most flawlessly by Camus in *The Stranger*. Writing moved outside "Literature," "Tradition," "Society." The human race lacks unity; the writer recognized the absence of a language of unity. He continues today to trace his personal mythic history, defeated even by his own successes: he renders his isolation only to find it debased as common currency.

But the dispersal of consciousness experienced by the younger generation in the United States goes further still. In the classic French myth, the center of consciousness is a clear eye, focusing on "clear, distinct ideas." "I *think*, therefore I am." Hence the painful clarity of French sensibility and consciousness. In the United States, in an ever growing sub-culture at least, the equivalent affirmation is simply: "I feel." No "therefore" is available, or needed. The eye of consciousness yields to affect, percept, kaleidoscope. The self is a recipient of stimuli in a darkened room. I know I am alive when a warm body is next to mine. Connections come through skin.

In the new civilization then, the primary sense of reality is shaped partly by parents and neighbors (local customs, raised eyebrows), partly by books ("the liberal tradition"), but mostly by cinema, television, and records. It is a civilization of massive dissolution.

Those whose sense of the meaningful, the relevant, and the real is not entirely shaped by the new media may feel themselves caught between two barbarisms. If they imagine the self to be a seeing eye, a fierce and mastering awareness—Reason—then they stand accused of the barbaric rationalization of human life that has yielded Dallas, airline terminals, body count, and painful inner emptiness. If they imagine the self to be a center of feeling, they will certainly be drawn to darkness, blood and destruction. (The "gentle revolution" is innocent when no threat faces it. The young have learned to cope when they are shown approval. Denied their will, their aspect is terrifying. Events, inevitably harsh, will surely make them bitter; filled with resentment, distrustful, they will feel trapped, a thousand times betrayed.) Apollo sheered from Dionysus yields two tribes of beasts.

The experience of nothingness in America, however, cuts across all networks: neighbor culture, book culture, electronic culture. In every part of America the sense of security has been undermined; nearly everything must be defended. All the more because the Republic was established to ensure our happiness, we find reality too much to bear. The experience of nothingness seeps into our awareness through a sieve.

Boredom is the first taste of nothingness. Today, boredom is the chief starting place of metaphysics. For boredom leads instantly to "killing time." And why is time a threat? Time, on the stage of consciousness, stands still. For the bored, no action is more attractive than any other. The self cannot be drawn into action; it lives by and for distractions; it waits. The world acts; the self is acted on. The fighter pilot whose skeleton is supported by the web straps of a plane crashed long ago in the jungles of Iwo Jima might today be supported by the web strap of a commuter train. Death seems continuous with death-in-life. Many have an overpowering urge to sleep. When Superman meets the social worker (Jules Feiffer), he learns that he is not an agent; he is acted on, his behavior has been determined. He loses strength. He droops.

Boredom: the discovery that everything is a game. A friend of mine decided that, short of suicide, one bulwark against time is a game sufficiently complicated to hold his attention until death. He made enough money as an electronics engineer (a specialist in game theory) to have free at least one year in every three. He determined to visit every town on the planet with a population over twenty-five thousand. During his working years he pored over maps; during his traveling years he concentrated on one continent after another. He often stayed in a town only long enough to lunch and to make a mark on his list. The beauty of it is, he told me, that a booming population, wars, and refugees guarantee an ever changing list.

Besides boredom, there is the collapse of a strongly inculcated set of values. I have heard students say with bitterness that high school is "enough betrayal for a lifetime." A seeing-eye God who turns out to be on the side of parents, society, philistinism, law and order, mind and dessication. But after that, what? Many search for a new social order, a new community of love. Without a vision they would perish; a utopia becomes their crutch, filling the psychological need once filled by God. Social scientists leap in to tell the adolescent that everything is relative, that everything is determined, and to suggest that the social system is the source of his inner emptiness. (The "system" plays, today, the role of devil.) Plato: the system is the self writ large; the alienation of the self comes from the system. The young are left with the inner helplessness they learned in grammar school. Their rage is legitimated; it is projected outward. They flail against "the dehumanization of the Ameri-

169

can way of life." Although the new imperative is "Humanize the system," it is impossible to discern the criteria for "humanization." No society in history ever met all the needs the young feel. Slowly the young learn that even warm, close lovers betray one another, and each discovers in himself count-less self-betrayals. Gone are the old firm values; gone also the innocent world that replaced them. Alienation projected onto the system is evasion. It evades a more terrifying emptiness.

Thirdly, there is helplessness. It is not only the large, impersonal bureauc-racy that engenders feelings of helplessness. It is not only the feeling that "I have no control over my life." It is also the recognition that those who wield power are also empty, and that I, too, if I had power over my life, am most confused about what I would do with it. The sense of helplessness today is not, in the end, political; power, even pressed down and running over, does not fill the void; it merely masks it. In the eyes of the successful leaders of the Students for a Democratic Society, as in those of the occupants of the White House, one may still see nothingness.

Fourthly, there is the betrayal by permissiveness, pragmatism, and value-neutral discourse. "To every child a childhood." The young have a right to learn a way of discriminating right from wrong, the posed from the authen-tic, the excellent from the mediocre, the brilliant from the philistine, the shoddy from the workmanlike. When no one with experience bothers to in-sist—to insist—on such discrimination, they rightly get the idea that discern-ment is not important, that no one cares, that no one cares either about such things—or about them. For it is demanding to teach children ethics, beauty, excellence; demanding in itself, and even more demanding to do so with authenticity. The laissez-faire attitude of American society in matters of the human spirit represents one of the greatest mass betrayals of responsibility by any civilization in human history. (Ironically, the young in their rebellion of-ten manifest in the form of "Do your own thing" precisely this profound sickness of their elders.)

Fifthly, there are drug experiences, and uncounted experiences with inti-macy unwanted but given anyway. The young are forced to live through the problems of technological consciousness, problems created by generations who built a rational, efficient society without calculating in advance its ef-fect upon human beings. The apocalypse may come, not by fire or flood, but by mass insanity. The civilization in and around New York City surely manifests insanity's advancing stages: everywhere there is hostility, bitterness, resentment—that grinding, bitter resentment of which Nietzsche and Scheler, warned. People lash out at one another. Parents ridicule children. Wives scream at husbands.

Everywhere there is the experience of mechanical relationships. Has any-one ever counted haw many persons in the United States are paid for telling lies? Has anyone ever counted the proportion of human transactions in which Americans are forced to treat one another impersonally, superficially, without interest? It is quite plain that Americans, the most nomadic people since the medieval Arabs, seldom grow organically into marriage. When they marry, they know only a small segment—hardly the least decisive—of their partners' lives. After they marry, the lives of husbands and wives are commonly attracted into separate orbits, sheering apart from one another. Nothing organic, nothing mutually rooted.

The enormous weight, meanwhile, put upon mutual sexual fulfillment is insupportable; intercourse is an organic expression of entire psyches, not a mechanical plugging in. Among young people, the weakening of cultural forms supporting sexual rituals and restraints deprives sexual intercourse of sustenance for the imagination and the spirit. It comes too cheaply: its intimacy is mainly fake; its symbolic power is reduced to the huddling warmth of kittens in the darkness—not to be despised, but open as a raw wound to the experience of nothingness. Close your eyes and plummet through the empty space where a lover ought to be.

A complete phenomenology of the experience of nothingness in our generation is neither possible nor desirable. There are as many ways for that unmistakable experience to break into one's consciousness as there are personal histories. Some feel its touch by way of sickness or disaster, some by way of external event and others by inner breakdown, some in the flush of power and others in irretrievable despair. The experience of nothingness comes uninvited; it may also be pursued. It is not found at the boundaries of life merely, at the broken places; it comes also from the very center, from the core of joy and pride and dignity. The strong nod at its voice with familiarity no less than the weak. The men and women from the lower middle class lack fancy words for it, but behind the skin of their faces it sits with the same mask it wears under the faces of television commentators.

Nor is the experience of nothingness accurately named *Angst* (Kierkegaard, Heidegger). Somehow the European hungers to possess his own being, to be the cause of his own existence, to be God. When he discovers that his own being is partial and invaded by nonbeing, he feels an icy threat. But the experience of nothingness in America is more often a peculiar and quiet vulnerability, a dead stillness at the center of activity, a lack of drive, an ignorance of Being and Life and Faith, a bafflement that a future that should have been so lovely turns out so bleak. The American experience of nothingness is a certain sadness. We do not have, despite our reputation, the European willfulness; behind our frenetic activity and self-assurance lurks a soft, purring, wounded kitten. We are not metaphysical but sentimental.

171

IN EUROPE: NIHILISM

One cannot, however, give the American experience voice without turning to its European background. European thinkers, of course, immediately turned the experience of nothingness, which began to "infect" Europeans with increasing frequency in the nineteenth century, into an "ism"; they spoke of it ideologically, as nihilism. They wrote from a history of unsurpassed intellectual energy. They had seen mythology, religion, and science express themselves in a brilliant sunrise of cultural history, each stage "higher" than the preceding; and then in the nineteenth century as they were stepping toward the peak of their achievement, on the threshold of a golden age, during nearly a century of relative world peace, they peered down into a fathomless abyss. Friedrich Nietzsche, like a tongue darting into a cavity, could not divert his attention. He asked himself again and again: "What does nihilism mean?" In a single felicitous sentence he answered: "The aim is lacking; 'why?' finds no answer."

The experience of nothingness is a mode of human consciousness; it occurs in human beings, not in cats or trees. It is, often, a kind of exhaustion of spirit that comes from seeking "meaning" too long and too ardently. It is accompanied by terror. It seems like a kind of death, an inertness, a paralysis. Meanwhile, the dark impulses of destruction find only thin resistance, they beat upon the doors for instantaneous release. The threshold of rage, suicide, and murder is frighteningly low. (Does death make any difference?) Yet even more vivid than the dark emotions are a desert-like emptiness, a malaise, an illness of the spirit and the stomach. One sees all too starkly the fraudulence of human arrangements. Every engagement seems so involved in half-truth, lie, and unimportance that the will to believe and the will to act collapse like ash.

Nietzsche distinguished three phases in the experience of nothingness, and it may be helpful to follow his notes on the subject, which are too long to quote in full. "Nihilism," he wrote, "will have to be reached, *first*, when we have sought in all events a 'meaning' that is not there." Nihilism, then, is a "recognition of the long *waste* of strength"; one is "ashamed in front of oneself, as if one had *deceived* oneself all too long." One had hoped to *achieve* something through one's actions, "and now one realizes that becoming aims at *nothing* and achieves *nothing*."

Nihilism "as a psychological state is reached, *secondly*," he writes, "when one has posited a totality," an organization, a unity "in all events, and underneath all events," so that a man will have "a deep feeling of standing in the context of, and being dependent on, some whole that is infinitely superior to him." This whole need not be God, but it is, at least, some scheme like that of progress, or the advance of science, or the fate of civilization, all

172

of which function as some form of deity. "But, behold, there is no such universal! At bottom, man has lost the faith in his own value when no infinitely valuable whole works through him; i.e., he conceived such a whole *in order to be able to believe in his own value.*"

The experience of nothingness has yet a third and last form:

> Given these two insights, that becoming has no goal and that underneath all becoming there is no grand unity in which the individual could immerse himself completely as in an element of supreme value, an escape remains: to pass sentence on this whole world of becoming as a deception and to invent a world beyond it, a *true* world. Having reached this standpoint, one grants the reality of becoming as the *only* reality, forbids oneself every kind of clandestine access to afterworlds and false divinities—*but cannot endure this world though one does not want to deny it.*
>
> What has happened, at bottom? The feeling of valuelessness was reached with the realization that the overall character of existence may not be interpreted by means of the concept of an "aim," the concept of "unity," or the concept of "truth." Existence has no goal or end; any comprehensive unity in the plurality of events is lacking: the character of existence is not "true," is *false*. One simply lacks any reason for convincing oneself that there is a *true* world. Briefly: the categories "aim," "unity," "being," which we used to project some values into the world—we *pull out* again; so the world looks valueless.

I recognize that I put structure into my own world. Such recognition is a necessary condition of the experience of nothingness. There is no "real" world out there, given, intact, full of significance. Consciousness is constituted by random, virtually infinite barrages of experience; these experiences are indistinguishably "inner" and "outer." The mad are aware of that buzzing confusion. The same have put structure into it. Structure *is put into experience by culture and the self*, and may also be pulled out again. Sociological consciousness recognizes such an insight under the rubric of "relativism." But the experience of nothingness casts doubt, also, on the reasons and methods of sociology (and every other science or philosophy). In its light they, too, seem like useless passions. The experience of nothingness is an experience beyond the limits of reason. It arises near the borderline of insanity. It is terrifying. It makes all attempts at speaking of purpose, goals, aims, meaning, importance, conformity, harmony, unity—it makes all such attempts seem doubtful and spurious. The person gripped by the experience of nothingness sees nearly everything *in reverse image*. What other persons call certain, he sees as pretend; what other persons call pragmatic or effective, he sees as a most ironical delusion. There is no real world out there, he says. Within human beings and outside them, there is only a great darkness, in which momentary beams of attention flash like fireflies. The experience of nothingness is an awareness of the multiplicity and polymorphousness of experience, and of the tide urging the conscious self to shape its own confusion by projecting myths.

Most people, of course, are instructed by their parents, schools, churches, economic and social roles, and other instruments of culture to shape their inner and outer confusion in clear, direct ways. A person who is "well brought up" is balanced, well adjusted, well rounded, purposive, dutiful, clear in his aims, views, and values. The well-brought-up person has been sheltered from the experience of nothingness. His feet are planted on solid ground. His perceptions of himself, others, and the world have been duly arranged. For him the question of reality has been settled. That is real which his culture says is real; that is of value which his culture values. His convictions about the aim of life have been formed in him by his culture. What he is to perceive and experience in life is determined in advance, and he *will* not allow himself to perceive or to experience otherwise.

To choose against the culture is not merely to disobey; it is to "die." Against what the culture knows is real, true, and good, one has chosen the evil, the false, and the unreal. To be or not to be, that is the question. To choose against the culture is to experience nothingness.

Nihilism is an ideological interpretation imposed on the experience of nothingness. Most writers on nihilism have placed the experience of nothingness in opposition to the values of the culture, as though that experience were a threat to it. I want to argue that the power of the experience of nothingness has been misperceived. Its root and source have not been detected, or else have been wrongly identified. The experience of nothingness was so new, so powerful, and so unexpected that it arrived *inconnu*. All who have since reflected upon it stand in the debt of Nietzsche and Heidegger, Freud and Sartre, but in probing for its source and power no one has yet driven an arrow into the center of the circle. The unassimilable horror of the regime of Adolf Hitler showed that the experience of nothingness may be put to the most horrible uses; the experience of nothingness may be murderous. Nevertheless, the experience of nothingness is now the point from which nearly every reflective man begins his adult life. We have seen too much blood to be astonished that Hitlers are possible. History, Hegel said, is a butcher's bench.

Still, the sorrows of this century have distorted our reflections on the experience of nothingness. That experience leads not only to murder; it is also the source of creativity and plenitude. We need not avert our eyes from the nihilism of the Fascists, or evade the ambiguities of nothingness. We can also reflect upon the preconditions and fertile possibilities of that experience, which in any case already occupies our hearts.

174

The source of the experience of nothingness lies in the deepest recesses of human consciousness, in its irrepressible tendency to ask questions. The necessary condition for the experience of nothingness is that everything can be questioned. Whatever the presuppositions of a culture or a way of life, questions can be addressed against them and other alternatives can be imagined. Whatever the massive solidity of institutions, cultural forms, or basic symbols, accurately placed questions can shatter their claims upon us. The drive to ask questions is the most persistent and basic drive of human consciousness. It is the principle of the experience of nothingness. By exercising that drive, we come to doubt the definitions of the real, the true, and the good that our culture presents to us. Without this drive, cultural change would not be possible. What was sacred once would for all time be locked in unchanging sacredness.

Because it is the principle of cultural change, the experience of nothingness is ambiguous, for cultural change is in itself of dubious value. Because it lies so near to madness, the experience of nothingness is a dangerous, possibly destructive experience. But when it leads to changes in cultural or personal consciousness that are liberating and joyful, it is called, deservedly, a "divine madness." Those whom the city must put to death for corrupting its youth sometimes fire the consciousness of many others with a madness that comes to define a new sanity, a corruption that becomes a new morality, a nothingness that yields a new being. And then the process may begin again.

When, meanwhile, the drive to raise questions makes us aware of its total range and depth, a feeling of formlessness, or nausea, or lassitude arises. When I perceive the drive to question in its purity, apart from the products to which it leads me, I perceive the ambiguity of my own conscious life. I recognize the formlessness, the aimlessness, and the disunity implicit in my own insignificance, my mortality, my ultimate dissolution. I peer into madness, chaos, and death. These insights are true insights. Not to experience them is to evade the character of one's own consciousness. It is to live a lie. The experience of nothingness bears the taste of honesty.

The truth of the human situation, however, remains to be decided. Is the character of human consciousness so inherently chaotic that the only genuine way to mirror our situation is insanity? Quite possibly. I wish to argue tentatively that the character of human consciousness is merely tragic; that is, that the experience of nothingness may be absorbed in full sanity; that a clear and troubling recognition of our fragility, our mortality, and our ignorance need not subvert our relation to the world in which we find ourselves. The experience of nothingness may lead either to madness or to wisdom. The man who shares it, however wise, appears to those who do not share it (and sometimes to himself) as mad. Wisdom lies on the edge of insanity, just as those who wish to see themselves as sane and well adjusted in this bloody and absurd world may be foolish and insane. Our lives seem to be tragic rather than absurd, but I am far from certain on that point. The issue falls one way rather than the other only by a hair.

FURTHER READING

There is much about "Alienation and The Death of Meaning" that is most tellingly expressed by the imagery and feeling of the poet. Matthew Arnold's "Dover Beach" was virtually prophetic, and T. S. Eliot's "The Love Song of J. Alfred Prufrock" (1917) and "The Hollow Men" (1925) were accurate portraits of men lost in a new age. In "The End of the World," by Archibald MacLeish (in *Poems 1924–1935*), the world is a circus whose top blows off to reveal above "nothing, nothing, nothing—nothing at all." The deep pessimism and cynicism of Robinson Jeffers are displayed in his description of man as the "King of Beasts" (*The Double Axe and Other Poems*, 1948).

The plays *Waiting for Godot* (1952) and *Krapp's Last Tape* (1958) are among the writings that won Samuel Beckett the Nobel Prize for literature in 1969. Sometimes grouped with Beckett in the "Theater of the Absurd" is Edward Albee, whose *The Zoo Story* (1958) is one of his best short plays.

Albert Camus, another Nobel laureate in literature (in 1957), wrote the classic existentialist novel *The Stranger* (1942) and discussed many of its themes in essay form in *The Myth of Sisyphus* (1942).

Norman Mailer described anomie and despair in an American setting in his great short story "The Man Who Studied Yoga" (in *Advertisements for Myself*, 1959). Alan Harrington told what it was like to "belong" to a giant corporation in America in the title essay in *Life in the Crystal Palace* (1959).

Two excellent anthologies are those edited by Eric and Mary Josephson, *Man Alone: Alienation in Modern Society* (1962), and Gerald Sykes, *Alienation: the Cultural Climate of Our Time* (2 vols., 1964). Colin Wilson's *The Outsider* (1956) amounts to another guide to fascinating literary, philosophical, and religious sources.

"The Present Age," the first part of William Barrett's *Irrational Man* (1958), is a philosophically perceptive survey of almost all the themes encountered in this chapter.

_*VALUES: DEFINING THE GOOD LIFE*

5

After all is said and done, it is the question of values that is central in philosophy. The deepest concern of every man is that he find and live "the good life"; he wants his existence to have the quality of "happiness." And the greatest challenge to philosophers has always been to define the values which comprise the good life.

We want more than to pass through an indistinguishable jumble of days and nights; we seek in the flux of events a sense of purpose. The phrase "a philosophy of life" and the current term "life style" refer primarily to holding a set of values. These values help us to discern the momentous from the trivial, and, in the words of Harold Taylor, "to make sense from the disorder of common experience."

The familiar question about the "practicality" of philosophy may be best answered in terms of philosophy's crucial involvement with values. First, the question is itself prompted by a prior judgment—that if philosophy is indeed worthwhile, one must be able to do something with it, or make some use of it—and it is one of the functions of philosophy to ascertain the validity of such judgments. Second, accepting the assumption of the question, philosophy may be said to be quite practical. It is even more practical than accounting or auto shop, insofar as it is one's philosophy which determines whether one goes into accounting or auto shop. Choices are reflections of our values, and we make choices, large and small, every day of our lives.

Illustrative of our natural immersion in philosophical matters is the reading selection by Sinclair Lewis. Here are values in their "raw" form—they comprise that body of preferences, judgments, prejudices, ideas, and ideals by which George F. Babbitt lives. Some of his ideas are inconsistent with one another, others are popular myths he has simply inherited, and many have persisted only because he has obviously never subjected them to critical appraisal. But these, nevertheless, are the values of the "non-philosophical" and even anti-intellectual Babbitt, whose fame has earned him a place in dictionaries as a model of narrow-mindedness and misguided self-satisfaction. "Aunt Arie," from The Foxfire Book, is an unaffected expression of other values (which would have horrified Babbitt). Arie Carpenter's values center primarily upon people—family and friends—and her mountain home. Hers is a life of simple pleasures and hard work on the land, and she has a refreshing disdain for money. It is a way of life which seems authentic, and its appeal today is reflected by the popularity of such publications as The Mother Earth News and Wood Heat Quarterly.

178

The ultimate disease of our time is valuelessness.

abraham maslow

Carl Rogers' approach to values stresses their growth in the life of the individual. The word "process" is important to Rogers. Debating in 1956 with B. F. Skinner, Rogers inveighed against "static attributes" and proposed that:

> we select a set of values that focuses on fluid elements of process. . . . We might then value: man as a process of becoming, as a process of achieving worth and dignity through the development of his potentialities; the individual human being as a self-actualizing process, moving on to more challenging and enriching experiences; the process by which the individual creatively adapts to an ever-new and changing world. . . .[1]

In the classic style of the philosopher, Aristotle was interested in looking beyond the many goods that swarm distractingly before us to determine what was the greatest good. "Are we not," he asks, "more likely to hit the mark if we have a target?" His is termed a teleological ethical system, that is, an end-oriented philosophy, which was typical of Greek thought and the long tradition which followed it.

Immanuel Kant, in abrupt contrast to Aristotle, holds a deontological ethical theory. The entire emphasis here shifts to a rule-oriented system: to act out of respect for what is right is man's foremost duty. It becomes risky, with Kant, to speak of his conception of the "good life" because moral action must be undertaken as an end in itself. If one's motive is another consideration (for example, a desire for the "good life" or even a natural inclination to be kind) that action is not properly termed "moral." Doing what is right means doing it because it is right and for no other reason. Value, for Kant, resides in the moral act.

John Stuart Mill proclaimed himself a hedonist. More specifically, it was that variety of hedonism he labeled utilitarianism. Happiness is defined as pleasure, and "pleasure and freedom from pain are the only things desirable as ends." His insistence, however, that there were different kinds of pleasures, some of them more desirable than others, suggests that there must be a criterion for ethical choices other than that of pleasure—and such a suggestion is heretical for a hedonist. Mill also differed from earlier hedonists in his view that the happiness to be sought for is not one's own, "but the greatest amount of happiness altogether."

[1] Carl R. Rogers and B. F. Skinner, "Some Issues Concerning the Control of Behavior: A Symposium," *Science* (Nov. 30, 1956), p. 1062.

179

Sinclair Lewis (1885–1951), the son of a country doctor, was born in Sauk Centre, Minnesota, in the midst of the provincialism he was later to satirize. Sauk Centre became the "Gopher Prairie" of Main Street, the novel that made a national celebrity of Lewis. He followed that novel with Babbitt, Arrowsmith, Elmer Gantry, *and* Dodsworth—*all published in the 1920s—and won the Nobel Prize for literature in 1930, the first American to be so honored. A tall, thin man with a deeply pock-marked face, Lewis had a sensitive, volatile, and sometimes difficult personality. He could be impulsive: he proposed marriage to his second wife, Dorothy Thompson, the very evening he met her at a party.*

"One of the livest banquets that has recently been pulled off occurred last night in the annual Get-Together Fest of the Zenith Real Estate Board, held in the Venetian Ball Room of the O'Hearn House. Mine host Gil O'Hearn had as usual done himself proud and those assembled feasted on such an assemblage of plates as could be rivaled nowhere west of New York, if there, and washed down the plenteous feed with the cup which inspired but did not inebriate in the shape of cider from the farm of Chandler Mott, president of the board and who acted as witty and efficient chairman.

"As Mr. Mott was suffering from slight infection and sore throat, G. F. Babbitt made the principal talk. Besides outlining the progress of Torrensing real estate titles, Mr. Babbitt spoke in part as follows:

" 'In rising to address you, with my impromptu speech carefully tucked into my vest pocket, I am reminded of the story of the two Irishmen, Mike and Pat, who were riding on the Pullman. Both of them, I forgot to say, were sailors in the Navy. It seems Mike had the lower berth and by and by he heard a terrible racket from the upper, and when he yelled up to find out what the trouble was, Pat answered, "Shure an' bedad an' how can I ever get a night's sleep at all, at all? I been trying to get into this darned little hammock ever since eight bells!"

" 'Now, gentlemen, standing up here before you, I feel a good deal like Pat, and maybe after I've spieled along for a while, I may feel so darn small that I'll be able to crawl into a Pullman hammock with no trouble at all, at all!

" 'Gentlemen, it strikes me that each year at this annual occasion when friend and foe get together and lay down the battle-ax and let the waves of good-fellowship waft them up the flowery slopes of amity, it behooves us, standing together eye to eye and shoulder to shoulder as fellow-citizens of the best city in the world, to consider where we are both as regards ourselves and the common weal.

"'It is true that even with our 361,000, or practically 362,000, population, there are, by the last census, almost a score of larger cities in the United States. But, gentlemen, if by the next census we do not stand at least tenth, then I'll be the first to request any knocker to remove my shirt and to eat the same, with the compliments of G. F. Babbitt, Esquire! It may be true that New York, Chicago, and Philadelphia will continue to keep ahead of us in size. But aside from these three cities, which are notoriously so overgrown that no decent white man, nobody who loves his wife and kiddies and God's good out-o'-doors and likes to shake the hand of his neighbor in greeting, would want to live in them—and let me tell you right here and now, I wouldn't trade a high-class Zenith acreage development for the whole length and breadth of Broadway or State Street!—aside from these three, it's evident to any one with a head for facts that Zenith is the finest example of American life and prosperity to be found anywhere.

"'I don't mean to say we're perfect. We've got a lot to do in the way of extending the paving of motor boulevards, for, believe me, it's the fellow with four to ten thousand a year, say, and an automobile and a nice little family in a bungalow on the edge of town, that makes the wheels of progress go round!

"'That's the type of fellow that's ruling America to-day; in fact, it's the ideal type to which the entire world must tend, if there's to be a decent, well-balanced, Christian, go-ahead future for this little old planet! Once in a while I just naturally sit back and size up this Solid American Citizen, with a whale of a lot of satisfaction.

"'Our Ideal Citizen—I picture him first and foremost as being busier than a bird-dog, not wasting a lot of good time in day-dreaming or going to sassiety teas or kicking about things that are none of his business, but putting the zip into some store or profession or art. At night he lights up a good cigar, and climbs into the little old 'bus, and maybe cusses the carburetor, and shoots out home. He mows the lawn, or sneaks in some practice putting, and then he's ready for dinner. After dinner he tells the kiddies a story, or takes the family to the movies, or plays a few fists of bridge, or reads the evening paper, and a chapter or two of some good lively Western novel if he has a taste for literature, and maybe the folks next-door drop in and they sit and visit about their friends and the topics of the day. Then he goes happily to bed, his conscience clear, having contributed his mite to the prosperity of the city and to his own bank-account.

"'In politics and religion this Sane Citizen is the canniest man on earth; and in the arts he invariably has a natural taste which makes him pick out the best, every time. In no country in the world will you find so many reproductions of the Old Masters and of well-known paintings on parlor walls as in these United States. No country has anything like our number of phonographs, with not only dance records and comic but also the best operas, such as Verdi, rendered by the world's highest-paid singers.

" 'In other countries, art and literature are left to a lot of shabby bums living in attics and feeding on booze and spaghetti, but in America the successful writer or picture-painter is indistinguishable from any other decent business man; and I, for one, am only too glad that the man who has the rare skill to season his message with interesting reading matter and who shows both purpose and pep in handling his literary wares has a chance to drag down his fifty thousand bucks a year, to mingle with the biggest executives on terms of perfect equality, and to show as big a house and as swell a car as any Captain of Industry! But, mind you, it's the appreciation of the Regular Guy who I have been depicting which has made this possible, and you got to hand as much credit to him as to the authors themselves.

" 'Finally, but most important, our Standardized Citizen, even if he is a bachelor, is a lover of the Little Ones, a supporter of the hearthstone which is the basic foundation of our civilization, first, last, and all the time, and the thing that most distinguishes us from the decayed nations of Europe.

" 'I have never yet toured Europe—and as a matter of fact, I don't know that I care to such an awful lot, as long as there's our own mighty cities and mountains to be seen—but, the way I figure it out, there must be a good many of our own sort of folks abroad. Indeed, one of the most enthusiastic Rotarians I ever met boosted the tenets of one-hundred-per-cent pep in a burr that smacked o' bonny Scutlond and all ye bonny braes o' Bobby Burns. But same time, one thing that distinguishes us from our good brothers, the hustlers over there, is that they're willing to take a lot off the snobs and journalists and politicians, while the modern American business man knows how to talk right up for himself, knows how to make it good and plenty clear that he intends to run the works. He doesn't have to call in some highbrow hired-man when it's necessary for him to answer the crooked critics of the sane and efficient life. He's not dumb, like the old-fashioned merchant. He's got a vocabulary and a punch.

" 'With all modesty, I want to stand up here as a representative business man and gently whisper, "Here's our kind of folks! Here's the specifications of the Standardized American Citizen! Here's the new generation of Americans: fellows with hair on their chests and smiles in their eyes and adding-machines in their offices. We're not doing any boasting, but we like ourselves first-rate, and if you don't like us, look out—better get under cover before the cyclone hits town!"

" 'So! In my clumsy way I have tried to sketch the Real He-man, the fellow with Zip and Bang. And it's because Zenith has so large a proportion of such men that it's the most stable, the greatest of our cities. New York also has its thousands of Real Folks, but New York is cursed with unnumbered foreigners. So are Chicago and San Francisco. Oh, we have a golden roster of cities—Detroit and Cleveland with their renowned factories, Cincinnati with its great machine-tool and soap products, Pittsburg and Birmingham with their steel, Kansas City and Minneapolis and Omaha that open their bountiful gates on the bosom of the ocean-like wheatlands, and countless other magnificent sister-cities, for, by the last census, there were no less than sixty-eight glorious American burgs with a population of over one hundred thousand! And all these cities stand together for power and purity, and against foreign ideas and communism—Atlanta with Hartford, Rochester with Denver, Milwaukee with Indianapolis, Los Angeles with Scranton, Portland, Maine, with Portland, Oregon. A good live wire from Baltimore or Seattle or Duluth is the twinbrother of every like fellow booster from Buffalo or Akron, Fort Worth or Oskaloosa!

" 'But it's here in Zenith, the home for manly men and womanly women and bright kids, that you find the largest proportion of these Regular Guys, and that's what sets it in a class by itself; that's why Zenith will be remembered in history as having set the pace for a civilization that shall endure when the old time-killing ways are gone forever and the day of earnest efficient endeavor shall have dawned all round the world!

" 'Some time I hope folks will quit handing all the credit to a lot of moth-eaten, mildewed, out-of-date, old, European dumps, and give proper credit to the famous Zenith spirit, that clean fighting determination to win Success that has made the little old Zip City celebrated in every land and clime, wherever condensed milk and pasteboard cartons are known! Believe me, the world has fallen too long for these worn-out countries that aren't producing anything but bootblacks and scenery and booze, that haven't got one bathroom per hundred people, and that don't know a loose-leaf ledger from a slip-cover; and it's just about time for some Zenithite to get his back up and holler for a show-down!

" 'I tell you, Zenith and her sister-cities are producing a new type of civilization. There are many resemblances between Zenith and these other burgs, and I'm darn glad of it! The extraordinary, growing, and sane standardization of stores, offices, streets, hotels, clothes, and newspapers throughout the United States shows how strong and enduring a type is ours.

" 'I always like to remember a piece that Chum Frink wrote for the newspapers about his lecture-tours. It is doubtless familiar to many of you, but if you will permit me, I'll take a chance and read it. It's one of the classic poems, like "If" by Kipling, or Ella Wheeler Wilcox's "The Man Worth While"; and I always carry this clipping of it in my note-book:

When I am out upon the road, a poet with a pedler's load I mostly sing a hearty song, and take a chew and hike along, a-handing out my samples fine of Cheero Brand of sweet sunshine, and peddling optimistic pokes and stable lines of japes and jokes to Lyceums and other folks, to Rotarys, Kiwanis' Clubs, and feel I ain't like other dubs. And then old Major Silas Satan, a brainy cuss who's always waitin', he gives his tail a lively quirk, and gets in quick his dirty work. He fills me up with mullygrubs; my hair the backward way he rubs; he makes me lonelier than a hound, on Sunday when the folks ain't round. And then b' gosh, I would prefer to never be a lecturer, a-ridin' round in classy cars and smoking fifty-cent cigars, and never more I want to roam; I simply want to be back home, a-eatin' flap-jacks, hash, and ham, with folks who savvy whom I am!

But when I get that lonely spell, I simply seek the best hotel, no matter in what town I be—St. Paul, Toledo, or K. C., in Washington, Schnectady, in Louisville or Albany. And at that inn it hits my dome that I again am right at home. If I should stand a lengthy spell in front of that first-class hotel, that to the drummers loves to cater, across from some big film theayter; if I should look around and buzz, and wonder in what town I was, I swear that I could never tell! For all the crowd would be so swell, in just the same fine sort of jeans they wear at home, and all the queens with spiffy bonnets on their beans, and all the fellows standing round a-talkin' always, I'll be bound, the same good jolly kind of guff, 'bout autos, politics and stuff and baseball players of renown that Nice Guys talk in my home town!

Then when I entered that hotel, I'd look around and say, "Well, well!" For there would be the same news-stand, same magazines and candies grand, same smokes of famous standard brand, I'd find at home, I'll tell! And when I saw the jolly bunch come waltzing in for eats at lunch, and squaring up in natty duds to platters large of French Fried spuds, why then I'd stand right up and bawl, "I've never left my home at all!" And all replete I'd sit me down beside some guy in derby brown upon a lobby chair of plush, and murmur to him in a rush, "Hello, Bill, tell me, good old scout, how is your stock a-holdin' out?" Then we'd be off, two solid pals, a-chatterin' like giddy gals of flivvers, weather, home, and wives, lodge-brothers then for all our lives! So when Sam Satan makes you blue, good friend, that's what I'd up and do, for in these States where'er you roam, you never leave your home sweet home.

" 'Yes, sir, these other burgs are our true partners in the great game of vital living. But let's not have any mistake about this. I claim that Zenith is the best partner and the fastest-growing partner of the whole caboodle. I trust I may be pardoned if I give a few statistics to back up my claims. If they are old stuff to any of you, yet the tidings of prosperity, like the good news of the Bible, never become tedious to the ears of a real hustler, no matter how oft the sweet story is told! Every intelligent person knows that Zenith manufactures more condensed milk and evaporated cream, more paper boxes, and more lighting-fixtures, than any other city in the United States, if not in the world. But it is not so universally known that we also stand second in the manufacture of package-butter, sixth in the giant realm of motors and automobiles, and somewhere about third in cheese, leather findings, tar roofing, breakfast food, and overalls!

" 'Our greatness, however, lies not alone in punchful prosperity but equally in that public spirit, that forward-looking idealism and brotherhood, which has marked Zenith ever since its foundation by the Fathers. We have a right, indeed we have a duty toward our fair city, to announce broadcast the facts about our high schools, characterized by their complete plants and the finest school-ventilating systems in the country, bar none; our magnificent new hotels and banks and the paintings and carved marble in their lobbies; and the Second National Tower, the second highest business building in any inland city in the entire country. When I add that we have an unparalleled number of miles of paved streets, bathrooms, vacuum cleaners, and all the other signs of civilization; that our library and art museum are well supported and housed in convenient and roomy buildings; that our park-system is more than up to par, with its handsome driveways adorned with grass, shrubs, and statuary, then I give but a hint of the all round unlimited greatness of Zenith!

" 'I believe, however, in keeping the best to the last. When I remind you that we have one motor car for every five and seven-eighths persons in the city, then I give a rock-ribbed practical indication of the kind of progress and braininess which is synonymous with the name Zenith!

" 'But the way of the righteous is not all roses. Before I close I must call your attention to a problem we have to face this coming year. The worst menace to sound government is not the avowed socialists but a lot of cowards who work under cover—the long-haired gentry who call themselves "liberals" and "radicals" and "non-partisan" and "intelligentsia" and God only knows how many other trick names! Irresponsible teachers and professors constitute the worst of this whole gang, and I am ashamed to say that several of them are on the faculty of our great State University! The U. is my own Alma Mater, and I am proud to be known as an alumni, but there are certain instructors there who seem to think we ought to turn the conduct of the nation over to hoboes and roustabouts.

" 'Those profs are the snakes to be scotched—they and all their milk-and-water ilk! The American business man is generous to a fault, but one thing he does demand of all teachers and lecturers and journalists: if we're going to pay them our good money, they've got to help us by selling efficiency and whooping it up for rational prosperity! And when it comes to these blab-mouth, fault-finding, pessimistic, cynical University teachers, let me tell you that during this golden coming year it's just as much our duty to bring influence to have those cusses fired as it is to sell all the real estate and gather in all the good shekels we can.

" 'Not till that is done will our sons and daughters see that the ideal of

American manhood and culture isn't a lot of cranks sitting around chewing the rag about their Rights and their Wrongs, but a God-fearing, hustling, successful, two-fisted Regular Guy, who belongs to some church with pep and piety to it, who belongs to the Boosters or the Rotarians or the Kiwanis, to the Elks or Moose or Red Men or Knights of Columbus or any one of a score of organizations of good, jolly, kidding, laughing, sweating, upstanding, lend-a-handing Royal Good Fellows, who plays hard and works hard, and whose answer to his critics is a square-toed boot that'll teach the grouches and smart alecks to respect the He-man and get out and root for Uncle Samuel, U. S. A.' "!

The Foxfire Book *grew out of materials assembled by students in a small high school in Georgia. Under the direction of their English teacher, Eliot Wigginton (who had proposed that they start a magazine rather than suffer together in a classroom), the students fanned out into the neighboring Southern Appalachians with notebooks, cameras, and tape recorders. They came back with fascinating mountain lore. "Building a Log Cabin," "Soapmaking," "Slaughtering Hogs," "Home Remedies," "Weather Signs," and "Moonshine as a Fine Art" were typical articles. The magazine* Foxfire *was quickly a success, and* The Foxfire Book *(edited by Eliot Wigginton), containing representative selections from the magazine, appeared in 1972.*

Aunt Arie Carpenter, whose tape-recorded words are transcribed below, was found far back in the mountains living alone in a log cabin. A widow, eighty-five years of age, she draws her water from a well, raises her own vegetables, and relies on a fireplace for heat. The students loved her. One of them, Jan Brown, wrote: "She is, to put it simply, just plain good. She is full of vitality and determination, and she radiates a warmth that few people have."

If I had plenty a'money, I'd put me in a short sink right here so I wouldn't have t'trot outdoors ever'time t'pour th' water out; but I guess I got just about what I'll have when I'm took away from here. Look like th' porch out there's gonna have t'be fixed; an' they want t'sell th' place so bad. I've already been offered lots fer't an' I wouldn't take it. This land goes over 'cross that mountain an' plumb on down on th' other side, an' th' government [government land] comes up there, an' they want that. I say I don't want'a sell it, an' they just looked up at me s'funny. Said, "What would I do with all that money?" You know, I don't care nothin' about money much.

My feet's gettin' sorta cold! (*We move to the living room where a fire is burning.*)

I was born an' raised on Hick'ry Knoll 'til I was eight years old. It'uz a hard livin'. I don't know how Poppy made it. Mommy never see'd a well day in her life. She was born with somethin' th' matter with her head—one side'a her head run from th' time she was born 'til she died. But I can tell y'one thing. In your life, don't never care a cent in this world t'wait on your mother, whether she's sick or not sick. When she's gone, you'll be glad y'did. Yes you will. 'Cause I've not got a thing in this world t'regret. I waited on my mother day and night—what I mean *day* and *night*. Many a night I been up waitin' on my mother when ever' body else was in th' bed asleep. I rejoice over that. God'll repay you for all that. God'll certainly bless y'fer it.

187

Poppy had a awful hard time, an' his daddy died a way 'fore he was born so he had a hard time t'begin with. Well, atter he's married he had a worse time *I'll* say, with all 'at sickness'n'ever'thing on 'im. Mommy did love wheat bread, an' he worked for a peck a'corn a day so he could get Mommy bread t'eat. Why, he'uz as good t'Mommy as a baby. Now Ulysses didn't believe this, an' I didn't care whether he did'r not—you know, if I tell anybody anything an' they believe it, it's all right; an' if they don't believe it, I don't care whether they do'r not—I never heard Poppy give Mommy a ill word in my life. Now we had some hogs, and one of our hogs got in a neighbor's corn patch an' eat some of his corn. And he come after Poppy an'told him t'come get his hog, an' he charged Poppy two dollers fer what it eat. Poppy's s'mad he didn't know what t'do. That'uz th' maddest I've ever seed Poppy in my life. An' Mommy—he called her Dink, that was her nickname—she said somethin' t'Poppy. "Now," he says, "Dink, don't you say a *word to* me while I'm mad." An' that was ever'thing's ever said about that. She hushed, of course. An' he never said nary another word. That was th' illest word I ever heered Poppy tell Mommy in my life.

It's a whole lot easier today. I've hoed corn many a day fer a quarter. *Many* a day. An' we used t'pick huckleberries, me'n m'brother did, an' swap two gallons a'huckleberries fer one gallon a'syrup. Had t'do somethin' t'make a livin'. But we always had plenty t'eat. We always had plenty a'what we had. We didn't have no great stuff that cost a lot. We never did buy that. Well, we just didn't have nothin't'pay fer't, an' we always tried t'pay as we went. You know, if y'get goin' in debt, next thing y'know you can't pay it t'save yore life. I'm scared t'death a debts. I owe fer this road now, an' it worries me t'death. Used t'be I didn't have enough money t'mail a letter with. An' you know how much candy I bought in my life 'fore I's married? I bought one nickel's worth a'candy in my life. I just didn't have nothin' t'buy *with*. Poppy hired a girl t'stay with Mommy 'til I got big enough t'do th' work, an' y'know how much he'd have t'pay? Seventy-five cents a week. They'd work all week fer seventy-five cents.

An' picked blackberries'n'strawberries. Always had something' t'eat. Pickled beans'n' ever'thin'. Why, we've pickled beans in a twenty gallon barrel; but I ain't got any this year. Groundhogs eat m'beans up an' I never had nary one t'pick. I had two bushel baskets full'a cans, an' I took 'em out there an' poured'em in th' groundhog's hole an' took a stick an' beat'em in. An' you know, that groundhog left an' never did come back. Couldn't bear them rattlin' things. Just couldn't stand'em (*laughing*).

An' we've raised high as seventy-five bushel a'Irish 'taters over'n'at field over there. Did'ja ever put up any sweet 'taters? Well, I'm gonna tell y'how. Law, I'uz s'glad t'know how I didn't know what t'do. Dig yer sweet 'taters an' sun'em 'til they gets just th' least bit swiveled, I call it; an' put 'em in pasteboard boxes an' cover'em up. They ain't nary one a'mine rotted yet. We kep'em in th'tater house. One day that 'tater house fell down—fell out, side of it did up there. I went t'get'taters an' they's th'biggest light in th'house, an' I said, "What in th' world's th' matter with th' tater house?" Here they was, th' side of it fell out.

Y'ever eat any lye hominy? Boys, 'at's th'best stuff ever you eat in yore life. It sure is. Boys, I've made many a pot full. And soap, law, I've made many a pot'a soap too. Had th' ash hopper, oak ashes. And bottomed chairs—I guess I bottomed 'bout ever'one a'these. He'ped to do it. I can't make th' splits. I bottom'em with white oak splits. Some people bottoms'em with bark, but I never did. Bark does easy t'what th' wood does. Course it don't last like wood. Tain't good like wood. (*We asked her to tell us more about the bark method.*) Use young poplar bark in th' spring a'th' year when th' sap rises; y'can't make it no other time. Only cut little poles certain lengths an'then peel'em an' use that while it's green. If y'wait 'til it gets all dried up, it'll break all t'pieces. An' always join th' ends under th' bottom. Never do jine'em on th' top a'th' chairs. On th' bottom so they won't bother nothin'.

An' I've made baskets. I've made lots'a baskets. I love t'fool wi'my hands. I just love t'fool with 'em. I made 'em with white oak splits, an' I've made some with willers. Willer baskets is hard 'cause y'have t'go off t'th' branch, an' we ain't got no willers grows on this place like a heap a'people has. Get'cha little willers, well, long as they grow. Ain't none of 'em big as yer finger. An' y'have t'have a big pot a'water by th' fire an' keep them willers soft in that. Didn't, they'd break all t'pieces. Put 'em in hot water an' th' bark just peels off like ever'thing. Gather'em when th' sap first rises on 'em pretty good, an y'can skin'em pretty well without scaldin'em; but if y'don't, y'have t'scald'em. I'd rather scald'em. They last longer I always think.

An' I've made foot mats out'a corn shucks—t'wipe yer feet on. That's easy, an' that's th' prettiest work! They make th' best foot mats. I ain't made none since m'hand's paralyzed. I reckon God just didn't intend fer me t'work my hand!

Used t'raise corn pones too. You ever eat any corn pones were raised? It's made out'a corn meal. Now hits another hard job, an' I love it better'n a cat loves sweet milk, I shore do. But I ain't raised none in a long time. Poppy always had me t'raise him a corn pone t'go t'Nantahaly. See, Poppy raised stock an'turned on Nantahaly range. Whenever th' time come, "I'm a goin' t'Nantahaly a certain day an' you raise me some corn pones," well, 'at's what I done. I had a big oven a'purpose t'bake'em in. Have t'cook'em on th' fireplace. An' Lester Mann, he found out I could do that, an'they's'good; why he a-a-a-always, when he started t'th' mountains, he always come an' I raised him a corn pone. Hit'd be five inches thick. An' you take that corn pone an' slice it an' lay it in grease an' fry it in a pan in th' mountains, an' that was hot bread, y'see? An' law, they thought that'uz th' greatest thing in th' world. I've raised many a one that's went t'Nantahaly.

I'll tell'y', be a neighbor and you'll have neighbors. Now I've tried that by experience. I do try t'be good t'ever'body, and I try t'treat ever'body just as I'd have them treat me. I don't care th' goodness you do, you'll always get repaid for it. Double. Fourfold. You children remember that. Th' more you do for people, th' more they'll do for you. Always remember, t'have a friend, be one.

Doesn't being here alone bother you sometimes?

Well, it's mighty lonesome. When it comes storms an'things like that, it's not s'good. And still I don't mind it a bit in th' world. Ain't only one thing I'm afraid of, an'that's snakes. When 'at big'n come in that big pile here awhile back, hit scared th' life out'a me just about. I like t'never got over it. But I ain't like this pore old woman lives over here. She's afraid of a bear an'carries a'axe with her ever'time she comes over here. Tickles me. A little old hand axe. I said, "What you goin' do wi'that?" She said, "Kill a bear." I've lived here eighty years an'never see'd a bear in my life. An' I'll tell you th' truth, I'm not bothered with one single thing in this world here. That groundhog's only thing in this world that bothers me. An th' fox. They won't let me have a chicken. I had twenty hens an' two roosters, an' they catched th'last one of 'em. I wanted t'get s'more, an' Ulysses said they wadn't no use.

We made a good life here, but we put in lots'a'time. Many an'many a night I've been workin' when two o'clock come in th' mornin'—cardin'n'spinnin'n' sewin'. They want me t'sell an'move away from here, but I won't do it. It's just home—'at's all. I spent my happiest days here.

190

carl r. rogers   # THE VALUING PROCESS
IN THE MATURE PERSON

*Carl R. Rogers (1902–   ) received both his M.A. and Ph.D. from Co-
lumbia University, and was associated with the Universities of Ohio and Chicago
as a clinical psychologist. More recently, he became a resident fellow at the
Center for Studies of the Person in La Jolla. A past president of the American
Association for Applied Psychologists, the American Psychological Association,
and the American Academy of Psychotherapists, he is the author of* Counseling
and Psychotherapy, Client-Centered Therapy, On Becoming a Person, *and* Freedom to Learn. *Among his many contributions to psychology has been a long
interest and involvement in the "intensive group experience"—T groups, encounter groups, sensitivity-training groups, and the like. The following essay was
published in 1964 in the* Journal of Abnormal and Social Psychology *(Vol. 68,
No. 2).*

There is a great deal of concern today with the problem of values. Youth,
in almost every country, is deeply uncertain of its value orientation; the
values associated with various religions have lost much of their influence;
sophisticated individuals in every culture seem unsure and troubled as to the
goals they hold in esteem. The reasons are not far to seek. The world
culture, in all its aspects, seems increasingly scientific and relativistic, and
the rigid, absolute views on values which come to us from the past appear
anachronistic. Even more important, perhaps, is the fact that the modern
individual is assailed from every angle by divergent and contradictory value
claims. It is no longer possible, as it was in the not too distant historical
past, to settle comfortably into the value system of one's forebears or one's
community and live out one's life without ever examining the nature and
the assumptions of that system.

In this situation it is not surprising that value orientations from the past
appear to be in a state of disintegration or collapse. Men question whether
there are, or can be, any universal values. It is often felt that we may have
lost, in our modern world, all possibility of any general or cross-cultural basis
for values. One natural result of this uncertainty and confusion is that there
is an increasing concern about, interest in, and a searching for, a sound or
meaningful value approach which can hold its own in today's world.

I share this general concern. As with other issues the general problem
faced by the culture is painfully and specifically evident in the cultural
microcosm which is called the therapeutic relationship, which is my sphere
of experience.

As a consequence of this experience I should like to attempt a modest theoretical approach to this whole problem. I have observed changes in the approach to values as the individual grows from infancy to adulthood. I observe further changes when, if he is fortunate, he continues to grow toward true psychological maturity. Many of these observations grow out of my experience as therapist, where I have had the mind stretching opportunity of seeing the ways in which individuals move toward a richer life. From these observations I believe I see some directional threads emerging which might offer a new concept of the valuing process, more tenable in the modern world. I have made a beginning by presenting some of these ideas partially in previous writings; I would like now to voice them more clearly and more fully.

SOME DEFINITIONS

Charles Morris has made some useful distinctions in regard to values. There are "operative values," which are the behaviors of organisms in which they show preference for one object or objective rather than another. The lowly earthworm, selecting the smooth arm of a **Y** maze rather than the arm which is paved with sandpaper, is giving an indication of an operative value.

There are also "conceived values," the preference of an individual for a symbolized object. "Honesty is the best policy" is such a conceived value.

There is also the term "objective value," to refer to what is objectively preferable, whether or not it is sensed or conceived of as desirable. I will be concerned primarily with operative or conceptualized values.

INFANT'S WAY OF VALUING

Let me first speak about the infant. The living human being has, at the outset, a clear approach to values. We can infer from studying his behavior that he prefers those experiences which maintain, enhance, or actualize his organism, and rejects those which do not serve this end. Watch him for a bit:

> Hunger is negatively valued. His expression of this often comes through loud and clear.
> Food is positively valued. But when he is satisfied, food is negatively valued, and the same milk he responded to so eagerly is now spit out, or the breast which seemed so satisfying is now rejected as he turns his head away from the nipple with an amusing facial expression of disgust and revulsion.
> He values security, and the holding and caressing which seem to communicate security.

He values new experience for its own sake, and we observe this in his obvious pleasure in discovering his toes, in his searching movements, in his endless curiosity.

He shows a clear negative valuing of pain, bitter tastes, sudden loud sounds.

All of this is commonplace, but let us look at these facts in terms of what they tell us about the infant's approach to values. It is first of all a flexible, changing, valuing *process*, not a fixed system. He likes food and dislikes the same food. He values security and rest, and rejects it for new experience. What is going on seems best described as an organismic valuing process, in which each element, each moment of what he is experiencing is somehow weighed, and selected or rejected, depending on whether, at that moment, it tends to actualize the organism or not. This complicated weighing of experience is clearly an organismic, not a conscious or symbolic function. These are operative, not conceived values. But this process can nonetheless deal with complex value problems. I would remind you of the experiment in which young infants had spread in front of them a score or more of dishes of natural (that is, unflavored) foods. Over a period of time they clearly tended to value the foods which enhanced their own survival, growth, and development. If for a time a child gorged himself on starches, this would soon be balanced by a protein "binge." If at times he chose a diet deficient in some vitamin, he would later seek out foods rich in this very vitamin. The physiological wisdom of his body guided his behavioral movements, resulting in what we might think of as objectively sound value choices.

Another aspect of the infant's approach to values is that the source or locus of the evaluating process is clearly within himself. Unlike many of us, he *knows* what he likes and dislikes, and the origin of these value choices lies strictly within himself. He is the center of the valuing process, the evidence for his choices being supplied by his own senses. He is not at this point influenced by what his parents think he should prefer, or by what the church says, or by the opinion of the latest "expert" in the field, or by the persuasive talents of an advertising firm. It is from within his own experiencing that his organism is saying in nonverbal terms, "This is good for me." "That is bad for me." "I like this." "I strongly dislike that." He would laugh at our concern over values, if he could understand it.

CHANGE IN THE VALUING PROCESS

What happens to this efficient, soundly based valuing process? By what sequence of events do we exchange it for the more rigid, uncertain, inefficient approach to values which characterizes most of us as adults? Let me try to state briefly one of the major ways in which I think this happens.

The infant needs love, wants it, tends to behave in ways which will bring a repetition of this wanted experience. But this brings complications. He pulls baby sister's hair, and finds it satisfying to hear her wails and protests. He then hears that he is "a naughty, bad boy," and this may be reinforced by a slap on the hand. He is cut off from affection. As this experience is repeated, and many, many others like it, he gradually learns that what "feels good" is often "bad" in the eyes of significant others. Then the next step occurs, in which he comes to take the same attitude toward himself which these others have taken. Now, as he pulls his sister's hair, he solemnly intones, "Bad, bad boy." He is introjecting the value judgment of another, taking it in as his own. To that degree he loses touch with his own organismic valuing process. He has deserted the wisdom of his organism, giving up the locus of evaluation, and is trying to behave in terms of values set by another, in order to hold love.

Or take another example at an older level. A boy senses, though perhaps not consciously, that he is more loved and prized by his parents when he thinks of being a doctor than when he thinks of being an artist. Gradually he introjects the values attached to being a doctor. He comes to want, above all, to be a doctor. Then in college he is baffled by the fact that he repeatedly fails in chemistry, which is absolutely necessary to becoming a physician, in spite of the fact that the guidance counselor assures him he has the ability to pass the course. Only in counseling interviews does he begin to realize how completely he has lost touch with his organismic reactions, how out of touch he is with his own valuing process.

Perhaps these illustrations will indicate that in an attempt to gain or hold love, approval, esteem, the individual relinquishes the locus of evaluation which was his in infancy, and places it in others. He learns to have a basic distrust for his own experiencing as a guide to his behavior. He learns from others a large number of conceived values, and adopts them as his own, even though they may be widely discrepant from what he is experiencing.

SOME INTROJECTED PATTERNS

It is in this fashion, I believe, that most of us accumulate the introjected value patterns by which we live. In the fantastically complex culture of today, the patterns we introject as desirable or undesirable come from a variety of sources and are often highly contradictory. Let me list a few of the introjections which are commonly held.

> Sexual desires and behaviors are mostly bad. The sources of this construct are many—parents, church, teachers.
> Disobedience is bad. Here parents and teachers combine with the mili-

194

tary to emphasize this concept. To obey is good. To obey without question is even better.

Making money is the highest good. The sources of this conceived value are too numerous to mention.

Learning an accumulation of scholarly facts is highly desirable. Education is the source.

Communism is utterly bad. Here the government is a major source.

To love thy neighbor is the highest good. This concept comes from the church, perhaps from the parents.

Cooperation and teamwork are preferable to acting alone. Here companions are an important source.

Cheating is clever and desirable. The peer group again is the origin.

Coca-Colas, chewing gum, electric refrigerators, and automobiles are all utterly desirable. From Jamaica to Japan, from Copenhagen to Kowloon, the "Coca-Cola culture" has come to be regarded as the acme of desirability.

This is a small and diversified sample of the myriads of conceived values which individuals often introject, and hold as their own, without ever having considered their inner organismic reactions to these patterns and objects.

COMMON CHARACTERISTICS OF ADULT VALUING

I believe it will be clear from the foregoing that the usual adult—I feel I am speaking for most of us—has an approach to values which has these characteristics:

✳ The majority of his values are introjected from other individuals or groups significant to him, but are regarded by him as his own.

The source or locus of evaluation on most matters lies outside of himself.

✳ The criterion by which his values are set is the degree to which they will cause him to be loved, accepted, or esteemed.

These conceived preferences are either not related at all, or not clearly related, to his own process of experiencing.

Often there is a wide and unrecognized discrepancy between the evidence supplied by his own experience, and these conceived values.

Because these conceptions are not open to testing in experience, he must hold them in a rigid and unchanging fashion. The alternative would be a collapse of his values. Hence his values are "right."

Because they are untestable, there is no ready way of solving contradictions. If he has taken in from the community the conception that money is the *summum bonum* and from the church the conception that love of one's neighbor is the highest value, he has no way of discovering which has more value for *him*. Hence a common aspect of modern life is living with absolutely contradictory values. We calmly discuss the possibility of dropping a hydrogen bomb on Russia, but find tears in our eyes when we see headlines about the suffering of one small child.

Because he has relinquished the locus of evaluation to others, and has lost touch with his own valuing process, he feels profoundly insecure and easily threatened in his values. If some of these conceptions were destroyed, what would take their place? This threatening possibility makes him hold his value conceptions more rigidly or more confusedly, or both.

FUNDAMENTAL DISCREPANCY

I believe that this picture of the individual, with values mostly introjected, held as fixed concepts, rarely examined or tested, is the picture of most of us. By taking over the conceptions of others as our own, we lose contact with the potential wisdom of our own functioning, and lose confidence in ourselves. Since these value constructs are often sharply at variance with what is going on in our own experiencing, we have in a very basic way divorced ourselves from ourselves, and this accounts for much of modern strain and insecurity. This fundamental discrepancy between the individual's concept and what he is actually experiencing, between the intellectual structure of his values and the valuing process going on unrecognized within— this is a part of the fundamental estrangement of modern man from himself.

RESTORING CONTACT WITH EXPERIENCE

Some individuals are fortunate in going beyond the picture I have just given, developing further in the direction of psychological maturity. We see this happen in psychotherapy where we endeavor to provide a climate favorable to the growth of the person. We also see it happen in life, whenever life provides a therapeutic climate for the individual. Let me concentrate on this further maturing of a value approach as I have seen it in therapy.

As the client senses and realizes that he is prized as a person he can slowly begin to value the different aspects of himself. Most importantly, he can begin, with much difficulty at first, to sense and to feel what is going on within him, what he is feeling, what he is experiencing, how he is reacting. He uses his experiencing as a direct referent to which he can turn in forming accurate conceptualizations and as a guide to his behavior. Gendlin (1961, 1962) has elaborated the way in which this occurs. As his experiencing becomes more and more open to him, as he is able to live more freely in the process of his feelings, then significant changes begin to occur in his approach to values. It begins to assume many of the characteristics it had in infancy.

INTROJECTED VALUES IN RELATION TO EXPERIENCING

Perhaps I can indicate this by reviewing a few of the brief examples of introjected values which I have given, and suggesting what happens to them as the individual comes closer to what is going on within him.

The individual in therapy looks back and realizes, "But I *enjoyed* pulling my sister's hair—and that doesn't make me a bad person."

The student failing chemistry realizes, as he gets close to his own experiencing, "I don't like chemistry; I don't value being a doctor, even though my parents do; and I am not a failure for having these feelings."

The adult recognizes that sexual desires and behavior may be richly satisfying and permanently enriching in their consequences, or shallow and temporary and less than satisfying. He goes by his own experiencing, which does not always coincide with social norms.

He recognizes freely that this communist book or person expresses attitudes and goals which he shares as well as ideas and values which he does not share.

He realizes that at times he experiences cooperation as meaningful and valuable to him, and that at other times he wishes to be alone and act alone.

VALUING IN THE MATURE PERSON

The valuing process which seems to develop in this more mature person is in some ways very much like that in the infant, and in some ways quite different. It is fluid, flexible, based on this particular moment, and the degree to which this moment is experienced as enhancing and actualizing. Values are not held rigidly, but are continually changing. The painting which last year seemed meaningful now appears uninteresting, the way of working with individuals which was formerly experienced as good now seems inadequate, the belief which then seemed true is now experienced as only partly true, or perhaps false.

Another characteristic of the way this person values experience is that it is highly differentiated, or as the semanticists would say, extensional. The examples in the preceding section indicate that what were previously rather solid monolithic introjected values now become differentiated, tied to a particular time and experience.

Another characteristic of the mature individual's approach is that the locus of evaluation is again established firmly within the person. It is his own experience which provides the value information or feedback. This does not mean that he is not open to all the evidence he can obtain from other sources. But it means that this is taken for what it is—outside evidence —and is not as significant as his own reactions. Thus he may be told by a friend that a new book is very disappointing. He reads two unfavorable reviews of the book. Thus his tentative hypothesis is that he will not value the book. Yet if he reads the book his valuing will be based upon the reactions it stirs in *him*, not on what he has been told by others.

There is also involved in this valuing process a letting oneself down into the immediacy of what one is experiencing, endeavoring to sense and to clarify all its complex meanings. I think of a client who, toward the close of therapy, when puzzled about an issue, would put his head in his hands and say, "Now what *is* it that I'm feeling? I want to get next to it. I want to learn what it is." Then he would wait, quietly and patiently, trying to listen to himself, until he could discern the exact flavor of the feelings he was experiencing. He, like others, was trying to get close to himself.

In getting close to what is going on within himself, the process is much more complex than it is in the infant. In the mature person it has much more scope and sweep. For there is involved in the present moment of experiencing the memory traces of all the relevant learnings from the past. This moment has not only its immediate sensory impact, but it has meaning growing out of similar experiences in the past. It has both the new and the old in it. So when I experience a painting or a person, my experiencing contains within it the learnings I have accumulated from past meetings with paintings or persons, as well as the new impact of this particular encounter. Likewise the moment of experiencing contains, for the mature adult, hypotheses about consequences. "It is not pleasant to express forthrightly my negative feelings to this person, but past experience indicates that in a continuing relationship it will be helpful in the long run." Past and future are both in this moment and enter into the valuing.

I find that in the person I am speaking of (and here again we see a similarity to the infant), the criterion of the valuing process is the degree to which the object of the experience actualizes the individual himself. Does it make him a richer, more complete, more fully developed person? This may sound as though it were a selfish or unsocial criterion, but it does not prove to be so, since deep and helpful relationships with others are experienced as actualizing.

Like the infant, too, the psychologically mature adult trusts and uses the wisdom of his organism, with the difference that he is able to do so knowingly. He realizes that if he can trust all of himself, his feelings and his intuitions may be wiser than his mind, that as a total person he can be, more sensitive and accurate than his thoughts alone. Hence he is not afraid to say, "I feel that this experience [or this thing, or this direction] is good. Later I will probably know *why* I feel it is good." He trusts the totality of himself, having moved toward becoming what Lancelot Whyte regards as "the unitary man."

It should be evident from what I have been saying that this valuing process in the mature individual is not an easy or simple thing. The process is complex, the choices often very perplexing and difficult, and there is no guarantee that the choice which is made will in fact prove to be self-actualizing. But because whatever evidence exists is available to the individual, and because he is open to his experiencing, errors are correctable. If this chosen course of action is not self-enhancing this will be sensed and

198

he can make an adjustment or revision. He thrives on a maximum feedback interchange, and thus, like the gyroscopic compass on a ship, can continually correct his course toward his true goal of self-fulfillment.

SOME PROPOSITIONS REGARDING THE VALUING PROCESS

Let me sharpen the meaning of what I have been saying by stating two propositions which contain the essential elements of this viewpoint. While it may not be possible to devise empirical tests of each proposition in its entirety, yet each is to some degree capable of being tested through the methods of psychological science. I would also state that though the following propositions are stated firmly in order to give them clarity, I am actually advancing them as decidedly tentative hypotheses.

Hypothesis I. There is an organismic base for an organized valuing process within the human individual.

It is hypothesized that this base is something the human being shares with the rest of the animate world. It is part of the functioning life process of any healthy organism. It is the capacity for receiving feedback information which enables the organism continually to adjust its behavior and reactions so as to achieve the maximum possible self-enhancement.

Hypothesis II. This valuing process in the human being is effective in achieving self-enhancement to the degree that the individual is open to the experiencing which is going on within himself.

I have tried to give two examples of individuals who are close to their own experiencing: the tiny infant who has not yet learned to deny in his awareness the processes going on within; and the psychologically mature person who has relearned the advantages of this open state.

There is a corollary to this second proposition which might be put in the following terms. One way of assisting the individual to move toward openness to experience is through a relationship in which he is prized as a separate person, in which the experiencing going on within him is empathically understood and valued, and in which he is given the freedom to experience his own feelings and those of others without being threatened in doing so.

This corollary obviously grows out of therapeutic experience. It is a brief statement of the essential qualities in the therapeutic relationship. There are already some empirical studies, of which the one by Barrett-Lennard is a good example, which give support to such a statement.

PROPOSITIONS REGARDING THE OUTCOMES OF THE VALUING PROCESS

I come now to the nub of any theory of values or valuing. What are its consequences? I should like to move into this new ground by stating bluntly two propositions as to the qualities of behavior which emerge from this valuing process. I shall then give some of the evidence from my experience as a therapist in support of these propositions.

Hypothesis III. In persons who are moving toward greater openness to their experiencing, there is an organismic commonality of value directions.

Hypothesis IV. These common value directions are of such kinds as to enhance the development of the individual himself, of others in his community, and to make for the survival and evolution of his species.

It has been a striking fact of my experience that in therapy, where individuals are valued, where there is greater freedom to feel and to be, certain value directions seem to emerge. These are not chaotic directions but instead exhibit a surprising commonality. This commonality is not dependent on the personality of the therapist, for I have seen these trends emerge in the clients of therapists sharply different in personality. This commonality does not seem to be due to the influences of any one culture, for I have found evidence of these directions in cultures as divergent as those of the United States, Holland, France, and Japan. I like to think that this commonality of value directions is due to the fact that we all belong to the same species—that just as a human infant tends, individually, to select a diet similar to that selected by other human infants, so a client in therapy tends, individually, to choose value directions similar to those chosen by other clients. As a species there may be certain elements of experience which tend to make for inner development and which would be chosen by all individuals if they were genuinely free to choose.

Let me indicate a few of these value directions as I see them in my clients as they move in the direction of personal growth and maturity.

> They tend to move away from façades. Pretense, defensiveness, putting up a front, tend to be negatively valued.
>
> They tend to move away from "oughts." The compelling feeling of "I ought to do or be thus and so" is negatively valued. The client moves away from being what he "ought to be," no matter who has set that imperative.
>
> They tend to move away from meeting the expectations of others. Pleasing others, as a goal in itself, is negatively valued.
>
> Being real is positively valued. The client tends to move toward being himself, being his real feelings, being what he is. This seems to be a very deep preference.
>
> Self-direction is positively valued. The client discovers an increasing pride and confidence in making his own choices, guiding his own life.
>
> One's self, one's own feelings come to be positively valued. From a point where he looks upon himself with contempt and despair, the client comes to value himself and his reactions as being of worth.
>
> Being a process is positively valued. From desiring some fixed goal, clients

come to prefer the excitement of being a process of potentialities being born.

Sensitivity to others and acceptance of others is positively valued. The client comes to appreciate others for what they are, just as he has come to appreciate himself for what he is.

Deep relationships are positively valued. To achieve a close, intimate, real, fully communicative relationship with another person seems to meet a deep need in every individual, and is very highly valued.

Perhaps more than all else, the client comes to value an openness to all of his inner and outer experience. To be open to and sensitive to his own *inner* reactions and feelings, the reactions and feelings of others, and the realities of the objective world—this is a direction which he clearly prefers. This openness becomes the client's most valued resource.

These then are some of the preferred directions which I have observed in individuals moving toward personal maturity. Though I am sure that the list I have given is inadequate and perhaps to some degree inaccurate, it holds for me exciting possibilities. Let me try to explain why.

I find it significant that when individuals are prized as persons, the values they select do not run the full gamut of possibilities. I do not find, in such a climate of freedom, that one person comes to value fraud and murder and thievery, while another values a life of self-sacrifice, and another values only money. Instead there seems to be a deep and underlying thread of commonality. I believe that when the human being is inwardly free to choose whatever he deeply values, he tends to value those objects, experiences, and goals which make for his own survival, growth, and development, and for the survival and development of others. I hypothesize that it is *characteristic* of the human organism to prefer such actualizing and socialized goals when he is exposed to a growth promoting climate.

A corollary of what I have been saying is that in *any* culture, given a climate of respect and freedom in which he is valued as a person, the mature individual would tend to choose and prefer these same value directions. This is a significant hypothesis which could be tested. It means that though the individual of whom I am speaking would not have a consistent or even a stable system of conceived values, the valuing process within him would lead to emerging value directions which would be constant across cultures and across time.

Another implication I see is that individuals who exhibit the fluid valuing process I have tried to describe, whose value directions are generally those I have listed, would be highly effective in the ongoing process of human evolution. If the human species is to survive at all on this globe, the human being must become more readily adaptive to new problems and situations, must be able to select that which is valuable for development and survival out of new and complex situations, must be accurate in his appreciation of reality if he is to make such selections. The psychologically mature person as I have described him has, I believe, the qualities which would cause him to value those experiences which would make for the survival and enhancement of the human race. He would be a worthy participant and guide in the process of human evolution.

Finally, it appears that we have returned to the issue of universality of values, but by a different route. Instead of universal values "out there," or a universal value system imposed by some group—philosophers, rulers, priests, or psychologists—we have the possibility of universal human value directions *emerging* from the experiencing of the human organism. Evidence from therapy indicates that both personal and social values emerge as natural, and experienced, when the individual is close to his own organismic valuing process. The suggestion is that though modern man no longer trusts religion or science or philosophy nor any system of beliefs to *give* him values, he may find an organismic valuing base within himself which, if he can learn again to be in touch with it, will prove to be an organized, adaptive, and social approach to the perplexing value issues which face all of us.

As a young man, Aristotle (384–322 B.C.) came to study at the Academy. Plato was by then approaching sixty, and Socrates had been dead for over thirty years. A brilliant student and scholar, Aristotle acquired an encyclopedic grasp of the knowledge of his day and went on to advance that knowledge in an astounding variety of fields. He founded the Lyceum, the second of the famous schools of Athens, conducted research into every area of thought, and wrote an enormous number of works. In the last year of his life he was charged with "impiety" on the basis of a poem written in honor of a friend. The charge was as groundless as were the political reasons that had prompted it, but, in contrast to Socrates, Aristotle left Athens. He said that he did not want "to give the Athenians a second chance of sinning against philosophy." His influence on later generations was such that in the thirteenth century the references by Thomas Aquinas to "The Philosopher" were to Aristotle, and in the seventeenth century his writings were cited in the attempt made to refute Galileo. Of all his contributions, the greatest was undoubtedly the Nicomachean Ethics, from which the following selection is taken.

BOOK ONE: CHAPTER I

It is thought that every activity, artistic or scientific, in fact every deliberate action or pursuit, has for its object the attainment of some good. We may therefore assent to the view which has been expressed that 'the good' is 'that at which all things aim.' Since modes of action involving the practised hand and the instructed brain are numerous, the number of their ends is proportionately large. For instance, the end of medical science is health; of military science, victory; of economic science, wealth. All skills of that kind which come under a single 'faculty'—a skill in making bridles or any other part of a horse's gear comes under the faculty or art of horsemanship, while horsemanship itself and every branch of military practice comes under the art of war, and in like manner other arts and techniques are subordinate to yet others—in all these the ends of the master arts are to be preferred to those of the subordinate skills, for it is the former that provide the motive for pursuing the latter.

CHAPTER II

Now if there is an end which as moral agents we seek for its own sake, and which is the cause of our seeking all the other ends—if we are not to go on choosing one act for the sake of another, thus landing ourselves in an infinite progression with the result that desire will be frustrated and ineffectual—it is clear that this must be the good, that is the absolutely good. May we not then argue from this that a knowledge of the good is a great advantage to us in the conduct of our lives? Are we not more likely to hit the mark if we have a target? If this be true, we must do our best to get at least a rough idea of what the good really is, and which of the sciences, pure or applied, is concerned with the business of achieving it. . . .

[*Let us resume our consideration of what is the end of political science. For want of a better word we call it 'Happiness.' People are agreed on the word but not on its meaning.*]

CHAPTER IV

To resume. Since every activity involving some acquired skill or some moral decision aims at some good, what do we take to be the end of politics —what is the supreme good attainable in our actions? Well, so far as the name goes there is pretty general agreement. 'It is happiness,' say both intellectuals and the unsophisticated, meaning by 'happiness' living well or faring well. But when it comes to saying in what happiness consists, opinions differ and the account given by the generality of mankind is not at all like that given by the philosophers. The masses take it to be something plain and tangible, like pleasure or money or social standing. Some maintain that it is one of these, some that it is another, and the same man will change his opinion about it more than once. When he has caught an illness he will say that it is health, and when he is hard up he will say that it is money. Conscious that they are out of their depths in such discussions, most people are impressed by anyone who pontificates and says something that is over their heads. Now it would no doubt be a waste of time to examine all these opinions; enough if we consider those which are most in evidence or have something to be said for them. Among these we shall have to discuss the view held by some that, over and above particular goods like those I have just mentioned, there is another which is good in itself and the cause of whatever goodness there is in all these others. . . .

[*A man's way of life may afford a clue to his genuine views upon the nature of happiness. It is therefore worth our while to glance at the different types of life.*]

CHAPTER V

. . . . There is a general assumption that the manner of a man's life is a clue to what he on reflection regards as the good—in other words happiness. Persons of low tastes (always in the majority) hold that it is pleasure. Accordingly they ask for nothing better than the sort of life which consists in having a good time. (I have in mind the three well-known types of life—that just mentioned, that of the man of affairs, that of the philosophic student.) The utter vulgarity of the herd of men comes out in their preference for the sort of existence a cow leads. Their view would hardly get a respectful hearing, were it not that those who occupy great positions sympathize with a monster of sensuality like Sardanapalus. The gentleman, however, and the man of affairs identify the good with honour, which may fairly be described as the end which men pursue in political or public life. Yet honour is surely too superficial a thing to be the good we are seeking. Honour depends more on those who confer than on him who receives it, and we cannot but feel that the good is something personal and almost inseparable from its possessor. Again, why do men seek honour? Surely in order to confirm the favourable opinion they have formed of themselves. It is at all events by intelligent men who know them personally that they seek to be honoured. And for what? For their moral qualities. The inference is clear; public men prefer virtue to honour. It might therefore seem reasonable to suppose that virtue rather than honour is the end pursued in the life of the public servant. But clearly even virtue cannot be quite the end. It is possible, most people think, to possess virtue while you are asleep, to possess it without acting under its influence during any portion of one's life. Besides, the virtuous man may meet with the most atrocious luck or ill-treatment; and nobody, who was not arguing for argument's sake, would maintain that a man with an existence of that sort was 'happy.' The third type of life is the 'contemplative,' and this we shall discuss later.

As for the life of the business man, it does not give him much freedom of action. Besides, wealth obviously is not the good we seek, for the sole purpose it serves is to provide the means of getting something else. So far as that goes, the ends we have already mentioned would have a better title to be considered the good, for they are desired on their own account. But in fact even their claim must be disallowed. We may say that they have furnished the ground for many arguments, and leave the matter at that. . . .

[*What then is the good? If it is what all men in the last resort aim at, it must be happiness. And that for two reasons: (1) happiness is everything it needs to be, (2) it has everything it needs to have.*]

CHAPTER VII

. . . . We may return to the good which is the object of our search. What is it? The question must be asked because good seems to vary with the art or pursuit in which it appears. It is one thing in medicine and another in strategy, and so in the other branches of human skill. We must enquire, then, what is the good which is the end common to all of them. Shall we say it is that for the sake of which everything else is done? In medicine this is health, in military science victory, in architecture a building, and so on—different ends in different arts; every consciously directed activity has an end for the sake of which everything that it does is done. This end may be described as its good. Consequently, if there be some one thing which is the end of all things consciously done, this will be the doable good; or, if there be more than one end, then it will be all of these. Thus the ground on which our argument proceeds is shifted, but the conclusion arrived at is the same.

I must try, however, to make my meaning clearer.

In our actions we aim at more ends than one—that seems to be certain —but, since we choose some (wealth, for example, or flutes and tools or instruments generally) as means to something else, it is clear that not all of them are ends in the full sense of the word, whereas the good, that is the supreme good, is surely such an end. Assuming then that there is some one thing which alone is an end beyond which there are no further ends, we may call *that* the good of which we are in search. If there be more than one such final end, the good will be that end which has the highest degree of finality. An object pursued for its own sake possesses a higher degree of finality than one pursued with an eye to something else. A corollary to that is that a thing which is never chosen as a means to some remoter object has a higher degree of finality than things which are chosen both as ends in themselves and as means to such ends. We may conclude, then, that something which is always chosen for its own sake and never for the sake of something else is without qualification a final end.

Now happiness more than anything else appears to be just such an end, for we always choose it for its own sake and never for the sake of some other thing. It is different with honour, pleasure, intelligence and good qualities generally. We choose them indeed for their own sake in the sense that we should be glad to have them irrespective of any advantage which might accrue from them. But we also choose them for the sake of our happiness in the belief that they will be instrumental in promoting that. On the other hand nobody chooses happiness as a means of achieving them or anything else whatsoever than just happiness.

The same conclusion would seem to follow from another consideration. It is a generally accepted view that the final good is self-sufficient. By 'self-sufficient' is meant not what is sufficient for oneself living the life of a solitary but includes parents, wife and children, friends and fellow-citizens in general. For man is a social animal. A self-sufficient thing, then, we take to be one which on its own footing tends to make life desirable and lacking in nothing. And we regard happiness as such a thing. Add to this that we regard it as the most desirable of all things without having it counted in with some other desirable thing. For, if such an addition were possible, clearly we should regard it as more desirable when even the smallest advantage was added to it. For the result would be an increase in the number of advantages, and the larger sum of advantages is preferable to the smaller.

Happiness then, the end to which all our conscious acts are directed, is found to be something final and self-sufficient.

[*But we desire a clearer definition of happiness. The way to this may be prepared by a discussion of what is meant by the 'function' of a man.*]

But no doubt people will say, 'To call happiness the highest good is a truism. We want a more distinct account of what it is.' We might arrive at this if we could grasp what is meant by the 'function' of a human being. If we take a flautist or a sculptor or any craftsman—in fact any class of men at all who have some special job or profession—we find that his special talent and excellence comes out in that job, and this is his function. The same thing will be true of man simply as man—that is of course if 'man' does have a function. But is it likely that joiners and shoemakers have certain functions or specialized activities, while man as such has none but has been left by Nature a functionless being? Seeing that eye and hand and foot and every one of our members has some obvious function, must we not believe that in like manner a human being has a function over and above these particular functions? Then what exactly is it? The mere act of living is not peculiar to man—we find it even in the vegetable kingdom—and what we are looking for is something peculiar to him. We must therefore exclude from our definition the life that manifests itself in mere nurture and growth. A step higher should come the life that is confined to experiencing sensations. But that we see is shared by horses, cows and the brute creation as a whole. We are left, then, with a life concerning which we can make two statements. First, it belongs to the rational part of man. Secondly, it finds expression in actions. The rational part may be either active or passive: passive in so far as it follows the dictates of reason, active in so far as it possesses and exercises the power of reasoning. A similar distinction can be drawn within the rational life; that is to say, the reasonable element in it may be active or passive. Let us take it that what we are concerned with here is the reasoning power in action, for it will be generally allowed that when we speak of 'reasoning' we really mean *exercising* our reasoning faculties. (This seems the more correct use of the word.) Now let us assume for the moment the truth of the following propositions. (*a*) The function of a man is the exercise of his non-corporeal faculties or 'soul' in accordance with, or at least not divorced from, a rational principle. (*b*) The function of an individual and of a *good* individual in the same class—a harp player, for example, and a good harp player, and so through the classes—is generically the same, except that we must add superiority in accomplishment to the function, the function of the harp player being merely to play on the harp, while the function of the good harp player is to play on it well. (c) The function of man is a certain form of life, namely an activity of the soul exercised in combination with a rational principle or reasonable ground of action. (d) The function of a good man is to exert such activity well. (e) A function is performed well when performed in accordance with the excellence proper to it.—If these assumptions are granted, we conclude that the good for man is 'an activity of soul in accordance with goodness' or (on the supposition that there may be more than one form of goodness) 'in accordance with the best and most complete form of goodness.'

[*Happiness is more than momentary bliss.*]

There is another condition of happiness; it cannot be achieved in less than a complete lifetime. One swallow does not make a summer; neither does one fine day. And one day, or indeed any brief period of felicity, does not make a man entirely and perfectly happy. . . .

BOOK TEN: CHAPTER VII

But if happiness is an activity in accordance with virtue, it is reasonable to assume that it will be in accordance with the highest virtue; and this can only be the virtue of the best part of us. Whether this be the intellect or something else—whatever it is that is held to have a natural right to govern and guide us, and to have an insight into what is noble and divine, either as being itself also divine or more divine than any other part of us—it is the activity of this part in accordance with the virtue proper to it that will be perfect happiness. Now we have seen already that this activity has a speculative or contemplative character. This is a conclusion which may be accepted as in harmony with our earlier arguments and with the truth. For 'contemplation' is the highest form of activity, since the intellect is the highest thing in us and the objects which come within its range are the highest that can be known. But it is also the most continuous activity, for we can think about intellectual problems more continuously than we can keep up any sort of physical action. Again, we feel sure that a modicum of pleasure must be one of the ingredients of happiness. Now it is admitted that activity along the lines of 'wisdom' is the pleasantest of all the good activities. At all events it is thought that philosophy ('the pursuit of wisdom') has pleasures marvellous in purity and duration, and it stands to reason that those who have knowledge pass their time more pleasantly than those who are engaged in its pursuit. . . .

immanuel kant   THE GOOD WILL

Immanuel Kant (1728–1804) was born, lived, and died in Königsberg, East Prussia. The uneventfulness of his life was its most remarkable feature. "He lived," wrote Heinrich Heine, "an abstract, mechanical, old-bachelor existence. . . . I do not believe that the great cathedral clock of this city accomplished its da;'ะ work in a less passionate and more regular way than its countryman, Immanuel Kant. Rising from bed, coffee-drinking, writing, lecturing, eating, walking, everything had its fixed time; and the neighbors knew that it must be exactly half past four when they saw Professor Kant, in his gray coat, with his cane in his hand, step out of his housedoor, and move toward the little lime tree avenue, which is named after him, the Philosopher's Walk." Kant's ideas comprised one of the great turning points in the history of philosophy: only a few philosophers of the stature of Plato and Aristotle compare with him. His major works include the Critique of Pure Reason, Prolegomena to Any Future Metaphysics, Critique of Practical Reason, Religion within the Limits of Reason Alone, *and* Critique of judgment. *The selection which follows is from* Fundamental Principles of the Metaphysics of Morals *(1785).*

Nothing can possibly be conceived in the world, or even out of it, which can be called good without qualification, except a *good will*. Intelligence, wit, judgment, and the other *talents* of the mind, however they may be named, or courage, resolution, perseverance, as qualities of temperament, are undoubtedly good and desirable in many respects; but these gifts of nature may also become extremely bad and mischievous if the will which is to make use of them, and which, therefore, constitutes what is called *character*, is not good. It is the same with the *gifts of fortune*. Power, riches, honor, even health, and the general well-being and contentment with one's condition which is called *happiness*, inspire pride, and often presumption, if there is not a good will to correct the influence of these on the mind, and with this also to rectify the whole principle of acting, and adapt it to its end. The sight of a being who is not adorned with a single feature of a pure and good will, enjoying unbroken prosperity, can never give pleasure to an impartial rational spectator. Thus a good will appears to constitute the indispensable condition even of being worthy of happiness.

There are even some qualities which are of service to this good will itself, and may facilitate its action, yet which have no intrinsic unconditional value, but always presuppose a good will, and this qualifies the esteem that we justly have for them, and does not permit us to regard them as absolutely good. Moderation in the affections and passions, self-control, and calm deliberation are not only good in many respects, but even seem to constitute part of the intrinsic worth of the person; but they are far from deserving to be called good without qualification, although they have been so unconditionally praised by the ancients. For without the principles of a good will, they may become extremely bad; and the coolness of a villain not only makes him far more dangerous, but also directly makes him more abominable in our eyes than he would have been without it.

A good will is good not because of what it performs or effects, not by its aptness for the attainment of some proposed end, but simply by virtue of the volition—that is, it is good in itself, and considered by itself is to be esteemed much higher than all that can be brought about by it in favor of any inclination, nay, even of the sum-total of all inclinations. Even if it should happen that, owing to special disfavor of fortune, or the niggardly provision of a step-motherly nature, this will should wholly lack power to accomplish its purpose, if with its greatest efforts it should yet achieve nothing, and there should remain only the good will (not, to be sure, a mere wish, but the summoning of all means in our power), then, like a jewel, it would still shine by its own light, as a thing which has its whole value in itself. Its usefulness or fruitlessness can neither add to nor take away anything from this value. It would be, as it were, only the setting to enable us to handle it the more conveniently in common commerce, or to attract to it the attention of those who are not yet connoisseurs, but not to recommend it to true connoisseurs, or to determine its value.

There is, however, something so strange in this idea of the absolute value of the mere will, in which no account is taken of its utility, that notwithstanding the thorough assent of even common reason to the idea, yet a suspicion must arise that it may perhaps really be the product of mere high-flown fancy, and that we may have misunderstood the purpose of nature in assigning reason as the governor of our will. Therefore we will examine this idea from this point of view.

In the physical constitution of an organized being, that is, a being adapted suitably to the purposes of life, we assume it as a fundamental principle that no organ for any purpose will be found but what is also the fittest and best adapted for that purpose. Now in a being which has reason and a will, if the proper object of nature were its *conservation*, its *welfare*, in a word, its *happiness*, then nature would have hit upon a very bad arrangement in selecting the reason of the creature to carry out this purpose. For all the actions which the creature has to perform with a view to this purpose, and the whole rule of its conduct, would be far more surely prescribed to it by instinct, and that end would have been attained thereby much more certainly than it ever can be by reason. Should reason have been communicated to this favored creature over and above, it must only have served it to contemplate the happy constitution of its nature, to admire it, to congratulate itself thereon, and to feel thankful for it to the beneficent cause, but not that it should subject its desires to that weak and delusive guidance, and meddle bunglingly with the purpose of nature. In a word, nature would have taken care that reason should not break forth into *practical exercise*, nor have the presumption, with its weak insight, to think out for itself the plan of happiness and of the means of attaining it. Nature would not only have taken on herself the choice of the ends but also of the means, and with wise foresight would have entrusted both to instinct.

And, in fact, we find that the more a cultivated reason applies itself with deliberate purpose to the enjoyment of life and happiness, so much the more does the man fail of true satisfaction. And from this circumstance there arises in many, if they are candid enough to confess it, a certain degree of *misology*, that is, hatred of reason, especially in the case of those who are most experienced in the use of it, because after calculating all the advantages they derive—I do not say from the invention of all the arts of common luxury, but even from the sciences (which seem to them to be after all only a luxury of the understanding)—they find that they have, in fact, only brought more trouble on their shoulders rather than gained in happiness; and they end by envying rather than despising the more common stamp of men who keep closer to the guidance of mere instinct, and do not allow their reason much influence on their conduct. And this we must admit, that the judgment of those who would very much lower the lofty eulogies of the advantages which reason gives us in regard to the happiness and satisfaction of life, or who would even reduce them below zero, is by no means morose or ungrateful to the goodness with which the world is governed, but that there lies at the root of these judgments the idea that our existence has a different and far nobler end, for which, and not for happiness, reason is properly intended, and which must, therefore, be regarded as the supreme condition to which the private ends of man must, for the most part, be postponed.

For as reason is not competent to guide the will with certainty in regard to its objects and the satisfaction of all our wants (which it to some extent even multiplies), this being an end to which an implanted instinct would have led with much greater certainty; and since, nevertheless, reason is imparted to us as a practical faculty, that is, as one which is to have influence on the *will*, therefore, admitting that nature generally in the distribution of her capacities has adapted the means to the end, its true destination must be to produce a *will*, not merely good as a *means* to something else, but *good in itself*, for which reason was absolutely necessary. This will then, though not indeed the sole and complete good, must be the supreme good and the condition of every other, even of the desire of happiness. Under these circumstances, there is nothing inconsistent with the wisdom of nature in the fact that the cultivation of the reason, which is requisite for the first and unconditional purpose, does in many ways interfere, at least in this life, with the attainment of the second, which is always conditional—namely, happiness. Nay, it may even reduce it to nothing, without nature thereby failing of her purpose. For reason recognizes the establishment of a good will as its highest practical destination, and in attaining this purpose is capable only of a satisfaction of its own proper kind, namely, that from the attainment of an end, which end again is determined by reason only, notwithstanding that this may involve many a disappointment to the ends of inclination.

We have then to develop the notion of a will which deserves to be highly esteemed for itself, and is good without a view to anything further, a notion which exists already in the sound natural understanding, requiring rather to be cleared up than to be taught, and which in estimating the value of our actions always takes the first place and constitutes the condition of all the rest. In order to do this, we will take the notion of duty, which includes that of a good will, although implying certain subjective restrictions and hindrances. These, however, far from concealing it or rendering it unrecognizable, rather bring it out by contrast and make it shine forth so much the brighter.

I omit here all actions which are already recognized as inconsistent with duty, although they may be useful for this or that purpose, for with these the question whether they are done *from duty* cannot arise at all, since they even conflict with it. I also set aside those actions which really conform to duty, but to which men have *no* direct *inclination*, performing them because they are impelled thereto by some other inclination. For in this case we can readily distinguish whether the action which agrees with duty is done *from duty* or from a selfish view. It is much harder to make this distinction when the action accords with duty, and the subject has besides a *direct* inclination to it. For example, it is always a matter of duty that a dealer should not overcharge an inexperienced purchaser; and wherever there is much commerce the prudent tradesman does not overcharge, but keeps a fixed price for everyone, so that a child buys of him as well as any other. Men are thus *honestly* served; but this is not enough to make us believe that the tradesman has so acted from duty and from principles of honesty; his own advantage required it; it is out of the question in this case to suppose that he might besides have a direct inclination in favor of the buyers, so that, as it were, from love he should give no advantage to one over another. Accordingly the action was done neither from duty nor from direct inclination, but merely with a selfish view.

On the other hand, it is a duty to maintain one's life; and, in addition, everyone has also a direct inclination to do so. But on this account the often anxious care which most men take for it has no intrinsic worth, and their maxim has no moral import. They preserve their life *as duty requires*, no doubt, but not *because duty requires*. On the other hand, if adversity and hopeless sorrow have completely taken away the relish for life, if the unfortunate one, strong in mind, indignant at his fate rather than desponding or dejected, wishes for death, and yet preserves his life without loving it—not from inclination or fear, but from duty—then his maxim has a moral worth.

To be beneficent when we can is a duty; and besides this, there are many minds so sympathetically constituted that, without any other motive of vanity or self-interest, they find a pleasure in spreading joy around them, and can take delight in the satisfaction of others so far as it is their own work. But I maintain that in such a case an action of this kind, however proper, however amiable it may be, has nevertheless no true moral worth, but is on a level with other inclinations, for example, the inclination to honor, which, if it is happily directed to that which is in fact of public utility and accordant with duty, and consequently honorable, deserves praise and encouragement, but not esteem. For the maxim lacks the moral import, namely, that such actions be done *from duty*, not from inclination. Put the case that the mind of that philanthropist was clouded by sorrow of his own, extinguishing all sympathy with the lot of others, and that while he still has the power to benefit others in distress, he is not touched by their trouble because he is absorbed with his own; and now suppose that he tears himself out of this dead insensibility and performs the action without any inclination to it, but simply from duty, then first has his action its genuine moral worth. Further still, if nature has put little sympathy in the heart of this or that man, if he, supposed to be an upright man, is by temperament cold and indifferent to the sufferings of others, perhaps because in respect of his own he is provided with the special gift of patience and fortitude, and supposes, or even requires, that others should have the same—and such a man would certainly not be the meanest product of nature—but if nature had not specially framed him for a philanthropist, would he not still find in himself a source from whence to give himself a far higher worth than that of a good-natured temperament could be? Unquestionably. It is just in this that the moral worth of the character is brought out which is incomparably the highest of all, namely, that he is beneficent, not from inclination, but from duty.

To secure one's own happiness is a duty, at least indirectly; for discontent with one's condition, under a pressure of many anxieties and amidst unsatisfied wants, might easily become a great *temptation to transgression of duty*. But here again, without looking to duty, all men have already the strongest and most intimate inclination to happiness, because it is just in this idea that all inclinations are combined in one total. But the precept of happiness is often of such a sort that it greatly interferes with some inclinations, and yet a man cannot form any definite and certain conception of the sum of satisfaction of all of them which is called happiness. It is not then to be wondered at that a single inclination, definite both as to what it promises and as to the time within which it can be gratified, is often able to overcome such a fluctuating idea, and that a gouty patient, for instance, can choose to enjoy what he likes, and to suffer what he may, since, according to his calculation, on this occasion at least, he has [only] not sacrificed the enjoyment of the present moment to a possibly mistaken expectation of a happiness which is supposed to be found in health. But even in this case, if the general desire for happiness did not influence his will, and supposing that in his particular case health was not a necessary element in this calculation, there yet remains in this, as in all other cases, this law—namely, that he should promote his happiness not from inclination but from duty, and by this would his conduct first acquire true moral worth.

It is in this manner, undoubtedly, that we are to understand those passages of Scripture also in which we are commanded to love our neighbor, even our enemy. For love, as an affection, cannot be commanded, but beneficence for duty's sake may, even though we are not impelled to it by an inclination—nay, are even repelled by a natural and unconquerable aversion. This is *practical* love, and not *pathological*—a love which is seated in the will, and not in the propensions of sense—in principles of action and not of tender sympathy; and it is this love alone which can be commanded.

The second proposition is: That an action done from duty derives its moral worth, *not from the purpose* which is to be attained by it, but from the maxim by which it is determined, and therefore does not depend on the realization of the object of the action, but merely on the *principle of volition* by which the action has taken place, without regard to any object of desire. It is clear from what precedes that the purposes which we may have in view in our actions, or their effects regarded as ends and springs of the will, cannot give to actions any unconditional or moral worth. In what, then, can their worth lie if it is not to consist in the will and in reference to its expected effect? It cannot lie anywhere but in the *principle of the will* without regard to the ends which can be attained by the action. For the will stands between its *a priori* principle, which is formal, and its *a posteriori* spring, which is material, as between two roads, and as it must be determined by something, it follows that it must be determined by the formal principle of volition when an action is done from duty, in which case every material principle has been withdrawn from it.

The third proposition, which is a consequence of the two preceding, I would express thus: *Duty is the necessity of acting from respect for the law.* I may have *inclination* for an object as the effect of my proposed action, but I cannot have *respect* for it just for this reason that it is an effect and not an energy of will. Similarly, I cannot have respect for inclination, whether my own or another's; I can at most, if my own, approve it; if another's, sometimes even love it, that is, look on it as favorable to my own interest. It is only what is connected with my will as a principle, by no means as an effect—what does not subserve my inclination, but overpowers it, or at least in case of choice excludes it from its calculation—in other words, simply the law of itself, which can be an object of respect, and hence a command. Now an action done from duty must wholly exclude the influence of inclination, and with it every object of the will, so that nothing remains which can determine the will except objectively the *law*, and subjectively *pure respect* for this practical law, and consequently the maxim that I should follow this law even to the thwarting of all my inclinations.

Thus the moral worth of an action does not lie in the effect expected from it, nor in any principle of action which requires to borrow its motive from this expected effect. For all these effects—agreeableness of one's condition, and even the promotion of the happiness of others—could have been also brought about by other causes, so that for this there would have been no need of the will of a rational being; whereas it is in this alone that the supreme and unconditional good can be found. The preeminent good which we call moral can therefore consist in nothing else than *the conception of law* in itself, *which certainly is only possible in a rational being*, in so far as this conception, and not the expected effect, determines the will. This is a good which is already present in the person who acts accordingly, and we have not to wait for it to appear first in the result.

But what sort of law can that be the conception of which must determine the will, even without paying any regard to the effect expected from it, in order that this will may be called good absolutely and without qualification? As I have deprived the will of every impulse which could arise to it from obedience to any law, there remains nothing but the universal conformity of its actions to law in general, which alone is to serve the will as a principle, that is, I am never to act otherwise than so *that I could also will that my maxim should become a universal law. . . .*

John Stuart Mill (1806–1873) received, under his father's tutelage, an early education that would put to shame the later education of most men. He began the study of Greek at the age of three and Latin at eight. By the time he was twelve he had read widely in the classics of the ancient world and had learned elementary geometry and algebra. He had also written a history of the Roman Government. Over a period of thirty-five years, Mill held increasingly responsible positions with the East India Company and was later elected to Parliament, but there seemed always to be time for his writing. His first major work, which was thirteen years in preparation, was A System of Logic. *It was followed by the* Principles of Political Economy, On Liberty, Representative Government, *and* The Subjection of Women. *Posthumously published were his* Autobiography *and* Three Essays on Religion. *The selection which follows is from* Utilitarianism *(1863).*

GENERAL REMARKS

. . . From the dawn of philosophy the question concerning the *summum bonum*, or, what is the same thing, concerning the foundation of morality, has been accounted the main problem in speculative thought, has occupied the most gifted intellects, and divided them into sects and schools, carrying on a vigorous warfare against one another. And after more than two thousand years the same discussions continue, philosophers are still ranged under the same contending banners, and neither thinkers nor mankind at large seem nearer to being unanimous on the subject than when the youth Socrates listened to the old Protagoras, and asserted (if Plato's dialogue be grounded on a real conversation) the theory of utilitarianism against the popular morality of the so-called Sophist. . . .

On the present occasion, I shall, without further discussion of the other theories, attempt to contribute something towards the understanding and appreciation of the Utilitarian or Happiness theory, and towards such proof as it is susceptible of. It is evident that this cannot be proof in the ordinary and popular meaning of the term. Questions of ultimate ends are not amenable to direct proof. Whatever can be proved to be good must be so by being shown to be a means to something admitted to be good without proof. The medical art is proved to be good, by its conducing to health; but how is it possible to prove that health is good? The art of music is good, for the reason, among others, that it produces pleasure; but what proof is it possible to give that pleasure is good? If, then, it is asserted that there is a comprehensive formula, including all things which are in themselves good, and that whatever else is good is not so as an end but as a mean, the formula may be accepted or rejected, but is not a subject of what is commonly understood by proof. We are not, however, to infer that its acceptance or rejection must depend on blind impulse or arbitrary choice. There is a larger meaning of the word proof, in which this question is as amenable to it as any other of the disputed questions of philosophy. The subject is within the cognizance of the rational faculty; and neither does that faculty deal with it solely in the way of intuition. Considerations may be presented capable of determining the intellect either to give or withhold its assent to the doctrine; and this is equivalent to proof. . . .

WHAT UTILITARIANISM IS

The creed which accepts as the foundation of morals, Utility, or the Greatest Happiness Principle, holds that actions are right in proportion as they tend to promote happiness, wrong as they tend to produce the reverse of happiness. By happiness is intended pleasure and the absence of pain; by unhappiness, pain and the privation of pleasure. To give a clear view of the moral standard set up by the theory much more requires to be said; in particular, what things it includes in the ideas of pain and pleasure; and to what extent this is left an open question. But these supplementary explanations do not affect the theory of life on which this theory of morality is grounded—namely, that pleasure and freedom from pain are the only things desirable as ends; and that all desirable things (which are as numerous in the utilitarian as in any other scheme) are desirable either for the pleasure inherent in themselves, or as means to the promotion of pleasure and the prevention of pain.

Now, such a theory of life excites in many minds, and among them in some of the most estimable in feeling and purpose, inveterate dislike. To suppose that life has (as they express it) no higher end than pleasure—no better and nobler object of desire and pursuit—they designate as utterly mean and grovelling; as a doctrine worthy only of swine, to whom the followers of Epicurus were, at a very early period, contemptuously likened; and modern holders of the doctrine are occasionally made the subject of equally polite comparisons by its German, French, and English assailants.

When thus attacked, the Epicureans have always answered that it is not they, but their accusers, who represent human nature in a degrading light; since the accusation supposes human beings to be capable of no pleasures except those of which swine are capable. If this supposition were true, the charge could not be gainsaid, but would then be no longer an imputation; for if the sources of pleasure were precisely the same to human beings and to swine, the rule of life which is good enough for the one would be good enough for the other. The comparison of the Epicurean life to that of beasts is felt as degrading, precisely because a beast's pleasures do not satisfy a human being's conceptions of happiness. Human beings have faculties more elevated than the animal appetites, and, when once made conscious of them, do not regard anything as happiness which does not include their gratification. I do not, indeed, consider the Epicureans to have been by any means faultless in drawing out their scheme of consequences from the utilitarian principle. To do this in any sufficient manner, many Stoic, as well as Christian, elements require to be included. But there is no known Epicurean theory of life which does not assign to the pleasures of the intellect, of the feelings and imagination, and of the moral sentiments, a much higher value as pleasures than to those of mere sensation.

It must be admitted, however, that utilitarian writers in general have placed the superiority of mental over bodily pleasures chiefly in the greater permanency, safety, uncostliness, etc., of the former—that is, in their circumstantial advantages rather than in their intrinsic nature. And on all these points utilitarians have fully proved their case; but they might have taken the other, and, as it may be called, higher ground, with entire consistency. It is quite compatible with the principle of utility to recognize the fact that some *kinds* of pleasure are more desirable and more valuable than others. It would be absurd that while, in estimating all other things, quality is considered as well as quantity, the estimation of pleasures should be supposed to depend on quantity alone.

If I am asked what I mean by difference of quality in pleasures, or what makes one pleasure more valuable than another, merely as a pleasure, except its being greater in amount, there is but one possible answer. Of two pleasures, if there be one to which all or almost all who have experience of both give a decided preference, irrespective of any feeling of moral obligation to prefer it, that is the more desirable pleasure. If one of the two is, by those who are competently acquainted with both, placed so far above the other that they prefer it, even though knowing it to be attended with a greater amount of discontent, and would not resign it for any quantity of the other pleasure of which their nature is capable, we are justified in ascribing to the preferred enjoyment a superiority in quality so far outweighing quantity as to render it, in comparison, of small account.

Now, it is an unquestionable fact that those who are equally acquainted with, and equally capable of appreciating and enjoying, both do give a most marked preference to the manner of existence which employs their higher faculties. Few human creatures would consent to be changed into any of the lower animals for a promise of the fullest allowance of a beast's pleasures; no intelligent human being would consent to be a fool, no instructed person would be an ignoramus, no person of feeling and conscience would be selfish and base, even though they should be persuaded that the fool, the dunce, or the rascal is better satisfied with his lot than they are with theirs. They would not resign what they possess more than he for the most complete satisfaction of all the desires which they have in common with him. If they ever fancy they would, it is only in cases of unhappiness so extreme that to escape from it they would exchange their lot for almost any other, however undesirable in their own eyes. A being of higher faculties requires more to make him happy, is capable probably of more acute suffering, and certainly accessible to it at more points, than one of an inferior type; but in spite of these liabilities, he can never really wish to sink into what he feels to be a lower grade of existence.

We may give what explanation we please of this unwillingness; we may attribute it to pride, a name which is given indiscriminately to some of the most and to some of the least estimable feelings of which mankind are capable; we may refer it to the love of liberty and personal independence, an appeal to which was with the Stoics one of the most effective means for the inculcation of it, to the love of power, or to the love of excitement, both of which do really enter into and contribute to it: but its most appropriate appellation is a sense of dignity, which all human beings possess in one form or another, and in some, though by no means in exact, proportion to their higher faculties, and which is so essential a part of the happiness of those in whom it is strong that nothing which conflicts with it could be, otherwise than momentarily, an object of desire to them. Whoever supposes that this preference takes place at a sacrifice of happiness—that the superior being, in anything like equal circumstances, is not happier than the inferior —confounds the two very different ideas, of happiness, and content. It is indisputable that the being whose capacities of enjoyment are low, has the greatest chance of having them fully satisfied; and a highly endowed being will always feel that any happiness which he can look for, as the world is constituted, is imperfect. But he can learn to bear its imperfections, if they are at all bearable; and they will not make him envy the being who is indeed unconscious of the imperfections, but only because he feels not at all the good which those imperfections qualify. It is better to be a human being dis-satisfied than a pig satisfied; better to be Socrates dissatisfied than a fool satisfied. And if the fool, or the pig, are of a different opinion, it is because they only know their own side of the question. The other party to the comparison knows both sides.

It may be objected that many who are capable of the higher pleasures, occasionally, under the influence of temptation, postpone them to the lower. But this is quite compatible with a full appreciation of the intrinsic superi-ority of the higher. Men often, from infirmity of character, make their elec-tion for the nearer good, though they know it to be the less valuable; and this no less when the choice is between two bodily pleasures than when it is between bodily and mental. They pursue sensual indulgences to the injury of health, though perfectly aware that health is the greater good.

It may be further objected that many who begin with youthful enthusiasm for everything noble, as they advance in years sink into indolence and selfishness. But I do not believe that those who undergo this very common change voluntarily choose the lower description of pleasures in preference to the higher. I believe that before they devote themselves exclusively to the one, they have already become incapable of the other. Capacity for the nobler feelings is in most natures a very tender plant, easily killed not only by hostile influences but by mere want of sustenance; and in the majority of young persons it speedily dies away if the occupations to which their position in life has devoted them, and the society into which it has thrown them, are not favourable to keeping that higher capacity in exercise. Men lose their high aspirations as they lose their intellectual tastes, because they have not time or opportunity for indulging them; and they addict themselves to inferior pleasures not because they deliberately prefer them, but because they are either the only ones to which they have access, or the only ones which they are any longer capable of enjoying. It may be questioned whether any one who has remained equally susceptible to both classes of pleasures ever knowingly and calmly preferred the lower; though many, in all ages, have broken down in an ineffectual attempt to combine both.

From this verdict of the only competent judges I apprehend there can be no appeal. On a question which is the best worth having of two pleasures, or which of two modes of existence is the most grateful to the feelings, apart from its moral attributes and from its consequences, the judgment of those who are qualified by knowledge of both, or, if they differ, that of the majority among them, must be admitted as final. And there needs be the less hesitation to accept this judgment respecting the quality of pleasures, since there is no other tribunal to be referred to even on the question of quantity. What means are there of determining which is the acuter of two pains, or the intenser of two pleasurable sensations, except the general suffrage of those who are familiar with both? Neither pains nor pleasures are homogeneous, and pain is always heterogeneous with pleasure. What is there to decide whether a particular pleasure is worth purchasing at the cost of a particular pain, except the feelings and judgment of the experienced? When, therefore, those feelings and judgment declare the pleasures derived from the higher faculties to be preferable *in kind*, apart from the question of intensity, to those of which the animal nature, disjoined from the higher faculties is susceptible, they are entitled on this subject to the same regard.

I have dwelt on this point, as being a necessary part of a perfectly just conception of Utility or Happiness, considered as the directive rule of human conduct. But it is by no means an indispensable condition to the acceptance of the utilitarian standard; for that standard is not the agent's own greatest happiness, but the greatest amount of happiness altogether; and, if it may possibly be doubted whether a noble character is always the happier for its nobleness, there can be no doubt that it makes other people happier, and that the world in general is immensely a gainer by it. Utilitarianism, therefore, could only attain its end by the general cultivation of nobleness of character, even if each individual were only benefited by the nobleness of others, and his own, so far as happiness is concerned, were a sheer deduction from the benefit. But the bare enunciation of such an absurdity as this last renders refutation superfluous.

According to the Greatest Happiness Principle, as above explained, the ultimate end, with reference to and for the sake of which all other things are desirable (whether we are considering our own good or that of other people), is an existence exempt as far as possible from pain, and as rich as possible in enjoyments, both in point of quantity and quality; the test of quality, and the rule for measuring it against quantity, being the preference felt by those who in their opportunities of experience, to which must be added their habits of self-consciousness and self-observation, are best furnished with the means of comparison. This, being, according to the utilitarian opinion, the end of human action, is necessarily also the standard of morality, which may accordingly be defined, the rules and precepts for human conduct, by the observance of which an existence such as has been described might be, to the greatest extent possible, secured to all mankind; and not to them only, but, so far as the nature of things admits, to the whole sentient creation. . . .

. . . When people who are tolerably fortunate in their outward lot do not find in life sufficient enjoyment to make it valuable to them, the cause generally is caring for nobody but themselves. To those who have neither public nor private affections, the excitements of life are much curtailed, and in any case dwindle in value as the time approaches when all selfish interests must be terminated by death; while those who leave after them objects of personal affection, and especially those who have also cultivated a fellow-feeling with the collective interests of mankind, retain as lively an interest in life on the eve of death as in the vigour of youth and health.

Next to selfishness, the principal cause which makes life unsatisfactory is want of mental cultivation. A cultivated mind—I do not mean that of a philosopher, but any mind to which the fountains of knowledge have been opened, and which has been taught, in any tolerable degree, to exercise its faculties—finds sources of inexhaustible interest in all that surrounds it: in the objects of nature, the achievements of art, the imaginations of poetry, the incidents of history, the ways of mankind, past and present, and their prospects in the future. It is possible, indeed, to become indifferent to all this, and that too without having exhausted a thousandth part of it; but only when one has had from the beginning no moral or human interest in these things, and has sought in them only the gratification of curiosity. . . .

FURTHER READING

The necessary sorting out of the issues and positions in value theory, is done very well in such chapters as "Ideals of Life" and "What Things Are Good?" in John Hospers, *Human Conduct* (1972).

The philosophy of hedonism advocates pleasure as the greatest good, and is itself a pleasure to read about. The relative simplicity of the philosophy makes it a good starting point. In addition to the philosophers (Aristippus, Epicurus, Bentham), see Edward Fitzgerald's translation of *The Rubaiyat of Omar Khayyam*, Walter Pater's "Conclusion" to his *Studies in the History of the Renaissance* (1873), and Chapter II of Sigmund Freud's *Civilization and Its Discontents* (1930).

Robert F. Davidson's *Philosophies Men Live By* (1952) is an unusually enjoyable description of the lives and ideas of representative philosophers, all done with an emphasis on values.

Thorough introductions and carefully edited readings are presented in *Great Traditions in Ethics* (2nd ed., 1969), edited by Ethel M. Albert, *et al.*

Basic readings from eight philosophers are included in Chapter 1, "What Is Worthwhile?" in Richard B. Brandt's *Value and Obligation* (1961).

Lucretius, Dante, and Goethe held different worldviews, each featuring a major value system; they are discussed in George Santayana's *Three Philosophical Poets* (1910).

For a change in pace, and an implicit rather than explicit presentation of a set of values, see *The Last Whole Earth Catalog* (1971), edited by Stewart Brand. Called an "Access to Tools," it was a best seller as much for the values it embodied as for the "tools" it recommended.

chapter six

THE ELUSIVE GROUND OF MORALITY

6

"If we had no moral sense," said the philosopher Clarence Irving Lewis, "philosophy would not give us one. But who can state, with complete satisfaction to himself, the adequate and consistent grounds of moral judgment?"[1] And such is the business of moral philosophy. It is certainly not the purpose of this area of philosophy to persuade men to be moral—men are moral, in the broadest sense of the term, because morality is inseparable from human choice and action. Nor is it the function of the moral philosopher to prescribe or preach a particular morality. His task is to seek out those grounds upon which morality is based. He attempts to formulate and evaluate those underlying principles of morality in order that they might be brought to bear upon the moral dilemmas which so frequently plague us.

That the reach of our moral concerns is broader than most of us tend to think is one of John Dewey's points in the essay which follows. "There is no act," he states, ". . . which may not have definitive moral significance." This is also the theme of the short story "In Dreams Begin Responsibilities," by Delmore Schwartz. In Schwartz's story a young man dreams of watching a film of a day in the life of his parents prior to their marriage. It was, in fact, the day they became engaged. The young couple are self-conscious and sometimes awkward with each other. They talk, try to impress one another, ride the merry-go-round, and there is the proposal of marriage. She sobs and accepts. They have their picture taken on the boardwalk, and they bicker over her desire to visit a fortune-teller. Throughout these commonplace but pregnant scenes, their future son is scarcely able to watch parts of the film. "What are they doing?" he cries out. "Don't they know what they are doing?" But the usher in the dream-theater admonishes him: "What are you doing? . . . You can't carry on like this, it is not right, you will find that out soon enough, everything you do matters too much."

Because what we do matters so much, and because all too often it is not entirely clear what we ought to do, we engage in deliberations over our

[1] *Mind and the World Order* (New York: Dover Publications, 1956), p. 3.

224

> The best lack all conviction, while the worst
> Are full of passionate intensity.

william butler yeats

actions. Moral theory, according to John Dewey, arises out of such deliberations: it is only an extension of that reflective thinking which is prompted by doubt about what is right.

Our unavoidable implication in moral issues and their urgency are stressed by Kenneth Fearing. The confession ("I have been guilty of ignorance, and talking with conviction. Of intolerable wisdom, and keeping silent.") is one which many of us might make. The "public-spirited citizen's" wish not to be involved only underscores how inexorable his involvement is. His shrill speech and desperate conception of his duty illustrate Erich Fromm's observation that "neurosis itself is, in the last analysis, a symptom of moral failure."[2]

But isn't morality relative? In "A Righteous Cockroach" Don Marquis's insect argues that it is. Modern men of course know that differing moral codes exist, and history shows that those codes change in time. Morality seems to depend upon time and place and what one thinks is right in the unique circumstances of each case. However, W. T. Stace, in his "Ethical Relativity," draws out the implications of that popular position and makes it appear somewhat less acceptable. If "right" means whatever people happen to think it means, then slavery was right for those who believed it so. This is the eternal debate between the relativists and the absolutists.

The questions raised in Plato's "Gyges' Ring" and Kurt Baier's "The Moral Point of View" are essentially the same. The argument in Plato's story is that men are moral only out of self-regarding necessity; it is in their own interest to avoid condemnation by society. Given the opportunity, however, to circumvent capture and punishment, men will be "unjust." Baier's task is to show, on the contrary, that there are grounds which overrule those of self-interest, even though taking "the moral point of view" may occasionally mean acting in a manner contrary to one's own interests.

---

[2] *Man for Himself* (New York: Rinehart and Company, 1947), p. viii.

delmore schwartz   IN DREAMS BEGIN
                                     RESPONSIBILITIES

Delmore Schwartz (1913–1966) was born in Brooklyn and took his B.A. in philosophy from New York University. He studied and taught at Harvard and worked as an editor for the Partisan Review *and* The New Republic. *As the style of the following short story may suggest, Schwartz was perhaps primarily a poet, and he was much honored as such. He received Guggenheim and Kenyon Review fellowships, two* Poetry *magazine awards, and the Bollinger poetry prize for 1959. His general theme, he once said, was "the wound of consciousness." He was himself troubled by mental illness for some twenty years. Schwartz's poetry is best represented in* Summer Knowledge: New and Selected Poems 1938–1958. *Short stories were collected in* The World Is a Wedding (1948) *and* Successful Love and Other Stories (1962). *"In Dreams Begin Responsibilities," from the former volume, magically recreates an earlier time and binds it to the present.*

I think it is the year 1909. I feel as if I were in a moving-picture theater, the long arm of light crossing the darkness and spinning, my eyes fixed upon the screen. It is a silent picture, as if an old Biograph one, in which the actors are dressed in ridiculously old-fashioned clothes, and one flash succeeds another with sudden jumps, and the actors, too, seem to jump about, walking too fast. The shots are full of rays and dots, as if it had been raining when the picture was photographed. The light is bad.

It is Sunday afternoon, June 12th, 1909, and my father is walking down the quiet streets of Brooklyn on his way to visit my mother. His clothes are newly pressed, and his tie is too tight in his high collar. He jingles the coins in his pocket, thinking of the witty things he will say. I feel as if I had by now relaxed entirely in the soft darkness of the theater; the organist peals out the obvious approximate emotions on which the audience rocks unknowingly. I am anonymous. I have forgotten myself: it is always so when one goes to a movie, it is, as they say, a drug.

My father walks from street to street of trees, lawns and houses, once in a while coming to an avenue on which a streetcar skates and yaws, progressing slowly. The motorman, who has a handlebar mustache, helps a young lady wearing a hat like a feathered bowl onto the car. He leisurely makes change and rings his bell as the passengers mount the car. It is obviously Sunday, for everyone is wearing Sunday clothes and the streetcar's noises emphasize the quiet of the holiday (Brooklyn is said to be the city of churches). The shops are closed and their shades drawn but for an occasional stationery store or drugstore with great green balls in the window.

226

My father has chosen to take this long walk because he likes to walk and think. He thinks about himself in the future and so arrives at the place he is to visit in a mild state of exaltation. He pays no attention to the houses he is passing, in which the Sunday dinner is being eaten, nor to the many trees which line each street, now coming to their full green and the time when they will enclose the whole street in leafy shadow. An occasional carriage passes, the horses' hooves falling like stones in the quiet afternoon, and once in a while an automobile, looking like an enormous upholstered sofa, puffs and passes.

My father thinks of my mother, of how lady-like she is, and of the pride which will be his when he introduces her to his family. They are not yet engaged and he is not yet sure that he loves my mother, so that, once in a while, he becomes panicky about the bond already established. But then he reassures himself by thinking of the big men he admires who are married: William Randolph Hearst and William Howard Taft, who has just become the President of the United States.

My father arrives at my mother's house. He has come too early and so is suddenly embarrassed. My aunt, my mother's younger sister, answers the loud bell with her napkin in her hand, for the family is still at dinner. As my father enters, my grandfather rises from the table and shakes hands with him. My mother has run upstairs to tidy herself. My grandmother asks my father if he has had dinner and tells him that my mother will be down soon. My grandfather opens the conversation by remarking about the mild June weather. My father sits uncomfortably near the table, holding his hat in his hand. My grandmother tells my aunt to take my father's hat. My uncle, twelve years old, runs into the house, his hair tousled. He shouts a greeting to my father, who has often given him nickels, and then runs upstairs, as my grandmother shouts after him. It is evident that the respect in which my father is held in this house is tempered by a good deal of mirth. He is impressive, but also very awkward.

II. Finally my mother comes downstairs and my father, being at the moment engaged in conversation with my grandfather, is made uneasy by her entrance, for he does not know whether to greet my mother or to continue the conversation. He gets up from his chair clumsily and says "Hello" gruffly. My grandfather watches this, examining their congruence, such as it is, with a critical eye, and meanwhile rubbing his bearded cheek roughly, as he always does when he reasons. He is worried; he is afraid that my father will not make a good husband for his oldest daughter. At this point something happens to the film, just as my father says something funny to my mother: I am awakened to myself and my unhappiness just as my interest has become most intense. The audience begins to clap impatiently. Then the trouble is

227

attended to, but the film has been returned to a portion just shown, and once more I see my grandfather rubbing his bearded cheek, pondering my father's character. It is difficult to get back into the picture once more and forget myself, but as my mother giggles at my father's words, the darkness drowns me.

My father and mother depart from the house, my father shaking hands with my grandfather once more, out of some unknown uneasiness. I stir uneasily also, slouched in the hard chair of the theater. Where is the older uncle, my mother's older brother? He is studying in his bedroom upstairs, studying for his final examinations at the College of the City of New York, having been dead of double pneumonia for the last twenty-one years. My mother and father walk down the same quiet streets once more. My mother is holding my father's arm and telling him of the novel she has been reading and my father utters judgments of the characters as the plot is made clear to him. This is a habit which he very much enjoys, for he feels the utmost superiority and confidence when he is approving or condemning the behavior of other people. At times he feels moved to utter a brief "Ugh," whenever the story becomes what he would call sugary. This tribute is the assertion of his manliness. My mother feels satisfied by the interest she has awakened; and she is showing my father how intelligent she is and how interesting.

They reach the avenue, and the streetcar leisurely arrives. They are going to Coney Island this afternoon, although my mother really considers such pleasures inferior. She has made up her mind to indulge only in a walk on the boardwalk and a pleasant dinner, avoiding the riotous amusements as being beneath the dignity of so dignified a couple.

My father tells my mother how much money he has made in the week just past, exaggerating an amount which need not have been exaggerated. But my father has always felt that actualities somehow fall short, no matter how fine they are. Suddenly I begin to weep. The determined old lady who sits next to me in the theater is annoyed and looks at me with an angry face, and being intimidated, I stop. I drag out my handkerchief and dry my face, licking the drop which has fallen near my lips. Meanwhile I have missed something, for here are my father and mother alighting from the streetcar at the last stop, Coney Island.

III. They walk toward the boardwalk and my mother commands my father to inhale the pungent air from the sea. They both breathe in deeply, both of them laughing as they do so. They have in common a great interest in health, although my father is strong and husky, and my mother is frail. They are both full of theories about what is good to eat and not good to eat, and sometimes have heated discussions about it, the whole matter ending in my

228

father's announcement, made with a scornful bluster, that you have to die sooner or later anyway. On the boardwalk's flagpole, the American flag is pulsing in an intermittent wind from the sea.

My father and mother go to the rail of the boardwalk and look down on the beach where a good many bathers are casually walking about. A few are in the surf. A peanut whistle pierces the air with its pleasant and active whine, and my father goes to buy peanuts. My mother remains at the rail and stares at the ocean. The ocean seems merry to her; it pointedly sparkles and again and again the pony waves are released. She notices the children digging in the wet sand, and the bathing costumes of the girls who are her own age. My father returns with the peanuts. Overhead the sun's lightning strikes and strikes, but neither of them are at all aware of it. The boardwalk is full of people dressed in their Sunday clothes and casually strolling. The tide does not reach as far as the boardwalk, and the strollers would feel no danger if it did. My father and mother lean on the rail of the boardwalk and absently stare at the ocean. The ocean is becoming rough; the waves come in slowly, tugging strength from far back. The moment before they somersault, the moment when they arch their backs so beautifully, showing white veins in the green and black, that moment is intolerable. They finally crack, dashing fiercely upon the sand, actually driving, full force downward, against it, bouncing upward and forward, and at last petering out into a small stream of bubbles which slides up the beach and then is recalled. The sun overhead does not disturb my father and my mother. They gaze idly at the ocean, scarcely interested in its harshness. But I stare at the terrible sun which breaks up sight, and the fatal merciless passionate ocean. I forget my parents. I stare fascinated, and finally, shocked by their indifference, I burst out weeping once more. The old lady next to me pats my shoulder and says: "There, there, young man, all of this is only a movie, only a movie," but I look up once more at the terrifying sun and the terrifying ocean, and being unable to control my tears I get up and go to the men's room, stumbling over the feet of the other people seated in my row.

IV. When I return, feeling as if I had just awakened in the morning sick for lack of sleep, several hours have apparently passed and my parents are riding on the merry-go-round. My father is on a black horse, my mother on a white one, and they seem to be making an eternal circuit for the single purpose of snatching the nickel rings which are attached to an arm of one of the posts. A hand-organ is playing; it is inseparable from the ceaseless circling of the merry-go-round.

For a moment it seems that they will never get off the carousel, for it will never stop, and I feel as if I were looking down from the fiftieth story of a building. But at length they do get off; even the hand-organ has ceased for a moment. There is a sudden and sweet stillness, as if the achievement of so much motion. My mother has acquired only two rings, my father, however, ten of them, although it was my mother who really wanted them.

They walk on along the boardwalk as the afternoon descends by imperceptible degrees into the incredible violet of dusk. Everything fades into a relaxed glow, even the ceaseless murmuring from the beach. They look for a place to have dinner. My father suggests the best restaurant on the boardwalk and my mother demurs, according to her principles of economy and housewifeliness.

However they do go to the best place, asking for a table near the window so that they can look out upon the boardwalk and the mobile ocean. My father feels omnipotent as he places a quarter in the waiter's hand in asking for a table. The place is crowded and here too there is music, this time from a kind of string trio. My father orders with a fine confidence.

As their dinner goes on, my father tells of his plans for the future and my mother shows with expressive face how interested she is, and how impressed. My father becomes exultant, lifted up by the waltz that is being played and his own future begins to intoxicate him. My father tells my mother that he is going to expand his business, for there is a great deal of money to be made. He wants to settle down. After all, he is twenty-nine, he has lived by himself since his thirteenth year, he is making more and more money, and he is envious of his friends when he visits them in the security of their homes, surrounded, it seems, by the calm domestic pleasures, and by delightful children, and then as the waltz reaches the moment when the dancers all swing madly, then, then with awful daring, then he asks my mother to marry him, although awkwardly enough and puzzled as to how he had arrived at the question, and she, to make the whole business worse, begins to cry, and my father looks nervously about, not knowing at all what to do now, and my mother says: "It's all I've wanted from the first moment I saw you," sobbing, and he finds all of this very difficult, scarcely to his taste, scarcely as he thought it would be, on his long walks over Brooklyn Bridge in the revery of a fine cigar, and it was then, at that point, that I stood up in the theater and shouted: "Don't do it! It's not too late to change your minds, both of you. Nothing good will come of it, only remorse, hatred, scandal, and two children whose characters are monstrous." The whole audience turned to look at me, annoyed, the usher came hurrying down the aisle flashing his searchlight, and the old lady next to me tugged me down into my seat, saying: "Be quiet. You'll be put out, and you paid thirty-five cents to come in." And so I shut my eyes because I could not bear to see what was happening. I sat there quietly.

230

V. But after a while I begin to take brief glimpses and at length I watch again with thirsty interest, like a child who tries to maintain his sulk when he is offered a bribe of candy. My parents are now having their picture taken in a photographer's booth along the boardwalk. The place is shadowed in the mauve light which is apparently necessary. The camera is set to the side on its tripod and looks like a Martian man. The photographer is instructing my parents in how to pose. My father has his arm over my mother's shoulder, and both of them smile emphatically. The photographer brings my mother a bouquet of flowers to hold in her hand, but she holds it at the wrong angle. Then the photographer covers himself with the black cloth which drapes the camera and all that one sees of him is one protruding arm and his hand with which he holds tightly to the rubber ball which he squeezes when the picture is taken. But he is not satisfied with their appearance. He feels that somehow there is something wrong in their pose. Again and again he comes out from his hiding place with new directions. Each suggestion merely makes matters worse. My father is becoming impatient. They try a seated pose. The photographer explains that he has his pride, he wants to make beautiful pictures, he is not merely interested in all of this for the money. My father says: "Hurry up, will you? We haven't got all night." But the photographer only scurries about apologetically, issuing new directions. The photographer charms me, and I approve of him with all my heart, for I know exactly how he feels, and as he criticizes each revised pose according to some obscure idea of rightness, I become quite hopeful. But then my father says angrily: "Come on, you've had enough time, we're not going to wait any longer." And the photographer, sighing unhappily, goes back into the black covering, and holds out his hand, saying: "One, two, three, Now!" and the picture is taken, with my father's smile turned to a grimace and my mother's bright and false. It takes a few minutes for the picture to be developed and as my parents sit in the curious light they become depressed.

VI. They have passed a fortune-teller's booth and my mother wishes to go in, but my father does not. They begin to argue about it. My mother becomes stubborn, my father once more impatient. What my father would like to do now is walk off and leave my mother there, but he knows that that would never do. My mother refuses to budge. She is near tears, but she feels an uncontrollable desire to hear what the palm-reader will say. My father consents angrily and they both go into the booth which is, in a way, like the photographer's, since it is draped in black cloth and its light is colored and shadowed. The place is too warm, and my father keeps saying that this is all nonsense, pointing to the crystal ball on the table. The fortune-teller, a short, fat woman garbed in robes supposedly exotic, comes into the room and greets them, speaking with an accent, but suddenly my father feels that the whole thing is intolerable; he tugs at my mother's arm but my mother refuses to budge. And then, in terrible anger, my father lets go of my mother's arm and strides out, leaving my mother stunned. She makes a movement as if to go after him, but the fortune-teller holds her and begs her not to do so, and I in my seat in the darkness am shocked and horrified. I feel as if I were walking a tight-rope one hundred feet over a circus audience and suddenly the rope is showing signs of breaking, and I get up from my seat and begin to shout once more the first words I can think of to communicate my terrible fear, and once more the usher comes hurrying down the aisle flashing his searchlight, and the old lady pleads with me, and the shocked audience has turned to stare at me, and I keep shouting: "What are they doing? Don't they know what they are doing? Why doesn't my mother go after my father and beg him not to be angry? If she does not do that, what will she do? Doesn't my father know what he is doing?" But the usher has seized my arm, and is dragging me away, and as he does so, he says: "What are *you* doing? Don't you know you can't do things like this, you can't do whatever you want to do, even if other people aren't about? You will be sorry if you do not do what you should do. You can't carry on like this, it is not right, you will find that out soon enough, everything you do matters too much," and as he said that, dragging me through the lobby of the theater, into the cold light, I woke up into the bleak winter morning of my twenty-first birthday, the window-sill shining with its lip of snow, and the morning already begun.

john dewey   THE NATURE OF MORAL THEORY

Among American philosophers, only Charles Pierce and William James can compare with John Dewey (1859–1952). Born into a family of modest means in rural Vermont, Dewey received his first degree from the University of Vermont. He taught briefly in a high school and small district school, and then went on for his Ph.D. from Johns Hopkins University. After holding teaching positions at the Universities of Michigan and Minnesota, he founded his famous experimental elementary school at the University of Chicago. When Dewey was eighty-two, it was reported that he had written 36 books and 815 articles and pamphlets. These included School and Society, Democracy and Education, Reconstruction in Philosophy, Human Nature and Conduct, The Quest for Certainty, Experience and Nature, *and* A Common Faith. *"The Nature of Moral Theory" was one of the chapters by Dewey in his and James H. Tufts' Ethics (1908, rev. ed., 1932).*

REFLECTIVE MORALITY AND ETHICAL THEORY

The intellectual distinction between customary and reflective morality is clearly marked. The former places the standard and rules of conduct in ancestral habit; the latter appeals to conscience, reason, or to some principle which includes thought. The distinction is as important as it is definite, for it shifts the center of gravity in morality. Nevertheless the distinction is relative rather than absolute. Some degree of reflective thought must have entered occasionally into systems which in the main were founded on social wont and use, while in contemporary morals, even when the need of critical judgment is most recognized, there is an immense amount of conduct that is merely accommodated to social usage. In what follows we shall, accordingly, emphasize the difference in *principle* between customary and reflective morals rather than try to describe different historic and social epochs. In principle a revolution was wrought when Hebrew prophets and Greek seers asserted that conduct is not truly conduct unless it springs from the heart, from personal desires and affections, or from personal insight and rational choice.

The change was revolutionary not only because it displaced custom from the supreme position, but even more because it entailed the necessity of criticizing existing customs and institutions from a new point of view. Standards which were regarded by the followers of tradition as the basis of duty and responsibility were denounced by prophet and philosopher as the source of moral corruption. These proclaimed the hollowness of outer conformity and insisted upon the cleansing of the heart and the clarifying of the mind as preconditions of any genuinely good conduct.

One great source of the abiding interest which Greek thought has for the western world is that it records so clearly the struggle to make the transition from customary to reflective conduct. In the Platonic dialogues for example Socrates is represented as constantly raising the question of whether morals can be taught. Some other thinker (like Protagoras in the dialogue of that name) is brought in who points out that habituation to existing moral traditions is actually taught. Parents and teachers constantly admonish the young "pointing out that one act is just, another unjust; one honorable and another dishonorable; one holy and another unholy." When a youth emerges from parental tutelage, the State takes up the task, for "the community compels them to learn laws and to live after the pattern of the laws and not according to their own fancies."

In reply, Socrates raises the question of the foundations of such teaching, of its right to be termed a genuine teaching of virtue, and in effect points out the need of a morality which shall be stable and secure because based upon constant and universal principles. Parents and teachers differ in their injunctions and prohibitions; different communities have different laws; the same community changes its habits with time and with transformation of government. How shall we know who among the teachers, whether individuals or States, is right? Is there no basis for morals except this fluctuating one? It is not enough to praise and blame, reward and punish, enjoin and prohibit. The essence of morals, it is implied, is to know the reason for these customary instructions; to ascertain the criterion which insures their being just. And in other dialogues, it is frequently asserted that even if the mass must follow custom and law without insight, those who make laws and fix customs should have sure insight into enduring principles, or else the blind will be leading the blind.

No fundamental difference exists between systematic moral theory . . . and the reflection an individual engages in when he attempts to find general principles which shall direct and justify his conduct. Moral theory begins, in germ, when any one asks "Why should I act thus and not otherwise? Why is this right and that wrong? What right has any one to frown upon this way of acting and impose that other way?" Children make at least a start upon the road of theory when they assert that the injunctions of elders are arbitrary, being simply a matter of superior position. Any adult enters the road when, in the presence of moral perplexity, of doubt as to what it is right or best to do, he attempts to find his way out through reflection which will lead him to some principle he regards as dependable.

Moral theory cannot emerge when there is positive belief as to what is right and what is wrong, for then there is no occasion for reflection. It emerges when men are confronted with situations in which different desires

234

promise opposed goods and in which incompatible courses of action seem to be morally justified. Only such a conflict of good ends and of standards and rules of right and wrong calls forth personal inquiry into the bases of morals. A critical juncture may occur when a person, for example, goes from a protected home life into the stress of competitive business, and finds that moral standards which apply in one do not hold in the other. Unless he merely drifts, accommodating himself to whatever social pressure is uppermost, he will feel the conflict. If he tries to face it in thought, he will search for a reasonable principle by which to decide where the right really lies. In so doing he enters into the domain of moral theory, even if he does so unwittingly.

For what is called moral theory is but a more conscious and systematic raising of the question which occupies the mind of any one who in the face of moral conflict and doubt seeks a way out through reflection. In short, moral theory is but an extension of what is involved in all reflective morality. There are two kinds of moral struggle. One kind, and that the most emphasized in moral writings and lectures, is the conflict which takes place when an individual is tempted to do something which he is convinced is wrong. Such instances are important practically in the life of an individual, but they are not the occasion of moral theory. The employee of a bank who is tempted to embezzle funds may indeed try to argue himself into finding reasons why it would not be wrong for him to do it. But in such a case, he is not really thinking, but merely permitting his desire to govern his beliefs. There is no sincere doubt in his mind as to what he should do when he seeks to find some justification for what he has made up his mind to do.

Take, on the other hand, the case of a citizen of a nation which has just declared war on another country. He is deeply attached to his own state. He has formed habits of loyalty and of abiding by its laws, and now one of its decrees is that he shall support war. He feels in addition gratitude and affection for the country which has sheltered and nurtured him. But he believes that this war is unjust, or perhaps he has a conviction that all war is a form of murder and hence wrong. One side of his nature, one set of convictions and habits, leads him to acquiesce in war; another deep part of his being protests. He is torn between two duties: he experiences a conflict between the incompatible values presented to him by his habits of citizenship and by his religious beliefs respectively. Up to this time, he has never experienced a struggle between the two; they have coincided and reënforced one another. Now he has to make a choice between competing moral loyalties and convictions. The struggle is not between a good which is clear to him and something else which attracts him but which he knows to be wrong. It is between values each of which is an undoubted good in its place but which now get in each other's way. He is forced to reflect in order to come to a decision. Moral theory is a generalized extension of the kind of thinking in which he now engages.

There are periods in history when a whole community or a group in a community finds itself in the presence of new issues which its old customs do not adequately meet. The habits and beliefs which were formed in the past do not fit into the opportunities and requirements of contemporary life. The age in Greece following the time of Pericles was of this sort; that of the Jews after their captivity; that following the Middle Ages when secular interests on a large scale were introduced into previous religious and ecclesiastic interests; the present is preëminently a period of this sort with the vast social changes which have followed the industrial expansion of the machine age.

Realization that the need for reflective morality and for moral theories grows out of conflict between ends, responsibilities, rights, and duties defines the service which moral theory may render, and also protects the student from false conceptions of its nature. The difference between customary and reflective morality is precisely that definite precepts, rules, definitive injunctions and prohibitions issue from the former, while they cannot proceed from the latter. Confusion ensues when appeal to rational principles is treated as if it were merely a substitute for custom, transferring the authority of moral commands from one source to another. Moral theory can (i) generalize the types of moral conflicts which arise, thus enabling a perplexed and doubtful individual to clarify his own particular problem by placing it in a larger context; it can (ii) state the leading ways in which such problems have been intellectually dealt with by those who have thought upon such matters; it can (iii) render personal reflection more systematic and enlightened, suggesting alternatives that might otherwise be overlooked, and stimulating greater consistency in judgment. But it does not offer a table of commandments in a catechism in which answers are as definite as are the questions which are asked. It can render personal choice more intelligent, but it cannot take the place of personal decision, which must be made in every case of moral perplexity. Such at least is the standpoint of the discussions which follow; the student who expects more from moral theory will be disappointed. The conclusion follows from the very nature of reflective morality; the attempt to set up ready-made conclusions contradicts the very nature of reflective morality.

THE NATURE OF A MORAL ACT

Since the change from customary to reflective morality shifts emphasis from conformity to prevailing modes of action over to personal disposition and attitudes, the first business of moral theory is to obtain in outline an idea

236

of the factors which constitute personal disposition. In its general features, the traits of a reflective moral situation have long been clear; doubts and disputes arise chiefly as to the relation which they bear to one another. The formula was well stated by Aristotle. The doer of the moral deed must have a certain "state of mind" in doing it. First, he must *know* what he is doing; secondly, he must *choose* it, and choose it for itself, and thirdly, the act must be the expression of a formed and stable *character*. In other words, the act must be *voluntary*; that is, it must manifest a choice, and for full morality at least, the choice must be an expression of the general tenor and set of personality. It must involve awareness of what one is about; a fact which in the concrete signifies that there must be a purpose, an aim, an end in view, something for the sake of which the particular act is done. The acts of infants, imbeciles, insane persons in some cases, have no moral quality; they do not know what they are about. Children learn early in life to appeal to accident, that is, absence of intention and purpose on their part, as an excuse for deeds that have bad consequences. When they exculpate themselves on the ground that they did not "mean" to do something they show a realization that intent is a normal part of a moral situation. Again, there is no choice, no implication of personal disposition, when one is coerced by superior physical power. Even when force takes the form of threats, rather than of immediate exercise of it, "duress" is at least a mitigating circumstance. It is recognized that fear of extreme harm to life and limb will overpower choice in all but those of heroic make-up.

An act must be the expression of a formed and stable character. But stability of character is an affair of degrees, and is not to be taken absolutely. No human being, however mature, has a completely formed character, while any child in the degree in which he has acquired attitudes and habits has a stable character to that extent. The point of including this qualification is that it suggests a kind of running scale of acts, some of which proceed from greater depths of the self, while others are more casual, more due to accidental and variable circumstances. We overlook acts performed under conditions of great stress or of physical weakness on the ground that the doer was "not himself" at the time. Yet we should not overdo this interpretation. Conduct may be eccentric and erratic just because a person in the past has formed that kind of disposition. An unstable character may be the product of acts deliberately chosen aforetime. A man is not himself in a state of intoxication. But a difference will be made between the case in which a usually temperate man is overcome by drink, and the case in which intoxication is so habitual as to be a sign of a habit formed by choice and of character.

May acts be voluntary, that is, be expressions of desire, intent, choice, and habitual disposition, and yet be morally neutral, indifferent? To all appearances the answer must be in the affirmative. We rise in the morning, dress, eat, and go about our usual business without attaching moral significance to what we are doing. These are the regular and normal things to do, and the acts, while many of them are performed intentionally and with a knowledge of what we are doing are a matter of course. So with the student's, merchant's, engineer's, lawyer's, or doctor's daily round of affairs. We feel that it would be rather morbid if a moral issue were raised in connection with each act; we should probably suspect some mental disorder if it were, at least some weakness in power of decision. On the other hand, we speak of the persons in question going about their daily round of *duties*. If we omitted from our estimate of moral character all the deeds done in the performance of daily tasks, satisfaction of recurrent needs, meeting of responsibilities, each slight perhaps in itself but enormous in mass, morality would be a weak and sickly thing indeed.

The inconsistency between these two points of view is only apparent. Many acts are done not only without thought of their *moral* quality but with practically no thought of any kind. Yet these acts are preconditions of other acts having significant value. A criminal on his way to commit a crime and a benevolent person on his way to a deed of mercy both have to walk or ride. Such acts, non-moral in isolation, derive moral significance from the ends to which they lead. If a man who had an important engagement to keep declined to get out of bed in the morning from sheer laziness, the indirect moral quality of a seemingly automatic act would be apparent. A vast number of acts are performed which seem to be trivial in themselves but which in reality are the supports and buttresses of acts in which definite moral considerations are present. The person who completely ignored the connection of the great number of more or less routine acts with the small number in which there is a clear moral issue would be an utterly independable person.

CONDUCT AND CHARACTER

These facts are implicitly recognized in common speech by the use of the word *conduct*. The word expresses continuity of action, an idea which we have already met in the conception of a stable and formed character. Where there is conduct there is not simply a succession of disconnected acts but each thing done carries forward an underlying tendency and intent, *conducting*, leading up, to further acts and to a final fulfillment or consummation. Moral development, in the training given by others and in the education one secures for oneself, consists in becoming aware that our acts are connected with one another; thereby an ideal of *conduct* is substituted for the blind and thoughtless performance of isolated acts. Even when a person has

238

attained a certain degree of moral stability, his temptations usually take the form of fancying that this particular act will not count, that it is an exception, that for this just one occasion it will not do any harm. His "temptation" is to disregard that continuity of sequence in which one act leads on to others and to a cumulative result.

We commence life under the influence of appetites and impulses, and of direct response to immediate stimuli of heat and cold, comfort and pain, lights, possessed of two different values, and he has to make a choice. The cent and natural. But he brings down reproach upon himself; he is told that he is unmannerly, inconsiderate, greedy; that he should wait till he is served, till his turn comes. He is made aware that his act has other connections than the one he had assigned to it: the immediate satisfaction of hunger. He learns to look at single acts not as single but as related links in a chain. Thus the idea of a *series*, an idea which is the essence of conduct, gradually takes the place of a mere succession of disconnected acts.

This idea of conduct as a serial whole solves the problem of morally indifferent acts. Every act has *potential* moral significance, because it is, through its consequences, part of a larger whole of behavior. A person starts to open a window because he feels the need of air—no act could be more "natural," more morally indifferent in appearance. But he remembers that his associate is an invalid and sensitive to drafts. He now sees his act in two different lights, possessed of two different values, and he has to make a choice. The potential moral import of a seemingly insignificant act has come home to him. Or, wishing to take exercise, there are two routes open to him. Ordinarily it would be a mere matter of personal taste which he would choose. But he recalls that the more pleasing of the two is longer, and that if he went that way he might be unable to keep an appointment of importance. He now has to place his act in a larger context of continuity and determine which ulterior consequence he prizes most: personal pleasure or meeting the needs of another. Thus while there is no single act which *must* under all circumstances have conscious moral quality, there is no act, since it is a part of conduct, which *may* not have definitive moral significance. There is no hard and fast line between the morally indifferent and the morally significant. Matthew Arnold expressed a prevailing idea when he said that conduct—in the moral sense—is three-fourths of life. Although he probably assigned it a higher ratio than most persons would, the statement expresses a widely shared idea, namely, that morality has to do with a clearly marked out portion of our life, leaving other things indifferent. Our conclusion is different. It is that *potentially* conduct is one hundred per cent of our conscious life. . . .

kenneth fearing   CONFESSION OVERHEARD
IN A SUBWAY

Kenneth Fearing (1902–1961) was born in Chicago and graduated from the University of Wisconsin. He worked as a reporter, salesman, mill-hand, and free-lance writer, and published his first volume of poetry, Angel Arms, *in 1929. There were some novels, including* The Big Clock, *but it was the tense, angry poetry that brought him a Guggenheim fellowship and critical acclaim. "This is not the first time,"* he wrote, *"nor will it be the last time the world has gone to hell." Some of the poetry collections include* Dead Reckoning, Afternoon of a Pawn-broker, Stranger on Coney Island, *and* The Loneliest Girl in the World. *"Confession Overheard in a Subway" is from his* Afternoon of a Pawnbroker and Other Poems (1943).

You will ask how I came to be eavesdropping, in the first place.
The answer is, I was not.
The man who confessed to these several crimes (call him John Doe) spoke
     into my right ear on a crowded subway train, while the man whom he
     addressed (call him Richard Roe) stood at my left.
Thus, I stood between them, and they talked, or sometimes shouted, quite
     literally straight through me.
How could I help but overhear?
Perhaps I might have moved away to some other strap. But the aisles were
     full.
Besides, I felt, for some reason, curious.

"I do not deny my guilt," said John Doe. "My own, first, and after that
     my guilty knowledge of still further guilt.
I have counterfeited often, and successfully.
I have been guilty of ignorance, and talking with conviction. Of intolerable
     wisdom, and keeping silent.
Through carelessness, or cowardice, I have shortened the lives of better men.
     And the name for that is murder.
All my life I have been a receiver of stolen goods."

"Personally, I always mind my own business," said Richard Roe. "Sensible
     people don't get into those scrapes."

I was not the only one who overheard this confession.
Several businessmen, bound for home, and housewives and mechanics, were
     within easy earshot.

240

A policeman sitting in front of us did not lift his eyes, at the mention of
   murder, from his paper.
Why should I be the one to report these crimes?
You will understand why this letter to your paper is anonymous. I will
   sign it: Public-Spirited Citizen, and hope that it cannot be traced.
But all the evidence, if there is any clamor for it, can be substantiated.
I have heard the same confession many times since, in different places.
And now that I come to think of it, I had heard it many times before.

"Guilt," said John, "is always and everywhere nothing less than guilt.
I have always, at all times, been a willing accomplice of the crass and the
   crude.
I have overheard, daily, the smallest details of conspiracies against the
   human race, vast in their ultimate scope, and conspired, daily, to launch
   my own.
You have heard of innocent men who died in the chair. It was my greed that
   threw the switch.
I helped, and I do not deny it, to nail that guy to the cross, and shall con-
   tinue to help.
Look into my eyes, you can see the guilt.
Look at my face, my hair, my very clothing, you will see guilt written
   plainly everywhere.
Guilt of the flesh. Of the soul. Of laughing, when others do not. Of breathing
   and eating and sleeping.
I am guilty of what? Of guilt. Guilty of guilt, that is all, and enough."

Richard Roe looked at his wristwatch and said: "We'll be twenty minutes
   late.
After dinner we might take in a show."

Now, who will bring John Doe to justice for his measureless crimes?
I do not, personally, wish to be involved.
Such nakedness of the soul belongs in some other province, probably the
   executioner's.
And who will bring the blunt and upright Richard Roe to the accuser's
   stand, where he belongs?
Or will he deny and deny his partnership?

I have done my duty, as a public-spirited citizen, in any case.

don marquis   A RIGHTEOUS COCKROACH

The speaker in "A Righteous Cockroach" is not named in this excerpt, but it is a very philosophical cockroach named Archy. He types at night in a deserted newspaper office by throwing himself head downward upon a key. Of course, he could not work the capital letters, and an hour's typing left him exhausted. Archy was the creation of Don Marquis (1878–1937) a hard-drinking newspaperman, poet, and playright of the old school who introduced Archy (and Mehitabel the cat) in his column in the New York Sun *in 1916. The columns were collected in* The Lives and Times of Archy and Mehitabel *(1930). The excerpt below is from the poem "Clarence the Ghost."*

the longer i live the more i
realize that everything is
relative even morality is
relative things you would not do
sometimes you would do other
times for instance i would not consider
it honorable in me as a
righteous cockroach to crawl into a
near sighted man s soup that
man would not have a sporting chance but
with a man with ordinarily good eye
sight i should say it was
up to him to watch his soup himself and
yet if i was very tired and hungry
i would crawl into even a near
sighted man s soup knowing all the
time it was wrong and my necessity would
keep me from reproaching myself too
bitterly afterwards you can
not make any hard and fast rule
concerning the morality of crawling into
soup nor anything else a certain
alloy of expediency improves the
gold of morality and makes
it wear all the longer . . .

Walter Terence Stace (1886–   ) was born in London and received degrees from Edinburgh and Trinity College in Dublin. For over thirty years, beginning in 1910, he led a dual life: he served in the British Civil Service in Ceylon, becoming a district judge and mayor of Colombo; and he pursued philosophical studies, publishing during these years A Critical History of Greek Philosophy, The Philosophy of Hegel, The Meaning of Beauty, *and* The Theory of Knowledge and Existence. *From 1932 until his retirement in 1955, he was a professor of philosophy at Princeton University. He served as president of the American Philosophical Association and wrote* The Destiny of Western Man, The Nature of the World, Time and Eternity, Religion and the Modern Mind, The Gate of Silence, *and* Mysticism and Philosophy. *"Ethical Relativity" is from* The Concept of Morals *(1937).*

There is an opinion widely current nowadays in philosophical circles which passes under the name of "ethical relativity." Exactly what this phrase means or implies is certainly far from clear. But unquestionably it stands as a label for the opinions of a group of ethical philosophers whose position is roughly on the extreme left wing among the moral theorizers of the day. And perhaps one may best understand it by placing it in contrast with the opposite kind of extreme view against which, undoubtedly, it has arisen as a protest. For among moral philosophers one may clearly distinguish a left and a right wing. Those of the left wing are the ethical relativists. They are the revolutionaries, the clever young men, the up to date. Those of the right wing we may call the ethical absolutists. They are the conservatives and the old-fashioned.

According to the absolutists there is but one eternally true and valid moral code. This moral code applies with rigid impartiality to all men. What is a duty for me must likewise be a duty for you. And this will be true whether you are an Englishman, a Chinaman, or a Hottentot. If cannibalism is an abomination in England or America, it is an abomination in central Africa, notwithstanding that the African may think otherwise. The fact that he sees nothing wrong in his cannibal practices does not make them for him morally right. They are as much contrary to morality for him as they are for us. The only difference is that he is an ignorant savage who does not know this. There is not one law for one man or race of men, another for another. There is not one moral standard for Europeans, another for Indians, another for Chinese. There is but one law, one standard, one morality, for all men. And this standard, this law, is absolute and unvarying.

Moreover, as the one moral law extends its dominion over all the corners of the earth, so too it is not limited in its application by any considerations of time or period. That which is right now was right in the centuries of Greece and Rome, nay, in the very ages of the cave man. That which is evil now was evil then. If slavery is morally wicked today, it was morally wicked among the ancient Athenians, notwithstanding that their greatest men accepted it as a necessary condition of human society. Their opinion did not make slavery a moral good for them. It only showed that they were, in spite of their otherwise noble conceptions, ignorant of what is truly right and good in this matter.

The ethical absolutist recognizes as a fact that moral customs and moral ideas differ from country to country and from age to age. This indeed seems manifest and not to be disputed. We think slavery morally wrong, the Greeks thought it morally unobjectionable. The inhabitants of New Guinea certainly have very different moral ideas from ours. But the fact that the Greeks or the inhabitants of New Guinea think something right does not make it right, even for them. Nor does the fact that we think the same things wrong make them wrong. They are *in themselves* either right or wrong. What we have to do is to discover which they are. What anyone thinks makes no difference. It is here just as it is in matters of physical science. We believe the earth to be a globe. Our ancestors may have thought it flat. This does not show that it *was* flat, and is *now* a globe. What it shows is that men having in other ages been ignorant about the shape of the earth have now learned the truth. So if the Greeks thought slavery morally legitimate, this does not indicate that it was for them and in that age morally legitimate, but rather that they were ignorant of the truth of the matter.

The ethical absolutist is not indeed committed to the opinion that his own, or our own, moral code is the true one. Theoretically at least he might hold that slavery is ethically justifiable, that the Greeks knew better than we do about this, that ignorance of the true morality lies with us and not with them. All that he is actually committed to is the opinion that, whatever the true moral code may be, it is always the same for all men in all ages. His view is not at all inconsistent with the belief that humanity has still much to learn in moral matters. . . .

Any ethical position which denies that there is a single moral standard which is equally applicable to all men at all times may fairly be called a species of ethical relativity. There is not, the relativist asserts, merely one moral law, one code, one standard. There are many moral laws, codes, standards. What morality ordains in one place or age may be quite different from what morality ordains in another place or age. The moral code of Chinamen is quite different from that of Europeans, that of African savages quite different from both. Any morality, therefore, is relative to the age, the

244

place, and the circumstances in which it is found. It is in no sense absolute.

This does not mean merely—as one might at first sight be inclined to suppose—that the very same kind of action which is *thought* right in one country and period may be *thought* wrong in another. This would be a mere platitude, the truth of which everyone would have to admit. Even the absolutist would admit this—would even wish to emphasize it—since he is well aware that different peoples have different sets of moral ideas, and his whole point is that some of these sets of ideas are false. What the relativist means to assert is, not this platitude, but that the very same kind of action which *is* right in one country and period may *be* wrong in another. And this, far from being a platitude, is a very startling assertion. . . .

Moral right *means* what people think morally right. It has no other meaning. What Frenchmen think right is, therefore, right *for Frenchmen*. And evidently one must conclude—though I am not aware that relativists are anxious to draw one's attention to such unsavoury but yet absolutely necessary conclusions from their creed—that cannibalism is right for people who believe in it, that human sacrifice is right for those races which practice it, and that burning widows alive was right for Hindus until the British stepped in and compelled the Hindus to behave immorally by allowing their widows to remain alive.

When it is said that, according to the ethical relativist, what is thought right in any social group is right for that group, one must be careful not to misinterpret this. The relativist does not, of course, mean that there actually is an objective moral standard in France and a different objective standard in England, and that French and British opinions respectively give us correct information about these different standards. His point is rather that there are no objectively true moral standards at all. There is no single universal objective standard. Nor are there a variety of local objective standards. All standards are subjective. People's subjective feelings about morality are the only standards which exist. . . .

THE CASE AGAINST ETHICAL RELATIVISM

First of all, then, ethical relativity, in asserting that the moral standards of particular social groups are the only standards which exist, renders meaningless all propositions which attempt to compare these standards with one another in respect of their moral worth. And this is a very serious matter indeed. We are accustomed to think that the moral ideas of one nation or social group may be "higher" or "lower" than those of another. We believe, for example, that Christian ethical ideals are nobler than those of the savage races of central Africa. Probably most of us would think that the Chinese moral standards are higher than those of the inhabitants of New

Guinea. In short we habitually compare one civilization with another and judge the sets of ethical ideas to be found in them to be some better, some worse. The fact that such judgments are very difficult to make with any justice, and that they are frequently made on very superficial and prejudiced grounds, has no bearing on the question now at issue. The question is whether such judgments have any *meaning*. We habitually assume that they have.

But on the basis of ethical relativity they can have none whatever. For the relativist must hold that there is no *common* standard which can be applied to the various civilizations judged. Any such comparison of moral standards implies the existence of some superior standard which is applicable to both. And the existence of any such standard is precisely what the relativist denies. According to him the Christian standard is applicable only to Christians, the Chinese standard only to Chinese, the New Guinea standard only to the inhabitants of New Guinea.

What is true of comparisons between the moral standards of different races will also be true of comparisons between those of different ages. It is not unusual to ask such questions as whether the standard of our own day is superior to that which existed among our ancestors five hundred years ago. And when we remember that our ancestors employed slaves, practiced barbaric physical tortures, and burnt people alive, we may be inclined to think that it is. At any rate we assume that the question is one which has meaning and is capable of rational discussion. But if the ethical relativist is right, whatever we assert on this subject must be totally meaningless. For here again there is no common standard which could form the basis of any such judgments. . . .

Thus the ethical relativist must treat all judgments comparing different moralities as either entirely meaningless; or, if this course appears too drastic, he has the alternative of declaring that they have for their meaning-content nothing except the vanity and egotism of those who pass them. We are asked to believe that the highest moral ideals of humanity are not really any better than those of an Australian bushman. But if this is so, why strive for higher ideals? Thus the heart is taken out of all effort, and the meaning out of all human ideals and aspirations.

The ethical relativist may perhaps say that he is being misjudged. It is not true that, on the basis of his doctrine, all effort for moral improvement is vain. For if we take such a civilization as our own, and if we assume that the standard of morals theoretically accepted by it is that of Christian ethics, then there is surely plenty of room for improvement and "progress" in the way of making our practice accord with our theory. Effort may legitimately be directed towards getting people to live up to whatever standards they profess to honour. Such effort will be, on the relativistic basis, perfectly meaningful;

for it does not imply a comparison of standards by reference to a common standard, but only a comparison of actual achievements with an admitted and accepted standard within a social group.

Now I do not believe that even this plea can be accepted. For as soon as it comes to be effectively realized that our moral standard is no better than that of barbarians, why should anyone trouble to live up to it? It would be much easier to adopt some lower standard, to preach it assiduously until everyone believes it, when it would automatically become right. But even if we waive this point, and admit that the exhortation to practice what we preach may be meaningful, this does not touch the issue which was raised above. It will still be true that efforts to improve moral *beliefs*, as distinguished from moral *practice*, will be futile. It will still be true that Jesus Christ would have done better had he tried only to persuade humanity to live up to the old barbaric standards than he did in trying to propagate among them a new and more enlightened moral code. It will still be true that any reformer in the future who attempts to make men see even more noble ideals than those which we have inherited from the reformers of the past will be wasting his time.

I come now to a second point. Up to the present I have allowed it to be taken tacitly for granted that, though judgments comparing different races and ages in respect of the worth of their moral codes are impossible for the ethical relativist, yet judgments of comparison between individuals living within the same social group would be quite possible. For individuals living within the same social group would presumably be subject to the same moral code, that of their group, and this would therefore constitute, as between these individuals, a common standard by which they could both be measured. We have not here, as we had in the other case, the difficulty of the absence of any common standard of comparison. It should therefore be possible for the ethical relativist to say quite meaningfully that President Lincoln was a better man than some criminal or moral imbecile of his own time and country, or that Jesus was a better man than Judas Iscariot.

But is even this minimum of moral judgment really possible on relativist grounds? It seems to me that it is not. For when once the whole of humanity is abandoned as the area covered by a single moral standard, what smaller areas are to be adopted as the *loci* of different standards? Where are we to draw the lines of demarcation? We can split up humanity, perhaps, —though the procedure will be very arbitrary—into races, races into nations, nations into tribes, tribes into families, families into individuals. . . .

If these arguments are valid, the ethical relativist cannot really maintain that there is anywhere to be found a moral standard binding upon anybody against his will. And he cannot maintain that, even within the social group, there is a common standard as between individuals. And if that is so, then even judgments to the effect that one man is morally better than another become meaningless. All moral valuation thus vanishes. There is nothing to prevent each man from being a rule unto himself. The result will be moral chaos and the collapse of all effective standards. . . .

Finally, not only is ethical relativity disastrous in its consequences for moral theory. It cannot be doubted that it must tend to be equally disastrous in its impact upon practical conduct. If men come really to believe that one moral standard is as good as another, they will conclude that their own moral standard has nothing special to recommend it. They might as well then slip down to some lower and easier standard. It is true that, for a time, it may be possible to hold one view in theory and to act practically upon another. But ideas, even philosophical ideas, are not so ineffectual that they can remain for ever idle in the upper chambers of the intellect. In the end they seep down to the level of practice. They get themselves acted on.

Speaking of the supposedly dangerous character of ethical relativity Westermarck says "Ethical subjectivism instead of being a danger is more likely to be an advantage to morality. Could it be brought home to people that there is no absolute standard in morality, they would perhaps be on the one hand more tolerant, and on the other hand more critical in their judgments." Certainly, if we believe that any one moral standard is as good as any other, we *are* likely to be more tolerant. We shall tolerate widow-burning, human sacrifice, cannibalism, slavery, the infliction of physical torture, or any other of the thousand and one abominations which are, or have been, from time to time approved by one moral code or another. But this is not the kind of toleration that we want, and I do not think its cultivation will prove "an advantage to morality."

These, then, are the main arguments which the antirelativist will urge against ethical relativity. And perhaps finally he will attempt a diagnosis of the social, intellectual, and psychological conditions of our time to which the emergence of ethical relativism is to be attributed. His diagnosis will be somewhat as follows.

We have abandoned, perhaps with good reason, the oracles of the past. Every age, of course, does this. But in our case it seems that none of us knows any more whither to turn. We do not know what to put in the place of that which has gone. What ought we, supposedly civilized peoples, to aim at? What are to be our ideals? What is right? What is wrong? What is beautiful? What is ugly? No man knows. We drift helplessly in this direction and that. We know not where we stand nor whither we are going.

There are, of course, thousands of voices frantically shouting directions. But they shout one another down, they contradict one another, and the upshot is mere uproar. And because of this confusion there creeps upon us an insidious scepticism and despair. Since no one knows what the truth is, we will deny that there is any truth. Since no one knows what right is, we will deny that there is any right. Since no one knows what the beautiful is, we will deny that there is any beauty. Or at least we will say—what comes to the same thing—that what people (the people of any particular age, region, society) think to be true is true *for them*; that what people think morally right is morally right *for them*; that what people think beautiful is beautiful *for them*. There is no common and objective standard in any of these matters. Since all the voices contradict one another, they must be all equally right (or equally wrong, for it makes no difference which we say). It is from the practical confusion of our time that these doctrines issue. When all the despair and defeatism of our distracted age are expressed in abstract concepts, are erected into a philosophy, it is then called relativism—ethical relativism, esthetic relativism, relativity of truth. Ethical relativity is simply defeatism in morals.

And the diagnosis will proceed. Perhaps, it will say, the current pessimism as to our future is unjustified. But there is undoubtedly a wide spread feeling that our civilization is rushing downwards to the abyss. If this should be true, and if nothing should check the headlong descent, then perhaps some historian of the future will seek to disentangle the causes. The causes will, of course, be found to be multitudinous and enormously complicated. And one must not exaggerate the relative importance of any of them. But it can hardly be doubted that our future historian will include somewhere in his list the failure of the men of our generation to hold steadfastly before themselves the notion of an (even comparatively) unchanging moral idea. He will cite that feebleness of intellectual and moral grasp which has led them weakly to harbour the belief that no one moral aim is really any better than any other, that each is good and true for those who entertain it. This meant, he will surely say, that men had given up in despair the struggle to attain moral truth. Civilization lives in and through its upward struggle. Whoever despairs and gives up the struggle, whether it be an individual or a whole civilization, is already inwardly dead.

And the philosophers of our age, where have they stood? They too, as is notorious, speak with many voices. But those who preach the various relativisms have taken upon themselves a heavy load of responsibility. By formulating abstractly the defeatism of the age they have made themselves the aiders and abettors of death. They are injecting poison into the veins of civilization. Their influence upon practical affairs may indeed be small. But it counts for something. And they cannot avoid their share of the general responsibility. They have failed to do what little they could to stem the tide. They have failed to do what Plato did for the men of his own age— find a way out of at least the intellectual confusions of the time. . . .

The story of Gyges is from the opening pages of Book II of The Republic, *the most reknowned of the* Dialogues of Plato *(see biographical note on p. 90). The speaker is the young and audacious Glaucon, who was one of Plato's older brothers, and he is addressing the problem to Socrates.*

Now that those who practise justice do so involuntarily and because they have not the power to be unjust will best appear if we imagine something of this kind: having given both to the just and the unjust power to do what they will, let us watch and see whither desire will lead them; then we shall discover in the very act the just and unjust man to be proceeding along the same road, following their interest, which all natures deem to be their good, and are only diverted into the path of justice by the force of law. The liberty which we are supposing may be most completely given to them in the form of such a power as is said to have been possessed by Gyges, the ancestor of Croesus the Lydian. According to the tradition, Gyges was a shepherd in the service of the king of Lydia; there was a great storm, and an earthquake made an opening in the earth at the place where he was feeding his flock. Amazed at the sight, he descended into the opening, where, among other marvels, he beheld a hollow brazen horse, having doors, at which he stooping and looking in saw a dead body of stature, as appeared to him, more than human, and having nothing on but a gold ring; this he took from the finger of the dead and reascended. Now the shepherds met together, according to custom, that they might send their monthly report about the flocks to the king; into their assembly he came having the ring on his finger, and as he was sitting among them he chanced to turn the collet of the ring inside his hand, when instantly he became invisible to the rest of the company and they began to speak of him as if he were no longer present. He was astonished at this, and again touching the ring he turned the collet outwards and reappeared; he made several trials of the ring, and always with the same result —when he turned the collet inwards he became invisible, when outwards he reappeared. Whereupon he contrived to be chosen one of the messengers who were sent to the court; where as soon as he arrived he seduced the queen, and with her help conspired against the king and slew him, and took the kingdom. Suppose now that there were two such magic rings, and the just put on one of them and the unjust the other; no man can be imagined to be of such an iron nature that he would stand fast in justice. No man would keep his hands off what was not his own when he could safely take what he liked out of the market, or go into houses and lie with any one at his pleasure, or kill or release from prison whom he would, and in all respects be like a god among men. Then the actions of the just would be as the actions of the unjust; they would both come at last to the same point. And this we may truly affirm to be a great proof that a man is just, not willingly or because he thinks that justice is any good to him individually, but of necessity, for wherever any one thinks that he can safely be unjust, there he is unjust. For all men believe in their hearts that injustice is far more profitable to the individual than justice, and he who argues as I have been supposing, will say that they are right. If you could imagine any one obtaining this power of becoming invisible, and never doing any wrong or touching what was another's, he would be thought by the lookers-on to be a most wretched idiot, although they would praise him to one another's faces, and keep up appearances with one another from a fear that they too might suffer injustice.

WHY SHOULD WE BE MORAL?

Kurt Baier (1917–   ) was born in Austria and holds degrees from the University of Vienna, the University of Melbourne, and Oxford University. He has taught at the University of Melbourne and Canberra University College, and was President of the Australian Association of Philosophy. Since 1962 he has been at the University of Pittsburgh. In addition to his many journal articles, he edited (with Nicholas Rescher) Values and the Future. *In the essay which follows, from* The Moral Point of View *(Abridged Edition, 1965), Baier raises one of the most basic questions in ethics. In his own words, "Should anyone do what is right when doing so is not to his advantage, and if so why?"*

SELF-INTEREST AS THE POINT OF VIEW OF MORALITY

Throughout the history of philosophy, by far the most popular candidate for the position of the moral point of view has been self-interest. There are obvious parallels between these two standpoints. Both aim at the good. Both are rational. Both involve deliberation, the surveying and weighing of reasons. The adoption of either yields statements containing the word 'ought.' Both involve the notion of self-mastery and control over the desires. It is, moreover, plausible to hold that a person could not have a reason for doing anything whatsoever unless his behavior was designed to promote his own good. Hence, if morality is to have the support of reason, moral reasons must be self-interested, hence the point of view of morality and self-interest must be the same. On the other hand, it seems equally obvious that morality and self-interest are very frequently opposed. Morality often requires us to refrain from doing what self-interest recommends or to do what self-interest forbids. Hence it seems that morality and self-interest cannot be the same points of view.

Can we save the doctrine that the moral point of view is that of self-interest? One way of circumventing the difficulty just mentioned is to draw a distinction between two senses of 'self-interest,' shortsighted and enlightened. The shortsighted egoist always follows his short-range interest without taking into consideration how this will affect others and how their reactions will affect him. The enlightened egoist, on the other hand, knows that he cannot get the most out of life unless he pays attention to the needs of others on whose good will he depends. On this view, the standpoint of (immoral) egoism differs from that of morality in that it fails to consider the interests of others even when the long-range benefits to oneself are likely to be greater than the short-range sacrifices.

252

This view can be made more plausible still if we distinguish between those egoists who consider each course of action on its own merits and those who, for convenience, adopt certain rules of thumb which they have found will promote their long-range interest. Slogans such as 'Honesty is the best policy,' 'Give to charity rather than to the Department of Internal Revenue,' 'Always give a penny to a beggar when you are likely to be watched by your acquaintances,' 'Treat your servants kindly and they will work for you like slaves,' 'Never be arrogant to anyone—you may need his services one day,' are maxims of this sort. They embody the "wisdom" of a given society. The enlightened long-range egoist may adopt these as rules of thumb, that is, as *prima-facie* maxims, as rules which he will observe unless he has good evidence that departing from them will pay him better than abiding by them. It is obvious that the rules of behavior adopted by the enlightened egoist will be very similar to those of a man who rigidly follows our own moral code.

Moreover, this sort of egoism does not appear to be contrary to reason but, rather, to be required by it. For in the first place, the consistent enlightened egoist satisfies the categorical imperative, or at least one version of it, 'Act only on that maxim whereby thou canst at the same time will that it should become a universal law.' And in the second place, it seems to be superior to other forms of reasoning. For, as Sidgwick puts it, "I quite admit that when the painful necessity comes for another man to choose between his own happiness and the general happiness, he must as a reasonable being prefer his own, i.e. it is right for him to do this on my principle."

Nevertheless it can be shown that this is not the point of view of morality. For those who adopt consistent egoism cannot make moral judgments. Moral talk is impossible for consistent egoists. But this amounts to a reductio ad absurdum of consistent egoism.

Let B and K be candidates for the presidency of a certain country and let it be granted that it is in the interest of either to be elected, but that only one can succeed. It would then be in the interest of B but against the interest of K if B were elected, and vice versa, and therefore in the interest of B but against the interest of K if K were liquidated, and vice versa. But from this it would follow that B ought to liquidate K, that it is wrong for B not to do so, that B has not "done his duty" until he has liquidated K; and vice versa. Similarly K, knowing that his own liquidation is in the interest of B and therefore anticipating B's attempts to secure it, ought to take steps to foil B's endeavors. It would be wrong for him not to do so. He would "not have done his duty" until he had made sure of stopping B. It follows that if K prevents B from liquidating him, his act must be said to be both wrong and not wrong—wrong because it is the prevention of what B ought to do, his duty, and wrong for B not to do it; not wrong because it is what K ought to do, his duty, and wrong for K not to do it. But one and the same act (logically) cannot be both morally wrong and not morally wrong. Hence in cases like these no moral judgments apply.

This is obviously absurd. For morality is designed to apply in just such cases, namely, those where interests conflict. But if the point of view of morality were that of self-interest, then there could *never* be moral solutions of conflicts of interest. However, when there are conflicts of interest, we always look for a "higher" point of view, one from which such conflicts can be settled. Consistent egoism makes everyone's private interest the "highest court of appeal." But by 'the moral point of view' we *mean* a point of view which furnishes a court of arbitration for conflicts of interest. Hence it cannot (logically) be identical with the point of view of the interest of any particular person or group of persons. . . .

THE HIERARCHY OF REASONS

How can we establish rules of superiority? It is a prima-facie reason for me to do something not only that *I* would enjoy it if *I* did it, but also that *you* would enjoy it if *I* did it. People generally would fare better if this fact were treated as a pro, for if this reason were followed, it would create additional enjoyment all round. But which of the two prima-facie reasons is superior when they conflict? How would we tell?

At first sight it would seem that these reasons are equally good, that there is nothing to choose between them, that no case can be made out for saying that people generally would fare better if the one or the other were treated as superior. But this is a mistake.

Suppose I could be spending half an hour in writing a letter to Aunt Agatha who would enjoy receiving one though I would not enjoy writing it, or alternatively in listening to a lecture which I would enjoy doing. Let us also assume that I cannot do both, that I neither enjoy writing the letter nor dislike it, that Aunt Agatha enjoys receiving the letter as much as I enjoy listening to the lecture, and that there are no extraneous considerations such as that I deserve especially to enjoy myself there and then, or that Aunt Agatha does, or that she has special claims on me, or that I have special responsibilities or obligations to please her.

In order to see which is the better of these two reasons, we must draw a distinction between two different cases: the case in which someone derives pleasure from giving pleasure to others and the case where he does not. Everyone is so related to certain other persons that he derives greater pleasure from doing something together with them than doing it alone because in doing so he is giving them pleasure. He derives pleasure not merely from the game of tennis he is playing but from the fact that in playing he is pleasing his partner. We all enjoy pleasing those we love. Many of us enjoy pleasing

254

even strangers. Some even enjoy pleasing their enemies. Others get very little enjoyment from pleasing anybody.

We must therefore distinguish between people with two kinds of natural make-up: on the one hand, those who need not always choose between pleasing themselves and pleasing others, who can please themselves *by* pleasing others, who can please themselves more by not merely pleasing themselves, and, on the other hand, those who always or often have to choose between pleasing themselves and pleasing others, who derive no pleasure from pleasing others, who do not please themselves more by pleasing not merely themselves.

If I belong to the first kind, then I shall derive pleasure from pleasing Aunt Agatha. Although writing her a letter is not enjoyable in itself, as listening to the lecture is, I nevertheless derive enjoyment from writing it because it is a way of pleasing her and I enjoy pleasing people. In choosing between writing the letter and listening to the lecture, I do not therefore have to choose between pleasing her and pleasing myself. I have merely to choose between two different ways of pleasing myself. If I am a man of the second kind, then I must choose between pleasing myself and pleasing her. When we have eliminated all possible moral reasons, such as standing in a special relationship to the person, then it would be strange for someone to prefer pleasing someone else to pleasing himself. How strange this is can be seen if we substitute for Aunt Agatha a complete stranger.

I conclude from this that the fact that I would enjoy it if *I* did x is a better reason for doing x than the fact that you would enjoy it if *I* did x. Similarly in the fact that I would enjoy doing x if I did it I have a reason for doing x which is better than the reason for doing y which I have in the fact that you would enjoy doing y as much as I would enjoy doing x. More generally speaking, we can say that self-regarding reasons are better than other-regarding ones. Rationally speaking, the old quip is true that everyone is his own nearest neighbor.

This is more obvious still when we consider the case of self-interest. Both the fact that doing x would be in my interest and the fact that it would be in someone else's interest are excellent prima-facie reasons for me to do x. But the self-interested reason is better than the altruistic one. Of course, interests need not conflict, and then I need not choose. I can do what is in both our interests. But sometimes interests conflict, and then it is in accordance with reason (prima facie) to prefer my own interest to someone else's. That my making an application for a job is in *my* interest is a reason for me to apply, which is better than the reason against applying, which I have in the fact that my not applying is in *your* interest.

There is no doubt that this conviction is correct for all cases. It is obviously better that everyone should look after his own interest than that everyone should neglect it in favor of someone else's. For whose interest should have precedence? It must be remembered that we are considering a case in which there are no special reasons for preferring a particular person's interests to one's own, as when there are no special moral obligations or emotional ties. Surely, in the absence of any *special* reasons for preferring someone else's interests, *everyone*'s interests are best served if *everyone* puts his own interests first. For, by and large, everyone is himself the best judge of what is in his own best interest, since everyone usually knows best what his plans, aims, ambitions, or aspirations are. Moreover, everyone is more diligent in the promotion of his own interests than that of others. Enlightened egoism is a possible, rational, orderly system of running things, enlightened altruism is not. Everyone can look after himself, no one can look after everyone else. Even if everyone had to look after only two others, he could not do it as well as looking after himself alone. And if he has to look after only one person, there is no advantage in making that person some one other than himself. On the contrary, he is less likely to know as well what that person's interest is or to be as zealous in its promotion as in that of his own interest.

For this reason, it has often been thought that enlightened egoism is a possible rational way of running things. Sidgwick, for instance, says that the principle of egoism, to have as one's ultimate aim one's own greatest happiness, and the principle of universal benevolence, to have as one's ultimate aim the greatest happiness of the greatest number, are equally rational. Sidgwick then goes on to say that these two principles may conflict and anyone who admits the rationality of both may go on to maintain that it is rational not to abandon the aim of one's own greatest happiness. On his view, there is a fundamental and ultimate contradiction in our apparent intuitions of what is reasonable in conduct. He argues that this can be removed only by the assumption that the individual's greatest happiness and the greatest happiness of the greatest number are both achieved by the rewarding and punishing activity of a perfect being whose sanctions would suffice to make it always everyone's interest to promote universal happiness to the best of his knowledge.

The difficulty which Sidgwick here finds is due to the fact that he regards reasons of self-interest as being no stronger and no weaker than moral reasons. This, however, is not in accordance with our ordinary convictions. It is generally believed that when reasons of self-interest conflict with moral reasons, then moral reasons override those of self-interest. It is our common conviction that moral reasons are superior to all others. Sidgwick has simply overlooked that although it is prima facie in accordance with reason to follow reasons of self-interest and also to follow moral reasons nevertheless, when there is a conflict between these two types of reason, when we have a self-interested reason for doing something and a moral reason against doing it, there need not be an ultimate and fundamental contradiction in what it is in accordance with reason to do. For one type of reason may be *stronger* or *better* than another so that, when two reasons of different types are in conflict, it is in accordance with reason to follow the stronger, contrary to reason to follow the weaker.

THE SUPREMACY OF MORAL REASONS

Are moral reasons really superior to reasons of self-interest as we all believe? Do we really have reason on our side when we follow moral reasons against self-interest? What reasons could there be for being moral? Can we really give an answer to 'Why should we be moral?' It is obvious that all these questions come to the same thing. When we ask, 'Should we be moral?' or 'Why should we be moral?' or 'Are moral reasons superior to all others?' we ask to be given a reason for regarding moral reasons as superior to all others. What is this reason?

Let us begin with a state of affairs in which reasons of self-interest are supreme. In such a state everyone keeps his impulses and inclinations in check when and only when they would lead him into behavior detrimental to his own interest. Everyone who follows reason will discipline himself to rise early, to do his exercises, to refrain from excessive drinking and smoking, to keep good company, to marry the right sort of girl, to work and study hard in order to get on, and so on. However, it will often happen that people's interests conflict. In such a case, they will have to resort to ruses or force to get their own way. As this becomes known, men will become suspicious, for they will regard one another as scheming competitors for the good things in life. The universal supremacy of the rules of self-interest must lead to what Hobbes called the state of nature. At the same time, it will be clear to everyone that universal obedience to certain rules overriding self-interest would produce a state of affairs which serves everyone's interest much better than his unaided pursuit of it in a state where everyone does the same. Moral rules are universal rules designed to override those of self-interest when following the latter is harmful to others. 'Thou shalt not kill,' 'Thou shalt not lie,' 'Thou shalt not steal' are rules which forbid the inflicting of harm on someone else even when this might be in one's interest.

The very *raison d'être* of a morality is to yield reasons which overrule the reasons of self-interest in those cases when everyone's following self-interest would be harmful to everyone. Hence moral reasons are superior to all others.

"But what does this mean?" it might be objected. "If it merely means that we do so regard them, then you are of course right, but your contention is useless, a mere point of usage. And how could it mean any more? If it

257

means that we not only do so regard them, but *ought* so to regard them, then there must be *reasons* for saying this. But there could not be any reasons for it. If you offer reasons of self-interest, you are arguing in a circle. Moreover, it cannot be true that it is always in my interest to treat moral reasons as superior to reasons of self-interest. If it were, self-interest and morality could never conflict, but they notoriously do. It is equally circular to argue that there are moral reasons for saying that one ought to treat moral reasons as superior to reasons of self-interest. And what other reasons are there?"

The answer is that we are now looking at the world from the point of view of *anyone*. We are not examining particular alternative courses of action before this or that person; we are examining two alternative worlds, one in which moral reasons are always treated by everyone as superior to reasons of self-interest and one in which the reverse is the practice. And we can see that the first world is the better world, because we can see that the second world would be the sort which Hobbes describes as the state of nature.

This shows that I ought to be moral, for when I ask the question 'What ought I to do?' I am asking, 'Which is the course of action supported by the best reasons?' But since it has just been shown that moral reasons are superior to reasons of self-interest, I have been given a reason for being moral, for following moral reasons rather than any other, namely, they are better reasons than any other.

But is this always so? Do we have a reason for being moral whatever the conditions we find ourselves in? Could there not be situations in which it is not true that we have reasons for being moral, that, on the contrary, we have reasons for ignoring the demands of morality? Is not Hobbes right in saying that in a state of nature the laws of nature, that is, the rules of morality, bind only *in foro interno*?[1]

Hobbes argues as follows.

(i) To live in a state of nature is to live outside society. It is to live in conditions in which there are no common ways of life and, therefore, no reliable expectations about other people's behavior other than that they will follow their inclination or their interest.

(ii) In such a state reason will be the enemy of co-operation and mutual trust. For it is too risky to hope that other people will refrain from protecting their own interests by the preventive elimination of probable or even possible dangers to them. Hence reason will counsel everyone to avoid these risks by preventive action. But this leads to war.

(iii) It is obvious that everyone's following self-interest leads to a state of

---

[1] "in the realm of conscience"

affairs which is desirable from no one's point of view. It is, on the contrary, desirable that everybody should follow rules overriding self-interest whenever that is to the detriment of others. In other words, it is desirable to bring about a state of affairs in which all obey the rules of morality.

(iv) However, Hobbes claims that in the state of nature it helps nobody if a single person or a small group of persons begins to follow the rules of morality, for this could only lead to the extinction of such individuals or groups. In such a state, it is therefore contrary to reason to be moral.

(v) The situation can change, reason can support morality, only when the presumption about other people's behavior is reversed. Hobbes thought that this could be achieved only by the creation of an absolute ruler with absolute power to enforce his laws. We have already seen that this is not true and that it can also be achieved if people live in a society, that is, if they have common ways of life, which are taught to all members and somehow enforced by the group. Its members have reason to expect their fellows generally to obey its rules, that is, its religion, morality, customs, and law, even when doing so is not, on certain occasions, in their interest. Hence they too have reason to follow these rules.

Is this argument sound? One might, of course, object to step (i) on the grounds that this is an empirical proposition for which there is little or no evidence. For how can we know whether it is true that people in a state of nature would follow only their inclinations or, at best, reasons of self-interest, when nobody now lives in that state or has ever lived in it?

However, there is some empirical evidence to support this claim. For in the family of nations, individual states are placed very much like individual persons in a state of nature. The doctrine of the sovereignty of nations and the absence of an effective international law and police force are a guarantee that nations live in a state of nature, without commonly accepted rules that are somehow enforced. Hence it must be granted that living in a state of nature leads to living in a state in which individuals act either on impulse or as they think their interest dictates. For states pay only lip service to morality. They attack their hated neighbors when the opportunity arises. They start preventive wars in order to destroy the enemy before he can deliver his knockout blow. Where interests conflict, the stronger party usually has his way, whether his claims are justified or not. And where the relative strength of the parties is not obvious, they usually resort to arms in order to determine "whose side God is on." Treaties are frequently concluded but, morally speaking, they are not worth the paper they are written on. Nor do the partners regard them as contracts binding in the ordinary way, but rather as public expressions of the belief of the governments concerned that for the time being their alliance is in the interest of the allies. It is well understood that such treaties may be canceled before they reach their predetermined end or simply broken when it suits one partner. In international affairs, there are very few examples of *Nibelungentreue*,[2] although statesmen whose countries have kept their treaties in the hope of profiting from them usually make such high moral claims.

It is, moreover, difficult to justify morality in international affairs. For suppose a highly moral statesman were to demand that his country adhere to a treaty obligation even though this meant its ruin or possibly its extinction. Suppose he were to say that treaty obligations are sacred and must be kept whatever the consequences. How could he defend such a policy? Perhaps one might argue that someone has to make a start in order to create mutual confidence in international affairs. Or one might say that setting a good example is the best way of inducing others to follow suit. But such a defense would hardly be sound. The less skeptical one is about the genuineness of the cases in which nations have adhered to their treaties from a sense of moral obligation, the more skeptical one must be about the effectiveness of such examples of virtue in effecting a change of international practice. Power politics still govern in international affairs.

We must, therefore, grant Hobbes the first step in his argument and admit that in a state of nature people, as a matter of psychological fact, would not follow the dictates of morality. But we might object to the next step that knowing this psychological fact about other people's behavior constitutes a reason for behaving in the same way. Would it not still be immoral for anyone to ignore the demands of morality even though he knows that others are likely or certain to do so, too? Can we offer as a justification for morality the fact that no one is entitled to do wrong just because someone else is doing wrong? This argument begs the question whether it *is* wrong for anyone in this state to disregard the demands of morality. It cannot be wrong to break a treaty or make preventive war if we have no reason to obey the moral rules. For to say that it is wrong to do so is to say that we ought not to do so. But if we have no reason for obeying the moral rule, then we have no reason overruling self-interest, hence no reason for keeping the treaty when keeping it is not in our interest, hence it is not true that we have a reason for keeping it, hence not true that we ought to keep it, hence not true that it is wrong not to keep it.

I conclude that Hobbes's argument is sound. Moralities are systems of principles whose acceptance by everyone as overruling the dictates of self-interest is in the interest of everyone alike, though following the rules of a morality is not of course identical with following self-interest. If it were, there could be no conflict between a morality and self-interest and no point in having moral rules overriding self-interest. Hobbes is also right in saying

---

[2] "extreme loyalty"

that the application of this system of rules is in accordance with reason only under social conditions, that is, when there are well-established ways of behavior.

The answer to our question 'Why should we be moral?' is therefore as follows. We should be moral because being moral is following rules designed to overrule reasons of self-interest whenever it is in the interest of everyone alike that such rules should be generally followed. This will be the case when the needs and wants and aspirations of individual agents conflict with one another and when, in the absence of such overriding rules, the pursuit of their ends by all concerned would lead to the attempt to eliminate those who are in the way. Since such rules will always require one of the rivals to abandon his pursuit in favor of the other, they will tend to be broken. Since, ex hypothesi it is in everyone's interest that they should be followed, it will be in everyone's interest that they should not only be taught as "superior to" other reasons but also adequately enforced, in order to reduce the temptation to break them. A person instructed in these rules can acknowledge that such reasons are superior to reasons of self-interest without having to admit that he is always or indeed ever attracted or moved by them.

But is it not self-contradictory to say that it is in a person's interest to do what is contrary to his interest? It certainly would be if the two expressions were used in exactly the same way. But they are not. We have already seen that an enlightened egoist can acknowledge that a certain course of action is in his enlightened long-term, but contrary to his narrow short-term interest. He can infer that it is "in his interest" and according to reason to follow enlightened long-term interest, and "against his interest" and contrary to reason to follow short-term interest. Clearly, "in his interest" and "against his interest" here are used in new ways. For suppose it is discovered that the probable long-rang consequences and psychological effects on others do not work out as predicted. Even so we need not admit that, in this new and extended sense, the line of action followed merely seemed but really was not in his interest. For we are now considering not merely a single action but a policy.

All the same, we must not make too much of this analogy. There is an all-important difference between the two cases. The calculations of the enlightened egoist properly allow for "exceptions in the agent's favor." After all, his calculus is designed to promote his interest. If he has information to show that in his particular circumstances it would pay to depart from a well-established general canon of enlightened self-interest, then it is proper for him to depart from it. It would not be a sign of the enlightened self-interest of a building contractor, let us say, if he made sacrifices for certain subcontractors even though he knew that they would or could not reciprocate, as subcontractors normally do. By contrast, such information is simply irrelevant in cases where moral reasons apply. Moral rules are not designed to serve the agent's interest directly. Hence it would be quite inappropriate for him to break them whenever he discovers that they do not serve his interest. They are designed to adjudicate primarily in cases where there is a conflict of interests so that from their very nature they are bound to be contrary to the interest of one of the persons affected. However, they are also bound to serve the interest of the other person, hence his interest in the other's observing them. It is on the assumption of the likelihood of a reversal of roles that the universal observation of the rule will serve everyone's interest. The principle of justice and other principles which we employ in improving the moral rules of a given society help to bring existing moralities closer to the ideal which is in the interest of everyone alike. Thus, just as following the canons of enlightened self-interest is in one's interest only if the assumptions underlying it are correct, so following the rules of morality is in everyone's interest only if the assumptions underlying it are correct, that is, if the moral rules come close to being true and are generally observed. Even then, to say that following them is in the interest of everyone alike means only that it is better for everyone that there should be a morality generally observed than that the principle of self-interest should be acknowledged as supreme. It does not of course mean that a person will not do better for himself by following self-interest than by doing what is morally right, when others are doing what is right. But of course such a person cannot *claim* that he is following a superior reason.

It must be added to this, however, that such a system of rules has the support of reason only where people live in societies, that is, in conditions in which there are established common ways of behavior. Outside society, people have no reason for following such rules, that is, for being moral. In other words, outside society, the very distinction between right and wrong vanishes.

FURTHER READING

"Moral philosophy arises when, like Socrates, we pass beyond the stage in which we are directed by traditional rules," says William K. Frankena, and his brief *Ethics* (1963) is a helpful map of the area.

Another quite brief introductory textbook, a reader in this case, is Mary Mothersill's *Ethics* (1965); it would be a fine companion volume to the Frankena book.

Alburey Castell's *An Elementary Ethics* (1954) is exactly what its title claims: a very basic survey of some main issues and philosophers including Paley, Bentham, Kant, Nietzsche, Dewey, and Ayer.

Three collections of essays grouped around particular moral questions such as suicide, violence, war, extramarital sex, punishment, and civil disobedience, are those edited by Robert N. Beck and John B. Orr, *Ethical Choice* (1970); James Rachels, *Moral Problems* (1971); and Harry K. Girvetz, *Contemporary Moral Issues* (2nd ed., 1968).

Very thorough expositions, with extensive bibliographies, are offered both by Richard B. Brandt in *Ethical Theory: The Problems of Normative and Critical Ethics* (1959) and by John Hospers, *Human Conduct: An Introduction to the Problems of Ethics* (1961).

Five "Syllabi" of the field of ethics—of its history, main types of theory, problems, polarities, and the "Ways of Life"—accompany the large selection of readings edited by W. T. Jones, *et al.*, in *Approaches to Ethics* (1962).

——————————*THE PROBLEM OF EVIL*

7

The problem of evil torments all religions and philosophies but especially those that are theistic. How is the evil in the world to be explained or justified if God is both good and omnipotent? David Hume pointed out that Epicurus' old questions remained: "Is he willing to prevent evil, but not able? then he is impotent. Is he able, but not willing? then he is malevolent. Is he both willing and able? whence then is evil?"

It is a problem that has obstinately stood in the path of believers, and there is no saying how many men have been led to reject belief in God because of it. In the debate over the existence of God, this issue has been one of the most telling arguments of the unbelievers. As old as the idea of God itself, the problem is very much alive today—perhaps even invigorated by the endless and meaningless cruelties of our century.

It is the personal tragedies one encounters that bring the problem of evil closest to us, and this was no doubt the case with Mark Twain. The author of Tom Sawyer must seem an unusual source; his homespun wit and talent for imaginative story-telling overshadowed the serious side of his nature. In the reading selection which follows, Twain's style is still that of the humorist. By interpreting the Bible in the most literal of terms (and by the addition of heretofore unrevealed details about those ancient events), Twain exaggerates for comic effect. But no one will laugh a great deal at this Twain. "Pleasure, Love, Fame, Riches," he wrote elsewhere, "they are but temporary disguises for lasting realities—Pain, Grief, Shame, Poverty." Here Twain claims that if there is a God, He must be a sadist; a world as menacing as ours could have been devised only by an ill-natured and ill-intentioned Being.

Albert Camus' "A Plague Death" relates the lengthy suffering and death-throes of a child. That it is a child dying is significant. It is rather difficult to imagine a child so sinful or crime-ridden that his pain might be deserved, and the death of one so young makes its very existence seem senseless. It might be argued that the child's agony serves a purpose in terms of those who witness it, but would that purpose justify using as a means an innocent being? Again, some will maintain that a future existence will appropriately compensate the child, but can "compensation" rectify what was done to the child? The

266

[The problem of] evil is the school in which we are made to put away the God of childhood.

michael novak

"Dr. Rieux" of the story speaks for Camus when he says, "I shall refuse to love a scheme of things in which children are put to torture."

"Theodicy" is the name given to attempts to vindicate the ways of God to men, and it is the title of an important work by Gottfried Wilhelm Leibniz. A theodicy was especially crucial for Leibniz, for it was he who argued that this is the best of all possible worlds. God's moral perfection could not allow for his creating anything less. Moving on those premises, Leibniz explains that metaphysical evil is mere privation or limitation, which is necessarily an aspect of a finite, created being. Moral evil, sin, is not willed by God, but only permitted. But in all cases, evil is necessary for the realization of ends superior to those that might be realized without the presence of evil.

J. L. Mackie's review of the problem focuses upon its logic, and on those grounds he holds that the theist is in an untenable position. The only adequate solutions to the question involve denying propositions essential to theism, and all other solutions, upon close examination, seem to be fallacious. Mackie's conclusion is that this issue shows the conventional form of belief in God to be "positively irrational."

John Hick also attempts to answer the problem of evil. He makes an important distinction between moral and non-moral evils: the former are attributable to man and the latter are those which occur in the workings of nature. Hick accounts for moral evils by holding them to be the consequence of man's freedom to choose to act wrongly—a solution rejected by Mackie (as Hick is aware). Non-moral evil, generally speaking, is a feature of the world which presents to man the genuine "trials and perils" appropriate to the purpose of "soul-making."

mark twain LETTERS FROM THE EARTH

Samuel Langhorne Clemens (1835–1910) *achieved early fame as a humorist both with his writing and speaking.* The Celebrated Jumping Frog of Calaveras County *was his first book, and* Innocents Abroad *was his bestselling book during his lifetime. For* The Adventures of Tom Sawyer *and* Life on the Mississippi *he drew upon his own boyhood days in Hannibal, Missouri, and his experiences as a riverboat pilot.* Huckleberry Finn *took on larger, epical dimensions, and there are critics who call it the great American novel. Twain named and ridiculed the "Gilded Age" but was himself the victim of an obsession for money; he had in particular a weakness for get-rich-quick schemes. In his later years a crushing bankruptcy and the deaths of two daughters and his wife led him into an increasingly bitter estimation of life. "Every man is a moon, and has a dark side which he never shows to anybody," he wrote. A large number of his writings were unpublished at his death, and his surviving daughter, Clara (who died in 1963), restricted the release of many materials.* Letters from the Earth (1962) *was prepared for publication by Bernard De Voto in 1939.*

SATAN'S LETTER

This is a strange place, an extraordinary place, and interesting. There is nothing resembling it at home. The people are all insane, the other animals are all insane, the earth is insane, Nature itself is insane. Man is a marvelous curiosity. When he is at his very very best he is a sort of low grade nickel-plated angel; at his worst he is unspeakable, unimaginable; and first and last and all the time he is a sarcasm. Yet he blandly and in all sincerity calls himself the "noblest work of God." This is the truth I am telling you. And this is not a new idea with him, he has talked it through all the ages, and believed it. Believed it, and found nobody among all his race to laugh at it.

Moreover—if I may put another strain upon you—he thinks he is the Creator's pet. He believes the Creator is proud of him; he even believes the Creator loves him; has a passion for him; sits up nights to admire him; yes, and watch over him and keep him out of trouble. He prays to Him, and thinks He listens. Isn't it a quaint idea? Fills his prayers with crude and bald and florid flatteries of Him, and thinks He sits and purrs over these extravagancies and enjoys them. He prays for help, and favor, and protection, every day; and does it with hopefulness and confidence, too, although no prayer of his has ever been answered. The daily affront, the daily defeat, do not discourage him, he goes on praying just the same. There is something almost fine about this perseverance. I must put one more strain upon you: he thinks he is going to heaven! . . .

LETTER III

[*Satan describes the contents of the Bible, which "has some noble poetry in it; and some clever fables; and some blood-drenched history; and some good morals; and a wealth of obscenity; and upwards of a thousand lies."*]

He made a man and a woman and placed them in a pleasant garden, along with the other creatures. They all lived together there in harmony and contentment and blooming youth for some time; then trouble came. God had warned the man and the woman that they must not eat of the fruit of a certain tree. And he added a most strange remark: he said that if they ate of it they should surely die. Strange, for the reason that inasmuch as they had never seen a sample of death they could not possibly know what he meant. Neither would he nor any other god have been able to make those ignorant children understand what was meant, without furnishing a sample. The mere word could have no meaning for them, any more than it would have for an infant of days.

Presently a serpent sought them out privately, and came to them walking upright, which was the way of serpents in those days. The serpent said the forbidden fruit would store their vacant minds with knowledge. So they ate it, which was quite natural, for a man is so made that he eagerly wants to know; whereas the priest, like God, whose imitator and representative he is, has made it his business from the beginning to keep him *from* knowing any useful thing.

Adam and Eve ate the forbidden fruit, and at once a great light streamed into their dim heads. They had acquired knowledge. What knowledge—useful knowledge? No—merely knowledge that there was such a thing as good, and such a thing as evil, and how to do evil. They couldn't do it before. Therefore all their acts up to this time had been without stain, without blame, without offense.

But now they could do evil—and suffer for it; now they had acquired what the Church calls an invaluable possession, the Moral Sense; that sense which differentiates man from the beast and sets him above the beast. Instead of below the beast—where one would suppose his proper place would be, since he is always foul-minded and guilty and the beast always clean-minded and innocent. It is like valuing a watch that must go wrong, above a watch that can't.

269

The Church still prizes the Moral Sense as man's noblest asset today, although the Church knows God had a distinctly poor opinion of it and did what he could in his clumsy way to keep his happy Children of the Garden from acquiring it. . . .

To proceed with the Biblical curiosities. Naturally you will think the threat to punish Adam and Eve for disobeying was of course not carried out, since they did not create themselves, nor their natures nor their impulses nor their weaknesses, and hence were not properly subject to anyone's commands, and not responsible to anybody for their acts. It will surprise you to know that the threat *was* carried out. Adam and Eve were punished, and that crime finds apologists unto this day. The sentence of death was executed.

As you perceive, the only person responsible for the couple's offense escaped; and not only escaped but became the executioner of the innocent.

In your country and mine we should have the privilege of making fun of this kind of morality, but it would be unkind to do it here. Many of these people have the reasoning faculty, but no one uses it in religious matters.

The best minds will tell you that when a man has begotten a child he is morally bound to tenderly care for it, protect it from hurt, shield it from disease, clothe it, feed it, bear with its waywardness, lay no hand upon it save in kindness and for its own good, and never in any case inflict upon it a wanton cruelty. God's treatment of his earthly children, every day and every night, is the exact opposite of all that, yet those best minds warmly justify these crimes, condone them, excuse them, and indignantly refuse to regard them as crimes at all, when *he* commits them. Your country and mine is an interesting one, but there is nothing there that is half so interesting as the human mind.

Very well, God banished Adam and Eve from the Garden, and eventually assassinated them. All for disobeying a command which he had no right to utter. But he did not stop there, as you will see. He has one code of morals for himself, and quite another for his children. He requires his children to deal justly—and gently—with offenders, and forgive them seventy-and-seven times; whereas he deals neither justly nor gently with anyone, and he did not forgive the ignorant and thoughtless first pair of juveniles even their first small offense and say, "You may go free this time, I will give you another chance."

On the contrary! He elected to punish *their* children, all through the ages to the end of time, for a trifling offense committed by others before they were born. He is punishing them yet. In mild ways? No, in atrocious ones.

You would not suppose that this kind of a Being gets many compliments. Undeceive yourself: the world calls him the All-Just, the All-Righteous, the All-Good, the All-Merciful, the All-Forgiving, the All-Truthful, the All-Loving, the Source of All Morality. These sarcasms are uttered daily, all over the

270

world. But not as conscious sarcasms. No, they are meant seriously: they are uttered without a smile.

LETTER V

Noah began to collect animals. There was to be one couple of each and every sort of creature that walked or crawled, or swam or flew, in the world of animated nature. We have to guess at how long it took to collect the creatures and how much it cost, for there is no record of these details. When Symmachus made preparation to introduce his young son to grown-up life in imperial Rome, he sent men to Asia, Africa and everywhere to collect wild animals for the arena-fights. It took the men three years to accumulate the animals and fetch them to Rome. Merely quadrupeds and alligators, you understand—no birds, no snakes, no frogs, no worms, no lice, no rats, no fleas, no ticks, no caterpillars, no spiders, no houseflies, no mosquitoes— nothing but just plain simple quadrupeds and alligators: and no quadrupeds except fighting ones. Yet it was as I have said: it took three years to collect them, and the cost of animals and transportation and the men's wages footed up $4,500,000.

How many animals? We do not know. But it was under five thousand, for that was the largest number *ever* gathered for those Roman shows, and it was Titus, not Symmachus, who made that collection. Those were mere baby museums, compared to Noah's contract. Of birds and beasts and fresh-water creatures he had to collect 146,000 kinds; and of insects upwards of two million species.

Thousands and thousands of those things are very difficult to catch, and if Noah had not given up and resigned, he would be on the job yet, as Leviticus used to say. However, I do not mean that he withdrew. No, he did not do that. He gathered as many creatures as he had room for, and then stopped.

If he had known all the requirements in the beginning, he would have been aware that what was needed was a fleet of Arks. But he did not know how many kinds of creatures there were, neither did his Chief. So he had no kangaroo, and no 'possum, and no Gila monster, and no ornithorhynchus, and lacked a multitude of other indispensable blessings which a loving Creator had provided for man and forgotten about, they having long ago wandered to a side of this world which he had never seen and with whose affairs he was not acquainted. And so everyone of them came within a hair of getting drowned.

They only escaped by an accident. There was not water enough to go around. Only enough was provided to flood one small corner of the globe— the rest of the globe was not then known, and was supposed to be nonexistent.

However, the thing that really and finally and definitely determined Noah to stop with enough species for purely business purposes and let the rest become extinct, was an incident of the last days: an excited stranger arrived with some most alarming news. He said he had been camping among some mountains and valleys about six hundred miles away, and he had seen a wonderful thing there: he stood upon a precipice overlooking a wide valley, and up the valley he saw a billowy black sea of strange animal life coming. Presently the creatures passed by, struggling, fighting, scrambling, screeching, snorting—horrible vast masses of tumultuous flesh! Sloths as big as an elephant; frogs as big as a cow; a megatherium and his harem huge beyond belief; saurians and saurians and saurians, group after group, family after family, species after species—a hundred feet long, thirty feet high, and twice as quarrelsome; one of them hit a perfectly blameless Durham bull a thump with its tail and sent it whizzing three hundred feet into the air and it fell at the man's feet with a sigh and was no more. The man said that these prodigious animals had heard about the Ark and were coming. Coming to get saved from the flood. And not coming in pairs, they were *all* coming: they did not know the passengers were restricted to pairs, the man said, and wouldn't care a rap for the regulations, anyway—they would sail in that Ark or know the reason why. The man said the Ark would not hold the half of them; and moreover they were coming hungry, and would eat up everything there was, including the menagerie and the family.

All these facts were suppressed, in the Biblical account. You find not a hint of them there. The whole thing is hushed up. Not even the names of those vast creatures are mentioned. It shows you that when people have left a reproachful vacancy in a contract they can be as shady about it in Bibles as elsewhere. Those powerful animals would be of inestimable value to man now, when transportation is so hard pressed and expensive, but they are all lost to him. All lost, and by Noah's fault. They all got drowned. Some of them as much as eight million years ago.

Very well, the stranger told his tale, and Noah saw that he must get away before the monsters arrived. He would have sailed at once, but the upholsterers and decorators of the housefly's drawing room still had some finishing touches to put on, and that lost him a day. Another day was lost in getting the flies aboard, there being sixty-eight billions of them and the Deity still afraid there might not be enough. Another day was lost in stowing forty tons of selected filth for the flies' sustenance.

Then at last, Noah sailed; and none too soon, for the Ark was only just sinking out of sight on the horizon when the monsters arrived, and added their lamentations to those of the multitude of weeping fathers and mothers and frightened little children who were clinging to the wave-washed rocks in the pouring rain and lifting imploring prayers to an All-Just and All-

Forgiving and All-Pitying Being who had never answered a prayer since those crags were builded, grain by grain out of the sands, and would still not have answered one when the ages should have crumbled them to sand again.

LETTER VI

On the third day, about noon, it was found that a fly had been left behind. The return voyage turned out to be long and difficult, on account of the lack of chart and compass, and because of the changed aspects of all coasts, the steadily rising water having submerged some of the lower landmarks and given to higher ones an unfamiliar look; but after sixteen days of earnest and faithful seeking, the fly was found at last, and received on board with hymns of praise and gratitude, the Family standing meanwhile uncovered, out of reverence for its divine origin. It was weary and worn, and had suffered somewhat from the weather, but was otherwise in good estate. Men and their families had died of hunger on barren mountain tops, but it had not lacked for food, the mulitudinous corpses furnishing it in rank and rotten richness. Thus was the sacred bird providentially preserved.

Providentially. That is the word. For the fly had not been left behind by accident. No, the hand of Providence was in it. There are no accidents. All things that happen, happen for a purpose. They are foreseen from the beginning of time, they are ordained from the beginning of time. From the dawn of Creation the Lord had foreseen that Noah, being alarmed and confused by the invasion of the prodigious brevet fossils, would prematurely fly to sea unprovided with a certain invaluable disease. He would have all the other diseases, and could distribute them among the new races of men as they appeared in the world, but he would lack one of the very best—typhoid fever; a malady which, when the circumstances are especially favorable, is able to utterly wreck a patient without killing him; for it can restore him to his feet with a long life in him, and yet deaf, dumb, blind, crippled, and idiotic. The housefly is its main disseminator, and is more competent and more calamitously effective than all the other distributors of the dreaded scourge put together. And so, by foreordination from the beginning of time, this fly was left behind to seek out a typhoid corpse and feed upon its corruptions and gaum its legs with the germs and transmit them to the repeopled world for permanent business. From that one housefly, in the ages that have since elapsed, billions of sickbeds have been stocked, billions of wrecked bodies sent tottering about the earth, and billions of cemeteries recruited with the dead. . . .

The human being is a machine. An automatic machine. It is composed of thousands of complex and delicate mechanisms, which perform their functions harmoniously and perfectly, in accordance with laws devised for their governance, and over which the man himself has no authority, no mastership, no control. For each one of these thousands of mechanisms the Creator has planned an enemy, whose office is to harass it, pester it, persecute it, damage it, afflict it with pains, and miseries, and ultimate destruction. Not one has been overlooked.

From cradle to grave these enemies are always at work; they know no rest, night or day. They are an army: an organized army; a besieging army; an assaulting army; an army that is alert, watchful, eager, merciless; an army that never relents, never grants a truce.

It moves by squad, by company, by battalion, by regiment, by brigade, by division, by army corps; upon occasion it masses its parts and moves upon mankind with its whole strength. It is the Creator's Grand Army, and he is the Commander-in-Chief. Along its battlefront its grisly banners wave their legends in the face of the sun: Disaster, Disease, and the rest.

Disease! That is the main force, the diligent force, the devastating force! It attacks the infant the moment is is born; it furnishes it one malady after another: croup, measles, mumps, bowel troubles, teething pains, scarlet fever, and other childhood specialties. It chases the child into youth and furnishes it some specialties for that time of life. It chases the youth into maturity, maturity into age, and age into the grave.

With these facts before you will you now try to guess man's chiefest pet name for this ferocious Commander-in-Chief? I will save you the trouble— but you must not laugh. It is Our Father in Heaven!

It is curious—the way the human mind works. The Christian begins with this straight proposition, this definite proposition, this inflexible and uncompromising proposition: *God is all-knowing, and all-powerful.*

This being the case, nothing can happen without his knowing beforehand that it is going to happen; nothing happens without his permission; nothing can happen that he chooses to prevent. . . .

Albert Camus (1913–1960) was a playwright, novelist, short story writer, and essayist whose preoccupations were mainly philosophical. "A novel," he once said, "is never anything but a philosophy put into images." Born in Algiers of a Spanish mother and a French father, Camus received a degree in philosophy from the University of Algiers. His father, whom he had never seen, was killed in World War I. During World War II, Camus wrote editorials for the underground Resistance newspaper Combat *and, wearing various disguises, helped deliver them on a bicycle. In 1957 he received the Nobel prize for literature, the second youngest (after Kipling) to be so honored. In 1960, at the age of only forty-seven, he was killed in an automobile accident. His novels are* The Stranger, The Plague, *and* The Fall. *A notable play is* The Possessed, *based upon Dostoyevsky's novel.* The Myth of Sisyphus *and* The Rebel *are long philosophical essays. "A Plague Death" is a chapter from* The Plague (1948).

Toward the close of October Castel's anti-plague serum was tried for the first time. Practically speaking, it was Rieux's last card. If it failed, the doctor was convinced the whole town would be at the mercy of the epidemic, which would either continue its ravages for an unpredictable period or perhaps die out abruptly of its own accord.

The day before Castel called on Rieux, M. Othon's son had fallen ill and all the family had to go into quarantine. Thus the mother, who had only recently come out of it, found herself isolated once again. In deference to the official regulations the magistrate had promptly sent for Dr. Rieux the moment he saw symptoms of the disease in his little boy. Mother and father were standing at the bedside when Rieux entered the room. The boy was in the phase of extreme prostration and submitted without a whimper to the doctor's examination. When Rieux raised his eyes he saw the magistrate's gaze intent on him, and, behind, the mother's pale face. She was holding a handkerchief to her mouth, and her big, dilated eyes followed each of the doctor's movements.

"He has it, I suppose?" the magistrate asked in a toneless voice.

"Yes." Rieux gazed down at the child again.

The mother's eyes widened yet more, but she still said nothing. M. Othon, too, kept silent for a while before saying in an even lower tone:

"Well, doctor, we must do as we are told to do."

Rieux avoided looking at Mme Othon, who was still holding her handkerchief to her mouth.

"It needn't take long," he said rather awkwardly, "if you'll let me use your phone."

The magistrate said he would take him to the telephone. But before going, the doctor turned toward Mme Othon.

"I regret very much indeed, but I'm afraid you'll have to get your things ready. You know how it is."

Mme Othon seemed disconcerted. She was staring at the floor.

Then, "I understand," she murmured, slowly nodding her head. "I'll set about it at once."

Before leaving, Rieux on a sudden impulse asked the Othons if there wasn't anything they'd like him to do for them. The mother gazed at him in silence. And now the magistrate averted his eyes.

"No," he said, then swallowed hard. "But—save my son."

In the early days a mere formality, quarantine had now been reorganized by Rieux and Rambert on very strict lines. In particular they insisted on having members of the family of a patient kept apart. If, unawares, one of them had been infected, the risks of an extension of the infection must not be multiplied. Rieux explained this to the magistrate, who signified his approval of the procedure. Nevertheless, he and his wife exchanged a glance that made it clear to Rieux how keenly they both felt the separation thus imposed on them. Mme Othon and her little girl could be given rooms in the quarantine hospital under Rambert's charge. For the magistrate, however, no accommodation was available except in an isolation camp the authorities were now installing in the municipal stadium, using tents supplied by the highway department. When Rieux apologized for the poor accommodation, M. Othon replied that there was one rule for all alike, and it was only proper to abide by it.

The boy was taken to the auxiliary hospital and put in a ward of ten beds which had formerly been a classroom. After some twenty hours Rieux became convinced that the case was hopeless. The infection was steadily spreading, and the boy's body putting up no resistance. Tiny, half-formed, but acutely painful buboes were clogging the joints of the child's puny limbs. Obviously it was a losing fight.

Under the circumstances Rieux had no qualms about testing Castel's serum on the boy. That night, after dinner, they performed the inoculation, a lengthy process, without getting the slightest reaction. At daybreak on the following day they gathered round the bed to observe the effects of this test inoculation on which so much hung.

The child had come out of his extreme prostration and was tossing about convulsively on the bed. From four in the morning Dr. Castel and Tarrou had been keeping watch and noting, stage by stage, the progress and remissions of the malady. Tarrou's bulky form was slightly drooping at the head of the bed, while at its foot, with Rieux standing beside him, Castel was seated, reading, with every appearance of calm, an old leather-bound book. One by one, as the light increased in the former classroom, the others arrived. Paneloux, the first to come, leaned against the wall on the opposite side of the bed to Tarrou. His face was drawn with grief, and the accumulated weariness of many weeks, during which he had never spared himself, had deeply seamed his somewhat prominent forehead. Grand came next. It was seven o'clock, and he apologized for being out of breath; he could only stay a moment, but wanted to know if any definite results had been observed. Without speaking, Rieux pointed to the child. His eyes shut, his teeth clenched, his features frozen in an agonized grimace, he was rolling his head from side to side on the bolster. When there was just light enough to make out the half-obliterated figures of an equation chalked on a blackboard that still hung on the wall at the far end of the room, Rambert entered. Posting himself at the foot of the next bed, he took a package of cigarettes from his pocket. But after his first glance at the child's face he put it back.

From his chair Castel looked at Rieux over his spectacles.

"Any news of his father?"

"No," said Rieux. "He's in the isolation camp."

The doctor's hands were gripping the rail of the bed, his eyes fixed on the small tortured body. Suddenly it stiffened, and seemed to give a little at the waist, as slowly the arms and legs spread out X-wise. From the body, naked under an army blanket, rose a smell of damp wool and stale sweat. The boy had gritted his teeth again. Then very gradually he relaxed, bringing his arms and legs back toward the center of the bed, still without speaking or opening his eyes, and his breathing seemed to quicken. Rieux looked at Tarrou, who hastily lowered his eyes.

They had already seen children die—for many months now death had shown no favoritism—but they had never yet watched a child's agony minute by minute, as they had now been doing since daybreak. Needless to say, the pain inflicted on these innocent victims had always seemed to them to be what in fact it was: an abominable thing. But hitherto they had felt its abomination in, so to speak, an abstract way; they had never had to witness over so long a period the death-throes of an innocent child.

And just then the boy had a sudden spasm, as if something had bitten him in the stomach, and uttered a long, shrill wail. For moments that seemed endless he stayed in a queer, contorted position, his body racked by convulsive tremors; it was as if his frail frame were bending before the fierce breath of the plague, breaking under the reiterated gusts of fever. Then the storm-wind passed, there came a lull, and he relaxed a little; the fever seemed to recede, leaving him gasping for breath on a dank, pestilential shore, lost in a languor that already looked like death. When for the third time the fiery wave broke on him, lifting him a little, the child curled himself up and shrank away to the edge of the bed, as if in terror of the flames advancing on him, licking his limbs. A moment later, after tossing his head wildly to and fro, he flung off the blanket. From between the inflamed eyelids big tears welled up and trickled down the sunken, leaden-hued cheeks. When the spasm had passed, utterly exhausted, tensing his thin legs and arms, on which, within forty-eight hours, the flesh had wasted to the bone, the child lay flat, racked on the tumbled bed, in a grotesque parody of crucifixion.

Bending, Tarrou gently stroked with his big paw the small face stained with tears and sweat. Castel had closed his book a few moments before, and his eyes were now fixed on the child. He began to speak, but had to give a cough before continuing, because his voice rang out so harshly.

"There wasn't any remission this morning, was there, Rieux?"

Rieux shook his head, adding, however, that the child was putting up more resistance than one would have expected. Paneloux, who was slumped against the wall, said in a low voice:

"So if he is to die, he will have suffered longer."

Light was increasing in the ward. The occupants of the other nine beds were tossing about and groaning, but in tones that seemed deliberately subdued. Only one, at the far end of the ward, was screaming, or rather uttering little exclamations at regular intervals, which seemed to convey surprise more than pain. Indeed, one had the impression that even for the sufferers the frantic terror of the early phase had passed, and there was a sort of mournful resignation in their present attitude toward the disease. Only the child went on fighting with all his little might. Now and then Rieux took his pulse—less because this served any purpose than as an escape from his utter helplessness—and when he closed his eyes, he seemed to feel its tumult mingling with the fever of his own blood. And then, at one with the tortured child, he struggled to sustain him with all the remaining strength of his own body. But, linked for a few moments, the rhythms of their heartbeats soon fell apart, the child escaped him, and again he knew his impotence. Then he released the small, thin wrist and moved back to his place.

The light on the whitewashed walls was changing from pink to yellow. The first waves of another day of heat were beating on the windows. They hardly heard Grand saying he would come back as he turned to go. All were waiting. The child, his eyes still closed, seemed to grow a little calmer. His clawlike fingers were feebly plucking at the sides of the bed. Then they rose, scratched at the blanket over his knees, and suddenly he doubled up his limbs, bringing his thighs above his stomach, and remained quite still. For the first time he opened his eyes and gazed at Rieux, who was standing immediately in front of him. In the small face, rigid as a mask of grayish clay, slowly the lips parted and from them rose a long, incessant scream, hardly varying with his respiration, and filling the ward with a fierce, indignant protest, so little childish that it seemed like a collective voice issuing from all the sufferers there. Rieux clenched his jaws, Tarrou looked away. Rambert went and stood beside Castel, who closed the book lying on his knees. Paneloux gazed down at the small mouth, fouled with the sordes of the plague and pouring out the angry death-cry that has sounded through the ages of mankind. He sank on his knees, and all present found it natural to hear him say in a voice hoarse but clearly audible across that nameless, never ending wail:

"My God, spare this child!"

But the wail continued without cease and the other suffers began to grow restless. The patient at the far end of the ward, whose little broken cries had gone on without a break, now quickened their tempo so that they flowed together in one unbroken cry, while the others' groans grew louder. A gust of sobs swept through the room, drowning Paneloux's prayer, and Rieux, who was still tightly gripping the rail of the bed, shut his eyes, dazed with exhaustion and disgust.

When he opened them again, Tarrou was at his side.

"I must go," Rieux said. "I can't bear to hear them any longer."

But then, suddenly, the other sufferers fell silent. And now the doctor grew aware that the child's wail, after weakening more and more, had fluttered out into silence. Around him the groans began again, but more faintly, like a far echo of the fight that now was over. For it was over. Castel had moved round to the other side of the bed and said the end had come. His mouth still gaping, but silent now, the child was lying among the tumbled blankets, a small, shrunken form, with the tears still wet on his cheeks.

Paneloux went up to the bed and made the sign of benediction. Then gathering up his cassock, he walked out by the passage between the beds.

"Will you have to start it all over again?" Tarrou asked Castel.

The old doctor nodded slowly, with a twisted smile.

"Perhaps. After all, he put up a surprisingly long resistance."

Rieux was already on his way out, walking so quickly and with such a strange look on his face that Paneloux put out an arm to check him when he was about to pass him in the doorway.

"Come, doctor," he began.

Rieux swung round on him fiercely.

"Ah! That child, anyhow, was innocent, and you know it as well as I do!"

He strode on, brushing past Paneloux, and walked across the school playground. Sitting on a wooden bench under the dingy, stunted trees, he wiped off the sweat that was beginning to run into his eyes. He felt like shouting imprecations—anything to loosen the stranglehold lashing his heart with steel. Heat was flooding down between the branches of the fig trees. A white haze, spreading rapidly over the blue of the morning sky, made the air yet more stifling. Rieux lay back wearily on the bench. Gazing up at the ragged branches, the shimmering sky, he slowly got back his breath and fought down his fatigue.

He heard a voice behind him. "Why was there that anger in your voice just now? What we'd been seeing was as unbearable to me as it was to you."

Rieux turned toward Paneloux.

"I know. I'm sorry. But weariness is a kind of madness. And there are times when the only feeling I have is one of mad revolt."

"I understand," Paneloux said in a low voice. "That sort of thing is revolting because it passes our human understanding. But perhaps we should love what we cannot understand."

Rieux straightened up slowly. He gazed at Paneloux, summoning to his gaze all the strength and fervor he could muster against his weariness. Then he shook his head.

"No, Father. I've a very different idea of love. And until my dying day I shall refuse to love a scheme of things in which children are put to torture."

A shade of disquietude crossed the priest's face. "Ah, doctor," he said sadly, "I've just realized what is meant by 'grace.' "

Rieux had sunk back again on the bench. His lassitude had returned and from its depths he spoke, more gently:

"It's something I haven't got; that I know. But I'd rather not discuss that with you. We're working side by side for something that unites us—beyond blasphemy and prayers. And it's the only thing that matters."

Paneloux sat down beside Rieux. It was obvious that he was deeply moved.

"Yes, yes," he said, "you, too, are working for man's salvation."

Rieux tried to smile.

"Salvation's much too big a word for me. I don't aim so high. I'm concerned with man's health; and for me his health comes first."

Paneloux seemed to hesitate. "Doctor—" he began, then fell silent. Down his face, too, sweat was trickling. Murmuring: "Good-by for the present," he rose. His eyes were moist. When he turned to go, Rieux, who had seemed lost in thought, suddenly rose and took a step toward him.

"Again, please forgive me. I can promise there won't be another outburst of that kind."

Paneloux held out his hand, saying regretfully:

"And yet—I haven't convinced you!"

"What does it matter? What I hate is death and disease, as you well know. And whether you wish it or not, we're allies, facing them and fighting them together." Rieux was still holding Paneloux's hand. "So you see"—but he refrained from meeting the priest's eyes—"God Himself can't part us now."

280

THE BEST OF ALL
POSSIBLE WORLDS

Gottfried Wilhelm Leibniz (1646–1716) was born in Leipzig and was formally trained in scholastic philosophy and law. But in his father's library he studied everything, and he published a significant treatise at the age of twenty. His motto is on his coffin: "As often as an hour is lost, a part of life perishes." Leibniz lost little time—he said once that he had been too busy all of his life to find time to marry. He sought to develop a universal language, was one of the founders of symbolic logic, and attempted to reconcile Protestantism and the Catholic Church. He and Newton discovered, independently, the differential calculus. There were contributions to the fields of physics, philology, jurisprudence, medicine, statistics, probability theory, history, and semantics. He was, Stuart Hampshire states, "perhaps the most universal genius of the modern world. . . . He was the last man who could hope to master the whole range of modern knowledge, and to be an encyclopedia in himself." The reading selection which follows was added to his Theodicy *(1710) as an "Abridgement of the Argument Reduced to Syllogistic Form."*

Some intelligent persons have desired that this supplement be made [to the Theodicy], and I have the more readily yielded to their wishes as in this way I have an opportunity again to remove certain difficulties and to make some observations which were not sufficiently emphasized in the work itself.

I. *Objection.* Whoever does not choose the best is lacking in power, or in knowledge, or in goodness.

God did not choose the best in creating this world.

Therefore, God has been lacking in power, or in knowledge, or in goodness.

Answer. I deny the minor, that is, the second premise of this syllogism; and our opponent proves it by this

Prosyllogism. Whoever makes things in which there is evil, which could have been made without any evil, or the making of which could have been omitted, does not choose the best.

God has made a world in which there is evil; a world, I say, which could have been made without any evil, or the making of which could have been omitted altogether.

Therefore, God has not chosen the best.

Answer. I grant the minor of this prosyllogism; for it must be confessed that there is evil in this world which God has made, and that it was possible to make a world without evil, or even not to create a world at all, for its creation has depended on the free will of God; but I deny the major, that is, the first of the two premises of the prosyllogism, and I might content myself with simply demanding its proof; but in order to make the matter clearer, I have wished to justify this denial by showing that the best plan is not always that which seeks to avoid evil, since it may happen that *the evil is accompanied by a greater good*. For example, a general of an army will prefer a great victory with a slight wound to a condition without wound and without victory. We have proved this more fully in the large work by making it clear, by instances taken from mathematics and elsewhere, that an imperfection in the part may be required for a greater perfection in the whole. In this I have followed the opinion of St. Augustine, who has said a hundred times, that God has permitted evil in order to bring about good, that is, a greater good; and that of Thomas Aquinas, that the permitting of evil tends to the good of the universe. I have shown that the ancients called Adam's fall *felix culpa*, a happy sin, because it had been retrieved with immense advantage by the incarnation of the Son of God, who has given to the universe something nobler than anything that ever would have been among creatures except for it. For the sake of a clearer understanding, I have added, following many good authors, that it was in accordance with order and the general good that God allowed to certain creatures the opportunity of exercising their liberty, even when he foresaw that they would turn to evil, but which he could so well rectify; because it was not fitting that, in order to hinder sin, God should always act in an extraordinary manner. To overthrow this objection, therefore, it is sufficient to show that a world with evil might be better than a world without evil; but I have gone even farther, in the work, and have even proved that this universe must be in reality better than every other possible universe. . . .

IV. *Objection.* Whoever can prevent the sin of another and does not do so, but rather contributes to it although he is well informed of it, is accessory to it.

God can prevent the sin of intelligent creatures; but he does not do so, and rather contributes to it by his concurrence and by the opportunities which he brings about, although he has a perfect knowledge of it.

Hence, etc.

Answer. I deny the major of this syllogism. For it is possible that one could prevent sin, but ought not, because he could not do it without himself committing a sin, or (when God is in question) without performing an unreasonable action. Examples have been given and the application to God himself has been made. It is possible also that we contribute to evil and that sometimes we even open the road to it, in doing things which we are obliged to do; and, when we do our duty or (in speaking of God) when, after thorough consideration, we do that which reason demands, we are not responsible for the results, even when we foresee them. We do not desire these evils; but we are willing to permit them for the sake of a greater good which we cannot reasonably help preferring to other considerations. And this is a *consequent* will, which results from *antecedent* wills by which we will the good. I know that some persons, in speaking of the antecedent and consequent will of God, have understood by the *antecedent* that which wills that all men should be saved; and by the *consequent*, that which wills, in consequence of persistent sin, that some should be damned. But these are merely illustrations of a more general idea, and it may be said for the same reason that God, by his antecedent will, wills that men should not sin; and by his consequent or final and decreeing will (that which is always followed by its effect), he wills to permit them to sin, this permission being the result of superior reasons. And we have the right to say in general that the antecedent will of God tends to the production of good and the prevention of evil, each taken in itself as if alone, according to the measure of the degree of each good and of each evil; but that the divine consequent or final or total will tends toward the production of as many goods as may be put together, the combination of which becomes in this way determined, and includes also the permission of some evils and the exclusion of some goods, as the best possible plan for the universe demands. Arminius, in his *Anti-perkinsus*, has very well explained that the will of God may be called consequent, not only in relation to the action of the creature considered beforehand in the divine understanding, but also in relation to other anterior divine acts of will. But this consideration of the passage cited from Thomas Aquinas, and that from Scotus, is enough to show that they make this distinction as I have done here. Nevertheless, if anyone objects to this use of terms let him substitute *deliberating* will, in place of antecedent, and *final* or decreeing will, in place of consequent. For I do not wish to dispute over words.

V. *Objection.* Whoever produces all that is real in a thing, is its cause.

God produces all that is real in sin.

Hence, God is the cause of sin.

Answer. I might content myself with denying the major or the minor, since the term *real* admits of interpretations which would render these propositions false. But in order to explain more clearly, I will make a distinction. *Real* signifies either that which is positive only, or, it includes also privative beings: in the first case, I deny the major and admit the minor; in the second case, I do the contrary. I might have limited myself to this, but I have chosen to proceed still farther and give the reason for this distinction. I have been very glad therefore to draw attention to the fact that every reality purely positive or absolute is a perfection; and that imperfection comes from limitation, that is, from the privative: for to limit is to refuse progress, or the greatest possible progress. Now God is the cause of all perfections and conse-

quently of all realities considered as purely positive. But limitations or priva-
tions result from the original imperfection of creatures, which limits their
receptivity. And it is with them as with a loaded vessel, which the river causes
to move more or less slowly according to the weight which it carries: thus
its speed depends upon the river, but the retardation which limits this
speed comes from the load. Thus in the *Theodicy*, we have shown how the
creature, in causing sin, is a defective cause; how errors and evil inclinations
are born of privation; and how privation is accidentally efficient; and I have
justified the opinion of St. Augustine who explains, for example, how God
makes the soul obdurate, not by giving it something evil, but because the effect of his good impression is limited by the soul's resistance and by the
circumstances which contribute to this resistance, so that he does not give it
all the good which would overcome its evil. But if God had wished to do
more, he would have had to make either other natures for creatures or
other miracles to change their natures, things which the best plan could not
admit. It is as if the current of the river must be more rapid than its fall
admitted or that the boats should be loaded more lightly, if it were necessary
to make them move more quickly. And the original limitation or imperfection of creatures requires that even the best plan of the universe could not
receive more good, and could not be exempt from certain evils, which, however, are to result in a greater good. There are certain disorders in the parts
which marvellously enhance the beauty of the whole; just as certain disson-
ances, when properly used, render harmony more beautiful. But this depends
on what has already been said in answer to the first objection.

VI. *Objection.* Whoever punishes those who have done as well as it was
in their power to do, is unjust.

God does so.

Hence, etc.

Answer. I deny the minor of this argument. And I believe that God always
gives sufficient aid and grace to those who have a good will, that is, to those
who do not reject this grace by new sin. Thus I do not admit the damnation
of infants who have died without baptism or outside of the church; nor the
damnation of adults who have acted according to the light which God
has given them. And I believe that if *any one has followed the light which
has been given him,* he will undoubtedly receive greater light when he has
need of it, as the late M. Hulseman, a profound and celebrated theologian at
Leipsig, has somewhere remarked; and if such a man has failed to receive it
during his lifetime he will at least receive it when at the point of death.

VII. *Objection.* Whoever gives only to some, and not to all, the means
which produces in them effectively a good will and salutary final faith, has
not sufficient goodness.

God does this.

Hence, etc.

Answer. I deny the major of this. It is true that God could overcome the greatest resistance of the human heart; and does it, too, sometimes, either by internal grace, or by external circumstances which have a great effect on souls; but he does not always do this. Whence comes this distinction? it may be asked, and why does his goodness seem limited? It is because, as I have already said in answering the first objection, it would not have been in order always to act in an extraordinary manner, and to reverse the connection of things. The reasons of this connection, by means of which one is placed in more favorable circumstances than another, are hidden in the depths of the wisdom of God: they depend upon the universal harmony. The best plan of the universe, which God could not fail to choose, made it so. We judge from the event itself; since God has made it, it was not possible to do better. Far from being true that this conduct is contrary to goodness, it is supreme goodness which led him to it. This objection with its solution might have been drawn from what was said in regard to the first objection; but it seemed useful to touch upon it separately.

VIII. *Objection.* Whoever cannot fail to choose the best, is not free.

God cannot fail to choose the best.

Hence, God is not free.

Answer. I deny the major of this argument; it is rather true liberty, and the most perfect, to be able to use one's free will for the best, and to always exercise this power, without ever being turned aside either by external force or by internal passions, the first of which causes slavery of the body, the second, slavery of the soul. There is nothing less servile, and nothing more in accordance with the highest degree of freedom, than to be always led toward the good, and always by one's own inclination, without any constraint and without any displeasure. And to object therefore that God had need of external things, is only a sophism. He created them freely; but having proposed to himself an end, which is to exercise his goodness, wisdom has determined him to choose the means best fitted to attain this end. To call this a *need*, is to take that term in an unusual sense which frees it from all imperfection, just as when we speak of the wrath of God.

Seneca has somewhere said that God commanded but once but that he obeys always, because he obeys laws which he willed to prescribe to himself. But he might better have said that God always commands and that he is always obeyed; for in willing, he always follows the inclination of his own nature, and all other things always follow his will. And as this will is always the same, it cannot be said that he obeys only that will which he formerly had. Nevertheless, although his will is always infallible and always tends toward the best, the evil, or the lesser good, which he rejects, does not cease to be possible in itself; otherwise the necessity of the good would be geometrical (so to speak), or metaphysical, and altogether absolute; the contingency of things would be destroyed, and there would be no choice. But this sort of necessity, which does not destroy the possibility of the contrary, has this name only by analogy; it becomes effective, not by the pure essence of things, but by that which is outside of them, above them, namely, by the will of God. This necessity is called moral, because, to the sage, *necessity* and *what ought to be* are equivalent things; and when it always has its effect, as it really has in the perfect sage, that is, in God, it may be said that it is a happy necessity. The nearer creatures approach to it, the nearer they approach to perfect happiness. Also this kind of necessity is not that which we try to avoid and which destroys morality, rewards and praise. For that which it brings, does not happen whatever we may do or will, but because we will it so. And a will to which it is natural to choose well, merits praise so much the more; also it carries its reward with it, which is sovereign happiness. And as this constitution of the divine nature gives entire satisfaction to him who possesses it, it is also the best and the most desirable for the creatures who are all dependent on God. If the will of God did not have for a rule the principle of the best, it would either tend toward evil, which would be the worst; or it would be in some way indifferent to good and to evil, and would be guided by chance: but a will which would allow itself always to act by chance, would not be worth more for the government of the universe than the fortuitous concourse of atoms, without there being any divinity therein. And even if God should abandon himself to chance only in some cases and in a certain way (as he would do, if he did not always work entirely for the best and if he were capable of preferring a lesser good to a greater, that is, an evil to a good, since that which prevents a greater good is an evil), he would be imperfect, as well as the object of his choice; he would not merit entire confidence; he would act without reason in such a case, and the government of the universe would be like certain games, equally divided between reason and chance. All this proves that this objection which is made against the choice of the best, perverts the notions of the free and of the necessary, and represents to use the best even as evil: which is either malicious or ridiculous.

J. L. Mackie (1917–   ) was born in Australia and taught at the University of Sydney. In England he was a professor of philosophy at the University of York; he is presently a Fellow of University College, Oxford. His many articles in the areas of ethics, the philosophy of religion, and the philosophy of science reflect his analytical skills. He is also the author of Contemporary Linguistic Philosophy *—Its Strength and Its Weakness. "Evil and Omnipotence" is an unusually thorough and incisive examination of the problem of evil, and it has been widely reprinted. It was originally published in the journal* Mind *(January 1955).*

The traditional arguments for the existence of God have been fairly thoroughly criticised by philosophers. But the theologian can, if he wishes, accept this criticism. He can admit that no rational proof of God's existence is possible. And he can still retain all that is essential to his position, by holding that God's existence is known in some other, non-rational way. I think, however, that a more telling criticism can be made by way of [the] traditional problem of evil. Here it can be shown, not that religious beliefs lack rational support, but that they are positively irrational, that the several parts of the essential theological doctrine are inconsistent with one another, so that the theologian can maintain his position as a whole only by a much more extreme rejection of reason than in the former case. He must now be prepared to believe, not merely what cannot be proved, but what can be *disproved* from other beliefs that he also holds.

The problem of evil, in the sense in which I shall be using the phrase, is a problem only for someone who believes that there is a God who is both omnipotent and wholly good. And it is a logical problem, the problem of clarifying and reconciling a number of beliefs: it is not a scientific problem that might be solved by further observations, or a practical problem that might be solved by a decision or an action. These points are obvious: I mention them only because they are sometimes ignored by theologians, who sometimes parry a statement of the problem with such remarks as "Well, can you solve the problem yourself?" or "This is a mystery which may be revealed to us later" or "Evil is something to be faced and overcome, not to be merely discussed."

In its simplest form the problem is this: God is omnipotent; God is wholly good; and yet evil exists. There seems to be some contradiction between these three propositions, so that if any two of them were true the third would be false. But at the same time all three are essential parts of most theological positions: the theologian, it seems, at once *must* adhere and *cannot consistently* adhere to all three. (The problem does not arise only for theists, but I shall discuss it in the form in which it presents itself for ordinary theism.)

However, the contradiction does not arise immediately; to show it we need some additional premises, or perhaps some quasi-logical rules connecting the terms 'good,' 'evil,' and 'omnipotent.' These additional principles are that good is opposed to evil, in such a way that a good thing always eliminates evil as far as it can, and that there are no limits to what an omnipotent thing can do. From these it follows that a good omnipotent thing eliminates evil completely, and then the propositions that a good omnipotent thing exists, and that evil exists, are incompatible.

ADEQUATE SOLUTIONS

Now once the problem is fully stated it is clear that it can be solved, in the sense that the problem will not arise if one gives up at least one of the propositions that constitute it. If you are prepared to say that God is not wholly good, or not quite omnipotent, or that evil does not exist, or that good is not opposed to the kind of evil that exists, or that there are limits to what an omnipotent thing can do, then the problem of evil will not arise for you.

There are, then, quite a number of adequate solutions of the problem of evil, and some of these have been adopted, or almost adopted, by various thinkers. For example, a few have been prepared to deny God's omnipotence, and rather more have been prepared to keep the term 'omnipotence' but severely to restrict its meaning, recording quite a number of things that an omnipotent being cannot do. Some have said that the evil is an illusion, perhaps because they held that the whole world of temporal, changing things is an illusion, and that what we call evil belongs only to this world, or perhaps because they held that although temporal things *are* much as we see them, those that we call evil are not really evil. Some have said that what we call evil is merely the privation of good, that evil in a positive sense, evil that would really be opposed to good, does not exist. Many have agreed with Pope that disorder is harmony not understood, and that partial evil is universal good. Whether any of these views is *true* is, of course, another question. But each of them gives an adequate solution of the problem of evil in the sense that if you accept it this problem does not arise for you, though you may, of course, have *other* problems to face.

But often enough these adequate solutions are only *almost* adopted. The thinkers who restrict God's power, but keep the term 'omnipotence,' may reasonably be suspected of thinking, in other contexts, that his power is really unlimited. Those who say that evil is an illusion may also be thinking, inconsistently, that this illusion is itself an evil. Those who say that "evil" is merely privation of good may also be thinking, inconsistently, that privation of good is an evil. (The fallacy here is akin to some forms of the "naturalistic fallacy" in ethics, where some think, for example, that "good" is just what contributes to evolutionary progress, and that evolutionary progress is itself good.) If Pope meant what he said in the first line of his couplet, that "disorder" is only harmony not understood, the "partial evil" of the second line must, for consistency, mean "that which, taken in isolation, falsely appears to be evil," but it would more naturally mean "that which, in isolation, really is "evil." The second line, in fact, hesitates between two views, that "partial evil" isn't really evil, since only the universal quality is real, and that "partial evil" is really an evil, but only a little one.

In addition, therefore, to adequate solutions, we must recognise unsatisfactory inconsistent solutions, in which there is only a half-hearted or temporary rejection of one of the propositions which together constitute the problem. In these, one of the constituent propositions is explicitly rejected, but it is covertly re-asserted or assumed elsewhere in the system.

FALLACIOUS SOLUTIONS

Besides these half-hearted solutions, which explicitly reject but implicitly assert one of the constituent propositions, there are definitely fallacious solutions which explicitly maintain all the constituent propositions, but implicitly reject at least one of them in the course of the argument that explains away the problem of evil.

There are, in face, many so-called solutions which purport to remove the contradiction without abandoning any of its constituent propositions. These must be fallacious, as we can see from the very statement of the problem, but it is not so easy to see in each case precisely where the fallacy lies. I suggest that in all cases the fallacy has the general form suggested above: in order to solve the problem one (or perhaps more) of its constituent propositions is given up, but in such a way that it appears to have been retained, and can therefore be asserted without qualification in other contexts. Sometimes there is a further complication: the supposed solution moves to and fro between, say, two of the constituent propositions, at one point asserting the first of these but covertly abandoning the second, at another point asserting the second but covertly abandoning the first. These fallacious solutions often turn upon some equivocation with the words 'good' and 'evil,' or upon some vagueness about the way in which good and evil are opposed to one another, or about how much is meant by 'omnipotence.' I propose to examine some of the so-called solutions, and to exhibit their fallacies in detail. Incidentally, I shall also be considering whether an adequate solution could be reached by a minor modification of one or more of the constituent propositions, which would, however, still satisfy all the essential requirements of ordinary theism.

1. *"Good cannot exist without evil"* or *"Evil is necessary as a counterpart to good."*

It is sometimes suggested that evil is necessary as a counterpart to good, that if there were no evil there could be no good either, and that this solves the problem of evil. It is true that it points to an answer to the question "Why should there be evil?" But it does so only by qualifying some of the propositions that constitute the problem.

First, it sets a limit to what God can do, saying that God *cannot* create good without simultaneously creating evil, and this means either that God is not omnipotent or that there are *some* limits to what an omnipotent thing can do. It may be replied that these limits are always presupposed, that omnipotence has never meant the power to do what is logically impossible, and on the present view the existence of good without evil would be a logical impossibility. This interpretation of omnipotence may, indeed, be accepted as a modification of our original account which does not reject anything that is essential to theism, and I shall in general assume it in the subsequent discussion. It is, perhaps, the most common theistic view, but I think that some theists at least have maintained that God can do what is logically impossible. Many theists, at any rate, have held that logic itself is created or laid down by God, that logic is the way in which God arbitrarily chooses to think. (This is, of course, parallel to the ethical view that morally right actions are those which God arbitrarily chooses to command, and the two views encounter similar difficulties). And *this* account of logic is clearly inconsistent with the view that God is bound by logical necessities—unless it is possible for an omnipotent being to bind himself, an issue which we shall consider later, when we come to the Paradox of Omnipotence. This solution of the problem of evil cannot, therefore, be consistently adopted along with the view that logic is itself created by God.

But, secondly, this solution denies that evil is opposed to good in our original sense. If good and evil are counterparts, a good thing will not "eliminate evil as far as it can." Indeed, this view suggests that good and evil are not strictly qualities of things at all. Perhaps the suggestion is that good and evil are related in much the same way as great and small. Certainly, when the term 'great' is used relatively as a condensation of 'greater than so-and-so,' and 'small' is used correspondingly, greatness and smallness are counterparts and cannot exist without each other. But in this sense greatness is not a quality, not an intrinsic feature of anything; and it would be absurd to think of a movement in favour of greatness and against smallness in this sense. Such a movement would be self-defeating, since relative greatness can be promoted only by a simultaneous promotion of relative smallness. I feel sure that no theists would be content to regard God's goodness as analogous to this—as if what he supports were not the *good* but the *better*, and as if he had the paradoxical aim that all things should be better than other things.

This point is obscured by the fact that 'great' and 'small' seem to have an absolute as well as a relative sense. I cannot discuss here whether there is absolute magnitude or not, but if there is, there could be an absolute sense for 'great,' it could mean of at least a certain size, and it would make sense to speak of all things getting bigger, of a universe that was expanding all over, and therefore it would make sense to speak of promoting greatness. But in *this* sense great and small are not logically necessary counterparts: either quality could exist without the other. There would be no logical impossibility in everything's being small or in everything's being great.

Neither in the absolute nor in the relative sense, then, of 'great' and 'small' do these terms provide an analogy of the sort that would be needed to support this solution of the problem of evil. In neither case are greatness and smallness *both* necessary counterparts *and* mutually opposed forces or possible objects for support and attack.

It may be replied that good and evil are necessary counterparts in the same way as any quality and its logical opposite: redness can occur, it is suggested, only if non-redness also occurs. But unless evil is merely the privation of good, they are not logical opposites, and some further argument would be needed to show that they are counterparts in the same way as genuine logical opposites. Let us assume that this could be given. There is still doubt of the correctness of the metaphysical principle that a quality must have a real opposite: I suggest that it is not really impossible that everything should be, say, red, that the truth is merely that if everything were red we should not notice redness, and so we should have no word 'red'; we observe and give names to qualities only if they have real opposites. If so, the principle that a term must have an opposite would belong only to our language or to our thought, and would not be an ontological principle, and, correspondingly, the rule that good cannot exist without evil would not state a logical necessity of a sort that God would just have to put up with. God might have made everything good, though *we* should not have noticed it if he had.

But, finally, even if we concede that this *is* an ontological principle, it will provide a solution for the problem of evil only if one is prepared to say, "Evil exists, but only just enough to serve as the counterpart of good." I doubt whether any theist will accept this. After all, the *ontological* requirement that nonredness should occur would be satisfied even if all the universe, except for a minute speck, were red, and, if there were a corresponding requirement for evil as a counterpart to good, a minute dose of evil would presumably do. But theists are not usually willing to say, in all contexts, that all the evil that occurs is a minute and necessary dose.

2. *"Evil is necessary as a means to good."*

It is sometimes suggested that evil is necessary for good not as a counterpart but as a means. In its simple form this has little plausibility as a solution of the problem of evil, since it obviously implies a severe restriction of God's power. It would be a *causal* law that you cannot have a certain end without a certain means, so that if God has to introduce evil as a means to good, he must be subject to at least some causal laws. This certainly conflicts with what a theist normally means by omnipotence. This view of God as limited by causal laws also conflicts with the view that causal laws are themselves made by God, which is more widely held than the corresponding view about the laws of logic. This conflict, would, indeed, be resolved if it were possible for an omnipotent being to bind himself, and this possibility has still to be considered. Unless a favourable answer can be given to this question, the suggestion that evil is necessary as a means to good solves the problem of evil only by denying one of its constituent propositions, either that God is omnipotent or that 'omnipotent' means what it says.

3. *"The universe is better with some evil in it than it could be if there were no evil."*

Much more important is a solution which at first seems to be a mere variant of the previous one, that evil may contribute to the goodness of a whole in which it is found, so that the universe as a whole is better as it is, with some evil in it, than it would be if there were no evil. This solution may be developed in either of two ways. It may be supported by an aesthetic analogy, by the fact that contrasts heighten beauty, that in a musical work, for example, there may occur discords which somehow add to the beauty of the work as a whole. Alternatively, it may be worked out in connexion with the notion of progress, that the best possible organisation of the universe will not be static, but progressive, that the gradual overcoming of evil by good is really a finer thing than would be the eternal unchallenged supremacy of good.

In either case, this solution usually starts from the assumption that the evil whose existence gives rise to the problem of evil is primarily what is called physical evil, that is to say, pain. In Hume's rather half-hearted presentation of the problem of evil, the evils that he stresses are pain and disease, and those who reply to him argue that the existence of pain and disease makes possible the existence of sympathy, benevolence, heroism, and the gradually successful struggle of doctors and reformers to overcome these evils. In fact, theists often seize the opportunity to accuse those who stress the problem of evil of taking a low, materialistic view of good and evil, equating these with pleasure and pain, and of ignoring the more spiritual goods which can arise in the struggle against evils.

But let us see exactly what is being done here. Let us call pain and misery 'first order evil' or 'evil (1).' What contrasts with this, namely, pleasure and happiness, will be called 'first order good' or 'good (1).' Distinct from this is 'second order good' or 'good (2)' which somehow emerges in a complex situation in which evil (1) is a necessary component—logically, not merely causally, necessary. (Exactly *how* it emerges does not matter: in the crudest version of this solution good (2) is simply the heightening of happiness by the contrast with misery, in other versions it includes sympathy with suffering, heroism in facing danger, and the gradual decrease of first order evil and increase of first order good.) It is also being assumed that second order good is more important than first order good or evil, in particular that it more than outweighs the first order evil it involves.

Now this is a particularly subtle attempt to solve the problem of evil. It defends God's goodness and omnipotence on the ground that (on a sufficiently long view) this is the best of all logically possible worlds, because it includes the important second order goods, and yet it admits that real evils, namely first order evils, exist. But does it still hold that good and evil are opposed? Not, clearly, in the sense that we set out originally: good does not tend to eliminate evil in general. Instead, we have a modified, a more complex pattern. First order good (*e.g.* happiness) *contrasts with* first order evil (*e.g.* misery): these two are opposed in a fairly mechanical way; some second order goods (*e.g.* benevolence) try to maximize first order good and minimise first order evil; but God's goodness is not this, it is rather the will to maximise *second* order good. We might, therefore, call God's goodness an example of a third order goodness, or good (3). While this account is different from our original one, it might well be held to be an improvement on it, to give a more accurate description of the way in which good is opposed to evil, and to be consistent with the essential theist position.

There might, however, be several objections to this solution.

First, some might argue that such qualities as benevolence—and *a fortiori* the third order goodness which promotes benevolence—have a merely derivative value, that they are not higher sorts of good, but merely means to good (1), that is, to happiness, so that it would be absurd for God to keep misery in existence in order to make possible the virtues of benevolence, heroism, etc. The theist who adopts the present solution must, of course, deny this, but he can do so with some plausibility, so I should not press this objection.

Secondly, it follows from this solution that God is not in our sense benevolent or sympathetic: he is not concerned to minimise evil (1), but only to promote good (2); and this might be a disturbing conclusion for some theists.

But, thirdly, the fatal objection is this. Our analysis shows clearly the possibility of the existence of a *second* order evil, an evil (2) contrasting with good (2) as evil (1) contrasts with good (1). This would include malevolence, cruelty, callousness, cowardice, and states in which good (1) is decreasing and evil (1) increasing. And just as good (2) is held to be the important kind of good, the kind that God is concerned to promote, so evil (2) will, by analogy, be the important kind of evil, the kind which God, if he were wholly good and omnipotent, would eliminate. And yet evil (2) plainly exists, and indeed most theists (in other contexts) stress its existence more than that of evil (1). We should, therefore, state the problem of evil in terms of second order evil, and against this form of the problem the present solution is useless.

An attempt might be made to use this solution again, at a higher level, to explain the occurrence of evil (2): indeed the next main solution that we shall examine does just this, with the help of some new notions. Without any fresh notions, such a solution would have little plausibility: for example, we could hardly say that the really important good was a good (3), such as the increase of benevolence in proportion to cruelty, which logically required for its occurrence the occurrence of some second order evil. But even if evil (2) could be explained in this way, it is fairly clear that there would be third order evils contrasting with this third order good: and we should be well on the way to an infinite regress, where the solution of a problem of evil, stated in terms of evil (*n*), indicated the existence of an evil (*n* + 1), and a further problem to be solved.

4. *"Evil is due to human freewill."*

Perhaps the most important proposed solution of the problem of evil is that evil is not to be ascribed to God at all, but to the independent actions of human beings, supposed to have been endowed by God with freedom of the will. This solution may be combined with the preceding one: first order evil (*e.g.* pain) may be justified as a logically necessary component in second order good (*e.g.* sympathy) while second order evil (*e.g.* cruelty) is not *justified*, but is so ascribed to human beings that God cannot be held responsible for it. This combination evades my third criticism of the preceding solution.

The freewill solution also involves the preceding solution at a higher level. To explain why a wholly good God gave men freewill although it would lead to some important evils, it must be argued that it is better on the whole that men should act freely, and sometimes err, than that they should be innocent automata, acting rightly in a wholly determined way. Freedom, that is to say, is now treated as a third order good, and as being more valuable than second order goods (such as sympathy and heroism) would be if they were deterministically produced, and it is being assumed that second order evils, such as cruelty, are logically necessary accompaniments of freedom, just as pain is a logically necessary pre-condition of sympathy.

I think that this solution is unsatisfactory primarily because of the incoherence of the notion of freedom of the will: but I cannot discuss this topic adequately here, although some of my criticisms will touch upon it.

First I should query the assumption that second order evils are logically necessary accompaniments of freedom. I should ask this: if God has made men such that in their free choices they sometimes prefer what is good and sometimes what is evil, why could he not have made men such that they always freely choose the good? If there is no logical impossibility in a man's freely choosing the good on one, or on several, occasions, there cannot be a logical impossibility in his freely choosing the good on every occasion. God was not, then, faced with a choice between making innocent automata and making beings who, in acting freely, would sometimes go wrong: there was open to him the obviously better possibility of making beings who would act freely but always go right. Clearly, his failure to avail himself of this possibility is inconsistent with his being both omnipotent and wholly good.

If it is replied that this objection is absurd, that the making of some wrong choices is logically necessary for freedom, it would seem that 'freedom' must here mean complete randomness or indeterminacy, including randomness with regard to the alternatives good and evil, in other words that men's choices and consequent actions can be 'free' only if they are not determined by their characters. Only on this assumption can God escape the responsibility for men's actions; for if he made them as they are, but did not determine their wrong choices, this can only be because the wrong choices are not determined by men as they are. But then if freedom is randomness, how can it be a characteristic of *will*? And, still more, how can it be the most important good? What value or merit would there be in free choices if these were random actions which were not determined by the nature of the agent?

I conclude that to make this solution plausible two different senses of 'freedom' must be confused, one sense which will justify the view that freedom is a third order good, more valuable than other goods would be without it, and another sense, sheer randomness, to prevent us from ascribing to God a decision to make men such that they sometimes go wrong when he might have made them such that they would always freely go right.

This criticism is sufficient to dispose of this solution. But besides this there is a fundamental difficulty in the notion of an omnipotent God creating men with free will, for if men's wills are really free this must mean that even God cannot control them, that is, that God is no longer omnipotent. It may be objected that God's gift of freedom to men does not mean that he *cannot* control their wills, but that he always *refrains* from controlling their wills. But why, we may ask, should God refrain from controlling evil wills? Why should he not leave men free to will rightly, but intervene when he sees them beginning to will wrongly? If God could do this, but does not, and if he is wholly good, the only explanation could be that even a wrong free act of will is not really evil, that its freedom is a value which outweighs its wrongness, so that there would be a loss of value if God took away the wrongness and the freedom together. But this is utterly opposed to what theists say about sin in other contexts. The present solution of the problem of evil, then, can be maintained only in the form that God has made men so free that he *cannot* control their wills.

This leads us to what I call the Paradox of Omnipotence: can an omnipotent being make things which he cannot subsequently control? Or, what is practically equivalent to this, can an omnipotent being make rules which then bind himself? (These are practically equivalent because any such rules could be regarded as setting certain things beyond his control, and *vice versa*.) The second of these formulations is relevant to the suggestions that we have already met, that an omnipotent God creates the rules of logic or causal laws, and is then bound by them.

It is clear that this is a paradox: the questions cannot be answered satisfactorily either in the affirmative or in the negative. If we answer "Yes," it follows that if God actually makes things which he cannot control, or makes rules which bind himself, he is not omnipotent once he has made them: there are *then* things which he cannot do. But if we answer "No," we are immediately asserting that there are things which he cannot do, that is to say that he is already not omnipotent.

It cannot be replied that the question which sets this paradox is not a proper question. It would make perfectly good sense to say that a human mechanic has made a machine which he cannot control: if there is any difficulty about the question it lies in the notion of omnipotence itself.

This, incidentally, shows that although we have approached this paradox from the free will theory, it is equally a problem for a theological determinist. No one thinks that machines have free will, yet they may well be beyond the control of their makers. The determinist might reply that anyone who makes anything determines its ways of acting, and so determines its subsequent behaviour: even the human mechanic does this by his *choice* of materials and structure for his machine, though he does not know all about either of these: the mechanic thus determines, though he may not foresee, his machine's actions. And since God is omniscient, and since his creation of things is total, he both determines and foresees the ways in which his creatures will act. We may grant this, but it is beside the point. The question is not whether God *originally* determined the future actions of his creatures, but whether he can *subsequently* control their actions, or whether he was able in his original creation to put things beyond his subsequent control. Even on determinist principles the answers "Yes" and "No" are equally irreconcilable with God's omnipotence.

Before suggesting a solution of this paradox, I would point out that there is a parallel Paradox of Sovereignty. Can a legal sovereign make a law restricting its own future legislative power? For example, could the British parliament make a law forbidding any future parliament to socialise banking, and also forbidding the future repeal of this law itself? Or could the British parliament, which was legally sovereign in Australia in, say, 1899, pass a valid law, or series of laws, which made it no longer sovereign in 1933? Again, neither the affirmative nor the negative answer is really satisfactory. If we were to answer "Yes," we should be admitting the validity of a law which, if it were actually made, would mean that parliament was no longer sovereign. If we were to answer "No," we should be admitting that there is a law, not logically absurd, which parliament cannot validly make, that is, that parliament is not now a legal sovereign. This paradox can be solved in the following way. We should distinguish between first order laws, that is laws governing the actions of individuals and bodies other than the legislature, and second order laws, that is laws about laws, laws governing the actions of the legislature itself. Correspondingly, we should distinguish two orders of sovereignty, first order sovereignty (sovereignty (1)) which is unlimited authority to make first order laws, and second order sovereignty (sovereignty (2)) which is unlimited authority to make second order laws. If we say that parliament is sovereign we might mean that any parliament at any time has sovereignty (1), or we might mean that parliament has both sovereignty (1) and sovereignty (2) at present, but we cannot without contradiction mean both that the present parliament has sovereignty (2) and that every parliament at every time has sovereignty (1), for if the present parliament has sovereignty (2) it may use it to take away the sovereignty (1) of later parliaments. What the paradox shows is that we cannot ascribe to any continuing institution legal sovereignty in an inclusive sense.

The analogy between omnipotence and sovereignty shows that the paradox of omnipotence can be solved in a similar way. We must distinguish between first order omnipotence (omnipotence (1), that is unlimited power to act, and second order omnipotence (omnipotence (2), that is unlimited power to determine what powers to act things shall have. Then we could consistently say that God all the time has omnipotence (1), but if so no beings at any time have powers to act independently of God. Or we could say that God at one time had omnipotence (2), and used it to assign independent powers to act to certain things, so that God thereafter did not have omnipotence (1). But what the paradox shows is that we cannot consistently ascribe to any continuing being omnipotence in an inclusive sense.

An alternative solution of this paradox would be simply to deny that God is a continuing being, that any times can be assigned to his actions at all. But on this assumption (which also has difficulties of its own) no meaning can be given to the assertion that God made men with wills so free that he could not control them. The paradox of omnipotence can be avoided by putting God outside time, but the freewill solution of the problem of evil cannot be saved in this way, and equally it remains impossible to hold that an omnipotent God *binds himself* by causal or logical laws.

CONCLUSION

Of the proposed solutions of the problem of evil which we have examined, none has stood up to criticism. There may be other solutions which require examination, but this study strongly suggests that there is no valid solution of the problem which does not modify at least one of the constituent propositions in a way which would seriously affect the essential core of the theistic position.

Quite apart from the problem of evil, the paradox of omnipotence has shown that God's omnipotence must in any case be restricted in one way or another, that unqualified omnipotence cannot be ascribed to any being that continues through time. And if God and his actions are not in time, can omnipotence, or power of any sort, be meaningfully ascribed to him?

*John Hick (1922–   ) received his M.A. from the University of Edinburgh
and his doctorate in philosophy from Oxford University. He was a Presbyterian
minister in rural Northumberland, England, before enlarging his audience with his
many articles and books. He has taught at Cornell University, was Stuart Professor
of Christian Philosophy at Princeton Theological Seminary, Lecturer in Divinity at
Cambridge, and Professor of Theology at the University of Birmingham. He is
the author of* Faith and Knowledge, *and he has edited* The Existence of God,
Faith and the Philosophers, *and* Classical and Contemporary Readings in the
Philosophy of Religion. *"The Problem of Evil" is from his* Philosophy of Religion
(1963). In a later volume, Evil and the God of Love *(1966), Hick reviewed
Christian attempts of the past to answer the problem of evil and presented in
greater detail his own position.*

To many, the most powerful positive objection to belief in God is the fact
of evil. Probably for most agnostics it is the appalling depth and extent of
human suffering, more than anything else, that makes the idea of a loving
Creator seem so implausible and disposes them toward one or another of the
various naturalistic theories of religion.

As a challenge to theism, the problem of evil has traditionally been posed
in the form of a dilemma: if God is perfectly loving, he must wish to abolish
evil; and if he is all-powerful, he must be able to abolish evil. But evil exists;
therefore God cannot be both omnipotent and perfectly loving.

Certain solutions, which at once suggest themselves, have to be ruled out
so far as the Judaic-Christian faith is concerned.

To say, for example (with contemporary Christian Science), that evil is
an illusion of the human mind, is impossible within a religion based upon
the stark realism of the Bible. Its pages faithfully reflect the characteristic
mixture of good and evil in human experience. They record every kind of
sorrow and suffering, every mode of man's inhumanity to man and of his
painfully insecure existence in the world. There is no attempt to regard evil
as anything but dark, menacingly ugly, heart-rending, and crushing. In the
Christian scriptures, the climax of this history of evil is the crucifixion of
Jesus, which is presented not only as a case of utterly unjust suffering, but
as the violent and murderous rejection of God's Messiah. There can be no
doubt, then, that for biblical faith, evil is unambiguously evil, and stands
in direct opposition to God's will.

Again, to solve the problem of evil by means of the theory (sponsored,
for example, by the Boston "Personalist" School) of a finite deity who does

the best he can with a material, intractable and co-eternal with himself, is to have abandoned the basic premise of Hebrew-Christian monotheism; for the theory amounts to rejecting belief in the infinity and sovereignty of God.

Indeed, any theory which would avoid the problem of the origin of evil by depicting it as an ultimate constituent of the universe, coordinate with good, has been repudiated in advance by the classic Christian teaching, first developed by Augustine, that evil represents the going wrong of something which in itself is good. Augustine holds firmly to the Hebrew-Christian conviction that the universe is *good*—that is to say, it is the creation of a good God for a good purpose. He completely rejects the ancient prejudice, widespread in his day, that matter is evil. There are, according to Augustine, higher and lower, greater and lesser goods in immense abundance and variety; but everything which has being is good in its own way and degree, except in so far as it may have become spoiled or corrupted. Evil—whether it be an evil will, an instance of pain, or some disorder or decay in nature— has not been set there by God, but represents the distortion of something that is inherently valuable. Whatever exists is, as such, and in its proper place, good; evil is essentially parasitic upon good, being disorder and perversion in a fundamentally good creation. This understanding of evil as something negative means that it is not willed and created by God; but it does not mean (as some have supposed) that evil is unreal and can be disregarded. Clearly, the first effect of this doctrine is to accentuate even more the question of the origin of evil.

Theodicy, as many modern Christian thinkers see it, is a modest enterprise, negative rather than positive in its conclusions. It does not claim to explain, nor to explain away, every instance of evil in human experience, but only to point to certain considerations which prevent the fact of evil (largely incomprehensible though it remains) from constituting a final and insuperable bar to rational belief in God.

In indicating these considerations it will be useful to follow the traditional division of the subject. There is the problem of *moral evil* or wickedness: why does an all-good and all-powerful God permit this? And there is the problem of the *non-moral evil* of suffering or pain, both physical and mental: why has an all-good and all-powerful God created a world in which this occurs?

Christian thought has always considered moral evil in its relation to human freedom and responsibility. To be a person is to be a finite center of freedom, a (relatively) free and self-directing agent responsible for one's own decisions. This involves being free to act wrongly as well as to act rightly. The idea of a person who can be infallibly guaranteed always to act rightly is self-contradictory. There can be no guarantee in advance that a genuinely free moral agent will never choose amiss. Consequently, the possibility of wrongdoing or sin is logically inseparable from the creation of finite persons, and to say that God should not have created beings who might sin amounts to saying that he should not have created people.

This thesis has been challenged in some recent philosophical discussions of the problem of evil, in which it is claimed that no contradiction is involved in saying that God might have made people who would be genuinely free and who could yet be guaranteed always to act rightly. A quote from one of these discussions follows:

> If there is no logical impossibility in a man's freely choosing the good on one, or on several occasions, there cannot be a logical impossibility in his freely choosing the good on every occasion. God was not, then, faced with a choice between making innocent automata and making beings who, in acting freely, would sometimes go wrong: there was open to him the obviously better possibility of making beings who would act freely but always go right. Clearly, his failure to avail himself of this possibility is inconsistent with his being both omnipotent and wholly good.[1]

A reply to this argument is suggested in another recent contribution to the discussion.[2] If by a free action we mean an action which is not externally compelled but which flows from the nature of the agent as he reacts to the circumstances in which he finds himself, there is, indeed, no contradiction between our being free and our actions being "caused" (by our own nature) and therefore being in principle predictable. There is a contradiction, however, in saying that God is the cause of our acting as we do but that we are free beings in relation to God. There is, in other words, a contradiction in saying that God has made us so that we shall of necessity act in a certain way, and that we are genuinely independent persons in relation to him. If all our thoughts and actions are divinely predestined, however free and morally responsible we may seem to be to ourselves, we cannot be free and morally responsible in the sight of God, but must instead be his helpless puppets. Such "freedom" is like that of a patient acting out a series of post-hypnotic suggestions: he appears, even to himself, to be free, but his volitions have actually been pre-determined by another will, that of the hypnotist, in relation to whom the patient is not a free agent.

A different objector might raise the question of whether or not we deny God's omnipotence if we admit that he is unable to create persons who are free from the risks inherent in personal freedom. The answer that has always been given is that to create such beings is logically impossible. It is no limitation upon God's power that he cannot accomplish the logically im-

---

[1] J. L. Mackie, "Evil and Omnipotence," *Mind* (April, 1955), 209. A similar point is made by Anthony Flew in "Divine Omnipotence and Human Freedom," *New Essays in Philosophical Theology*. An important critical comment on these arguments is offered by Ninian Smart in "Omnipotence, Evil and Supermen," *Philosophy* (April, 1961), with replies by Flew (January, 1962) and Mackie (April, 1962).

[2] Flew, in *New Essays in Philosophical Theology*.

possible, since there is nothing here to accomplish, but only a meaningless conjunction of words—in this case "person who is not a person." God is able to create beings of any and every conceivable kind; but creatures who lack moral freedom, however superior they might be to human beings in other respects, would not be what we mean by persons. They would constitute a different form of life which God might have brought into existence instead of persons. When we ask why God did not create such beings in place of persons, the traditional answer is that only persons could, in any meaningful sense, become "children of God," capable of entering into a personal relationship with their Creator by a free and uncompelled response to his love.

When we turn from the possibility of moral evil as a correlate of man's personal freedom to its actuality, we face something which must remain inexplicable even when it can be seen to be possible. For we can never provide a complete causal explanation of a free act; if we could, it would not be a free act. The origin of moral evil lies forever concealed within the mystery of human freedom.

The necessary connection between moral freedom and the possibility, now actualized, of sin throws light upon a great deal of the suffering which afflicts mankind. For an enormous amount of human pain arises either from the inhumanity or the culpable incompetence of mankind. This includes such major scourges as poverty, oppression and persecution, war, and all the injustice, indignity, and inequity which occur even in the most advanced societies. These evils are manifestations of human sin. Even disease is fostered to an extent, the limits of which have not yet been determined by psychosomatic medicine, by moral and emotional factors seated both in the individual and in his social environment. To the extent that all of these evils stem from human failures and wrong decisions, their possibility is inherent in the creation of free persons inhabiting a world which presents them with real choices which are followed by real consequences.

We may now turn more directly to the problem of suffering. Even though the major bulk of actual human pain is traceable to man's misused freedom as a sole or part cause, there remain other sources of pain which are entirely independent of the human will, for example, earthquake, hurricane, storm, flood, drought, and blight. In practice, it is often impossible to trace a boundary between the suffering which results from human wickedness and folly and that which falls upon mankind from without. Both kinds of suffering are inextricably mingled together in human experience. For our present purpose, however, it is important to note that the latter category does exist and that it seems to be built into the very structure of our world. In response to it, theodicy, if it is wisely conducted, follows a negative path. It is not possible to show positively that each item of human pain serves the divine purpose of good; but, on the other hand, it does seem possible to show that the divine purpose as it is understood in Judaism and Christianity could not be forwarded in a world which was designed as a permanent hedonistic paradise.

An essential premise of this argument concerns the nature of the divine purpose in creating the world. The skeptic's assumption is that man is to be viewed as a completed creation and that God's purpose in making the world was to provide a suitable dwelling-place for this fully-formed creature. Since God is good and loving, the environment which he has created for human life to inhabit is naturally as pleasant and comfortable as possible. The problem is essentially similar to that of a man who builds a cage for some pet animal. Since our world, in fact, contains sources of hardship, inconvenience, and danger of innumerable kinds, the conclusion follows that this world cannot have been created by a perfectly benevolent and all-powerful deity.

Christianity, however, has never supposed that God's purpose in the creation of the world was to construct a paradise whose inhabitants would experience a maximum of pleasure and a minimum of pain. The world is seen, instead, as a place of "soul-making" in which free beings, grappling with the tasks and challenges of their existence in a common environment, may become "children of God" and "heirs of eternal life." A way of thinking theologically of God's continuing creative purpose for man was suggested by some of the early Hellenistic Fathers of the Christian Church, especially Irenaeus. Following hints from St. Paul, Irenaeus taught that man has been made as a person in the image of God but has not yet been brought as a free and responsible agent into the finite likeness of God, which is revealed in Christ. Our world, with all its rough edges, is the sphere in which this second and harder stage of the creative process is taking place.

This conception of the world (whether or not set in Irenaeus' theological framework) can be supported by the method of negative theodicy. Suppose, contrary to fact, that this world were a paradise from which all possibility of pain and suffering were excluded. The consequences would be very far-reaching. For example, no one could ever injure anyone else: the murderer's knife would turn to paper or his bullets to thin air; the bank safe, robbed of a million dollars, would miraculously become filled with another million dollars (without this device, on however large a scale, proving inflationary); fraud, deceit, conspiracy, and treason would somehow always leave the fabric of society undamaged. Again, no one would ever be injured by accident: the mountain-climber, steeplejack, or playing child falling from a height would float unharmed to the ground; the reckless driver would never meet with disaster. There would be no need to work, since no harm could result from avoiding work; there would be no call to be concerned for others in time of need or danger, for in such a world there could be no real needs or dangers.

To make possible this continual series of individual adjustments, nature would have to work by "special providences" instead of running according to general laws which men must learn to respect on penalty of pain or death. The laws of nature would have to be extremely flexible: sometimes gravity would operate, sometimes not; sometimes an object would be hard and solid, sometimes soft. There could be no sciences, for there would be no enduring world structure to investigate. In eliminating the problems and hardships of an objective environment, with its own laws, life would become like a dream in which, delightfully but aimlessly, we would float and drift at ease.

One can at least begin to imagine such a world. It is evident that our present ethical concepts would have no meaning in it. If, for example, the notion of harming someone is an essential element in the concept of a wrong action, in our hedonistic paradise there could be no wrong actions— nor any right actions in distinction from wrong. Courage and fortitude would have no point in an environment in which there is, by definition, no danger or difficulty. Generosity, kindness, the *agape* aspect of love, prudence, unselfishness, and all other ethical notions which presuppose life in a stable environment, could not even be formed. Consequently, such a world, however well it might promote pleasure, would be very ill adapted for the development of the moral qualities of human personality. In relation to this purpose it would be the worst of all possible worlds.

It would seem, then, that an environment intended to make possible the growth in free beings of the finest characteristics of personal life, must have a good deal in common with our present world. It must operate according to general and dependable laws; and it must involve real dangers, difficulties, problems, obstacles, and possibilities of pain, failure, sorrow, frustration, and defeat. If it did not contain the particular trials and perils which—subtracting man's own very considerable contribution—our world contains, it would have to contain others instead.

To realize this is not, by any means, to be in possession of a detailed theodicy. It is to understand that this world, with all its "heartaches and the thousand natural shocks that flesh is heir to," an environment so manifestly not designed for the maximization of human pleasure and the minimization of human pain, may be rather well adapted to the quite different purpose of "soul-making."

These considerations are related to theism as such. Specifically, Christian theism goes further in the light of the death of Christ, which is seen paradoxically both (as the murder of the divine Son) as the worst thing that has ever happened and (as the occasion of man's salvation) as the best thing that has ever happened. As the supreme evil turned to supreme good, it provides the paradigm for the distinctively Christian reaction to evil. Viewed from the standpoint of Christian faith, evils do not cease to be evils; and certainly, in view of Christ's healing work, they cannot be said to have been sent by God. Yet, it has been the persistent claim of those seriously and wholeheartedly committed to Christian discipleship that tragedy, though truly tragic, may nevertheless be turned, through a man's reaction to it, from a cause of despair and alienation from God to a stage in the fulfillment of God's loving purpose for that individual. As the greatest of all evils, the crucifixion of Christ, was made the occasion of man's redemption, so good can be won from other evils. As Jesus saw his execution by the Romans as an experience which God desired him to accept, an experience which was to be brought within the sphere of the divine purpose and made to serve the divine ends, so the Christian response to calamity is to accept the adversities, pains, and afflictions which life brings, in order that they can be turned to a positive spiritual use.

At this point, theodicy points forward in two ways to the subject of life after death.

First, although there are many striking instances of good being triumphantly brought out of evil through a man's or a woman's reaction to it, there are many other cases in which the opposite has happened. Sometimes obstacles breed strength of character, dangers evoke courage and unselfishness, and calamities produce patience and moral steadfastness. But sometimes they lead, instead, to resentment, fear, grasping selfishness, and disintegration of character. Therefore, it would seem that any divine purpose of soul-making which is at work in earthly history must continue beyond this life if it is ever to achieve more than a very partial and fragmentary success.

Second, if we ask whether the business of soul-making is worth all the toil and sorrow of human life, the Christian answer must be in terms of a future good which is great enough to justify all that has happened on the way to it.

The conclusion of this chapter is thus parallel to the conclusion of the preceding one. There it appeared that we cannot decisively prove the existence of God; here it appears that neither can we decisively disprove his existence.

FURTHER READING

Voltaire's short novel *Candide* (1759) ridicules Leibniz and his optimism about this being the best of worlds; it is also a delightful masterpiece in its own right.

Michael Novak sides with God but acknowledges that "the fact of evil cuts the believer's faith very deeply. . . ." See Chapter VI, "God or Evil," in *Belief and Unbelief* (1965).

Ivan Karamazov is one of those overcome by the presence of evil and injustice in the world. See Book V, Chapter IV, "Rebellion," in Fyodor Dostoyevsky's *The Brothers Karamazov* (1880).

Wilmon Henry Sheldon presents a reasoned defense of the theistic position in the chapter entitled "The Problem of Evil," in *God and Polarity* (1954).

David Hume, *Dialogues Concerning Natural Religion* (published posthumously in 1779). Parts X and XI comprise a classic discussion of the problem of evil by the great Scottish skeptic.

The Archbishop of Canterbury, William Temple, attempts to resolve the question of moral evil in Lecture XIV, "Finitude and Evil," in *Nature, Man, and God* (1934), the Gifford Lectures of 1932–1934.

A fine collection of materials appears in *The Voice Out of the Whirlwind: The Book of Job* (1960), edited by Ralph E. Hone. Included are the relevant portions of the Bible and items by Calvin, Kierkegaard, Newman, William Blake, Josiah Royce, Robert Frost, Archibald MacLeish, Reinhold Niebuhr, and others.

Walter Kaufmann offers a spirited critique of the Bible (and many other writings) in Chapter VI, "Suffering and the Bible," in *The Faith of a Heretic* (1959).

chapter eight

RELIGIOUS VISIONS

8

There are insurmountable difficulties that await anyone who would attempt to distinguish sharply between religion and philosophy. We speak, after all, of religious philosophies and of philosophical religions. Any number of philosophers have also been Christians, Jews, Hindus, or Buddhists; the best theologians are at the same time philosophers. There are religions that do not mention God, and the initial assumptions of the philosopher look very much like the faith of the religious believer. Karl Popper, for example, arguing for the rationalist attitude, has admitted that adopting that attitude involves acting on an "irrational faith in reason."

Illustrating the same point is Nicolas Berdyaev, who speaks in the pages that follow of his having a "conversion to the search for the truth" and of being convinced that "there is no religion above Truth." He is called a Christian existentialist (or existentialist Christian), a label that aptly indicates the coincidence of his religious and philosophical concerns. Berdyaev's starting point is a belief in a radical freedom, and his faith is grounded in an awareness of man's existential predicament. Part of that predicament is that certitude is not possible: the existentialist believes that the conditions of knowing are such that man can never know whether he has the truth or not. Every belief and every action is a risk-taking, and only the fool is ever comfortable. Thus, "All my life anguish never left me," Berdyaev writes, and his anguish points both to God and to "the distance, the yawning gulf that exists between man and the transcendent."

Taoism, described here by Huston Smith, comes to us from ancient China. Although its precise origins are obscure, it is clear that Taoism was old when Christianity was born. Centering upon a nameless, ineffable, impersonal Absolute that both transcends and pervades nature, it is a religion that quietly suggests that man learn to live in harmony with the forces that flow through life. This is the "Way," and it stands in stark contrast to the spirit of aggressiveness and struggle that characterizes so much of Western man and his religion. The "counterculture" in our society has a great deal in common with Taoism. So did Thoreau, who went to Walden Pond saying that "a man is rich in proportion to the number of things he can afford to let alone."

> *Religion—a daughter of Hope and Fear, explaining to Ignorance the nature of the Unknowable.*
>
> ambrose bierce

William James' "Mysticism" reports phenomena which occur with striking similarity in all of the major religions of the world, though in the West mystics have received considerably less attention than in the East. The term "mysticism," as James points out, suggests to many of us a nebulous and ill-grounded species of the occult, but mysticism can in fact claim to be based upon certain types of experience. *The religious experiences of the mystic, it is true, are private and thus not open to objective verification. Mystics have difficulty even describing what occurs during the mystical state of consciousness. Nevertheless, the experience is such that he who has it feels assured of its validity. There is no call here for faith, no need to assent to belief in religious creeds or documents. The focal point of mysticism is the "reality" of direct and immediate experience.*

Bertrand Russell's "A Free Man's Worship" is bluntly atheistic—but by no means nonreligious (as its title suggests). Science, Russell says, has revealed the world to be purposeless and meaningless; man is only the result of chance combinations of atoms in a blind cosmos, and his destiny is simply to die. Feeling hopelessly impotent, man creates gods to worship and placate. But then there is Russell's own religion of humanism, and it finds eloquent expression in these pages. Even in an indifferent universe and in spite of the finality of death, there are human *values that can be cherished. "Let us preserve," he urges, "our respect for truth, for beauty, for the ideal of perfection. . . ." We can strive to live with dignity and fortitude, and there is love that can be realized.*

Paul Tillich has been referred to as the "Apostle of the Skeptics," and the title is appropriate. His work constitutes a reinterpretation of what it means to be religious—in terms relevant to a skeptical age. He redefined faith to incorporate modern doubt and argued that the forms of courage which enable one to participate or to be oneself are limiting when compared to the "courage to be," which has its source in the very ground of being. The different forms of theism (and their accompanying forms of atheism) are rejected as being either too narrowly conceived, too partisan, or simply erroneous. The "old" God whose death Nietzsche announced is to be transcended, for there is "the God above God."

309

Nicolas Berdyaev (1874–1948) was born and educated in Russia. Unorthodox and rebellious, he has said that freedom was the basis of his philosophy, and a variety of authorities responded accordingly. As a student at the University of Kiev he was arrested and briefly exiled. In 1917 he was headed toward another exile at the hands of the Russian Orthodox Church when the Revolution cut short the proceedings. In 1920 he was a professor at the University of Moscow; in 1921 he was deported. There was a short period of work in Berlin, but in 1924 Paris became and remained his home. His writing, lecturing, and energetic participation in religious and philosophical organizations were interrupted only by the restrictions of the Nazis during their occupation of Paris in World War II. Among his titles are Freedom and the Spirit, The Meaning of History, The Destiny of Man, Slavery and Freedom, The Divine and the Human, The Beginning and the End, *and* Truth and Revelation. *The following selection is from his autobiography* Dream and Reality.

There is a rhythmic quality in the life of every human being, which I have experienced in my own life. The successiveness of temporal moments and periods as experienced by man derives from his inability to contain the fulness of life and to remain on the summits of inspiration. I have known periods of great inspiration which bordered on ecstasy; but I also knew times of dullness and heaviness of heart and mind when the creative flame faded and I felt deprived of spiritual strength.

As I look back on my spiritual path I do not discern any experience which could be properly described as a 'conversion. I know of no point in my life at which I underwent a decisive crisis, partly perhaps because my whole life was a series of continuous crises. 'Conversion' plays altogether a far greater rôle amongst the Roman Catholics and Protestants than among the Orthodox; and Western Christians are apt to exaggerate its importance. Even if we do experience it, we are reluctant to drag it into the day or to proclaim it from the housetops. I shall speak of my religious experience at another stage of this autobiography: now I only want to dwell on one particular point which accounts for a rather important event in my inner life.

I have few childhood memories of traditional Orthodox beliefs and practices: I had no occasion to fall away from, or to return to, a traditional faith. The fact that no such memories remained with me, that, as a child, I was nurtured by no Orthodox religious environment, was of enormous significance for my entire spiritual make-up. I see two initial motives in man's inner life: the search for meaning and the search for the eternal. The search for meaning preceded in me the search for God, and the search for the eternal was prior to the search for redemption. Once, on the threshold of adolescence, I was shaken to the depths by the thought that, even though there may be no such thing as a meaning in life, the very search for meaning would render life significant and meaningful. It is to this that I desired passionately to dedicate my life. This insight marked a true inner revolution which changed my whole outlook. There followed a time of great vision and inspiration: I even wrote an account of this inner change in me, but the manuscript was taken away from me when I was arrested for the first time in Russia, and I never saw it again. I should have liked now to read what I wrote then, so as to re-live and re-capture a first initiation into the mystery of life. This was undoubtedly a kind of conversion—the most powerful and perhaps the only one in my life. It was the conversion to the search for truth: a search which itself implied faith in the existence of truth; a search for truth and meaning which conflicted with commonplace and meaningless actuality. But the change was not evidence of a conversion to any religious confession, either to Orthodoxy or even to Christianity in general. It was above all a re-orientation towards spirit and spirituality.

Henceforth I was convinced that there is no religion above Truth (a statement, by the way, which has been much used and misused in theosophy); and the awareness of this supremacy of Truth has put a lasting stamp on my spiritual and intellectual development. This 'spiritualism' became the ground and framework of my whole philosophical attitude and probably of my very existence. As I understand it, however, the word spiritualism does not denote any philosophical or mystical or, indeed, any occult school of thought, but an existential awareness. I came to believe in the primary reality of the spirit at a level which is deeper than, and transcends, the sphere of discursive reasoning, for this latter has a secondary, derivative nature and belongs to the 'symbolic' and 'reflected' world of externality. . . .

. . . All my life anguish never left me, although my awareness of it varied and was more or less intense at different stages of my inner development. It is necessary to distinguish between anguish, fear, and tedium. Anguish points to the world above and is associated with the experience of the insignificance, precariousness and transitoriness of this world. Anguish bears witness to the transcendent and, at the same time, to the distance, the yawning gulf that exists between man and the transcendent. Anguish is also a longing for another world, for that which is beyond the boundaries of this finite world of ours. It spells solitude in face of the transcendent; it is the point of greatest conflict between my existence in the world and the transcendent. Anguish can awake my awareness of God, but it can also signify my God-forsakenness. It intervenes, as it were, between the transcendent and the abyss of non-being, of void.

Fear and tedium, on the other hand, consign me to the nether world. Fear is evidence of danger, coming from the lower world; and tedium denotes this world's triviality and emptiness. There is nothing more frightful and hopeless than the tedious and wearisome void of life. Anguish admits of hope, but tedium is devoid of hope. There is no issue out of tedium, unless it be in the act of creation. Fear is always associated with external danger and must be distinguished from terror, which is an experience in the depths of spirit and concerns the transcendent realities of being and non-being. Kierkegaard draws a distinction between *Angst* and *Furcht*; and for him *Angst* is a primordial religious phenomenon. Anguish and terror are related experiences; but the experience of terror is the more poignant, the more intense and overpowering, while anguish is the gentler, the more tranquil and untroubled. Terror may deliver man from tedium, and, when it turns to anguish, man's diseased condition ceases to be acute and becomes chronic.

It is easier to endure anguish and terror than sadness of heart and sorrow, and I always sought to escape from these as quickly as possible. I felt helpless in face of anything that stirred my emotions: I was too deeply sensitive and impressionable. Sadness, which is of the heart, looks towards the past. Terror, which is of the spirit, looks towards the eternal. Turgenyev is the artist of sadness *par excellence*; Dostoevsky is the artist of terror. Sadness has a poetical quality; terror is inherently dramatic. I knew anguish and terror and bore them with fortitude; but it seemed to me that if I were to surrender to sadness, I would pass away. Sadness is often associated with the sensation of pity, which I have always feared, knowing the power that it is apt to acquire over my soul. I was driven to raise barriers against sadness and pity, as indeed I did against anything that moved my emotions. But I was powerless to resist anguish, and it had no such destructive effects on me. To use an old-fashioned and rather inaccurate distinction, I combined in myself two types of temperament, commonly considered incompatible: I am at once sanguine and melancholic; and the sanguine element in me was perhaps even more pronounced than the melancholic. I was very easily roused, and my quick reaction issued, amongst other things, in the irascibility of which I have already spoken. But melancholy in me had deeper roots. Sometimes I suffered agonies of nostalgia and was driven by pessimistic moods, even when I appeared outwardly cheerful and content.

It is interesting, perhaps, that at the time of my spiritual awakening it was the philosophy of Schopenhauer rather than the Bible which impressed me—a fact which may have had far-reaching consequences for my later life. I found it difficult to recognize the alleged 'goodness' of creation. It is strange that I should have suffered most acutely from anguish during the so-called happy moments of life, if indeed it is at all possible to speak of such moments. I have always been afraid of happy, joyful experiences, for they have always brought me the most vivid memories of the agony of life. On great feast-days I almost invariably felt anguish, perhaps because I was awaiting some miraculous transformation of ordinary, workaday life: but it never came. The tragedy is that I was unable to idealize and romanticize, as some succeeded in doing, the painful condition of man—his anguish, his despair, his doubts, his sufferings and conflicts. I often thought of this condition as a frightful betrayal of life.

There is anguish which is characteristic of adolescence. In my youth I have known greater anguish than in later and more mature years: this anguish springs from an abundance of unrealized powers, from doubts and uncertainty as to the possibility of realizing them. Youth lives in the hope of a life rich, colourful, momentous and eventful; but there is disparity and contrast between life as it presents itself to hope and life as actually lived, life distorted and betrayed by untold disappointments, injustices, suffering and pain. It is a mistake to think that anguish is born of weakness: on the contrary, it is born of abundant strength. In life's very intensity there is contained an element of anguish. I believe that the young endure more of the anguish and longing of life than others are generally ready to admit. But different people experience this in different ways. I was myself particularly prone to anguish at moments which are commonly said to be joyful; for there is agony in the joy of the given moment when it is experienced against the background of life as a whole, pervaded as this is by tragedy and torment.

Anguish is always evidence of longing for eternity, of inability to come to terms with time. When we face the future we are moved not only by hope but also by anguish; for, in the end, the future carries death within itself and thus gives rise to anguish. Both future and past are hostile to eternity. I have often experienced a burning anguish under a wonderful starry or moonlit sky or on a glorious sunny day; in the quiet of a blossoming garden or in the silent immensity of the steppes; on looking into the face of a beautiful woman or at the moment of the awakening of love. Such moments called forth a vision of contrast between these and the darkness, decay and ugliness which fill the world to overflowing.

I was always struck by the unspeakable pain and destructiveness of time: I always foresaw the end in imagination and found no strength or desire to adapt myself to the process which led up to it. I was impatient. Love in particular seemed to me to carry within itself the seed of anguish, and I have frequently been amazed that people could experience the exultation of love as sheer joy and happiness. *Eros* is in anguish, for it is concerned

313

with, and deeply rooted in, the mystery of time and eternity: it concerns time athirst for eternal fulfilment, and yet never attaining it. Likewise, there is anguish in sex, which does not merely denote a passion for satisfaction of desire, but also bears the signature of the fallen nature of man. It is impossible to quench the thirst of sex in the conditions of this fallen life, for this thirst gives rise to illusions which make man the tool of an inhuman, biological process. Dionysos, the god of dying and rising life, gives birth to tragedy, from which sex cannot ever extricate itself: Dionysos and Pluto are one. Sex shows man wounded, fallen apart and never able to attain true fulness through union. It bids man go out into another; but he returns once more into himself and the anguish of his longing for unity continues unrelieved. The desire for wholeness inherent in men cannot be satisfied, least of all in sexual passion, which indeed only serves to deepen the wounds of disunity. Sex is, in its very nature, unwholesome, unchaste: it is evidence of the divided nature of man: only true love prevails over the division and attains wholeness and chastity. This is a profoundly tragic problem, on which I shall dwell at a later stage.

I have known anguish at unusual times and in unusual circumstances. Summer twilight in the streets of a big city, especially in Petersburg and Paris, with their drifting, half-formed images, has frequently inspired anguish in me. I have always found it hard to bear the hour of twilight. It is the hour of transition between life and darkness—a time when the fount of daylight is already spent, and when the other light, which springs from the starry mystery of night, or when the man-made artificial light, by which we try to protect ourselves against the power of darkness, has not as yet illumined human existence. Twilight intensifies the longing for eternity, for eternal life. It is also at the hour of twilight, in the ghostly atmosphere of a large town, that the veil over the nightmares and the evil of human life is drawn aside. But the anguish of twilight is different from the anguish of night: the latter has a depth, a transcendence unknown to the former. I have known both: I have known the anguish of misty twilight and the anguish of night which turns into terror and which no human language can convey or express. But this experience vanished in time. There were periods when I could not wake or sleep in darkness, and I was haunted by terrifying dreams and nightmares. Dreams have altogether been a source of torment to me, although I have sometimes had remarkable dreams of great illumination for me. Night conveyed to me some alien presence which terrified and pursued me into daylight. Thus we would go, four of us, for a walk in the country, into forests or fields; and I would suddenly have a sense of the presence of a fifth, come I know not whence, and I would forget how many of us there were. I can see no other source of these experiences but this mysterious and unaccountable anguish.

Modern psychoanalysis describes these phenomena as having their origin in the sub-conscious, but this explains little and elucidates nothing. I am deeply convinced that the transcendent is present in human life: it allures man and acts in human existence. I have known the depth and power of the sub-conscious and the subterranean, but I have also known that other and greater deep which is transcendence. Anguish is present in the very fabric of so-called life (though it may be unknown to those who take this life for granted and ask no questions), and all living beings are imbued with its deadly poison.

It has been said that 'green is the tree of life and grey the theory of life.' Paradoxical though it may seem, I am inclined to think that the reverse is true: 'grey is the tree of life and green the theory thereof.' But I must explain, lest this should give rise to misunderstandings. Have I not always been a declared enemy of scholastic conceptualism and the desiccated theories of discursive reason? Have I not always been a Faust rather than a Wagner? What is known as 'life,' however, is as often as not an embodiment of the commonplace and consists of nothing but the cares of workaday existence. 'Theory,' on the other hand, may be understood as creative vision, as the Greek *theoria*, which raises us above the habits of daily life. Philosophy, the 'green theory of life,' is free of anguish and boredom. I became a philosopher and a servant of 'theory' that I might renounce and be relieved of this unspeakable anguish. Philosophical thinking had always freed me from life's ugliness and corruption. To 'being' I have always opposed 'creativity,' that is to say, not 'life,' but the breaking through and flight from 'life' into 'existence,' from the finite into the infinite and transcendent.

Anguish, then, takes its rise in 'life'—in the twilight and the mists of life —and drives man toward the transcendent; while creativity is that very movement towards transcendence and the evocation of the image of the wholly other in relation to this life. In the realm of creativity all things acquire depth, meaning, character and interest, in contrast to the shallowness, insignificance, fortuitousness and insipidity peculiar to the realm of tedious external fact. A world endowed with beauty, unknown to this objective world where ugliness reigns supreme, unfolded itself before me, and called upon my creative spirit.

Has tedium, which rises from the waste and vacant regions of being, ever filled my heart? I have hardly ever been bored, and time never seemed to suffice for the accomplishment of my life's work and the fulfilment of my vocation; nor have I ever wasted time. And yet many, all too many, things have bored me. I have been bored by the views and opinions of the majority of men; by politics; by ideologies; by the affairs of state and nation. The commonplace in life, the repetitions and imitations, the fetters and repressions of life have produced in me a sense of tedium and drawn me into a void of nothingness. Indeed, when man submits, through weakness or through ignorance, to the pressure of these things, the world becomes flat and empty, devoid of depth and meaning, and tedium comes into its own, in anticipation of that kingdom of utter emptiness which is hell. The final and infernal limit of tedium is reached when man says to himself that nothing is. Suffering is, no doubt, a relief and a salvation in such a human condition, for it is a way of regaining the depth of life. Anguish too may bring salvation. There are people who feel happy in the midst of their own and the world's emptiness, and this state may well be the supreme instance of triviality and the commonplace.

Many people are, or say they are, in love with life. But I have never been able to feel or, indeed, to understand this. I could only be 'in love' with creativity and with the rapture of the creative act. I could never escape the feeling of anguish when confronted with life in its inexorable finality, and always believed that man's stature and significance is in proportion to that in him which breaks through to infinity. This issued in my inability ever to master the art of living and to profit by life. 'The misfortune of man,' says Carlyle in *Sartor Resartus*, 'has its source in his greatness; for there is something infinite in him, and he cannot succeed in burying himself completely in the finite.' The 'objective' world and 'objective' life are indeed buried in the finite; and burial is the most fitting thing that can happen in the finite world. 'Life,' then, is, as it were, the dying of the infinite into the finite, of the eternal into the temporal. There is in me a strong anarchist instinct: I revolt against the power of the finite, the circumscribed and the limitatively determined. The commonplace, which is the epitome of finiteness in the life of man and of the world, has either struck me by its utter insignificance, or it has roused me to revolt; and any attempt to ascribe a sacred character to finite things was repulsive to me.

Anguish can denote a religious experience. Religious anguish involves longing for immortality and eternal life, for redemption of the finitude of existence. Similarly, art appeared to me as imbued with anguish and, therefore, as evidence of the longing for transcendence. The magic of art is its power to wrench out the roots of finitude and to turn man's gaze to the eternal, archetypal forms and images of existence.

Anguish has persistently weakened my activity in the world: I thought to withdraw, whilst life was there to be re-shaped and transformed. That is, perhaps, why happiness and the sense of satisfaction were denied to me. From time to time it seemed to me that I would have known joy and happiness, had the cause of some particular pain at a particular moment been removed. But when this did happen the sense of anguish would persist and intensify some new and hitherto unknown torment. Nothing gave me a feeling of complete satisfaction and sufficiency; indeed these very states betrayed to me their fundamentally sinful character.

Huston Smith (1919–   ) was born in Soochow, China. His parents were missionaries to China for forty-one years, and Smith himself lived there for seventeen years. He received his Ph.D. from the University of Chicago and taught philosophy at the University of Denver, Washington University, and (since 1958) the Massachusetts Institute of Technology. He is the author of The Purposes of Higher Education, The Search for America, *and* Condemned to Meaning. *In* The Religions of Man *(1958), from which "Taoism" is taken, Smith explained that he had deliberately sought out what was of positive value in the religions, but he cautioned his readers to realize that "the full story of religion is not rose-colored. It is not all insight and inspiration. . . . A balanced view of man's religions would record its perversities as well as its glories. It would include human sacrifice and scapegoating, fanaticism and persecution, the Christian Crusades and the holy wars of Islam. It would include witch hunts in Massachusetts, monkey trials in Tennessee, and snake worship in the Ozarks—the list would have no end."*

THE OLD MASTER

According to tradition, Taoism (pronounced Dowism) originated with a man named Lao Tzu, said to have been born about 604 B.C. Some scholars date his life as much as three centuries later than this; some doubt that he ever lived. If he did we know almost nothing about him. We don't even know his name, Lao Tzu—which can be translated "the Old Boy," "the Old Fellow," or "the Grand Old Master"—being obviously a title of endearment and respect. All we really have is a mosaic of legends. Some of these are fantastic: that he was immaculately conceived by a shooting star; carried in his mother's womb for eighty-two years; and born already a wise old man with white hair. Other parts of the story have the ring of authenticity: that his occupation was that of keeper of the archives in his native western state; and that around this occupation he lived a simple and undemanding life. Estimates of his personality have been based almost entirely on one slim volume attributed to him. From this it has been surmised by some that he must have been a solitary recluse wound up in his personal occult meditations; others picture him as "the everlasting neighbor," as natural, genial, and homely as Lincoln with Lincoln's sense of humor and proportion as well. The one purportedly contemporary portrait speaks only of the enigmatic impression he left—the sense that here were depths that defied ready comprehension. Confucius, intrigued by what he had heard of Lao Tzu, once visited him. His description suggests that he was baffled by the strange man yet came away respecting him. "Of birds," he told his disciples, "I know that they have wings to fly with, of fish that they have fins to swim with, of wild beasts that they have feet to run with. For feet there are traps, for fins nets, for wings arrows. But who knows how dragons surmount wind and cloud into heaven. This day I have seen Lao Tzu. Today I have seen a dragon."

Saddened by men's disinclination to cultivate the natural goodness he advocated, and seeking greater personal solitude for his closing years, Lao Tzu is said at length to have climbed on a water buffalo and ridden westward toward what is now Tibet. At the Hankao Pass a gatekeeper sensing the unusual character of the truant tried to persuade him to turn back. Failing this, he asked the "Old Boy" if he would not at least leave a record of his beliefs to the civilization he was deserting. This Lao Tzu consented to do. He retired for three days and returned with a slim volume of 5000 characters titled *Tao Te Ching*, or "The Way and Its Power." A testament to man's at-home-ness in the universe, it can be read, as one chooses, in half an hour or a lifetime and remains to this day the basic text of all Taoist thought.

What a curious life this was for the supposed founder of a religion. He didn't preach; he didn't organize a church. He wrote a few pages, rode off on a water buffalo, and that (as far as he was concerned) was the end of the matter. How unlike Buddha who trudged the dusty roads of India for forty-five years to make his point. How unlike Confucius who hit the capitols for thirteen years trying to gain an administrative foothold for his philosophy. Here was a man so little concerned with the success of his own ideas, to say nothing of fame and fortune, that he didn't even stay around to answer questions. And yet, whether the story of this life be fact or fiction, it is so true to Taoist values that it will remain a part of the religion forever.

THE THREE MEANINGS OF TAO

On opening Taoism's bible, the *Tao Te Ching*, we sense at once that everything revolves around the pivotal concept of *Tao* itself. Literally this word means "path" or "way." There are three senses, however, in which this "way" can be understood.

First, *Tao* is the *way of ultimate reality*. This *Tao* cannot be perceived for it exceeds the reach of the senses. If it were to reveal itself in all its sharpness, fullness, and glory, mortal man would not be able to bear the vision. Not only does it exceed the senses, however; it exceeds all thoughts and imaginings as well. Hence words cannot describe nor define it. The *Tao Te Ching* opens by stating this point categorically: "The Tao which can be conceived is not the real Tao." Ineffable and transcendent, this ultimate *Tao* is the ground of all existence. It is behind all and beneath all, the womb from which all life springs and to which it again returns. Overawed by the very thought of it, the author of the *Tao Te Ching* bursts recurrently into hymns of praise, for he is face to face with life's "basic mystery, the mystery of mysteries, the entrance into the mystery of all life." "How clear and quiet it is! It must be something eternally existing!" "Of all great things, surely Tao is the greatest." *Tao* in this first and basic sense can be known, but only through mystical insight which cannot be translated into words—hence Taoism's teasing epigram, "Those who know don't say, and those who say don't know."

Though *Tao* ultimately is transcendent, it is also immanent. In this secondary sense it is *the way of the universe*; the norm, the rhythm, the driving power in all nature, the ordering principle behind all life. Behind, but likewise in the midst of, for when *Tao* enters this second form it "assumes flesh" and informs all things. It "adapts its vivid essence, clarifies its manifold fullness, subdues its resplendent lustre, and assumes the likeness of dust." Basically spirit rather than matter it cannot be exhausted; the more it is drawn upon the richer the fountain will gush. There are about it the marks of inevitability; when autumn comes "no leaf is spared because of its beauty, no flower because of its fragrance." Yet ultimately it is benign. Graceful instead of abrupt, flowing rather than hesitant, it is infinitely generous. Giving as it does without stint to nature and man, "it may be called the Mother of the World." As nature's agent, *Tao* bears a resemblance to Bergson's *élan vital*; as her orderer, it parallels to some extent the *lex aeterna* of the Classical West, the eternal law of nature in accord with which the universe operates. Darwin's colleague Roames could have been speaking of it when he referred to "the integrating principle of the whole—the Spirit, as it were, of the universe—instinct with contrivance, which flows with purpose."

In its third sense *Tao* refers to *the way man should order his life* to gear in with the way the universe operates. Most of what follows in this chapter will detail what Taoism suggests this way of life should be. First, however, it is necessary to point out that there have been in China not one Taoism but three.

THREE INTERPRETATIONS OF POWER AND THE DIFFERENT TAOISMS TO WHICH THEY LED

Tao Te Ching, the title of Taoism's basic text, may be translated *The Way and Its Power*. We have seen that the first of these substantive terms, the Way, can be taken in three senses. We must now add that this is also true of the second. According to the three ways *Te* or "power" can be conceived, there have arisen in China three species of Taoism so dissimilar that it is an anomaly that a common name and handbook should link them even formally.

One way to approach the basic power of the universe is through magic. From this approach to the power of *Tao* comes Popular Taoism, the Taoism of the masses. Popular Taoism is not a pretty sight. We have already said enough about the original doctrine of *Tao* to indicate that it was a concept too subtle to be grasped by the average mind or spirit. It was perhaps inevitable that when the concept was translated to make contact with the average villager and institutionalized around this translation it would be rendered in cruder and eventually perverted terms. To pass from the lofty heights of the *Tao Te Ching* to the priestcraft of Popular Taoism is like passing from a crystal mountain spring to the thick, fetid waters of a stagnant canal. Mysticism becomes mystification and religion is perverted into necromancy and sorcery. There have been long epochs in China's history when Taoism in its popular form could be characterized as little more than a funeral racket.

A second approach to the power of the universe is mystical. From this approach to *Tao*'s power came a second form of Taoism which, because it was more or less a covert doctrine, we may label Esoteric Taoism. Though it barely survived into the Christian era and left little mark on Chinese culture as a whole, it deserves mention for its instrinsic interest.

Originating at about the same time, Esoteric Taoism like Confucius was concerned with *Te*, the power that holds society together. Instead of granting Confucius' contention that such power was generated by moral example, however, the Esoteric Taoists maintained that it was basically psychic in nature. By cultivating "stillness" through yogic practices paralleling if not actually derived from India—"sitting with a blank mind," practicing "the dawn breath"—a few key individuals in each community could become perfect receptacles for *Tao*, the basic power of the universe. Thereafter these persons would radiate a kind of healing, harmonious psychic influence over the communities in which they lived. Though they would do nothing overt or dramatic and hence remain completely anonymous, the social health of the community would depend entirely on their presence.

Behind Esoteric Taoism lay a fascination with the inner as contrasted with the outer man. Every human being can be considered either externally according to what he says and does and the surface emotions he displays, or from within in which case he is approached as a subjective center of self-consciousness. As a child is not aware of this second internal aspect of his being, neither is early man. Esoteric Taoism arose as the Chinese mind was first discovering its inward dimension and was captivated by it. So wonderful was spirit that matter suffered by comparison; so sublime was the interior life that the exterior was dismissed as shell and accretion. Successive de-

320

posits of toil and worry had so silted up the soul that it was necessary to work back through their layers until "man as he was meant to be" was reached. Pure consciousness would then be struck; at last the individual would see not merely "things perceived" but "that by which we perceive."

To arrive at this inwardness it was necessary to reverse all self-seeking and cultivate perfect cleanliness of thought and body. Pure spirit can be known only in a life that is "garnished and swept." "Only where all is clean" will it reveal itself, therefore "put self aside." Perturbing emotions must likewise be quelled. Ruffling the surface of the mind they prevent introspection from seeing past them to the springs of consciousness beneath. Desire and revulsion, grief and joy, delight and annoyance—each must subside if the mind is to return to its original purity, for in the end only peace and stillness are good for it. Let anxiety be dispelled and harmony between the mind and its cosmic source will come unsought.

> It is close at hand, stands indeed at our very side; yet is intangible, a thing that by reaching for cannot be got. Remote it seems as the furthest limits of the Infinite. Yet it is not far off; every day we use its power. For . . . the Way of the Vital Spirit . . . fills out whole frames, yet man cannot keep track of it. It goes, yet has not departed. It comes, yet is not here. It is muted, makes no note that can be heard, yet of a sudden we find that it is there in the mind. It is dim and dark, showing no outward form, yet in a great stream it flowed into us at our birth.[1]

Selflessness, cleanliness, and emotional calm are the preliminaries to arriving at full self-knowledge, but they must be climaxed by deep meditation. "Bide in silence, and the radiance of the spirit shall come in and make its home." For this to happen, all outward impressions must be stilled and the senses withdrawn to a completely interior point of focus. Postures paralleling the Indian *asanas* are recommended and the breath must be similarly controlled—it must be as soft and light as that of an infant, or even an embryo in the womb. The result will be a condition of alert waiting known as "sitting with a blank mind."

And when the realization comes, what then? With it come truth, joy, and power. The climactic insight of Esoteric Taoism came with the impact of finality, everything at last having fallen into place. The condition could not be described as merely pleasurable. The direct perception of the source of one's awareness as "serene and immovable, like a monarch on a throne" brought an absolute joy completely unlike any that hitherto had been experienced. The social utility of the condition, however, lay in the extraordinary power it provided over people and things, a power in fact which

[1] Quoted by Arthur Waley, *The Way and Its Power*, pp. 48–49.

"could shift Heaven and Earth." "To the mind that is still the whole universe surrenders." As Waley points out this concept of psychic power has not been confined to the East. St. John of the Cross offers an identical promise: "Without labor you shall subject the peoples, and things shall be subject to you." Without lifting a finger overtly, a ruler who was adept in "stillness" could order a whole people with his mystical-moral power. A ruler who is desireless himself and has this much psychic power automatically turns his subjects from their unruly desires. He rules without even being known to rule.

> The Sage relies on actionless activity, . . .
> Puts himself in the background; but is always to the fore.
> Remains outside; but is always there.
> Is it not just because he does not strive for any personal end
> That all his personal ends are fulfilled?[2]

The Esoteric Taoists recognized that they could not hope for their abstruse and demanding perspective to take hold among the populace as a whole, and they made no attempt to publicize their position. When they did write, their words tended to be veiled and cryptic, open to one interpretation by initiates and another by the general public. Doubtless they wrote this way because they were sensitive to the lampooning to which mysticism so readily lends itself when the uncongenial get wind of it. So Chuang Tzu, burlesquing their breathing exercises reported that these people "expel the used air with great energy and inhale the fresh air. Like bears, they climb trees in order to breathe with greater ease." Mencius joined the fun by likening psychic short-cuts to social order to the impatient farmer who, grieved that his crops grew so slowly, went out nightly to help them along by pulling at the stalks. Despite such ridicule from outsiders, Esoteric Taoism had an appreciable core of devotees during the first five centuries before Christ. Arthur Waley considers it the basic perspective from which the *Tao Te Ching* was written.

This may be true. If so, it is proof of its veiled language. For the *Tao Te Ching* lends itself to a third reading in which the *Tao*'s power is interpreted as neither magical (as in Popular Taoism) nor mystical (as in Esoteric Taoism) but philosophical. In this third sense, the power of *Tao* is the power that enters a life that has reflectively and intuitively geared itself in with the Way of the Universe. More a perspective than an organized movement, a point of view which has had a profound influence on Chinese life, Philosophical Taoism will be the focus of the remainder of this chapter. Esoteric Taoism has vanished; Popular Taoism is corrupt; but Philosophical Taoism continues to shape Chinese character in the direction of serenity and grace.

[2] *Tao Te Ching* (Waley tr.), Chs. 2, 7.

CREATIVE QUIETUDE

The basic quality of life in tune with the universe is *wu wei*. This concept is often translated as a do-nothingness or inaction, but this (suggesting as it does a vacant attitude of passive abstention) misses the point. A better rendering is "creative quietude."

Creative quietude combines within a single individual two seemingly incompatible conditions—supreme activity and supreme relaxation. These seeming incompatibles can coexist because man is not a self-enclosed entity. He rides on an unbounded sea of *Tao* which feeds him, as we may say, through his subliminal mind. One way to create is through following the calculated directives of the conscious mind. The results of this mode of action, however, are seldom impressive; they tend to smack more of sorting and arranging than of genuine creation. Genuine creation, as every artist has discovered, comes when the more abundant resources of the subliminal self are somehow released. But for this to happen a certain dissociation from the surface self is needed. The conscious mind must relax, stop standing in its own light, let go. Only so is it possible to break through the law of reversed effort in which the more we try the more our efforts boomerang.

Wu wei is the supreme action, the precious suppleness, simplicity, and freedom that flows from us, or rather through us, when our private egos and conscious efforts yield to a power not their own. In a way it is virtue approached from a direction diametrically opposite to that of Confucius. With Confucius every effort was turned to building up a complete pattern of ideal responses which might thereafter be consciously imitated. Taoism's approach is the opposite—to get the foundations of the self in tune with *Tao* and let behavior flow spontaneously. Action follows being; new action, wiser action, stronger action will follow new being, wiser being, stronger being. The *Tao Te Ching* puts this point without wasting a single word. "The way to do," it says simply, "is to be."

How are we to describe the action that flows from a life that is grounded directly in *Tao*? Nurtured by a force that is infinitely subtle, infinitely intricate, it is a consummate gracefulness born from an abundant vitality that has no need for abruptness or violence. One simply lets *Tao* flow in and flow out again until all life becomes an even dance in which there is neither imbalance nor feverishness. *Wu wei* is life lived above tension:

> Keep stretching a bow
> You repent of the pull,
> A whetted saw
> Goes thin and dull. (Ch. 9)[3]

[3] Chapter references are to the *Tao Te Ching*, Bynner translation.

Far from inaction, however, it is the pure embodiment of suppleness, simplicity, and freedom—a kind of pure effectiveness in which no motion is wasted on outward show.

> One may move so well that a foot-print never shows,
> Speak so well that the tongue never slips,
> Reckon so well that no counter is needed. (Ch. 27)

Effectiveness of this order obviously requires an extraordinary skill, a point conveyed in the Taoist story of the fisherman who was able to land enormous fish with a thread because it was so delicately made that it had no weakest point at which to break. But Taoist skill is seldom noticed, for viewed externally *wu wei*—never forcing, never under strain—seems quite without effort. The secret here lies in the way it seeks out the empty spaces in life and nature and moves through these. Chuang Tzu, the greatest popularizer of Philosophical Taoism, makes this point with his story of a butcher whose cleaver did not get dull for twenty years. Pressed for his secret the butcher replied, "Between the bones of every joint there is always some space, otherwise there could be no movement. By seeking out this space and passing through it my cleaver lays wide the bones without touching them."

The natural phenomenon which the Taoists saw as bearing the closest resemblance to *Tao* itself was water. They were struck by the way it would support objects and carry them effortlessly on its tide. The Chinese characters for swimmer, deciphered, mean literally "one who knows the nature of water." Similarly one who knows the nature of the basic life-force knows that it will sustain him if he will only stop his thrashing and flailing and trust it to buoy him and carry him gently forward.

> Those who flow as life flows know
> They need no other force:
> They feel no wear, they feel no tear,
> They need no mending, no repair. (Ch. 15)

Water, then, was the closest parallel to *Tao* in the natural world. But it was also the prototype of *wu wei*.

The Taoists were struck by the way it adapts itself to its surroundings and seeks out the lowest places. So too,

> Man at his best, like water,
> Serves as he goes along:
> Like water he seeks his own level,
> The common level of life. (Ch. 8)

324

Yet despite its accommodation, water holds a power unknown to hard and brittle things. In a stream it follows the stones' sharp edges only to turn them in the end into pebbles, rounded to conform to its streamlined flow. It works its way past frontiers and under dividing walls. Its gentle current melts rock and carries away the proud hills we call eternal.

> What is more fluid, more yielding than water?
> Yet back it comes again, wearing down the tough strength
> Which cannot move to withstand it.
> So it is that the strong yield to the weak,
> The haughty to the humble.
> This we know
> But never learn. (Ch. 78)

Infinitely supple yet incomparably strong—these virtues of water are precisely those of *wu wei* as well. The man who embodies this condition, says the *Tao Te Ching*, "works without working." He acts without strain, persuades without argument, is eloquent without flourish, and makes his point without violence, coercion, or pressure. Though as an individual he may be scarcely noticed, his influence is in fact decisive.

> A leader is best
> When people barely know that he exists.
> . . . Of a good leader, who talks little,
> When his work is done, his aim fulfilled,
> They will all say, "We did this ourselves." (Ch. 17)

A final characteristic of water that makes it an appropriate analogue to *wu wei* is the clarity it attains through being still. "Muddy water let stand," says the *Tao Te Ching*, "will clear." If you want to study the stars after being in a brightly lit room, you have to wait twenty minutes for your eyes to dilate for their new assignment. There must be similar periods of waiting if the focal length of the mind is to be readjusted from the world's external glare to the internal recesses of the soul.

> The five colors can blind,
> The five tones deafen,
> The five tastes cloy.
> The race, the hunt, can drive men mad
> And their booty leave them no peace.
> Therefore a sensible man
> Prefers the inner to the outer eye. (Ch. 12)

Clarity can come to the inner eye, however, only in so far as man's life attains a quiet equaling that of a deep and silent pool.

OTHER TAOIST VALUES

Still following the analogy of water, the Taoists rejected all forms of self-assertiveness and competition. The world is full of people who are determined to be somebody or give trouble. They want to get ahead, to stand out. Taoism has little use for such ambition. "The ax falls first on the tallest tree."

> Standing tiptoe a man loses balance,
> Admiring himself he does so alone. . . .
> At no time in the world will a man who is sane
> Over-reach himself,
> Over-spend himself,
> Over-rate himself. (Ch. 24, 29)

Their almost reverential attitude toward humility led the Taoists to honor hunchbacks and cripples because of the way they typified meekness and self-effacement. They were fond of pointing out that the value of cups, windows, and doorways lies precisely in the parts of them that are empty. "Selfless as melting ice" is one of their descriptive figures.

The Taoists' refusal to clamber for position sprang from a profound disinterest in the things the world prizes. The point comes out in the story of Chuang Tzu's visit to the minister of a neighboring state. Someone told the minister that Chuang Tzu was coming in the hope of replacing him. The minister was severely alarmed. But when Chuang Tzu heard of the rumor he said to the minister: "In the South there is a bird. It is called *yuan-ch'u*. Have you heard of it? This *yuan-ch'u* starts from the southern ocean and flies to the northern ocean. During its whole journey it perches on no tree save the sacred Wo-tung, eats no fruit save that of the Persian Lilac, drinks only at the Magic Well. It happened that an owl that had got hold of the rotting carcass of a rat looked up as this bird flew by, and terrified lest the *yuan-ch'u* should stop and snatch at the succulent morsel, it screamed, 'Shoo! Shoo!' And now I am told that you are trying to 'Shoo' me off from this precious Ministry of yours."

So it is with most of the world's prides. They are not the true values they are thought to be.

> Surrounded with treasure
> You lie ill at ease,
> Proud beyond measure
> You come to your knees:

> Do enough, without vieing,
> Be living, not dying. (Ch. 9)

What is the point of competition or assertiveness? *Tao* seems to get along very well without them.

> Nature does not have to insist,
> Can blow for only half a morning,
> Rain for only half a day. (Ch. 23)

Man should avoid being strident and aggressive not only toward other men but also toward nature. How should man relate himself to nature? On the whole the modern Western attitude has been to regard nature as an antagonist, something to be squared off against, dominated, controlled, conquered. Taoism's attitude toward nature tends to be the precise opposite of this. There is a profound naturalism in Taoist thought, but it is the naturalism of Rousseau, Wordsworth, Thoreau rather than that of Galileo or Bacon.

> Those who would take over the earth
> And shape it to their will
> Never, I notice, succeed.
> The earth is like a vessel so sacred
> That at the mere approach of the profane
> It is marred
> And when they reach out their fingers it is gone. (Ch. 29)

Nature is to be befriended. When Mount Everest was scaled the phrase commonly used in the West to describe the feat was "the conquest of Everest." An Oriental whose writings have been deeply influenced by Taoism remarked, "We would put the matter differently. We would speak of 'the befriending of Everest.'" Taoism seeks to be in tune with nature. Its approach is basically ecological, a characteristic that has led Joseph Needham to point out that despite China's backwardness in scientific theory she early developed "an organic philosophy of nature . . . closely resembling that which modern science has been forced to adopt after three centuries of mechanical materialism." This ecological approach of Taoism has made it one of the inspirations of Frank Lloyd Wright. Taoist temples do not stand out from the landscape. They are nestled against the hills, back under the trees, blending in with the environment. At best man too blends in with nature. His highest achievement is to identify himself with the *Tao* and let it work through him.

This Taoist approach to nature has made a deep impression on Chinese art. It is no accident that the seventeenth century "Great Period" of Chinese art coincided with a great surge of Taoist influence on the Chinese sentiment and imagination. Painters took nature as their subject, and before assuming brush and silk would go out to nature, lose themselves in it, and become one with it. They would sit for half a day or fourteen years before making a stroke. The Chinese word for landscape painting is composed of the radicals for mountain and water, one of which suggests vastness and solitude, the other pliability, endurance, and continuous movement. Man's part in that vastness is small, so we have to look closely for him in the paintings if we find him at all. Usually he is climbing with his bundle, riding a buffalo, or poling a boat—man with his journey to make, his burden to carry, his hill to climb, his glimpse of beauty through the parting mists. He is not as formidable as a mountain; he does not live as long as a pine; yet he too belongs in the scheme of things as surely as the birds and the clouds. And through him as through the rest of the world flows the rhythmic movement of *Tao*.

Taoist naturalism was combined with a propensity for naturalness as well. Pomp and extravagance were regarded as pointless accretions. When Chuang Tzu's followers asked permission to give him a grand funeral he replied: "Heaven and earth are my inner and outer coffins. The sun, moon, and stars are my drapery, and the whole creation my funeral procession. What more do I want?" As with Rousseau, civilization tended to be condemned and the simplicity of primitive society idealized. "Let us have a small country with few inhabitants," said Lao Tzu. "Let the people return to the use of knotted cords [for keeping records]. Let them obtain their food sweet, their clothing beautiful, their homes comfortable, their rustic tasks pleasurable." Travel should be discouraged as pointless and conducive to idle curiosity. "The neighboring state might be so near at hand that one could hear the cocks crowing in it and dogs barking. But the people would grow old and die without ever having been there."

This drive toward simplicity most separated the Taoists from the Confucianists. The basic values of the two schools did not differ widely, but the Taoists had small patience with the Confucian approach to securing them. All formalism, show, and ceremony left them cold. What could be hoped from punctiliousness or the meticulous observance of propriety? The whole approach was artificial, a lacquered surface which was bound to prove brittle and repressive. Confucianism here was but one instance of man's general tendency to approach life in the wrong mode. All calculated systems, every attempt to arrange life in neat apple-pie order, is pointless. Different ways of slicing the same reality, in the end none of them comes to more than Three in the Morning. And what is Three in the Morning? Once in the state of Sung hard times forced a keeper of monkeys to reduce the ration of nuts he could give his charges. "From now on," he announced, "it will be three in the morning and four in the evening." At once the monkeys howled a furious protest. The keeper agreed to reconsider. When he returned he said to them, "I see your point and have revised my proposal to accommodate it. It will be four in the morning and three in the evening." The monkeys accepted with delight.

Another feature of Taoism is its notion of the relativity of all values and, as the correlate of this principle, the identity of contraries. Here Taoism tied in with the traditional Chinese symbolism of *yang* and *yin*, pictured as follows:

This polarity sums up all life's basic oppositions: good-evil, active-passive, positive-negative, light-dark, summer-winter, male-female, etc. But though its principles are in tension, they are not flatly opposed. They complement and counterbalance each other. Each invades the other's hemisphere and establishes itself in the very center of its opposite's territory. In the end both are resolved in an all-embracing circle, symbol of the final unity of *Tao*. Constantly turning and interchanging places, the opposites are but phases of a revolving wheel. Life does not move onward and upward towards a fixed pinnacle or pole. It turns and bends back upon itself until the self comes full-circle and knows that at center all things are one.

Those who meditate upon this profoundly symbolic figure, Taoists maintain, will find that it affords better access to the world's secrets than any length of words or philosophies. Faithful to it, Taoism eschews all clean-cut dichotomies. No perspective in this relative world can be considered as absolute. Who knows when the longest way around will prove the shortest way home? Or consider the relativity of dream and wakefulness. Chuang Tzu dreamed that he was a butterfly, and during the dream had no notion that he had ever been anything else. When he awoke, however, he was astonished to find that he was Chuang Tzu. But this left him with a question.

329

Was he really Chuang Tzu who had dreamed he was a butterfly, or was he a butterfly now dreaming he was Chuang Tzu?

All values and concepts, then, are ultimately relative to the mind that entertains them. When it was suggested to the wren and cicada that there are birds that fly hundreds of miles without alighting, both quickly agreed that such a thing was impossible. "You and I know very well," they said, "that the furthest one can ever get even by the most tremendous effort is that elm-tree over there; and even this one can not be sure of reaching every time. Often one finds oneself dragged back to earth long before one gets there. All these stories about flying hundreds of miles at a stretch are sheer nonsense."

In Taoist perspective even good and evil lose their absolute character. The West, encouraged in the last few centuries by puritanism, has tended to draw categorical distinctions between the two. Taoists are seldom this positive. They buttress their reticence with the story about a farmer whose horse ran away. His neighbor commiserated only to be told, "Who knows what's good or bad?" It was true. The next day the horse returned, bringing with it a drove of wild horses it had befriended in its wanderings. The neighbor came over again, this time to congratulate the farmer on his wind-fall. He was met with the same observation: "Who knows what is good or bad?" True this time too; the next day the farmer's son tried to mount one of the wild horses and fell off breaking his leg. Back came the neighbor, this time with more commiserations, only to encounter for the third time the same response, "Who knows what is good or bad?" And once again the farmer's point was well taken, for the following day soldiers came by commandeering for the army and because of his injury the son was not drafted. If this all sounds very much like Zen, it should; for Indian Buddhism processed through Chinese Taoism becomes Japanese Zen.

Taoism follows its principle of relativity to its logical limit, life and death themselves being regarded as relative phases of the Tao's embracing continuum. When Chuang Tzu's wife died, a friend came to join in the rites of mourning. He was surprised to find Chuang Tzu drumming upon an inverted rice bowl and singing a song.

"After all," said his friend, "she lived with you, brought up your children, grew old along with you. That you should not mourn for her is bad enough; but to let your friends find you drumming and singing—that is going too far!"

"You misjudge me," said Chuang Tzu. "When she died I was in despair, as any man well might be. But soon, pondering on what had happened, I told myself that in death no strange new fate befalls us. . . . If some one is tired and has gone to lie down, we do not pursue him with hooting and bawling. She whom I have lost has lain down to sleep for awhile in the

Great Inner Room. To break in upon her rest with the noise of lamentation would but show that I know nothing of nature's Sovereign Law. That is why I ceased to mourn."

Elsewhere Chuang Tzu expressed his confidence in the face of death directly:

> There is the globe,
> The foundation of my bodily existence.
> It wears me out with work and duties,
> It gives me rest in old age,
> It gives me peace in death.
> For the one who supplied me with what I needed in life
> Will also give me what I need in death.[4]

It is no surprise to find an outlook as averse to violence as Taoism verging on strict pacifism in its attitude toward war. There are passages in the *Tao Te Ching* that read almost like the *Sermon on the Mount*.

> One who would guide a leader of men in the uses of life
> Will warn him against the use of arms for conquest.
> Even the finest arms are an instrument of evil:
> An army's harvest is a waste of thorns.
>
> In time of war men civilized in peace
> Turn from their higher to their lower nature.
> But triumph is not beautiful
> He who thinks triumph beautiful
> Is one with a will to kill.
> The death of a multitude is cause for mourning:
> Conduct your triumph as a funeral. (Chs. 30, 31, rearranged.)

That in traditional China the scholar ranked at the top of the social scale may be the doing of Confucius, but Taoism is fully as responsible for placing the soldier at the bottom. "The way for a vital man to go is not the way of a soldier." Only the man "who recognizes all men as members of his own body is a sound man to guard them. . . . Heaven arms with compassion those whom she would not see destroyed."

War is a solemn matter, and Taoism spoke to life's solemn issues. Yet it always retained in its approach to every problem a quality of lightness verging on gaiety. There is a sophistication, an urbanity, a charm about the perspective which is infectious. "He who feels punctured," observes the *Tao Te Ching*, "must once have been a bubble." The economy, directness, and

[4] Quoted in K. L. Richelt, *Meditation and Piety in the Far East* (New York: Harper and Row, 1954), p. 102.

fundamental good humor of such a statement is typical of its entire outlook. In its freedom from the tortured, heavy-booted approach to life it is at one with the rest of China; but it is also, as we have seen, free of the Confucian tendency toward rigidity and formalism. Taoist literature is full of dialogues with Confucianists in which the latter are shown up as stuffy and pompous. An instance is the story of Chuang Tzu (the Taoist) and Hui Tzu (the Confucianist) who were strolling one day on a bridge over the Hao river. Observed Chuang Tzu:

"Look how the minnows dart hither and thither at will. Such is the pleasure fish enjoy."

"You are not a fish," responded Hui Tzu. "How do you know what gives pleasure to fish?"

"You are not I," said Chuang Tzu. "How do you know I do not know what gives pleasure to fish?"

William James (1842–1910) was born in New York into wealth and a cos-
mopolitan, intellectual environment. His father, Henry James, Senior, moved his
children through a long succession of private schools in the United States and
Europe. James, however, had difficulties finding himself and his work, and during
his twenties there were problems with his health and even more serious periods
of depression. He was graduated from Harvard with a degree in medicine, but
it was not until he was thirty that he began his teaching career as an instructor of
anatomy and physiology at Harvard. The good years followed: there was a happy
marriage and five children, and eleven years of work culminated in his Principles
of Psychology. At Harvard he progressed to psychology and finally to philosophy.
James wrote in a style that reflected his warm, very natural, and sometimes restless
personality. An informal and engaging teacher, he "seemed hardly imposing
enough for a great man." But in the classroom "the spirit would sometimes come
upon him, and, leaning his head on his hand, he would let fall golden words,
picturesque, fresh from the heart, full of the knowledge of good and evil."[1] Among
his books are The Will to Believe, Pragmatism, The Meaning of Truth, and A
Pluralistic Universe. "Mysticism" is from The Varieties of Religious Experience
(1902).

. . . One may say truly, I think, that personal religious experience has its
root and centre in mystical states of consciousness; so for us, who in these
lectures are treating personal experience as the exclusive subject of our
study, such states of consciousness ought to form the vital chapter from which
the other chapters get their light. Whether my treatment of mystical states
will shed more light or darkness, I do not know, for my own constitution
shuts me out from their enjoyment almost entirely, and I can speak of them
only at second hand. But though forced to look upon the subject so externally, I will be as objective and receptive as I can; and I think I shall at
least succeed in convincing you of the reality of the states in question, and
of the paramount importance of their function.

First of all, then, I ask, What does the expression 'mystical states of
consciousness' mean? How do we part off mystical states from other states?

The words 'mysticism' and 'mystical' are often used as terms of mere reproach, to throw at any opinion which we regard as vague and vast and
sentimental, and without a base in either facts or logic. For some writers a
'mystic' is any person who believes in thought-transference, or spirit-return.

[1] George Santayana, *Character and Opinion in the United States* (New York: Doubleday Anchor Books, 1954), p. 59.

Employed in this way the word has little value: there are too many less ambiguous synonyms. So, to keep it useful by restricting it, I will do what I did in the case of the word 'religion,' and simply propose to you four marks which, when an experience has them, may justify us in calling it mystical for the purpose of the present lectures. In this way we shall save verbal disputation, and the recriminations that generally go therewith.

1. *Ineffability.* The handiest of the marks by which I classify a state of mind as mystical is negative. The subject of it immediately says that it defies expression, that no adequate report of its contents can be given in words. It follows from this that its quality must be directly experienced; it cannot be imparted or transferred to others. In this peculiarity mystical states are more like states of feeling than like states of intellect. No one can make clear to another who has never had a certain feeling, in what the quality or worth of it consists. One must have musical ears to know the value of a symphony; one must have been in love one's self to understand a lover's state of mind. Lacking the heart or ear, we cannot interpret the musician or the lover justly, and are even likely to consider him weak-minded or absurd. The mystic finds that most of us accord to his experiences an equally incompetent treatment.

2. *Noetic quality.* Although so similar to states of feeling, mystical states seem to those who experience them to be also states of knowledge. They are states of insight into depths of truth unplumbed by the discursive intellect. They are illuminations, revelations, full of significance and importance, all inarticulate though they remain; and as a rule they carry with them a curious sense of authority for after-time.

These two characters will entitle any state to be called mystical, in the sense in which I use the word. Two other qualities are less sharply marked, but are usually found. These are:

3. *Transiency.* Mystical states cannot be sustained for long. Except in rare instances, half an hour, or at most an hour or two, seems to be the limit beyond which they fade into the light of common day. Often, when faded, their quality can but imperfectly be reproduced in memory; but when they recur it is recognized; and from one recurrence to another it is susceptible of continuous development in what is felt as inner richness and importance.

4. *Passivity.* Although the oncoming of mystical states may be facilitated by preliminary voluntary operations, as by fixing the attention, or going through certain bodily performances, or in other ways which manuals of mysticism prescribe; yet when the characteristic sort of consciousness once has set in, the mystic feels as if his own will were in abeyance, and indeed sometimes as if he were grasped and held by a superior power. This latter peculiarity connects mystical states with certain definite phenomena of secondary or alternative personality, such as prophetic speech, automatic

writing, or the mediumistic trance. When these latter conditions are well pronounced, however, there may be no recollection whatever of the phenomenon, and it may have no significance for the subject's usual inner life, to which, as it were, it makes a mere interruption. Mystical states, strictly so called, are never merely interruptive. Some memory of their content always remains, and a profound sense of their importance. They modify the inner life of the subject between the times of their recurrence. . . .

Nitrous oxide and ether, especially nitrous oxide, when sufficiently diluted with air, stimulate the mystical consciousness in an extraordinary degree. Depth beyond depth of truth seems revealed to the inhaler. This truth fades out, however, or escapes, at the moment of coming to; and if any words remain over in which it seemed to clothe itself, they prove to be the veriest nonsense. Nevertheless, the sense of a profound meaning having been there persists; and I know more than one person who is persuaded that in the nitrous oxide trance we have a genuine metaphysical revelation.

Some years ago I myself made some observations on this aspect of nitrous oxide intoxication, and reported them in print. One conclusion was forced upon my mind at that time, and my impression of its truth has ever since remained unshaken. It is that our normal waking consciousness, rational consciousness as we call it, is but one special type of consciousness, whilst all about it, parted from it by the filmiest of screens, there lie potential forms of consciousness entirely different. We may go through life without suspecting their existence; but apply the requisite stimulus, and at a touch they are there in all their completeness, definite types of mentality which probably somewhere have their field of application and adaptation. No account of the universe in its totality can be final which leaves these other forms of consciousness quite disregarded. How to regard them is the question, for they are so discontinuous with ordinary consciousness. Yet they may determine attitudes though they cannot furnish formulas, and open a region though they fail to give a map. At any rate, they forbid a premature closing of our accounts with reality. Looking back on my own experiences, they all converge towards a kind of insight to which I cannot help ascribing some metaphysical significance. The keynote of it is invariably a reconciliation. It is as if the opposites of the world, whose contradictoriness and conflict make all our difficulties and troubles, were melted into unity. . . .

[*An instance of the mystical experience is taken from the Autobiography of J. Trevor:*]

One brilliant Sunday morning, my wife and boys went to the Unitarian Chapel in Macclesfield. I felt it impossible to accompany them—as though to leave the sunshine on the hills, and go down there to the chapel, would be for the time an act of spiritual suicide. And I felt such need for new inspiration and expansion in my life. So, very reluctantly and sadly, I left my wife and boys to go down into the town, while I went further up into the hills with my stick and my dog. In the loveliness of the morning, and the beauty of the hills and valleys, I soon lost my sense of sadness and, regret. For nearly an hour I walked along the road to the 'Cat and Fiddle,' and then returned. On the way back, suddenly, without warning, I felt that I was in Heaven—an inward state of peace and joy and assurance indescribably intense, accompanied with a sense of being bathed in a warm glow of light, as though the external condition had brought about the internal effect —a feeling of having passed beyond the body, though the scene around me stood out more clearly and as if nearer to me than before, by reason of the illumination in the midst of which I seemed to be placed. This deep emotion lasted, though with decreasing strength, until I reached home, and for some time after, only gradually passing away.[1]

The writer adds that having had further experiences of a similar sort, he now knows them well.

The spiritual life, [he writes], justifies itself to those who live it; but what can we say to those who do not understand? This, at least, we can say, that it is a life whose experiences are proved real to their possessor, because they remain with him when brought closest into contact with the objective realities of life. Dreams cannot stand this test. We wake from them to find that they are but dreams. Wanderings of an overwrought brain do not stand this test. These highest experiences that I have had of God's presence have been rare and brief—flashes of consciousness which have compelled me to exclaim with surprise—God is *here!*—or conditions of exaltation and insight, less intense, and only gradually passing away. I have severely questioned the worth of these moments. To no soul have I named them, lest I should be building my life and work on mere phantasies of the brain. But I find that, after every questioning and test, they stand out to-day as the most real experiences of my life, and experiences which have explained and justified and unified all past experiences and all past growth. Indeed, their reality and their far-reaching significance are ever becoming more clear and evident. When they came, I was living the fullest, strongest, sanest, deepest life. I was not seeking them. What I was seeking, with resolute determination, was to live more intensely my own life, as against what I knew would be the adverse judgment of the world. It was in the most real seasons that the Real Presence came, and I was aware that I was immersed in the infinite ocean of God.[2]

. . . A Canadian psychiatrist, Dr. R. M. Bucke, gives to the more distinctly characterized of these phenomena the name of cosmic consciousness. "Cos-

[1] My Quest for God, London, 1897, pp. 268, 269, abridged.
[2] Op. cit., pp. 256, 257, abridged.

mic consciousness in its more striking instances is not," Dr. Bucke says, "simply an expansion or extension of the self-conscious mind with which we are all familiar, but the superaddition of a function as distinct from any possessed by the average man as *self*-consciousness is distinct from any function possessed by one of the higher animals."

> The prime characteristic of cosmic consciousness is a consciousness of the cosmos, that is, of the life and order of the universe. Along with the consciousness of the cosmos there occurs an intellectual enlightenment which alone would place the individual on a new plane of existence—would make him almost a member of a new species. To this is added a state of moral exaltation, an indescribable feeling of elevation, elation, and joyousness, and a quickening of the moral sense, which is fully as striking, and more important than is the enhanced intellectual power. With these come what may be called a sense of immortality, a consciousness of eternal life, not a conviction that he shall have this, but the consciousness that he has it already.[3]

It was Dr. Bucke's own experience of a typical onset of cosmic consciousness in his own person which led him to investigate it in others. He has printed his conclusions in a highly interesting volume, from which I take the following account of what occurred to him:—

> I had spent the evening in a great city, with two friends, reading and discussing poetry and philosophy. We parted at midnight. I had a long drive in a hansom to my lodging. My mind, deeply under the influence of the ideas, images, and emotions called up by the reading and talk, was calm and peaceful. I was in a state of quiet, almost passive enjoyment, not actually thinking, but letting ideas, images, and emotions flow of themselves, as it were, through my mind. All at once, without warning of any kind, I found myself wrapped in a flame-colored cloud. For an instant I thought of fire, an immense conflagration somewhere close by in that great city; the next, I knew that the fire was within myself. Directly afterward there came upon me a sense of exultation, of immense joyousness accompanied or immediately followed by an intellectual illumination impossible to describe. Among other things, I did not merely come to believe, but I saw that the universe is not composed of dead matter, but is, on the contrary, a living Presence; I became conscious in myself of eternal life. It was not a conviction that I would have eternal life, but a consciousness that I possessed eternal life then; I saw that all men are immortal; that the cosmic order is such that without any peradventure all things work together for the good of each and all; that the foundation principle of the world, of all the worlds, is what we call love, and that the happiness of each and all is in the long run absolutely certain.

[3] Cosmic Consciousness: a study in the evolution of the human Mind, Philadelphia, 1901, p. 2.

The vision lasted a few seconds and was gone; but the memory of it and the sense of the reality of what it taught has remained during the quarter of a century which has since elapsed. I knew that what the vision showed was true. I had attained to a point of view from which I saw that it must be true. That view, that conviction, I may say that consciousness, has never, even during periods of the deepest depression, been lost.[4]

We have now seen enough of this cosmic or mystic consciousness, as it comes sporadically. We must next pass to its methodical cultivation as an element of the religious life. Hindus, Buddhists, Mohammedans, and Christians all have cultivated it methodically.

In India, training in mystical insight has been known from time immemorial under the name of yoga. Yoga means the experimental union of the individual with the divine. It is based on persevering exercise; and the diet, posture, breathing, intellectual concentration, and moral discipline vary slightly in the different systems which teach it. The yogi, or disciple, who has by these means overcome the obscurations of his lower nature sufficiently, enters into the condition termed *samâdhi*, "and comes face to face with facts which no instinct or reason can ever know." He learns—

> That the mind itself has a higher state of existence, beyond reason, a superconscious state, and that when the mind gets to that higher state, then this knowledge beyond reasoning comes. . . . All the different steps in yoga are intended to bring us scientifically to the superconscious state or samâdhi. . . . Just as unconscious work is beneath consciousness, so there is another work which is above consciousness, and which, also, is not accompanied with the feeling of egoism. . . . There is no feeling of *I*, and yet the mind works, desireless, free from restlessness, objectless, bodiless. Then the Truth shines in its full effulgence, and we know ourselves—for Samâdhi lies potential in us all—for what we truly are, free, immortal, omnipotent, loosed from the finite, and its contrasts of good and evil altogether, and identical with the Atman or Universal Soul.[5]

The Vedantists say that one may stumble into superconsciousness sporadically, without the previous discipline, but it is then impure. Their test of its purity, like our test of religion's value, is empirical: its fruits must be good for life. When a man comes out of Samâdhi, they assure us that he remains "enlightened, a sage, a prophet, a saint, his whole character changed, his life changed, illumined.". . .

[4] Loc. cit., pp. 7, 8. My quotation follows the privately printed pamphlet which preceded Dr. Bucke's larger work, and differs verbally a little from the text of the latter.

[5] My quotations are from VIVEKANANDA, Raja Yoga, London, 1896. The completest source of information on Yoga is the work translated by VIHARI LALA MITRA: Yoga Vasishta Maha Ramayana, 4 vols., Calcutta, 1891–99.

In the Christian church there have always been mystics. Although many of them have been viewed with suspicion, some have gained favor in the eyes of the authorities. The experiences of these have been treated as precedents, and a codified system of mystical theology has been based upon them, in which everything legitimate finds its place. The basis of the system is 'orison' or meditation, the methodical elevation of the soul towards God. Through the practice of orison the higher levels of mystical experience may be attained. It is odd that Protestantism, especially evangelical Protestantism, should seemingly have abandoned everything methodical in this line. Apart from what prayer may lead to, Protestant mystical experience appears to have been almost exclusively sporadic. It has been left to our mind-curers to reintroduce methodical meditation into our religious life.

The first thing to be aimed at in orison is the mind's detachment from outer sensations, for these interfere with its concentration upon ideal things. Such manuals as Saint Ignatius's Spiritual Exercises recommend the disciple to expel sensation by a graduated series of efforts to imagine holy scenes. The acme of this kind of discipline would be a semi-hallucinatory mono-ideism—an imaginary figure of Christ, for example, coming fully to occupy the mind. Sensorial images of this sort, whether literal or symbolic, play an enormous part in mysticism. But in certain cases imagery may fall away entirely, and in the very highest raptures it tends to do so. The state of consciousness becomes then insusceptible of any verbal description. Mystical teachers are unanimous as to this. Saint John of the Cross, for instance, one of the best of them, thus describes the condition called the 'union of love," which, he says, is reached by 'dark contemplation.' In this the Deity compenetrates the soul, but in such a hidden way that the soul—

finds no terms, no means, no comparison whereby to render the sublimity of the wisdom and the delicacy of the spiritual feeling with which she is filled. . . . We receive this mystical knowledge of God clothed in none of the kinds of images, in none of the sensible representations, which our mind makes use of in other circumstances. Accordingly in this knowledge, since the senses and the imagination are not employed, we get neither form nor impression, nor can we give any account or furnish any likeness, although the mysterious and sweet-tasting wisdom comes home so clearly to the inmost parts of our soul. Fancy a man seeing a certain kind of thing for the first time in his life. He can understand it, use and enjoy it, but he cannot apply a name to it, nor communicate any idea of it, even though all the while it be a mere thing of sense. How much greater will be his powerlessness when it goes beyond the senses! This is the peculiarity of the divine language. The more infused, intimate, spiritual, and supersensible it is, the more does it exceed the senses, both inner and outer, and impose silence upon them. . . . The soul then feels as if placed in a vast and profound solitude, to which no created thing has access, in an immense and boundless desert, desert the more delicious the more solitary it is. There, in this abyss of wisdom, the soul grows by what it drinks in from the well-springs of the comprehension of love, . . . and recognizes, however sublime and learned may be the terms we employ, how utterly vile, insignificant, and improper they are, when we seek to discourse of divine things by their means.[6]

I cannot pretend to detail to you the sundry stages of the Christian mystical life. Our time would not suffice, for one thing; and moreover, I confess that the subdivisions and names which we find in the Catholic books seem to me to represent nothing objectively distinct. So many men, so many minds: I imagine that these experiences can be as infinitely varied as are the idiosyncrasies of individuals.

The cognitive aspects of them, their value in the way of revelation, is what we are directly concerned with, and it is easy to show by citation how strong an impression they leave of being revelations of new depths of truth. Saint Teresa is the expert of experts in describing such conditions, so I will turn immediately to what she says of one of the highest of them, the 'orison of union.'

In the orison of union [says Saint Teresa], the soul is fully awake as regards God, but wholly asleep as regards things of this world and in respect of herself. During the short time the union lasts, she is as it were deprived of every feeling, and even if she would, she could not think of any single thing. Thus she needs to employ no artifice in order to arrest the use of her understanding: it remains so stricken with inactivity that she neither knows what she loves, nor in what manner she loves, nor what she wills. In short, she is utterly dead to the things of the world and lives solely in God. . . . I do not even know whether in this state she has enough life left to breathe. It seems to me she has not; or at least that if she does breathe, she is unaware of it. Her intellect would fain understand something of what is going on within her, but it has so little force now that it can act in no way whatsoever. So a person who falls into a deep faint appears as if dead. . . .

Thus does God, when he raises a soul to union with himself, suspend the natural action of all her faculties. She neither sees, hears, nor understands, so long as she is united with God. But this time is always short, and it seems even shorter than it is. God establishes himself in the interior of this soul in such a way, that when she returns to herself, it is wholly impossible for her to doubt that she has been in God, and God in her. This truth

[6] Saint John of the Cross: The Dark Night of the Soul, book ii. ch. xvii., in Vie et Œuvres, 3me édition, Paris 1893, iii. 428–432. Chapter xi, of book ii. of Saint John's Ascent of Carmel is devoted to showing the harmfulness for the mystical life of the use of sensible imagery.

remains so strongly impressed on her that, even though many years should pass without the condition returning, she can neither forget the favor she received, nor doubt of its reality. If you, nevertheless, ask how it is possible that the soul can see and understand that she has been in God, since during the union she has neither sight nor understanding, I reply that she does not see it then, but that she sees it clearly later, after she has returned to herself, not by any vision, but by a certitude which abides with her and which God alone can give her. I knew a person who was ignorant of the truth that God's mode of being in everything must be either by presence, by power, or by essence, but who, after having received the grace of which I am speaking, believed this truth in the most unshakable manner. So much so that, having consulted a half-learned man who was as ignorant on this point as she had been before she was enlightened, when he replied that God is in us only by 'grace,' she disbelieved his reply, so sure she was of the true answer; and when she came to ask wiser doctors, they confirmed her in her belief, which much consoled her. . . .

But how, you will repeat, *can* one have such certainty in respect to what one does not see? This question, I am powerless to answer. These are secrets of God's omnipotence which it does not appertain to me to penetrate. All that I know is that I tell the truth; and I shall never believe that any soul who does not possess this certainty has ever been really united to God.[7] . . .

. . . There are many similar pages in her autobiography. Where in literature is a more evidently veracious account of the formation of a new centre of spiritual energy, than is given in her description of the effects of certain ecstasies which in departing leave the soul upon a higher level of emotional excitement?

Often, infirm and wrought upon with dreadful pains before the ecstasy, the soul emerges from it full of health and admirably disposed for action . . . as if God had willed that the body itself, already obedient to the soul's desires, should share in the soul's happiness. . . . The soul after such a favor is animated with a degree of courage so great that if at that moment its body should be torn to pieces for the cause of God, it would feel nothing but the liveliest comfort. Then it is that promises and heroic resolutions spring up in profusion in us, soaring desires, horror of the world, and the clear perception of our proper nothingness. . . . What empire is comparable to that of a soul who, from this sublime summit to which God has raised her, sees all the things of earth beneath her feet, and is captivated by no one of them? How ashamed she is of her former attachments! How amazed at her blindness! What lively pity she feels for those whom she recognizes still shrouded in the darkness! . . . She groans at having ever been sensitive to points of honor, at the illusion that made her ever see as honor what the

[7] The Interior Castle, Fifth Abode, ch. i., in Œuvres, translated by BOUIX, iii. 421–424.

world calls by that name. Now she sees in this name nothing more than an immense lie of which the world remains a victim. She discovers, in the new light from above, that in genuine honor there is nothing spurious, that to be faithful to this honor is to give our respect to what deserves to be respected really, and to consider as nothing, or as less than nothing, whatsoever perishes and is not agreeable to God. . . . She laughs when she sees grave persons, persons of orison, caring for points of honor for which she now feels profoundest contempt. It is suitable to the dignity of their rank to act thus, they pretend, and it makes them more useful to others. But she knows that in despising the dignity of their rank for the pure love of God they would do more good in a single day than they would effect in ten years by preserving it. . . . She laughs at herself that there should ever have been a time in her life when she made any case of money, when she ever desired it. . . . Oh! if human beings might only agree together to regard it as so much useless mud, what harmony would then reign in the world! With what friendship we would all treat each other if our interest in honor and in money could but disappear from earth! For my own part, I feel as if it would be a remedy for all our ills.[8] . . .

This overcoming of all the usual barriers between the individual and the Absolute is the great mystic achievement. In mystic states we both become one with the Absolute and we become aware of our oneness. This is the everlasting and triumphant mystical tradition, hardly altered by differences of clime or creed. In Hinduism, in Neoplatonism, in Sufism, in Christian mysticism, in Whitmanism, we find the same recurring note, so that there is about mystical utterances an eternal unanimity which ought to make a critic stop and think, and which brings it about that the mystical classics have, as has been said, neither birthday nor native land. Perpetually telling of the unity of man with God, their speech antedates languages, and they do not grow old.

'That art Thou!' say the Upanishads, and the Vedantists add: 'Not a part, not a mode of That, but identically That, that absolute Spirit of the World.' "As pure water poured into pure water remains the same, thus, O Gautama, is the Self of a thinker who knows. Water in water, fire in fire, ether in ether, no one can distinguish them; likewise a man whose mind has entered into the Self." " 'Every man,' says the Sufi Gulshan-Râz, 'whose heart is no longer shaken by any doubt, knows with certainty that there is no being save only One. . . . In his divine majesty the *me*, the *we*, the *thou*, are not found, for in the One there can be no distinction. Every being who is annulled and entirely separated from himself, hears resound outside of him this voice and this echo: *I am God*: he has an eternal way of existing, and is no longer subject to death.' " In the vision of God, says Plotinus,

[8] Vie, pp. 200, 229, 231–233, 243.

342

"what sees is not our reason, but something prior and superior to our reason. . . . He who thus sees does not properly see, does not distinguish or imagine two things. He changes, he ceases to be himself, preserves nothing of himself. Absorbed in God, he makes but one with him, like a centre of a circle coinciding with another centre." "Here," writes Suso, "the spirit dies, and yet is all alive in the marvels of the Godhead . . . and is lost in the stillness of the glorious dazzling obscurity and of the naked simple unity. It is in this modeless *where* that the highest bliss is to be found.". . .

A FREE MAN'S WORSHIP

No justice can be done in such few words to the long and illustrious career of Bertrand Russell (1871–1970). In his ninety-seven years he wrote some 60 books and an estimated 2000 articles, and was intensely involved in controversial political and social causes. He was imprisoned during World War I for pacifist activities and was arrested at the age of eighty-seven for demonstrating against nuclear armaments. In a case in 1940, a court decreed that he was not to teach at the City College of New York: it was feared that Russell, like Socrates, would corrupt the young. His genius and integrity in the world of ideas was expressed in writing noted for its clarity, and in 1950 he was awarded the Nobel prize for literature. "Three passions," he wrote in his Autobiography, *"simple but overwhelmingly strong, have governed my life: the longing for love, the search for knowledge, and unbearable pity for the suffering of mankind." Indicating the range of his interests, some of his titles include* A Critical Exposition of the Philosophy of Leibniz, The Problems of Philosophy, Our Knowledge of the External World, Roads to Freedom, Marriage and Morals, The Scientific Outlook, Education and the Social Order, *and* A History of Western Philosophy. *"A Free Man's Worship" was originally published in 1903.*

To Dr. Faustus in his study Mephistopheles told the history of the Creation, saying:

> The endless praises of the choirs of angels had begun to grow wearisome; for, after all, did he not deserve their praise? Had he not given them endless joy? Would it not be more amusing to obtain undeserved praise, to be worshiped by beings whom he tortured? He smiled inwardly, and resolved that the great drama should be performed.
>
> For countless ages the hot nebula whirled aimlessly through space. At length it began to take shape, the central mass threw off planets, the planets cooled, boiling seas and burning mountains heaved and tossed, from black masses of cloud hot sheets of rain deluged the barely solid crust. And now the first germ of life grew in the depths of the ocean, and developed rapidly in the fructifying warmth into vast forest trees, huge ferns springing from the damp mold, sea monsters breeding, fighting, devouring, and passing away. And from the monsters, as the play unfolded itself, Man was born, with the power of thought, the knowledge of good and evil, and the cruel thirst for worship. And Man saw that all is passing in this mad, monstrous world, that all is struggling to snatch, at any cost, a few brief moments of life before Death's inexorable decree. And Man said: 'There is a hidden purpose, could we but fathom it, and the purpose is good; for we must reverence something, and in the visible world there is nothing worthy of

344

reverence.' And Man stood aside from the struggle, resolving that God intended harmony to come out of chaos by human efforts. And when he followed the instincts which God had transmitted to him from his ancestry of beasts of prey, he called it Sin, and asked God to forgive him. But he doubted whether he could be justly forgiven, until he invented a divine Plan by which God's wrath was to have been appeased. And seeing the present was bad, he made it yet worse, that thereby the future might be better. And he gave God thanks for the strength that enabled him to forgo even the joys that were possible. And God smiled; and when he saw that Man had become perfect in renunciation and worship, he sent another sun through the sky, which crashed into Man's sun; and all returned again to nebula.

"Yes," he murmured, "It was a good play; I will have it performed again."

Such, in outline, but even more purposeless, more void of meaning, is the world which Science presents for our belief. Amid such a world, if anywhere, our ideals henceforth must find a home. That Man is the product of causes which had no prevision of the end they were achieving; that his origin, his growth, his hopes and fears, his loves and his beliefs, are but the outcome of accidental collocations of atoms; that no fire, no heroism, no intensity of thought and feeling, can preserve an individual life beyond the grave; that all the labors of the ages, all the devotion, all the inspiration, all the noonday brightness of human genius, are destined to extinction in the vast death of the solar system, and that the whole temple of Man's achievement must inevitably be buried beneath the débris of a universe in ruins—all these things, if not quite beyond dispute, are yet so nearly certain, that no philosophy which rejects them can hope to stand. Only within the scaffolding of these truths, only on the firm foundation of unyielding despair, can the soul's habitation henceforth be safely built.

How, in such an alien and inhuman world, can so powerless a creature as Man preserve his aspirations untarnished? A strange mystery it is that Nature, omnipotent but blind, in the revolutions of her secular hurryings through the abysses of space, has brought forth at last a child, subject still to her power, but gifted with sight, with knowledge of good and evil, with the capacity of judging all the works of his unthinking Mother. In spite of Death, the mark and seal of the parental control, Man is yet free, during his brief years, to examine, to criticize, to know, and in imagination to create. To him alone, in the world with which he is acquainted, this freedom belongs; and in this lies his superiority to the resistless forces that control his outward life.

The savage, like ourselves, feels the oppression of his impotence before the powers of Nature; but having in himself nothing that he respects more than Power, he is willing to prostrate himself before his gods, without inquiring

345

whether they are worthy of his worship. Pathetic and very terrible is the long history of cruelty and torture, of degradation and human sacrifice, endured in the hope of placating the jealous gods: surely, the trembling believer thinks, when what is most precious has been freely given, their lust for blood must be appeased, and more will not be required. The religion of Moloch—as such creeds may be generically called—is in essence the cringing submission of the slave, who dare not, even in his heart, allow the thought that his master deserves no adulation. Since the independence of ideals is not yet acknowledged, Power may be freely worshiped, and receive an unlimited respect, despite its wanton infliction of pain.

But gradually, as morality grows bolder, the claim of the ideal world begins to be felt; and worship, if it is not to cease, must be given to gods of another kind than those created by the savage. Some, though they feel the demands of the ideal, will still consciously reject them, still urging that naked Power is worthy of worship. Such is the attitude inculcated in God's answer to Job out of the whirlwind: the divine power and knowledge are paraded, but of the divine goodness there is no hint. Such also is the attitude of those who, in our own day, base their morality upon the struggle for survival, maintaining that the survivors are necessarily the fittest. But others, not content with an answer so repugnant to the moral sense, will adopt the position which we have become accustomed to regard as specially religious, maintaining that, in some hidden manner the world of fact is really harmonious with the world of ideals. Thus Man creates God, all-powerful and all-good, the mystic unity of what is and what should be.

But the world of fact, after all, is not good; and, in submitting our judgment to it, there is an element of slavishness from which our thoughts must be purged. For in all things it is well to exalt the dignity of Man, by freeing him as far as possible from the tyranny of non-human Power. When we have realized that Power is largely bad, that man, with his knowledge of good and evil, is but a helpless atom in a world which has no such knowledge, the choice is again presented to us: Shall we worship Force, or shall we worship Goodness? Shall our God exist and be evil or shall he be recognized as the creation of our own conscience?

The answer to this question is very momentous, and affects profoundly our whole morality. The worship of Force, to which Carlyle and Nietzsche and the creed of Militarism have accustomed us, is the result of failure to maintain our own ideals against a hostile universe: it is itself a prostrate submission to evil, a sacrifice of our best to Moloch. If strength indeed is to be respected, let us respect rather the strength of those who refuse that false "recognition of facts" which fails to recognize that facts are often bad. Let us admit that, in the world we know, there are many things that would be better otherwise, and that the ideals to which we do and must adhere are not realized in the realm of matter. Let us preserve our respect for truth, for beauty, for the ideal of perfection which life does not permit us to attain, though none of these things meet with the approval of the unconscious universe. If Power is bad, as it seems to be, let us reject it from our hearts. In this lies Man's true freedom: in determination to worship only the God created by our own love of the good, to respect only the heaven which inspires the insight of our best moments. In action, in desire, we must submit perpetually to the tyranny of outside forces; but in thought, in aspiration, we are free, free from our fellow-men, free from the petty planet on which our bodies impotently crawl, free even, while we live, from the tyranny of death. Let us learn, then, that energy of faith which enables us to live constantly in the vision of the good; and let us descend, in action, into the world of fact, with that vision always before us.

When first the opposition of fact and ideal grows fully visible, a spirit of fiery revolt, of fierce hatred of the gods, seems necessary to the assertion of freedom. To defy with Promethean constancy a hostile universe, to keep its evil always in view, always actively hated, to refuse no pain that the malice of Power can invent, appears to be the duty of all who will not bow before the inevitable. But indignation is still a bondage, for it compels our thoughts to be occupied with an evil world; and in the fierceness of desire from which rebellion springs there is a kind of self-assertion which it is necessary for the wise to overcome. Indignation is a submission of our thoughts, but not of our desires; the Stoic freedom in which wisdom consists is found in the submission of our desires, but not of our thoughts. From the submission of our desires springs the virtue of resignation; from the freedom of our thoughts springs the whole world of art and philosophy, and the vision of beauty by which, at last, we half reconquer the reluctant world. But the vision of beauty is possible only to unfettered contemplation, to thoughts not weighted by the load of eager wishes; and thus Freedom comes only to those who no longer ask of life that it shall yield them any of those personal goods that are subject to the mutations of Time.

Although the necessity of renunciation is evidence of the existence of evil, yet Christianity, in preaching it, has shown a wisdom exceeding that of the Promethean philosophy of rebellion. It must be admitted that, of the things we desire, some, though they prove impossible, are yet real goods; others, however, as ardently longed for, do not form part of a fully purified ideal. The belief that what must be renounced is bad, though sometimes false, is far less often false than untamed passion supposes; and the creed of religion, by providing a reason for proving that it is never false, has been the means of purifying our hopes by the discovery of many austere truths.

But there is in resignation a further good element: even real goods, when they are unattainable, ought not to be fretfully desired. To every man comes, sooner or later, the great renunciation. For the young, there is nothing unattainable; a good thing desired with the whole force of a passionate will, and yet impossible, is to them not credible. Yet, by death, by illness, by poverty, or by the voice of duty, we must learn, each one of us, that the world was not made for us, and that, however beautiful may be the things we crave, Fate may nevertheless forbid them. It is the part of courage, when misfortune comes, to bear without repining the ruin of our hopes, to turn away our thoughts from vain regrets. This degree of submission to Power is not only just and right: it is the very gate of wisdom.

But passive renunciation is not the whole of wisdom; for not by renunciation alone can we build a temple for the worship of our own ideals. Haunting foreshadowings of the temple appear in the realm of imagination, in music, in architecture, in the untroubled kingdom of reason, and in the golden sunset magic of lyrics, where beauty shines and glows, remote from the touch of sorrow, remote from the fear of change, remote from the failures and disenchantments of the world of fact. In the contemplation of these things the vision of heaven will shape itself in our hearts, giving at once a touchstone to judge the world about us, and an inspiration by which to fashion to our needs whatever is not incapable of serving as a stone in the sacred temple.

Except for those rare spirits that are born without sin, there is a cavern of darkness to be traversed before that temple can be entered. The gate of the cavern is despair, and its floor is paved with the gravestones of abandoned hopes. There Self must die; there the eagerness, the greed of untamed desire must be slain, for only so can the soul be freed from the empire of Fate. But out of the cavern the Gate of Renunciation leads again to the daylight of wisdom, by whose radiance a new insight, a new joy, a new tenderness, shine forth to gladden the pilgrim's heart.

When, without the bitterness of impotent rebellion, we have learnt both to resign ourselves to the outward rule of Fate and to recognize that the non-human world is unworthy of our worship, it becomes possible at last so to transform and refashion the unconscious universe, so to transmute it in the crucible of imagination, that a new image of shining gold replaces the old idol of clay. In all the multiform facts of the world—in the visual shapes of trees and mountains and clouds, in the events of the life of man, even in the very omnipotence of Death—the insight of creative idealism can find the reflection of a beauty which its own thoughts first made. In this way mind asserts its subtle mastery over the thoughtless forces of Nature. The more evil the material with which it deals, the more thwarting to untrained desire, the greater is its achievement in inducing the reluctant rock to yield up its hidden treasures, the prouder its victory in compelling the opposing forces to swell the pageant of its triumph. Of all the arts, Tragedy is the proudest, the most triumphant; for it builds its shining citadel in the very center of the enemy's country, on the very summit of his highest mountain; from its impregnable watch-towers, his camps and arsenals, his columns and forts, are all revealed; within its walls the free life continues, while the legions of Death and Pain and Despair, and all the servile captains of tyrant Fate, afford the burghers of that dauntless city new spectacles of beauty. Happy those sacred ramparts, thrice happy the dwellers on that all-seeing eminence. Honor to those brave warriors who, through countless ages of warfare, have preserved for us the priceless heritage of liberty, and have kept undefiled by sacrilegious invaders the home of the unsubdued.

But the beauty of Tragedy does but make visible a quality which, in more or less obvious shapes, is present always and everywhere in life. In the spectacle of Death, in the endurance of intolerable pain, and in the irrevocableness of a vanished past, there is a sacredness, an overpowering awe, a feeling of the vastness, the depth, the inexhaustible mystery of existence, in which, as by some strange marriage of pain, the sufferer is bound to the world by bonds of sorrow. In these moments of insight, we lose all eagerness of temporary desire, all struggling and striving for petty ends, all care for the little trivial things that, to a superficial view, make up the common life of day by day; we see, surrounding the narrow raft illumined by the flickering light of human comradeship, the dark ocean on whose rolling waves we toss for a brief hour; from the great night without, a chill blast breaks in upon our refuge; all the loneliness of humanity amid hostile forces is concentrated upon the individual soul, which must struggle alone, with what of courage it can command, against the whole weight of a universe that cares nothing for its hopes and fears. Victory, in this struggle with the powers of darkness, is the true baptism into the glorious company of heroes, the true initiation into the overmastering beauty of human existence. From that awful encounter of the soul with the outer world, renunciation, wisdom, and charity are born; and with their birth a new life begins. To take into the inmost shrine of the soul the irresistible forces whose puppets we seem to be—Death and change, the irrevocableness of the past and the powerlessness of man before the blind hurry of the universe from vanity to vanity—to feel these things and know them is to conquer them.

This is the reason why the Past has such magical power. The beauty of its motionless and silent pictures is like the enchanted purity of late autumn, when the leaves, though one breath would make them fall, still glow against the sky in golden glory. The Past does not change or strive; like Duncan, after life's fitful fever it sleeps well; what was eager and grasping, what was petty and transitory, has faded away, the things that were beautiful and eternal shine out of it like stars in the night. Its beauty, to a soul not worthy of it, is unendurable; but to a soul which has conquered Fate it is the key of religion.

The life of Man, viewed outwardly, is but a small thing in comparison with the forces of Nature. The slave is doomed to worship Time and Fate and Death, because they are greater than anything he finds in himself, and because all his thoughts are of things which they devour. But, great as they are, to think of them greatly, to feel their passionless splendor, is greater still. And such thought makes us free men; we no longer bow before the inevitable in Oriental subjection, but we absorb it, and make it a part of ourselves. To abandon the struggle for private happiness, to expel all eagerness of temporary desire, to burn with passion for eternal things—this is emancipation, and this is the free man's worship. And this liberation is effected by a contemplation of Fate; for Fate itself is subdued by the mind which leaves nothing to be purged by the purifying fire of Time.

United with his fellow-men by the strongest of all ties, the tie of a common doom, the free man finds that a new vision is with him always, shedding over every daily task the light of love. The life of Man is a long march through the night, surrounded by invisible foes, tortured by weariness and pain, towards a goal that few can hope to reach, and where none may tarry long. One by one, as they march, our comrades vanish from our sight, seized by the silent orders of omnipotent Death. Very brief is the time in which we can help them, in which their happiness or misery is decided. Be it ours to shed sunshine on their path, to lighten their sorrows by the balm of sympathy, to give them the pure joy of a never-tiring affection, to strengthen failing courage, to instill faith in hours of despair. Let us not weigh in grudging scales their merits and demerits, but let us think only of their need— of the sorrows, the difficulties, perhaps the blindnesses, that make the misery of their lives; let us remember that they are fellow-sufferers in the same darkness, actors in the same tragedy with ourselves. And so, when their day is over, when their good and their evil have become eternal by the immortality of the past, be it ours to feel that, where they suffered, where they failed, no deed of ours was the cause; but wherever a spark of the divine fire kindled in their hearts, we were ready with encouragement, with sympathy, with brave words in which high courage glowed.

Brief and powerless is Man's life; on him and all his race the slow, sure doom falls pitiless and dark. Blind to good and evil, reckless of destruction, omnipotent matter rolls on its relentless way; for Man, condemned to-day to lose his dearest, to-morrow himself to pass through the gate of darkness, it remains only to cherish, ere yet the blow falls, the lofty thoughts that ennoble his little day; disdaining the coward terrors of the slave of Fate, to worship at the shrine that his own hands have built; undismayed by the empire of chance, to preserve a mind free from the wanton tyranny that rules his outward life; proudly defiant of the irresistible forces that tolerate, for a moment, his knowledge and his condemnation, to sustain alone, a weary but unyielding Atlas, the world that his own ideals have fashioned despite the trampling march of unconscious power.

paul tillich   THE GOD ABOVE GOD

Paul Tillich (1886–1965), *the son of a Lutheran minister, was born in Germany and was himself ordained an Evangelical Lutheran minister in 1912. His orthodoxy, however, began to crumble in World War I (he served as a German Army chaplain) and during the difficult years that followed. He taught at universities in Berlin, Dresden, Leipzig, and Frankfort, and was outspoken in his criticism of the rising Nazi movement. In 1933, while at the University of Frankfort, he "had the honor," as he worded it, "to be the first non-Jewish philosopher fired from a German university." Moving to the United States, he became a naturalized citizen in 1940 and taught at Union Theological Seminary, Harvard University, and finally at the University of Chicago. Among his books are* The Protestant Era, The Shaking of the Foundations, The New Being, The Dynamics of Faith, *and* Biblical Religion and the Search for Ultimate Reality. The three-volume Systematic Theology *is his major work. The selection which follows is from* The Courage to Be (1952).

THEISM TRANSCENDED

The courage to take meaninglessness into itself presupposes a relation to the ground of being which we have called "absolute faith." It is without a special content, yet it is not without content. The content of absolute faith is the "God above God." Absolute faith and its consequence, the courage that takes the radical doubt, the doubt about God, into itself, transcends the theistic idea of God.

Theism can mean the unspecified affirmation of God. Theism in this sense does not say what it means if it uses the name of God. Because of the traditional and psychological connotations of the word God such an empty theism can produce a reverent mood if it speaks of God. Politicians, dictators, and other people who wish to use rhetoric to make an impression on their audience like to use the word God in this sense. It produces the feeling in their listeners that the speaker is serious and morally trustworthy. This is especially successful if they can brand their foes as atheistic. On a higher level people without a definite religious commitment like to call themselves theistic, not for special purposes but because they cannot stand a world without God, whatever this God may be. They need some of the connotations of the word God and they are afraid of what they call atheism. On the highest level of this kind of theism the name of God is used as a poetic or practical symbol, expressing a profound emotional state or the highest ethical idea. It is a theism which stands on the boundary line between the second type of theism and what we call "theism transcended." But it is still too indefinite to cross this boundary line. The atheistic negation of this whole type of theism is as vague as the theism itself. It may produce an irreverent mood and angry reaction of those who take their theistic affirmation seriously. It may even be felt as justified against the rhetorical-political abuse of the name God, but it is ultimately as irrelevant as the theism which it negates. It cannot reach the state of despair any more than the theism against which it fights can reach the state of faith.

Theism can have another meaning, quite contrary to the first one: it can be the name of what we have called the divine-human encounter. In this case it points to those elements in the Jewish-Christian tradition which emphasize the person-to-person relationship with God. Theism in this sense emphasizes the personalistic passages in the Bible and the Protestant creeds, the personalistic image of God, the word as the tool of creation and revelation, the ethical and social character of the kingdom of God, the personal nature of human faith and divine forgiveness, the historical vision of the universe, the idea of a divine purpose, the infinite distance between creator and creature, the absolute separation between God and the world, the conflict between holy God and sinful man, the person-to-person character of prayer and practical devotion. Theism in this sense is the nonmystical side of biblical religion and historical Christianity. Atheism from the point of view of this theism is the human attempt to escape the divine-human encounter. It is an existential—not a theoretical—problem.

Theism has a third meaning, a strictly theological one. Theological theism is, like every theology, dependent on the religious substance which it conceptualizes. It is dependent on theism in the first sense insofar as it tries to prove the necessity of affirming God in some way; it usually develops the so-called arguments for the "existence" of God. But it is more dependent on theism in the second sense insofar as it tries to establish a doctrine of God which transforms the person-to-person encounter with God into a doctrine about two persons who may or may not meet but who have a reality independent of each other.

Now theism in the first sense must be transcended because it is irrelevant, and theism in the second sense must be transcended because it is one-sided. But theism in the third sense must be transcended because it is wrong. It is bad theology. This can be shown by a more penetrating analysis. The God of theological theism is a being beside others and as such a part of the whole of reality. He certainly is considered its most important part, but as a part and therefore as subjected to the structure of the whole. He is supposed to be beyond the ontological elements and categories which constitute reality. But every statement subjects him to them. He is seen as a self which has a world, as an ego which is related to a thou, as a cause which is separated from its effect, as having a definite space and an endless time. He is a being, not being-itself. As such he is bound to the subject-object structure of reality, he is an object for us as subjects. At the same time we are objects for him as a subject. And this is decisive for the necessity of transcending theological theism. For God as a subject makes me into an object which is nothing more than an object. He deprives me of my subjectivity because he is all-powerful and all-knowing. I revolt and try to make *him* into an object, but the revolt fails and becomes desperate. God appears as the invincible tyrant, the being in contrast with whom all other beings are without freedom and subjectivity. He is equated with the recent tyrants who with the help of terror try to transform everything into a mere object, a thing among things, a cog in the machine they control. He becomes the model of everything against which Existentialism revolted. This is the God Nietzsche said had to be killed because nobody can tolerate being made into a mere object of absolute knowledge and absolute control. This is the deepest root of atheism. It is an atheism which is justified as the reaction against theological theism and its disturbing implications. It is also the deepest root of the Existentialist despair and the widespread anxiety of meaninglessness in our period.

Theism in all its forms is transcended in the experience we have called absolute faith. It is the accepting of the acceptance without somebody or something that accepts. It is the power of being-itself that accepts and gives the courage to be. This is the highest point to which our analysis has brought us. It cannot be described in the way the God of all forms of theism can be described. It cannot be described in mystical terms either. It transcends both mysticism and personal encounter, as it transcends both the courage to be as a part and the courage to be as oneself.

THE GOD ABOVE GOD AND THE COURAGE TO BE

The ultimate source of the courage to be is the "God above God"; this is the result of our demand to transcend theism. Only if the God of theism is transcended can the anxiety of doubt and meaninglessness be taken into the courage to be. The God above God is the object of all mystical longing, but mysticism also must be transcended in order to reach him. Mysticism does not take seriously the concrete and the doubt concerning the concrete. It plunges directly into the ground of being and meaning, and leaves the concrete, the world of finite values and meanings, behind. Therefore it does not solve the problem of meaninglessness. In terms of the present religious situation this means that Eastern mysticism is not the solution of the problems of Western Existentialism, although many people attempt this solution. The God above the God of theism is not the devaluation of the meanings which doubt has thrown into the abyss of meaninglessness; he is their potential restitution. Nevertheless absolute faith agrees with the faith implied in mysticism in that both transcend the theistic objectivation of a God who is a being. For mysticism such a God is not more real than any finite being, for the courage to be such a God has disappeared in the abyss of meaninglessness with every other value and meaning.

The God above the God of theism is present, although hidden, in every divine-human encounter. Biblical religion as well as Protestant theology are aware of the paradoxical character of this encounter. They are aware that if God encounters man God is neither object nor subject and is therefore above the scheme into which theism has forced him. They are aware that personalism with respect to God is balanced by a transpersonal presence of the divine. They are aware that foregiveness can be accepted only if the power of acceptance is effective in man—biblically speaking, if the power of grace is effective in man. They are aware of the paradoxical character of every prayer, of speaking to somebody to whom you cannot speak because he is not "somebody," of asking somebody of whom you cannot ask anything because he gives or gives not before you ask, of saying "thou" to somebody who is nearer to the I than the I is to itself. Each of these paradoxes drives the religious consciousness toward a God above the God of theism.

The courage to be which is rooted in the experience of the God above the God of theism unites and transcends the courage to be as a part and the courage to be as oneself. It avoids both the loss of oneself by participation and the loss of one's world by individualization. The acceptance of the God above the God of theism makes us a part of that which is not also a part but is the ground of the whole. Therefore our self is not lost in a larger whole, which submerges it in the life of a limited group. If the self participates in the power of being-itself it receives itself back. For the power of being acts through the power of the individual selves. It does not swallow them as every limited whole, every collectivism, and every conformism does. This is why the Church, which stands for the power of being-itself or for the God who transcends the God of the religions, claims to be the mediator of the courage to be. A church which is based on the authority of the God of theism cannot make such a claim. It inescapably develops into a collectivist or semi-collectivist system itself.

But a church which raises itself in its message and its devotion to the God above the God of theism without sacrificing its concrete symbols can mediate a courage which takes doubt and meaninglessness into itself. It is the Church under the Cross which alone can do this, the Church which preaches the Crucified who cried to God who remained his God after the God of confidence had left him in the darkness of doubt and meaninglessness. To be as a part in such a church is to receive a courage to be in which one cannot lose one's self and in which one receives one's world.

Absolute faith, or the state of being grasped by the God beyond God, is not a state which appears beside other states of the mind. It never is something separated and definite, an event which could be isolated and described. It is always a movement in, with, and under other states of the mind. It is the situation of the boundary of man's possibilities. It *is* this boundary. Therefore it is both the courage of despair and the courage in and above every courage. It is not a place where one can live, it is without the safety of words and concepts, it is without a name, a church, a cult, a theology. But it is moving in the depth of all of them. It is the power of being, in which they participate and of which they are fragmentary expressions.

One can become aware of it in the anxiety of fate and death when the traditional symbols, which enable men to stand the vicissitudes of fate and the horror of death have lost their power. When "providence" has become a superstition and "immortality" something imaginary that which once was the power in these symbols can still be present and create the courage to be in spite of the experience of a chaotic world and a finite existence. The Stoic courage returns but not as the faith in universal reason. It returns as the absolute faith which says Yes to being without seeing anything concrete which could conquer the nonbeing in fate and death.

And one can become aware of the God above the God of theism in the anxiety of guilt and condemnation when the traditional symbols that enable men to withstand the anxiety of guilt and condemnation have lost their power. When "divine judgment" is interpreted as a psychological complex and forgiveness as a remnant of the "father-image," what once was the power in those symbols can still be present and create the courage to be in spite of the experience of an infinite gap between what we are and what we ought to be. The Lutheran courage returns but not supported by the faith in a judging and forgiving God. It returns in terms of the absolute faith which says Yes although there is no special power that conquers guilt. The courage to take the anxiety of meaninglessness upon oneself is the boundary line up to which the courage to be can go. Beyond it is mere non-being. Within it all forms of courage are re-established in the power of the God above the God of theism. *The courage to be is rooted in the God who appears when God has disappeared in the anxiety of doubt.*

FURTHER READING

Six very short religious tales are presented and interpreted by the Jewish philosopher and scholar Martin Buber in "The Way of Man According to the Teachings of Hasidism" (1949).

"It is wrong always, everywhere, and for everyone, to believe anything upon insufficient evidence," states William Kingdom Clifford in his essay "The Ethics of Belief" (1877).

Both of the preceding items appear in Walter Kaufmann's outstanding anthology *Religion from Tolstoy to Camus* (1961). Also included are Nietzsche, Freud, Tillich, Schweitzer, Maritain, James, and others.

The Spanish philosopher Miguel de Unamuno wrote unusually good fiction. One of his best short stories, about faith and doubt, is "Saint Emmanuel the Good Martyr" in *Abel Sanchez and Other Stories* (1958).

C. S. Lewis was an Oxford scholar, one of the most adept defenders of Christianity, and an artist with words. *Surprised by Joy* (1956) tells of his own early years and turn to faith.

W. T. Stace presents readings from Hindu, Buddhist, Taoist, Christian, Islamic, and Jewish mystics, with abundant comment of his own, in *The Teachings of the Mystics* (1960).

Huston Smith's *The Religions of Man* (1958) is the best introduction to the world's major religions for the general reader. The chapters on Hinduism, Buddhism (includes Zen), and Confucianism are especially recommended.

"Religion is solitariness," wrote Alfred North Whitehead, "and if you are never solitary, you are never religious." His *Religion in the Making* (1926) consists of four short and provocative lectures.

Søren Kierkegaard, profoundly Christian and one of the nineteenth century forerunners of existentialism, is sometimes difficult to read. The Anchor Books edition of *Fear and Trembling and The Sickness Unto Death* (1954), translated with introductions by Walter Lowrie, is a good starting point.

_____*RELIGION: MOVING ON*

9

"The sun is new every day," said Heraclitus, and so it is with religion. There may be an ultimate truth about religion, and it may be unchanging, but man's conception of that truth is constantly assuming new forms. Bibles abound and prophets come and go, sects rising and falling in their wake. The old religions change as they move into new ages, and every individual brings to his religion a unique perspective which transmutes everything it touches. And we too are new every day. For all practical purposes, Heraclitus was right; change is the law of the land.

The recent upheavals in Christian theology are intimated by Nels F. S. Ferré in the essay which follows. He welcomes and elaborates upon the "radical revolt against God that is dragging to destruction the false ideas of God that have been embedded in our main Christian tradition." The gods of deism, pantheism, atheism, and theism ought not be confused, Ferré argues, with the God of Christianity. God "is not a being, or even the supreme Being" because such terms imply that He is a being among other beings. When God is conceived in terms of substance, one is led to believe that God must be somewhere ("up there" or "out there"). But the God of Christianity is not a being or a thing—he is no thing and no where. He is larger than those terms. God is Spirit, the Infinite, the source of Being; He is "the Living God of Nowhere and Nothing" who is everywhere.

Ferré is only one of a small army of theologians and religious leaders who have been rethinking the premises and renovating the forms of traditional religion. But the religious views of many Americans have moved beyond the traditional altogether. "Significant though it is," writes Jacob Needleman, "the revolution that is striking the established religious institutions of the West is only part of a spiritual phenomenon that promises to transform everything modern man has thought about God and human possibility. The contemporary disillusionment with religion has revealed itself to be a religious disillusionment." [1] There has been, for one thing, a vast surge of interest in the religions of the East. Among these "new" religions is Zen. Its history reaches back to Gautama Buddha and India; over the centuries it drifted through China to Japan, where it has flourished since the twelfth century. In San Francisco there is now a "Zen Center," described in these pages by Needleman.

[1] *The New Religions* (New York: Doubleday & Co., 1970), p. xi.

358

> Ethiopians have gods with snub noses and black hair; Thracians have gods with gray eyes and red hair.

> xenophanes

Studies undertaken by psychologist Abraham Maslow led him to theorize that people may be divided into two groups: "peakers" are those who have had the peak-experience—an intense, private, transcendent experience of illumination or revelation about their identity, God, or the world. "Non-peakers" either have not had such experiences or have suppressed them. The two types of people may be observed in many areas—in philosophy, there are the non-peaking analytical philosophers and the peaking existentialists. In religion the peak-experience is the core-religious experience; it is what lies at the heart of religion, most notably in the insights of the great prophets and seers. The non-peakers are the organizers, the legalists, and the followers who have no essential understanding of the real basis of their religion.

Those within the "Jesus movement" of recent years would no doubt include themselves among Maslow's peakers—as would those who are into the other enthusiasms of the times (drugs, astrology, encounter groups, etc.) The Age of Anxiety may be superseded by the Age of Revelatory Experiences. But is every peak-experience "valid"? I can readily imagine a member of the Ku Klux Klan peaking ecstatically on a night ride. Can Zen-peakers and Jesus-peakers be equally correct? How are the proliferating claims of truth and salvation to be authenticated?

Peter Marin, for one, has grave doubts about the Jesus-cults. "The age itself is a chamber of yearning" in which "every passing idea is turned zealously into a faith." The chaos and confusion of the times have spawned a generation with a desperate need for order and certainty. The Jesus-cults offer a comprehensive package—everything from "instantaneous and push-button forgiveness" to a new family. However, Marin feels this package is grounded mostly in fear, leading to a retreat from life.

In "Rain and the Rhinoceros" Thomas Merton, a Trappist monk, writes of withdrawing to solitude in a cabin in the woods. "What a thing it is to sit absolutely alone, in the forest, at night. . . ." He celebrates the festival of rain, and his thoughts lead to a meditation on man and God. In the city there is the deathly pursuit of "fun" and the purchasing of illusions; the city (which is a state of mind, needless to say) suffers from rhinoceritis—the compulsive and brutal charging here and there of a monstrous herd. When man is alone rain can be listened to and "our capacities for joy, peace, and truth" can be liberated.

359

nels f. s. ferré   # THE LIVING GOD OF
NOWHERE AND NOTHING

*Born in Sweden, Nels F. S. Ferré (1908–1971) came to the United States in
1921 and became a naturalized citizen in 1931. He received degrees from Boston
University (A.B.), Andover Newton Theological Seminary (B.D.), and Harvard
University (M.A., Ph.D.). Most of his teaching career was spent at Andover
Newton Theological Seminary. From 1965–1968 he was Scholar-in-Residence at
Parsons College, a position which left him free for research and writing. For the
last few years of his life he was at the College of Wooster. Among his many
books are* Faith and Reason, Evil and the Christian Faith, The Christian Understanding of God, God's New Age, *and* Reason in Religion. *The reading selection
which follows is from* The Living God of Nowhere and Nothing *(1966).*

Mixed drinks can cause malaise; a far more serious malady results from mixed
theological perspectives. The modern age suffers from such a mixture, resulting in confusion, sappage of meaning and enervated motivation. We are not
sure of God, that he is, who he is, and what he wills. Nor should we be, in
the light of the inconsistencies we have been accepting in his place, and in
the face of the guilt of our wicked and frivolous days. Our day is doomed.
We cannot keep disintegrating and not perish. Yet disintegrate we must
until we find the faith that holds us steady by its truth and ready for its living.

I hail the radical revolt against God that is dragging to destruction the
false ideas of God that have been embedded in our main Christian tradition. It is not God but the sacred cows we have put in his place that are
being sacrificed. Therefore, even more boldly and confidently, I await the
coming of a new and better day in Christian theology. In order to present a
clear and convincing view of God and what that view involves for faith, I
shall at the outset analyse traditional doctrines of God in an attempt to show
that the living God must go beyond them all to provide the full focus for a
consistent Christian standpoint. A focal centre of this nature, however, is so
dynamic, touching all life with vibrant movement, that to live and look from
it can no more be standing still than can an astronaut on a space platform.
Upon reaching it we find that our very resting moves with the space-speed of
God. I believe that only such a view of God and such a follow-through in
life and thought of what this view involves can supply both the courage and
the resources for a new creative day.

The traditional ideas of God may be roughly grouped under four headings: theism, deism, pantheism and atheism. Any discussion of the nature of God necessarily depends upon the terms used. Many misunderstandings arise simply from dearth of analysis, indefiniteness of terms and a general lack of communication that, while sometimes purposeful, is often the result of carelessness.

I am going to reject 'theism' as an unchristian term, but in order to do so I must first assign definite meaning to the term. In fairness to numerous theists I observe that they are using the word in a wider sense than I. I also admit that a good deal of historical usage is on their side. Throughout its history, however, 'theism' has been so often connected with a certain philosophy (albeit one not necessary to it) that it has become difficult to think of one without the other. Because of this nearly constant association, while granting that others have a right to use 'theism' in a broader sense, I want to dissociate myself from the term.

The philosophy that has become so closely and constantly associated with theism as to make it nearly impossible to use the term without using the philosophy is, of course, substance philosophy. In this view, which I shall consider more fully later, reality consists of discrete, or separate substances, or things such as sun and stars, rocks and trees; these are real in themselves, just being there, needing no explanation in terms of anything else. Simple or compound, static or dynamic, these things are basically what they are in themselves. On this basis God would be the supreme instance of substance, the supreme Being. The Christian faith, however, cannot hold that there is a supreme Being in the sense of substance. In this sense the Christian must reject theism. To make clear the reason for rejection let us first discuss the other choices among the previously mentioned traditional ideas of God.

1. Deism holds God to be a separate, self-sufficient Being who has created the world, but has since left it alone. If such a god enters the world or works in it he must necessarily interfere in the world's now self-sufficient workings. He must intrude as an alien power. Such an understanding of God has never been a real option for the Christian faith, with its view of Incarnation and Providence. There have been periods, like the Enlightenment, when such a conception has had enormous appeal and much acceptance. Even today, some thinkers would like to believe that they can still be considered to hold a Christian position if they declare that somehow God may be responsible for the original hydrogen molecules, which are presupposed by prominent modern views of creation, but that there is no need to resort to God for any explanation apart from his having provided, so to speak, the start of our cosmic process. Such a view of God, however, is only an accommodation to scientism. Christian faith thus rejects deism.

2. Pantheism is the position that God is the spirit of the whole universe.

361

He is no separate being, creating or coming into the world. He is the soul of the world. He is the world bethinking itself. He is the process directing itself. The pronoun 'he,' to be sure, in spite of common usage, is meaningless, for in pantheism God is not a personal being distinct from the world or the process, but the inner directedness of the world or the process itself. The world has, so to speak, its mental aspect, even its evaluational capacity, not as separate from the world but as a function of its own total being. This view of God is nature creating, shall we say, so that we can even speak of 'God or nature.'

Pantheism cannot, of course, be nailed down to one limited understanding. Like all other views of the whole it is a mood and a method as well as an ontology or a theory of being. Whitehead and Tillich have both told me at times that they would prefer, in contradistinction from theism, to be called pantheists. In our latest talk in 1965, however, Tillich disclaimed the term, calling pantheism a 'swear word.' Pantheism can be a high and holy view of God. It does not have to approach the caricatures of it that charge that the god of pantheism is equally manure and a rose, or equally good and evil. The process can even be alive, seeking to further and to enhance existence from within its dimension of depth. Nevertheless pantheism is not a Christian position, lacking as it does, God the creator, a doctrine of personal providence, and capacity for Incarnation.

A variation of this view is 'panentheism,' which tries to understand God as within the total process and yet as somehow distinct from it. At times Tillich, for instance, has preferred this view. But on the assumptions of substance philosophy (that is, of any thinking that makes being ultimate) God either is or is not a separate being. If he is, the view is theism. Panentheism's assumption, when viewed in the light of substance philosophy, that God could be a distinct being and yet work from within the world, is, as we shall see, simply theism.

If God is not genuinely a separate being, on the other hand, but merely the logical presupposition for existence or whatever necessity obtains within it, or possibly some ultimate meaning without existence in ultimate terms, panentheism becomes by and large an empty and meaningless term. It no longer has theism in it! When substance philosophy is presupposed, panentheism, in fact, is a misnomer. Unless God is in the world in some sense, we have deism. If God is more, and therefore other than the world and yet in it, we have theism. Panentheism as a term merely confuses and beclouds the issue. In one sense the Christian faith, by definition in terms of its primitive or essential claim, is theistic. The reason I nevertheless disown the term theism, as will become increasingly clear, is its close, almost inseparable connection with substance philosophy, which has arbitrarily defined God in its own terms. Substance philosophy, posing under the name of a theology of being,

362

alone provides modern critics with the right to deny the existence of God. On their presuppositions these critics have the right to claim that for honest, competently trained modern man God is dead. But only, as we shall see, on their presuppositions! Panentheism, however, in this context is a red herring.

3. It remains to discuss the classical view of atheism. Technically atheism merely rejects theism. It is a-theism. If theism stands for God as a general category, to be an atheist is simply to deny entirely the reality of God. If, however, theism stands for a particular view of God, namely that God is the supreme Being, a person can call himself an atheist and still believe in God. Much confusion comes from this indefinite use of the term theism. Some reject theism and call themselves religious atheists simply because they do not believe that God is a *static* being, but that as the Ground of Being he is, rather, *dynamic* being. They are merely radically revolting against the traditional association of theism with substance philosophy in a narrow sense.

Many claim, however, that no one can be an atheist because God is whatever for us is ultimate, and that all of us inescapably have such an ultimate. To live is unavoidably to have some unprovable presupposition; a presupposition obviously cannot be proved. Therefore, they aver, no one living can be an atheist. Notice that they are using the term 'theist' in the general rather than in the particular sense, not only beyond the identification of theism with substance philosophy but also beyond any definitely specifiable or distinguishable reality of God. The many definitions of theism result in, on the one hand, both honest confusion and plain lack of analysis, and, on the other, dishonest avoidance of the question of God altogether a hiding behind the ambiguities of definition. Crooked thinking is like a zigzag rail fence that seems forever trying to be on both sides at once! Too facilely the use of the term keeps shifting to fit the company or the argument.

To make our definition clear and precise, I repeat that the term 'theism' has become so associated with substance philosophy as to be no longer practically available for general constructive usage. If by espousing theism one means merely that one is neither a deist, a pantheist, nor a general denier of God in some such sense as humanism or naturalism, as a Christian one obviously has to be a theist. Definitionally there is no other choice. The Christian faith as an historic entity stands or falls with its worship of the living God who is more and other than the ordinary world and who is yet naturally present in it and working through it. But the term 'theism' has taken on the very substance of the philosophy that bears that name. For this reason I hold that the Christian faith is not theistic in the common use of the term with all its natural associations.

The only reason that the charge can be made that God is not a being, or even the supreme Being (for in such case he would be *a* being among other beings) is simply that being has itself been made into an ultimate category in terms of substance. God is, of course, not a finite object among other finite objects, God is certainly not a thing among things. God obviously cannot be objectified without being made finite. God can never be considered as a concrete entity. Defining God in terms of some such philosophical ultimate as being gives us in a final sense two ultimates: God and being. Mathematics may allow many infinities but two infinite beings cannot exist. There cannot be two infinite realms in terms of substance. The choice, therefore, is either to make philosophy in this sense ultimate, with an ultimate ontology or a doctrine of being as such, in which case the living God of the New Testament, the Spirit of Love, cannot be ultimate (and then theology cannot be a subject dealing with ultimates); or to make theology ultimate, saying then that God is God, the inevitable tautology of the definition of the ultimate, in which case we much define being in terms of God, not God in terms of being. The living God is ultimately *not* Being, but self-revealed as Spirit, Love and Father. We cannot have it both ways.

To call God the supreme Being, therefore, is either an impossible dualism or a mistake. It is to define the ultimate God in terms of another or a second ultimate. Either we mean simply that being has to be defined ultimately or supremely in terms of God (in which case we should not classify him by definition in terms of being) or else we define God in terms of some independent realm of being, i.e. substance (in which case he is not God but only the supreme instance of some philosophical rather than theological ultimate). If God is Love ultimately, he cannot ultimately *be* being. It is right to say that God *is*. We cannot avoid discussion of being in this merely analytical sense. But then, who or what God is, is left open. To say that God is being, however, is either to say superfluously that God is *is* or that God is substance, a category of being in its own right. Then the question of being is no longer merely analytical but a matter of content. I reject the theism that defines God in terms of being. In this sense God is not the supreme Being. God is God who cannot be defined in terms of any category that would permit him to be finite. God cannot be defined except in terms of himself. (For more sustained analysis of this topic the reader may wish to consult *Reason in Religion* or *The Christian Understanding of God*.)

This kind of substance philosophy has bedevilled the history of theology. Christian theology has languished long in the dungeon of Greek philosophy. Thus imprisoned it has starved and withered into impotence. One marvels that the Christian faith has managed to live in spite of being shackled to the wall of substance thinking. Only for illustration, we can mention how theologians have worried about God's relation to the world. If he is absolute, they have pondered, he cannot be relative, for to be relative is to have relations. Therefore God, being ultimate and not relative, cannot have real relations to the world, or at best his relating himself to the world is a dark and deep secret called paradox. All such paradoxes or denials add up to no more than wrong and superficial thinking, an attempt to think the Christian faith within a framework that cannot possibly fit it. What fun, for instance, such a keen critic of theism as Ronald Hepburn has with such thinking in his *Christianity and Paradox*.

In the same way, Tillich dismisses theism in the sense that God cannot be 'a' god because, if he were, the supreme being would be conditioned either as outside the world by being related to it, or, as inside the world, by being confined and made relative by it. With regard to the kind of theism that is based on substance philosophy, Tillich is right in his analysis; but with regard to the Christian faith that espouses the living God in terms of Spirit who is both more and other than the world but who is yet also in control of it and working within it, he takes the wrong path. He dismisses not only theism but the living personal God. And many a student, minister or university professor does not know the difference, sometimes because they have not been informed and sometimes because they prefer not to know.

In the name of the theism of the Christian faith a multitude of similar problems have been approached from the point of view of substance philosophy. The resulting formulations are poison for Christian thinkers to swallow. For instance, God is supposed to be unchangeable or unable to suffer. That there is some truth in such assertions is undeniable, for practically all falsehoods are part-truths, distorted out of context or parts made into wholes; but the unvarnished fact is that all such problems (as to whether God changes or suffers) dissolve when the Christian faith is seen from within its own truth. They are pseudo-problems springing from our attempt to couch the Christian faith in terms of an alien philosophy. The simplest way out now, therefore, is an outright rejection of theism for what it has become in the history of Christian faith.

Theism has also been accused of using comparative language for God, whereas God cannot be in a class with anything else or be compared to anything else. On the basis of theism as substance philosophy this charge is correct, for then God is the unique being among other beings who can be known only externally. But we have no way of knowing anything that is totally different from all else. The finite as such cannot contain the infinite; the finite as such is not capable of the infinite. If our language is couched in terms of things we know, we cannot proceed to know God in such terms, for by definition he is qualitatively different. If, on the contrary, we try to define him in no terms that we know, we are left with no knowledge of him as well. No knowledge leaves us in agnosticism; and faith can have neither substance nor language for its life. Along such lines we are forced to a *via negativa* which, however consistently we walk in it, leads us nowhere. When the Christian faith is understood from within its own presuppositions, however, there is no such dilemma between what is technically called univocal or equivocal language.

Under substance philosophy, too, revelation becomes impossible. In so far as revelation comes through experience and words of our understanding, it cannot be proved to be from God. If, however, revelation comes as God in human form, all we can be sure of knowing is the human form, for what is above the human is unique, alien, ungraspable. Even so, whatever God in human form is supposed to have done cannot be demonstrated to be a revelation of God but is no more than an assertion that deeds of the same kind as ours, which we can therefore understand, were done in an exceptional way. Since, however, strictly speaking, comparisons are impossible in the case of God, we can claim such deeds to be revelation only by an arbitrary faith which either cannot or does not dare to analyse its own presuppositions.

Enough! If theism is defined in terms of substance philosophy we cannot use comparative human language; yet without such language and comparison we can have neither knowledge of God nor an authentic way of communicating knowledge of him. If God is a self-sufficient, unique supreme Being, some unique supernatural substance, he obviously cannot be known in terms of anything human or natural, but we know nothing else. Because of substance philosophy, Aristotle, himself the formulator of substance philosophy *par excellence*, long ago rejected the basic approach of theism. How tragic that Christian thinkers, by taking for granted this kind of Greek philosophy, set up the impossible problems of Christian theism. God is not the supreme Being of the Christian faith. God is, rather, the living God, the all-pervasive, all-relating Spirit, in terms of and in relation to whom all else must ultimately be understood, and understood, at that, in terms of internal as well as of external relations.

There should be little need to stress that substance philosophy occasioned spatial thinking. God, if not 'up there,' was 'out there.' Somehow God had to be localized. If God is a being, he is somewhere. Theism assumed spatialization by its very way of thinking. But the living God, as Jesus pointed out, is Spirit, and Spirit dwells neither on mountain-tops nor in temples. The steeples of substance philosophy can crumble and fall and yet the bells of the Spirit can ring on. God does not dwell in temples made by hands. In one sense the Christian claim is obvious. But it is altogether obvious? Do we not subtly assume the theism of substance philosophy? Surely, we think, God is 'somewhere.' If we say merely that he is equally 'everywhere,' we are spatial pantheists. Or, to say that God is 'nowhere' is for most people equivalent to saying that he does not exist; and to say that he does not 'exist' is the same as saying that there is no God!

The living God of the Christian faith, however, is precisely nowhere. The living God is the God of the spatial nowhere. But then how can anything at all be 'there' if it is nowhere at all? That is the point. God is not anything. He is precisely no thing. Therefore he exists nowhere. But if he is nowhere and nothing, how can he be the living God? If he is not in heaven, at least must he not be a condition of the human heart? Is he not in our imagination, if not in our legitimate thinking of reality? No; we must change our way of looking at the problem.

God is no thing, in this sense, literally nothing; and he is no where, in this sense, nowhere. All things exist in God even as all time is in God; thus God is never in space or in time. Space and time are adjectival to God's work. Things, persons, relations, times stand out from God as creations of his love for his own purposes. Is not God, then, at least the centre, at least some dynamic substance from which all things and times come, and to which they are related and kept in being? Only if time and space are in some way real in themselves can such be the case. But both space and time, are adjectival both to God and to his activity; they have no being except for his purposes. They come for his temporary and limited purposes 'out of' the womb of the unlimited, unbounded, unlocalized, non-temporal reality of God. Space and time become dimensions of what is objectified, aspects of what is 'reified,' or made into events. Space and time themselves appear as time-and-space-bounded events 'from out of' the creative womb of God, the invisible, unlocalized, non-temporal Spirit.

To say even this much, however, is to drag God into that which is bounded in terms of our negative definitions. The world of things and time is actual, but not real. It is for God's purpose, but not *as* God's purpose. The conditions of eternal Spirit are unimaginable except through God's love for us in this kind of existence. We can imagine through sound and colour, through space and time, and thus come to know through Incarnation a conclusive Life in time and space, the Spirit of Love on whom we can depend. God is faithful. We can trust him as unconditional or all-conditional Love. We can try to imagine God as the Source not only of all significance but also of all being; but when we say that God is *in* the world or *with* us, we use our own mode of understanding, speak under our objectified conditions. By so doing we really make ourselves central and define God in terms of creation. We make real and normative what we ourselves know and can partially control.

The opposite is true: God as Spirit, the Infinite, is nothing and nowhere, no event in space-time; and precisely therefore he is the Living God of eternity. He forgives us not only our unwitting arrogance but our human limitation when we rob him of final reality by using such language as 'the God who inhabits eternity.' Even biblical writers had to use such language, comparable to 'The sun rose.' There is no eternity to dwell in! Eternity is adjectival to God, *God's time*. God is continually creating eternity. God is continually creating being. God is continually creating space. They come to be because he is the living God, and they exist only for his love as the constituents of a temporarily objectified, pedagogical process for our sake. Through lack of language, therefore, we say they come *from* him. But God, being nothing and nowhere, cannot be the supreme Being. Unable, therefore, to be a theist in the traditional sense, I choose, rather, the living God of the Christian faith.

jacob needleman   ZEN CENTER

After his graduation from Harvard, Jacob Needleman (1934–   ) studied in Europe for three years. There was a Fulbright scholarship for graduate work at the University of Freiburg and a Fels Foundation fellowship for research in Munich. He returned to the United States for a Ph.D. in philosophy from Yale, spent a year as a trainee in clinical psychology, and was a research fellow at the Rockefeller Institute for another year. Since 1962 he has been with the philosophy department at San Francisco State College. In 1967–1968 he was a visiting scholar at Union Theological Seminary. In addition to his journal articles, he is author of The New Religions *(1970), from which "Zen Center" is taken, and he edited* Being-in-the-World: Selected Papers of Ludwig Binswanger. *In progress is* A Conscious Universe *and he is editing* Religion for a New Generation.

THE EMBRACE OF ZEN BUDDHISM

When it first became known in America, Zen Buddhism brought with it a picture of the fierce teacher with his strange laughter and incomprehensible responses, the explosive moment of enlightenment called *satori*, the breath-taking irreverence and contempt for what was tradition-bound and intellectual. There were the stories of blows and shoutings. There were the koans, superriddles designed to break through the tyranny of thought. From the East had come an approach that turned askew all our concepts of religion. No talk of morality, God, immortality, love, duty, faith, sacrifice or sin. No prescriptions, no commandments, no judgments. Only the constant and unfathomable call for man to see into his own nature.

In trying to understand such an approach, our minds were assaulted by one negation after another and we swam in an ocean of the unsaid. We simply could not figure out what Zen was. We never accepted it; yet we never really rejected it.

Not even when others seemed to grasp it so quickly and easily—too quickly and too easily! Even when the koans and haiku poems were flying thick and fast, when the Beat generation was flinging Zen in our faces and drumming our heads with it and when so many others were using it as a whip to beat every dog, real and imaginary, that existed in our culture and traditions—even then, Zen itself (whatever it was) commanded a corner of our respect.

Instinctively, we felt there was a difference between Zen and those who were shouting about it.

At the very least, the Zen stories were excellent theater. The monk striving and straining for illumination, the countless obstacles, the false successes, the despair, the hopelessness, and yet the persistence, and then, finally, the climax, *satori!* All of this in flesh and blood, with spontaneity, and a certain light touch, rescued the idea of a spiritual search from the doldrums. Masters and monks were not what we pictured as the gaunt, somewhat inhuman Christian mystics, and their struggle was for a life and vitality that we ourselves could recognize and wish for. Zen was showing us that the life of the spirit, and its reality, was not less but perhaps more interesting and dramatic than our own lives and the reality we lived in.

Quietly and persistently, the writings of D. T. Suzuki and a few others survived their long flash of popularity to take a solid place in the important thought of our time. Zen became the paradigm of practical, tough-minded religion. It outstripped even the existentialist writers in its impatience with thought that had no bearing on the everyday realities and crises of life. It went even further than psychoanalysis in emphasizing the emotional, experiential basis of insight. About nature it was more unsentimental than even the most positivistic scientist, yet, in some extraordinary way, as sensitive and alive to nature as any artist or poet among us.

It was unprecedented that people whose orientations toward life seemed mutually antagonistic all drew inspiration from the same source: humanists as well as psychoanalysts, scientists as well as artists. Amid all of its innumerable negations, Zen rejected nothing. Consequently, no one among us felt compelled to reject it. Zen made no enemies.

True, the place of Zen was only in our minds. Very few of us practiced it, or even dreamed of practicing it. From what we had read and heard, that would have meant renouncing everything to go off to Japan to search, we knew not where or how, for some monastery and teacher who might either reject our suit or demand intolerable demonstrations of sincerity. We had been very impressed by stories such as that of the monk who was made to stand in the snow for months before being admitted.

We thus felt no need to chase Zen from our minds when we saw that we could not put it into practice. We could accept it without expecting ourselves to live it or even understand it. Within the individual psyche, too, Zen made no enemies.

Some would complain about this, that it was *only* in our minds, but the extraordinary thing, reflecting the particular genius of Zen, was that it *stayed* in our minds without prompting us to do much of anything about it. It was a kind of miracle that the Zen approach, which undercut everything the Western world lived by, faced it so little as a challenge, provoked so little in the way of resistance and interpretation.

The way Zen appeared in the West is an intimation of the way it seems to act upon the individuals who now do pactice it in America. Perhaps we could call it the method of intrapsychic non-violence. In order to understand something about this, it is best to look first at what is termed Soto Zen, that sort of Zen which has now taken root as practice in the city of San Francisco and in a monastic setting in the midst of a California wilderness.

"JUST SITTING"

There are two main sects of Zen: Rinzai and Soto. Both present themselves as methods by means of which the individual may directly experience the truth about his own nature: that it is, at any instant, the completely real. Without this experience, human life is at every moment generated by the sense that something necessary is lacking. This is the state of desire. What we call the particular desires, fears, feelings and the thinking associated with them, result from this basic state. According to Buddhism, the only thing really lacking in man is the experience that nothing is lacking.

Unenlightened man is characterized as lacking the experience of what is. His experience of what is, of the real, is mixed with thought that is in the service of desire. This thought, or judging, is not an experience, but is itself an aspect of the real. It, too, is something to be experienced. But unenlightened man rarely, if ever, turns simply to experience his thought or his feelings as such. Thus, he desires instead of experiencing his desires. Now desire (and hence the thought which serves it) is part of the effort to change what exists, make it better, more pleasing, and so forth. Unenlightened man, therefore, never experiences reality.

According to the Buddhist tradition, there is that in a man which is able, quietly and directly, to experience rather than desire. This is called the Buddha-nature. Life submerged in desire and its thought can itself be experienced. The awakening of this experience is thus an important element in what is called the realization of the Buddha-nature. Zen Buddhism is a means to help an individual come to this awakening of experience.

Soto Zen differs from the Rinzai in that it does not emphasize use of the koan* to bring about this awakening. In fact, almost the entire picture which we Westerners have of Zen is based on reports about Rinzai practice and not Soto.

My first investigations of Zen Center, which practices the Soto way, were therefore something of a shock. The same is true for many of the Americans who later become practicing members. They come geared for the koans, the "anti-rationality," the "demandingness" and existential warfare that is part of their picture of Zen practice. Instead of this they receive some simple instructions in posture and are told to "just sit." For this sitting, or *zazen*, they

* Such as the now famous "What is the sound of one hand clapping?"

are invited to join the other students at Zen Center early each morning and in the evening.

"Just sit": hardly a gauntlet thrown at the feet of the aspirant! But, in its way, this is the great koan of Soto Zen: "Just sit." Only it does not manifest immediately as a challenge, nor does it correspond to the student's preconceived idea of a test: some external difficulty which he must overcome to obtain what is desirable. Such "tests," which face all men throughout their lives, leave the individual basically unchanged. One passes or fails, one gets what one wants or one does not. But the wanting, the desiring, itself remains: unexperienced, unknown except as the object of a kind of thinking which is itself in the service of another desire in the "ego."

The students come before sunrise to an old synagogue in the center of San Francisco's Japanese section. Inside the building little has been changed. It is extraordinarily clean and quiet. In the main auditorium, some figures of the Buddha have replaced the ark of the covenant, and upstairs the large meeting room now serves as a *zendo*, the main room for the sitting. *Zafus*, the small, nearly spherical black sitting cushions, are lined against the wall in fresh precision, tatami mats cover the floor and at the head of the room is an altar holding figures of the Buddha and Bodhisattvas. Small black cushions are also arranged outside the zendo in the balcony of the auditorium. In Orthodox synagogues, the balcony is the place reserved for women, but now this one is used for the newer students practicing their zazen.

This is, then, very much a Western building, but one touched by a Far Eastern light. As this book was going to press, the students moved to a large new building where they are all housed together, and where the Master now also resides with them. Strange to say, the Star of David also decorates this building which was a residence club for young Jewish women. The reader is free to draw his own conclusions about the interlocking *karma* of Judaism and Buddhism in America. In the history of the spread of Buddhism, it has always been so: as Buddhism moved out of India to China, Tibet, Japan, and throughout the rest of Asia, it was not its way to replace the traditional forms and structures of the culture it was entering. It seems never to have arrived as a substitute for anything, never as a new religion. In this, of course, it is unlike the well-known aspects of Western religious-missionary activity. Nor does Buddhism seem to come as a synthesis, or bringing-together of the various traditions in a culture.

It is true that there are many rigorous forms of practice connected with Zen Center, most of which are obviously rooted deep in the traditions of Japanese-Zen practice. The picture before our eyes will, therefore, be this: American men and women, many of them young; their faces are our faces and the faces of our children; their manner, their dress, their walk—far from the self-indulgence of an escapist. Except for a lack of extremeness in their behavior and talk, they seem quite ordinary and varied.

Yet there they are in California, seated in the lotus posture, monotonously chanting—in Japanese—"Form is emptiness, emptiness is form," words and concepts we simply cannot understand. Then there is the extraordinarily detailed "ritual" of taking meals together, the unwrapping and wrapping of the bowls, the bowing as each portion is served. Is this not the process of institutionalizing a new structure of ritual forms? In a way, the answer must be *yes*. But, in a much more interesting sense, it is really not so. For the center, the axis around which all the forms revolve, and for which all the forms are instrumental, is just: *sitting*.

All the ritual forms are means to an end; one might very well call them practical aids toward the awakening of experience. Such a goal is strange to the average man because he usually seeks a certain *kind* of experience, whereas the goal of Zen practice is the experiencing itself, no matter what it is experience of.

Our well-known Western religious rituals, for example, provide a certain kind of experience, and most of us participate in them in order to have such experiences: the experience of God, of repentance, of consolation, of being understood or accepted, of harmony, of awe. But the Zen teaching is that we err in expecting these future experiences to make us complete and whole. In fact, when we are "having" these experiences, we are not really having them at all. Even in the midst of these rituals, we are still seeking the experience that awaits us in the next minute or hour. We are always seeking for the completing experience, and when certain pleasant feelings finally arise in us, our minds merely label them as the experience we looked for. In a word, something makes us unable to have the experiences we seek, because something makes us unable to have experience itself. We are always seeking, expecting.

This is the basis of what appears to be the anti-religious nature of much Zen writing. If religion strengthens, instead of dissolves, the mental habit of expecting, it ceases to operate as a means of realization or "salvation."

When such ideas first appeared in contemporary America, many people —especially the young—took them as sanctioning a sort of libertinism. But they obviously provide no such sanction, since libertinism under any name is equally the seeking for certain kinds of experience. . . .

WHAT IS A MASTER?

Shunryu Suzuki is the man through whom the work at Zen Center is sustained and guided. He is called *Roshi*, meaning "master" or "teacher." Short and slight, he appears to be in his early sixties; his head is shaved, and he wears the robes of a priest. One's overwhelming first impression is of openness and warmth. He laughs often, noiselessly—and when I was with him, trying to discuss "profound questions," I found myself laughing with him throughout the interview. Beneath the lightness and the gentleness, however, one feels as well his tremendous rigor; more than one student has called him "awesome."

But apart from describing him further, the question naturally arises: *what* does a Zen Master teach?

In order to approach that question, one must, I think, ask another question first: *whom* does a Zen Master teach?

When, for example, Roshi first came to the United States in 1959, it was as a priest of the Japanese Zen Buddhist congregation in San Francisco. Only when he was sought out by some young Americans did he respond with Zen instruction geared to their minds and backgrounds. The development of Zen Center, from its very slight beginnings with a handful of students to its present scale of activity, can only be understood as Suzuki Roshi's *response* to the sincerity of his American pupils. The fact that he now devotes so much of his time and energies to the Americans—more so, now, than to the Japanese—is a measure of that sincerity.

Said one student:

> I came because I was desperate. People come and stay because they're desperate. Not in an insane way. Desperate, not disturbed. Roshi says that if you're disturbed, you can't sit.
> There's a piece of wood at Tassajara with a Japanese inscription on it, and, roughly translated, it says "Pardon me, but Zen is a matter of life and death."

Another young man, comparing the American pupils with some of the San Francisco Japanese community, said the Japanese are where the Americans were twenty-five years ago: "hung-up on cars, success, material things."

> It's amazing who Roshi takes under his wing. Some of his closest disciples are people who if you looked at them you wouldn't believe it. People you'd think were pathetic, or inept. And he gives them some responsible position or something. It's wonderful what he's able to see in people; he sees their potential, he sees something in them that the rest of us don't see.

Whatever it is which a master like Suzuki teaches, it can only exist as a response to this quality of sincerity or desperation. If the desperation is deep and persistent, then the process of teaching is deep and persistent. When some of the older students say that Roshi is "always teaching," it means that he is always responding to their sincerity. Of course, this responding can be rather subtle and is certainly invisible to an outsider or even to a student whose need is not quite so intense. Such a student will receive a response appropriate to the degree of his sincerity.

Now, the remarkable thing is that this sincerity is not necessarily manifested in the intellect, or consciousness, what Suzuki calls "the thinking mind." Suzuki has said that man has more than one mind, and that the thinking mind in the head (which we usually identify as *the* mind and even the "self") is, as it were, only a "branch office" of the more fundamental mind known as the *hara* centered in the abdomen. Thus, a man may be in despair without "thinking" or "knowing" it in any simple or clear way. Conversely, a man may believe he is seeking Zen practice and instruction, but this search may be only an idea in the thinking mind.

The process of teaching is not directed primarily to the thinking mind. One might say it is directed to the unconscious mind, but nowadays such an expression is associated with certain psychoanalytic concepts which are themselves products of the thinking mind. In any event, the teaching is not done mainly with words. Thus, to the degree that a man is identified with verbal or conceptual formulations, the process of teaching is either incomprehensible or invisible. For those without sincerity or desperation, it is even unreceivable.

> Roshi is a teacher because he lives what he says.
> In his presence everything is different. Whatever he does or says to you, in passing or just very lightly, it gets you right in the gut.

Saying this, the student, a man in his forties, pounded his fist against his belly. "Like a sword," he said.

In *The Wind Bell*, the students wrote:

> One of the most helpful experiences for the students was to work with him or just watch him working . . . But it was not just his skill in moving huge stones to direct the course of the stream, or in shaping stones to rebuild the large supporting wall under the bridge that affected the students so directly. It was the energy and attention with which he did his work. He seemed able to work without rest all day long, even when moving bigger stones than anyone else, and by midday to completely tire out the strapping students who were working with him. One student who was helping him finally observed that Roshi was always at rest, unless he was directly pushing on a stone, and that even when he fell he was relaxed and found his balance naturally. Suzuki Roshi is very modest, even embarrassed about this and says that he is too attached to hard work; but to the students he is what they hoped a Zen Master would be like.

Equally instructive—perhaps more so—for the students is Roshi's ability to live the instantaneous self-acceptance of the enlightened, whether he is coughing, sneezing, or even dozing during zazen. In this sense, he teaches by example, by what he is—not so much by what he says. This, plus the quality of immediate and appropriate response to sincere need, plus no doubt many other things of which I am not aware, helps the student to practice zazen right there on the spot. It is as though his presence is, for the sincere student, a continuous and varied reminder that he, the student, is the Buddha.

Such a reminder is no balm for the ego. Quite the contrary. Since most emotional crises of our daily life manifest as the desire for something external—be it words of praise, or a material thing—this reminder is a call to discover within oneself the strength and freedom to experience the crises, rather than to resolve them. Thus the famous Zen saying: "I owe everything to my teacher because he taught me nothing."

It is not an easeful thing to live in the presence of such a teacher. . . .

AN AMERICAN ZEN MONASTERY

Zen Mountain Center—*Zenshinji*, meaning Zen mind/heart temple in Japanese—is now the center of gravity of Zen practice in America, and, perhaps, the whole Western world. It is situated within some five hundred acres of rugged mountain land about one hundred and fifty miles south of San Francisco. By car it can be reached only by driving over twenty miles of precipitous, winding dirt road that is impassable to ordinary traffic eight months out of the year. The only other access is by foot over the mountain trails of Los Padres National Forest which surrounds it. For American Zen students, it is a dream come true.

Before its purchase by Zen Center in 1966, it was known as Tassajara Hot Springs and was the site of a secluded resort hotel which catered to a clientele seeking the refreshment of woods and stream, and intense starry nights. The owner of the hotel, seeking to preserve its natural beauty, held back from selling until he found a buyer who shared his feeling for the area. Zen Center was that buyer.

The students immediately set to work raising a large sum of money in the form of benefit performances by dozens of artists and entertainers and by donations from well-wishers throughout the country. When the money appeared, a huge amount, it was a concrete indication of how the ground had already been prepared in America. America was very much "Zen conscious."

At the same time, other students began the task of putting Tassajara into physical order. They rebuilt the large stone-and-stucco house, redesigned the porches to fit the natural curves of the clear, winding creek. Partitions were removed, hardwood floors put in, door openings walled up, windows replaced, redwood lamps installed, and the interior furnished anew with furniture carved from old fence posts.

Another building, an old slatestone dining room dating from the late 1890s, was converted into a zendo (meditation and dining hall) by removing the bar and constructing an altar over the open hearth. The many cabins on the premises were painted and reshingled. The cold springs and hot springs reservoirs and the springs themselves were reroofed and an old bathhouse by the pool was torn down. The area around all the buildings was cleared of fire-hazardous brush, a vegetable garden was planted, landscaping started, and root-infested pipes were replaced.

Quoting again from *The Wind Bell*:

> (The) beginner's spirit pervades the practice and activity in San Francisco and Tassajara. Everything is done by the students and there is little distinction between leaders and workers. We grow as much of our food as is possible, cook for and serve ourselves, repair, maintain and build the facilities, raise the money to purchase them, administer the monastery, and develop the practice there. We had learned how to find our own way by having experienced eight years of taking care of Zen Center in San Francisco. By not having many explanations from Suzuki Roshi on how many sesshins there should be, how often we should meditate each day, or as to why we bowed, chanted or meditated in a certain way, we developed over the years an independence and an understanding of our own practice and how to take care of group practice. Thus we knew something of how to approach the development of Tassajara, and to come to our own determination about the need for strictness and freedom in Zen practice.

The need for intensive group practice and prolonged periods of exposure to the master was, of course, the central and closest reason for the development of Zen Mountain Center. To see it in operation and to observe its effects on the students raises some interesting general questions about the nature and function of monastic life in all religions.

WHAT IS A MONK?

In modern times, most Westerners have come to accept this rather grim picture of a monk: not quite strong enough for the pressures of ordinary society, he retreats to a secluded and protected place where he and others like him may devote their lives to God. It is a picture of a man starving himself existentially, cutting himself off from the vital forces of life, a man "holier" than we, but less human as well. Granting him his slightly questionable mystical communion, he is envied by us only in those moments when the press of life seems unendurable. In such moments we ourselves dream of "going off to a monastery or something." It is one step short of wishing ourselves dead; at best it is very much like the need for rest and respite. One recognizes that the life of a monk is not easy; he rises early, he labors hard at some physical or mental task, he eats little, etc. But, in our moments of stress or disillusionment—and only in such moments—this seems a small price to pay for the luxury of being told what to do.

At Tassajara, however, one comes to see monasticism not as a flight from society, but to society. The principle difference between the monastic society and ours is surely not that ours is more real, but that in this monastery everyone has a common aim. Moreover, this aim is for themselves: each to awaken to his true nature, each to "find his own way."

In such a community, there exists the constant danger that in the name of charity and kindness someone will find my way for me, will directly or indirectly tell me what to do, what is good and what bad. As a result, I may find a way, but not my own way; I will discover a nature, but not necessarily my own nature.

This "danger" is rooted in an overwhelming force inherent in human nature: to put in Buddhist terms it is the deep-rooted belief that inwardly we are incomplete and can reach completeness and actualization only by acquiring something external to ourselves: be it material things, "love," "knowledge," "respect," etc. The hardness and unsentimentality of the Zen community, called the *sangha*, is based on a precise awareness of this tendency in man and on the axioms that man is both essentially alone and essentially complete.

But what is complete is the Buddha-nature—not what we may now call the human-nature. This distinction is crucial, at least for a long time along the way. The experiencing of our human nature, of our faults and weaknesses, our wavering and anxiety, our desires and fears, is in itself a complete experience, a complete actualization of the Buddha-mind. The Buddhist way is lost when what is wished for is completion and perfection of the human-nature. This explains, to some degree, why the hardness of the Zen community also manifests itself in the teacher's acceptance of whatever the monk does, so long as he knows the monk is maintaining the aim of finding his own way. But this acceptance can be the hardest thing to bear to our human nature which constantly seeks external support.

The sense of how Buddhism should exist in America was in sharp focus during the first practice period when we (the students) were faced over and over again with details like: Do we wear robes or not, and what kind of robes? Shall this ceremony be simplified? How? Shall it be in English? Should we chant in English or Japanese? Japanese has more resonance but English we can understand. Should there be three, five or seven days of tangaryo? How much zazen, study time, work time should there be? Should the organization and spirit of the practice be along the lines of original Buddhism, or present-day Buddhism in Japan, or what combination of these? How strict should the practice be made? Should we follow the Soto way completely, or should we apply the approaches of various schools according to the needs of the students? To what extent should the experiences of zazen, koans, mantras, and the other techniques of Buddhism be used? These questions . . . suggested guidelines that pervaded our whole practice, and perhaps prepared some of the ground for Buddhism in America.

abraham h. maslow   PEAK-EXPERIENCES

Abraham Maslow (1908–1970) was born in Brooklyn and received his A.B.,
M.A., and Ph.D. degrees from the University of Wisconsin. He taught for some
ten years at Brooklyn College and then moved to Brandeis University, with which
he was still associated until shortly before his death. Maslow was "Mr. Human-
ist," a prime mover of the humanist movement in psychology. He liked to call it
the "Third Force" in psychology (in distinction from Freudian and behaviorist
psychology). An independent and innovative thinker, he was disturbed at being
elected president of the American Psychological Association, fearing he must
have betrayed that independence he prized. Typical of Maslow himself was his
emphasis upon man's need for self-actualization, his desire "to become every-
thing that one is capable of becoming." Among his many writings are Motivation
and Personality, Toward a Psychology of Being, The Psychology of Science, *and*
Eupsychian Management. *The selection which follows is from* Religions, Values,
and Peak-Experiences *(1964).*

The very beginning, the intrinsic core, the essence, the universal nucleus
of every known high religion (unless Confucianism is also called a religion)
has been the private, lonely, personal illumination, revelation, or ecstasy of
some acutely sensitive prophet or seer. The high religions call themselves
revealed religions and each of them tends to rest its validity, its function, and
its right to exist on the codification and the communication of this original
mystic experience or revelation from the lonely prophet to the mass of human beings in general.

But it has recently begun to appear that these "revelations" or mystical
illuminations can be subsumed under the head of the "peak-experiences" or
"ecstasies" or "transcendent" experiences which are now being eagerly in-
vestigated by many psychologists. That is to say, it is very likely, indeed almost certain, that these older reports, phrased in terms of supernatural
revelation, were, in fact, perfectly natural, human peak-experiences of the
kind that can easily be examined today, which, however, were phrased in
terms of whatever conceptual, cultural, and linguistic framework the particular seer had available in his time.

In a word, we can study today what happened in the past and was then ex-
plainable in supernatural terms only. By so doing, we are enabled to examine religion in all its facets and in all its meanings in a way that makes it a
part of science rather than something outside and exclusive of it.

Also this kind of study leads us to another very plausible hypothesis: to the
extent that all mystical or peak-experiences are the same in their essence and

have always been the same, all religions are the same in their essence and always have been the same. They should, therefore, come to agree in principle on teaching that which is common to all of them, i.e., whatever it is that peak-experiences teach in common (whatever is *different* about these illuminations can fairly be taken to be localisms both in time and space, and are, therefore, peripheral, expendable, not essential). This something common, this something which is left over after we peel away all the localisms, all the accidents of particular languages or particular philosophies, all the ethnocentric phrasings, all those elements which are *not* common, we may call the "core-religious experience" or the "transcendent experience."

To understand this better, we must differentiate the prophets in general from the organizers or legalists in general as (abstracted) types. (I admit that the use of pure, extreme types which do not really exist can come close to the edge of caricature; nevertheless, I think it will help all of us in thinking through the problem we are here concerned with.) The characteristic prophet is a lonely man who has discovered his truth about the world, the cosmos, ethics, God, and his own identity from within, from his own personal experiences, from what he would consider to be a revelation. Usually, perhaps always, the prophets of the high religions have had these experiences when they were alone.

Characteristically the abstraction-type of the legalist-ecclesiastic is the conserving organization man, an officer and arm of the organization, who is loyal to the structure of the organization which has been built up on the basis of the prophet's original revelation in order to make the revelation available to the masses. From everything we know about organizations, we may very well expect that people will become loyal to it, as well as to the original prophet and to his vision; or at least they will become loyal to the organization's version of the prophet's vision. I may go so far as to say that characteristically (and I mean not only the religious organizations but also parallel organizations like the Communist Party or like revolutionary groups) these organizations can be seen as a kind of punch card or IBM version of an original revelation or mystical experience or peak-experience to make it suitable for group use and for administrative convenience.

It will be helpful here to talk about a pilot investigation, still in its beginnings, of the people I have called non-peakers. In my first investigations, in collaboration with Gene Nameche, I used this word because I thought some people had peak-experiences and others did not. But as I gathered information, and as I became more skillful in asking questions, I found that a higher and higher percentage of my subjects began to report peak-experiences. . . . I finally fell into the habit of expecting everyone to have peak-experiences and of being rather surprised if I ran across somebody who could report none at all. Because of this experience, I finally began to use the word "non-peaker" to describe, not the person who is unable to have peak-experiences, but rather the person who is afraid of them, who suppresses them, who denies them, who turns away from them, or who "forgets" them. My preliminary investigations of the reasons for these negative reactions to peak-experiences have led me to some (unconfirmed) impressions about why certain kinds of people renounce their peak-experiences.

Any person whose character structure (or Weltanschauung, or way of life) forces him to try to be extremely or completely rational or "materialistic" or mechanistic tends to become a non-peaker. That is, such a view of life tends to make the person regard his peak- and transcendent experiences as a kind of insanity, a complete loss of control, a sense of being overwhelmed by irrational emotions, etc. The person who is afraid of going insane and who is, therefore, desperately hanging on to stability, control, reality, etc., seems to be frightened by peak-experiences and tends to fight them off. For the compulsive-obsessive person, who organizes his life around the denying and the controlling of emotion, the fear of being overwhelmed by an emotion (which is interpreted as a loss of control) is enough for him to mobilize all his stamping-out and defensive activities against the peak-experience. I have one instance of a very convinced Marxian who denied—that is, who turned away from—a legitimate peak-experience, finally classifying it as some kind of peculiar but unimportant thing that had happened but that had best be forgotten because this experience conflicted with her whole materialistic mechanistic philosophy of life. I have found a few non-peakers who were ultra-scientific, that is, who espoused the nineteenth-century conception of science as an unemotional or anti-emotional activity which was ruled entirely by logic and rationality and who thought anything which was not logical and rational had no respectable place in life. (I suspect also that extremely "practical," i.e., exclusively means-oriented, people will turn out to be non-peakers, since such experiences earn no money, bake no bread, and chop no wood. So also for extremely other-directed people, who scarcely know what is going on inside themselves. Perhaps also people who are reduced to the concrete à la Goldstein, etc. etc.) Finally, I should add that, in some cases, I could not come to any explanation for non-peaking.

If you will permit me to use this developing but not yet validated vocabulary, I may then say simply that the relationship between the prophet and the ecclesiastic, between the lonely mystic and the (perfectly extreme) religious-organization man may often be a relationship between peaker and non-peaker. Much theology, much verbal religion through history and throughout the world, can be considered to be the more or less vain efforts to put into communicable words and formulae, and into symbolic rituals and ceremonies, the original mystical experience of the original prophets. In a word, organized religion can be thought of as an effort to communicate peak-experiences to non-peakers, to teach them, to apply them, etc. Often, to make it more difficult, this job falls into the hands of non-peakers. On the whole we now would expect that this would be a vain effort, at least so far as much of mankind is concerned. The peak-experiences and their experiential reality ordinarily are not transmittable to non-peakers, at least not by words alone, and certainly not by non-peakers. What happens to many people, especially the ignorant, the uneducated, the naïve, is that they simply concretize all of the symbols, all of the words, all of the statues, all of the ceremonies, and by a process of functional autonomy make *them*, rather than the original revelation, into the sacred things and sacred activities. That is to say, this is simply a form of the idolatry (or fetishism) which has been the curse of every large religion. In idolatry the essential original meaning gets so lost in concretizations that these finally become hostile to the original mystical experiences, to mystics, and to prophets in general, that is, to the very people that we might call from our present point of view the truly religious people. Most religions have wound up denying and being antagonistic to the very ground upon which they were originally based.

If you look closely at the internal history of most of the world religions, you will find that each one very soon tends to divide into a left-wing and a right-wing, that is, into the peakers, the mystics, the transcenders, or the privately religious people, on the one hand, and, on the other, into those who concretize the religious symbols and metaphors, who worship little pieces of wood rather than what the objects stand for, those who take verbal formulas literally, forgetting the original meaning of these words, and, perhaps most important, those who take the organization, the church, as primary and as more important than the prophet and his original revelations. These men, like many organization men who tend to rise to the top in any complex bureaucracy, tend to be non-peakers rather than peakers. Dostoevski's famous Grand Inquisitor passage, in his *Brothers Karamazov*, says this in a classical way.

This cleavage between the mystics and the legalists, if I may call them that, remains at best a kind of mutual tolerance, but it has happened in some churches that the rulers of the organization actually made a heresy out of the mystic experiences and persecuted the mystics themselves. This may be an old story in the history of religion, but I must point out that it is also an old story in other fields. For instance, we can certainly say today that professional philosophers tend to divide themselves into the same kind of characterologically based left-wing and right-wing. Most official, orthodox philosophers today are the equivalent of legalists who reject the problems and the data of transcendence as "meaningless." That is, they are positivists, atomists, analysts, concerned with means rather than with ends. They sharpen tools rather than discovering truths. These people contrast sharply with another group of contemporary philosophers, the existentialists and the phenomenologists. These are the people who tend to fall back on experiencing as the primary datum from which everything starts.

A similar split can be detected in psychology, in anthropology, and, I am quite sure, in other fields as well, perhaps in *all* human enterprises. I often suspect that we are dealing here with a profoundly characterological or constitutional difference in people which may persist far into the future, a human difference which may be universal and may continue to be so. The job then will be to get these two kinds of people to understand each other, to get along well with each other, even to love each other. This problem is paralleled by the relations between men and women who are so different from each other and yet who *have to* live with each other and even to love each other. (I must admit that it would be almost impossible to achieve this with poets and literary critics, composers and music critics, etc.)

To summarize, it looks quite probable that the peak-experience may be the model of the religious revelation or the religious illumination or conversion which has played so great a role in the history of religions. But, because peak-experiences are in the natural world and because we can research with them and investigate them, and because our knowledge of such experiences is growing and may be confidently expected to grow in the future, we may now fairly hope to understand more about the big revelations, conversions, and illuminations upon which the high religions were founded.

(Not only this, but I may add a new possibility for scientific investigation of transcendence. In the last few years it has become quite clear that certain drugs called "psychedelic," especially LSD and psilocybin, give us some possibility of control in this realm of peak-experiences. It looks as if these drugs often produce peak-experiences in the right people under the right circumstances, so that perhaps we needn't wait for them to occur by good fortune. Perhaps we can actually produce a private personal peak-experience under observation and whenever we wish under religious or non-religious circumstances. We may then be able to study in its moment of birth the experience of illumination or revelation. Even more important, it may be that these drugs, and perhaps also hypnosis, could be used to produce a peak-experience, with core-religious revelation, in non-peakers, thus bridging the chasm between these two separated halves of mankind.)

To approach this whole discussion from another angle, in effect what I have been saying is that the evidence from the peak-experiences permits us to talk about the essential, the intrinsic, the basic, the most fundamental religious or transcendent experience as a totally private and personal one which can hardly be shared (except with other "peakers"). As a consequence, all the paraphernalia of organized religion—buildings and specialized personnel, rituals, dogmas, ceremonials, and the like—are to the "peaker" secondary, peripheral, and of doubtful value in relation to the intrinsic and essential religious or transcendent experience. Perhaps they may even be very harmful in various ways. From the point of view of the peak-experiencer, each person has his own private religion, which he develops out of his own private revelations in which are revealed to him his own private myths and symbols, rituals and ceremonials, which may be of the profoundest meaning to him personally and yet completely idiosyncratic, i.e., of no meaning to anyone else. But to say it even more simply, each "peaker" discovers, develops, and retains his own religion. . . .

In addition, what seems to be emerging from this new source of data is that this essential core-religious experience may be embedded either in a theistic, supernatural context or in a non-theistic context. This private religious experience is shared by all the great world religions including the atheistic ones like Buddhism, Taoism, Humanism, or Confucianism. As a matter of fact, I can go so far as to say that this intrinsic core-experience is a meeting ground not only, let us say, for Christians and Jews and Mohammedans but also for priests and atheists, for communists and anti-communists, for conservatives and liberals, for artists and scientists, for men and for women, and for different constitutional types, that is to say, for athletes and for poets, for thinkers and for doers. I say this because our findings indicate that all or almost all people have or can have peak-experiences. Both men and women have peak-experiences, and all kinds of constitutional types have peak-experiences, but, although the content of the peak-experiences is approximately as I have described for all human beings . . . , the situation or the trigger which sets off peak-experience, for instance in males and females, can be quite different. These experiences can come from different sources, but their content may be considered to be very similar. To sum it up, from this point of view, the two religions of mankind tend to be the peakers and the non-peakers, that is to say, those who have private, personal, transcendent, core-religious experiences easily and often and who accept them and make use of them, and, on the other hand, those who have never had them or who repress or suppress them and who, therefore, cannot make use of them for their personal therapy, personal growth, or personal fulfillment.

peter marin   MEDITATIONS ON THE
                                           JESUS MOVEMENT

---

*Peter Marin (1933–   ) is a sympathetic student of the emerging life styles
of the young. In his notable introduction to* The Free People *(a book of photo-
graphs by Anders Holmquist) he wrote, "It is clear to me now that the rapid
and unfamiliar changes now in the world will make themselves known to us as
new persons, new natures: sequential waves of lovers and comrades whose natures
will be different enough to enlarge and enchant us and demand that we change."
A severe critic of traditional schools, Marin has been a fellow at the Center for
the Study of Democratic Institutions. He served as director of Pacific High
School, an experimental school, and was the editor of the* New Schools Exchange
Newsletter. *He is the co-author of* Understanding Drug Use: An Adult's Guide
to Drugs and the Young. *The essay which follows was published in the* Saturday
Review *(May 6, 1972).*

These days I keep pinned to my wall a note from a friend. "Ah, Peter, the
distances are so great, my paralysis so nearly complete. I feel like a grim,
weary animal on the banks of a river as it is moving on." Though my friend
is Jewish, as am I, and still unmoved by the revivalism of the times, his note
is as good a place as any to begin talking of the New Christians. He has been
through it all: the free-speech movement, civil rights, hash and acid, traditional and communal marriage, fatherhood and a book, and even a hint of
fame. What he has learned from it all is summed up by one of his favorite
phrases: the long march. What he means by that is simply that we have
barely begun a journey it will take us decades to complete. Our "new" consciousness has not released us from the demons of the age but has simply
brought us face to face with them.

In his exhaustion, vision, and hope, he is one of those souls the Zohar, the
Jewish *Book of Splendor*, calls "children from the chamber of yearning"—
those compelled to suffer in their privacies and nightmares the confusion
of the age. I understand, as do some of my comrades and most of the
young, the loneliness and exhaustion he feels, for the condition is not his
alone. It is a natural one. The age itself is a chamber of yearning; what
disappears in the midst of it is the sense of any hold on life, any touch with
the physical world, any feeling of ease or belonging.

The new "millennialism" of the young is a desperate response to this mixture of public chaos and private isolation. What moves the young is only
in part the desire for the simple life, religious ecstasy, and justification. There

is a more desolate and organic need, the need to reduce the nightmare complexity of things to a manageable form. The Jesus revolution is simply the most recent, popular, and obvious expression of that need. One can find among the young dozens of other disciplines and creeds—Krishna-consciousness, Subud, Zen, Yoga, transcendental meditation—and, beyond those, the whole hazy landscape of pop therapies and enthusiasms. Every passing idea is turned zealously into a faith. The *I Ching*, the Tarot cards, the *Whole Earth Catalog*, and the ephemerides become fundamentalist texts.

In all these zealotries the driving need is for certainty and purity, for a transcendence of the self. The Jesus-cults are more popular than others have been because they offer the young what other faiths do not—an instantaneous and push-button forgiveness, an apparent and abrupt end to guilt and self-disgust. They are familial, offer an authoritative Father, brothers, and sisters for company. Though ultimately triumphant, they can explain and justify present suffering. Though ultimately millennial, they are comfortably regressive, a denial of the probable future and its crises. One becomes a child again. The world is defused, depoliticized. *Jesus is coming.* First the necessary catastrophe, then the New World. There is little one can do save render the State its due and prepare oneself for the Second Coming.

Much of the need for refuge is, of course, the direct result of civic terror and individual impotence. Perhaps the cruelest legacy of the past decade has been the steady demoralization of the young. Whatever private avenues have opened for them—sex, drugs, mobility—have all been overshadowed by the growing sense that men and women are not really free in America, if they ever have been. In face of that realization, the young were driven first to protest and then to violence. But on the furthest edge of things, they found the State ready to murder them. Those unwilling to resist with comparable violence were forced to withdraw, not into the "system," but into a disconsolate quietism that has become boredom for some and despair for others. Terrorized, some were radicalized and deepened by it all. Others have become, for the moment, members of a middle-class version of what the radical South American educator, Paolo Freire, calls the "silent culture" —a class that is so disheartened by its victimization that it retreats into passivity and silence.

But that is not all there is to their retreat. Deeper down something else is going on, something that cannot be explained in simple sociological terms. It is a kind of cultural involution occurring in many young people at the deepest levels of private experience. They have entered an internal evolutionary maelstrom in which they undergo radical changes and trials. They are surrounded by adults who seem unable to live passionately or effectively in the world, unable to understand or aid them. The adult hopes they hear voiced around them—"reformation of the system," "social engineering," "hu-

387

man potential"—must seem to the young both desperate and self-delusive, shrill tunes whistled in the dark. The young are left in their own gravid darkness to fabricate little myths and fancies. The poignant result is what one sees among the young—brittle, innocent, and millennial fantasies, a mixture of half-truths and insights garbled by fear. They salvage shreds of past beliefs and patch them together to give to the age an ostensible purpose and end.

One evening I talk to a newly converted Christian. "I'd just got outta jail. Met a girl on the beach, and we started for the New Mexican communes but ended up here. When I first saw the house, I said, O *Christ, Jesus freaks,* but after a while I saw they'd gotten it together, and nobody else I knew had done it. Now I been here six months, baptized and everything."

"And before?"

"I hustled and dealt. Lived on the street. Got into some shit that was wrong."

"Wrong?"

"Yeah, shit I know was wrong. I mean, I was hanging out with a black dude, and one of his friends got killed by the pigs. So we went out one night with this shotgun and found a pig sitting alone in his squad car. Stuck the gun through the window and blew him wide open."

His face is open and scrubbed, and he says all this casually in a weedy southern drawl. We are standing on a leafy, suburban street, late on a quiet American night, but you can hear in his words the disorder that lies beneath them. He is a member of a new marginal class, the lumpen-young. They drift across immense internal and external distances, seeking solace, meaning, and contact, all dispossessed, mobile, and pained, all without ways to feel useful, potent, or good. They have come in their own lives to an edge of the world, and they have come to it crippled by isolation. Though the surface taboos have apparently been broken, there remains in their lives an undertow of doubt and self-disgust. There is an inability to find any pleasure in sensation, any satisfaction in experience.

They are both the victims and products of one of the century's many botched revolutions—the partial release of libido, of Lawrence's "dark gods," and our fumbled attempts to confront those gods. Under our surface *yes* to sensation, we have not yet learned how to stop saying *no* to life. Our new patterns of behavior allow us increased experience. We are driven toward sensation by a shrill mental need. But we also suffer in the flesh a contaminating guilt, a fear and detachment that empty whatever we do of significance. If there is among the young a slant toward ecstasy or carnal delight, it is riddled at the moment with more hysteria and fear than one finds in their parents. In this no man's land of the psyche, the young experience an inexplicable hurt. There is a sense of bewilderment, betrayal, and humiliation.

388

That is where salvation comes in—and the divine and resurrected Christ. Conversion means a new life for these children, not merely a deepening or an integration of feeling, but a new beginning altogether. It is not the exemplary Jesus they follow, not Jesus the man in and of the world. It is instead the miraculous, sacrificing, risen Son of God whose death and divine resurrection mean forgiveness for our sins. Their faith is a Pauline faith in a Christ devoid of mystery and human ambiguity, a Christ denied his manhood. Paul wrote to the Romans, "If thou shalt confess with thy mouth the Lord Jesus and shall believe in thine heart that God has raised him from the dead, thou shalt be saved."

In this rawly fundamentalist approach to Christ, one professes and converts, and the past is left behind. Many of the new Christians were at one time deeply involved with drugs, destructively into a passive and pleasureless sexuality. Others were merely adrift and purposeless. Conversion offers them an alternative to those pasts, an absolute therapy. The past is neither explored nor analyzed. It is simply left behind, forgiven and forgotten, at the very moment one embraces Jesus.

Trying to come to terms with it all, I visit with some local Christians at their weekly prayer meeting. The participants are all in their teens and twenties, some in couples, a few married, all clean and smiling. As they arrive, they are greeted by exclamations of thanksgiving. "O praise Jesus, brother. O praise the Lord." There is no leader. There is no service. In other groups there is sometimes a leader or a sermon of sorts or speaking in tongues. But here it is simpler—testimony and singing. Someone hands out a hymnbook. A few of the hymns are traditional, but most of them are newly written to familiar tunes. One of the tunes is *Lend an Ear*. Another is *Chopsticks*. A third is *Dixie*. Its refrain is *look within, look within, look within for Jesus Christ*. The hymns are interspersed with spontaneous outbursts of enthusiasm and testimony. Most of the members testify about their daily lives—how Jesus has found them a job, or has settled a fight between roommates, or has improved a floundering marriage. There is a continuous round of exhortation and praise, all of it colored by a curious and heady mixture of the humility of the meek and the smugness of the redeemed.

Someone cries out: "Gonna join you, Lord. We're knocking at the gate."

Another: "You're our master, Jesus, our only King."

Another: "Gonna rise right up out of slavery, Jesus, gonna sit on God's throne."

And another: "Thank you, Jesus, thank you. We're no longer under the thumb of the world."

It is all so antiseptic, so hygienic, so humorless, so innocent and distressing at the same time—a roomful of shiny pennies stamped with the same date. But one can hear underneath all the snuffling and scuttling of small animals seeking a place to hide. There is a kind of nostalgia to the meeting, an old-fashioned boosterism and a curious oscillation between zeal and fear. It is as if the last night of summer camp were being held in the hold of the sinking *Titanic*.

These are the "good" children, those who do not want to burn or smash the world but merely desire to shut their eyes and wish it out of existence. I remember talking to a recently converted friend of mine about a man I thought had learned, by the end of his days, to face life bravely and with gentleness. "Maybe so," she shrugged, "but he wasn't, after all, a true Christian." What she meant was that his warmth, courage, and tenderness could mean nothing unless it fell within the limits of her world. This is America after all, and these are middle-class American children, as ready as ever to diminish whatever fails to fit their dream of things.

I remember, too, watching a friend argue with a few evangelical young Christians. In a patient way he insisted that Buddha and Muhammad were also adequate models and gods and that most religions could bring one to a sense of the divine. But the new Christians would have none of it. Christ, they insisted, was the only way. Those who chose other paths were damned. In the face of my friend's quiet persistence they began to rage, and finally one of them shouted: "No! No! Jesus is the way. Compared to him what you believe is nothing. Nothing!"

What moves these children is fright. What terrifies them is what seems to bewilder us all these days: something beneath political disorder and social chaos, a peculiar kind of psychic event occurring at the center of the soul, an event for which we have no precedents, theories, or laws. We have only the sense of boundaries given way, of a kind of nakedness, of distances shrinking and yet increasing at the same speeds—as if we have lost all sense of privacy but are still absolutely isolated from the world.

Somewhere at the heart of it all lies the end of the Renaissance "person," of the whole structure and experience of the self as we have known it. From the Renaissance onward, we have held, in one form or another, a hard-edged image of man fundamentally independent and self-contained. Now our ladderlike image of self as superego, ego, and id—a skeletal but a highly charged model—has become something else altogether, a kind of porous sieve, less of a structure and more of a field, a curious, hybrid puddle of sensation. The self lacks hard edges and melts into the world around it, is easily swept by the world's currents and waves.

What I am talking about is a fundamental change in the way we experience our relation to the world. What is occurring now is a process of psychic collectivization that comes close to what some have called a "retribalization." But it is actually radically different. What tribes share is a visceral world view, a physical sense of the shared sources of communal power and physical reality—a connection of *flesh and blood*. What we share is something else altogether: a loss of touch with physical nature and a connection of *consciousness*, something far more electric and mental, a soup of inexplicable and contagious sensations and moods in which the physical world is somehow forgotten—and with it the primacy and value of the *person*.

What the collectivization produces is not the state of ecstasy Norman Brown envisioned in *Love's Body*, but the kind of condition Blake described in *Milton:* "No human form but only a fibrous vegetation, a polypus of soft affections without Vision or Thought." The self becomes a vast and vulnerable suggestibility. Nothing is generated from within. Instead, impulses flow in from the outside in a kind of perpetual "imprinting" at odds with all ripening.

What one often sees, working or living with the young, is a peculiar condition of personality, an expansiveness and release at the surface, but beneath, a self held in suspension and closed defensively against the world like a fist or a fetus, struggling to maintain some sort of identity. Though there is, in general, an ache for transcendence, there is in many of the young little sense of, or love for, the reality to be transcended. There is an impatience with both ego and thought, but there is no fully developed ego to be set aside. Usually, what takes the place of thought is neither ecstasy nor imagination, but merely superstition. There is a sweet hollowness, an undercurrent of anger, a gentle impulse toward potency and touch, but not yet the hard daring and resilience it takes to survive in the world.

All of that is probably transitional, a direct result of the confusions of the age, but for the time being many young persons are struggling to survive. Sex, drugs, and motion are all seemingly expansive and liberating, but only if one is at home in the world or whole enough to make use of their ambiguous lessons. Survival depends upon a resonance and depth of self, the existence at the center of experience of *someone*, a self strong enough to absorb the strains. But too often a center seems to be missing. Unable to deal adequately with the unceasing rush of experience, the young are forced to armor themselves against it with abstract systems and beliefs.

The irony, of course, is that the systems they choose to bring them closer to life are inevitably those that divorce them from it. The "new" Christianity is merely another shape of our habitual cultural rejection of the truth of our own lives. To reject the State and its institutions and choose instead the dogma of the Resurrected Christ is merely to replace one web of evasions with another. As Erich Gutkind argued in *The Absolute Collective*, mysticism and nationalism are forms of the same panicked impulse. Of course, there are always men and women who live their lives in the "white heat of God," but for most of us creedal mysticism and idealism are simply refined forms of spiritual jingoism—the same old American refrain set to a different tune. They leave men and women in the same closed box, clinging to abstraction and evasion for the sense of contact or meaning that it would be too painful to wrest from the world.

The Jesus-cults are in reality an ironic extension of what Henry Miller once called the "universe of Death," the grid of compulsive moral abstractions that separates us from experience. They are the latest resurgence of a recurrent theme in Western and American experience: the compulsive search for a transcendental consciousness, a disembodied and pure awareness, a "love" to lift us beyond the physicality we cannot tolerate or love. We use our spirituality in much the same way we use our technology, as a defense against life. It is no accident that we are drawn to both, for they offer us the same gifts: an end not only to pain, age, and death but also to the complexities of "personhood." In both realms we struggle to escape or subdue whatever seems to us mysterious, alien, or wild; we are driven to control or transcend because we are afraid to enter or inhabit. "We are like balloons held down by strings of ego," says one of my Sufi friends. "We can cut ourselves loose. We can be high *all* the time."

A knowledgeable friend of mine calls our new faiths the "emerging schizoid ethic"—an attempt to rationalize dis-ease into a system of values. For we still suffer the grievous condition we have inherited from the past, not simply the split between body and mind, but the more awful separation between being and meaning. The history of Western religion is the history of that separation, a record of the monopolization of meaning by religion, the substitution of a divine and distant significance for an earthly one. The world and the flesh are denied; there is a sacred and a profane, and the profane is always the world, always the flesh—unless redeemed from above. Meaning, once separated from the world, must be begged back or earned from Heaven.

But that won't work. What we need is not a new or higher "consciousness" but a renewal of the raw stuff that moves beneath consciousness, of the substance of things, of the underpinnings of life, of our ability as fleshed creatures to come warmly and fully to the world. Only such great renegade Christians as Blake and Lawrence understood that meaning is nothing "spiritual," nothing transcendent. It is instead a kind of heat and light, the natural result of felt contact with life, of a passionate receptivity to the world. What we forget in our zeal and belief is that meaning and value are incarnate. "Love, Mercy, Pity, Peace," as Blake said, "have a human form divine." They reside in each of us as the meaning released when we make real contact with the world. All we are, all self is, is life in touch with life. But when we fail to make that touch, we are prey to both a feeling of deadness and the dream of salvation.

But why bother to rage about it all? As I sit here writing, making it all so important, it suddenly seems unimportant. The sun is hot this afternoon.

The sky is clear. A warm breeze moves through these mountains, and the eucalyptus leaves brush against one another. The physical world is still here. It has not disappeared. My daughter, sitting nude on the table, smiles a gap-toothed, Gatsby-like smile and pastes blue-chip stamps to her feet in a rite of some kind of magic. These are hard times, and why begrudge to anyone the fancies and extremes he needs to save himself? Some of us take consolation in independence, others have the university or the corporation, and some cling still to possessions, or professions, or an idealized dream of the future.

These days I keep muttering to myself: "How great a need." Like all of us, the new Christians seek and improvise what they need, and the hard truth is that many of them can find no consolation elsewhere. If they have left behind the flag, the university, and the two parties, only to replace them with astrology, yoga, and Jesus, well, that is the way we progress from age to age.

The trouble, of course, is that we may not progress at all, but merely mark time and substitute one set of delusions for another. There is a change in values but no deepening of life. The world stays flat. These days offer nothing less than the chance for a resignification of being, a chance to re-create some kind of meaning in the world. But it is a turbulent task, and it will be decades before we emerge on the other side of this chaos with any sense of belonging or ease in the world. The young will cling, before we are through, to dozens of millennial enthusiasms. They will seek meaning in new systems and creeds, forgetting, as we always do, that meaning is never assigned to the world, is never found. It is created by the depth of imagination and feeling we bring to the world.

What matters after all, especially in times such as ours, is never how saved or whole one is, but the extent to which one restores to others, through presence and passion, a sense of possibility and independence. As for myself, what I prize among my comrades these days has nothing to do with enlightenment or heightened consciousness. It is instead a fierceness, an animal tenacity, a sense one sometimes gets from others of a complex, evolving person, of a rare and lusty insistence on a complex, honest, solitary privacy that protects life in the flesh against abstractions, ideals, and even salvation itself. The most difficult task of all is to steer between exhaustion and illusion, between resignation and an escape into dogma.

Those who try it will find—like my friend from the chamber of learning —a kind of grimness and weariness, a kind of loneliness. But if they are lucky, they will also get a glimpse here and there of light and depth, an occasional sense of freedom and potency, a few good comrades to hold in their thoughts or arms.

thomas merton   RAIN AND THE RHINOCEROS

Thomas Merton (1915–1968) was born in France, his mother an American and his artist-father originally from New Zealand. Merton attended French schools and Clare College, Cambridge, but received his A.B. and M.A. degrees from Columbia University. He was converted to Catholicism in 1939 and in 1941 became a Trappist monk, entering the "Our Lady of Gethsemani" monastery in Kentucky. ("Trappist" is the popular name for those within an austere and contemplative reform movement that originated in the seventeenth century in the Cistercian Order of the Catholic Church.) Among his many volumes of poetry and meditations are Thoughts in Solitude, The Silent Life, Seeds of Contemplation, No Man Is an Island, The Ascent to Truth, *and* Mystics and Zen Masters. *He wrote a best-selling autobiography,* The Seven Storey Mountain, *in 1948. "Rain and the Rhinoceros" is from* Raids on the Unspeakable (1965).

Let me say this before rain becomes a utility that they can plan and distribute for money. By "they" I mean the people who cannot understand that rain is a festival, who do not appreciate its gratuity, who think that what has no price has no value, that what cannot be sold is not real, so that the only way to make something *actual* is to place it on the market. The time will come when they will sell you even your rain. At the moment it is still free, and I am in it. I celebrate its gratuity and its meaninglessness.

The rain I am in is not like the rain of cities. It fills the woods with an immense and confused sound. It covers the flat roof of the cabin and its porch with insistent and controlled rhythms. And I listen, because it reminds me again and again that the whole world runs by rhythms I have not yet learned to recognize, rhythms that are not those of the engineer.

I came up here from the monastery last night, sloshing through the cornfield, said Vespers, and put some oatmeal on the Coleman stove for supper. It boiled over while I was listening to the rain and toasting a piece of bread at the log fire. The night became very dark. The rain surrounded the whole cabin with its enormous virginal myth, a whole world of meaning, of secrecy, of silence, of rumor. Think of it: all that speech pouring down, selling nothing, judging nobody, drenching the thick mulch of dead leaves, soaking the trees, filling the gullies and crannies of the wood with water, washing out the places where men have stripped the hillside! What a thing it is to sit absolutely alone, in the forest, at night, cherished by this wonderful, unintelligible, perfectly innocent speech, the most comforting speech in the world, the talk that rain makes by itself all over the ridges, and the talk of the watercourses everywhere in the hollows!

394

Nobody started it, nobody is going to stop it. It will talk as long as it wants, this rain. As long as it talks I am going to listen.

But I am also going to sleep, because here in this wilderness I have learned how to sleep again. Here I am not alien. The trees I know, the night I know, the rain I know. I close my eyes and instantly sink into the whole rainy world of which I am a part, and the world goes on with me in it, for I am not alien to it. I am alien to the noises of cities, of people, to the greed of machinery that does not sleep, the hum of power that eats up the night. Where rain, sunlight and darkness are contemned, I cannot sleep. I do not trust anything that has been fabricated to replace the climate of woods or prairies. I can have no confidence in places where the air is first fouled and then cleansed, where the water is first made deadly and then made safe with other poisons. There is nothing in the world of buildings that is not fabricated, and if a tree gets in among the apartment houses by mistake it is taught to grow chemically. It is given a precise reason for existing. They put a sign on it saying it is for health, beauty, perspective; that it is for peace, for prosperity; that it was planted by the mayor's daughter. All of this is mystification. The city itself lives on its own myth. Instead of waking up and silently existing, the city people prefer a stubborn and fabricated dream; they do not care to be a part of the night, or to be merely of the world. They have constructed a world outside the world, against the world, a world of mechanical fictions which contemn nature and seek only to use it up, thus preventing it from renewing itself and man.

Of course the festival of rain cannot be stopped, even in the city. The woman from the delicatessen scampers along the sidewalk with a newspaper over her head. The streets, suddenly washed, became transparent and alive, and the noise of traffic becomes a plashing of fountains. One would think that urban man in a rainstorm would *have* to take account of nature in its wetness and freshness, its baptism and its renewal. But the rain brings no renewal to the city, only to tomorrow's weather, and the glint of windows in tall buildings will then have nothing to do with the new sky. All "reality" will remain somewhere inside those walls, counting itself and selling itself with fantastically complex determination. Meanwhile the obsessed citizens plunge through the rain bearing the load of their obsessions, slightly more vulnerable than before, but still only barely aware of external realities. They do not see that the streets shine beautifully, that they themselves are walking on stars and water, that they are running in skies to catch a bus or a taxi, to shelter somewhere in the press of irritated humans, the faces of advertisements and the dim, cretinous sound of unidentified music. But they must know that there is wetness abroad. Perhaps they even *feel* it. I cannot say. Their complaints are mechanical and without spirit.

Naturally no one can believe the things they say about the rain. It all implies one basic lie: *only the city is real.* That weather, not being planned, not being fabricated, is an impertinence, a wen on the visage of progress. (Just a simple little operation, and the whole mess may become relatively tolerable. Let business *make* the rain. This will give it meaning.)

Thoreau sat in *his* cabin and criticized the railways. I sit in mine and wonder about a world that has, well, progressed. I must read *Walden* again, and see if Thoreau already guessed that he was part of what he thought he could escape. But it is not a matter of "escaping." It is not even a matter of protesting very audibly. Technology is here, even in the cabin. True, the utility line is not here yet, and so G.E. is not here yet either. When the utilities and G.E. enter my cabin arm in arm it will be nobody's fault but my own. I admit it. I am not kidding anybody, even myself. I will suffer their bluff and patronizing complacencies in silence. I will let them think they know what I am doing here.

They are convinced that *I am having fun.*

This has already been brought home to me with a wallop by my Coleman lantern. Beautiful lamp: It burns white gas and sings viciously but gives out a splendid green light in which I read Philoxenos, a sixth-century Syrian hermit. Philoxenos fits in with the rain and the festival of night. Of this, more later. Meanwhile: what does my Coleman lantern tell me? (Coleman's philosophy is printed on the cardboard box which I have (guiltily) not shellacked as I was supposed to, and which I have tossed in the woodshed behind the hickory chunks.) Coleman says that the light is good, and has a reason: it *"Stretches days to give more hours of fun."*

Can't I just be in the woods without any special reason? Just being in the woods, at night, in the cabin, is something too excellent to be justified or explained! It just *is*. There are always a few people who are in the woods at night, in the rain (because if there were not the world would have ended), and I am one of them. We are not having fun, we are not "having" anything, we are not *"stretching our days,"* and if we had fun it would not be measured by hours. Though as a matter of fact that is what fun seems to be: a state of diffuse excitation that can be measured by the clock and "stretched" by an appliance.

There is no clock that can measure the speech of this rain that falls all night on the drowned and lonely forest.

Of course at three-thirty A.M. the SAC plane goes over, red light winking low under the clouds, skimming the wooded summits on the south side of the valley, loaded with strong medicine. Very strong. Strong enough to burn up all these woods and stretch our hours of fun into eternities.

And that brings me to Philoxenos, a Syrian who had fun in the sixth century, without benefit of appliances, still less of nuclear deterrents.

Philoxenos in his ninth *memra* (on poverty) to dwellers in solitude, says that there is no explanation and no justification for the solitary life, since it is without a law. To be a contemplative is therefore to be an outlaw. As was Christ. As was Paul.

One who is not "alone," says Philoxenos, has not discovered his identity. He seems to be alone, perhaps, for he experiences himself as "individual." But because he is willingly enclosed and limited by the laws and illusions of collective existence, he has no more identity than an unborn child in the womb. He is not yet conscious. He is alien to his own truth. He has senses, but he cannot use them. He has life, but no identity. To have an identity, he has to be awake, and aware. But to be awake, he has to accept vulnerability and death. Not for their own sake: not out of stoicism or despair —only for the sake of the invulnerable inner reality which we cannot recognize (which we can only *be*) but to which we awaken only when we see the unreality of our vulnerable shell. The discovery of this inner self is an act and affirmation of solitude.

Now if we take our vulnerable shell to be our true identity, if we think our mask is our true face, we will protect it with fabrications even at the cost of violating our own truth. This seems to be the collective endeavor of society: the more busily men dedicate themselves to it, the more certainly it becomes a collective illusion, until in the end we have the enormous, obsessive, uncontrollable dynamic of fabrications designed to protect mere fictitious identities—"selves," that is to say, regarded as objects. Selves that can stand back and see themselves having fun (an illusion which reassures them that they are real).

Such is the ignorance which is taken to be the axiomatic foundation of all knowledge in the human collectivity: in order to experience yourself as real, you have to suppress the awareness of your contingency, your unreality, your state of radical need. This you do by creating an awareness of yourself as *one who has no needs that he cannot immediately fulfill*. Basically, this is an illusion of omnipotence: an illusion which the collectivity arrogates to itself, and consents to share with its indivdual members in proportion as they submit to its more central and more rigid fabrications.

You have needs; but if you behave and conform you can participate in the collective power. You can then satisfy all your needs. Meanwhile, in order to increase its power over you, the collectivity increases your needs. It also tightens its demand for conformity. Thus you can become all the more committed to the collective illusion in proportion to becoming more hopelessly mortgaged to collective power.

How does this work? The collectivity informs and shapes your will to happiness ("have fun") by presenting you with irresistible images of yourself as you would like to be: having *fun that is so perfectly credible that it allows no interference of conscious doubt.* In theory such a good time can be so convincing that you are no longer aware of even a remote possibility that it might change into something less satisfying. In practice, expensive fun always admits of a doubt, which blossoms out into another full-blown need, which then calls for a still more credible and more costly refinement of satisfaction, which again fails you. The end of the cycle is despair.

Because we live in a womb of collective illusion, our freedom remains abortive. Our capacities for joy, peace, and truth are never liberated. They can never be used. We are prisoners of a process, a dialectic of false promises and real deceptions ending in futility.

"The unborn child," says Philoxenos, "is already perfect and fully constituted in his nature, with all his senses, and limbs, but he cannot make use of them in their natural functions, because, in the womb, he cannot strengthen or develop them for such use."

Now, since all things have their season, there is a time to be unborn. We must begin, indeed, in the social womb. There is a time for warmth in the collective myth. But there is also a time to be born. He who is spiritually "born" as a mature identity is liberated from the enclosing womb of myth and prejudice. He learns to think for himself, guided no longer by the dictates of need and by the systems and processes designed to create artificial needs and then "satisfy" them.

This emancipation can take two forms: first that of the active life, which liberates itself from enslavement to necessity by considering and serving the needs of others, without thought of personal interest or return. And second, the contemplative life, which must not be construed as an escape from time and matter, from social responsibility and from the life of sense, but rather, as an advance into solitude and the desert, a confrontation with poverty and the void, a renunciation of the empirical self, in the presence of death, and nothingness, in order to overcome the ignorance and error that spring from the fear of "being nothing." The man who dares to be alone can come to see that the "emptiness" and "usefulness" which the collective mind fears and condemns are necessary conditions for the encounter with truth.

It is in the desert of loneliness and emptiness that the fear of death and the need for self-affirmation are seen to be illusory. When this is faced, then anguish is not necessarily overcome, but it can be accepted and understood. Thus, in the heart of anguish are found the gifts of peace and understanding: not simply in personal illumination and liberation, but by commitment and empathy, for the contemplative must assume the universal anguish and the inescapable condition of mortal man. The solitary, far from enclosing himself in himself, becomes every man. He dwells in the solitude, the poverty, the indigence of every man.

It is in this sense that the hermit, according to Philoxenos, imitates Christ. For in Christ, God takes to Himself the solitude and dereliction of man: every man. From the moment Christ went out into the desert to be tempted, the loneliness, the temptation and the hunger of every man became the loneliness, temptation and hunger of Christ. But in return, the gift of truth with which Christ dispelled the three kinds of illusion offered him in his temptation (security, reputation and power) can become also our own truth, if we can only accept it. It is offered to us also in temptation. "You too go out into the desert," said Philoxenos, "having with you nothing of the world, and the Holy Spirit will go with you. See the freedom with which Jesus has gone forth, and go forth like Him—see where he has left the rule of men; leave the rule of the world where he has left the law, and go out with him to fight the power of error."

And where is the power of error? We find it was after all not in the city, but in *ourselves*.

Today the insights of a Philoxenos are to be sought less in the tracts of theologians than in the meditations of the existentialists and in the Theater of the Absurd. The problem of Berenger, in Ionesco's *Rhinoceros*, is the problem of the human person stranded and alone in what threatens to become a society of monsters. In the sixth century Berenger might perhaps have walked off into the desert of Scete, without too much concern over the fact that all his fellow citizens, all his friends, and even his girl Daisy, had turned into rhinoceroses.

The problem today is that there are no deserts, only dude ranches.

The desert islands are places where the wicked little characters in the *Lord of the Flies* come face to face with the Lord of the Flies, form a small, tight, ferocious collectivity of painted faces, and arm themselves with spears to hunt down the last member of their group who still remembers with nostalgia the possibilities of rational discourse.

When Berenger finds himself suddenly the last human in a rhinoceros herd he looks into the mirror and says, humbly enough, "After all, man is not as bad as all that, is he?" But his world now shakes mightily with the stampede of his metamorphosed fellow citizens, and he soon becomes aware that the very stampede itself is the most telling and tragic of all arguments. For when he considers going out into the street "to try to convince them," he realizes that he "would have to learn their language." He looks in the mirror and sees that *he no longer resembles anyone*. He searches madly for a photograph of people as they were before the big change. But now humanity itself has become incredible, as well as hideous. To be the last man in the rhinoceros herd is, in fact, to be a monster.

Such is the problem which Ionesco sets us in his tragic irony: solitude and dissent become more and more impossible, more and more absurd. That Berenger finally accepts his absurdity and rushes out to challenge the whole herd only points up the futility of a commitment to rebellion. At the same time in *The New Tenant* (*Le Nouveau Locataire*) Ionesco portrays the absurdity of a logically consistent individualism which, in fact, is a self-isolation by the pseudo-logic of proliferating needs and possessions.

Ionesco protested that the New York production of *Rhinoceros* as a farce was a complete misunderstanding of his intention. It is a play not merely against *conformism* but about *totalitarianism*. The rhinoceros is not an amiable beast, and with him around the fun ceases and things begin to get serious. Everything has to make sense and be totally useful to the totally obsessive operation. At the same time Ionesco was criticized for not giving the audience "something positive" to take away with them, instead of just "refusing the human adventure." (Presumably "rhinoceritis" is the latest in human adventure!) He replied: "They [the spectators] leave in a void— and that was my intention. It is the business of a free man to pull himself out of this void by his own power and not by the power of other people!" In this Ionesco comes very close to Zen and to Christian eremitism.

"In all the cities of the world, it is the same," says Ionesco. "The universal and modern man is the man in a rush (i.e. a rhinoceros), a man who has no time, who is a prisoner of necessity, who cannot understand that *a thing might perhaps be without usefulness*; nor does he understand that, at bottom, it is the useful that may be a useless and back-breaking burden. If one does not understand the usefulness of the useless and the uselessness of the useful, one cannot understand art. And a country where art is not understood is a country of slaves and robots. . . ." (*Notes et Contre Notes*, p. 129) Rhinoceritis, he adds, is the sickness that lies in wait "for those who *have lost the sense and the taste for solitude*."

The love of solitude is sometimes condemned as "hatred of our fellow men." But is this true? If we push our analysis of collective thinking a little further we will find that the dialectic of power and need, of submission and satisfaction, ends by being a dialectic of hate. Collectivity needs not only to absorb everyone it can, but also implicitly to hate and destroy whoever cannot be absorbed. Paradoxically, one of the needs of collectivity is to reject certain classes, or races, or groups, in order to strengthen its own self-awareness by hating them instead of absorbing them.

Thus the solitary cannot survive unless he is capable of loving everyone, without concern for the fact that he is likely to be regarded by all of them as a traitor. Only the man who has fully attained his own spiritual identity can live without the need to kill, and without the need of a doctrine that permits him to do so with a good conscience. There will always be a place, says Ionesco, *"for those isolated consciences who have stood up for the universal conscience"* as against the mass mind. But their place is solitude. They have no other. Hence it is the solitary person (whether in the city or in the desert) who does mankind the inestimable favor of reminding it of its true capacity for maturity, liberty and peace.

It sounds very much like Philoxenos to me.

And it sounds like what the rain says. We still carry this burden of illusion because we do not dare to lay it down. We suffer all the needs that society demands we suffer, because if we do not have these needs we lose our "usefulness" in society—the usefulness of suckers. We fear to be alone, and to be ourselves, and so to remind others of the truth that is in them.

"I will not make you such rich men as have need of many things," said Philoxenos (putting the words on the lips of Christ), "but I will make you true rich men who have need of nothing. Since it is not he who has many possessions that is rich, but he who has no needs." Obviously, we shall always have *some* needs. But only he who has the simplest and most natural needs can be considered to be without needs, since the only needs he has are real ones, and the real ones are not hard to fulfill if one is a free man!

The rain has stopped. The afternoon sun slants through the pine trees: and how those useless needles smell in the clear air!

A dandelion, long out of season, has pushed itself into bloom between the smashed leaves of last summer's day lilies. The valley resounds with the totally uninformative talk of creeks and wild water.

Then the quails begin their sweet whistling in the wet bushes. Their noise is absolutely useless, and so is the delight I take in it. There is nothing I would rather hear, not because it is a better noise than other noises, but because it is the voice of the present moment, the present festival.

Yet even here the earth shakes. Over at Fort Knox the Rhinoceros is having fun.

FURTHER READING

Two recent essays which survey contemporary trends in religion are those by philosophy professor Marcia Cavel, "Visions of a New Religion," *Saturday Review* (December 19, 1970) and Sara Davidson, "The Rush for Instant Salvation," *Harpers* (July 1971).

Jacob Needleman's *The New Religions* (1970) is a study of the "explosion" of Eastern religious thought in America. Among its topics are Transcendental Meditation, Meher Baba, Subud, Tibetan Buddhism, and Gurd-jieff.

Frank Waters' *Book of the Hopi* (1963) and *Black Elk Speaks* (1932; Pocket Books edition, 1972), as told through John G. Neihardt, are two of the best books about the American Indian, whose view of life was always religious.

The Japanese scholar and Zen Master D. T. Suzuki, as someone else has surely said, was almost single-handedly responsible for introducing Zen to the West. His work is sampled in *Zen Buddhism: Selected Writings of D. T. Suzuki* (1956) edited by William Barrett.

The theologian-pastor Dietrich Bonhoeffer, who was involved in the plot to assassinate Hitler, was executed in 1945. His "non-religious" Christianity was evolving in his *Letters and Papers from Prison* (rev. ed., 1967).

Thomas J. J. Altizer and William Hamilton, *Radical Theology and the Death of God* (1966). Radical theology, the authors write in their preface, is "an attempt to set an atheist point of view within the spectrum of Christian possibilities."

The New Christianity (1967), edited by William Robert Miller, is a more broadly based anthology than its title suggests. Nietzsche, Feuerbach, and Freud are included, as well as Schleiermacher, Bonhoeffer, and Harvey Cox.

Donald A. Wells *God, Man, and the Thinker* (1962) is a most readable and unbiased introduction to the philosophy of religion.

chapter ten

THE DEBATE OVER DETERMINISM

10

The problem of freedom versus determinism is a tantalizing one; the arguments on both sides of the dispute are strong and convincing. And yet, as William James writes in the pages that follow, "The truth must lie with one side or the other, and its lying with the one side makes the other false."

At issue is whether or not men are sometimes capable of free choice. No one thinks that men are always free, or even free most of the time. The extent to which we are subject to the circumstances of our birth and environment is obvious to all. But are there ever choices that are not determined by antecedent conditions?

The determinist believes that man's thoughts and actions are, without exception, the necessary effects of prior causes. He contends, in short, that men are governed by the laws of nature (particularly the law of cause and effect), just as is everything else in this world. We think we are free, of course, but the determinist attributes that to our ignorance of all the external and internal factors at work upon us.

The indeterminist (sometimes "libertarian") argues that freedom is a fact of our immediate experience. Holding a pencil in my hand, I definitely feel I can choose whether to put it down or not; I have no sense of being compelled to choose one alternative over the other. (A determinist would reply that it would make as much sense to think that a tree can choose to sway or not to sway in a breeze.) Then there is our moral sense, which presupposes free will; an action is deemed right or wrong only when the actor had a choice about performing it. Feelings of obligation, remorse, and responsibility imply that choices are real. Our assigning of rewards and punishments assume a free agent who might have behaved differently. Most of the religions of the world, especially insofar as they are involved in morality, are indeterministic.

The idea of fatalism is an unsophisticated, pre-philosophical form of determinism. It played a role in Greek and Roman thought and was a prominent feature of their literature. Fatalism holds that certain crucial events—a great love, murder, death—are determined either by the gods or by an impersonal Fate. W. Somerset Maugham's vignette of a servant's encounter with Death in "Appointment in Samarra," is a typical expression of fatalism: *a man is generally free, but at an appointed time and place fate will strike.*

Predestination is a religious variety of determinism. Usually less thoroughgoing than determinism, it maintains principally that God has decreed (from the beginning of time) an individual's final destiny—whether he will enjoy heaven or suffer the agonies of hell. Luther, for example, basing his thinking on passages in Paul's writings in the New Testament, insisted that a man must realize "that his salvation is utterly beyond his own powers, counsel, endeavours, will, and works, and absolutely depending on the will, counsel, pleasure, and work of another, that is, of God only." St. Augustine, John Calvin, Jonathan Edwards, and others accepted predestination as a theological fact of life.

There can be little doubt about our feelings with regard to determinism. In Richard Wilbur's short story "A Game of Catch," a boy infuriates his friends by claiming that he is making them do whatever he wants them to do. But the question of what our reaction might be if determinism were proven to be true is a curious one, because in that case our reaction would itself be determined.

In support of its contentions determinism can lay claim to large bodies of scientific research. The evidence is not all in, by any means, but the research being done on the brain and on our behavior leans heavily in favor of determinism. Much under the influence of his own scientific background, Dean E. Wooldridge has drawn his analogy between "Computers and the Brain." Elsewhere in the same volume from which this selection was taken Wooldridge writes that "with a degree of confidence not less than that which we feel in other well-established scientific theories, we can today assert that biology is indeed a branch of physical science and that man is only a complex kind of machine."

William James and Ledger Wood marshal philosophical arguments for and against free-will. Though neither of them claims to have presented a conclusive case, each is persuaded that his position is the more reasonable. "What divides us into possibility men and anti-possibility men," James points out, "is different faiths of postulates—postulates of rationality." James' faith led him to defend indeterminism; Wood's culminates in his conclusion that free-will is "a philosophical absurdity."

405

w. somerset maugham   APPOINTMENT IN
                                                SAMARRA

W. Somerset Maugham (1874–1965) studied medicine but became a prolific and enormously popular author—one of the world's richest. He traveled widely, collected art, and lived in a twenty-room villa in France. Cynical and generally disillusioned, Maugham had survived a miserable childhood and suffered from an embarrassing stutter all of his life. He believed life to be meaningless. Of Human Bondage *is regarded as his best novel;* Cakes and Ale *was his own favorite. He also wrote* The Moon and Sixpence *and* The Razor's Edge.

Death speaks: There was a merchant in Bagdad who sent his servant to market to buy provisions and in a little while the servant came back, white and trembling, and said, Master, just now when I was in the market-place I was jostled by a woman in the crowd and when I turned I saw it was Death that jostled me. She looked at me and made a threatening gesture; now, lend me your horse, and I will ride away from this city and avoid my fate. I will go to Samarra and there Death will not find me. The merchant lent him his horse, and the servant mounted it, and he dug his spurs in its flanks and as fast as the horse could gallop he went. Then the merchant went down to the market-place and he saw me standing in the crowd and he came to me and said, Why did you make a threatening gesture to my servant when you saw him this morning? That was not a threatening gesture, I said, it was only a start of surprise. I was astonished to see him in Bagdad, for I had an appointment with him tonight in Samarra.

richard wilbur   A GAME OF CATCH

*Richard Wilbur (1921–   ) is known for his poetry, for which he has re-
ceived the Pulitzer Prize and the National Book Award (both in 1957). Born in
New York, he was graduated from Amherst College in 1942, served overseas in
the infantry during World War II, and in 1947 received his M.A. from Harvard.
He has taught at Harvard, Wellesley College, and Wesleyan University, and he
has twice been the recipient of Guggenheim grants. His poetry collections include* Beautiful Changes and Other Poems, Things of This World, *and* Advice
to a Prophet and Other Poems. *"A Game of Catch" was first published in* The
New Yorker *(July 15, 1953).*

Monk and Glennie were playing catch on the side lawn of the firehouse
when Scho caught sight of them. They were good at it, for seventh-graders,
as anyone could see right away. Monk, wearing a catcher's mitt, would lean
easily sidewise and back, with one leg lifted and his throwing hand almost
down to the grass, and then lob the white ball straight up into the sunlight.
Glennie would shield his eyes with his left hand and, just as the ball fell
past him, snag it with a little dart of his glove. Then he would burn the
ball straight toward Monk, and it would spank into the round mitt and
sit, like a still-life apple on a plate, until Monk flipped it over into his
right hand and, with a negligent flick of his hanging arm, gave Glennie a
fast grounder.

They were going on and on like that, in a kind of slow, mannered,
luxurious dance in the sun, their faces perfectly blank and entranced, when
Glennie noticed Scho dawdling along the other side of the street and called
hello to him. Scho crossed over and stood at the front edge of the lawn,
near an apple tree, watching.

"Got your glove?" asked Glennie after a time. Scho obviously hadn't.

"You could give me some easy grounders," said Scho. "But don't burn
'em."

"All right," Glennie said. He moved off a little, so the three of them
formed a triangle, and they passed the ball around for about five minutes,
Monk tossing easy grounders to Scho, Scho throwing to Glennie, and Glennie burning them in to Monk. After a while, Monk began to throw them
back to Glennie once or twice before he let Scho have his grounder, and
finally Monk gave Scho a fast, bumpy grounder that hopped over his shoulder and went into the brake on the other side of the street.

"Not so hard," called Scho as he ran across to get it.

"You should've had it," Monk shouted.

It took Scho a little while to find the ball among the ferns and dead leaves, and when he saw it, he grabbed it up and threw it toward Glennie. It struck the trunk of the apple tree, bounced back at an angle, and rolled steadily and stupidly onto the cement apron in front of the firehouse, where one of the trucks was parked. Scho ran hard and stopped it just before it rolled under the truck, and this time he carried it back to his former position on the lawn and threw it carefully to Glennie.

"I got an idea," said Glennie. "Why don't Monk and I catch for five minutes more, and then you can borrow one of our gloves?"

"That's all right with me," said Monk. He socked his fist into his mitt, and Glennie burned one in.

"All right," Scho said, and went over and sat under the tree. There in the shade he watched them resume their skillful play. They threw lazily fast or lazily slow—high, low, or wide—and always handsomely, their expressions serene, changeless, and forgetful. When Monk missed a low backhand catch, he walked indolently after the ball and, hardly even looking, flung it sidearm for an imaginary put-out. After a good while of this, Scho said, "Isn't it five minutes yet?"

"One minute to go," said Monk, with a fraction of a grin.

Scho stood up and watched the ball slap back and forth for several minutes more, and then he turned and pulled himself up into the crotch of the tree.

"Where you going?" Monk asked.

"Just up the tree," Scho said.

"I guess he doesn't want to catch," said Monk.

Scho went up and up through the fat light-gray branches until they grew slender and bright and gave under him. He found a place where several supple branches were knit to make a dangerous chair, and sat there with his head coming out of the leaves into the sunlight. He could see the two other boys down below, the ball going back and forth between them as if they were bowling on the grass, and Glennie's crew-cut head looking like a sea urchin.

"I found a wonderful seat up here," Scho said loudly. "If I don't fall out." Monk and Glennie didn't look up or comment, and so he began jouncing gently in his chair of branches and singing, "Yo-ho, heave ho" in an exaggerated way.

"Do you know what, Monk?" he announced in a few moments. "I can make you two guys do anything I want. Catch that ball, Monk! Now you catch it, Glennie!"

"I was going to catch it anyway," Monk suddenly said. "You're not making anybody do anything when they're already going to do it anyway."

· "I made you say what you just said," Scho replied joyfully.

"No, you didn't," said Monk, still throwing and catching but now less serenely absorbed in the game.

"That's what I wanted you to say," Scho said.

The ball bounded off the rim of Monk's mitt and plowed into a gladiolus bed beside the firehouse, and Monk ran to get it while Scho jounced in his treetop and sang, "I wanted you to miss that. Anything you do is what I wanted you to do."

"Let's quit for a minute," Glennie suggested.

"We might as well, until the peanut gallery shuts up." Monk said.

They went over and sat cross-legged in the shade of the tree. Scho looked down between his legs and saw them on the dim, spotty ground, saying nothing to one another. Glennie soon began abstractedly spinning his glove between his palms; Monk pulled his nose and stared out across the lawn.

"I want you to mess around with your nose, Monk," said Scho, giggling. Monk withdrew his hand from his face.

"Do that with your glove, Glennie," Scho persisted. "Monk, I want you to pull up hunks of grass and chew on it."

Glennie looked up and saw a self-delighted, intense face staring down at him through the leaves. "Stop being a dope and come down and we'll catch for a few minutes," he said.

Scho hesitated, and then said, in a tentatively mocking voice, "That's what I wanted you to say."

"All right, then, nuts to you," said Glennie.

"Why don't you keep quiet and stop bothering people?" Monk asked.

"I made you say that," Scho replied, softly.

"Shut up," Monk said.

"I made you say that, and I want you to be standing there looking sore. And I want you to climb up the tree. I'm making you do it!"

Monk was scrambling up through the branches, awkward in his haste, and getting snagged on twigs. His face was furious and foolish, and he kept telling Scho to shut up, shut up, shut up, while the other's exuberant and panicky voice poured down upon his head.

"*Now* you shut up or you'll be sorry," Monk said, breathing hard as he reached up and threatened to shake the cradle of slight branches in which Scho was sitting.

"*I want*—" Scho screamed as he fell. Two lower branches broke his rustling, crackling fall, but he landed on his back with a deep thud and lay still, with a strangled look on his face and his eyes clenched. Glennie knelt down and asked breathlessly, "Are you O.K., Scho? Are you O.K.?," while Monk swung down through the leaves crying that honestly he hadn't even

409

touched him, the crazy guy just let go. Scho doubled up and turned over on his right side, and now both the other boys knelt beside him, pawing at his shoulder and begging to know how he was.

Then Scho rolled away from them and sat partly up, still struggling to get his wind but forcing a species of smile onto his face.

"I'm sorry, Scho," Monk said. "I didn't mean to make you fall."

Scho's voice came out weak and gravelly, in gasps. "I meant—you to do it. You—had to. You can't do—anything—unless I want—you to."

Glennie and Monk looked helplessly at him as he sat there, breathing a bit more easily and smiling fixedly, with tears in his eyes. Then they picked up their gloves and the ball, walked over to the street, and went slowly away down the sidewalk, Monk punching his fist into the mitt, Glennie juggling the ball between glove and hand.

From under the apple tree, Scho, still bent over a little for lack of breath, croaked after them in triumph and misery, "I want you to do whatever you're going to do for the whole rest of your life!"

dean e. wooldridge   COMPUTERS AND THE BRAIN

Dean E. Wooldridge (1913–   ) was graduated from high school at four-teen, majored in physics at the University of Oklahoma for his A.B. and M.A. degrees, and received his Ph.D. from the California Institute of Technology. A career in electronics research and development began at the Bell Telephone Laboratories and culminated in his presidency of the Ramo-Wooldridge Cor-poration. He has also been a Research Associate in Engineering at the California Institute of Technology and is the author of The Machinery of the Brain *and* The Machinery of Life. *"Computers and the Brain" is from his* Mechanical Man: The Physical Basis of Intelligent Life *(1968).*

During each second of the seventy-year life span of the average human being, tens of millions of pulses of electricity arrive over long fibers from millions of sensory neurons to bring his brain information about the internal conditions of his body and its external environment. Special receptors in muscles and glands regularly report the configuration and state of activity of his parts and organs; optic nerve cells send in information about the sur-rounding patterns of light; neurons in the auditory system provide data on the ambient sounds; olfactory, taste, touch, temperature, and pressure-sensitive neurons continually transmit electric signals related to other as-pects of his environment. And during each same second, tens of millions of pulses of electricity also leave his brain over the long fibers of millions of effector neurons to control the glands and muscles that in turn regulate his internal health and external activity. If he is Paderewski, the external activity resulting from the complex pattern of outgoing nerve signals may include the extraordinarily skillful manipulation of the keys of a piano. If he is an Einstein, the conspicuous output may be the muscular control of a pen to write, or of the throat muscles to speak, profound new scientific deductions. Explanation of such phenomena, in our terms, requires no less than the demonstration that *the lifelong sequence of such external, intel-ligent actions is completely and in detail the consequence of the operation of the ordinary laws of physical science in the material of the brain cells, under the continuing stimulus provided by the lifelong sequence of incom-ing neuronal signals.*

One of the striking curiosities of modern biology is the fact that nearly all of the significant evidence for such a physical basis of intelligence has emerged from research in a nonbiological field: computer science. To make the results of this research logically available to our present considerations, we must first examine the case for the family relationship of electronic digital computers and brains.

THE COMPUTER/BRAIN HYPOTHESIS

Nothing is easier, or has more frequently been done, than to draw a certain kind of parallel between digital-computer installations and the nervous systems of men and animals. Consider, for example, an industrial process-control computer system—one which directs the activities of, say, a chemical plant. There is an obvious analogy between the devices that derive electric indications of pressure and temperature for use by the central computer of such a chemical control installation and the pressure and temperature receptors in the periphery of the body, with their nerve-fiber connections to the brain. And a similar analogy exists between the actuators that open and close valves to implement the commands of the computer and the muscles by means of which the body obeys the dictates of the brain. Inevitably, therefore, we find it easy to infer a general analogy between the centralized process-control computer that receives data and generates commands and the centralized brain, which receives similar-seeming data and generates similar-seeming commands.

This kind of analogy provides encouragement for a scrutiny of the two kinds of central data processors in search of significant elements of similarity. And encouragement is needed, for there is much about the electronic digital computer which seems irrelevant to biological structures. Its punched cards, rotating disks, and flashing lights appear as far removed as anything could be from the quiet assemblage of interconnected nerve cells that we believe to constitute the working machinery of the brain. But modern engineering has provided many examples of devices that, while markedly different in physical structure, are functionally equivalent. The same symphony concert can be recorded either on a magnetic tape or on a grooved wax disk, and both may ultimately be supplanted by an entirely different recording medium as technology develops in directions we cannot now foresee. In general, the particular devices and techniques our engineers find most suitable for attaining a functional result are transient and changeable. The important similarities between computers and brains, if there are any, must relate to their basic principles of operation rather than to the kinds of components used in their construction.

It is therefore pertinent to ask, "What is the *essence* of an electronic digital computer? What is the fundamental nature of its operation?" Fortunately, there is a clear-cut answer. When its performance is reduced to basic essentials, it can be shown that a digital computer obtains its impressive results solely by means of a sequence of complex switching

412

operations. The computer contains a number of input terminals and a number of output terminals, on each of which an electric voltage may be either present or absent. In each switching operation voltage is applied to some input terminals of the computer and not to others, as a result of which voltage appears on some output terminals but not on others. The pattern of output voltage is rigidly determined by the pattern of applied input voltage, the internal wiring of the computer, and the electrical state in which each of its components has been left by any preceding switching episodes.

Indeed, if we ignore such practical matters as cost and size, it can be shown that any digital computer could be constructed in its entirety from a large number of electrically actuated switches. Each switch would be designed so that voltage would appear on its single output, or "power," terminal only on application of a suitable pattern of voltages to its several input, or "actuating," terminals. A few of the actuating terminals would also double as computer inputs; similarly, a small fraction of the power terminals of the assemblage of switches would serve as computer outputs. But the vast majority of the interconnections within the computer would be governed by a very simple scheme: the power terminal of each switch would be connected to one of the actuating terminals of each of a number of other switches. To be sure, the details of such interconnections would have to be carefully worked out, in order to enforce the desired relationship between the sequence of output voltage patterns generated by the network and the sequence of input voltage patterns supplied to it. But this would be the only complication; the computer would still be properly described as consisting solely of multiply interconnected, electrically actuated, switches.

Our interest, of course, is in whether there is anything in this basic switching nature of computers to justify ascribing to them relevance to the study of brain function. An affirmative answer is strongly suggested by the similarity between the essential switching-network structure of the basic computer and the anatomy of the brain. We have just seen that one can be described as a large number of multiply interconnected electric switches, arranged so that the output of each is determined by the pattern of impulses that comes to it from the other switches and input devices with which it is connected. But the other can be described as a large number of multiply interconnected neurons, arranged so that the output of each is determined by the pattern of impulses that comes to it from the other neurons and input sensory cells with which it is connected. Such resemblance between the anatomy of a basic electronic computer and that of the nervous system would alone be enough to suggest a strong family relationship, even if there were no more fundamental reason to relate computers and the brain.

However, there *is* a more fundamental reason. It arises from a certain powerful general capability that has been rigorously proved to be possessed by complex switching systems: if enough switching elements are used (and the number can be formidable), it is possible to interconnect them so as to enforce absolutely *any* detailed relationship between the sequence of voltage patterns appearing on the output terminals and the sequence previously applied to the input terminals, provided only that rules determining such a relationship can be expressed clearly and unambiguously.

But this is remarkable. In terms of our interests it can be paraphrased as follows: *If there is any kind of definite cause-and-effect relationship between the lifelong sequence of electric pulses leaving the brain and the lifelong sequence of pulses entering the brain, it can be precisely implemented by a switching network of the type that is known to underlie the design of all electronic digital computers and that at least appears to underlie the design of the brain.* It would be hard to imagine a discovery that would point more strongly both to the likelihood that the brain does achieve its results by purely physical means and to the probability that computers and brains are basically similar kinds of devices.

Before proceeding further along this exciting line of inference, we must observe that there is nothing here that requires anything like *identity* in the details of operation of brains and computers. Such a requirement would of course be untenable, even with reference to the basic, switch-only, type of computer. There are substantial differences among the electrochemical properties of the electronic and the neuronal components: a neuron is a much more complex device than a switch, and the nature of the signal propagated over its axon is by no means identical with the electric content of the wire that interconnects two switches. Indeed, most neurons rarely if ever operate as simple on/off switches. In computer terminology, a neuron possesses a combination of digital and analog characteristics: like a digital switching element, it does not ordinarily fire (except for an occasional random discharge) until it receives an adequate pattern of stimulation on its input terminals; nevertheless, when it does fire, the amount of stimulus it propagates to other elements over its long axon is not a fixed quantity, but depends on the magnitude of its own inputs. There is also evidence that bulk chemical and electrical effects can modify the response characteristics of the neurons and thereby influence the overall operation of large regions of the brain.

But in terms of our interests, such complications are probably not very fundamental. It is true that the powerful general capabilities of switching networks have been derived by application of physical principles only to arrangements of the on/off components appearing in man-made digital computers. However, it seems certain that the same physical principles would attribute at least equal capabilities to the nervous system if the scientists were able to solve the much more difficult analytic problems that the greater operational sophistication of the natural components presents. To be sure, the optimization of the design of a network to take maximum advantage of the properties of the versatile neurons—and therefore the actual evolutionarily developed design of the brain—would be expected to involve details of interconnection of the components greatly different from those of existing computers. But again, although of enormous importance to those actually engaged in the design of improved computers, such practical differences between computers and brains do not greatly concern us. It is only necessary to remember that when henceforth we characterize the brain as a switching network, nothing so limited is implied as simple on/off switches interconnected like the components of an electronic digital computer of today.

EXPERIMENTAL TEST OF THE COMPUTER/BRAIN HYPOTHESIS

The chain of inference developed to this point runs about as follows: We set out in search of a purely physical explanation of intelligence. We observed that this required that the brain's output signals be causally related to its input signals through the operation of the ordinary laws of physics in the neuronal material. We then saw that the anatomy of the brain looks remarkably like that of the switching-network equivalent of electronic digital computers. We next learned of a powerful general theorem proving the ability of such switching networks to establish just the kind of cause-and-effect relationship between input and output that our initial assumption required. We therefore concluded not only that there is at least inferential support for the physical basis of brain function, but that also there is good reason to suspect that brains and computers employ similar operating principles.

But this argument clearly implies that it should be possible to design a computer with performance characteristics indistinguishable from those of a real brain. Such a computer, if provided with the same lifelong sequence of voltage pulses on its millions of input terminals as that brought to Einstein's brain over his incoming nerve fibers, would then provide at its millions of output terminals a lifelong sequence of voltage pulses indistinguishable from those which actually appeared in his motor-control nerves. Such a computer-generated sequence would, among other things, be able to direct the muscles of the fingers to write, and those of the throat to speak, all the details of the theory of relativity that Einstein did in fact write and speak during his lifetime.

It is likely that the construction and demonstration of a computer with such properties would convince nearly everyone that brains owe their impressive capabilities to the operation of physical principles essentially similar to those governing the performance of man-made electronic machines. However, severe practical problems stand in the way of such a convincing demonstration of computer intelligence. There are two main reasons why today's engineers could not be expected to build devices with properties approaching those of the natural articles. First there is the matter of *equipment* complexity. It is true that successive generations of machines have grown in complexity (and therefore in capability) until today hundreds of thousands or even a few millions of diodes, transistors, magnetic-core memory elements, and other electronic components may be employed in a single digital computer. But these numbers are still insignificant compared with the ten billion nerve cells each of us carries around inside his skull. In addition, as we have already observed, research has shown that each nerve cell is a device of considerable sophistication, when compared with the simple circuit elements of the computer designer.

The second impediment to the construction of brainlike computers arises from the *design* complexity of the problem. To specify the precise relationship between output and input that the general network theorem assumes to be known when it assures us that a corresponding computer can be designed, we would first have to solve some such problem as the following: "Given ten billion neurons with (presumed) known physical properties and (presumed) known interconnections, apply the known laws of physics to derive an expression describing the pattern of voltage found at any time on the millions of output neurons in terms of the preceding lifelong sequence of voltage patterns provided by the millions of input neurons." Even if we knew enough (which we don't) about the physical properties of the neurons and the details of their interconnections, the enormity of such a network problem places its rigorous solution well outside current capabilities. Not even the remarkable enhancement of design power that can be achieved by putting large mathematically programmed digital computers to work on the task of designing still more complex computers is enough, today, to permit the problem to be solved.

Thus whatever may be the future potential of man-made computers, we must not expect too much of them now. Rather, we should bear in mind that their current inability to compete favorably with human brains in the performance of most intellectual chores may be indicative only of the very early stage of their evolutionary development. After all, the brain has had the advantage of a billion years of design improvement by nature's evolutionary processes; by comparison, the computer era is hardly more than twenty years old. While progress has been remarkable, it is probably not unreasonable for the engineers to ask for at least a hundred years or so to catch up with the advanced state of the art of such a competitor.

r. buckminster fuller   WHAT'S A MAN?

R. Buckminster Fuller (1895–   ) is an engineer, architect, essayist, poet, inventor, and all-round visonary. Educated at Harvard and the United States Naval Academy, Fuller had a long career in industry and has lectured at Yale, Harvard, and a host of other universities. He designed the geodesic dome and invented the Dymaxion three-wheeled automobile in the 1930s. His books include No More Secondhand God, Education Automation, Ideas and Integrities, The Unfinished Epic Poem of Industrialization, *and* An Operating Manual for Spaceship Earth. *The excerpt which follows is from* Nine Chains to the Moon *(1939).*

"What is that, mother?"
"It's a man, darling."
"What's a man?"

Man?
A self-balancing, 28-jointed adapter-base biped; an electrochemical reduction-plant, integral with segregated stowages of special energy extracts in storage batteries, for subsequent actuation of thousands of hydraulic and pneumatic pumps, with motors attached; 62,000 miles of capillaries; millions of warning signal, railroad and conveyor systems; crushers and cranes (of which the arms are magnificent 23-jointed affairs with self-surfacing and lubricating systems, and a universally distributed telephone system needing no service for 70 years if well managed); the whole, extraordinarily complex mechanism guided with exquisite precision from a turret in which are located telescopic and microscopic self-registering and recording range finders, a spectroscope, *et cetera*, the turret control being closely allied with an air conditioning intake-and-exhaust, and a main fuel intake.

Within the few cubic inches housing the turret mechanisms, there is room, also, for two sound-wave and sound-direction-finder recording diaphragms, a filing and instant reference system, and an expertly devised analytical laboratory large enough not only to contain minute records of every last and continual event of up to 70 years' experience, or more, but to extend, by computation and abstract fabrication, this experience with relative accuracy into all corners of the observed universe. There is, also, a forecasting and tactical plotting department for the reduction of future possibilities and probabilities to generally successful specific choice.

william james   THE DILEMMA OF DETERMINISM

It is hard to imagine a thesis better designed to cross the grain of William James than that of determinism. James (see biographical note on p. 333) was himself a thorough-going "possibility" man, while determinism holds that there is only "necessity." The world envisioned by James was always open; truth was something that evolved in experience. Arguing for faith, for example, in his essay "Is Life Worth Living?" James said, "You make one or the other of two possible universes true by your trust or mistrust, both universes having been only maybes. . . ."

Originally an address to the Harvard Divinity Students, "The Dilemma of Determinism" was first published in the Unitarian Review *(September 1884).*

A common opinion prevails that the juice has ages ago been pressed out of the free-will controversy, and that no new champion can do more than warm up stale arguments which every one has heard. This is a radical mistake. I know of no subject less worn out, or in which inventive genius has a better chance of breaking open new ground—not, perhaps, of forcing a conclusion or of coercing assent, but of deepening our sense of what the issue between the two parties really is, of what the ideas of fate and of free will imply. . . .

What does determinism profess?

It professes that those parts of the universe already laid down absolutely appoint and decree what the other parts shall be. The future has no ambiguous possibilities hidden in its womb: the part we call the present is compatible with only one totality. Any other future complement than the one fixed from eternity is impossible. The whole is in each and every part, and welds it with the rest into an absolute unity, an iron block, in which there can be no equivocation or shadow of turning.

> With earth's first clay they did the last man knead,
> And there of the last harvest sowed the seed.
> And the first morning of creation wrote
> What the last dawn of reckoning shall read.

Indeterminism, on the contrary, says that the parts have a certain amount of loose play on one another, so that the laying down of one of them does not necessarily determine what the others shall be. It admits that possibilities may be in excess of actualities, and that things not yet revealed to our knowledge may really in themselves be ambiguous. Of two alternative futures which we conceive, both may now be really possible; and the one become impossible only at the very moment when the other excludes it by becoming real itself. Indeterminism thus denies the world to be one unbending unit of fact. It says there is a certain ultimate pluralism in it; and, so saying, it corroborates our ordinary unsophisticated view of things. To that view, actualities seem to float in a wider sea of possibilities from out of which they are chosen; and, *somewhere*, indeterminism says, such possibilities exist, and form a part of truth.

Determinism, on the contrary, says they exist *nowhere*, and that necessity on the one hand and impossibility on the other are the sole categories of the real. Possibilities that fail to get realized are, for determinism, pure illusions: they never were possibilities at all. There is nothing inchoate, it says, about this universe of ours, all that was or is or shall be actual in it having been from eternity virtually there. The cloud of alternatives our minds escort this mass of actuality withal is a cloud of sheer deceptions, to which "impossibilities" is the only name that rightfully belongs.

The issue, it will be seen, is a perfectly sharp one, which no eulogistic terminology can smear over or wipe out. The truth *must* lie with one side or the other, and its lying with one side makes the other false.

The question relates solely to the existence of possibilities, in the strict sense of the term, as things that may, but need not, be. Both sides admit that a volition, for instance, has occurred. The indeterminists say another volition might have occurred in its place: the determinists swear that nothing could possibly have occurred in its place. Now, can science be called in to tell us which of these two point-blank contradicters of each other is right? Science professes to draw no conclusions but such as are based on matters of fact, things that have actually happened; but how can any amount of assurance that something actually happened give us the least grain of information as to whether another thing might or might not have happened in its place? Only facts can be proved by other facts. With things that are possibilities and not facts, facts have no concern. If we have no other evidence than the evidence of existing facts, the possibility-question must remain a mystery never to be cleared up.

And the truth is that facts practically have hardly anything to do with making us either determinists or indeterminists. Sure enough, we make a flourish of quoting facts this way or that; and if we are determinists, we talk about the infallibility with which we can predict one another's conduct; while if we are indeterminists, we lay great stress on the fact that it is just because we cannot foretell one another's conduct, either in war or statecraft or in any of the great and small intrigues and businesses of men, that life is so intensely anxious and hazardous a game. But who does not see the wretched insufficiency of this so-called objective testimony on both sides? What fills up the gaps in our minds is something not objective, not external. What divides us into *possibility* men and *anti-possibility* men is different faiths or postulates—postulates of rationality. To this man the world seems more rational with possibilities in it—to that man more rational with possibilities excluded; and talk as we will about having to yield to evidence, what makes us monists or pluralists, determinists or indeterminists, is at bottom always some sentiment like this.

The stronghold of the deterministic sentiment is the antipathy to the idea of chance. As soon as we begin to talk indeterminism to our friends, we find a number of them shaking their heads. This notion of alternative possibility, they say, this admission that any one of several things may come to pass, is, after all, only a round-about name for chance; and chance is something the notion of which no sane mind can for an instant tolerate in the world. What is it, they ask, but barefaced crazy unreason, the negation of intelligibility and law? And if the slightest particle of it exist anywhere, what is to prevent the whole fabric from falling together, the stars from going out, and chaos from recommencing her topsy-turvy reign? . . .

The sting of the word "chance" seems to lie in the assumption that it means something positive, and that if anything happens by chance, it must needs be something of an intrinsically irrational and preposterous sort. Now, chance means nothing of the kind. It is a purely negative and relative term, giving us no information about that of which it is predicated, except that it happens to be disconnected with something else—not controlled, secured, or necessitated by other things in advance of its own actual presence. As this point is the most subtle one of the whole lecture, and at the same time the point on which all the rest hinges, I beg you to pay particular attention to it. What I say is that it tells us nothing about what a thing may be in itself to call it "chance." It may be a bad thing, it may be a good thing. It may be lucidity, transparency, fitness incarnate, matching the whole system of other things, when it has once befallen, in an unimaginably perfect way. All you mean by calling it "chance" is that this is not guaranteed, that it may also fall out otherwise. For the system of other things has no positive hold on the chance-thing. Its origin is in a certain fashion negative: it escapes, and says, Hands off! coming, when it comes, as a free gift, or not at all.

This negativeness, however, and this opacity of the chance-thing when thus considered *ab extra*,[1] or from the point of view of previous things or distant things, do not preclude its having any amount of positiveness and luminosity from within, and at its own place and moment. All that its chance-character asserts about it is that there is something in it really of its own, something that is not the unconditional property of the whole. If the whole wants this property, the whole must wait till it can get it, if it be a matter of chance.

[1] "from without"

That the universe may actually be a sort of joint-stock society of this sort, in which the sharers have both limited liabilities and limited powers, is of course a simple and conceivable notion.

Nevertheless, many persons talk as if the minutest dose of disconnectedness of one part with another, the smallest modicum of independence, the faintest tremor of ambiguity about the future, for example, would ruin everything, and turn this goodly universe into a sort of insane sand-heap or nulliverse—no universe at all. Since future human volitions are as a matter of fact the only ambiguous things we are tempted to believe in, let us stop for a moment to make ourselves sure whether their independent and accidental character need be fraught with such direful consequences to the universe as these.

What is meant by saying that my choice of which way to walk home after the lecture is ambiguous and matter of chance as far as the present moment is concerned? It means that both Divinity Avenue and Oxford Street are called; but that only one, and that one *either* one, shall be chosen. Now, I ask you seriously to suppose that this ambiguity of my choice is real; and then to make the impossible hypothesis that the choice is made twice over, and each time falls on a different street. In other words, imagine that I first walk through Divinity Avenue, and then imagine that the powers governing the universe annihilate ten minutes of time with all that it contained, and set me back at the door of this hall just as I was before the choice was made. Imagine then that, everything else being the same, I now make a different choice and traverse Oxford Street. You, as passive spectators, look on and see the two alternative universes—one of them with me walking through Divinity Avenue in it, the other with the same me walking through Oxford Street. Now, if you are determinists you believe one of these universes to have been from eternity impossible: you believe it to have been impossible because of the intrinsic irrationality or accidentality somewhere involved in it. But looking outwardly at these universes, can you say which is the impossible and accidental one, and which the rational and necessary one? I doubt if the most iron-clad determinist among you could have the slightest glimmer of light on this point. In other words, either universe *after the fact* and once there would, to our means of observation and understanding, appear just as rational as the other. There would be absolutely no criterion by which we might judge one necessary and the other matter of chance. Suppose now we relieve the gods of their hypothetical task and assume my choice, once made, to be made forever. I go through Divinity Avenue for good and all. If, as good determinists, you now begin to affirm, what all good determinists punctually do affirm, that in the nature of things I *couldn't* have gone through Oxford Street—had I done so it would have been chance, irrationality, insanity, a horrid gap in nature—I simply call your attention to this, that your affirmation is what the Germans call a *Macht-spruch*, a mere conception fulminated as a dogma and based on no insight into details. Before my choice, either street seemed as natural to you as to me. Had I happened to take Oxford Street, Divinity Avenue would have figured in your philosophy as the gap in nature; and you would have so proclaimed it with the best deterministic conscience in the world.

But what a hollow outcry, then, is this against a chance which, if it were present to us, we could by no character whatever distinguish from a rational necessity! I have taken the most trivial of examples, but no possible example could lead to any different result. For what are the alternatives which, in point of fact, offer themselves to human volition? What are those futures that now seem matters of chance? Are they not one and all like the Divinity Avenue and Oxford Street of our example? Are they not all of them *kinds* of things already here and based in the existing frame of nature? Is any one ever tempted to produce an *absolute* accident, something utterly irrelevant to the rest of the world? Do not all the motives that assail us, all the futures that offer themselves to our choice, spring equally from the soil of the past . . . ?

And this at last brings us within sight of our subject. We have seen what determinism means: we have seen that indeterminism is rightly described as meaning chance; and we have seen that chance, the very name of which we are urged to shrink from as from a metaphysical pestilence, means only the negative fact that no part of the world, however big, can claim to control absolutely the destinies of the whole. But although, in discussing the word "chance," I may at moments have seemed to be arguing for its real existence, I have not meant to do so yet. We have not yet ascertained whether this be a world of chance or no; at most, we have agreed that it seems so. And I now repeat what I said at the outset, that, from any strict theoretical point of view, the question is insoluble. To deepen our theoretic sense of the *difference* between a world with chances in it and a deterministic world is the most I can hope to do; and this I may now at last begin upon, after all our tedious clearing of the way.

I wish first of all to show you just what the notion that this is a deterministic world implies. The implications I call your attention to are all bound up with the fact that it is a world in which we constantly have to make what I shall, with your permission, call judgments of regret. Hardly an hour passes in which we do not wish that something might be otherwise; and happy indeed are those of us whose hearts have never echoed the wish of Omar Khayam—

> That we might clasp, ere closed, the book of fate,
> And make the writer on a fairer leaf
> Inscribe our names, or quite obliterate.
> Ah! Love, could you and I with fate conspire

> To mend this sorry scheme of things entire,
>   Would we not shatter it to bits, and then
> Remould it nearer to the heart's desire?

Now, it is undeniable that most of these regrets are foolish, and quite on a par in point of philosophic value with the criticisms on the universe of that friend of our infancy, the hero of the fable "The Atheist and the Acorn"—

> Fool! had that bough a pumpkin bore,
> Thy whimsies would have worked no more, etc.

Even from the point of view of our own ends, we should probably make a botch of remodelling the universe. How much more then from the point of view of ends we cannot see! Wise men therefore regret as little as they can. But still some regrets are pretty obstinate and hard to stifle—regrets for acts of wanton cruelty or treachery, for example, whether performed by others or by ourselves. Hardly any one can remain *entirely* optimistic after reading the confession of the murderer at Brockton the other day: how, to get rid of the wife whose continued existence bored him, he inveigled her into a desert spot, shot her four times, and then, as she lay on the ground and said to him, "You didn't do it on purpose, did you, dear?" replied, "No, I didn't do it on purpose," as he raised a rock and smashed her skull. Such an occurrence, with the mild sentence and self-satisfaction of the prisoner, is a field for a crop of regrets, which one need not take up in detail. We feel that, although a perfect mechanical fit to the rest of the universe, it is a bad moral fit, and that something else would really have been better in its place.

But for the deterministic philosophy the murder, the sentence, and the prisoner's optimism were all necessary from eternity; and nothing else for a moment had a ghost of a chance of being put into their place. To admit such a chance, the determinists tell us, would be to make a suicide of reason; so we must steel our hearts against the thought. And here our plot thickens, for we see the first of those difficult implications of determinism and monism which it is my purpose to make you feel. If this Brockton murder was called for by the rest of the universe, if it had to come at its preappointed hour, and if nothing else would have been consistent with the sense of the whole, what are we to think of the universe? Are we stubbornly to stick to our judgment of regret, and say, though it *couldn't* be, yet it *would* have been a better universe with something different from this Brockton murder in it? That, of course, seems the natural and spontaneous thing for us to do; and yet it is nothing short of deliberately espousing a kind of pessimism. The judgment of regret calls the murder bad. Calling a thing bad means, if it mean anything at all, that the thing ought not to be, that something else ought to be in its stead. Determinism, in denying that anything else can be in its stead, virtually defines the universe as a place in which what ought to be is impossible—in other words, as an organism whose constitution is afflicted with an incurable taint, an irremediable flaw. The pessimism of a Schopenhauer says no more than this—that the murder is a symptom; and that it is a vicious symptom because it belongs to a vicious whole, which can express its nature no otherwise than by bringing forth just such a symptom as that at this particular spot. Regret for the murder must transform itself, if we are determinists and wise, into a larger regret. It is absurd to regret the murder alone. Other things being what they are, *it* could not be different. What we should regret is that whole frame of things of which the murder is one member. I see no escape whatever from this pessimistic conclusion if, being determinists, our judgment of regret is to be allowed to stand at all.

The only deterministic escape from pessimism is everywhere to abandon the judgment of regret. That this can be done, history shows to be not impossible. The devil, *quoad existentiam*,[2] may be good. That is, although he be a *principle* of evil, yet the universe, with such a principle in it, may practically be a better universe than it could have been without. On every hand, in a small way, we find that a certain amount of evil is a condition by which a higher form of good is brought. There is nothing to prevent anybody from generalizing this view, and trusting that if we could but see things in the largest of all ways, even such matters as this Brockton murder would appear to be paid for by the uses that follow in their train. An optimism *quand même*,[3] a systematic and infatuated optimism like that ridiculed by Voltaire in his *Candide*, is one of the possible ideal ways in which a man may train himself to look on life. Bereft of dogmatic hardness and lit up with the expression of a tender and pathetic hope, such an optimism has been the grace of some of the most religious characters that ever lived.

> Throb thine with Nature's throbbing breast,
> And all is clear from east to west.

Even cruelty and treachery may be among the absolutely blessed fruits of time, and to quarrel with any of their details may be blasphemy. The only real blasphemy, in short, may be that pessimistic temper of the soul which lets it give way to such things as regrets, remorse, and grief.

Thus, our deterministic pessimism may become a deterministic optimism at the price of extinguishing our judgments of regret.

But does not this immediately bring us into a curious logical predicament? Our determinism leads us to call our judgments of regret wrong, because they

[2] "as far as existence is concerned"
[3] "anyway" or "in spite of everything"

are pessimistic in implying that what is impossible yet ought to be. But how then about the judgments of regret themselves? If they are wrong, other judgments, judgments of approval presumably, ought to be in their place. But as they are necessitated, nothing else *can* be in their place; and the universe is just what it was before—namely, a place in which what ought to be appears impossible. We have got one foot out of the pessimistic bog, but the other one sinks all the deeper. We have rescued our actions from the bonds of evil, but our judgments are now held fast. When murders and treacheries cease to be sins, regrets are theoretic absurdities and errors. The theoretic and the active life thus play a kind of see-saw with each other on the ground of evil. The rise of either sends the other down. Murder and treachery cannot be good without regret being bad: regret cannot be good without treachery and murder being bad. Both, however, are supposed to have been foredoomed; so something must be fatally unreasonable, absurd, and wrong in the world. It must be a place of which either sin or error forms a necessary part. . . .

Ledger Wood (1901–1970) was born in Colorado; he received his A.B. from the University of California and a Ph.D. from Cornell University, at which school he first taught. He spent a year teaching at Stanford University and in 1927 began his long and distinguished association with Princeton University. Over the years he became a Professor of Philosophy, Chairman of the Department, and Director of Graduate Studies. In 1941–1942 he was the Sterling Fellow in Philosophy at Yale University; he has also been a visiting professor of philosophy at New York University. He is the author of The Analysis of Knowledge *and (with Frank Thilly)* A History of Philosophy. *Among his many journal articles is the following, from* Philosophy *(Vol. 16, 1941).*

Few philosophical controversies have been waged with greater acrimony than the controversy between the libertarians and the determinists; the vigour with which both sides of the question have been espoused is due not only to the metaphysical importance of the issue—which is indeed considerable—but more especially to its moral and religious implications. No other philosophical issues, with the exception of those pertaining to God and the immortality of the soul, are of greater ethical and theological moment. So thoroughly has the question been debated that further consideration of it may seem futile. Has not the evidence been so completely canvassed on both sides of the controversy that further discussion will be a fruitless reiteration of long familiar arguments? The free-will problem is considered by many contemporary thinkers an admittedly unsolved but completely outmoded problem to which they respond with impatience or complete indifference. This attitude toward the problem is quite indefensible since the question of the freedom of the will is one of those perennially significant philosophical issues which takes on new meaning in every age and is particularly significant in the context of contemporary science and philosophy. Recent psychology, in large measure through the influence of Freud, has achieved a more penetrating analysis of human motivation by bringing to the fore certain hitherto obscure factors which are operative in volition. The psychology of the subconscious by filling in apparent gaps in the psychological causation of volition has furthered the case for determinism. Furthermore, behaviouristic psychology by subjecting all human behaviour, including so-called volitional acts, to a mechanistic formula bears directly on the free-will issue and like the Freudian psychology seems to strengthen the deterministic position. Recent developments in the physical sciences are not without their significance for the free-will issue; the principle of indeterminacy in quantum mechanics has been eagerly seized upon by the libertarians in the belief that it affords a physical foundation for their position. Finally, in philosophy proper the progress of philosophical analysis and of the philosophical theory of meaning renders possible a more exact statement of the free-will issue and permits a more just appraisal of the traditional arguments on both sides of the free-will controversy than has hitherto been possible. The concepts of determinacy, indeterminacy, compulsion, choice, etc., are elucidated by analysis in accordance with the theory of meaning of recent positivism and radical empiricism. It is for these reasons that a contemporary re-examination of the free-will issue is not only legitimate but most imperative.

The question of the freedom of the will, reduced to its barest essentials, is simply this: *Are all human acts of will causally produced by antecedent conditions or are at least some volitional actions exempt from causal determination?* The determinist insists that all actions, even the most carefully planned and deliberate, can be causally explained and that if we knew enough about a man's hereditary traits and the environmental influences which have moulded his character, we could predict just how he would behave under any specified set of circumstances. The free-willist or libertarian, on the other hand, asserts that there are at least some human actions of the volitional type in which the individual by the exercise of his will-power, acts independently of conditioning factors—that he, so to speak, "lifts himself up by his boot-straps."

The freedom of caprice (the traditional *liberum arbitrium*) when precisely defined means that some, and perhaps all, volitional acts are causally indeterminate, that is to say, are not conjoined in any uniform way with antecedent conditions. The uniform antecedents of free acts are, on this view, undiscoverable for the simple reason that they do not exist. Free-acts are the products of pure chance and, therefore, remain unexplained because they are inherently inexplicable; they are, in the strict sense of the word, miracles—a miracle being defined as any occurrence which cannot be brought within the compass of natural law. The freedom of chance, conceived in this extreme fashion, would, if it existed, utterly disrupt social intercourse, for, no one could possibly anticipate when another, or even himself, might act freely, or in other words, miraculously. Perhaps the closest approximation to a capricious free-will is to be found in a lunatic—but even his acts are not genuinely free, since a psychiatrist can, at least ideally, explain and even predict them. The maniac's actions, however strange they may seem when judged by the sane man's standards of normal behaviour, are psychologically explicable; they conform to certain uniform patterns of abnormal psychology, which, in turn, are assimilable to the laws of general psychology. The free-willist—however much he may seek to disguise the fact—introduces an element of indeterminacy into human behaviour; he admits an effect, namely, the volitional action, without a sufficient and adequate natural cause. The free-will of man, according to the extreme defenders of the free-will doctrine, swoops down from above and injects into the volitional situation an arbitrary, capricious, and incalculable factor.

I propose to give a brief résumé of the free-will controversy, examining first the arguments for the freedom of the will and then stating the case for determinism. Although the position taken throughout the present paper is avowedly deterministic, the attempt will be made to state with fairness the case for and against both of the rival positions and on the basis of these arguments, to give a just appraisal of the two positions. The strength of the deterministic position will be found to lie not only in the positive evidence which may be adduced to support it, but also in its easy ability to meet the arguments advanced by the free-willists.

ARGUMENTS FOR THE FREEDOM OF THE WILL

The arguments of the free-willist are for the most part humanistic and non-scientific in character and may be conveniently considered under the following heads:

(1) the introspective or psychological argument,
(2) the moral and religious arguments,
(3) the argument from physical indeterminacy.

(1) *The Introspective or Psychological Argument.* Most advocates of the free-will doctrine believe that the mind is directly aware of its freedom in the very act of making a decision, and thus that freedom is an immediate datum of our introspective awareness. "I feel myself free, *therefore*, I am free," runs the simplest and perhaps the most compelling of the arguments for freedom. In the elaboration of his argument, the free-willist offers a detailed description of what, in his opinion, is introspectively observable whenever the self makes a free choice. Suppose I find myself forced to choose between conflicting and incompatible lines of action. At such a time, I stand, so to speak, at the moral cross-roads, I deliberate, and finally by some mysterious and inexplicable power of mind, I decide to go one way rather than the other. Deliberative decision, if this description is correct, is analysable into these three constituents: (*a*) the envisaging of two or more incompatible courses of action, (*b*) the review of considerations favourable and unfavourable to each of the conflicting possibilities of action, and (*c*) the choice among the alternative possibilities.

Deliberative, or so-called "moral" decisions, are fairly numerous in the lives of all of us and are made on the most trivial occasions, as well as on matters of grave import. The university undergraduate's resolution of the conflict between his desire to see the latest cinema at the local playhouse and his felt obligation to devote the evening to his studies, trivial and inconsequential as it may seem, is the *type* of all moral decisions and differs in no essential respect from such a momentous decision as his choice of a life career. Each of these decisions to the extent that it is truly deliberative involves (*a*) the imaginative contemplation of alternative actions, (*b*) the weighing of considerations *for* and *against* the several alternatives involving, perhaps, an appeal to ideals and values approved by the moral agent, and finally (*c*) the choice between the several possibilities of action. At the moment of making the actual decision, the mind experiences a *feeling* of self-assertion and of independence of determining influences both external and internal. The libertarian rests his case for free-will on the authenticity of this subjective feeling of freedom.

The phenomenon of decision after deliberation is an indubitable *fact* which determinist and free-willist alike must acknowledge, but the real issue is whether this fact warrants the *construction* which the free-willist puts upon it. The determinist, replying to the introspective argument, urges that the *feeling* of freedom is nothing but a sense of relief following upon earlier tension and indecision. After conflict and uncertainty, the pent-up energies of the mind—or rather of the underlying neural processes—are released and this process is accompanied by an inner sense of power. Thus the feeling of freedom or of voluntary control over one's actions is a mere subjective illusion which cannot be considered evidence for psychological indeterminacy.

Besides the direct appeal to the sense of freedom, there is a psychological argument which *infers* freedom from the mind's ability to resolve an equilibrium of opposing motives. The allegedly "prerogative" or "critical" instance of free-will, is that in which the will makes a choice between two or more actions which are equally attractive, or equally objectionable. If, after a careful weighing of all the considerations *for* and *against* each of the alternative actions, the mind finds the rival claimants exactly equal, a decision is possible, argues the libertarian, only by a free act of will. We weigh the motives against one another, find the scale balanced, and then, in the words of William James, . . . "we feel, in deciding as if we ourselves by our wilful act inclined the beam." This argument from the equilibrium of motives is indeed plausible, but the determinist has a ready reply. *If* the motives really had been exactly equal and opposite, then the mind would have remained indefinitely in a state of suspended judgment and consequent inaction or would, in Hamlet fashion, have oscillated between the two incompatibles, never able to yield to one or to the other. The analogy of the balanced scale would lead one to expect the will under these circumstances to do just this. Indeed, there are undoubtedly some pathological minds

429

which are in a perpetual tug-of-war between conflicting tendencies of action and whose wills, as a consequence, are completely paralysed. But in normal minds the motives on the one side or the other become momentarily stronger because of some new external factor injected into the situation or because of the inner reorganization of forces and then action immediately ensues. Often the decision is determined by accidental and contingent circumstances —a literal flip of the coin—or perhaps one allows one's action to be decided by a chance idea or impulse, that is to say, by a "mental flip of the coin." In any case the fact that a decision is actually made testifies to the eventual inequality of the opposing forces. Under no circumstances is it necessary to resort to a mysterious, inner force of will to "incline the beam" one way rather than the other.

Still another introspective fact cited by the libertarian in support of his doctrine is that the moral agent is in retrospect convinced that he might, *if he had chosen*, have followed a course of action different from that which he actually pursued. The belief that there are genuine alternatives of action and that the choice between them is indeterminate is usually stronger in prospect and in retrospect than at the time of actual decision. The alternatives exist in prospect as imaginatively envisaged possibilities of action and in retrospect as the memory of the state of affairs before the agent had, so to speak, "made up his mind." Especially in retrospect does the agent recall his earlier decision with remorse and repentance, dwelling sorrowfully upon rejected possibilities of action which now loom up as opportunities missed. How frequently one hears the lament: "I regret that decision; I should, and I could, have acted otherwise." Now the contemplation of supposed alternatives of action along with the sentiment of regret produces the illusion of indeterminate choice between alternatives, but a careful analysis of the import of the retrospective judgment, "I could have acted otherwise than I did," will, I believe, disclose it to be an empirically meaningless statement. If I decided in favour of this alternative, rather than that, it can only mean that the circumstances being what they were, and I in the frame of mind I was at the time, no other eventuation was really possible. My statement that I could have acted differently expresses only my memory of an earlier state of suspense, indecision, and uncertainty, intensified by my present remorse and the firm determination that if, in the future, I am faced with a similar choice, I shall profit by my earlier mistake. There is, however, in the deliberate situation no evidence of genuine alternatives of action, or the indeterminacy of my choice between them.

(2) *The Moral and Religious Arguments.* The moral argument assumes a variety of forms, but they all agree in their attempt to infer volitional freedom of the moral agent from some feature of the moral situation. The most characteristic feature of moral action is that it seems to be directed

toward the realization of an ideal or the fulfilment of an obligation. But, argues the free-willest, it is of the very nature of an ideal or an obligation that it shall be *freely* embraced; the acceptance or rejection of a moral ideal and the acknowledgement of an obligation as binding can only be accounted for on the assumption of the agent's free choice. The very existence of moral ideals, norms, or standards which, though *coercive* or not *compulsive*, testifies to the freedom of the agent who acknowledges them. Thus did Kant in his famous formula: "I ought, therefore I can" directly infer the agent's freedom from his recognition of moral obligation.

The moral argument is so loose in its logic that unable to put one's finger on its fallacy one is tempted to resort to the logicians' "catch-all," and call it a *non sequitur*. A moral agent's adoption of a moral ideal or recognition of a moral obligation simply does *not* imply that he possesses a free-will in the sense of psychological indeterminacy. An adequate critique of the moral argument would require a detailed psychological account of the genesis of moral ideals and duties without recourse to freedom of the libertarian sort and I am convinced that such an account is forthcoming. The emergence of ideals in the mind of an individual moral agent along with the feeling that such ideals are coercive is largely non-volitional and even when it rises to the volitional level and represents a choice between competing ideals, there is even then no reason for abandoning psychological determinism. The moral argument for freedom is found, on close examination, to be the psychological argument in disguise and like it, is introspectively false; there is no indication of volitional freedom either in the original adoption of moral standards nor in subsequent moral decisions in accordance with those standards once they have been embraced.

The moral argument for freedom has sometimes been stated from the point of view not of the moral agent but of the moral critic who passes judgment on the action of another or even upon his own actions. A judgment of praise or blame, or approval or condemnation, so the argument runs, imputes freedom to the agent whose action is judged. When I praise your unselfish and benevolent acts, I imply that you could, if you had chosen, have been cruel and selfish instead. Condemnation of another's conduct seems even more surely to suggest that he acted willingly, or rather "willfully." Otherwise, would it not be in order to pity rather than condemn the wrong-doer? Should we not say with condescension, "Poor misguided fool, he can't help what he does, he is simply that kind of man"? Instead, we reprove his action and by so doing implicitly acknowledge that he is a free moral agent. A novel variant of this argument is contained in William James's essay "The Dilemma of Determinism." The determinist, so James argues, finds himself in a curious logical predicament whenever he utters a judgment of regret. If I, a determinist, pass an adverse judgment on my own or another's actions, I thereby acknowledge that they ought not to have been, that others ought to have been performed in their place. But how can I meaningfully make such a statement if these particular actions, and no others, were possible? "What sense can there be in condemning ourselves for taking the wrong way, unless the right way was open to us as well?" James advanced the moral argument, not as an absolute *proof* of freedom (he admits that it is not intellectually coercive), but rather as a belief to be *freely* embraced. As a pragmatically effective, moral fiction, freedom has much to be said in its favour: the belief in freedom no doubt fosters moral earnestness, whereas the belief in determinism may, at least in certain persons, induce moral lassitude. Most defenders of the free-will doctrine do not, however, share James's cautious restraint; they advance the moral argument as a conclusive proof of an indeterminate free-will. The fallacy again can only be described as a *non sequitur*. Moral appraisal has nothing to do with the freedom of the will; the mere fact that *I* approve certain of *your* actions because I consider them good and condemn others as wrong may give some indication of *my* moral make-up, but it proves nothing whatsoever regarding the freedom of *your* will. Your moral acts, even though completely determined, may be judged in accordance with prevailing standards to be laudable or reprehensible. I praise your good conduct and condemn your bad conduct even though both are inexorably determined and—the determinist would add—I too am determined to judge them as I do. Hence the freedom of a moral agent cannot possibly be inferred from the judgments of approbation and disapprobation passed upon him by a moral critic.

The determinist finds no difficulty in assimilating to his deterministic scheme the facts of moral approval and disapproval. Moral valuation is not the detached and disinterested judgment of a moral critic, but is an instrumentality for the social propagation of norms of conduct. Morality is essentially a social phenomenon; society has gradually evolved its patterns of social behaviour which it imposes upon its individual members by means of various sanctions including the favourable or adverse judgments which members of society pass upon one another. Judgments of moral valuation rest upon the socially constituted norms of action and are the media through which these norms are communicated from individual to individual. I reprove your unsocial or antisocial behaviour in the belief that my adverse judgment may influence you to desist therefrom. When I pass a moral judgment on another, far from implying his free-will, I tacitly assume that my judgment of him, in so far as he takes cognizance of it, operates as a determining influence on his conduct. Thus moral criticism when interpreted naturalistically harmonizes with the theory of moral determinism.

Another moral argument, closely paralleling the argument from obligation, stresses the concept of moral responsibility. The free-willist considers freedom a *sine qua non* of responsibility; his argument runs: "Without freedom, there can be no responsibility, but there *must* be responsibility, hence man is free." There are *two* ways of attacking this argument: (1) we may pertinently ask: "But *why* must there be responsibility?", or, (2) we may challenge the underlying assumption of the argument, namely, that freedom is an indispensable condition of responsibility. The first criticism is a rejection of the minor and usually tacit premise of the free-willist's argument, the conviction, namely, that there must be responsibility. The conviction prevalent among moralists that responsibility, obligation, etc., because they are morally significant must actually exist, would seem to be the outcome of a curiously perverse ontological argument. Whatever is morally useful and significant must actually exist. But why must it? What assurance have we that reality is constituted so as to satisfy the insistent demands of our moral nature? Even if responsibility could be shown to be an indispensable adjunct of genuine morality, this would not suffice to guarantee its factuality. There is only one way of establishing the fact of responsibility, and that is by exhibiting actual instances of morally responsible actions. The concept of moral responsibility no doubt admits of precise empirical definition and exmplification; there is a real distinction between responsible and irresponsible actions. But when responsibility is analysed in this empirical and positivistic fashion, it will be found in no wise to imply volitional freedom. A careful analysis of responsible actions will show them to be if anything no more indeterminate than non-responsible and irresponsible actions. And this brings us to the second criticism of the argument from responsibility: *viz.*, the failure to establish the alleged implication of the concept of freedom by the concept of responsibility. The concepts of freedom and responsibility are by no means indissolubly connected; on the contrary, the freedom of indeterminacy, far from guaranteeing responsibility, would, if it existed, actually be prejudicial to it. If freedom is the complete divorce of the will from antecedent conditions, including my moral character, I cannot then be held accountable for my actions. A will which descends upon me like "a bolt from the blue" is not *my* will and it is manifestly unfair to take me to task for its caprices.

Closely allied with—perhaps in the last analysis indistinguishable from—the moral argument is the *religious* argument for free-will. The free-will dogma is deeply rooted in the Hebraic-Christian theology. The essential connection between freedom and responsibility to God is the real theme of the Book of *Genesis:* Man's freedom is necessary to insure what William James has aptly referred to as man's "forensic responsibility before God." Were man not free, he could not be held accountable for his action, but he *must* be held accountable, therefore, man is free. The Hebraic doctrine of

433

the freedom of the will arises from a paternalistic conception of the relation between God and man. On this view, moral principles are the commandments of God to which man yields as does the child to parental authority. But, just as a recalcitrant child may defy his father, so man may, at his own peril, rebel against the divine moral code. The principles of morality are authoritative in that they emanate from God, but they are not compulsive since man may or may not choose to conform to them. The paternalism of the Hebraic conception of God is embodied in the myth of creation. God created Adam and endowed him with a will, free to choose between good and evil. Adam yielded to temptation and his original sin has been transmitted to all his descendants. The story of the fall of man is a highly symbolic expression of the theological doctrine that man is accountable for his actions only on the assumption that they are free. Incidentally, the ascription of a free-will to man, absolves God from any responsibility for the sins of mankind and thus affords an easy solution to one of the most perplexing of theological problems, the problem of evil.

The religious argument may be dismissed quite summarily by rejecting outright the conception of God as a task-master who maintains discipline over humanity by conferring upon him a freedom which shall insure his responsibility and justify his punishment. If the Hebraic conception of an austere and vengeful God be renounced, the religious argument for freedom loses all force; it then reduces to the simple moral argument from responsibility to freedom, the fallacies of which have already been exposed. The determinist by his rejection of this particular conception of divinity is not necessarily committed to atheism. Determinism and theology in certain of its forms are entirely compatible; thus the theological doctrine of predestination, though of course very different in its emphasis from physical and psychological determinism of the naturalistic sort, is by no means inconsistent with the latter. There is then no strictly theological argument proof for freedom and theological considerations can at best serve to reinforce the moral argument for freedom.

(3) *The Argument from Physical Indeterminacy.* Free-willists have recently derived not a little encouragement from the advent of the principle of physical indeterminacy which even if it does not suffice to demonstrate freedom of the will, at least seems to remove a serious obstacle to its acceptance. If there is a real indeterminacy at the subatomic level of quantum mechanics, this affords at least the *possibility* of the physiological and ultimately of the psychological indeterminacy which constitutes the freedom of the will. Recent quantum theory seems on the surface to afford a physical basis for a volitional indeterminacy much as the swerve of the atoms invoked by the ancient Epicureans seemed to justify their free-will doctrine. But the contemporary argument is defective and in very much the same respects as its historic prototype.

434

Against the modern version of the indeterminacy argument, it may be urged in the first place that the physical theory of indeterminacy merely expresses an observational difficulty encountered in the attempt to determine both the position and the velocity of an electron and that consequently it posits a methodological and not the physical or ontological indeterminacy which is requisite for the purposes of the free-will doctrine. But secondly, even supposing that the indeterminacy principle is physical and not merely methodological, it has not been shown that this subatomic indeterminacy manifests itself in the behaviour of ordinary mass-objects and in particular that it is exemplified in just those neural processes which are supposedly the basis of the act of free-will. The psycho-physical correlation of a neural indeterminacy with its psychological counterpart, could be effected only by the introspective observation of the volitional indeterminacy along with the underlying physical indeterminacy, and thus the evidence of introspection is an essential link in the argument from physical indeterminacy. The physical theory of indeterminacy is at the present time far from demonstrating the existence of or giving a complete picture of the *modus operandi* of a free-will and thus the freedom of indeterminacy remains, even on the background of physical indeterminacy, a more speculative possibility.

THE CASE FOR DETERMINISM

Whereas the evidence for the free-will doctrine is largely humanistic and moralistic, the case for determinism is an appeal to scientific evidence; the determinist finds that the sciences of *physiology*, *psychology*, and *sociology* afford evidence that human behaviour is no exception to the causal uniformity of nature.

(1) *Physiological Evidence.* The more we know about the physiological and neural processes which go on inside the human organism, even when it reacts to the most complicated of stimuli, the more evident it becomes that there is no break in the continuous chain of causation. Physiology gives us a reasonably clear picture of the mechanism of human behaviour. The behaviourists, the most recent recruits to the cause of determinism, have with infinite patience applied the objective method of the physiologist to human conduct; they have described in the minutest detail the mechanism of reflexes and the manner of their conditioning. There seems to remain no missing link in the causal chain from stimulus to ultimate response—even when that response is long "delayed." Delayed responses are mediated by very complex neural processes which on their subjective side are called conflict, indecision, and deliberation, but they are no exception to the behaviouristic formula.

(2) *Psychological Evidence.* While the deterministic thesis receives its

most obvious support from physiology and behaviouristic psychology, introspective psychology makes its contribution also. An unbiased introspective examination of volition supports the theory of psychological determinism. The more carefully I scrutinize my decisions, the more clearly do I discern the motives which determine them. If one's powers of introspection were sufficiently developed, one could presumably after any decision discover the exact psychological influences which rendered that particular decision inevitable. Doubtless for a complete explanation of certain decisions it is necessary in addition to the conscious antecedents of the volitional act to recover the more recondite sub-conscious and unconscious influences; the extensive researches of the Freudians into the submerged factors in human motivation provide the explanation of otherwise inexplicable mental acts and therefore tend to supply the missing links in the chain of psychic causation. Indeed, the existence of consciously inexplicable conscious events was one of the most compelling reasons for the original positing of an unconscious or subconscious mind. It remains true, however, that a fairly complete account of the psychological causation of volitional decisions is possible even without recourse to an unconscious mind.

Perhaps the best classical statement of the case for psychological determinism was given by David Hume. Hume, whose introspective subtlety has rarely been surpassed, commits himself unequivocally to psychological determinism in his assertion that "There is a great uniformity among the actions of men. . . . *The same motives always produce the same actions.*" Every historian, as Hume points out, appeals to this principle in judging the accuracy of historical documents; he asks himself whether the reported actions conform to what is known of human nature. And we might add, the same criterion is appealed to even in the evaluation of works of fiction. The novelist or the playwright gives a portrayal of his characters; he places them in definite situations, and then describes how they act. If his account of their behaviour under these precisely defined circumstances violates any of the recognized laws of human motivation, his literary and dramatic artistry is to that extent defective. Thus the principle of psychological determinism serves as a recognized canon on historical, literary, and dramatic criticism, and while this does not "prove" the correctness of psychological determinism, it does afford confirmation of it from an unsuspected quarter.

(3) *Sociological Evidence.* The social sciences yield abundant evidence for a deterministic view of human behaviour. The fact that the conduct of large aggregates of individuals is expressible in terms of statistical law, although it is by no means a conclusive proof of individual determinism, certainly points in that direction. I may not be able to predict how you as an individual will behave in any specified circumstances, but I can formulate a statistical law applicable to a large group of individuals of which you are a

436

member. It is difficult to reconcile the possibility of the laws of groups or mass action with individual free-will.

The conclusion reached as a result of the survey of the arguments on both sides of the free-will controversy is that the strength of the deterministic position lies not only in the overwhelming array of psychological, physiological, and sociological evidence for the uniformity of human behaviour, but also in its ability to meet the psychological, moral, and religious "proofs" of free-will. Accordingly, we seem fully justified in concluding that a capricious free-will, that is to say, a will capable of acting independently of antecedent conditions, psychological or physiological, is a philosophical absurdity.

FURTHER READING

B. F. Skinner's famous novel *Walden Two* (1948) is predicated on his determinism; Chapter 29 contains an interesting dialogue which explicitly raises the question of man's freedom. The Harvard behaviorist's most recent book, *Beyond Freedom and Dignity* (1971) continues his longtime advocacy of a "technology of behavior."

A. H. Compton, a Nobel prize winner in physics, argues that "physical laws, which at one stage seemed so exact and compelling, are now found to leave open a wide range of possibilities." See "Science and Man's Freedom" in *The Atlantic Monthly* (October, 1957).

In *The Age of Adventure* (1956), edited by Giorgio de Santillana, are fascinating excerpts from essays by Erasmus and Luther, who debated heatedly the doctrine of predestination.

Robert Coughlan's "Behavior by Electronics" in *Life* (March 8, 1963) is a report for the layman on research underway on the brain. The implications are strongly deterministic. More thorough and more recent is Albert Rosenfeld's *The Second Genesis: The Coming Control of Life* (1969), in which Part III, "Control of the Brain and Behavior," is especially pertinent.

Sidney Hook collected in *Determinism and Freedom in the Age of Modern Science* (1958) a large number of papers by contemporary philosophers. Note in particular John Hospers' "What Means This Freedom?"

Sigmund Freud's determinism was an outgrowth of his convictions about the role of the unconscious mind in our conscious thoughts and behavior. Chapter XII, "Determinism—Chance—and Superstitious Beliefs," in his

Psychopathology of Everyday Life (1904) is one of his discussions of this topic.

Corliss Lamont's position is stated in his title in *Freedom of Choice Affirmed* (1967), a non-technical and most readable volume. His first chapter, "The Perennial Debate," notes many writers who have spoken to the issue down through the ages.

FACT OR FICTION, DREAM OR REALITY?

11

In a memorable passage in his An Essay Concerning Human Understanding (1690), John Locke explained very simply what led him to ponder the problems of knowledge:

> Were it fit to trouble thee with the history of this *Essay*, I should tell thee, that five or six friends, meeting at my chamber, and discoursing on a subject very remote from this, found themselves quickly at a stand by the difficulties that rose on every side. After we had awhile puzzled ourselves, without coming any nearer a resolution of those doubts which perplexed us, it came into my thoughts that we took a wrong course; and that, before we set ourselves upon inquiries of that nature, it was necessary to examine our own abilities, and see what *objects* our understandings were, or were not, fitted to deal with.

The question Locke had raised was not new—the Greeks had wrestled with it long before—but Locke moved it to center stage. Since his time, the study of the problem of knowledge, epistemology, has been a primary concern of most philosophers.

The questions here are many, and they are all difficult. What are our sources of knowledge? What are the faculties of the mind, and how reliable are they? What is the nature of knowledge itself? If there is a reality independent of mind, can we acquire knowledge of it? Does knowledge always have a subjective cast to it? What is truth? How are knowledge claims to be verified? Is it possible to know anything with certainty?

Some of these issues are posed by Ryūnosuke Akutagawa's cryptic story "In a Grove." Most obviously, there is the matter of conflicting testimony: which (if any) witness is to be believed? Even if some of the witnesses or participants believe themselves to be telling the truth, are their reports necessarily trustworthy? Or, on the other hand, are all of the accounts of the events in question "true" for those who hold them? How can fact and fiction be distinguished, if indeed there is a difference?

Carl L. Becker observes that "we talk much about the 'hard facts' and the 'cold facts,' about 'not being able to get around the facts,'" and many of us suppose that historical facts are among the hardest and coldest of them all. That supposition is annihilated by Becker's essay. It is, he says, "an intangible world, re-created imaginatively, and present in our minds." What is imagination and what is not?

What, in fact, is dream and what is reality? Or, as Jerome Shaffer puts it, "How do I know I am not now dreaming?" And his answer is that there is

440

> *Nothing exists; and if it did, no one could know it; but even if he knew it, he could not communicate it.*
>
> gorgias

no way of knowing when one is dreaming or not dreaming. But in the light of Akutagawa's story and Becker's essay, perhaps the disjunction "dreaming or not dreaming" is too sharp. Don't dreams have a reality of their own, and how much much of our "real" lives is, in Shakespeare's words, "such stuff/As dreams are made of"?

Such questions and considerations as the foregoing prompted René Descartes to elevate doubt to a methodological principle. He attempted to call everything into question, to scrutinize every article of knowledge and belief. It was a harrowing experience. Descartes writes that it was "as if I had of a sudden fallen into very deep water, I am so disconcerted that I can neither make certain of setting my feet on the bottom, nor can I swim and so support myself on the surface." His goal was to discover what there was that was certain, or to learn "for certain that there is nothing in the world that is certain." Descartes finally found indubitable the proposition "I think, therefore I am" and constructed a philosophy on that foundation. Most later philosophers found it possible to doubt Descartes.

It was David Hume who made the method of doubt his very own. Writing with a clarity and grace that almost belied his profound skepticism, he

> might be said to have undermined the whole edifice of human knowledge: first, science and common sense, by his penetrating analysis of causality and induction; second, religion, by his decisive criticism of certain arguments for the existence of God . . . ; third, our sense of reality, by his treatment of the claim that we have knowledge of an external world; and finally, even our sense of ourselves, by his analysis of substance and personal identity.[1]

The tradition of rationalism (to which Descartes was pledged) and the tradition of empiricism (to which Hume belonged) have dominated Western thought. Among the fruits of these modes of knowing and thinking has been the growth of science and technology, and an entire way of life which Theodore Roszak has termed the "technocracy." The overriding objectivity and rationality of this worldview have relegated mystics, poets, and visionaries to the status of mere curiosities. Yet theirs is the domain of art and magic, of feeling and of the person, and it is Roszak's contention that that domain must be restored. We need the shaman with his "non-intellective sources of the personality"—his eyes of fire—to lead us back to life and to ourselves.

[1] Alexander Sesonske and Noel Fleming, eds., *Human Understanding: Studies in the Philosophy of David Hume* (Belmont, California: Wadsworth Publishing Company, Inc., 1965), p. 1.

ryūnosuke akutagawa   IN A GROVE

*Ryūnosuke Akutagawa (1892–1927) was born in Tokyo and lived there all of
his life. He studied English literature at the Tokyo Imperial University and
while still a student attracted attention with his earliest stories. There were also
poems, essays, and a novel, but the short stories—some 150 of them—were his
best efforts. "The Beautiful and the Grotesque" was a subtitle for one of the
collections of his stories, and it was just such uneasy juxtapositions of themes
that characterized his work. He frequently found the ideas for his stories in Japanese legends and folklore. A frail, neurotic, acutely sensitive, and sometimes
melancholy man, Akutagawa committed suicide at the age of thirty-five. Before
doing so, he wrote enigmatic notes explaining the action, mentioning a "vague
uneasiness" and listing notable suicides of the past. In 1951 Akiro Kurosawa
converted two of Akutagawa's stories ("Rashomon" and "In a Grove") into the
unforgettable motion picture* Rashomon, *and Western interest in Akutagawa
grew rapidly. Several collections of his stories have now appeared in English, including* Japanese Short Stories, Exotic Japanese Stories, *and* Hell Screen and
Other Stories. *"In a Grove" is from* Rashomon and Other Stories *(1952).*

THE TESTIMONY OF A WOODCUTTER QUESTIONED
BY A HIGH POLICE COMMISSIONER

Yes, sir. Certainly, it was I who found the body. This morning, as usual, I
went to cut my daily quota of cedars, when I found the body in a grove in
a hollow in the mountains. The exact location? About 150 meters off the
Yamashina stage road. It's an out-of-the-way grove of bamboo and cedars.

The body was lying flat on its back dressed in a bluish silk kimono and a
wrinkled head-dress of the Kyoto style. A single sword-stroke had pierced the
breast. The fallen bamboo-blades around it were stained with bloody
blossoms. No, the blood was no longer running. The wound had dried up, I
believe. And also, a gadfly was stuck fast there, hardly noticing my footsteps.

You ask me if I saw a sword or any such thing?

No, nothing, sir. I found only a rope at the root of a cedar near by. And
. . . well, in addition to a rope, I found a comb. That was all. Apparently
he must have made a battle of it before he was murdered, because the grass
and fallen bamboo-blades had been trampled down all around.

"A horse was near by?"

No, sir. It's hard enough for a man to enter, let alone a horse.

442

THE TESTIMONY OF A TRAVELING BUDDHIST PRIEST QUESTIONED BY A HIGH POLICE COMMISSIONER

The time? Certainly, it was about noon yesterday, sir. The unfortunate man was on the road from Sekiyama to Yamashina. He was walking toward Sekiyama with a woman accompanying him on horseback, who I have since learned was his wife. A scarf hanging from her head hid her face from view. All I saw was the color of her clothes, a lilac-colored suit. Her horse was a sorrel with a fine mane. The lady's height? Oh, about four feet five inches. Since I am a Buddhist priest, I took little notice about her details. Well, the man was armed with a sword as well as a bow and arrows. And I remember that he carried some twenty odd arrows in his quiver.

Little did I expect that he would meet such a fate. Truly human life is as evanescent as the morning dew or a flash of lightning. My words are inadequate to express my sympathy for him.

THE TESTIMONY OF A POLICEMAN QUESTIONED BY A HIGH POLICE COMMISSIONER

The man that I arrested? He is a notorious brigand called Tajomaru. When I arrested him, he had fallen off his horse. He was groaning on the bridge at Awataguchi. The time? It was in the early hours of last night. For the record, I might say that the other day I tried to arrest him, but unfortunately he escaped. He was wearing a dark blue silk kimono and a large plain sword. And, as you see, he got a bow and arrows somewhere. You say that this bow and these arrows look like the ones owned by the dead man? Then Tajomaru must be the murderer. The bow wound with leather strips, the black lacquered quiver, the seventeen arrows with hawk feathers—these were all in his possession I believe. Yes, sir, the horse is, as you say, a sorrel with a fine mane. A little beyond the stone bridge I found the horse grazing by the roadside, with his long rein dangling. Surely there is some providence in his having been thrown by the horse.

Of all the robbers prowling around Kyoto, this Tajomaru has given the most grief to the women in town. Last autumn a wife who came to the mountain back of the Pindora of the Toribe Temple, presumably to pay a visit, was murdered, along with a girl. It has been suspected that it was his doing. If this criminal murdered the man, you cannot tell what he may have done with the man's wife. May it please your honor to look into this problem as well.

THE TESTIMONY OF AN OLD WOMAN QUESTIONED BY A HIGH POLICE COMMISSIONER

Yes, sir, that corpse is the man who married my daughter. He does not come from Kyoto. He was a samurai in the town of Kokufu in the province of Wakasa. His name was Kanazawa no Takehiko, and his age was twenty-six. He was of a gentle disposition, so I am sure he did nothing to provoke the anger of others.

My daughter? Her name is Masago, and her age is nineteen. She is a spirited, fun-loving girl, but I am sure she has never known any man except Takehiko. She has a small, oval, dark-complected face with a mole at the corner of her left eye.

Yesterday Takehiko left for Wakasa with my daughter. What bad luck it is that things should have come to such a sad end! What has become of my daughter? I am resigned to giving up my son-in-law as lost, but the fate of my daughter worries me sick. For heaven's sake leave no stone unturned to find her. I hate that robber Tajomaru, or whatever his name is. Not only my son-in-law, but my daughter . . . (Her later words were drowned in tears.)

TAJOMARU'S CONFESSION

I killed him, but not her. Where's she gone? I can't tell. Oh, wait a minute. No torture can make me confess what I don't know. Now things have come to such a head, I won't keep anything from you.

Yesterday a little past noon I met that couple. Just then a puff of wind blew, and raised her hanging scarf, so that I caught a glimpse of her face. Instantly it was again covered from my view. That may have been one reason; she looked like a Bodhisattva. At that moment I made up my mind to capture her even if I had to kill her man.

Why? To me killing isn't a matter of such great consequence as you might think. When a woman is captured, her man has to be killed anyway. In killing, I use the sword I wear at my side. Am I the only one who kills people? You, you don't use your swords. You kill people with your power, with your money. Sometimes you kill them on the pretext of working for their good. It's true they don't bleed. They are in the best of health, but all the same you've killed them. It's hard to say who is a greater sinner, you or me. (An ironical smile.)

But it would be good if I could capture a woman without killing her man. So, I made up my mind to capture her, and do my best not to kill him. But it's out of the question on the Yamashina stage road. So I managed to lure the couple into the mountains.

It was quite easy. I became their traveling companion, and I told them there was an old mound in the mountain over there, and that I had dug it open and found many mirrors and swords. I went on to tell them I'd buried the things in a grove behind the mountain, and that I'd like to sell them at a low price to anyone who would care to have them. Then . . . you see, isn't greed terrible? He was beginning to be moved by my talk before he knew it.

444

In less than half an hour they were driving their horse toward the mountain with me.

When he came in front of the grove, I told them that the treasures were buried in it, and I asked them to come and see. The man had no objection—he was blinded by greed. The woman said she would wait on horseback. It was natural for her to say so, at the sight of a thick grove. To tell you the truth, my plan worked just as I wished, so I went into the grove with him, leaving her behind alone.

The grove is only bamboo for some distance. About fifty yards ahead there's a rather open clump of cedars. It was a convenient spot for my purpose. Pushing my way through the grove, I told him a plausible lie that the treasures were buried under the cedars. When I told him this, he pushed his laborious way toward the slender cedar visible through the grove. After a while the bamboo thinned out, and we came to where a number of cedars grew in a row. As soon as we got there, I seized him from behind. Because he was a trained, sword-bearing warrior, he was quite strong, but he was taken by surprise, so there was no help for him. I soon tied him up to the root of a cedar. Where did I get a rope? Thank heaven, being a robber, I had a rope with me, since I might have to scale a wall at any moment. Of course it was easy to stop him from calling out by gagging his mouth with fallen bamboo leaves.

When I disposed of him, I went to his woman and asked her to come and see him, because he seemed to have been suddenly taken sick. It's needless to say that this plan also worked well. The woman, her sedge hat off, came into the depths of the grove, where I led her by the hand. The instant she caught sight of her husband, she drew a small sword. I've never seen a woman of such violent temper. If I'd been off guard, I'd have got a thrust in my side. I dodged, but she kept on slashing at me. She might have wounded me deeply or killed me. But I'm Tajomaru. I managed to strike down her small sword without drawing my own. The most spirited woman is defenseless without a weapon. At least I could satisfy my desire for her without taking her husband's life.

Yes, . . . without taking his life. I had no wish to kill him. I was about to run away from the grove, leaving the woman behind in tears, when she frantically clung to my arm. In broken fragments of words, she asked that either her husband or I die. She said it was more trying than death to have her shame known to two men. She gasped out that she wanted to be the wife of whichever survived. Then a furious desire to kill him seized me. (Gloomy excitement.)

Telling you in this way, no doubt I seem a crueler man than you. But that's because you didn't see her face. Especially her burning eyes at that moment. As I saw her eye to eye, I wanted to make her my wife even if I were to be struck by lightning. I wanted to make her my wife . . . this single desire filled my mind. This was not only lust, as you might think. At that time if I'd had no other desire than lust, I'd surely not have minded knocking her down and running away. Then I wouldn't have stained my sword with his blood. But the moment I gazed at her face in the dark grove, I decided not to leave there without killing him.

But I didn't like to resort to unfair means to kill him. I untied him and told him to cross swords with me. (The rope that was found at the root of the cedar is the rope I dropped at the time.) Furious with anger, he drew his thick sword. And quick as thought, he sprang at me ferociously, without speaking a word. I needn't tell you how our fight turned out. The twenty-third stroke . . . please remember this. I'm impressed with this fact still. Nobody under the sun has ever clashed swords with me twenty strokes. (A cheerful smile.)

When he fell, I turned toward her, lowering my blood-stained sword. But to my great astonishment she was gone. I wondered to where she had run away. I looked for her in the clump of cedars. I listened, but heard only a groaning sound from the throat of the dying man.

As soon as we started to cross swords, she may have run away through the grove to call for help. When I thought of that, I decided it was a matter of life and death to me. So, robbing him of his sword, and bow and arrows, I ran out to the mountain road. There I found her horse still grazing quietly. It would be a mere waste of words to tell you the later details, but before I entered town I had already parted with the sword. That's all my confession. I know that my head will be hung in chains anyway, so put me down for the maximum penalty. (A defiant attitude.)

THE CONFESSION OF A WOMAN WHO HAS COME TO THE *SHIMIZU* TEMPLE

That man in the blue silk kimono, after forcing me to yield to him, laughed mockingly as he looked at my bound husband. How horrified my husband must have been! But no matter how hard he struggled in agony, the rope cut into him all the more tightly. In spite of myself I ran stumblingly toward his side. Or rather I tried to run toward him, but the man instantly knocked me down. Just at that moment I saw an indescribable light in my husband's eyes. Something beyond expression . . . his eyes make me shudder even now. That instantaneous look of my husband, who couldn't speak a word, told me all his heart. The flash in his eyes was neither anger nor sorrow . . . only a cold light, a look of loathing. More struck by the look in his eyes than by the blow of the thief, I called out in spite of myself and fell unconscious.

In the course of time I came to, and found that the man in blue silk was gone. I saw only my husband still bound to the root of the cedar. I raised myself from the bamboo-blades with difficulty, and looked into his face; but the expression in his eyes was just the same as before.

Beneath the cold contempt in his eyes, there was hatred. Shame, grief, and anger . . . I don't know how to express my heart at that time. Reeling to my feet, I went up to my husband.

"Takejiro," I said to him, "since things have come to this pass, I cannot live with you. I'm determined to die, . . . but you must die, too. You saw my shame. I can't leave you alive as you are."

This was all I could say. Still he went on gazing at me with loathing and contempt. My heart breaking, I looked for his sword. It must have been taken by the robber. Neither his sword nor his bow and arrows were to be seen in the grove. But fortunately my small sword was lying at my feet. Raising it over head, once more I said, "Now give me your life. I'll follow you right away."

When he heard these words, he moved his lips with difficulty. Since his mouth was stuffed with leaves, of course his voice could not be heard at all. But at a glance I understood his words. Despising me, his look said only, "Kill me." Neither conscious nor unconscious, I stabbed the small sword through the lilac-colored kimono into his breast.

Again at this time I must have fainted. By the time I managed to look up, he had already breathed his last—still in bonds. A streak of sinking sunlight streamed through the clump of cedars and bamboos, and shone on his pale face. Gulping down my sobs, I untied the rope from his dead body. And . . . and what has become of me since I have no more strength to tell you. Anyway I hadn't the strength to die. I stabbed my own throat with the small sword, I threw myself into a pond at the foot of the mountain, and I tried to kill myself in many ways. Unable to end my life, I am still living in dishonor. (A lonely smile.) Worthless as I am, I must have been forsaken even by the most merciful Kwannon. I killed my own husband. I was violated by the robber. Whatever can I do? Whatever can I . . . I . . . (Gradually, violent sobbing.)

THE STORY OF THE MURDERED MAN, AS TOLD
THROUGH A MEDIUM

After violating my wife, the robber, sitting there, began to speak comforting words to her. Of course I couldn't speak. My whole body was tied fast to the root of a cedar. But meanwhile I winked at her many times, as much as to say "Don't believe the robber." I wanted to convey some such meaning to her. But my wife, sitting dejectedly on the bamboo leaves, was looking hard at her lap. To all appearances, she was listening to his words. I was agonized by jealousy. In the meantime the robber went on with his clever talk, from one subject to another. The robber finally made his bold, brazen proposal. "Once your virtue is stained, you won't get along well with your husband, so won't you be my wife instead? It's my love for you that made me be violent toward you."

While the criminal talked, my wife raised her face as if in a trance. She had never looked so beautiful as at that moment. What did my beautiful wife say in answer to him while I was sitting bound there? I am lost in space, but I have never thought of her answer without burning with anger and jealousy. Truly she said, . . . "Then take me away with you wherever you go."

This is not the whole of her sin. If that were all, I would not be tormented so much in the dark. When she was going out of the grove as if in a dream, her hand in the robber's, she suddenly turned pale, and pointed at me tied to the root of the cedar, and said, "Kill him! I cannot marry you as long as he lives." "Kill him!" she cried many times, as if she had gone crazy. Even now these words threaten to blow me headlong into the bottomless abyss of darkness. Has such a hateful thing come out of a human mouth ever before? Have such cursed words ever struck a human ear, even once? Even once such a . . . (A sudden cry of scorn.) At these words the robber himself turned pale. "Kill him," she cried, clinging to his arms. Looking hard at her, he answered neither yes nor no . . . but hardly had I thought about his answer before she had been knocked down into the bamboo leaves. (Again a cry of scorn.) Quietly folding his arms, he looked at me and said, "What will you do with her? Kill her or save her? You have only to nod. Kill her?" For these words alone I would like to pardon his crime.

While I hesitated, she shrieked and ran into the depths of the grove. The robber instantly snatched at her, but he failed even to grasp her sleeve.

After she ran away, he took up my sword, and my bow and arrows. With a single stroke he cut one of my bonds. I remember his mumbling, "My fate is next." Then he disappeared from the grove. All was silent after that. No, I heard someone crying. Untying the rest of my bonds, I listened carefully, and I noticed that it was my own crying. (Long silence.)

I raised my exhausted body from the root of the cedar. In front of me there was shining the small sword which my wife had dropped. I took it up and stabbed it into my breast. A bloody lump rose to my mouth, but I didn't feel any pain. When my breast grew cold, everything was as silent as the dead in their graves. What profound silence! Not a single bird-note was heard in the sky over this grave in the hollow of the mountains. Only a lonely light lingered on the cedars and mountains. By and by the light gradually grew fainter, till the cedars and bamboo were lost to view. Lying there, I was enveloped in deep silence.

Then someone crept up to me. I tried to see who it was. But darkness had already been gathering round me. Someone . . . that someone drew the small sword softly out of my breast in its invisible hand. At the same time once more blood flowed into my mouth. And once and for all I sank down into the darkness of space.

Translated by Takashi Kojima

carl l. becker   WHAT ARE HISTORICAL FACTS?

In his essay "Frederick Jackson Turner" Carl L. Becker (1873–1945) tells how he went to the University of Wisconsin as a naive eighteen-year-old country boy from Iowa to study under the historian "old Freddie Turner" (who was thirty-three at the time). Before he was through with Wisconsin and Turner, Becker was a student of history; he went on to become one of America's most distinguished historians and men of letters. He taught at Pennsylvania State College, Dartmouth, the Universities of Kansas and Minnesota, and from 1917 until his death, at Cornell University. Such volumes as The Declaration of Independence, Modern Democracy, *and* Freedom and Responsibility in the American Way of Life *reflect his concern for the cause of freedom and democracy.* The Heavenly City of the Eighteenth-Century Philosophers *is his most highly praised work. "What Are Historical Facts?" was written in 1926 but not published until after his death; it expresses a theme Becker returned to in 1932 with his often reprinted "Everyman His Own Historian."*

History is a venerable branch of knowledge, and the writing of history is an art of long standing. Everyone knows what history is, that is, everyone is familiar with the word, and has a confident notion of what it means. In general, history has to do with the thought and action of men and women who lived in past times. Everyone knows what the past is too. We all have a comforting sense that it lies behind us, like a stretch of uneven country we have crossed; and it is often difficult to avoid the notion that one could easily, by turning round, walk back into this country of the past. That, at all events, is what we commonly think of the historian as doing: he works in the past, he explores the past in order to find out what men did and thought in the past. His business is to discover and set forth the "facts" of history.

When anyone says "facts" we are all there. The word gives us a sense of stability. We know where we are when, as we say, we "get down to the facts" —as, for example, we know where we are when we get down to the facts of the structure of the atom, or the incredible movement of the electron as it jumps from one orbit to another. It is the same with history. Historians feel safe when dealing with the facts. We talk much about the "hard facts" and the "cold facts," about "not being able to get around the facts," and about the necessity of basing our narrative on a "solid foundation of fact." By virtue of talking in this way, the facts of history come in the end to seem something solid, something substantial like physical matter (I mean matter in the common sense, not matter defined as "a series of events in the ether"), something possessing definite shape, and clear persistent outline—like bricks

450

or scantlings; so that we can easily picture the historian as he stumbles about in the past, stubbing his toe on the hard facts if he doesn't watch out. That is his affair of course, a danger he runs; for his business is to dig out the facts and pile them up for someone to use. Perhaps he may use them himself; but at all events he must arrange them conveniently so that someone—perhaps the sociologist or the economist—may easily carry them away for use in some structural enterprise.

Such (with no doubt a little, but not much, exaggeration to give point to the matter) are the common connotations of the words historical facts, as used by historians and other people. Now, when I meet a word with which I am entirely unfamiliar, I find it a good plan to look it up in the dictionary and find out what someone thinks it means. But when I have frequently to use words with which everyone is perfectly familiar—words like "cause" and "liberty" and "progress" and "government"—when I have to use words of this sort which everyone knows perfectly well, the wise thing to do is to take a week off and think about them. The result is often astonishing; for as often as not I find that I have been talking about words instead of real things. Well, "historical fact" is such a word; and I suspect it would be worthwhile for us historians at least to think about this word more than we have done. For the moment therefore, leaving the historian moving about in the past piling up the cold facts, I wish to inquire whether the historical fact is really as hard and stable as it is often supposed to be.

And this inquiry I will throw into the form of three simple questions. I will ask the questions, I can't promise to answer them. The questions are: (1) What is the historical fact? (2) Where is the historical fact? (3) When is the historical fact? Mind I say *is* not *was*. I take it for granted that if we are interested in, let us say, the fact of the Magna Carta, we are interested in it for our own sake and not for its sake; and since we are living now and not in 1215 we must be interested in the Magna Carta, if at all, for what it is and not for what it was.

First then, What is the historical fact? Let us take a simple fact, as simple as the historian often deals with, viz.: "In the year 49 B.C. Caesar crossed the Rubicon." A familiar fact this is, known to all, and obviously of some importance since it is mentioned in every history of the great Caesar. But is this fact as simple as it sounds? Has it the clear, persistent outline which we commonly attribute to simple historical facts? When we say that Caesar crossed the Rubicon we do not of course mean that Caesar crossed it alone, but with his army. The Rubicon is a small river, and I don't know how long it took Caesar's army to cross it; but the crossing must surely have been accompanied by many acts and many words and many thoughts of many men. That is to say, a thousand and one lesser "facts" went to make up the one simple fact that Caesar crossed the Rubicon; and if we had someone, say James Joyce, to know and relate all these facts, it would no doubt require a book of 794 pages to present this one fact that Caesar crossed the Rubicon. Thus the simple fact turns out to be not a simple fact at all. It is the statement that is simple—a simple generalization of a thousand and one facts.

Well, anyhow Caesar crossed the Rubicon. But what of it? Many other people at other times crossed the Rubicon. Why charge it up to Caesar? Why for two thousand years has the world treasured this simple fact that in the year 49 B.C. Caesar crossed the Rubicon? What of it indeed? If I, as historian, have nothing to give you but this fact taken by itself with its clear outline, with no fringes or strings tied to it, I should have to say, if I were an honest man, why nothing of it, nothing at all. It may be a fact but it is nothing to us. The truth is, of course, that this simple fact *has* strings tied to it, and that is why it has been treasured for two thousand years. It is tied by these strings to innumerable other facts, so that it can't mean anything except by losing its clear outline. It can't mean anything except as it is absorbed into the complex web of circumstances which brought it into being. This complex web of circumstances was the series of events growing out of the relation of Caesar to Pompey, and the Roman Senate, and the Roman Republic, and all the people who had something to do with these. Caesar had been ordered by the Roman Senate to resign his command of the army in Gaul. He decided to disobey the Roman Senate. Instead of resigning his command, he marched on Rome, gained the mastery of the Republic, and at last, as we are told, bestrode the narrow world like a colossus. Well, the Rubicon happened to be the boundary between Gaul and Italy, so that by the act of crossing the Rubicon with his army Caesar's treason became an accomplished fact and the subsequent great events followed in due course. Apart from these great events and complicated relations, the crossing of the Rubicon means nothing, is not an historical fact properly speaking at all. In itself it is nothing for us; it becomes something for us, not in itself, but as a symbol of something else, a symbol standing for a long series of events which have to do with the most intangible and immaterial realities, viz.: the relation between Caesar and the millions of people of the Roman world.

Thus the simple historical fact turns out to be not a hard, cold something with clear outline, and measurable pressure, like a brick. It is so far as we can know it, only a *symbol*, a simple statement which is a generalization of a thousand and one simpler facts which we do not for the moment care to use, and this generalization itself we cannot use apart from the wider facts and generalizations which it symbolizes. And generally speaking, the more simple an historical fact is, the more clear and definite and provable it is, the less use it is to us in and for itself. . . .

What then is the historical fact? Far be it from me to define so illusive and intangible a thing! But provisionally I will say this: the historian may be interested in anything that has to do with the life of man in the past—any act or event, any emotion which men have expressed, any idea, true or false, which they have entertained. Very well, the historian is interested in some event of this sort. Yet he cannot deal directly with this event itself, since the event itself has disappeared. What he can deal with directly is a *statement about the event*. He deals in short not with the event, but with a statement which affirms *the fact that the event occurred*. When we really get down to the hard facts, what the historian is always dealing with is an *affirmation*— an affirmation of the fact that something is true. There is thus a distinction of capital importance to be made: the distinction between the ephemeral event which disappears, and the affirmation about the event which persists. For all practical purposes it is this affirmation about the event that constitutes for us the historical fact. If so the historical fact is not the past event, but a symbol which enables us to recreate it imaginatively. Of a symbol it is hardly worthwhile to say that it is cold or hard. It is dangerous to say even that it is true or false. The safest thing to say about a symbol is that it is more or less appropriate.

This brings me to the second question—Where is the historical fact? I will say at once, however brash it sounds, that the historical fact is in someone's mind or it is nowhere. To illustrate this statement I will take an event familiar to all. "Abraham Lincoln was assassinated in Ford's Theater in Washington on the 14th of April, 1865." That *was* an actual event, occurrence, fact at the moment of happening. But speaking now, in the year 1926, we say it *is* an historical fact. We don't say that it *was* an historical fact, for that would imply that it no longer is one. We say that it *was* an actual event, but *is now* an historical fact. The actual occurrence and the historical fact, however closely connected, are two different things. Very well, if the assassination of Lincoln is an historical fact, where is this fact now? Lincoln is not being assassinated now in Ford's Theater, or anywhere else (except perhaps in propagandist literature!). The actual occurrence, the event, has passed, is gone forever, never to be repeated, never to be again experienced or witnessed by any living person. Yet this is precisely the sort of thing the historian is concerned with—events, acts, thoughts, emotions that have forever vanished as actual occurrences. How can the historian deal with vanished realities? He can deal with them because these vanished realities give place to pale reflections, impalpable images or ideas of themselves, and these pale reflections, and impalpable images which cannot be touched or handled are all that is left of the actual occurrence. These are therefore what the historian deals with. These are his "material." He has to be satisfied with these, for the very good reason that he has nothing else. Well then, where are they—these pale reflections and impalpable images of the actual? Where are these facts? They are, as I said before, in his mind, or in somebody's mind, or they are nowhere.

Ah, but they are in the records, in the sources, I hear someone say. Yes, in a sense, they are in the sources. The historical fact of Lincoln's assassination is in the records—in contemporary newspapers, letters, diaries, etc. In a sense the fact is there, but in what sense? The records are after all only paper, over the surface of which ink has been distributed in certain patterns. And even these patterns were not made by the actual occurrence, the assassination of Lincoln. The patterns are themselves only "histories" of the event, made by someone who had in *his* mind an image or idea of Lincoln's assassination. Of course we, you and I, can, by looking at these inky patterns, form in *our* minds images or ideas more or less like those in the mind of the person who made the patterns. But if there were now no one in the world who could make any meaning out of the patterned records or sources, the fact of Lincoln's assassination would cease to be an historical fact. You might perhaps call it a dead fact; but a fact which is not only dead, but not known ever to have been alive, or even known to be now dead, is surely not much of a fact. At all events, the historical facts lying dead in the records can do nothing good or evil in the world. They become historical facts, capable of doing work, of making a difference, only when someone, you or I, brings them alive in our minds by means of pictures, images, or ideas of the actual occurrence. For this reason I say that the historical fact is in someone's mind, or it is nowhere, because when it is in no one's mind it lies in the records inert, incapable of making a difference in the world.

But perhaps you will say that the assassination of Lincoln has made a difference in the world, and that this difference is now effectively working, even if, for a moment, or an hour or a week, no one in the world has the image of the actual occurrence in mind. Quite obviously so, but why? Quite obviously because after the actual event people remembered it, and because ever since they have continued to remember it, by repeatedly forming images of it in their mind. If the people of the United States had been incapable of enduring memory, for example, like dogs (as I assume; not being a dog I can't be sure) would the assassination of Lincoln be now doing work in the world, making a difference? If everyone had forgotten the occurrence after forty-eight hours, what difference would the occurrence have made, then or since? It is precisely because people have long memories, and have constantly formed images in their minds of the assassination of Lincoln, that the universe contains the historical fact which persists as well as the actual event which does not persist. It is the persisting historical fact, rather than the ephemeral actual event, which makes a difference to us now; and the historical fact makes a difference only because it is, and so far as it is, in human minds.

Now for the third question—When is the historical fact? If you agree with what has been said (which is extremely doubtful) the answer seems simple enough. If the historical fact is present, imaginatively, in someone's mind, then it is now, a part of the present. But the word present is a slippery word, and the thing itself is worse than the word. The present is an indefinable point in time, gone before you can think it; the image or idea which I have now present in mind slips instantly into the past. But images or ideas of past events are often, perhaps always, inseparable from images or ideas of the future. Take an illustration. I awake this morning, and among the things my memory drags in to enlighten or distress me is a vague notion that there was something I needed particularly to remember but cannot—a common experience surely. What is it that I needed to remember I cannot recall; but I can recall that I made a note of it in order to jog my memory. So I consult my little pocket memorandum book—a little Private Record Office which I carry about, filled with historical sources. I take out my memorandum book in order to do a little historical research; and there I find the dead historical fact—"Pay Smith's coal bill today: $1,016." The image of the memorandum book now drops out of mind, and is replaced by another image—an image of what? Why an image, an idea, a picture (call it what you will) made up of three things more or less inseparable. First the image of myself ordering coal from Smith last summer; second, the image of myself holding the idea in mind that I must pay the bill; third, the image of myself going down to Smith's office at four o'clock to pay it. The image is partly of things done in the past, and partly of things to be done in the future; but it is more or less all one image now present in mind.

Someone may ask, "Are you talking of history or of the ordinary ills of every day that men are heir to?" Well, perhaps Smith's coal bill is only my personal affair, of no concern to anyone else, except Smith to be sure. Take then another example. I am thinking of the Congress of Berlin, and that is without doubt history—the real thing. The historical facts of the Congress of Berlin I bring alive in memory, imaginatively. But I am making an image of the Congress of Berlin for a purpose; and indeed without a purpose no one would take the trouble to bring historical facts to mind. My purpose happens to be to convey this image of the Congress of Berlin to my class in History 42, in Room C, tomorrow afternoon at 3 o'clock. Now I find that inseparable from this image of the Congress of Berlin, which occurred in the past, are flitting images of myself conveying this image of the Congress of Berlin to my class tomorrow in Room C. I picture myself standing there monotonously talking, I hear the labored sentences painfully issuing forth, I picture the students' faces alert or bored as the case may be; so that images of this future event enter into the imagined picture of the Congress of Berlin, a past event; enter into it, coloring and shaping it too, to the end that the performance may do credit to me, or be intelligible to immature minds, or be compressed within the limits of fifty minutes, or to accomplish some other desired end. Well, this living historical fact, this mixed image of the coal bill or the Congress of Berlin—is it past, present, or future? I cannot say. Perhaps it moves with the velocity of light, and is timeless. At all events it is real history to me, which I hope to make convincing and real to Smith, or to the class in Room C.

I have now asked my three questions, and have made some remarks about them all. I don't know whether these remarks will strike you as quite beside the mark, or as merely obvious, or as novel. If there is any novelty in them, it arises, I think, from our inveterate habit of thinking of the world of history as part of the external world, and of historical facts as actual events. In truth the actual past is gone; and the world of history is an intangible world, re-created imaginatively, and present in our minds.

jerome a. shaffer   HOW DO I KNOW I AM
                                       NOT NOW DREAMING?

*Jerome A. Shaffer (1929–   ) was born in Brooklyn and earned his A.B. at
Cornell University. He was awarded Wilson and Proctor fellowships and received his Ph.D. from Princeton University. A Fulbright scholar in 1952–1953,
he taught for a few years at Swarthmore College and in 1958 moved to the
University of Connecticut. The author of* The Philosophy of Mind *as well as of
journal articles, he was a Fellow at the Center for Advanced Study in the Behavioral Sciences at Stanford. The selection which follows is from* Reality, Knowledge, and Value: A Basic Introduction to Philosophy (1971).

Let us start our investigation into metaphysics and epistemology by raising
a specific question: How do I know I am not now dreaming? This question
was posed by Plato and, later, by the father of modern philosophy, Descartes,
who published his *Meditations on First Philosophy* in 1641. How do I
know I am not now dreaming? Well, everything certainly *seems* perfectly
normal. The book that I am looking at now *seems* clear and sharp to me. The
room I am in *seems* perfectly normal and real. There is nothing particularly
strange or unusual going on right now. It certainly *seems* that I am wide
awake. But still we must remember that people frequently have very realistic
dreams—dreams in which everything *seems* to be quite normal. If dreams
didn't seem so real to us, then things that happen in dreams would never
frighten us. But as we know, we sometimes get quite frightened by a dream
because it does seem to be so real. Perhaps I am at this very minute in bed
having a most realistic dream, dreaming that I am sitting at my desk, reading
a philosophy book. It is certainly possible that there might be a dream just
like this. How do I know that *this* is not such a dream?

If I seriously raised the question, How do I know I am not now dreaming?
—I might feel that there are things I could do to determine whether it is a
dream or not. For example, I could try pinching myself, slapping myself in the
face, getting up and stretching, or reciting "Abou Ben Adhem." Yet what
would this show? For is it not quite possible that I should *dream* that I am
pinching myself, slapping my face, getting up and stretching, or reciting
"Abou Ben Adhem"? One can imagine that kind of dream occurring. How
do I know that this is not that kind of dream? Suppose I try to do a little
experiment. I seem to remember writing my name in the front of this book,
and I predict that it will still be there. So, if I look in the front of the book
and find it there, this will confirm my seeming to remember that I did

write it there, and perhaps that will show that I am now awake. But suppose I look and I see my name in the front of the book. What does this show? Surely I can dream that I put my name there, surely I can dream that I am now checking, and surely I can dream that I am now finding my name there. We have still not broken out of the dream world. Suppose I try to remember something difficult—the names of all the states, for example. Can I not also dream that I am remembering them? Suppose that I try doing a mathematical problem in my head. Can I not dream that I am trying to do a mathematical problem in my head? Can I not dream that I have solved it successfully? It does not seem that any test that I try to perform will prove anything, because I can never be sure whether I am actually performing the test or merely dreaming that I am performing it; and I can never be sure whether the outcome of the test is successful or whether I am only dreaming that the outcome of the test is successful. So, in general, it looks as though there is no way of showing that I am now awake and not dreaming.

The following thought may occur to you: I grant that I cannot be *sure*, cannot *prove* that I am now awake, but I can at least make it *probable* that I am awake. But this thought would miss the fundamental point of our problem. It is not that I cannot *prove* that I am awake; it is that there does not seem to be even *the slightest reason* for thinking that I am now awake. All of the apparent evidence that I have—the way things appear to be now—have no weight at all if I am only dreaming them. No matter how much like waking life all of this seems to me to be, the fact remains that I may well be dreaming that everything is going on normally. So the fact that everything seems to be going on normally gives not the slightest weight to the supposition that I am awake. For all I know, this may be a very realistic dream, and I cannot infer from the realistic appearances that it is *not* a realistic dream.

"Well," you might say, "what does it matter? If it is a very realistic dream, then that is just the same as being awake, so who cares whether it is a dream or waking life?" But it obviously does matter. If this is all a dream, then, for example, you are not awake and studying now, so that you are not getting your philosophy assignment done. You may find yourself waking up in the next few minutes to discover that you have overslept and missed your class. Here the importance of deciding whether it is a dream or not is based on the importance of having some reasonable expectations about what is going to happen next. Of course, it is true that even if this is a dream, it is a pleasant enough dream—let us hope even an interesting dream. But suppose that in the next few minutes things begin to get more unpleasant. Suppose your roommate rushes in with some bad news. Suppose you suddenly notice a person creeping toward you with a knife. Then it will be quite important whether it is a dream or not—whether you are really in danger or not. Of course, we can't go through our lives constantly asking ourselves, Is this a dream or not? But this does not mean that we should *never* raise the question. Here is one comparatively convenient time to raise this question, and we have seen that once it is raised, it does not seem very easy to answer.

The problem we have been discussing so far is a problem in epistemology. That is to say, it is a problem concerned with what can be known and how it is to be known, if it can be known. We can see connected with this epistemological problem a metaphysical problem, that is, a problem concerned with the nature of reality. The metaphysical problem would be this: How are the things that happen in dreams different in their basic nature from the things that happen in "real life"? We have already seen that the difference cannot lie in whether what happens is normal or ordinary or "realistic," since dreams may be exactly like real life in their content. In fact, that is what makes us believe during the dream that these things are really happening. So the difference between dreams and real life cannot be in the content of each. It must be something else. But what is the difference, then, between something that happens in a dream and something that happens in real life? Might the difference consist only in this: What we call "real life" is simply an elaborate, consistent, prolonged dream; and what we call "a dream" is a comparatively short sequence that does not fit in with the longer part? Here is another possibility. Perhaps each person in the world is having his own dream, but all the dreams are in phase, so that when you dream you are speaking with your roommate, he at the same time is dreaming that he is speaking with you. Here would be a case where there was a common world to some degree, although each of us existed only in his dream world.

There are a number of different possibilities here. All of these would be somewhat different metaphysical schemes. Each would give us a somewhat different account of the ultimate nature of things. We see how intertwined epistemology and metaphysics are when we notice that each of these metaphysical schemes is possible and that the epistemological question of whether we have any reason for believing that our world is one way rather than another is always pertinent.

René Descartes (1596–1650) is a pivotal figure in the history of philosophy: his emphasis upon rational methods of inquiry (carefully delineated in his "Rules for the Direction of the Mind") has led to his being credited with initiating the period of modern philosophy. Born into a notable family and some wealth in France, he was well educated at a Jesuit college, had a brief fling at Parisian social life, and then served in three European armies as a professional soldier over a period of twelve years. At the same time, apparently having ample time for his own interests, he became one of the prominent mathematicians of his day. Settling finally in Holland, where there was relative freedom of thought, he produced his most important works: The Discourse on Method, The Meditations of First Philosophy, The Principles of Philosophy, *and* The Passions of the Soul. *A man of a retiring nature, Descartes valued privacy and time for solitary thinking and writing; he enjoyed remaining in bed until midday. In 1649, Queen Christina of Sweden persuaded him to visit her: he did so, only to find himself commanded to discuss philosophy with her daily at five in the morning. "This unphilosophic hour of rising," commented Bertrand Russell, "at dead of night in a Swedish winter was more than Descartes could endure. He took ill and died. . . ."*

I. OF THE THINGS WHICH MAY BE BROUGHT WITHIN THE SPHERE OF THE DOUBTFUL

It is now some years since I detected how many were the false beliefs that I had from my earliest youth admitted as true, and how doubtful was everything I had since constructed on this basis; and from that time I was convinced that I must once for all seriously undertake to rid myself of all the opinions which I had formerly accepted, and commence to build anew from the foundation, if I wanted to establish any firm and permanent structure in the sciences. But as this enterprise appeared to be a very great one, I waited until I had attained an age so mature that I could not hope that at any later date I should be better fitted to execute my design. This reason caused me to delay so long that I should feel that I was doing wrong were I to occupy in deliberation the time that yet remains to me for action. To-day, then, since very opportunely for the plan I have in view I have delivered my mind from every care [and am happily agitated by no passions] and since I have procured for myself an assured leisure in a peaceable retirement, I shall at last seriously and freely address myself to the general upheaval of all my former opinions.

Now for this object it is not necessary that I should show that all of these are false—I shall perhaps never arrive at this end. But inasmuch as reason already persuades me that I ought no less carefully to withhold my assent from matters which are not entirely certain and indubitable than from those which appear to me manifestly to be false, if I am able to find in each one some reason to doubt, this will suffice to justify my rejecting the whole. And for that end it will not be requisite that I should examine each in particular, which would be an endless undertaking; for owing to the fact that the destruction of the foundations of necessity brings with it the downfall of the rest of the edifice, I shall only in the first place attack those principles upon which all my former opinions rested.

All that up to the present time I have accepted as most true and certain I have learned either from the senses or through the senses; but it is sometimes proved to me that these senses are deceptive, and it is wiser not to trust entirely to any thing by which we have once been deceived.

But it may be that although the senses sometimes deceive us concerning things which are hardly perceptible, or very far away, there are yet many others to be met with as to which we cannot reasonably have any doubt, although we recognise them by their means. For example, there is the fact that I am here, seated by the fire, attired in a dressing gown, having this paper in my hands and other similar matters. And how could I deny that these hands and this body are mine, were it not perhaps that I compare myself to certain persons, devoid of sense, whose cerebella are so troubled and clouded by the violent vapours of black bile, that they constantly assure us that they think they are kings when they are really quite poor, or that they are clothed in purple when they are really without covering, or who imagine that they have an earthenware head or are nothing but pumpkins or are made of glass. But they are mad, and I should not be any the less insane were I to follow examples so extravagant.

At the same time I must remember that I am a man, and that consequently I am in the habit of sleeping, and in my dreams representing to myself the same things or sometimes even less probable things, than do those who are insane in their waking moments. How often has it happened to me that in the night I dreamt that I found myself in this particular place, that I was dressed and seated near the fire, whilst in reality I was lying undressed in bed! At this moment it does indeed seem to me that it is with eyes awake that I am looking at this paper; that this head which I move is not asleep, that it is deliberately and of set purpose that I extend my hand and perceive it; what happens in sleep does not appear so clear nor so distinct as does all this. But in thinking over this I remind myself that on many occasions I have in sleep been deceived by similar illusions, and in dwelling carefully on this reflection I see so manifestly that there are no certain indications by which we may clearly distinguish wakefulness from sleep that I am lost in astonishment. And my astonishment is such that it is almost capable of persuading me that I now dream.

Now let us assume that we are asleep and that all these particulars, e.g. that we open our eyes, shake our head, extend our hands, and so on, are but false delusions; and let us reflect that possibly neither our hands nor our whole body are such as they appear to us to be. At the same time we must at least confess that the things which are represented to us in sleep are like painted representations which can only have been formed as the counterparts of something real and true, and that in this way those general things at least, i.e. eyes, a head, hands, and a whole body, are not imaginary things, but things really existent. For, as a matter of fact, painters, even when they study with the greatest skill to represent sirens and satyrs by forms the most strange and extraordinary, cannot give them natures which are entirely new, but merely make a certain medley of the members of different animals; or if their imagination is extravagant enough to invent something so novel that nothing similar has ever before been seen, and that then their work represents a thing purely fictitious and absolutely false, it is certain all the same that the colours of which this is composed are necessarily real. And for the same reason, although these general things, to wit, [a body], eyes, a head, hands, and such like, may be imaginary, we are bound at the same time to confess that there are at least some other objects yet more simple and more universal, which are real and true; and of these just in the same way as with certain real colours, all these images of things which dwell in our thoughts, whether true and real or false and fantastic, are formed.

To such a class of things pertains corporeal nature in general, and its extension, the figure of extended things, their quantity or magnitude and number, as also the place in which they are, the time which measures their duration, and so on.

That is possibly why our reasoning is not unjust when we conclude from this that Physics, Astronomy, Medicine and all other sciences which have as their end the consideration of composite things, are very dubious and uncertain; but that Arithmetic, Geometry and other sciences of that kind which only treat of things that are very simple and very general, without taking great trouble to ascertain whether they are actually existent or not, contain some measure of certainty and an element of the indubitable. For whether I am awake or asleep, two and three together always form five, and the square can never have more than four sides, and it does not seem possible that truths so clear and apparent can be suspected of any falsity [or uncertainty].

Nevertheless I have long had fixed in my mind the belief that an all-powerful God existed by whom I have been created such as I am. But how do I know that He has not brought it to pass that there is no earth, no heaven, no extended body, no magnitude, no place, and that nevertheless [I possess the perceptions of all these things and that] they seem to me to exist just exactly as I now see them? And, besides, as I sometimes imagine that others deceive themselves in the things which they think they know best, how do I know that I am not deceived every time that I add two and three, or count the sides of a square, or judge of things yet simpler, if anything simpler can be imagined? But possibly God has not desired that I should be thus deceived, for He is said to be supremely good. If, however, it is contrary to His goodness to have made me such that I constantly deceive myself, it would also appear to be contrary to His goodness to permit me to be sometimes deceived, and nevertheless I cannot doubt that He does permit this.

There may indeed be those who would prefer to deny the existence of a God so powerful, rather than believe that all other things are uncertain. But let us not oppose them for the present, and grant that all that is here said of a God is a fable; nevertheless in whatever way they suppose that I have arrived at the state of being that I have reached—whether they attribute it to fate or to accident, or make out that it is by a continual succession of antecedents, or by some other method—since to err and deceive oneself is a defect, it is clear that the greater will be the probability of my being so imperfect as to deceive myself ever, as is the Author to whom they assign my origin the less powerful. To these reasons I have certainly nothing to reply, but at the end I feel constrained to confess that there is nothing in all that I formerly believed to be true, of which I cannot in some measure doubt, and that not merely through want of thought or through levity, but for reasons which are very powerful and maturely considered; so that henceforth I ought not the less carefully to refrain from giving credence to these opinions than to that which is manifestly false, if I desire to arrive at any certainty [in the sciences].

But it is not sufficient to have made these remarks, we must also be careful to keep them in mind. For these ancient and commonly held opinions still revert frequently to my mind, long and familiar custom having given them the right to occupy my mind against my inclination and rendered them almost masters of my belief; nor will I ever lose the habit of deferring to them or of placing my confidence in them, so long as I consider them as they really are, i.e. opinions in some measure doubtful, as I have just shown, and at the same time highly probable, so that there is much more reason to believe in than to deny them. That is why I consider that I shall not be acting amiss, if, taking of set purpose a contrary belief, I allow myself to be deceived, and for a certain time pretend that all these opinions are entirely false and imaginary, until at last, having thus balanced any former prejudices with my latter [so that they cannot divert my opinions more to one side than to the other], my judgment will no longer be dominated by bad usage or turned away from the right knowledge of the truth. For I am assured that there can be neither peril nor error in this course, and that I cannot at present yield too much to distrust, since I am not considering the question of action, but only of knowledge.

I shall then suppose, not that God who is supremely good and the fountain of truth, but some evil genius not less powerful than deceitful, has employed his whole energies in deceiving me; I shall consider that the heavens, the earth, colours, figures, sound, and all other external things are nought but the illusions and dreams of which this genius has availed himself in order to lay traps for my credulity; I shall consider myself as having no hands, no eyes, no flesh, no blood, nor any senses, yet falsely believing myself to possess all these things; I shall remain obstinately attached to this idea, and if by this means it is not in my power to arrive at the knowledge of any truth, I may at least do what is in my power [i.e. suspend my judgment], and with firm purpose avoid giving credence to any false thing, or being imposed upon by this arch deceiver, however powerful and deceptive he may be. But this task is a laborious one, and insensibly a certain lassitude leads me into the course of my ordinary life. And just as a captive who in sleep enjoys an imaginary liberty, when he begins to suspect that his liberty is but a dream, fears to awaken, and conspires with these agreeable illusions that the deception may be prolonged, so insensibly of my own accord I fall back into my former opinions, and I dread awakening from this slumber, lest the laborious wakefulness which would follow the tranquility of this repose should have to be spent not in daylight, but in the excessive darkness of the difficulties which have just been discussed.

II. OF THE NATURE OF THE HUMAN MIND . . .

The Meditation of yesterday filled my mind with so many doubts that it is no longer in my power to forget them. And yet I do not see in what manner I can resolve them; and, just as if I had all of a sudden fallen into very deep water, I am so disconcerted that I can neither make certain of setting my feet on the bottom, nor can I swim and so support myself on the surface. I shall nevertheless make an effort and follow anew the same path as that on which I yesterday entered, i.e. I shall proceed by setting aside all that in which the least doubt could be supposed to exist, just as if I had discovered that it was absolutely false; and I shall ever follow in this road until I have met with something which is certain, or at least, if I can do nothing else, until I have learned for certain that there is nothing in the world that is certain. Archimedes, in order that he might draw the terrestrial globe out of its place, and transport it elsewhere, demanded only that one point should be fixed and immoveable; in the same way I shall have the right to conceive high hopes if I am happy enough to discover one thing only which is certain and indubitable.

I suppose, then, that all the things that I see are false; I persuade myself that nothing has ever existed of all that my fallacious memory represents to me. I consider that I possess no senses; I imagine that body, figure, extension, movement and place are but the fictions of my mind. What, then, can be esteemed as true? Perhaps nothing at all, unless that there is nothing in the world that is certain.

But how can I know there is not something different from those things that I have just considered, of which one cannot have the slightest doubt? Is there not some God, or some other being by whatever name we call it, who puts these reflections into my mind? That is not necessary, for is it not possible that I am capable of producing them myself? I myself, am I not at least something? But I have already denied that I had senses and body. Yet I hesitate, for what follows from that? Am I so dependent on body and senses that I cannot exist without these? But I was persuaded that there was nothing in all the world, that there was no heaven, no earth, that there were no minds, nor any bodies: was I not then likewise persuaded that I did not exist? Not at all; of a surety I myself did exist since I persuaded myself of something [or merely because I thought of something]. But there is some deceiver or other, very powerful and very cunning, who ever employs his ingenuity in deceiving me. Then without doubt I exist also if he deceives me, and let him deceive me as much as he will, he can never cause me to be nothing so long as I think that I am something. So that after having reflected well and carefully examined all things, we must come to the definite conclusion that this proposition: I am, I exist, is necessarily true each time that I pronounce it, or that I mentally conceive it.

But I do not yet know clearly enough what I am, I who am certain that I am; and hence I must be careful to see that I do not imprudently take some other object in place of myself, and thus that I do not go astray in respect of this knowledge that I hold to be the most certain and most evident of all that I have formerly learned. That is why I shall now consider anew what I believed myself to be before I embarked upon these last reflections; and of my former opinions I shall withdraw all that might even in a small degree be invalidated by the reasons which I have just brought forward, in order that there may be nothing at all left beyond what is absolutely certain and indubitable.

What then did I formerly believe myself to be? Undoubtedly I believed myself to be a man. But what is a man? Shall I say a reasonable animal? Certainly not; for then I should have to inquire what an animal is, and what is reasonable; and thus from a single question I should insensibly fall into an infinitude of others more difficult; and I should not wish to waste the little time and leisure remaining to me in trying to unravel subtleties like these. But I shall rather stop here to consider the thoughts which of themselves spring up in my mind, and which were not inspired by anything beyond my own nature alone when I applied myself to the consideration of my being. In the first place, then, I considered myself as having a face, hands, arms, and all that system of members composed of bones and flesh as seen in a corpse which I designated by the name of body. In addition to this I considered that I was nourished, that I walked, that I felt, and that I thought, and I referred all these actions to the soul: but I did not stop to consider what the soul was, or if I did stop, I imagined that it was something extremely rare and subtle like a wind, a flame, or an ether, which was spread throughout my grosser parts. As to body I had no manner of doubt about its nature, but thought I had a very clear knowledge of it; and if I had desired to explain it according to the notions that I had then formed of it, I should have described it thus: By the body I understand all that which can be defined by a certain figure: something which can be confined in a certain place, and which can fill a given space in such a way that every other body will be excluded from it; which can be perceived either by touch, or by sight, or by hearing, or by taste, or by smell: which can be moved in many ways not, in truth, by itself, but by something which is foreign to it, by which it is touched [and from which it receives impressions]: for to have the power of self-movement, as also of feeling or of thinking, I did not consider to appertain to the nature of body: on the contrary, I was rather astonished to find that faculties similar to them existed in some bodies.

But what am I, now that I suppose that there is a certain genius which is extremely powerful, and, if I may say so, malicious, who employs all his powers in deceiving me? Can I affirm that I possess the least of all those things which I have just said pertain to the nature of body? I pause to consider, I revolve all these things in my mind, and I find none of which I can say that it pertains to me. It would be tedious to stop to enumerate them. Let us pass to the attributes of soul and see if there is any one which is in me? What of nutrition or walking [the first mentioned]? But if it is so that I have no body it is also true that I can neither walk nor take nourishment. Another attribute is sensation. But one cannot feel without body, and besides I have thought I perceived many things during sleep that I recognised in my waking moments as not having been experienced at all. What of thinking? I find here that thought is an attribute that belongs to me: it alone cannot be separated from me. I am, I exist, that is certain. But how often? Just when I think; for it might possibly be the case if I ceased entirely to think, that I should likewise cease altogether to exist. I do not now admit anything which is not necessarily true: to speak accurately I am not more than a thing which thinks, that is to say a mind or a soul, or an understanding, or a reason, which are terms whose significance was formerly unknown to me. I am, however, a real thing and really exist; but what thing? I have answered: a thing which thinks.

And what more? I shall exercise my imagination [in order to see if I am not something more]. I am not a collection of members which we call the human body: I am not a subtle air distributed through these members, I am not a wind, a fire, a vapour, a breath, nor anything at all which I can imagine or conceive; because I have assumed that all these were nothing. Without changing that supposition I find that I only leave myself certain of the fact that I am somewhat. But perhaps it is true that these same things which I supposed were non-existent because they are unknown to me, are really not different from the self which I know. I am not sure about this, I shall not dispute about it now; I can only give judgment on things that are known to me. I know that I exist, and I inquire what I am, I whom I know to exist. But it is very certain that the knowledge of my existence taken in its precise significance does not depend on things whose existence is not yet known to me; consequently it does not depend on those which I can feign in imagination. And indeed the very term *feign* in imagination proves to me my error, for I really do this if I image myself a something, since to imagine is nothing else than to contemplate the figure or image of a corporeal thing. But I already know for certain that I am, and that it may be that all these images, and, speaking generally, all things that relate to the nature of body are nothing but dreams [and chimeras]. For this reason I see clearly that I have as little reason to say, 'I shall stimulate my imagination in order to know more distinctly what I am,' than if I were to say, 'I am now awake, and I perceive somewhat that is real and true: but because I do not yet perceive it distinctly enough, I shall go to sleep of express purpose, so that my dreams may represent the perception with greatest truth and evidence.' And, thus, I know for certain that nothing of all that I can understand by means of my imagination belongs to this knowledge which I have of myself, and that it is necessary to recall the mind from this mode of thought with the utmost diligence in order that it may be able to know its own nature with perfect distinctness.

But what then am I? A thing which thinks. What is a thing which thinks? It is a thing which doubts, understands, [conceives], affirms, denies, wills, refuses, which also imagines and feels.

Certainly it is no small matter if all these things pertain to my nature. But why should they not so pertain? Am I not that being who now doubts nearly everything, who nevertheless understands certain things, who affirms that one only is true, who denies all the others, who desires to know more, is averse from being deceived, who imagines many things, sometimes indeed despite his will, and who perceives many likewise, as by the intervention of the bodily organs? Is there nothing in all this which is as true as it is certain that I exist, even though I should always sleep and though he who has given me being employed all his ingenuity in deceiving me? Is there likewise any one of these attributes which can be distinguished from my thought, or which might be said to be separated from myself? For it is so evident of itself that it is I who doubts, who understands, and who desires, that there is no reason here to add anything to explain it. And I have certainly the power of imagining likewise; for although it may happen (as I formerly supposed) that none of the things which I imagine are true, nevertheless this power of imagining does not cease to be really in use, and it forms part of my thought. Finally, I am the same who feels, that is to say, who perceives certain things, as by the organs of sense, since in truth I see light, I hear noise, I feel heat. But it will be said that these phenomena are false and that I am dreaming. Let it be so; still it is at least quite certain that it seems to me that I see light, that I hear noise and that I feel heat. That cannot be false; properly speaking it is what is in me called feeling, and used in this precise sense that is no other thing than thinking.

From this time I begin to know what I am with a little more clearness and distinction than before; but nevertheless it still seems to me, and I cannot prevent myself from thinking, that corporeal things, whose images are framed by thought, which are tested by the senses, are much more distinctly known than that obscure part of me which does not come under the imagination. Although really it is very strange to say that I know and understand more distinctly these things whose existence seems to me dubious, which are unknown to me, and which do not belong to me, than others of the truth of which I am convinced, which are known to me and which pertain to my real nature, in a word, than myself. But I see clearly how the case stands: my mind loves to wander, and cannot yet suffer itself to be retained within the just limits of truth. Very good, let us once more give it the freest rein, so that, when afterwards we seize the proper occasion for pulling up, it may the more easily be regulated and controlled.

Let us begin by considering the commonest matters, those which we believe to be the most distinctly comprehended, to wit, the bodies which we touch and see; not indeed bodies in general, for these general ideas are usually a little more confused, but let us consider one body in particular. Let us take, for example, this piece of wax: it has been taken quite freshly from the hive, and it has not yet lost the sweetness of the honey which it contains; it still retains somewhat of the odour of the flowers from which it has been culled; its colour, its figure, its size are apparent; it is hard, cold, easily handled, and if you strike it with the finger, it will emit a sound. Finally all the things which are requisite to cause us distinctly to recognise a body, are met with in it. But notice that while I speak and approach the fire what remained of the taste is exhaled, the smell evaporates, the colour alters, the figure is destroyed, the size increases, it becomes liquid, it heats, scarcely can one handle it, and when one strikes it, no sound is emitted. Does the same wax remain after this change? We must confess that it remains; none would judge otherwise. What then did I know so distinctly in this piece of wax? It could certainly be nothing of all that the senses brought to my notice, since all these things which fall under taste, smell, sight, touch, and hearing, are found to be changed, and yet the same wax remains.

Perhaps it was what I now think, viz. that this wax was not that sweetness of honey, nor that agreeable scent of flowers, nor that particular whiteness, nor that figure, nor that sound, but simply a body which a little while before appeared to me as perceptible under these forms, and which is now perceptible under others. But what, precisely, is it that I imagine when I form such conceptions? Let us attentively consider this, and, abstracting from all that does not belong to the wax, let us see what remains. Certainly nothing remains excepting a certain extended thing which is flexible and movable. But what is the meaning of flexible and movable? Is it not that I imagine that this piece of wax being round is capable of becoming square and of passing from a square to a triangular figure? No, certainly it is not that, since I imagine it admits of an infinitude of similar changes, and I nevertheless do not know how to compass the infinitude by my imagination, and consequently this conception which I have of the wax is not brought about by the faculty of imagination. What now is this extension? Is it not also unknown? For it becomes greater when the wax is melted, greater when it is boiled, and greater still when the heat increases; and I should not conceive [clearly] according to truth what wax is, if I did not think that even this piece that we are considering is capable of receiving more variations in extension than I have ever imagined. We must then grant that I could not even understand through the imagination what this piece of wax is, and that it is my mind alone which perceives it. I say this piece of wax in particular, for as to wax in general it is yet clearer. But what is this piece of wax which cannot be understood excepting by the [understanding or] mind? It is certainly the same that I see, touch, imagine, and finally it is the same which I have always believed it to be from the beginning. But what must particularly be observed is that its perception is neither an act of vision, nor of touch, nor of imagination, and has never been such although it may have appeared formerly to be so, but only an intuition of the mind, which may be imperfect and confused as it was formerly, or clear and distinct as it is at present, according as my attention is more or less directed to the elements which are found in it, and of which it is composed.

Yet in the meantime I am greatly astonished when I consider [the great feebleness of mind] and its proneness to fall [insensibly] into error; for although without giving expression to my thoughts I consider all this in my own mind, words often impede me and I am almost deceived by the terms of ordinary language. For we say that we see the same wax, if it is present, and not that we simply judge that it is the same from its having the same colour and figure. From this I should conclude that I knew the wax by means of vision and not simply by the intuition of the mind; unless by chance I remember that, when looking from a window and saying I see men who pass in the street, I really do not see them, but infer that what I see is men, just as I say that I see wax. And yet what do I see from the window but hats and coats which may cover automatic machines? Yet I judge these to be men. And similarly solely by the faculty of judgment which rests in my mind, I comprehend that which I believed I saw with my eyes.

A man who makes it his aim to raise his knowledge above the common should be ashamed to derive the occasion for doubting from the forms of speech invented by the vulgar; I prefer to pass on and consider whether I had a more evident and perfect conception of what the wax was when I first perceived it, and when I believed I knew it by means of the external senses or at least by the common sense as it is called, that is to say by the imaginative faculty, or whether my present conception is clearer now that I have most carefully examined what it is, and in what way it can be known. It would certainly be absurd to doubt as to this. For what was there in this first perception which was distinct? What was there which might not as well have been perceived by any of the animals? But when I distinguish the wax from its external forms, and when, just as if I had taken from it its vestments, I consider it quite naked, it is certain that although some error may still be found in my judgment, I can nevertheless not perceive it thus without a human mind.

But finally what shall I say of this mind, that is, of myself, for up to this point I do not admit in myself anything but mind? What then, I who seem to perceive this piece of wax so distinctly, do I not know myself, not only with much more truth and certainty, but also with much more distinctness and clearness? For if I judge that the wax is or exists from the fact that I see it, it certainly follows much more clearly that I am or that I exist myself from the fact that I see it. For it may be that what I see is not really wax, it may also be that I do not possess eyes with which to see anything; but it cannot be that when I see, or (for I no longer take account of the distinction) when I think I see, that I myself who think am nought. So if I judge that the wax exists from the fact that I touch it, the same thing will follow, to wit, that I am; and if I judge that my imagination, or some other cause, whatever it is, persuades me that the wax exists, I shall still conclude the same. And what I have here remarked of wax may be applied to all other things which are external to me [and which are met with outside of me]. And further, if the [notion or] perception of wax has seemed to me clearer and more distinct, not only after the sight or the touch, but also after many other causes have rendered it quite manifest to me, with how much more [evidence] and distinctness must it be said that I now know myself, since all the reasons which contribute to the knowledge of wax, or any other body whatever, are yet better proofs of the nature of my mind! And there are so many other things in the mind itself which may contribute to the elucidation of its nature, that those which depend on body such as these just mentioned, hardly merit being taken into account.

But finally here I am, having insensibly reverted to the point I desired, for, since it is now manifest to me that even bodies are not properly speaking known by the senses or by the faculty of imagination, but by the understanding only, and since they are not known from the fact that they are seen or touched, but only because they are understood, I see clearly that there is nothing which is easier for me to know than my mind. But because it is difficult to rid oneself so promptly of an opinion to which one was accustomed for so long, it will be well that I should halt a little at this point, so that by the length of my meditation I may more deeply imprint on my memory this new knowledge.

In a short but delightful sketch entitled "My Own Life," David Hume (1711–1776) described himself as "a man of mild dispositions, of command of temper, of an open, social, and cheerful humor, capable of attachment, but little susceptible of enmity, and of great moderation in all my passions. . . . My company was not unacceptable to the young and careless, as well as to the studious and literary; and as I took a particular pleasure in the company of modest women, I had no reason to be displeased with the reception I met with from them."

Born and educated in Edinburgh, Hume published his Treatise of Human Nature *when he was only twenty-seven, but it attracted little notice.* An Inquiry Concerning Human Understanding *came a decade later, followed by* An Inquiry Concerning the Principles of Morals. *His fame, however, first resulted from his* Political Discourses *and* History of England. *The* Dialogues Concerning Natural Religion *was published (by Hume's choice) posthumously.*

The reading selection which follows is from Section IV of An Inquiry Concerning Human Understanding *(1748).*

PART I

All the objects of human reason or inquiry may naturally be divided into two kinds, to wit, "Relations of Ideas," and "Matters of Fact." Of the first kind are the sciences of Geometry, Algebra, and Arithmetic, and, in short, every affirmation which is either intuitively or demonstratively certain. *That the square of the hypotenuse is equal to the square of the two sides* is a proposition which expresses a relation between these figures. *That three times five is equal to the half of thirty* expresses a relation between these numbers. Propositions of this kind are discoverable by the mere operation of thought, without dependence on what is anywhere existent in the universe. Though there never were a circle or triangle in nature, the truths demonstrated by Euclid would forever retain their certainty and evidence.

Matters of fact, which are the second objects of human reason, are not ascertained in the same manner, nor is our evidence of their truth, however great, of a like nature with the foregoing. The contrary of every matter of fact is still possible, because it can never imply a contradiction and is conceived by the mind with the same facility and distinctness as if ever so conformable to reality. *That the sun will not rise tomorrow* is no less intelligible a proposition and implies no more contradiction than the affirmation *that it will rise.* We should in vain, therefore, attempt to demonstrate its falsehood. Were it demonstratively false, it would imply a contradiction and could never be distinctly conceived by the mind.

It may, therefore, be a subject worthy of curiosity to inquire what is the nature of that evidence which assures us of any real existence and matter of fact beyond the present testimony of our senses or the records of our memory. This part of philosophy, it is observable, had been little cultivated either by the ancients or moderns; and, therefore, our doubts and errors in the prosecution of so important an inquiry may be the more excusable while we march through such difficult paths without any guide or direction. They may even prove useful by exciting curiosity and destroying that implicit faith and security which is the bane of all reasoning and free inquiry. The discovery of defects in the common philosophy, if any such there be, will not, I presume, be a discouragement, but rather an incitement, as is usual, to attempt something more full and satisfactory than has yet been proposed to the public.

All reasonings concerning matter of fact seem to be founded on the relation of *cause* and *effect*. By means of that relation alone we can go beyond the evidence of our memory and senses. If you were to ask a man why he believes any matter of fact which is absent, for instance, that his friend is in the country or in France, he would give you a reason, and this reason would be some other fact: as a letter received from him or the knowledge of his former resolutions and promises. A man finding a watch or any other machine in a desert island would conclude that there had once been men in that island. All our reasonings concerning fact are of the same nature. And here it is constantly supposed that there is a connection between the present fact and that which is inferred from it. Were there nothing to bind them together, the inference would be entirely precarious. The hearing of an articulate voice and rational discourse in the dark assures us of the presence of some person. Why? Because these are the effects of the human make and fabric, and closely connected with it. If we anatomize all the other reasonings of this nature, we shall find that they are founded on the relation of cause and effect, and that this relation is either near or remote, direct or collateral. Heat and light are collateral effects of fire, and the one effect may justly be inferred from the other.

If we would satisfy ourselves, therefore, concerning the nature of that evidence which assures us of matters of fact, we must inquire how we arrive at the knowledge of cause and effect.

I shall venture to affirm, as a general proposition which admits of no exception, that the knowledge of this relation is not, in any instance, attained by reasonings *a priori*, but arises entirely from experience, when we find that any particular objects are constantly conjoined with each other. Let an object be presented to a man of ever so strong natural reason and abilities—if that object be entirely new to him, he will not be able, by the most accurate examination of its sensible qualities, to discover any of its causes or effects.

Adam, though his rational faculties be supposed, at the very first, entirely perfect, could not have inferred from the fluidity and transparency of water that it would suffocate him, or from the light and warmth of fire that it would consume him. No object ever discovers, by the qualities which appear to the senses, either the causes which produced it or the effects which will arise from it; nor can our reason, unassisted by experience, ever draw any inference concerning real existence and matter of fact.

This proposition, *that causes and effects are discoverable, not by reason, but by experience,* will readily be admitted with regard to such objects as we remember to have once been altogether unknown to us, since we must be conscious of the utter inability which we then lay under of foretelling what would arise from them. Present two smooth pieces of marble to a man who has no tincture of natural philosophy; he will never discover that they will adhere together in such a manner as to require great force to separate them in a direct line, while they make so small a resistance to a lateral pressure. Such events as bear little analogy to the common course of nature are also readily confessed to be known only by experience, nor does any man imagine that the explosion of gunpowder or the attraction of a loadstone could ever be discovered by arguments *a priori*. In like manner, when an effect is supposed to depend upon an intricate machinery or secret structure of parts, we make no difficulty in attributing all our knowledge of it to experience. Who will assert that he can give the ultimate reason why milk or bread is proper nourishment for a man, not for a lion or tiger?

But the same truth may not appear at first sight to have the same evidence with regard to events which have become familiar to us from our first appearance in the world, which bear a close analogy to the whole course of nature, and which are supposed to depend on the simple qualities of objects without any secret structure of parts. We are apt to imagine that we could discover these effects by the mere operation of our reason without experience. We fancy that, were we brought on a sudden into this world, we could at first have inferred that one billiard ball would communicate motion to another upon impulse, and that we needed not to have waited for the event in order to pronounce with certainty concerning it. Such is the influence of custom that where it is strongest it not only covers our natural ignorance but even conceals itself, and seems not to take place, merely because it is found in the highest degree.

But to convince us that all the laws of nature and all the operations of bodies without exception are known only by experience, the following reflections may perhaps suffice. Were any object presented to us, and were we required to pronounce concerning the effect which will result from it without consulting past observation, after what manner, I beseech you, must the mind proceed in this operation? It must invent or imagine some event which it ascribes to the object as its effect; and it is plain that this invention must be entirely arbitrary. The mind can never possibly find the effect in the supposed cause by the most accurate scrutiny and examination. For the effect is totally different from the cause, and consequently can never be discovered in it. Motion in the second billiard ball is a quite distinct event from motion in the first, nor is there anything in the one to suggest the smallest hint of the other. A stone or piece of metal raised into the air and left without any support immediately falls. But to consider the matter *a priori,* is there anything we discover in this situation which can beget the idea of a downward rather than an upward or any other motion in the stone or metal?

And as the first imagination or invention of a particular effect in all natural operations is arbitrary where we consult not experience, so must we also esteem the supposed tie or connection between the cause and effect which binds them together and renders it impossible that any other effect could result from the operation of that cause. When I see, for instance, a billiard ball moving in a straight line toward another, even suppose motion in the second ball should by accident be suggested to me as the result of their contact or impulse, may I not conceive that a hundred different events might as well follow from that cause? May not both these balls remain at absolute rest? May not the first ball return in a straight line or leap off from the second in any line or direction? All these suppositions are consistent and conceivable. Why, then, should we give the preference to one which is no more consistent or conceivable than the rest? All our reasonings *a priori* will never be able to show us any foundation for this preference.

In a word, then, every effect is a distinct event from its cause. It could not, therefore, be discovered in the cause, and the first invention or conception of it, *a priori,* must be entirely arbitrary. And even after it is suggested, the conjunction of it with the cause must appear equally arbitrary, since there are always many other effects which, to reason, must seem fully as consistent and natural. In vain, therefore, should we pretend to determine any single event or infer any cause or effect without the assistance of observation and experience.

Hence we may discover the reason why no philosopher who is rational and modest has ever pretended to assign the ultimate cause of any natural operation, or to show distinctly the action of that power which produces any single effect in the universe. It is confessed that the utmost effort of human reason is to reduce the principles productive of natural phenomena to a greater simplicity, and to resolve the many particular effects into a few general causes, by means of reasonings from analogy, experience, and observation. But as to the causes of these general causes, we should in vain attempt their discovery, nor shall we ever be able to satisfy ourselves by any particular explication of them. These ultimate springs and principles are totally shut up from human curiosity and inquiry. Elasticity, gravity, cohesion of parts, communication of motion by impulse—these are probably the ultimate causes and principles which we shall ever discover in nature; and we may esteem ourselves sufficiently happy if, by accurate inquiry and reasoning, we can trace up the particular phenomena to, or near to, these general principles. The most perfect philosophy of the natural kind only staves off our ignorance a little longer, as perhaps the most perfect philosophy of the moral or metaphysical kind serves only to discover larger portions of it. Thus the observation of human blindness and weakness is the result of all philosophy, and meets us, at every turn, in spite of our endeavors to elude or avoid it.

Nor is geometry, when taken into the assistance of natural philosophy, ever able to remedy this defect or lead us into the knowledge of ultimate causes by all that accuracy of reasoning for which it is so justly celebrated. Every part of mixed mathematics proceeds upon the supposition that certain laws are established by nature in her operations, and abstract reasonings are employed either to assist experience in the discovery of these laws or to determine their influence in particular instances where it depends upon any precise degree of distance and quantity. Thus it is a law of motion, discovered by experience, that the moment or force of any body in motion is in the compound ratio or proportion of its solid contents and its velocity, and, consequently, that a small force may remove the greatest obstacle or raise the greatest weight if by any contrivance or machinery we can increase the velocity of that force so as to make it an overmatch for its antagonist. Geometry assists us in the application of this law by giving us the just dimensions of all the parts and figures which can enter into any species of machine, but still the discovery of the law itself is owing merely to experience; and all the abstract reasonings in the world could never lead us one step toward the knowledge of it. When we reason *a priori* and consider merely any object or cause as it appears to the mind, independent of all observation, it never could suggest to us the notion of any distinct object, such as its effect, much less show us the inseparable and inviolable connection between them. A man must be very sagacious who could discover by reasoning that crystal is the effect of heat, and ice of cold, without being previously acquainted with the operation of these qualities.

PART II

But we have not yet attained any tolerable satisfaction with regard to the question first proposed. Each solution still gives rise to a new question as difficult as the foregoing and leads us on to further inquiries. When it is asked,

What is the nature of all our reasonings concerning matter of fact? the proper answer seems to be, That they are founded on the relation of cause and effect. When again it is asked, *What is the foundation of all our reasonings and conclusions concerning that relation?* it may be replied in one word, *experience*. But if we still carry on our sifting humor and ask, *What is the foundation of all conclusions from experience?* this implies a new question which may be of more difficult solution and explication. Philosophers that give themselves airs of superior wisdom and sufficiency have a hard task when they encounter persons of inquisitive dispositions, who push them from every corner to which they retreat, and who are sure at last to bring them to some dangerous dilemma. The best expedient to prevent this confusion is to be modest in our pretensions and even to discover the difficulty ourselves before it is objected to us. By this means we may make a kind of merit of our very ignorance.

I shall content myself in this section with an easy task and shall pretend only to give a negative answer to the question here proposed. I say, then, that even after we have experience of the operations of cause and effect, our conclusions from that experience are *not* founded on reasoning or any process of the understanding. This answer we must endeavor both to explain and to defend.

It must certainly be allowed that nature has kept us at a great distance from all her secrets and has afforded us only the knowledge of a few superficial qualities of objects, while she conceals from us those powers and principles on which the influence of these objects entirely depends. Our senses inform us of the color, weight, and consistency of bread, but neither sense nor reason can ever inform us of those qualities which fit it for the nourishment and support of the human body. Sight or feeling conveys an idea of the actual motion of bodies, but as to that wonderful force or power which would carry on a moving body forever in a continued change of place, and which bodies never lose but by communicating it to others, of this we cannot form the most distant conception. But notwithstanding this ignorance of natural powers and principles, we always presume when we see like sensible qualities that they have like secret powers, and expect that effects similar to those which we have experienced will follow from them. If a body of like color and consistency with that bread which we have formerly eaten be presented to us, we make no scruple of repeating the experiment and foresee with certainty like nourishment and support. Now this is a process of the mind or thought of which I would willingly know the foundation. It is allowed on all hands that there is no known connection between the sensible qualities and the secret powers, and, consequently, that the mind is not led to form such a conclusion concerning their constant and regular conjunction by anything which it knows of their nature. As to past *experience*, it can be allowed to give *direct* and *certain* information of those precise objects only, and that precise period of time which fell under its cognizance: But why this experience should be extended to future times and to other objects which, for aught we know, may be only in appearance similar, this is the main question on which I would insist. The bread which I formerly ate nourished me; that is, a body of such sensible qualities was, at that time, endued with such secret powers. But does it follow that other bread must also nourish me at another time, and that like sensible qualities must always be attended with like secret powers? The consequence seems nowise necessary. At least, it must be acknowledged that there is here a consequence drawn by the mind that there is a certain step taken, a process of thought, and an inference which wants to be explained. These two propositions are far from being the same: *I have found that such an object has always been attended with such an effect*, and *I forsee that other objects which are in appearance similar will be attended with similar effects*. I shall allow, if you please, that the one proposition may justly be inferred from the other: I know, in fact, that it always is inferred. But if you insist that the inference is made by a chain of reasoning, I desire you to produce that reasoning. The connection between these propositions is not intuitive. There is required a medium which may enable the mind to draw such an inference, if indeed it be drawn by reasoning and argument. What that medium is I must confess passes my comprehension; and it is incumbent on those to produce it who assert that it really exists and is the original of all our conclusions concerning matter of fact.

This negative argument must certainly, in process of time, become altogether convincing if many penetrating and able philosophers shall turn their inquiries this way, and no one be ever able to discover any connecting proposition or intermediate step which supports the understanding in this conclusion. But as the question is yet new, every reader may not trust so far to his own penetration as to conclude, because an argument escapes his inquiry, that therefore it does not really exist. For this reason it may be requisite to venture upon a more difficult task, and, enumerating all the branches of human knowledge, endeavor to show that none of them can afford such an argument.

All reasonings may be divided into two kinds, namely, demonstrative reasoning, or that concerning relations of ideas, and moral reasoning, or that concerning matter of fact and existence. That there are no demonstrative arguments in the case seems evident, since it implies no contradiction that the course of nature may change and that an object, seemingly like those which we have experienced, may be attended with different or contrary effects. May I not clearly and distinctly conceive that a body, falling from the clouds and which in all other respects resembles snow, has yet the taste of salt or feeling of fire? Is there any more intelligible proposition than to affirm that all the trees will flourish in December and January, and will decay in May and June? Now, whatever is intelligible and can be distinctly conceived implies no contradiction and can never be proved false by any demonstrative argument or abstract reasoning *a priori*.

If we be, therefore, engaged by arguments to put trust in past experience and make it the standard of our future judgment, these arguments must be probable only, or such as regard matter of fact and real existence, according to the division above mentioned. But that there is no argument of this kind must appear if our explication of that species of reasoning be admitted as solid and satisfactory. We have said that all arguments concerning existence are founded on the relation of cause and effect, that our knowledge of that relation is derived entirely from experience, and that all our experimental conclusions proceed upon the supposition that the future will be conformable to the past. To endeavor, therefore, the proof of this last supposition by probable arguments, or arguments regarding existence, must be evidently going in a circle and taking that for granted which is the very point in question.

In reality, all arguments from experience are founded on the similarity which we discover among natural objects, and by which we are induced to expect effects similar to those which we have found to follow from such objects. And though none but a fool or madman will ever pretend to dispute the authority of experience or to reject that great guide of human life, it may surely be allowed a philosopher to have so much curiosity at least as to examine the principle of human nature which gives this mighty authority to experience and makes us draw advantage from that similarity which nature has placed among different objects. From causes which appear similar, we expect similar effects. This is the sum of all our experimental conclusions. Now it seems evident that, if this conclusion were formed by reason, it would be as perfect at first, and upon one instance, as after ever so long a course of experience; but the case is far otherwise. Nothing so like as eggs, yet no one, on account of this appearing similarity, expects the same taste and relish in all of them. It is only after a long course of uniform experiments in any kind that we attain a firm reliance and security with regard to a particular event. Now, where is that process of reasoning which, from one instance, draws a conclusion so different from that which it infers from a hundred instances that are nowise different from that single one? This question I propose as much for the sake of information as with an intention of raising difficulties. I cannot find, I cannot imagine any such reasoning. But I keep my mind still open to instruction if anyone will vouchsafe to bestow it on me.

Should it be said that, from a number of uniform experiments, we *infer*

479

a connection between the sensible qualities and the secret powers, this, I must confess, seems the same difficulty, couched in different terms. The question still occurs, On what process of argument is this *inference* founded? Where is the medium, the interposing ideas which join propositions so very wide of each other? It is confessed that the color, consistency, and other sensible qualities of bread appear not of themselves to have any connection with the secret powers of nourishment and support; for otherwise we could infer these secret powers from the first appearance of these sensible qualities without the aid of experience, contrary to the sentiment of all philosophers, and contrary to plain matter of fact. Here, then, is our natural state of ignorance with regard to the powers and influence of all objects. How is this remedied by experience? It only shows us a number of uniform effects resulting from certain objects, and teaches us that those particular objects, at that particular time, were endowed with such powers and forces. When a new object endowed with similar sensible qualities is produced, we expect similar powers and forces, and look for a like effect. From a body of like color and consistency with bread, we expect like nourishment and support. But this surely is a step or progress of the mind which wants to be explained. When a man says, *I have found, in all past instances, such sensible qualities, conjoined with such secret powers*, and when he says, *similar sensible qualities will always be conjoined with similar secret powers*, he is not guilty of a tautology, nor are these propositions in any respect the same. You say that the one proposition is an inference from the other; but you must confess that the inference is not intuitive, neither is it demonstrative. Of what nature is it then? To say it is experimental is begging the question. For all inferences from experience suppose, as their foundation, that the future will resemble the past and that similar powers will be conjoined with similar sensible qualities. If there be any suspicion that the course of nature may change, and that the past may be no rule for the future, all experience becomes useless and can give rise to no inference or conclusion. It is impossible, therefore, that any arguments from experience can prove this resemblance of the past to the future, since all these arguments are founded on the supposition of that resemblance. Let the course of things be allowed hitherto ever so regular, that alone, without some new argument or inference, proves not that for the future it will continue so. In vain do you pretend to have learned the nature of bodies from your past experience. Their secret nature, and consequently all their efforts and influence, may change without any change in their sensible qualities. This happens sometimes, and with regard to some objects. Why may it not happen always, and with regard to all objects? What logic, what process of argument secures you against this supposition? My practice, you say, refutes my doubts. But you mistake the purport of my question. As an agent, I am quite satisfied in the point; but as a philosopher who has some share of curiosity, I will not say skepticism, I want to learn the foundation of this inference. No reading, no inquiry has yet been able to remove my difficulty or give me satisfaction in a matter of such importance. Can I do better than propose the difficulty to the public, even though, perhaps, I have small hopes of obtaining a solution? We shall at least, by this means, be sensible of our ignorance, if we do not augment our knowledge.

I must confess that a man is guilty of unpardonable arrogance who concludes, because an argument has escaped his own investigation, that therefore it does not really exist. I must also confess that, though all the learned, for several ages, should have employed themselves in fruitless search upon any subject, it may still, perhaps, be rash to conclude positively that the subject must therefore pass all human comprehension. Even though we examine all the sources of our knowledge and conclude them unfit for such a subject, there may still remain a suspicion that the enumeration is not complete or the examination not accurate. But with regard to the present subject, there are some considerations which seem to remove all this accusation of arrogance or suspicion of mistake.

It is certain that the most ignorant and stupid peasants, nay infants, nay even brute beasts, improve by experience and learn the qualities of natural objects by observing the effects which result from them. When a child has felt the sensation of pain from touching the flame of a candle brought on a sudden into this world; he would, indeed, immediately observe a continual succession of objects and one event following another, but he would not be able to discover anything further. He would not at first, by any reasoning, be able to reach the idea of cause and effect, since the particular powers by which all natural operations are performed never appear to the senses; nor is it reasonable to conclude, merely because one event in one instance precedes another, that therefore the one is the cause, the other the effect. The conjunction may be arbitrary and casual. There may be no reason to infer the existence of one from the appearance of the other: and, in a word, such a person without more experience could never employ his conjecture or reasoning concerning any matter of fact or be assured of anything beyond what was immediately present to his memory or senses.

Suppose again that he has acquired more experience and has lived so long in the world as to have observed similar objects or events to be constantly conjoined together—what is the consequence of this experience? He immediately infers the existence of one object from the appearance of the other, yet he has not, by all his experience, acquired any idea or knowledge of the secret power by which the one object produces the other, nor is it by any process of reasoning he is engaged to draw this inference; but still he finds himself determined to draw it, and though he should be convinced that his understanding has no part in the operation, he would nevertheless continue in the same course of thinking. There is some other principle which determines him to form such a conclusion.

This principle is *custom* or *habit*. For wherever the repetition of any particular act or operation produces a propensity to renew the same act or operation without being impelled by any reasoning or process of the understanding, we always say that this propensity is the effect of *custom*. By employing that word we pretend not to have given the ultimate reason of such a propensity. We only point out a principle of human nature which is universally acknowledged, and which is well known by its effects. Perhaps we can push our inquiries no further or pretend to give the cause of this cause, but must rest contented with it as the ultimate principle which we can assign of all our conclusions from experience. It is sufficient satisfaction that we can go so far without repining at the narrowness of our faculties, because they will carry us no further. And it is certain we here advance a very intelligible proposition at least, if not a true one, when we assert that after the constant conjunction of two objects, heat and flame, for instance, weight and solidity, we are determined by custom alone to expect the one from the appearance of the other. This hypothesis seems even the only one which explains the difficulty why we draw from a thousand instances an inference which we are not able to draw from one instance that is in no respect different from them. Reason is incapable of any such variation. The conclusions which it draws from considering one circle are the same which it would form upon surveying all the circles in the universe. But no man, having seen only one body move after being impelled by another, could infer that every other body will move after a like impulse. All inferences from experience, therefore, are effects of custom, not of reasoning.

Custom, then, is the great guide of human life. It is that principle alone which renders our experience useful to us and makes us expect, for the future, a similar train of events with those which have appeared in the past. Without the influence of custom we should be entirely ignorant of every matter of fact beyond what is immediately present to the memory and senses. We should never know how to adjust means to ends or to employ our natural powers in the production of any effect. There would be an end at once of all action as well as of the chief part of speculation.

But here it may be proper to remark that though our conclusions from experience carry us beyond our memory and senses and assure us of matters of fact which happened in the most distant places and most remote ages, yet some fact must always be present to the senses or memory from which we may first proceed in drawing these conclusions. A man who should find in a desert country the remains of pompous buildings would conclude that the country had, in ancient times, been cultivated by civilized inhabitants; but did nothing of this nature occur to him, he could never form such an inference. We learn the events of former ages from history, but then we must peruse the volume in which this instruction is contained, and thence carry up our inferences from one testimony to another, till we arrive at the eye-witnesses and spectators of these distant events. In a word, if we proceed not upon some fact present to the memory or senses, our reasonings would be merely hypothetical; and however the particular links might be connected with each other, the whole chain of inferences would have nothing to support it, nor could we ever, by its means, arrive at the knowledge of any real existence. If I ask why you believe any particular matter of fact which you relate, you must tell me some reason; and this reason will be some other fact connected with it. But as you cannot proceed after this manner *in infinitum*, you must at last terminate in some fact which is present to your memory or senses or must allow that your belief is entirely without foundation.

What, then, is the conclusion of the whole matter? A simple one, though, it must be confessed, pretty remote from the common theories of philosophy. All belief of matter of fact or real existence is derived merely from some object present to the memory or senses and a customary conjunction between that and some other object; or, in other words, having found, in many instances, that any two kinds of objects, flame and heat, snow and cold, have always been conjoined together: if flame or snow be presented anew to the senses, the mind is carried by custom to expect heat or cold, and to *believe* that such a quality does exist and will discover itself upon a nearer approach. This belief is the necessary result of placing the mind in such circumstances. It is an operation of the soul, when we are so situated, as unavoidable as to feel the passion of love, when we receive benefits; or hatred, when we meet with injuries. All these operations are a species of natural instincts, which no reasoning or process of the thought and understanding is able either to produce or to prevent. . . .

theodore roszak   EYES OF FLESH, EYES OF FIRE

Theodore Roszak (1933–   ) has a Ph.D. from Princeton and has taught history at Stanford and at California State College at Hayward. His feelings about the educational establishment are, to say the very least, mixed. He is the editor of (and contributor to) The Dissenting Academy, *a volume which vigorously attacks the typical academician and his school on several counts. However, Roszak was hopeful about the phenomena he described in* The Making of a Counter Culture (1968), *from which the following selection is taken. He has also contributed frequently to* The Nation *and has recently edited* Sources: An Anthology of Contemporary Materials Useful for Preserving Personal Sanity While Braving the Great Technological Wilderness—*a title which is emblematic of where Roszak stands.*

"What," it will be Question'd, "When the Sun rises, do you not see a round disk of fire somewhat like a Guinea?" O no, no, I see an Innumerable company of the Heavenly host crying, "Holy, Holy is the Lord God Almighty."

—William Blake

What are we to say of the man who fixes his eye on the sun and does not see the sun, but sees instead a chorus of flaming seraphim announcing the glory of God? Surely we shall have to set him down as mad . . . unless he can coin his queer vision into the legal tender of elegant verse. Then, perhaps, we shall see fit to assign him a special status, a pigeonhole: call him "poet" and allow him to validate his claim to intellectual respectability by way of metaphorical license. Then we can say, "He did not *really* see what he says he saw. No, not at all. He only put it that way to lend color to his speech . . . as poets are in the professional habit of doing. It is a lyrical turn of phrase, you see: just that and nothing more." And doubtless all the best, all the most objective scholarship on the subject would support us in our perfectly sensible interpretation. It would tell us, for example, that the poet Blake, under the influence of Swedenborgian mysticism, developed a style based on esoteric visionary correspondences and was, besides, a notorious, if gifted, eccentric. Etc. Etc. Footnote.

In such fashion, we confidently discount and denature the visionary experience, and the technocratic order of life rolls on undeterred, obedient to the scientific reality principle. From such militant rationality the technocracy must permit no appeal.

Yet, if there is to be an alternative to the technocracy, there *must* be an appeal from this reductive rationality which objective consciousness dictates. This, so I have argued, is the primary project of our counter culture: to proclaim a new heaven and a new earth so vast, so marvelous that the inordinate claims of technical expertise must of necessity withdraw in the presence of such splendor to a subordinate and marginal status in the lives of men. To create and broadcast such a consciousness of life entails nothing less than the willingness to open ourselves to the visionary imagination on its own demanding terms. We must be prepared to entertain the astonishing claim men like Blake lay before us: that here are eyes which see the world not as commonplace sight or scientific scrutiny sees it, but see it transformed, made lustrous beyond measure, and in seeing the world so, see it as it really is. Instead of rushing to downgrade the rhapsodic reports of our enchanted seers, to interpret them at the lowest and most conventional level, we must be prepared to consider the scandalous possibility that wherever the visionary imagination grows bright, magic, that old antagonist of science, renews itself, transmuting our workaday reality into something bigger, perhaps more frightening, certainly more adventurous than the lesser rationality of objective consciousness can ever countenance.

But to speak of magic is to summon up at once images of vaudeville prestidigitators and tongue-in-cheek nature-fakers: tricksters who belong to the tawdry world of the stage. We have learned in this enlightened age to tolerate magicians only as an adjunct of the entertainment industry, where it is strictly understood by performer and audience alike that a trick is no more than a trick, a practised effort to baffle us. When the impossible appears to happen on stage, we know better than to believe that it has really happened. What we applaud is the dexterity with which the illusion has been created. If the magician were to claim that his deed was more than an illusion, we would consider him a lunatic or a charlatan, for he would be asking us to violate our basic conception of reality; and this we would not tolerate. While there are many, surprisingly many, who remain willing to take spiritualists, faith healers, fortunetellers, and such seriously, the scientific skeptic is forced to discount all these phenomena as atavistic and to insist stubbornly on the primacy of a coherent world view. The skeptical mind argues doggedly that we live in the midst of a nature that has been explained and exploited by science. The vaccines we inject into our bodies, the electricity that goes to work for us at the flick of a switch, the airplanes and automobiles that transport us: these and the ten thousand more technological devices we live among and rely upon derive from the scientist's, not the charlatan's, conception of nature. How shall we, with intellectual conscience, enjoy so much of what science has with an abundance of empirical demonstration brought us, and then deny the essential truth of its world view?

It is a challenge before which even our clergy have had to yield ground. Reportedly, more than one hundred million Americans attend religious services every Sunday. But if the religion they found in their churches were anything more than such timid gestures, inspirational verbiage, and comfortable socializing as are compatible with the world of science and reason which they inhabit for the next six days, how many of them would continue to attend? The last place any respectable, right-thinking citizen or enlightened clergyman wants to find himself these days is on William Jennings Bryan's side of another monkey trial.

But magic has not always belonged to the province of the carnival or the vulgar occultist. Behind these debased versions there stretches a tradition which reaches back to a noble origin. The stage magician who calls for a drum roll to catch our skeptical attention is but our latter-day form of the old tribal shaman beating his animal skin tom-tom to invoke the communal spirits. It would perhaps seem strange to many in our society to refer to this as a "noble" exemplar of the magical arts. Witch doctor, medicine man, voodoo priest . . . the very names invite savage and comic stereotypes: bone rattles and macabre masks, mumbo jumbo and blood rituals, superstitious spells and charms and incantations that never work. In the classic Hollywood encounter, the tribal magician, a figure both sinister and absurd, quickly exhausts his inane bag of tricks; and then the great white hunter steps forward to cure the sick with wonder drugs or to amaze the bug-eyed natives with pocket watch or flashlight. The white man's magic wins because it is, after all, the product of science. It wins especially when it arrives in the form of gunpowder, armed colonization, and massive material investment, the standard vehicles of civilization.

But before we dismiss the ludicrous old shaman as readily as we do the side-show sleight-of-hand man, let us spend another moment contemplating some of his less comic features—if with no other attitude of mind than the noblesse oblige of the self-styled superior culture which is well on its way to forcing the shamans of the world into rapid extinction. Soon their drums will be silent forever, superseded in every quarter of the globe by the sonic boom and the chatter of ever more intelligent computers. Perhaps the old magician's image will be replaced even in our children's literature as the Merlins of the fairy stories give place to the heroes of science fiction and fact. If it means anything very interesting to be "civilized," it means to possess the willingness to consider as instructive examples all the human possibilities that lie within our intellectual horizon—including those that conventional wisdom tells us are hopelessly obsolescent.

When we look more closely at the shaman, we discover that the contribution this exotic character has made to human culture is nearly inestimable. Indeed, the shaman might properly lay claim to being the culture hero *par excellence*, for through him creative forces that approach the superhuman seem to have been called into play. In the shaman, the first figure to have established himself in human society as an individual personality, several great talents were inextricably combined that have since become specialized professions. It is likely that men's first efforts at pictorial art—and brilliant efforts they were as they survive in the form of the great paleolithic cave paintings—were the work of shamans practising a strange, graphic magic. In the shaman's rhapsodic babbling we might once have heard the first rhythms and euphonics of poetic utterance. In his inspired taletelling we might find the beginnings of mythology, and so of literature; in his masked and painted impersonations, the origin of the drama; in his entranced gyrations, the first gestures of the dance. He was—besides being artist, poet, dramatist, dancer—his people's healer, moral counsellor, diviner, and cosmologer. Among his many skills, nearly the whole repertory of the modern circus entertainer could be found in its primordial form: ventriloquism, acrobatics, contortionism, juggling, fire eating, sword swallowing, sleight of hand. Still today, we find, among surviving primitives, shamans who are proficient in most of these talents, combining in their ancient craft things we consider high art and religion with things we consider profane diversions.

Sorted out into its several surviving traditions, the shaman's craft speaks for itself as a human achievement. But if we look for the creative thrust that once unified these skills and arts, we find the most important thing the shaman has to teach us, which is the meaning of magic in its pristine form: magic not as a repertory of clever stunts, but as a form of experience, a way of addressing the world. Those who still find themselves confronted by something of the unaccountably marvelous in the talents of artists and performers have perhaps been touched by a faint, lingering spark of the ancient shamanistic world view and have, to that extent, glimpsed an alternative reality.

Magic, as the shaman practices it, is a matter of communing with the forces of nature as if they were mindful, intentional presences, as if they possessed a will that requires coaxing, argument, imprecation. When he conjures, divines, or casts spells, the shaman is addressing these presences as one addresses a person, playing the relationship by ear, watching out for the other's moods, passions, attitudes—but always respectful of the other's dignity. For the shaman, the world is a place alive with mighty, invisible personalities; these have their own purposes, which, like those of any person, are apt to be ultimately mysterious. The shaman is on intimate terms with the presences he addresses; he strives to find out their ways and to move with the grain of them. He speaks of them as "you," not "it."

Here, for example, is Sivoangnag, an Eskimo shaman, directing a weather incantation to the unseen forces behind wind and wave:

Come, he says, thou outside there; come, he says,
   thou outside there.
Come, he says, thou outside there; come, he says,
   thou outside there.
Thy Sivoangnag bids thou come,
Tells thou to enter into him.
Come, he says, thou outside there.[1]

What is this but an invitation extended respectfully to an old friend? Or here is a Wintu (California) Indian describing the contrasting relationship of her shamanistic culture and that of the white man to a common environment:

> The white people never cared for land or deer or bear. When we Indians kill meat, we eat it all up. When we dig roots, we make little holes. . . . We shake down acorns and pinenuts. We don't chop down the trees. We only use dead wood. But the white people plow up the ground, pull up the trees, kill everything. The tree says, "Don't. I am sore. Don't hurt me." But they chop it down and cut it up. The spirit of the land hates them. . . . The Indians never hurt anything, but the white people destroy all. They blast rocks and scatter them on the ground. The rock says "Don't! You are hurting me." But the white people pay no attention. When the Indians use rocks, they take little round ones for their cooking. . . . How can the spirit of the earth like the white man? . . . Everywhere the white man has touched it, it is sore."[2]

"The tree says . . . ," "the rock says . . .": nothing could more easily express the difference between the scientific and the magical visions of nature. The Indian woman has been taught to hear the voices of plant and stone; we have been taught to "pay no attention." The essence of magic lies in just this sense that man and not-man can stand on communicable terms with one another. The relationship is not that of In-Here impassively observing Out-There, but of man carrying on a personal transaction with forces in his environment which are known to be turbulently, perhaps menacingly alive. The shaman enters into the field of these forces warmly, sensuously; and because he approaches with respect, they welcome him and permit him to strive and bargain with them.

It is not a relationship the presences accept with all comers. Unlike the scientific experiment, which is depersonalized and so should work for anyone who performs it, the magical relationship is available only to those

[1] *Report of the Canadian Arctic Expedition, 1913–1918*: Vol. 14: "Eskimo Songs" (Ottawa, 1925), p. 486.
[2] Lee, *Freedom and Culture*, p. 163.

chosen by the presences themselves. The shaman is ordinarily one who discovers his vocation upon being seized up by powers beyond his comprehension. He does not initially train for the position as for a prefabricated office; this is a development that ensues when the shaman's calling becomes routinized into the formal role of the priest. Rather, like the prophets of Israel to whom so much of the primitive tradition clings, the shaman is ambushed by the divine and called forth by surprise. The prophet Amos—protesting significantly in this case to the official temple priest—explains:

> I was no prophet, neither was I a prophet's son; but I was an herdsman, and a gatherer of sycamore fruit; And the Lord took me as I followed the flock, and the Lord said unto me, Go, prophesy unto my people Israel. (Amos 7:14–15)

And prophesy he did, with an eloquence that defies explanation in one from so humble an origin.

Communion with the transcendent powers, then, is not a feat that can be achieved by anyone; it is a mystery peculiar to the one elected, and is therefore through and through personal in character. For this reason, the shaman ordinarily becomes one who stands apart from his people—not in a position of institutional authority, but in a position of talented uniqueness. The respect felt for him is the respect many of us still feel for the especially gifted person, the artist or performer whose uncanny influence over us does not lie in any office he holds but in his own manifest skill.

In order to heighten that skill, the shaman devotes himself to a life of severe discipline and solitude. He fasts, he prays, he meditates; he isolates himself in order that he may watch out for such signs as the presences make visible for his education. Above all, he becomes adept in cultivating those exotic states of awareness in which a submerged aspect of his personality seems to free itself from his surface consciousness to rove among the hidden powers of the universe. The techniques by which shamans undertake their psychic adventures are many; they may make use of narcotic substances, dizziness, starvation, smoke inhalation, suffocation, hypnotic drum and dance rhythms, or even the holding of one's breath. One recognizes at once in this trance-inducing repertory a number of practices which underlie the many mystical traditions of the world: the practices of oracles, dervishes, yogis, sibyls, prophets, druids, etc.—the whole heritage of mystagoguery toward which the beat-hip wing of our counter culture now gravitates.

By such techniques, the shaman cultivates his rapport with the non-intellective sources of the personality as assiduously as any scientist trains himself to objectivity, a mode of consciousness at the polar extreme from that of the shaman. Thus the shaman is able to diffuse his sensibilities through his environment, assimilating himself to the surrounding universe. He enters wholly into the grand symbiotic system of nature, letting its currents and nuances flow through him. He may become a keener student of his environment than any scientist. He may be able to taste rain or plague on the wind. He may be able to sense the way the wild herds will move next or how the planting will go in the season to come.

The shaman, then, is one who knows that there is more to be seen of reality than the waking eye sees. Besides our eyes of flesh, there are eyes of fire that burn through the ordinariness of the world and perceive the wonders and terrors beyond. In the superconsciousness of the shaman, nothing is simply a dead object, a stupid creature; rather, all the things of this earth are swayed by sacred meanings. " 'Primitive man,' " Martin Buber observes, "is a naive pansacramentalist. Everything is to him full of sacramental substance, everything. Each thing and each function is ever ready to light up into a sacrament for him."

FURTHER READING

Aldous Huxley, of *Brave New World* fame, reported his experiences with mescaline in *The Doors of Perception* (1954) and in the process raised profound questions about man's senses and mind.

In *Saturday Review*'s Science sections of August 6, 1966, September 3, 1966, October 1, 1966, and February 4, 1967, there appeared articles by John Lear and others about Unidentified Flying Objects. The claims and counter-claims pose dramatically the problems of the reliability of testimony, of what constitutes evidence, and of what *truth* consists.

An essay in substantial agreement with Roszak's "Eyes of Flesh, Eyes of Fire" is Norman O. Brown's "Apocalypse: The Place of Mystery in the Life of the Mind," *Harpers* (May, 1961). The controversial Brown (the author of *Love's Body*) urges us to find again the "holy madness" which is possible outside of the scientific-rationalistic tradition.

Chapter VIII, "Problems Concerning the Scope and Extent of Knowledge," in John Herman Randall and Justus Buchler's *Philosophy: An Introduction* (1942), is a clear and brief statement of the problems of epistemology. Roderick M. Chisholm's *Theory of Knowledge* (1966) is a more extended (113-page) and studious introductory text.

In *An Introduction to Modern Philosophy* (2nd ed., 1963) Alburey Castell provides a great deal of interpretative commentary with judiciously selected readings from Locke, Hume, Kant, Comte, Vaihinger, and Collingwood. See Topic Three, "An Epistemological Problem."

John W. Yolton's *Theory of Knowledge* (1965) offers twelve key readings with an introductory essay by Yolton. The entire volume is limited to 119 pages.

John Locke's *An Essay Concerning Human Understanding* (1690) was in most respects the beginning of modern epistemology. George Berkeley's *A Treatise Concerning the Principles of Human Knowledge* (1710) is another landmark in the field. The best parts of Locke's *Essay* and all of Berkeley's *Treatise*, as well as Hume's *An Inquiry Concerning Human Understanding* in its entirety, are included in *The English Philosophers from Bacon to Mill* (Modern Library, 1939), edited by E. A. Burtt.

chapter twelve

IDENTITY AND FREEDOM

12

It is only in the context of human lives and institutions that the themes of identity and freedom take on form and reality. The two themes are joined in this chapter because they are hardly separable: to the degree that freedom is exercised, there is a sense of identity; and where men are autonomous, freedom exists and is prized.

It is the bond between freedom and identity that suggests the significance of Paul Goodman's essay "Freedom and Learning." His recommendation is that the young be allowed to choose the contents of their education; nothing can be learned under compulsion anyway, and "freedom is the only way toward authentic citizenship and real, rather than verbal, philosophy." The existing educational establishment, at its worst, is largely irrelevant to the young, and breeds apathy and resentment. Goodman's proposals for new kinds of schools rest on his conviction that the individuality of children must be recognized and permitted to grow. This can be accomplished only in an atmosphere of freedom.

Betty Friedan is concerned with the place and role of women in society. "The feminine mystique" demands that they become wives and mothers; it is understood that their place is in the home. Thus young women must put aside personal, professional, or career interests, make certain that they marry, and then settle down to housewifery. While men are expected to grapple with the question of their identity, women are assigned functions (by virtue of their anatomy, no less) which forestall the realization of their own potentialities as human beings. The freedom to choose or to create an identity, to choose oneself, is necessary "simply to become fully human."

Lerone Bennett writes of the slavery of both black men and white men, on all levels of society. He writes, in other words, of the slavery of America. It is a slavery to machines, poverty and wealth, class, fear—to that entire chain of concerns that shackles the lives of most of us. Racism is an outgrowth of this larger oppression: it is "a confused and alienated protest against a suffocating reality," a protest against the quality of our lives. What is required, therefore, is a reappraisal of every aspect of life, of all that which has brought upon us "the whole sick syndrome surrounding real

494

estate, status, greed, and human pettiness." Hanging in the balance is
the creation of man, Bennett says, because that creation is dependent upon
the condition of freedom.

Herbert Marcuse sees in modern industrial society forms of control more
covert and vicious than those of the past. The problem here is that massive
corporate forces, geared for ever-increasing growth and efficiency, repress the
individual. This is a new kind of totalitarianism, a "non-terroristic
economic-technical coordination which operates through the manipulation
of needs by vested interests." Because the individual has the material comforts of a technological society, and because he is further pacified by small,
meaningless liberties (for the purchaser to choose, for example, among
brands), he succumbs to a repressiveness so total that not even consciousness of the repression remains.

Charles Reich optimistically believes that a revolution is now underway,
that the younger generation has started the turn toward a more humane
and authentic community of men. The problems that have culminated in
loss of self, a sense of powerlessness, and confusion about the nature of the
entire dilemma are being confronted by a new consciousness in the young.
They are involved in a new life style that affirms a "liberation of each
individual in which he is enabled to grow toward the highest possibilities
of the human spirit."

Jiddu Krishnamurti has written elsewhere that his "only concern is to
set men absolutely, unconditionally free," and in the essay presented here
he suggests how this is accomplished. Whereas Western philosophers tend
to look at the external conditions of life that encourage or inhibit personal
freedom, the Easterner Krishnamurti looks within. Desires and fears and
our very processes of thought must be understood; self-knowledge must be
acquired. Then one may become free. And this is the way one changes the
world, for you are the world.

The struggle for freedom is invariably against discouraging odds. "It is
not as easy as people think to be a free man," said Albert Camus. "In truth,
the only ones who assert that it is easy are those who have decided to
forego freedom." And to forego themselves.

495

paul goodman   FREEDOM AND LEARNING

*Paul Goodman (1911–72) has been a novelist, TV critic, university pro-
fessor, poet, playwright, short story writer, literary critic, and so forth, but it has
been his very influential and effective criticism of schools and society that has
brought him fame—or notoriety, as some of his critics would have it. Regimentation, conformity, bureaucracy, and the "moral suffocation" of corporate America
are among his favorite topics.*

*Born in New York, Goodman was graduated from the City College of New
York and holds a Ph.D. from the University of Chicago. His titles include* Grow-
ing Up Absurd, The Community of Scholars, Making Do, Compulsory Mis-
Education, *and* Five Years. *His most recent book is* New Reformation: Notes of
a Neolithic Conservative. *"Freedom and Learning" is from the* Saturday Review
(May 18, 1968).

The belief that a highly industrialized society requires twelve to twenty
years of prior processing of the young is an illusion or a hoax. The evidence
is strong that there is no correlation between school performance and life
achievement in any of the professions, whether medicine, law, engineering,
journalism, or business. Moreover, recent research shows that for more
modest clerical, technological, or semi-skilled factory jobs there is no advantage in years of schooling or the possession of diplomas. We were not exactly
savages in 1900 when only 6 per cent of adolescents graduated from high
school.

Whatever the deliberate intention, schooling today serves mainly for
policing and for taking up the slack in youth unemployment. It is not
surprising that the young are finally rebelling against it, especially since
they cannot identify with the goals of so much social engineering—for
instance, that 86 per cent of the federal budget for research and development is for military purposes.

We can, I believe, educate the young entirely in terms of their free
choice, with no processing whatever. Nothing can be efficiently learned, or,
indeed, learned at all—other than through parroting or brute training, when
acquired knowledge is promptly forgotten after the examination—unless it
meets need, desire, curiosity, or fantasy. Unless there is a reaching from
within, the learning cannot become "second nature," as Aristotle called
true learning. It seems stupid to decide a priori what the young ought to
know and then to try to motivate them, instead of letting the initiative
come from them and putting information and relevant equipment at their
service. It is false to assert that this kind of freedom will not serve society's

496

needs—at least those needs that should humanly be served; freedom is the only way toward authentic citizenship and real, rather than verbal, philosophy. Free choice is not random but responsive to real situations; both youth and adults live in a nature of things, a polity, an ongoing society, and it is these, in fact, that attract interest and channel need. If the young, as they mature, can follow their bent and choose their topics, times, and teachers, and if teachers teach what they themselves consider important—which is all they can skillfully teach anyway—the needs of society will be adequately met; there will be more lively, independent, and inventive people; and in the fairly short run there will be a more sensible and efficient society.

It is not necessary to argue for free choice as a metaphysical proposition; it is what is indicated by present conditions. Increasingly, the best young people resolutely resist authority, and we will let them have a say or lose them. And more important, since the conditions of modern social and technological organization are so pervasively and rigidly conforming, it is necessary, in order to maintain human initiative, to put our emphasis on protecting the young from top-down direction. The monkish and academic methods which were civilizing for wild shepherds create robots in a period of high technology. The public schools which did a good job of socializing immigrants in an open society now regiment individuals and rigidify class stratification.

Up to age twelve, there is no point to formal subjects or a prearranged curriculum. With guidance, whatever a child experiences is educational. Dewey's idea is a good one: It makes no difference *what* is learned at this age, so long as the child goes on wanting to learn something further. Teachers for this age are those who like children, pay attention to them, answer their questions, enjoy taking them around the city and helping them explore, imitate, try out, and who sing songs with them and teach them games. Any benevolent grownup—literate or illiterate—has plenty to teach an eight-year-old; the only profitable training for teachers is a group therapy and, perhaps, a course in child development.

We see that infants learn to speak in their own way in an environment where there is speaking and where they are addressed and take part. If we tried to teach children to speak according to our own theories and methods and schedules, as we try to teach reading, there would be as many stammerers as there are bad readers. Besides, it has been shown that whatever is useful in the present eight-year elementary curriculum can be learned in four months by a normal child of twelve. If let alone, in fact, he will have learned most of it by himself.

Since we have communities where people do not attend to the children as a matter of course, and since children must be rescued from their homes, for most of these children there should be some kind of school. In a proposal for mini-schools in New York City, I suggested an elementary group of twenty-eight children with four grownups: a licensed teacher, a housewife who can cook, a college senior, and a teen-age school dropout. Such a group can meet in any store front, church basement, settlement house, or housing project; more important, it can often go about the city, as is possible when the student-teacher ratio is 7 to 1. Experience at the First Street School in New York has shown that the cost for such a little school is less than for the public school with a student-teacher ratio of 30 to 1. (In the public system, most of the money goes for administration and for specialists to remedy the lack of contact in the classroom.) As A. S. Neill has shown, attendance need not be compulsory. The school should be located near home so the children can escape from it to home, and from home to it. The school should be supported by public money but administered entirely by its own children, teachers, and parents.

In the adolescent and college years, the present mania is to keep students at their lessons for another four to ten years as the only way of their growing up in the world. The correct policy would be to open as many diverse paths as possible, with plenty of opportunity to backtrack and change. It is said by James Conant that about 15 per cent learn well by books and study in an academic setting, and these can opt for high school. Most, including most of the bright students, do better either on their own or as apprentices in activities that are for keeps, rather than through lessons. If their previous eight years had been spent in exploring their own bents and interests, rather than being continually interrupted to do others' assignments on others' schedules, most adolescents would have a clearer notion of what they are after, and many would have found their vocations.

For the 15 per cent of adolescents who learn well in schools and are interested in subjects that are essentially academic, the present catch-all high schools are wasteful. We would do better to return to the small preparatory academy, with perhaps sixty students and three teachers—one in physical sciences, one in social sciences, one in humanities—to prepare for college board examinations. An academy could be located in, and administered by, a university and staffed by graduate students who like to teach and in this way might earn stipends while they write their theses. In such a setting, without dilution by nonacademic subjects and a mass of uninterested fellow students, an academic adolescent can, by spending three hours a day in the classroom, easily be prepared in three or four years for college.

Forcing the nonacademic to attend school breaks the spirit of most and foments alienation in the best. Kept in tutelage, young people, who are necessarily economically dependent, cannot pursue the sexual, adventurous, and political activities congenial to them. Since lively youngsters insist on these anyway, the effect of what we do is to create a gap between them and the oppressive adult world, with a youth subculture and an arrested development.

School methods are simply not competent to teach all the arts, sciences, professions, and skills the school establishment pretends to teach. For some professions—e.g., social work, architecture, pedagogy—trying to earn academic credits is probably harmful because it is an irrelevant and discouraging obstacle course. Most technological know-how has to be learned in actual practice in offices and factories, and this often involves unlearning what has been laboriously crammed for exams. The technical competence required by skilled and semiskilled workmen and average technicians can be acquired in three weeks to a year on the job, with no previous schooling. The importance of even "functional literacy" is much exaggerated; it is the attitude, and not the reading ability, that counts. Those who are creative in the arts and sciences almost invariably go their own course and are usually hampered by schools. Modern languages are best learned by travel. It is pointless to teach social sciences, literary criticism, and philosophy to youngsters who have had no responsible experience in life and society.

Most of the money now spent for high schools and colleges should be devoted to the support of apprenticeships; travel; subsidized browsing in libraries and self-directed study and research; programs such as VISTA, the Peace Corps, Students for a Democratic Society, or the Student Non-violent Coordinating Committee; rural reconstruction; and work camps for projects in conservation and urban renewal. It is a vast sum of money—but it costs almost $1,500 a year to keep a youth in a blackboard jungle in New York; the schools have become one of our major industries. Consider one kind of opportunity. Since it is important for the very existence of the republic to countervail the now overwhelming national corporate style of information, entertainment, and research, we need scores of thousands of small independent television stations, community radio stations, local newspapers that are more than gossip notes and ads, community theaters, highbrow or dissenting magazines, small design offices for neighborhood renewal that is not bureaucratized, small laboratories for science and invention that are not centrally directed. Such enterprises could present admirable opportunities for bright but unacademic young people to serve as apprentices.

Ideally, the polis itself is the educational environment; a good community consists of worthwhile, attractive, and fulfilling callings and things to do, to grow up into. The policy I am proposing tends in this direction rather than away from it. By multiplying options, it should be possible to find an interesting course for each individual youth, as we now do for only some of the emotionally disturbed and the troublemakers. Voluntary adolescent choices are often random and foolish and usually transitory;

but they are the likeliest ways of growing up reasonably. What is most essential is for the youth to see that he is taken seriously as a person, rather than fitted into an institutional system. I don't know if this tailor-made approach would be harder or easier to administer than standardization that in fact fits nobody and results in an increasing number of recalcitrants. On the other hand, as the Civilian Conservation Corps showed in the Thirties, the products of willing youth labor can be valuable even economically, whereas accumulating Regents blue-books is worth nothing except to the school itself.

(By and large, it is not in the adolescent years but in later years that, in all walks of life, there is need for academic withdrawal, periods of study and reflection, synoptic review of the texts. The Greeks understood this and regarded most of our present college curricula as appropriate for only those over the age of thirty or thirty-five. To some extent, the churches used to provide a studious environment. We do these things miserably in hurried conferences.)

We have similar problems in the universities. We cram the young with what they do not want at the time and what most of them will never use; but by requiring graded diplomas we make it hard for older people to get what they want and can use. Now, paradoxically, when so many are going to school, the training of authentic learned professionals is proving to be a failure, with dire effects on our ecology, urbanism, polity, communications, and even the direction of science. Doing others' lessons under compulsion for twenty years does not tend to produce professionals who are autonomous, principled, and ethically responsible to client and community. Broken by processing, professionals degenerate to mere professional-personnel. Professional peer groups have become economic lobbies. The licensing and maintenance of standards have been increasingly relinquished to the state, which has no competence.

In licensing professionals, we have to look more realistically at functions, drop mandarin requirements of academic diplomas that are irrelevant, and rid ourselves of the ridiculous fad of awarding diplomas for every skill and trade whatever. In most professions and arts there are important abstract parts that can best be learned academically. The natural procedure is for those actually engaged in a professional activity to go to school to learn what they now know they need; re-entry into the academic track, therefore, should be made easy for those with a strong motive.

Universities are primarily schools of learned professions, and the faculty should be composed primarily not of academics but of working professionals who feel duty-bound and attracted to pass on their tradition to apprentices of a new generation. Being combined in a community of scholars, such professionals teach a noble apprenticeship, humane and with vision toward a more ideal future. It is humane because the disciplines communicate

500

with one another; it is ideal because the young are free and questioning. A good professional school can be tiny. In *The Community of Scholars* I suggest that 150 students and ten professionals—the size of the usual medieval university—are enough. At current faculty salaries, the cost per student would be a fourth of that of our huge administrative machines. And, of course, on such a small scale contact between faculty and students is sought for and easy.

Today, because of the proved incompetence of our adult institutions and the hypocrisy of most professionals, university students have a right to a large say in what goes on. (But this, too, is medieval.) Professors will, of course, teach what they please. My advice to students is that given by Prince Kropotkin, in "A Letter to the Young": "Ask what kind of world do you want to live in? What are you good at and want to work at to build that world? What do you need to know? Demand that your teachers teach you that." Serious teachers would be delighted by this approach.

The idea of the liberal arts college is a beautiful one: to teach the common culture and refine character and citizenship. But it does not happen; the evidence is that the college curriculum has little effect on underlying attitudes, and most cultivated folk do not become so by this route. School friendships and the community of youth do have lasting effects, but these do not require ivied clubhouses. Young men learn more about the theory and practice of government by resisting the draft than they ever learned in Political Science 412.

Much of the present university expansion, needless to say, consists in federal- and corporation-contracted research and other research and has nothing to do with teaching. Surely such expansion can be better carried on in the Government's and corporations' own institutes, which would be unencumbered by the young, except those who are hired or attach themselves as apprentices.

Every part of education can be open to need, desire, choice, and trying out. Nothing needs to be compelled or extrinsically motivated by prizes and threats. I do not know if the procedure here outlined would cost more than our present system—though it is hard to conceive of a need for more money than the school establishment now spends. What would be saved is the pitiful waste of youthful years—caged, daydreaming, sabotaging, and cheating—and the degrading and insulting misuse of teachers.

It has been estimated by James Coleman that the average youth in high school is really "there" about ten minutes a day. Since the growing-up of the young into society to be useful to themselves and others, and to do God's work, is one of the three or four most important functions of any society, no doubt we ought to spend even more on the education of the young than we do; but I would not give a penny to the present administrators, and I would largely dismantle the present school machinery.

betty friedan THE CRISIS IN WOMAN'S
IDENTITY

Betty Friedan (1921–   ) was graduated from Smith College and then (in keeping with the dictates of the feminine mystique) married in 1947 to become a suburban housewife and mother of three children. Ten years later she began to become aware of "the problem that has no name," and The Feminine Mystique *resulted. In 1966 she founded and became president of the National Organization for Women (NOW), the largest of the feminist organizations. She stepped down from the presidency of NOW in 1970 and organized the nation-wide Women's Strike for Equality of August 26, 1970.*

The selection which follows is from The Feminine Mystique, *which was an immediate best-seller in 1963. It has been translated into thirteen languages.*

I discovered a strange thing, interviewing women of my own generation over the past ten years. When we were growing up, many of us could not see ourselves beyond the age of twenty-one. We had no image of our own future, of ourselves as women.

I remember the stillness of a spring afternoon on the Smith campus in 1942, when I came to a frightening dead end in my own vision of the future. A few days earlier, I had received a notice that I had won a graduate fellowship. During the congratulations, underneath my excitement, I felt a strange uneasiness; there was a question that I did not want to think about.

"Is this really what I want to be?" The question shut me off, cold and alone, from the girls talking and studying on the sunny hillside behind the college house. I thought I was going to be a psychologist. But if I wasn't sure, what did I want to be? I felt the future closing in—and I could not see myself in it at all. I had no image of myself, stretching beyond college. I had come at seventeen from a Midwestern town, an unsure girl; the wide horizons of the world and the life of the mind had been opened to me. I had begun to know who I was and what I wanted to do. I could not go back now. I could not go home again, to the life of my mother and the women of our town, bound to home, bridge, shopping, children, husband, charity, clothes. But now that the time had come to make my own future, to take the deciding step, I suddenly did not know what I wanted to be.

I took the fellowship, but the next spring, under the alien California sun of another campus, the question came again, and I could not put it out of my mind. I had won another fellowship that would have committed me to research for my doctorate, to a career as professional psychologist. "Is this really what I want to be?" The decision now truly terrified me. I lived in a terror of indecision for days, unable to think of anything else.

The question was not important, I told myself. No question was important to me that year but love. We walked in the Berkeley hills and a boy said: "Nothing can come of this, between us. I'll never win a fellowship like yours." Did I think I would be choosing, irrevocably, the cold loneliness of that afternoon if I went on? I gave up the fellowship, in relief. But for years afterward, I could not read a word of the science that once I had thought of as my future life's work; the reminder of its loss was too painful.

I never could explain, hardly knew myself, why I gave up this career. I lived in the present, working on newspapers with no particular plan. I married, had children, lived according to the feminine mystique as a suburban housewife. But still the question haunted me. I could sense no purpose in my life, I could find no peace, until I finally faced it and worked out my own answer.

I discovered, talking to Smith seniors in 1959, that the question is no less terrifying to girls today. Only they answer it now in a way that my generation found, after half a lifetime, not to be an answer at all. These girls, mostly seniors, were sitting in the living room of the college house, having coffee. It was not too different from such an evening when I was a senior, except that many more of the girls wore rings on their left hands. I asked the ones around me what they planned to be. The engaged ones spoke of weddings, apartments, getting a job as a secretary while husband finished school. The others, after a hostile silence, gave vague answers about this job or that, graduate study, but no one had any real plans. A blonde with a ponytail asked me the next day if I had believed the things they had said. "None of it was true," she told me. "We don't like to be asked what we want to do. None of us know. None of us even like to think about it. The ones who are going to be married right away are the lucky ones. They don't have to think about it."

But I noticed that night that many of the engaged girls, sitting silently around the fire while I asked the others about jobs, had also seemed angry about something. "They don't want to think about not going on," my ponytailed informant said. "They know they're not going to use their education. They'll be wives and mothers. You can say you're going to keep on reading and be interested in the community. But that's not the same. You won't really go on. It's a disappointment to know you're going to stop now, and not go on and use it."

In counterpoint, I heard the words of a woman, fifteen years after she left college, a doctor's wife, mother of three, who said over coffee in her New England kitchen:

The tragedy was, nobody ever looked us in the eye and said you have to decide what you want to do with your life, besides being your husband's wife and children's mother. I never thought it through until I was thirty-six, and my husband was so busy with his practice that he couldn't entertain me every night. The three boys were in school all day. I kept on trying to have babies despite an Rh discrepancy. After two miscarriages, they said I must stop. I thought that my own growth and evolution were over. I always knew as a child that I was going to grow up and go to college, and then get married, and that's as far as a girl has to think. After that, your husband determines and fills your life. It wasn't until I got so lonely as the doctor's wife and kept screaming at the kids because they didn't fill my life that I realized I had to make my own life. I still had to decide what I wanted to be. I hadn't finished evolving at all. But it took me ten years to think it through.

The feminine mystique permits, even encourages, women to ignore the question of their identity. The mystique says they can answer the question "Who am I?" by saying "Tom's wife . . . Mary's mother." But I don't think the mystique would have such power over American women if they did not fear to face this terrifying blank which makes them unable to see themselves after twenty-one. The truth is—and how long it has been true, I'm not sure, but it was true in my generation and it is true of girls growing up today— an American woman no longer has a private image to tell her who she is, or can be, or wants to be.

The public image, in the magazines and television commercials, is designed to sell washing machines, cake mixes, deodorants, detergents, rejuvenating face creams, hair tints. But the power of that image, on which companies spend millions of dollars for television time and ad space, comes from this: American women no longer know who they are. They are sorely in need of a new image to help them find their identity. As the motivational researchers keep telling the advertisers, American women are so unsure of who they should be that they look to this glossy public image to decide every detail of their lives. They look for the image they will no longer take from their mothers.

In my generation, many of us knew that we did not want to be like our mothers, even when we loved them. We could not help but see their disappointment. Did we understand, or only resent, the sadness, the emptiness, that made them hold too fast to us, try to live our lives, run our fathers' lives, spend their days shopping or yearning for things that never seemed to satisfy them, no matter how much money they cost? Strangely, many mothers who loved their daughters—and mine was one—did not want their daughters to grow up like them either. They knew we needed something more.

504

But even if they urged, insisted, fought to help us educate ourselves, even if they talked with yearning of careers that were not open to them, they could not give us an image of what we could be. They could only tell us that their lives were too empty, tied to home; that children, cooking, clothes, bridge, and charities were not enough. A mother might tell her daughter, spell it out, "Don't be just a housewife like me." But that daughter, sensing that her mother was too frustrated to savor the love of her husband and children, might feel: "I will succeed where my mother failed, I will fulfill myself as a woman," and never read the lesson of her mother's life.

Recently, interviewing high-school girls who had started out full of promise and talent, but suddenly stopped their education, I began to see new dimensions to the problem of feminine conformity. These girls, it seemed at first were merely following the typical curve of feminine adjustment. Earlier interested in geology or poetry, they now were interested only in being popular; to get boys to like them, they had concluded, it was better to be like all the other girls. On closer examination, I found that these girls were so terrified of becoming like their mothers that they could not see themselves at all. They were afraid to grow up. They had to copy in identical detail the composite image of the popular girl—denying what was best in themselves out of fear of femininity as they saw it in their mothers. One of these girls, seventeen years old, told me:

> I want so badly to feel like the other girls. I never get over this feeling of being a neophyte, not initiated. When I get up and have to cross a room, it's like I'm a beginner, or have some terrible affliction, and I'll never learn. I go the local hangout after school and sit there for hours talking about clothes and hairdos and the twist, and I'm not that interested, so it's an effort. But I found out I could make them like me—just do what they do, dress like them, talk like them, not do things that are different. I guess I even started to make myself not different inside.
>
> I used to write poetry. The guidance office says I have this creative ability and I should be at the top of the class and have a great future. But things like that aren't what you need to be popular. The important thing for a girl is to be popular.
>
> Now I go out with boy after boy, and it's such an effort because I'm not myself with them. It makes you feel even more alone. And besides, I'm afraid of where it's going to lead. Pretty soon, all my differences will be smoothed out, and I'll be the kind of girl that could be a housewife.
>
> I don't want to think of growing up. If I had children, I'd want them to stay the same age. If I had to watch them grow up, I'd see myself growing older, and I wouldn't want to. My mother says she can't sleep at night, she's sick with worry over what I might do. When I was little, she wouldn't let me cross the street alone, long after the other kids did.
>
> I can't see myself as being married and having children. It's as if I

wouldn't have any personality myself. My mother's like a rock that's been smoothed by the waves, like a void. She's put so much into her family that there's nothing left, and she resents us because she doesn't get enough in return. But sometimes it seems like there's nothing there. My mother doesn't serve any purpose except cleaning the house. She isn't happy, and she doesn't make my father happy. If she didn't care about us children at all, it would have the same effect as caring too much. It makes you want to do the opposite. I don't think it's really love. When I was little and I ran in all excited to tell her I'd learned how to stand on my head, she was never listening.

Lately, I look into the mirror, and I'm so afraid I'm going to look like my mother. It frightens me, to catch myself being like her in gestures or speech or anything. I'm not like her in so many ways, but if I'm like her in this one way, perhaps I'll turn out like my mother after all. And that terrifies me.

And so the seventeen-year-old was so afraid of being a woman like her mother that she turned her back on all the things in herself and all the opportunities that would have made her a different woman, to copy from the outside the "popular" girls. And finally, in panic at losing herself, she turned her back on her own popularity and defied the conventional good behavior that would have won her a college scholarship. For lack of an image that would help her grow up as a woman true to herself, she retreated into the beatnik vacuum.

Another girl, a college junior from South Carolina told me:

I don't want to be interested in a career I'll have to give up.

My mother wanted to be a newspaper reporter from the time she was twelve, and I've seen her frustration for twenty years. I don't want to be interested in world affairs. I don't want to be interested in anything beside my home and being a wonderful wife and mother. Maybe education is a liability. Even the brightest boys at home want just a sweet, pretty girl. Only sometimes I wonder how it would feel to be able to stretch and stretch and stretch, and learn all you want, and not have to hold yourself back.

Her mother, almost all our mothers, were housewives, though many had started or yearned for or regretted giving up careers. Whatever they told us, we, having eyes and ears and mind and heart, knew that their lives were somehow empty. We did not want to be like them, and yet what other model did we have?

The only other kind of women I knew, growing up, were the old-maid high-school teachers; the librarian; the one woman doctor in our town, who cut her hair like a man; and a few of my college professors. None of these women lived in the warm center of life as I had known it at home. Many had not married or had children. I dreaded being like them, even the ones who taught me truly to respect my own mind and use it, to feel that I had a part in the world. I never knew a woman, when I was growing up, who used her mind, played her own part in the world, and also loved, and had children.

I think that this has been the unknown heart of woman's problem in America for a long time, this lack of a private image. Public images that defy reason and have very little to do with women themselves have had the power to shape too much of their lives. These images would not have such power, if women were not suffering a crisis of identity.

The strange, terrifying jumping-off point that American women reach—at eighteen, twenty-one, twenty-five, forty-one—has been noticed for many years by sociologists, psychologists, analysts, educators. But I think it has not been understood for what it is. It has been called a "discontinuity" in cultural conditioning; it has been called woman's "role crisis." It has been blamed on the education which made American girls grow up feeling free and equal to boys—playing baseball, riding bicycles, conquering geometry and college boards, going away to college, going out in the world to get a job, living alone in an apartment in New York or Chicago or San Francisco, testing and discovering their own powers in the world. All this gave girls the feeling they could be and do whatever they wanted to, with the same freedom as boys, the critics said. It did not prepare them for their role as women. The crisis comes when they are forced to adjust to this role. To-day's high rate of emotional distress and breakdown among women in their twenties and thirties is usually attributed to this "role crisis." If girls were educated for their role as women, they would not suffer this crisis, the adjusters say.

But I think they have seen only half the truth.

What if the terror a girl faces at twenty-one, when she must decide who she will be, is simply the terror of growing up—growing up, as women were not permitted to grow before? What if the terror a girl faces at twenty-one is the terror of freedom to decide her own life, with no one to order which path she will take, the freedom and the necessity to take paths women before were not able to take? What if those who choose the path of "feminine adjustment"—evading this terror by marrying at eighteen, losing themselves in having babies and the details of housekeeping—are simply refusing to grow up, to face the question of their own identity?

Mine was the first college generation to run head-on into the new mystique of feminine fulfillment. Before then, while most women did indeed end up as housewives and mothers, the point of education was to discover the life of the mind, to pursue truth and to take a place in the world. There was a sense, already dulling when I went to college, that we

507

would be New Women. Our world would be much larger than home. Forty per cent of my college class at Smith had career plans. But I remember how, even then, some of the seniors, suffering the pangs of that bleak fear of the future, envied the few who escaped it by getting married right away.

The ones we envied then are suffering that terror now at forty. "Never have decided what kind of woman I am. Too much personal life in college. Wish I'd studied more science, history, government, gone deeper into philosophy," one wrote on an alumnae questionnaire, fifteen years later. "Still trying to find the rock to build on. Wish I had finished college. I got married instead." "Wish I'd developed a deeper and more creative life of my own and that I hadn't become engaged and married at nineteen. Having expected the ideal in marriage, including a hundred-per-cent devoted husband, it was a shock to find this isn't the way it is," wrote a mother of six.

Many of the younger generation of wives who marry early have never suffered this lonely terror. They thought they did not have to choose, to look into the future and plan what they wanted to do with their lives. They had only to wait to be chosen, marking time passively until the husband, the babies, the new house decided what the rest of their lives would be. They slid easily into their sexual role as women before they knew who they were themselves. It is these women who suffer most the problem that has no name.

It is my thesis that the core of the problem for women today is not sexual but a problem of identity—a stunting or evasion of growth that is perpetuated by the feminine mystique. It is my thesis that as the Victorian culture did not permit women to accept or gratify their basic sexual needs, our culture does not permit women to accept or gratify their basic need to grow and fulfill their potentialities as human beings, a need which is not solely defined by their sexual role.

Biologists have recently discovered a "youth serum" which, if fed to young caterpillars in the larva state, will keep them from ever maturing into moths; they will live out their lives as caterpillars. The expectations of feminine fulfillment that are fed to women by magazines, television, movies, and books that popularize psychological half-truths, and by parents, teachers and counselors who accept the feminine mystique, operate as a kind of youth serum, keeping most women in the state of sexual larvae, preventing them from achieving the maturity of which they are capable. And there is increasing evidence that woman's failure to grow to complete identity has hampered rather than enriched her sexual fulfillment, virtually doomed her to be castrative to her husband and sons, and caused neuroses, or problems as yet unnamed as neuroses, equal to those caused by sexual repression.

There have been identity crises for man at all the crucial turning points in human history, though those who lived through them did not give them

508

that name. It is only in recent years that the theorists of psychology, sociology and theology have isolated this problem, and given it a name. But it is considered a man's problem. It is defined, for man, as the crisis of growing up, of choosing his identity, "the decision as to what one is and is going to be," in the words of the brilliant psychoanalyst Erik H. Erikson:

> I have called the major crisis of adolescence the identity crisis; it occurs in that period of the life cycle when each youth must forge for himself some central perspective and direction, some working unity, out of the effective remnants of his childhood and the hopes of his anticipated adulthood; he must detect some meaningful resemblance between what he has come to see in himself and what his sharpened awareness tells him others judge and expect him to be. . . . In some people, in some classes, at some periods in history, the crisis will be minimal; in other people, classes and periods, the crisis will be clearly marked off as a critical period, a kind of "second birth," apt to be aggravated either by widespread neuroticisms or by pervasive ideological unrest.[1]

In this sense, the identity crisis of one man's life may reflect, or set off, a rebirth, or new stage, in the growing up of mankind. "In some periods of his history, and in some phases of his life cycle, man needs a new ideological orientation as surely and sorely as he must have air and food," said Erikson, focusing new light on the crisis of the young Martin Luther, who left a Catholic monastery at the end of the Middle Ages to forge a new identity for himself and Western man.

The search for identity is not new, however, in American thought—though in every generation, each man who writes about it discovers it anew. In America, from the beginning, it has somehow been understood that men must thrust into the future; the pace has always been too rapid for man's identity to stand still. In every generation, many men have suffered misery, unhappiness, and uncertainty because they could not take the image of the man they wanted to be from their fathers. The search for identity of the young man who can't go home again has always been a major theme of American writers. And it has always been considered right in America, good, for men to suffer these agonies of growth, to search for and find their own identities. The farm boy went to the city, the garment-maker's son became a doctor, Abraham Lincoln taught himself to read—these were more than rags-to-riches stories. They were an integral part of the American dream. The problem for many was money, race, color, class, which barred

[1] Erik H. Erikson, *Young Man Luther, A Study in Psychoanalysis and History,* New York, 1958, pp. 15 ff. See also Erikson, *Childhood and Society,* New York, 1950, and Erikson, "The Problem of Ego Identity." *Journal of the American Psychoanalytical Association,* Vol. 4, 1956, pp. 56–121.

them from choice—not what they would be if they were free to choose.

Even today a young man learns soon enough that he must decide who he wants to be. If he does not decide in junior high, in high school, in college, he must somehow come to terms with it by twenty-five or thirty, or he is lost. But this search for identity is seen as a greater problem now because more and more boys cannot find images in our culture—from their fathers or other men—to help them in their search. The old frontiers have been conquered, and the boundaries of the new are not so clearly marked. More and more young men in America today suffer an identity crisis for want of any image of man worth pursuing, for want of a purpose that truly realizes their human abilities.

But why have theorists not recognized this same identity crisis in women? In terms of the old conventions and the new feminine mystique women are not expected to grow up to find out who they are, to choose their human identity. Anatomy is woman's destiny, say the theorists of femininity; the identity of women is determined by her biology.

But is it? More and more women are asking themselves this question. As if they were waking from a coma, they ask, "Where am I . . . what am I doing here?" For the first time in their history, women are becoming aware of an identity crisis in their own lives, a crisis which began many generations ago, has grown worse with each succeeding generation, and will not end until they, or their daughters, turn an unknown corner and make of themselves and their lives the new image that so many women now so desperately need.

In a sense that goes beyond any one woman's life, I think this is the crisis of women growing up—a turning point from an immaturity that has been called femininity to full human identity. I think women had to suffer this crisis of identity, which began a hundred years ago, and have to suffer it still today, simply to become fully human.

lerone bennett   BLACK AND WHITE FREEDOM

Lerone Bennett, Jr. (1928–   ) was born in Mississippi. In Jackson he worked on his high school newspaper and edited the local weekly, The Mississippi Enterprise. *During his college years at Morehouse College in Atlanta there was more work in journalism, including the editorship of the student newspaper. After his graduation he was first a reporter and then city editor for the* Atlanta Daily World. *In 1953 he became an associate editor of* Jet *and* Ebony; *in 1960 he became the latter magazine's first senior editor. Bennett is the author of* Before the Mayflower: A History of the Negro in America, 1619–1966; The Negro Mood and Other Essays; What Manner of Man (*a biography of Martin Luther King*); and Confrontation: Black and White. *The essay which follows was first published in the* Negro Digest (*March 1967*).

There has never been a free people, a free country, a real democracy on the face of this earth.

In a city of some 300,000 slaves and 90,000 so-called free men, Plato sat down and praised freedom in exquisitely elegant phrases.

In a colony of 500,000 slaves and thousands of white indentured servants, Thomas Jefferson, a wealthy slaveowner, sat down and wrote the memorable words of the Declaration of Independence.

In a country with 10 million second-class citizens and millions on millions of poverty-stricken whites, Woodrow Wilson segregated the toilets in Washington, D. C., and went forth to make the world safe for democracy.

There has never been a free people, a free country, a real democracy in the recorded history of man.

The great masses of men have always lived in suburbs of hell.

The great masses of men and almost all women have always been anvils for the hammers of the few.

We have gathered therefore to talk about a subject which has no past, insofar as mankind is concerned, and which can have no future, unless it is visualized and made concrete in the body of mankind. And it seems to me that one forfeits the right to talk about freedom unless one is prepared to face that fact and to do something about it.

Almost 200 years ago, at a time of revolutionary turbulence not unlike the present, Tom Paine held that unpalatable truth up to the unseeing eyes of his contemporaries. "Freedom," he said, hath been hunted around the Globe . . . O! receive the fugitive, and prepare in time an asylum for mankind." Today, after a thousand evasions, after a thousand proclamations and manifestoes, freedom is still a fugitive—in America as well as in Russia, in Portugal as well as in Angola, in England as well as in Rhodesia, in Boston as well as in Mississippi.

We live in a world where two-thirds of the people are hungry.

We live in a world where most of the peoples are diseased and illiterate.

In such a world, who has the effrontery—who has the gall—to praise the state of freedom?

The whole problem of freedom in the white and nonwhite worlds must be placed first in this larger context, for henceforth it will be impossible to speak of freedom in terms of the concerns of the tiny minority of men who live in Europe and North America. We must note, moreover, that freedom in Western Europe and North America is abstract, negative and largely illusory. And even in these areas, millions live on the edge of despair, and millions more are slaves to their skin or to their omnivorous machines.

It will be my argument here that the truth of freedom in the world is the truth of the truly disinherited. And by that I mean that the state of freedom is most accurately reflected in the lives of the men on the bottom. The men on the top and the men in the middle can remain ignorant of what they do and of what they are. But the men on the bottom experience the truth of society irremediably. They are the truth of every society. In them, we can see what we are, and what we have become. In the mirror of their eyes, we can measure the depth of our alienation from freedom and from man.

To be even more explicit and to bring the matter closer to home, I intend to maintain here that racism is the best index of the failure of American society to create a human and equitable society *for white people*. My argument here is the very simple one that the depth of racism is a measure of the unfreedom in the white community. And from that premise, we can conclude that black men are not free because white men are not free. And by all this we must understand that when the Emancipation Proclamation finally comes it will be most of all an emancipation of white people from the fears and frailties that cruelly twist and goad their lives.

Before pursuing that argument, let us pause for a moment and examine the meaning and implications of the word that everybody praises and few people live. As we all know, freedom lends itself to numerous interpretations. In the white Western world, it is usually defined negatively as "freedom from." This definition finds its truth in certain abstract liberties: freedom of speech, freedom of association, *et cetera*. To define freedom thusly, and to stop there, is, in my opinion, a perversion of freedom, for freedom also means "freedom to." And this positive definition finds its truth in concrete possibilities created in the social field, in the right to work, in the right to eat, in the right to shelter, in the right to be.

There is still another definition of freedom, a psychological one, which stresses the act of willing or choosing. And this definition, in turn, is linked to a fourth one which contends that man—by his ability to rise above or transcend a situation, any situation, by his ability to say No—is the measure and the meaning of freedom in the world.

In my opinion, no definition of freedom is adequate in today's world which does not embrace all these meanings—freedom from, freedom to transcendence—in a concrete context linked to conditions that open or close real possibilities to concrete men in their social and historical situation. Such a definition would recognize the existentialist truth that man *is* freedom and would recognize that the alienation of the world from freedom is a measure of its alienation from man and the possibilities of man. It would also recognize the truth that man has not yet been created and that the creation of man—black man as well as white man—awaits the winning of real, concrete freedom for all men.

Here and there, across the great wastelands of time, little knots of men have glimpsed the terrifying possibilities of that paradox. I think particularly of African village democracy and other free forms developed by American Indians and other communal groups. But these groups were hemmed in by material limitations and it was left to Western Europe to free man from feudal restrictions and to hoist high the standards of individuality and personal autonomy. But Europe, in its lunge toward freedom, made three fatal errors. First of all, and most important of all, Europe experienced its newfound freedom as the untrammelled exercise of the ego. And in pursuit of the goal of possessive individualism, it drew a circle around itself, excluding and enslaving three-fourths of mankind.

Second, out of sheer terror, Europe cut freedom into two parts, separating man into positive and negative poles, the mind and the body, reason and emotion, sex and the soul. Refusing to recognize the full force of freedom, which manifests itself in sex as well as in prayer, Europe facilitated that manic process by which men project their rejected freedom onto the scapegoats and outcasts of society.

In the third place, Europe refused to admit the full logic of its own idea. With few exceptions, Europeans and the sons of Europeans found it difficult to extend the idea of freedom to poor whites and impossible to extend it to nonwhites. In Europe and in the extensions of Europe, freedom became a function of the skin and of property.

Despite the huge achievements of European technology and science, European freedom, beautiful as it was, was not freedom. Or better still: it was not yet freedom. Having freed man from arbitrary restraints, Europe stopped halfway, leaving man tied to the chains of caste, class and passion. Having expelled man from his tribal and feudal Eden, Europe retreated, in terror, from Nietzsche's lucid question:

"Not free from what, but free for what?"

America inherited Europe's immense achievements and its immense failures and extended both. The history of America, like the history of Europe, has been a history of a magnificent evasion of the multiple meanings of freedom. The most obvious example of that failure is the black American. But the failure to integrate black people into the American community is only a part of our culture's general inability to create a just and human environment.

Despite our alleged affluence, 30 to 40 million Americans, many of them white, live in abject poverty, and millions more live lives of harrowing economic insecurity.

Despite our extraordinary mechanical ability, which cannot be praised too highly, we have failed to create a truly human community. Machines are more real here than human beings—and vastly more important. In a society of machines, by machines and for machines, we are increasingly powerless, and a nihilistic individualism has made conformists—and cowards—of us all. Dehumanized, depersonalized, distracted by bread and television, we have almost lost sight of man. Mystified by an ethic which confuses the verb to be with the verb to have, we try to staunch the running wound of our lives by adding layers and layers of mechanical band-aids. We lack passion, we lack purpose, and we decide nothing. The great alternatives are formulated by others, and in our name and without our assent men, women, and little children are killed in poverty-stricken countries. Increasingly irresponsible as our choices become fewer, and as the world becomes more threatening, we whirl around and in a materialistic inferno between collective madness and collective self-destruction.

And we are afraid.

We are afraid of our neighbors, of Negroes, of Chinese, of Communists, of four-letter words, sex, fluoridation—we are afraid, in a word, of ourselves.

Because we fear ourselves and others, because we are dominated by machines and things, because we are not in control of our destiny, we are neither happy nor free.

"If one probes beneath the chrome-plated surface," Senator J. W. Fulbright says, "he comes inescapably to the conclusion that the American people by and large are not happy. . . . I believe . . . that America's trouble is basically one of aimlessness at home and frustration abroad."

As you have probably guessed by now, I believe America's trouble is at a deeper level. The problem, in my opinion, is structural, that is, institutional. We have not created a single community here. We have not even created a single community for white people. Men tell me that white people ought to love black people. But it is clear to me that white people don't love each other, not to speak of the fact that an incredibly large number of white Americans don't love themselves.

514

Racism in America is a reflection of this structural problem. As I have said elsewhere, we misunderstand racism completely if we do not see it as a confused and alienated protest against a suffocating reality. On the level of power, racism is used by men to effect magical solutions of the unresolved social problems in the white community. On a personal level, particularly among lower-income and middle-income whites, racism is an avenue of flight, a cry for help from desperate men stifling in the prisons of their skins. Viewed in this perspective, racism is a flight from freedom, a flight from the self, a flight from the intolerable burdens of being a man in a mechanized world.

There is considerable evidence that America's stress on possessive individualism induces exaggerated anxieties which are displaced onto the area of race relations. The fear of failure, the fear of competitors, the fear of losing status, of not living in the right neighborhood, of not having the right friends or the right gadgets: these fears weigh heavily on the minds of millions of Americans and lead to a search for avenues on the escape. And so the factory worker or the poor farmer who finds himself at a dead end with a nagging wife, a problem child and a past-due bill uses the black man as a screen to hide himself from himself and intolerable reality.

To adapt the perceptive words of Richard Wright, social discontent assumes many guises, and the social commentator who focuses on the police blotter misses the real clues to contemporary reality. By this I mean that it is possible to know, *before it happens*, that certain forms of violence will occur. It can be known, *before it happens*, that a native-born American, educated, healthy, with a pretty wife, a split-level house and two cars, with all the abstract liberties *but devoid of basic human satisfactions*, will seize upon a powerless black man and derive deep feelings of pleasure from hacking him to death with a chain. "But," as Wright said, "to know that a seemingly normal, ordinary American is capable of such brutality implies making a judgment about the nature and quality of our everyday American experiences which most Americans simply cannot do, FOR, TO ADMIT THAT OUR INDIVIDUAL EXPERIENCES ARE OF SO LOW A QUALITY . . . AS TO PRECLUDE THE DEEP, ORGANIC SATISFACTIONS NECESSARY FOR CIVILIZED, PEACEFUL LIVING, IS TO CONDEMN THE SYSTEM THAT PROVIDES THOSE EXPERIENCES."

The real question in America is how we build a society in which apparently normal people do not need scapegoats or whipping boys to build their egos and to maintain their dignity?

How can we build a society that will enhance freedom and integrity and obviate the need for racism?

First of all, we have to condemn the system.

And we have to condemn the system in the name of that America, of that Commonwealth of Silence, which was written, which was promised, and which has never existed. I am suggesting here that we must initiate a sustained dialogue on the foundations of our society. And we must demand the right to subject every institution to the claims of freedom.

Let me say immediately that I don't have all the answers. The only thing I know is that everything must be rethought again. We need a new definition of work embracing any act of value that a man brings to society and a new definition of politics embracing the full and effective participation of all men in formulating the alternatives and choosing between the alternatives of the political, economic and social decisions that affect their lives. We also need a new definition of sex which would free women for equal roles in the church, in labor unions, in the professions and every other institution of our society. I often say to my wife that women, not Negroes, are the most brainwashed people in the Western world. Of course, in this regard, I am very much like Thomas Jefferson. I want women to have absolute freedom everywhere right now—but I hope that the revolution starts with somebody else's wife.

But wherever the revolution starts, I am prepared to welcome it, for I believe that the future of freedom in America is dependent upon the formulation of a broader definition of freedom and of man and of woman than our society is based upon. And it seems to me that it is necessary to set liberty in the context of equality with the understanding that every individual is entitled to the space and the chance to fulfill himself, which is only another way of saying that every individual is entitled to the instruments that will permit him to go to the boundaries of himself.

This, I believe, is a precondition for black and white freedom in America. For if we want black men and white men to cooperate, we must create conditions that will make it possible for them to cooperate. In other words, we must change the conditions that lead white men to see black men as threats to their homes, to their jobs, to their masculinity. And to do this we must modify the situation of the white man from top to bottom. For to demand that white men give up their irrational responses to black reality is to demand that a situation which requires irrational responses be abolished.

We must conceive and organize in this country programs that will make it impossible for one man to profit by another man's fall.

We must conceive and organize in this community, and in every other community, programs that will relieve the economic pressures on all men so that some men will not find it to their short-term economic interest to keep other men down.

In other words, we must take the profit out of bigotry.

The first steps in this direction would be a guaranteed annual income, the extension of Medicare to all citizens, the elimination of regressive taxes, and housing and educational subsidies to lower- and middle-income groups.

Ultimately, however, such an effort would require a reevaluation of our dominant myths, including the myth of possessive individuality, which is the greatest single obstacle to individuality, and the myth of property, which is the greatest single obstacle to the free enjoyment of property by all men.

Let there be no misunderstanding here: I am not saying that property in itself is evil—what I'm saying is that property masquerading as God is the major roadblock to freedom in the world today. Men need a certain amount of property to validate themselves and their freedom, but freedom becomes unfreedom and life loses its meaning when property becomes an inhuman idol, when anything and everything is sacrificed to an abstract Thing.

There was an interesting article on this subject in the New York Post which I would like to quote at some length. The article referred to the summer marches by Dr. Martin Luther King, Jr., and his supporters through the Gage Park area of Chicago. Peter Hamill visited the neighborhood and wrote the following words:

"This was the way the Hollywood hustlers used to put their cardboard America together, in a time more innocent than ours.

"Children played in the streets, or burbled from baby carriages. Young boys mowed lawns which still smelled sweetly from the morning rains. Housewives pushed strollers to the grocery stores, or drove the family cars to the supermarkets. A man on vacation nailed a brass numeral to his front door. A lot of people seemed to be polishing automobiles with an almost reverent devotion. Gage Park on Monday afternoon seemed as innocuous as anyplace where Doris Day had ever lived on film.

"But underneath, past the front doors of those two-story houses, in the secret places behind those lawns and those automobiles and those smiling children, Gage Park was like a tray of summer worms. By the time the thing that is crawling through Gage Park has hooked its last inhabitant, that neighborhood is almost certainly going to murder someone. It is going to murder someone because of the accident of color. It is going to murder someone over the combination of wood, metal and concrete which the inhabitants fondly describe as their property."

The same animal is crawling through the Gage Parks of Boston and New York and California. And if we don't confront it soon, an unspeakably horrible disaster is going to happen here. It's going to happen because our churches and schools have not taught people that no thing is higher than man. It's going to happen because our civilization has not yet learned that men are important, whether they own property or not.

To a great extent, racism in America is grounded on the whole sick syndrome surrounding real estate, status, greed, and human pettiness. If we are serious about freedom, we are going to have to come to grips with that syndrome.

We hear a great deal about freedom and property, but we must have the courage to say that words cannot be prostituted with impunity. Freedom is a fine word, but it has its boundaries. Men who say the community is free when it is enslaved, men who say the sky is black when it is blue, are debasing reality and preparing the way for tyranny.

We can respect freedom only when it is intended for freedom. A freedom that denies freedom must be denied in the name of freedom. For to be free is not to have the power to do anything you want to do. I am oppressed if I am denied the right of free movement, but I am not oppressed if I am denied the right to deny my neighbor freedom of movement.

Beyond all that, we must note that the idea of one-class, one-kind neighborhoods is in and of itself a clear and present danger to American democracy. The standardized neighborhoods, the standardized houses, the standardized minds and the standardized fears which stretch from one end of America to another is a denial of the movement of life which advances by integrating differences. As Chardin has said: "Joy lies not in exclusiveness and isolation, but in variety which is the reservoir of experience and emotion." On the other hand, uniformity, sameness, standardization make for cultural stagnation and, as sure as night follows day, regimentation and eventually neo-Fascism.

In order to deal with the anti-democratic ideas, which have made deep inroads in American life, we must make revolutionary changes at every level of our lives. We confront, in a word, the need for not a law here or a law there but for a vital change in the whole spirit of our civilization.

All signs indicate that we are moving toward a critical point in American history. The rise of the Radical Right, the deepening despair in the ghetto, the deepening fear in the white community, the explicit avowals of *apartheid* in the recent elections: all these bespeak the seriousness of the moment.

This is an important moment in the history of the Commonwealth. There stretch out before us now two roads and two roads only. America must now become America or something else, a Fourth Reich perhaps or a Fourth Reich of the spirit. To put the matter bluntly—we must become what we say we are or give in to the secret dream that blights our hearts.

Let us rejoice that it has come to this.

Now that freedom is dangerous, perhaps men will stop prostituting it. Now that freedom is exploding in broad open daylight in the streets of America and Vietnam, perhaps we will be able to recognize her true friends.

As individuals, we are called upon to make a creative response to this challenge by assuming our own freedom and validating it in social acts designed to create spaces in which the seeds of freedom can grow.

In a very real sense, the struggle in America is a struggle to free white Americans or, to be quite precise, it is a struggle to put them in the presence of their freedom. And it seems to me that it is the duty of this convocation to send abroad the good news that one can be free, even in Boston or Chicago or New York.

Freedom isn't something you can buy on the installment plan. It is not a gift from anybody—it is a priceless possession that must be reclaimed and rewon every day. As Silone has said: "One can be free even under a dictatorship. All you have to do is to struggle against it." He who thinks with his own head and acts with his own heart is free. He who is not afraid of his neighbors is free. He who struggles for what he believes in is a free man. On the other hand: If you live in the richest Boston suburb and if you are lazy, timid, conformist, you are not free, but a slave.

Because men deny the tiny bit of psychological freedom at their disposal, it is necessary to awaken them by social movements in which wills confront each other. This is the meaning of the Black Revolution, which is inviting us to become ourselves by going to the limits of ourselves. This revolution defines the state of freedom in America today, and it tells us that freedom has no future in America if the black man does not have a future in freedom.

More than 100 years ago, Walt Whitman told Ralph Waldo Emerson: "Master, I am a man who has perfect faith. But Master, we have not come through centuries, caste, heroism, fables, to halt in this land today."

The spirit of Walt Whitman is marching today in the Harlems in our mind. Men and women made in Whitman's image are saying to us: "Fellow Americans, we have perfect faith. But Fellow Americans, we have not come through slavery, segregation, degradation, blood, cotton, roaches, rats, to halt in this land today."

Black Americans, by daring to claim their freedom, are daring us to claim our own.

And the movement which expresses that thrust will continue despite the recent revelations of the depth and extent of racism in America. Whatever the problems, whatever the setbacks, whatever the dangers, oppression must be rejected at any cost. For, as Du Bois said, the price of freedom is always less than the cost of oppression.

In the Black Revolution, America comes hard up against a new fact: *the color of the world has changed.* And with that change, a terrifying freedom has become the burden of all men, especially those men who were tyrannized for so long by the arbitrary limitations of their skin. If white men come forward now to claim their own freedom and individuality, if they abandon their trenches and come out into the open, America will become the America that was dreamed.

This is the real meaning of the Black Revolution, which is a desperate attempt to place before our freedom the burning alternatives history is offering us.

Walt Whitman said:

"We have not come through centuries, caste, fables, to halt in this land today."

Black Americans are saying:

"We have not come through slavery, segregation, degradation to halt in this land today."

And the question now is:

What do you say?

herbert marcuse   THE NEW FORMS OF CONTROL

Herbert Marcuse (1898–   ) has had the distinction of being condemned by such diverse critics as Pravda and the American Legion. The latter group raised $20,000 in 1968 in an attempt "to buy up his contract" at the University of California at San Diego. During that same year, with exquisite timing, the Pacific Division of the American Philosophical Association unanimously elected him its president.

Born of Jewish parents in Germany, Marcuse earned his Ph.D. at the University of Freiburg but left Germany in 1933 because of the Nazis. He taught at Columbia University, became a naturalized citizen, and served during World War II in the Office of Strategic Services. After the war he worked for the State Department and in 1951 returned to teaching at Columbia. From there he moved to Harvard, then to Brandeis, and in 1965 to San Diego.

He is the author of Reason and Revolution, Eros and Civilization, Soviet Marxism, *and* An Essay on Liberation. *The essay which follows is from his most popular book,* One-Dimensional Man *(1964).*

A comfortable, smooth, reasonable, democratic unfreedom prevails in advanced industrial civilization, a token of technical progress. Indeed, what could be more rational than the suppression of individuality in the mechanization of socially necessary but painful performances; the concentration of individual enterprises in more effective, more productive corporations; the regulation of free competition among unequally equipped economic subjects; the curtailment of prerogatives and national sovereignties which impede the international organization of resources. That this technological order also involves a political and intellectual coordination may be a regrettable and yet promising development.

The rights and liberties which were such vital factors in the origins and earlier stages of industrial society yield to a higher stage of this society: they are losing their traditional rationale and content. Freedom of thought, speech, and conscience were—just as free enterprise, which they served to promote and protect—essentially *critical* ideas, designed to replace an obsolescent material and intellectual culture by a more productive and rational one. Once institutionalized, these rights and liberties shared the fate of the society of which they had become an integral part. The achievement cancels the premises.

To the degree to which freedom from want, to concrete substance of all freedom, is becoming a real possibility, the liberties which pertain to a state of lower productivity are losing their former content. Independence of thought, autonomy, and the right to political opposition are being deprived of their basic critical function in a society which seems increasingly capable of satisfying the needs of the individuals through the way in which it is organized. Such a society may justly demand acceptance of its principles and institutions, and reduce the opposition to the discussion and promotion of alternative policies *within* the status quo. In this respect, it seems to make little difference whether the increasing satisfaction of needs is accomplished by an authoritarian or a non-authoritarian system. Under the conditions of a rising standard of living, non-conformity with the system itself appears to be socially useless, and the more so when it entails tangible economic and political disadvantages and threatens the smooth operation of the whole. Indeed, at least in so far as the necessities of life are involved, there seems to be no reason why the production and distribution of goods and services should proceed through the competitive concurrence of individual liberties.

Freedom of enterprise was from the beginning not altogether a blessing. As the liberty to work or to starve, it spelled toil, insecurity, and fear for the vast majority of the population. If the individual were no longer compelled to prove himself on the market, as a free economic subject, the disappearance of this kind of freedom would be one of the greatest achievements of civilization. The technological processes of mechanization and standardization might release individual energy into a yet uncharted realm of freedom beyond necessity. The very structure of human existence would be altered; the individual would be liberated from the work world's imposing upon him alien needs and alien possibilities. The individual would be free to exert autonomy over a life that would be his own. If the productive apparatus could be organized and directed toward the satisfaction of the vital needs, its control might well be centralized; such control would not prevent individual autonomy, but render it possible.

This is a goal within the capabilities of advanced industrial civilization, the "end" of technological rationality. In actual fact, however, the contrary trend operates: the apparatus imposes its economic and political requirements for defense and expansion on labor time and free time, on the material and intellectual culture. By virtue of the way it has organized its technological base, contemporary industrial society tends to be totalitarian. For "totalitarian" is not only a terroristic political coordination of society, but also a nonterroristic economic-technical coordination which operates through the manipulation of needs by vested interests. It thus precludes the emergence of an effective opposition against the whole. Not only a specific form of government or party rule makes for totalitarianism, but also a specific system of production and distribution which may well be compatible with a "pluralism" of parties, newspapers, "countervailing powers," etc.

522

Today political power asserts itself through its power over the machine process and over the technical organization of the apparatus. The government of advanced and advancing industrial societies can maintain and secure itself only when it succeeds in mobilizing, organizing, and exploiting the technical, scientific, and mechanical productivity available to industrial civilization. And this productivity mobilizes society as a whole, above and beyond any particular individual or group interests. The brute fact that the machine's physical (only physical?) power surpasses that of the individual, and of any particular group of individuals, makes the machine the most effective political instrument in any society whose basic organization is that of the machine process. But the political trend may be reversed; essentially the power of the machine is only the stored-up and projected power of man. To the extent to which the work world is conceived of as a machine and mechanized accordingly, it becomes the *potential* basis of a new freedom for man.

Contemporary industrial civilization demonstrates that it has reached the stage at which "the free society" can no longer be adequately defined in the traditional terms of economic, political, and intellectual liberties, not because these liberties have become insignificant, but because they are too significant to be confined within the traditional forms. New modes of realization are needed, corresponding to the new capabilities of society.

Such new modes can be indicated only in negative terms because they would amount to the negation of the prevailing modes. Thus economic freedom would mean freedom *from* the economy—from being controlled by economic forces and relationships; freedom from the daily struggle for existence, from earning a living. Political freedom would mean liberation of the individuals *from* politics over which they have no effective control. Similarly, intellectual freedom would mean the restoration of individual thought now absorbed by mass communication and indoctrination, abolition of "public opinion" together with its makers. The unrealistic sound of these propositions is indicative, not of their utopian character, but of the strength of the forces which prevent their realization. The most effective and enduring form of warfare against liberation is the implanting of material and intellectual needs that perpetuate obsolete forms of the struggle for existence.

The intensity, the satisfaction and even the character of human needs, beyond the biological level, have always been preconditioned. Whether or not the possibility of doing or leaving, enjoying or destroying, possessing or rejecting something is seized as a *need* depends on whether or not it can be seen as desirable and necessary for the prevailing societal institutions and interests. In this sense, human needs are historical needs and, to the extent to which the society demands the repressive development of the individual,

523

his needs themselves and their claim for satisfaction are subject to overriding critical standards.

We may distinguish both true and false needs. "False" are those which are superimposed upon the individual by particular social interests in his repression: the needs which perpetuate toil, aggressiveness, misery, and injustice. Their satisfaction might be most gratifying to the individual, but this happiness is not a condition which has to be maintained and protected if it serves to arrest the development of the ability (his own and others) to recognize the disease of the whole and grasp the chances of curing the disease. The result then is euphoria in unhappiness. Most of the prevailing needs to relax, to have fun, to behave and consume in accordance with the advertisements, to love and hate what others love and hate, belong to this category of false needs.

Such needs have a societal content and function which are determined by external powers over which the individual has no control; the development and satisfaction of these needs is heteronomous. No matter how much such needs may have become the individual's own, reproduced and fortified by the conditions of his existence; no matter how much he identifies himself with them and finds himself in their satisfaction, they continue to be what they were from the beginning—products of a society whose dominant interest demands repression.

The prevalence of repressive needs is an accomplished fact, accepted in ignorance and defeat, but a fact that must be undone in the interest of the happy individual as well as all those whose misery is the price of his satisfaction. The only needs that have an unqualified claim for satisfaction are the vital ones—nourishment, clothing, lodging at the attainable level of culture. The satisfaction of these needs is the prerequisite for the realization of *all* needs, of the unsublimated as well as the sublimated ones.

For any consciousness and conscience, for any experience which does not accept the prevailing societal interest as the supreme law of thought and behavior, the established universe of needs and satisfactions is a fact to be questioned—questioned in terms of truth and falsehood. These terms are historical throughout, and their objectivity is historical. The judgment of needs and their satisfaction, under the given conditions, involves standards of *priority*—standards which refer to the optimal development of the individual, of all individuals, under the optimal utilization of the material and intellectual resources available to man. The resources are calculable. "Truth" and "falsehood" of needs designate objective conditions to the extent to which the universal satisfaction of vital needs and, beyond it, the progressive alleviation of toil and poverty, are universally valid standards. But as historical standards, they do not only vary according to area and stage of development, they also can be defined only in (greater or lesser) *contra-*

diction to the prevailing ones. What tribunal can possibly claim the authority of decision?

In the last analysis, the question of what are true and false needs must be answered by the individuals themselves, but only in the last analysis; that is, if and when they are free to give their own answer. As long as they are kept incapable of being autonomous, as long as they are indoctrinated and manipulated (down to their very instincts), their answer to this question cannot be taken as their own. By the same token, however, no tribunal can justly arrogate to itself the right to decide which needs should be developed and satisfied. Any such tribunal is reprehensible, although our revulsion does not do away with the question: how can the people who have been the object of effective and productive domination by themselves create the conditions of freedom?

The more rational, productive, technical, and total the repressive administration of society becomes, the more unimaginable the means and ways by which the administered individuals might break their servitude and seize their own liberation. To be sure, to impose Reason upon an entire society is a paradoxical and scandalous idea—although one might dispute the righteousness of a society which ridicules this idea while making its own population into objects of total administration. All liberation depends on the consciousness of servitude, and the emergence of this consciousness is always hampered by the predominance of needs and satisfactions which, to a great extent, have become the individual's own. The process always replaces one system of preconditioning by another; the optimal goal is the replacement of false needs by true ones, the abandonment of repressive satisfaction.

The distinguishing feature of advanced industrial society is its effective suffocation of those needs which demand liberation—liberation also from that which is tolerable and rewarding and comfortable—while it sustains and absolves the destructive power and repressive function of the affluent society. Here, the social controls exact the overwhelming need for the production and consumption of waste; the need for stupefying work where it is no longer a real necessity; the need for modes of relaxation which soothe and prolong this stupefication; the need for maintaining such deceptive liberties as free competition at administered prices, a free press which censors itself, free choice between brands and gadgets.

Under the rule of a repressive whole, liberty can be made into a powerful instrument of domination. The range of choice open to the individual is not the decisive factor in determining the degree of human freedom, but *what* can be chosen and what *is* chosen by the individual. The criterion for free choice can never be an absolute one, but neither is it entirely relative. Free election of masters does not abolish the masters or the slaves. Free choice among a wide variety of goods and services does not signify freedom if these goods and services sustain social controls over a life of toil and fear— that is, if they sustain alienation. And the spontaneous reproduction of superimposed needs by the individual does not establish autonomy; it only testifies to the efficacy of the controls.

Our insistence on the depth and efficacy of these controls is open to the objection that we overrate greatly the indoctrinating power of the "media," and that by themselves the people would feel and satisfy the needs which are now imposed upon them. The objection misses the point. The pre-conditioning does not start with the mass production of radio and television and with the centralization of their control. The people enter this stage as preconditioned receptacles of long standing; the decisive difference is in the flattening out of the contrast (or conflict) between the given and the possible, between the satisfied and the unsatisfied needs. Here, the so-called equalization of class distinctions reveals its ideological function. If the worker and his boss enjoy the same television program and visit the same resort places, if the typist is as attractively made up as the daughter of her employer, if the Negro owns a Cadillac, if they all read the same newspaper, then this assimilation indicates not the disappearance of classes, but the extent to which the needs and satisfactions that serve the preservation of the Establishment are shared by the underlying population.

Indeed, in the most highly developed areas of contemporary society, the transplantation of social into individual needs is so effective that the difference between them seems to be purely theoretical. Can one really distinguish between the mass media as instruments of information and entertainment, and as agents of manipulation and indoctrination? Between the automobile as nuisance and as convenience? Between the horrors and the comforts of functional architecture? Between the work for national defense and the work for corporate gain? Between the private pleasure and the commercial and political utility involved in increasing the birth rate?

We are again confronted with one of the most vexing aspects of ad-vanced industrial civilization: the rational character of its irrationality. Its productivity and efficiency, its capacity to increase and spread comforts, to turn waste into need, and destruction into construction, the extent to which this civilization transforms the object world into an extension of man's mind and body makes the very notion of alienation questionable. The people recognize themselves in their commodities; they find their soul in their automobile, hi-fi set, split-level home, kitchen equipment. The very mechanism which ties the individual to his society has changed, and social control is anchored in the new needs which it has produced.

The prevailing forms of social control are technological in a new sense. To be sure, the technical structure and efficacy of the productive and destructive apparatus has been a major instrumentality for subjecting the population to the established social division of labor throughout the modern period. Moreover, such integration has always been accompanied by more obvious forms of compulsion: loss of livelihood, the administration of justice, the police, the armed forces. It still is. But in the contemporary period, the technological controls appear to be the very embodiment of Reason for the benefit of all social groups and interests—to such an extent that all contradiction seems irrational and all counteraction impossible.

No wonder then that, in the most advanced areas of this civilization, the social controls have been introjected to the point where even individual protest is affected at its roots. The intellectual and emotional refusal "to go along" appears neurotic and impotent. This is the socio-psychological aspect of the political event that marks the contemporary period: the passing of the historical forces which, at the preceding stage of industrial society, seemed to represent the possibility of new forms of existence.

But the term "introjection" perhaps no longer describes the way in which the individual by himself reproduces and perpetuates the external controls exercised by his society. Introjection suggests a variety of relatively spontaneous processes by which a Self (Ego) transposes the "outer" into the "inner." Thus introjection implies the existence of an inner dimension distinguished from and even antagonistic to the external exigencies—an individual consciousness and an individual unconscious *apart from* public opinion and behavior. The idea of "inner freedom" here has its reality: it designates the private space in which man may become and remain "himself."

Today this private space has been invaded and whittled down by technological reality. Mass production and mass distribution claim the *entire* individual, and industrial psychology has long since ceased to be confined to the factory. The manifold processes of introjection seem to be ossified in almost mechanical reactions. The result is, not adjustment but *mimesis:* an immediate identification of the individual with *his* society and, through it, with the society as a whole.

This immediate, automatic identification (which may have been characteristic of primitive forms of association) reappears in high industrial civilization; its new "immediacy," however, is the product of a sophisticated, scientific management and organization. In this process, the "inner" dimension of the mind in which opposition to the status quo can take root is whittled down. The loss of this dimension, in which the power of negative thinking—the critical power of Reason—is at home, is the ideological counterpart to the very material process in which advanced industrial society silences and reconciles the opposition. The impact of progress turns

Reason into submission to the facts of life, and to the dynamic capability of producing more and bigger facts of the same sort of life. The efficiency of the system blunts the individuals' recognition that it contains no facts which do not communicate the repressive power of the whole. If the individuals find themselves in the things which shape their life, they do so, not by giving, but by accepting the law of things—not the law of physics but the law of their society.

I have just suggested that the concept of alienation seems to become questionable when the individuals identify themselves with the existence which is imposed upon them and have in it their own development and satisfaction. This identification is not illusion but reality. However, the reality constitutes a more progressive stage of alienation. The latter has become entirely objective; the subject which is alienated is swallowed up by its alienated existence. There is only one dimension, and it is everywhere and in all forms. The achievements of progress defy ideological indictment as well as justification; before their tribunal, the "false consciousness" of their rationality becomes the true consciousness.

This absorption of ideology into reality does not, however, signify the "end of ideology." On the contrary, in a specific sense advanced industrial culture is *more* ideological than its predecessor, inasmuch as today the ideology is in the process of production itself. In a provocative form, this proposition reveals the political aspects of the prevailing technological rationality. The productive apparatus and the goods and services which it produces "sell" or impose the social system as a whole. The means of mass transportation and communication, the commodities of lodging, food, and clothing, the irresistible output of the entertainment and information industry carry with them prescribed attitudes and habits, certain intellectual and emotional reactions which bind the consumers more or less pleasantly to the producers and, through the latter, to the whole. The products indoctrinate and manipulate; they promote a false consciousness which is immune against its falsehood. And as these beneficial products become available to more individuals in more social classes, the indoctrination they carry ceases to be publicity; it becomes a way of life. It is a good way of life—much better than before—and as a good way of life, it militates against qualitative change. Thus emerges a pattern of *one-dimensional thought and behavior* in which ideas, aspirations, and objectives that, by their content, transcend the established universe of discourse and action are either repelled or reduced to terms of this universe. They are redefined by the rationality of the given system and of its quantitative extension.

The trend may be related to a development in scientific method: operationalism in the physical, behaviorism in the social sciences. The

528

common feature is a total empiricism in the treatment of concepts; their meaning is restricted to the representation of particular operations and behavior. The operational point of view is well illustrated by P. W. Bridgman's analysis of the concept of length:

> We evidently know what we mean by length if we can tell what the length of any and every object is, and for the physicist nothing more is required. To find the length of an object, we have to perform certain physical operations. The concept of length is therefore fixed when the operations by which length is measured are fixed: that is, the concept of length involves as much and nothing more than the set of operations by which length is determined. In general, we mean by any concept nothing more than a set of operations; *the concept is synonymous with the corresponding set of operations.*

Bridgman has seen the wide implications of this mode of thought for the society at large:

> To adopt the operational point of view involves much more than a mere restriction of the sense in which we understand 'concept,' but means a far-reaching change in all our habits of thought, in that we shall no longer permit ourselves to use as tools in our thinking concepts of which we cannot give an adequate account in terms of operations.

Bridgman's prediction has come true. The new mode of thought is today the predominant tendency in philosophy, psychology, sociology, and other fields. Many of the most seriously troublesome concepts are being "eliminated" by showing that no adequate account of them in terms of operations or behavior can be given. The radical empiricist onslaught . . . thus provides the methodological justification for the debunking of the mind by the intellectuals—a positivism which, in its denial of the transcending elements of Reason, forms the academic counterpart of the socially required behavior.

Outside the academic establishment, the "far-reaching change in all our habits of thought" is more serious. It serves to coordinate ideas and goals with those exacted by the prevailing system, to enclose them in the system, and to repel those which are irreconcilable with the system. The reign of such a one-dimensional reality does not mean that materialism rules, and that the spiritual, metaphysical, and bohemian occupations are petering out. On the contrary, there is a great deal of "Worship together this week," "Why not try God," Zen, existentialism, and beat ways of life, etc. But such modes of protest and transcendence are no longer contradictory to the status quo and no longer negative. They are rather the ceremonial part of practical behaviorism, its harmless negation, and are quickly digested by the status quo as part of its healthy diet.

One-dimensional thought is systematically promoted by the makers of politics and their purveyors of mass information. Their universe of discourse is populated by self-validating hypotheses which, incessantly and monopolistically repeated, become hypnotic definitions or dictations. For example, "free" are the institutions which operate (and are operated on) in the countries of the Free World; other transcending modes of freedom are by definition either anarchism, communism, or propaganda. "Socialistic" are all encroachments on private enterprises not undertaken by private enterprise itself (or by government contracts), such as universal and comprehensive health insurance, or the protection of nature from all too sweeping commercialization, or the establishment of public services which may hurt private profit. This totalitarian logic of accomplished facts has its Eastern counterpart. There, freedom is the way of life instituted by a communist regime, and all other transcending modes of freedom are either capitalistic, or revisionist, or leftist sectarianism. In both camps, non-operational ideas are non-behavioral and subversive. The movement of thought is stopped at barriers which appear as the limits of Reason itself.

Such limitation of thought is certainly not new. Ascending modern rationalism, in its speculative as well as empirical form, shows a striking contrast between extreme critical radicalism in scientific and philosophic method on the one hand, and an uncritical quietism in the attitude toward established and functioning social institutions. Thus Descartes' *ego cogitans*[1] was to leave the "great public bodies" untouched, and Hobbes held that "the present ought always to be preferred, maintained, and accounted best." Kant agreed with Locke in justifying revolution *if and when* it has succeeded in organizing the whole and in preventing subversion.

However, these accommodating concepts of Reason were always contradicted by the evident misery and injustice of the "great public bodies" and the effective, more or less conscious rebellion against them. Societal conditions existed which provoked and permitted real dissociation from the established state of affairs; a private as well as political dimension was present in which dissociation could develop into effective opposition, testing its strength and the validity of its objectives.

With the gradual closing of this dimension by the society, the self-limitation of thought assumes a larger significance. The interrelation between scientific-philosophical and societal processes, between theoretical and practical Reason, asserts itself "behind the back" of the scientists and

[1] "the thinking I," a reference to Descartes' "I think, therefore I am."

530

philosophers. The society bars a whole type of oppositional operations and behavior; consequently, the concepts pertaining to them are rendered illusory or meaningless. Historical transcendence appears as metaphysical transcendence, not acceptable to science and scientific thought. The operational and behavioral point of view, practiced as a "habit of thought" at large, becomes the view of the established universe of discourse and action, needs and aspirations. The "cunning of Reason" works, as it so often did, in the interest of the powers that be. The insistence on operational and behavioral concepts turns against the efforts to free thought and be- havior *from* the given reality and *for* the suppressed alternatives. Theoretical and practical Reason, academic and social behaviorism meet on common ground: that of an advanced society which makes scientific and technical progress into an instrument of domination.

"Progress" is not a neutral term; it moves toward specific ends, and these ends are defined by the possibilities of ameliorating the human condition. Advanced industrial society is approaching the stage where continued progress would demand the radical subversion of the prevailing direction and organization of progress. This stage would be reached when material production (including the necessary services) becomes automated to the extent that all vital needs can be satisfied while necessary labor time is re- duced to marginal time. From this point on, technical progress would transcend the realm of necessity, where it served as the instrument of domination and exploitation which thereby limited its rationality; technology would become subject to the free play of faculties in the struggle for the pacification of nature and of society.

Such a state is envisioned in Marx's notion of the "abolition of labor." The term "pacification of existence" seems better suited to designate the historical alternative of a world which—through an international conflict which transforms and suspends the contradictions within the established societies—advances on the brink of a global war. "Pacification of existence" means the development of man's struggle with man and with nature, under conditions where the competing needs, desires, and aspirations are no longer organized by vested interests in domination and scarcity—an organization which perpetuates the destructive forms of this struggle.

Today's fight against this historical alternative finds a firm mass basis in the underlying population, and finds its ideology in the rigid orientation of thought and behavior to the given universe of facts. Validated by the ac- complishments of science and technology, justified by its growing produc- tivity, the status quo defies all transcendence. Faced with the possibility of pacification on the grounds of its technical and intellectual achievements, the mature industrial society closes itself against this alternative. Oper- ationalism, in theory and practice, becomes the theory and practice of *containment.* Underneath its obvious dynamics, this society is a thoroughly static system of life: self-propelling in its oppressive productivity and in its beneficial coordination. Containment of technical progress goes hand in hand with its growth in the established direction. In spite of the political fetters imposed by the status quo, the more technology appears capable of creating the conditions for pacification, the more are the minds and bodies of man organized against this alternative.

The most advanced areas of industrial society exhibit throughout these two features: a trend toward consummation of technological rationality, and intensive efforts to contain this trend within the established institutions. Here is the internal contradiction of this civilization: the irrational element in its rationality. It is the token of its achievements. The industrial society which makes technology and science its own is organized for the ever-more-effective domination of man and nature, for the ever-more-effective utilization of its resources. It becomes irrational when the success of these efforts opens new dimensions of human realization. Organization for peace is different from organization for war; the institutions which served the struggle for existence cannot serve the pacification of existence. Life as an end is qualitatively different from life as a means.

Such a qualitatively new mode of existence can never be envisaged as the mere by-product of economic and political changes, as the more or less spontaneous effect of the new institutions which constitute the necessary prerequisite. Qualitative change also involves a change in the *technical* basis on which this society rests—one which sustains the economic and political institutions through which the "second nature" of man as an aggressive object of administration is stabilized. The techniques of industrialization are political techniques; as such, they prejudge the possibilities of Reason and Freedom.

To be sure, labor must precede the reduction of labor, and industrialization must precede the development of human needs and satisfactions. But as all freedom depends on the conquest of alien necessity, the realization of freedom depends on the *techniques* of this conquest. The highest productivity of labor can be used for the perpetuation of labor, and the most efficient industrialization can serve the restriction and manipulation of needs.

When this point is reached, domination—in the guise of affluence and liberty—extends to all spheres of private and public existence, integrates all authentic opposition, absorbs all alternatives. Technological rationality reveals its political character as it becomes the great vehicle of better domination, creating a truly totalitarian universe in which society and nature, mind and body are kept in a state of permanent mobilization for the defense of this universe.

532

charles a. reich   THE COMING AMERICAN
                                                   REVOLUTION

*Charles A. Reich (1928–   ) summed up his earlier years rather sarcastically:
"New York private school, college, Yale Law School, I did everything right. I
was editor of The Law Journal at Yale. . . ." And for a time he went on doing
the "right" things: he served as a law clerk for Supreme Court Justice Hugo L.
Black, joined the law firm of Arnold, Fortas, and Porter, and began teaching at
Yale Law School in 1960. But then his thinking turned in the direction of what
Roszak termed the "counter culture," and he initiated an immensely popular
undergraduate course called "The Individual in America." In 1970 he published
The Greening of America, in which "The Coming American Revolution" is the
first chapter. Reich concluded his book by expressing his debts to many writers
and friends, and he added, "Much of the book was written in the Stiles-Morse
dining hall at Yale, and the encouragement, the coffee, the warmth of all the
people of the dining hall, are a part of it."*

America is dealing death, not only to people in other lands, but to its own
people. So say the most thoughtful and passionate of our youth, from
California to Connecticut. This realization is not limited to the new
generation. Talk to a retired school teacher in Mendocino, a judge in
Washington, D. C., a housewife in Belmont, Massachusetts, a dude rancher
in the Washington Cascades. We think of ourselves as an incredibly rich
country, but we are beginning to realize that we are also a desperately poor
country—poor in most of the things that throughout the history of mankind have been cherished as riches.

There is a revolution coming. It will not be like revolutions of the past.
It will originate with the individual and with culture, and it will change
the political structure only as its final act. It will not require violence to
succeed, and it cannot be successfully resisted by violence. It is now spreading with amazing rapidity, and already our laws, institutions and social
structure are changing in consequence. It promises a higher reason, a more
human community, and a new and liberated individual. Its ultimate
creation will be a new and enduring wholeness and beauty—a renewed
relationship of man to himself, to other men, to society, to nature, and to
the land.

This is the revolution of the new generation. Their protest and rebellion,
their culture, clothes, music, drugs, ways of thought, and liberated life-style
are not a passing fad or a form of dissent and refusal, nor are they in any
sense irrational. The whole emerging pattern, from ideals to campus demon-

533

strations to beads and bell bottoms to the Woodstock Festival, makes sense and is part of a consistent philosophy. It is both necessary and inevitable, and in time it will include not only youth, but all people in America.

The logic and necessity of the new generation—and what they are so furiously opposed to—must be seen against a background of what has gone wrong in America. It must be understood in light of the betrayal and loss of the American dream, the rise of the Corporate State of the 1960's, and the way in which that State dominates, exploits, and ultimately destroys both nature and man. Its rationality must be measured against the insanity of existing "reason"—reason that makes impoverishment, dehumanization, and even war appear to be logical and necessary. Its logic must be read from the fact that Americans have lost control of the machinery of their society, and only new values and a new culture can restore control. Its emotions and spirit can be comprehended only by seeing contemporary America through the eyes of the new generation.

The meaning and the future of the revolution emerge from a perspective on America. The revolution is a movement to bring man's thinking, his society, and his life to terms with the revolution of technology and science that has already taken place. Technology demands of man a new mind—a higher, transcendent reason—if it is to be controlled and guided rather than to become an unthinking monster. It demands a new individual responsibility for values, or it will dictate all values. And it promises a life that is more liberated and more beautiful than any man has known, if man has the courage and the imagination to seize that life.

The transformation that is coming invites us to reexamine our own lives. It confronts us with a personal and individual choice: are we satisfied with how we have lived; how would we live differently? It offers us a recovery of self. It faces us with the fact that this choice cannot be evaded, for as the freedom is already there, so must the responsibility be there.

At the heart of everything is what we shall call a change of consciousness. This means a "new head"—a new way of living—a new man. This is what the new generation has been searching for, and what it has started achieving. Industrialism produced a new man, too—one adapted to the demands of the machine. In contrast, today's emerging consciousness seeks a new knowledge of what it means to be human, in order that the machine, having been built, may now be turned to human ends; in order that man once more can become a creative force, renewing and creating his own life and thus giving life back to his society.

It is essential to place the American crisis and this change within individuals in a philosophic perspective, showing how we got to where we are, and where we are going. Current events are so overwhelming that we only see from day to day, merely responding to each crisis as it comes, seeing only immediate evils, and seeking inadequate solutions such as merely ending the war, or merely changing our domestic priorities. A longer-range view is necessary.

What is the nature of the present American crisis? Most of us see it as a collection of problems, not necessarily related to each other, and, although profoundly troubling, nevertheless within the reach of reason and reform. But if we list these problems, not according to topic, but as elements of larger issues concerning the structure of our society itself, we can see that the present crisis is an organic one, that it arises out of the basic premises by which we live and that no mere reform can touch it.

1. *Disorder, corruption, hypocrisy, war.* The front pages of newspapers tell of the disintegration of the social fabric and the resulting atmosphere of anxiety and terror in which we all live. Lawlessness is most often associated with crime and riots, but there is lawlessness and corruption in all the major institutions of our society—matched by an indifference to responsibility and consequences, and a pervasive hypocrisy that refuses to acknowledge the facts that are everywhere visible. Both lawlessness and evasion found expression in the Vietnam War, with its unprincipled destruction of everything human, and its random, indifferent, technological cruelty.

2. *Poverty, distorted priorities, and law-making by private power.* America presents a picture of drastic poverty amid affluence, an extremity of contrast unknown in other industrial nations. Likewise there is a superabundance of some goods, services, and activities such as defense manufacture, while other needs, such as education and medical care, are at a starvation level for many. These closely related kinds of inequality are not the accidents of a free economy, they are intentionally and rigidly built into the laws of our society by those with powerful influence; an example is the tax structure which subsidizes private wealth and production of luxuries and weapons at the direct expense of impoverished people and impoverished services. The nation has a planned economy, and the planning is done by the exercise of private power without concern for the general good.

3. *Uncontrolled technology and the destruction of environment.* Technology and production can be great benefactors of man, but they are mindless instruments; if undirected they roll along with a momentum of their own. In our country they pulverize everything in their path: the landscape, the natural environment, history and tradition, the amenities and civilities, the privacy and spaciousness of life, beauty, and the fragile, slow-growing social structures which bind us together. Organization and bureaucracy, which are applications of technology to social institutions, increasingly dictate how we shall live our lives, with the logic of organization taking precedence over any other values.

4. *Decline of democracy and liberty; powerlessness.* The Constitution and Bill of Rights have been weakened, imperceptibly but steadily. The nation has gradually become a rigid managerial hierarchy, with a small elite and a great mass of the disenfranchised. Democracy has rapidly lost ground as power is increasingly captured by giant managerial institutions and corporations, and decisions are made by experts, specialists, and professionals safely insulated from the feelings of the people. Most governmental power has shifted from Congress to administrative agencies, and corporate power is free to ignore both stockholders and consumers. As regulation and administration have grown, liberty has been eroded and bureaucratic discretion has taken the place of the rule of law. Today both dissent and efforts at change are dealt with by repression. The pervasiveness of police, security men, the military, and compulsory military service show the changed character of American liberty.

5. *The artificiality of work and culture.* Work and living have become more and more pointless and empty. There is no lack of meaningful projects that cry out to be done, but our working days are used up in work that lacks meaning: making useless or harmful products, or servicing the bureaucratic structures. For most Americans, work is mindless, exhausting, boring, servile, and hateful, something to be endured while "life" is confined to "time off." At the same time our culture has been reduced to the grossly commercial; all cultural values are for sale, and those that fail to make a profit are not preserved. Our life activities have become plastic, vicarious, and false to our genuine needs, activities fabricated by others and forced upon us.

6. *Absence of community.* America is one vast, terrifying anti-community. The great organizations to which most people give their working day, and the apartments and suburbs to which they return at night, are equally places of loneliness and alienation. Modern living has obliterated place, locality, and neighborhood, and given us the anonymous separateness of our existence. The family, the most basic social system, has been ruthlessly stripped to its functional essentials. Friendship has been coated over with a layer of impenetrable artificiality as men strive to live roles designed for them. Protocol, competition, hostility, and fear have replaced the warmth of the circle of affection which might sustain man against a hostile universe.

7. *Loss of self.* Of all of the forms of impoverishment that can be seen or felt in America, loss of self, or death in life, is surely the most devastating. It is, even more than the draft and the Vietnam War, the source of discontent and rage in the new generation. Beginning with school, if not before, an individual is systematically stripped of his imagination, his creativity, his heritage, his dreams, and his personal uniqueness, in order to style him into a productive unit for a mass, technological society. Instinct,

feeling, and spontaneity are repressed by overwhelming forces. As the individual is drawn into the meritocracy, his working life is split from his home life, and both suffer from a lack of wholeness. Eventually, people virtually become their professions, roles, or occupations, and are thenceforth strangers to themselves. Blacks long ago felt their deprivation of identity and potential for life. But white "soul" and blues are just beginning. Only a segment of youth is articulately aware that they too suffer an enforced loss of self—they too are losing the lives that could be theirs.

What has caused the American system to go wrong in such an organic way? The first crucial fact is the existence of a universal sense of powerlessness. We seem to be living in a society that no one created and that no one wants. The feeling of powerlessness extends even to the inhabitants of executive offices. Yet, paradoxically, it is also a fact that we have available to us the means to begin coping with virtually all of the problems that beset us. Most people would initially deny this, but reflection shows how true it is. We know what causes crime and social disorder, and what can be done to eliminate those causes. We know the steps that can be taken to create greater economic equality. We are in possession of techniques to fashion and preserve more livable cities and environments. Our problems are vast, but so is our store of techniques; it is simply not being put to use.

Urban riots offer a well-documented case in point for the late 1960's. They were predictable and they were predicted. Their causes and the appropriate remedies (which include education, housing, and jobs) have been known and described for many years by students of social problems. After the riots took place, a presidential commission reviewed the events, and their findings gave wide publicity to the same knowledge; the commission's recommendations were not acted upon, just as the preexisting knowledge had not been acted upon. Response was either nonexistent, absurdly inadequate, or childishly irrational (such as the proposal to deprive looters of jobs with public agencies).

The American crisis, then, seems clearly to be related to an inability to act. But what is the cause of this paralysis? Why, in the face of every warning, have we been unable to act? Why have we not used our resources more wisely and justly? We tell ourselves that social failure comes down to an individual moral failure: we must have the will to act; we must first find concern and compassion in our hearts. The theme is deep in America, from Hawthorne to E. B. White, from the Puritans to Richard Nixon, from *Time* to *The New York Times*. But this diagnosis is not good enough. It is contradicted by the *experience* of powerlessness that is encountered by so many people today. In 1968 a majority of the people certainly wanted peace, but they could not turn their individual wills into action by society. It is

537

not that we do not will action, but that we are unable to act, unable to put existing knowledge to use. Is something wrong with the machinery of society? It apparently no longer works, or we no longer know how to make it work.

What is the machinery that we rely upon to turn our wishes into realities? In the private sphere, the market system. In the public sphere, the public version of the market system: voter democracy, or democratic pluralism. In both spheres, a system of administration and law, resting ultimately on the Constitution. Could it be that the American crisis results from a structure that is obsolete? All of the other machinery we use becomes obsolete in a short time. A social institution, which is, after all, only another type of machinery, is not necessarily immune from the same laws of obsolescence. The ideals or principles of a society might remain valid, but the means for applying the principles could lose their effectiveness.

If we seek to explain the American crisis in terms of obsolete structure, we might find an illustration in the ideal and the machinery of free speech. The ideal or principle is that every opinion must be expressed freely in order that truth be arrived at. But the machinery for carrying out this ideal was designed for a very different society than ours, a society of small villages, town meetings, and face-to-face discussions. The First Amendment furnishes no workable means for the public to be adequately informed about complex issues. News is cut down into a commodity by the mass media, a staccato piece of show business, and no one who only watches television and reads a typical newspaper could possibly know enough to be an intelligent voter. The vital decisions of the private sector of the economy receive even less adequate coverage and reporting. Moreover, the media systematically deny any fundamentally different or dissenting point of view a chance to be heard at all—it is simply kept off the air and out of the newspapers. The opinion that does get on television is commercially sponsored and thus heavily subsidized by government tax policies; the opinion that is not allowed is sometimes heavily penalized by the same tax laws (thus: the Georgia-Pacific Lumber Company's advertising is tax deductible; conservation advertising may not be). In short, our machinery for free speech is hopelessly ineffectual in the light of the way society is organized today, and this illustrates the plight of most of our democratic machinery which has not adapted to changing realities.

To explain the American crisis only in the above terms is, however, far from adequate. For one thing, it fails to take account of the whole Marxist analysis of capitalism. Those who analyze society in terms of class interests point out that there are powerful and privileged groups that profit greatly by the status quo. This power elite, and the monopolistic corporations it represents, has long exploited both people and environment. It profits from poverty, inequality, and war; it has a well-founded fear of democracy, liberty, and communal solidarity. The Marxists would argue that our government machinery is not naïvely obsolete; it has been captured by class interests. The same free speech illustration we used above would also illustrate a Marxist analysis: the media only disseminate the opinions that serve the interests of monopoly capital.

The Marxist analysis of the American crisis seems convincing. But is it a satisfactory explanation? The difficulty is that in focusing so strongly on economic interest, it does not take into account the vital factors of bureaucracy, organization, and technology which so dominate America today. These factors have a powerful momentum of their own that may not be inconsistent with class interests, but may well be indifferent to them. Thus we may be in the grip, not of capitalist exploiters, but of mindless, impersonal forces that pursue their own, non-human logic. A great deal of evidence supports this view.

Can the American crisis be defined, then, in terms of obsolete structure, monopoly capitalism, mindless technology, or perhaps some combination of the three? The question that we started with still remains: why are we unable to do anything to solve our problems? Government machinery can be overhauled; monopoly capitalism may be subjected to social regulation, as it has been in not only the communist countries but in the moderate-socialist countries; and technology is, after all, only a tool. There is something even deeper behind the crisis of structure and the crisis of inaction.

Whenever any attempt is made to begin confronting America's problems, we encounter a profound lack of understanding. This lack of understanding is not merely a phenomenon of the masses, for it extends to the powerful, the well educated, and the elite; it is not simply a lack of knowledge, for it includes many people who possess more than enough information. Its basis is a pervasive unreality. Our picture of our economy, of how we are governed, of how our culture is made, of how we may be threatened at home or abroad, is fantastically out of keeping with contemporary realities. Indeed, the central fact about America in 1970 is the discrepancy between the realities of our society and our beliefs about them. The gap is even greater in terms of our failure to understand the possibilities and potential of American life.

Unreality is the true source of powerlessness. What we do not understand, we cannot control. And when we cannot comprehend the major forces, structures, and values that pervade our existence, they must inevitably come to dominate us. Thus a true definition of the American crisis would say this: we no longer understand the system under which we live, hence the structure has become obsolete and we have become powerless; in turn, the system has been permitted to assume unchallenged power to dominate our lives, and now rumbles along, unguided and therefore indifferent to human ends.

What is this "understanding" that holds such a key place in our contemporary situation? Clearly the word "understanding" is inadequate, for we are talking about something much broader and deeper than "understanding" usually connotes. To describe what we are talking about, we propose to use the term "consciousness." It is a term that already has several meanings, including an important one in Marx, a medical one, a psychoanalytic one, a literary or artistic one, and one given us by users of hallucinogenic drugs. Our use of the term "consciousness" will not be exactly like any of these, but it gains meaning from all of them, and is consistent with all of them.

Consciousness, as we are using the term, is not a set of opinions, information, or values, but a total configuration in any given individual, which makes up his whole perception of reality, his whole world view. It is a common observation that once one has ascertained a man's beliefs on one subject, one is likely to be able to predict a whole range of views and reactions. Ask a stranger on a bus or airplane about psychiatry or redwoods or police or taxes or morals or war, and you can guess with fair accuracy his views on all the rest of these topics and many others besides, even though they are seemingly unrelated. If he thinks wilderness areas should be "developed" he is quite likely to favor punitive treatment for campus disruptions. If he is enthusiastic about hunting wild animals, he probably believes that the American economic system rests on individual business activity, and has an aversion to people with long hair.

It is apparent that the particular views we have mentioned really are related, and that an individual's opinions, understanding, and values are all part of some invisible whole. It is also apparent that consciousness is in substantial degree (but not necessarily entirely) socially determined. One evidence of this is the fact that many people have consciousnesses that are roughly similar, especially members of the same generation with the same social backgrounds. Also, when one hears a person's views and opinions, one can often tell something about his background, experience, and social role. The unity of consciousness in any individual is also revealed by the way in which it resists change, even in the smallest detail, and maintains a remarkable cohesion. Quite evidently the individual cannot allow any part of his consciousness to be challenged without feeling that the whole configuration is threatened. Thus a person who believes in "free enterprise" as part of his total perception of reality may resist, despite an overwhelming showing, the conclusion that "free enterprise" no longer serves to produce the same social consequences that it used to. Such a conclusion might undermine all of the assumptions under which this person has lived. Similarly, the violent reaction of some older people to long hair on boys shows that the adults feel a threat to the whole reality that they have constructed and lived by. An argument between people who are on different levels of consciousness often goes nowhere; there is no common ground on which they can meet.

Included within the idea of consciousness is a person's background, education, politics, insight, values, emotions, and philosophy, but consciousness is more than these or even the sum of them. It is the whole man; his "head"; his way of life. It is that by which he creates his own life and thus creates the society in which he lives.

As a mass phenomenon, consciousness is formed by the underlying economic and social conditions. There was a consciousness that went with peasant life in the Middle Ages, and a consciousness that went with small town, preindustrial life in America. Culture and government interact with consciousness; they are its products but they also help to form it. While consciousness is the creator of any social system, it can lag behind a system, once created, and even be manipulated by that system. Lag and manipulation are the factors that produce a consciousness characterized by unreality. If we believe in free enterprise, but the nation has become an interlocking corporate system, we are living in unreality as the victims of lag, and we are powerless to cope with the existing corporate system.

To show how this has worked out in America, and to show the true meaning of the new generation, we have attempted to classify three general types of consciousness. These three types predominate in America today. One was formed in the nineteenth century, the second in the first half of this century, the third is just emerging. Consciousness I is the traditional outlook of the American farmer, small businessman, and worker who is trying to get ahead. Consciousness II represents the values of an organizational society. Consciousness III is the new generation. The three categories are, of course, highly impressionistic and arbitrary; they make no pretense to be scientific. And, since each type of consciousness is a construct, we would not expect any real individual to exhibit in symmetrical perfection all the characteristics of one type of consciousness.

The concept of consciousness gives us the elements from which we can fashion an argument about what has happened and what is happening to America. For the chaos we have just described is not chaos at all, but part of a coherent pattern of history, values, and thought. In the paragraphs that follow, we set forth the logic that emerges from behind the crisis of our contemporary life.

The great question of these times is how to live in and with a technological society; what mind and what way of life can preserve man's humanity and his very existence against the domination of the forces he has created. This question is at the root of the American crisis, beneath all the immediate issues of lawlessness, poverty, meaninglessness, and war. It is this question to which America's new generation is beginning to discover an answer, an answer based on a renewal of life that carries the hope of restoring us to our sources and ourselves.

At the opening of the industrial era, Western society underwent a major change of values in which scientific technique, materialism, and the market system became ascendant over other, more humanistic values. Although the contradiction was not recognized at the time, these industrial values were inconsistent with the democratic and spiritual ideas of the new American nation, and they soon began to undermine these American ideals.

Every stage of human civilization is accompanied by, and also influenced by, a consciousness. When civilization changes slowly, the existing consciousness is likely to be in substantial accord with underlying material realities. But industrialism brought sudden uprooting and a rapidly accelerating rate of change. Consciousness then began to lag increasingly far behind reality, or to lose touch with a portion of reality altogether. Today a large segment of the American people still have a consciousness which was appropriate to the nineteenth-century society of small towns, face-to-face relationships, and individual economic enterprise. Another large segment of the people have a consciousness formed by organized technological and corporate society, but far removed from the realities of human needs.

In the second half of the twentieth century, this combination of an anachronistic consciousness characterized by myth, and an inhuman consciousness dominated by the machine-rationality of the Corporate State, have, between them, proved utterly unable to manage, guide, or control the immense apparatus of technology and organization that America has built. In consequence, this apparatus of power has become a mindless juggernaut, destroying the environment, obliterating human values, and assuming domination over the lives and minds of its subjects. To the injustices and exploitation of the nineteenth century, the Corporate State has added depersonalization, meaninglessness, and repression, until it has threatened to destroy all meaning and all life.

Faced with this threat to their very existence, the inhabitants of America have begun, as a matter of urgent biological necessity, to develop a new consciousness appropriate to today's realities and therefore capable of mastering the apparatus of power and bringing it under human control. This new consciousness is based on the present state of technology, and could not have arisen without it. And it represents a higher, transcendent form of reason; no lesser consciousness could permit us to exist, given the present state of our technology.

This transcendent reason has made its first appearance among the youth

542

of America. It is the product of the contradictions, failures, and exigencies of the Corporate State itself, not of any force external to the State. It is now in the process of rapidly spreading to wider and wider segments of youth, and by degrees to older people, as they experience the recovery of self that marks conversion to a different consciousness. The new consciousness is also in the process of revolutionizing the structure of our society. It does not accomplish this by direct political means, but by changing culture and the quality of individual lives, which in turn change politics and, ultimately, structure.

When the new consciousness has achieved its revolution and rescued us from destruction, it must go about the task of learning how to live in a new way. This new way of life presupposes all that modern science can offer. It tells us how to make technology and science work for, and not against, the interests of man. The new way of life proposes a concept of work in which quality, dedication, and excellence are preserved, but work is non-alienated, is the free choice of each person, is integrated into a full and satisfying life, and expresses and affirms each individual being. The new way of life makes both possible and necessary a culture that is nonartificial and nonalienated, a form of community in which love, respect, and a mutual search for wisdom replace the competition and separation of the past, and a liberation of each individual in which he is enabled to grow toward the highest possibilities of the human spirit.

The task of learning how to live in this way represents the chief philosophic undertaking for man after he saves himself from his present danger. It requires man to create a reality—a fiction based on what can offer men the best hope of a life that is both satisfying and beautiful.

jiddu krishnamurti   YOU ARE THE WORLD

It was evident even in his youth that Jiddu Krishnamurti (1895–   ) had remarkable qualities of mind, and over his long lifetime he has won world-wide respect for his integrity and perceptive, selfless teaching. He was only thirteen when Theosophist Annie Besant named him the most recent incarnation of Maitreya—the new Buddha—and the Order of the Star in the East was formed with Krishnamurti as its spiritual head. But in 1929 he renounced his role as a religious leader on the grounds that no man can lead another to the truth. And the Order was also repudiated: "The important thing," he said, "is to free your mind of envy, hate and violence; and for that you don't need an organization, do you? So-called religious organizations never liberate the mind, they only make it conform to a certain creed or belief." Thereafter Krishnamurti traveled throughout the world lecturing to (or, better, talking with) enormous numbers of people. He has also written voluminously. Among his titles are The Only Revolution, The Pool of Wisdom, The First and Last Freedom, Education and the Significance of Life, *and* Commentaries on Living. *The selection which follows is from* You Are the World *(1972).*

Considering the chaos and disorder in the world—both outwardly and inwardly—seeing all this misery, starvation, war, hatred, brutality—many of us must have asked what one can do. As a human being confronted with this confusion, what can I or you do? When we put that question, we feel we must be committed to some kind of political or sociological action, or some kind of religious search and discovery. One feels one must be committed, and throughout the world this desire to be committed has become very important. Either one is an activist, or one withdraws from this social chaos and pursues a vision. I think it is far more important not to be committed at all, but to be totally involved in the whole structure and nature of life. When you commit yourself, you are committed to a part and therefore the part becomes important and that creates division. Whereas, when one is involved completely, totally, with the whole problem of living, action is entirely different. Then action is not only inward, but also outward; it is in relationship with the whole problem of life. To be involved implies total relationship with every problem, with every thought and feeling of the human mind. And when one is so completely involved in life and not committed to any particular part or fragment of it, then one has to see what one can actually do as a human being.

For most of us, action is derived from an ideology. First we have an idea about what we should do, the idea being an ideology, a concept, a formula. Having formulated what we should do, we act according to that ideology. So there is always a division, and hence a conflict between action and what you have formulated that action should be. And as most of one's life is a series of conflicts, struggles, one inevitably asks oneself whether one can live in this world being completely involved with it, not in some isolated monastery.

Inevitably this brings about another question, which is: What is relationship? Because it is in that that we are involved—man in relationship with another man—that is the whole of life. If there were no relationship at all, if one actually lived completely in isolation, life would cease. Life is a movement in relationship. To understand that relationship and to end the conflict in that relationship is our entire problem. It is to see whether man can live at peace not only within himself, but also outwardly. Because then behaviour is righteous and we are concerned with behaviour, which is action. You might ask, 'What can one individual, one human being do, confronted with this immense problem of life with its confusion, wars, hatred, agony, suffering?' What can one human being do to bring about a change, a revolution, a radical state, a new way of looking, living? I think that is a wrong question, to say, 'What can I do to affect this total confusion and disorder.' If you put that question, 'What can I do, confronted with this disorder,' then you have already answered it; you can't do anything. Therefore it is a wrong question. But if you are concerned, not with what you can do confronted with this enormity of misery, but with how you can live a totally different life, then you will find that your relationship with man, with the whole community, with the world, undergoes a change. Because after all, you and I as human beings, we are the entire world—I'm not saying this rhetorically, but actually: I and you are the entire world. What one thinks, what one feels, the agony, the suffering, the ambition, the envy, the extraordinary confusion one is in, that is the world. There must be a change in the world, a radical revolution, one can't live as one is living, a bourgeois life, a life of superficiality, a life of shoddy existence from day to day, indifferent to what is happening. If you and I, as human beings, can change totally, then whatever we do will be righteous. Then we will not bring about a conflict within ourselves and therefore outwardly. So that is the problem. That is what the speaker wants to talk over with you this evening. Because as we said, how one conducts one's life, what one does in daily life—not at a moment of great crisis but actually every day—is of the highest importance. Relationship *is* life, and this relationship is a constant movement, a constant change.

So our question is: How am I, or you, to change so fundamentally, that tomorrow morning you wake up as a different human being meeting any problem that arises, resolving it instantly and not carrying it over as a burden, so that there is great love in your heart and you see the beauty of the hills and the light on the water? To bring about this change, obviously one must understand oneself, because self-knowledge, not theoretically but actually, whatever you are, is of the highest importance.

You know, when one is confronted with all these problems, one is deeply moved; not by words, not by the description, because the word is not the thing, the description is not the described. When one observes oneself as one actually is, then either one is moved to despair because one considers oneself as hopeless, ugly, miserable; or one looks at oneself without any judgment. And to look at oneself without any judgment is of the greatest importance, because that is the only way you can understand yourself and know about yourself. And in observing oneself objectively—which is not a process of self-centeredness, or self-isolation, or cutting oneself off from the whole of mankind or from another human being—one realises how terribly one is conditioned: by the economic pressures, by the culture in which one has lived, by the climate, by the food one eats, by the propaganda of the so-called religious organisations or by the Communists. This conditioning is not superficial but it goes down very deeply and so one asks whether one can ever be free of it, because if one is not free, then one is a slave, then one lives in incessant conflict and battle, which has become the accepted way of life.

I hope you are listening to the speaker, not merely to the words but using the words as a mirror to observe yourself. Then communication between the speaker and yourself becomes entirely different, then we are dealing with facts and not suppositions, or opinions, or judgments, then we are both concerned with this problem of how the mind can be unconditioned, changed completely. As we said, this understanding of oneself is only possible by becoming aware of our relationships. In relationship alone can one observe oneself; there all the reactions, all the conditionings are exposed. So in relationship one becomes aware of the actual state of oneself. And as one observes, one becomes aware of this immense problem of fear.

One sees the mind is always demanding to be certain, to be secure, to be safe. A mind that is safe, secure, is a bourgeois mind, a shoddy mind. Yet that is what all of us want: to be completely safe. And psychologically there is no such thing. See what takes place outwardly—it's quite interesting if you observe it—each person wants to be safe, secure. And yet psychologically he does everything to bring about his own destruction. You can see this. As long as there are nationalities with their sovereign governments, with their armies and navies and so on, there must be war. And yet psychologically we are conditioned to accept that we are a particular group, a particular nation, belonging to a particular ideology, or religion. I do not know if you have ever observed what mischief the religious organisations have done in the world, how they have divided man. You are a Catholic, I am a Protestant. To us the label is much more important than the actual state of affection, love, kindliness. Nations have divided us, nationalities have divided us. One can observe this division, which is our conditioning and which brings about fear.

So we are going to go into the question of what to do with fear. Unless we resolve this fear we live in darkness, we live in violence. A man who is not afraid is not aggressive, a man who has no sense of fear of any kind is really a free, a peaceful man. As human beings we must resolve this problem, because if we cannot, we cannot possibly live righteously. Unless one understands behaviour, conduct in which is involved virtue—you may spit on that word—and unless one is totally free of fear, the mind can never discover what truth is, what bliss is, and if there is such a thing as a timeless state. When there is fear you want to escape, and that escape is quite absurd, immature. So we have this problem of fear. Can the mind be free of it entirely, both at the conscious as well as at the so-called unconscious, deeper levels of the mind? That is what we are going to talk over this evening, because without understanding this question of fear and resolving it, the mind can never be free. And it is only in freedom that you can explore, discover. It is very important, it is essential, that the mind be free of fear. So shall we go into it?

Now first of all do please bear in mind that the description is not the described, so don't be caught by the description, by the words. The word, the description, is merely a means of communicating. But if you are held by the word you cannot go very far. One has to be aware not only of the meaning of the word, but also one has to realise that the word is not actually the thing. So what is fear? I hope we are going to do it together. Please don't just listen and disregard it; be involved, entirely live it. Because it is *your* fear, it's not mine. We are taking a journey together into this very conplex problem of fear. If one doesn't understand it and become free of it, relationship is not possible: relationship remains conflict, travail, misery.

What is fear? One is afraid of the past, of the present, or of something that might happen tomorrow. Fear involves time. One is afraid of death; that is in the future. Or one is afraid of something that has happened. Or one is afraid of the pain one has had when one was ill. Please follow this closely. Fear implies time: one is afraid of something—of some pain that one has had and which might happen again. One is afraid of something that might take place tomorrow, in the future. Or one is afraid of the present. All that involves time. Psychologically speaking, if there were no yesterday, today and tomorrow, there would be no fear. Fear is not only of time but it is the product of thought. That is, in thinking about what happened yesterday—which was painful—I am thinking that it might happen again tomorrow.

Thought produces this fear. Thought breeds fear: thinking about the pain, thinking about death, thinking about the frustrations, the fulfilments, what might happen, what should be, and so on. Thought produces fear and gives vitality to the continuance of fear. And thought, by thinking about what has given you pleasure yesterday, sustains that pleasure, gives it duration. So thought produces, sustains, nourishes, not only fear but also pleasure. Please observe it in yourself, see what actually goes on within you.

You have had a pleasurable or so-called enjoyable experience and you think about it. You want to repeat it, whether it is sex or any other experience. Thinking about that thing which has given a pleasurable moment, you want that pleasure repeated, continued. So thought is not only responsible for fear, but also for pleasure. One sees the truth of this, the actual fact that thought sustains pleasure and nourishes fear. Thought breeds both fear and pleasure; the two are not separate. Where there is the demand for pleasure, there must also be fear; the two are unavoidable because they are both the product of thought.

Please let's bear in mind that I am not persuading you of anything, I'm not making propaganda. God forbid! Because to make propaganda is to lie; if someone is trying to convince you of something, don't be convinced. We are dealing with something much more serious than being convinced, or with offering opinions and judgments. We are dealing with realities, with facts. And facts, which you observe, don't need an opinion. You haven't got to be told what the fact is, it is there, if you are capable of observing it.

So one sees that thought sustains and nourishes fear as well as pleasure. We want pleasure continued, we want more and more pleasure. The ultimate pleasure for man is to find out if there is a permanent state in heaven which is God; to him God is the highest form of pleasure. And if you observe, all social morality—which is really immoral—is based on pleasure and fear, reward and punishment.

Then one asks, when one sees this actual fact—not the description, not the word, but the thing described, the actual state of how thought brings this about: 'Is it possible for thought to come to an end?' The question sounds rather crazy, but it is not. You saw a sunset yesterday, the hills were extraordinarily lit in the evening sun and there was a glory, a beauty that gave you great enjoyment. Can one enjoy it so completely that it comes to an end, so that thought doesn't carry it over to tomorrow? And can one face fear, if there is such a thing as fear? This is only possible when you understand the whole structure and nature of thought. So one asks, 'What is thinking?'

For most of us thinking has become extraordinarily important. We never realise that thought is always old, thought is never new, thought can never be free. We were talking about freedom of thought, which is sheer nonsense, which means you may express what you want, say what you like; but thought in itself is never free, because thought is the response of memory. One can observe this for oneself. Thought is the response of memory, experience, knowledge. Knowledge, experience, memory, are always old and so thought is always old. Therefore thought can never see anything new. Can the mind look at the problem of fear without the interference of thought? Do you understand, Sirs?

I am afraid. There is fear of what one has done. Be completely aware of it without the interference of thought—and then is there fear? As we said, fear is brought about through time; time is thought. This is not philosophy, not some mystical experience; just observe it in yourself, you will see. One realises thought must function objectively, efficiently, logically, healthily. When you go to the office, or whatever you do, thought must operate, otherwise you cannot do anything. But the moment thought breeds or sustains pleasure and fear, then thought becomes inefficient. Thought then breeds inefficiency in relationship and therefore causes conflict. So one asks whether there can be an ending of thought in one direction, and yet with thought functioning in its highest capacity. We are concerned with whether thought can be absent when the mind sees the sunset in all its beauty. It is only then that you see the beauty of the sunset, not when your mind is full of thoughts, problems, violence. That is, if you have observed it, at the moment of seeing the sunset thought is absent. You look at this extraordinary light on the mountain, it is a great delight and at that moment thought has no place in it at all. But the next moment thought says: 'How marvellous that was, how beautiful, I wish I could paint it, I wish I could write a poem about it, I wish I could tell my friends what a lovely thing it is.' Or thought says: 'I would like to see that sunset again tomorrow.' Then thought begins its mischief. Because thought then says: 'Tomorrow I will have that pleasure again,' and when you don't have it there is pain. This is very simple, and because of its very simplicity it gets lost. We all want to be terribly clever, we are all so sophisticated, intellectual, we read such a lot. The whole psychological history of mankind (not who was king and what kind of wars there were and all the absurdity of nationalities) is within oneself. When you can read that in yourself you have understood. Then you are a light to yourself, then there is no authority, then you are actually free.

So our question is: Can thought cease to interfere? And it is this interference that produces time. Do you understand? Take death. There is great beauty in what is involved in death, and it is not possible to understand that beauty if there is any form of fear. We are just showing how frightened we are of death, because it might happen in the future and it is inevitable. So thought thinks about it and shuts it out. Or thought thinks about the fear that you have had, the pain, the anxiety, and that it might be repeated. We are caught in the mischief made by thought. Yet one also realises the extraordinary importance of thought. When you go to the office, when you do something technological, you must use thought and knowledge. Seeing the whole process of it from the beginning of this talk till now—seeing the whole of that—one asks, 'Can thought be silent?' Can one look at the sunset and be completely involved in the beauty of that sunset, without thought bringing into it the question of pleasure? Please follow this. Then conduct becomes righteous. Conduct becomes virtuous only when thought does not cultivate what it considers to be virtue, which then becomes unholy and ugly. Virture is not of time or of thought; which means virtue is not a product of pleasure or of fear. So now the question is: How is it possible to look at the sunset without thought weaving round it pleasure or pain? Can one look at this sunset with such attention, with such complete involvement in that beauty, so that when you have seen that sunset it is ended and not taken over by thought, as pleasure, for tomorrow?

Are we communicating with each other? Are we? (*Audience: Yes, yes.*) Good, I'm glad, but don't be so quick in answering 'Yes.' (*Laughter*) For this is quite a difficult problem. To watch the sunset without the interference of thought demands tremendous discipline; not the discipline of conformity, not the discipline of suppression or control. The word 'discipline' means 'to learn'—not to conform, not to obey—to learn about the whole process of thinking and its place. The negation of thought needs great observation. And to observe there must be freedom. In this freedom one knows the movement of thought, and then learning is active.

What do we mean by learning? When one goes to school or college one learns a great deal of information, perhaps not of great importance, but one learns. That becomes knowledge and from that knowledge we act, either in the technological field, or in the whole field of consciousness. So one must understand very deeply what that word 'to learn' means. The word 'to learn' obviously is an active present. There is learning all the time. But when that learning becomes a means to the accumulation of knowledge, then it is quite a different thing. That is, I have learned from past experience that fire burns. That is knowledge. I have learned it, therefore I don't go near the fire. I have ceased to learn. And most of us, having learned, act from there. Having gathered information about ourselves (or about another) this becomes knowledge; then that knowledge becomes almost static and from that we act. Therefore action is always old. So learning is something entirely different.

If one has listened this evening with attention, one has learned the nature of fear and pleasure; one has learned it and from that one acts. You see the difference, I hope. Learning implies a constant action. There is learning all the time. And the very act of learning is doing. The doing is not separate from learning. Whereas for most of us the doing is separate from the knowledge. That is, there is the ideology or the ideal, and according to that ideal we act, approximating the action only to that ideal. Therefore action is always old.

Learning, like seeing, is a great art. When you see a flower, what takes place? Do you see the flower actually, or do you see it through the image you have of that flower? The two things are entirely different. When you look at a flower, at a colour, without naming it, without like or dislike, without any screen between you and the thing you see as a flower, without the word, without thought, then the flower has an extraordinary colour and beauty. But when you look at the flower through botanical knowledge, when you say: 'This is a rose,' you have already conditioned your looking. Seeing and learning is quite an art, but you don't go to college to learn it. You can do it at home. You can look at a flower and find out how you look at it. If you are sensitive, alive, watching, then you will see that the space between you and the flower disappears and when that space disappears you see the thing so vitally, so strongly! In the same way when you observe yourself without that space (not as 'the observer' and 'the thing observed') then you will see there is no contradiction and therefore no conflict. In seeing the structure of fear, one also sees the structure and nature of pleasure. The seeing is the learning about it and therefore the mind is not caught in the pursuit of pleasure. Then life has quite a different meaning. One lives —not in search of pleasure.

Wait a minute before you ask questions. I would like to ask you a question: What have you got out of this talk? Don't answer me, please. Find out whether you got words, descriptions, ideas, or if you got something that is true, that is irrevocable, indestructible, because you yourself have seen it. Then you are a light to yourself and therefore you will not light your candle at any other light; you are that light yourself. If that is a fact, not a hypocritical assumption, then a gathering of this kind has been worthwhile. Now, perhaps, would you like to ask questions?

As we said yesterday, you are asking questions to find out, not to show that you are more intelligent than the speaker. A person who compares is not intelligent; an intelligent man never compares. Either you ask a question because by asking you would reveal yourself, expose yourself to yourself and thereby learn, or you ask a question to trip up the speaker—which you are perfectly welcome to do. Or you ask a question to have a wider view, to open the door. So it depends on you what kind and what quality of question you are going to ask. Which doesn't mean, please, that the speaker does not want you to ask questions.

Questioner: What is one to do when one notices the sunset and at the same time thought is coming into it?

KRISHNAMURTI: What is one to do? Please understand the significance of the question. That is, you see the sunset, thought interferes with it, and then you say 'What is one to do?' Who is the questioner who says 'What is one to do?' Is it thought that says what am I to do? Do you understand the question? Let me put it this way. There is the sunset, the beauty of it, the extraordinary colour, the feeling of it, the love of it; then thought comes along and I say to myself: 'Here it is, what am I to do?' Do listen to it carefully, do go into it. Is it not thought also that says 'What am I to do?' The 'I' who says 'What am I to do?', is the result of thought. So thought, seeing what is interfering with this beauty, says: 'What am I to do?'

Don't do anything! (*Laughter*) If you *do* something, you bring conflict into it. But when you see the sunset and thought comes in, *be aware* of it. Be aware of the sunset and the thought that comes into it. Don't chase thought away. Be choicelessly aware of this whole thing: the sunset and thought coming into it. Then you will find, if you are so aware, without any desire to suppress thought, to struggle against the interference of thought, if you don't do any of those things then thought becomes quiet. Because it is thought itself that is saying 'What am I to do?' That is one of the tricks of thought. Don't fall into the trap, but observe this whole structure of what is happening.

Questioner: We are conditioned how to look at the sunset, we are conditioned how we listen to you as the speaker. So through our conditioning we look at everything and listen to everything. How is one to be free of this conditioning?

KRISHNAMURTI: When are you aware of this conditioning, of any conditioning? Do please follow it a little bit. When are you aware that you are conditioned? Are you aware that you are conditioned as an American, as a Hindu, as a Catholic, Protestant, Communist, this and that? Are you aware that you are so conditioned, or are you aware of it because somebody has told you? If you are aware because someone has pointed out to you that you are conditioned, then that is one kind of awareness. But if you are aware that you are conditioned without being told, then it has a different quality. If you are told that you are hungry, that is one thing; but if you are actually hungry that is another. Now find out which it is: whether you were told you are conditioned and therefore you realise it; or, because you are aware, because you are involved in this whole process of living, and because of that awareness you realise for yourself, without being told, that you are conditioned. Then that has a vitality, then it becomes a problem that you have to understand very deeply. One sees that one is conditioned, not because one is told. The obvious reaction to it is to throw away that conditioning, if you are intelligent. Becoming aware of a particular conditioning, you revolt against it, as the present generation is revolting—which is merely a reaction. Revolt against a conditioning forms another kind of conditioning. One becomes aware of one's conditioning as a Communist, a Protestant, a Democrat, or a Republican. What takes place when there is no reaction but only awareness of what this conditioning actually is? What takes place when you are choicelessly aware of this conditioning, which you have found for yourself? There is no reaction. Then you are learning about this conditioning, why it comes into being. Two thousand years of propaganda have made you believe in a particular form of religious dogma. You are aware of how the church through centuries upon centuries, through tradition, repetition, through various rituals and entertainments, has conditioned our minds. There has been the repetition day after day, month after month, from childhood on; we are baptised and all the rest of it. And another form of the same thing takes place in other countries like India, China and so on.

Now when you become aware of it, what happens? You see how quickly the mind is influenced. The mind being pliable, young, innocent, is conditioned as a Communist, Catholic, Protestant and so on. Why is it conditioned? Why is it so shaped by propaganda? Are you following this? Why are you persuaded by propaganda to buy certain things, to believe in certain things, why? Not only is there this constant pressure from the outside, but also one wants to belong to something, one wants to belong to a group, because belonging to a group is safe. One wants to be a tribal entity. And behind that there is fear, fear of being alone, of being left out—left out not only psychologically, but also one may not get a job. All that is involved in it and then you ask whether the mind can be free of conditioning. When you see the danger of conditioning, as you see the danger of a precipice or of a wild animal, then it drops away from you without any effort. But we don't see the danger of being conditioned. We don't see the danger of nationalism, how it separates man from man. If you saw the danger of it intensely, vitally, then you would drop it instantly.

So the question then is: Is it possible to be so intensely aware of conditioning that you see the truth of it?—not whether you like or dislike it, but the fact that you are conditioned and therefore have a mind incapable of freedom. Because only the free mind knows what love is.

FURTHER READING

Henry David Thoreau's **Walden** (1854) has grown increasingly relevant. Even more so today do "the mass of men lead lives of quiet desperation."

Edgar Z. Friedberg studied the forces of conformity among the young in *Coming of Age in America* (1965). Note the chapter "The Cradle of Liberty," a damning account of standard operating procedures in high schools.

Shirley Jackson's famous and horrifying short story "The Lottery" (in the volume *The Lottery*, 1949) portrays a community enslaved by a grotesque tradition.

The significance for the individual of a free society has never been more eloquently stated than in John Stuart Mill's *On Liberty* (1859).

Only a handful of novels in this century have attracted as much attention as George Orwell's *1984* (1949), in which both freedom and identity have been lost in a totalitarian state.

Richard E. Farson included "the Right to be Unique, to be different, to be autonomous" in his "Bill of Rights for 1984," reprinted in Maryjane Dunstan and Patricia W. Garlan (eds.), *Worlds in the Making* (1970).

Kate Millet's *Sexual Politics* (1970) features insight, wit, and an analysis of the subjection of women as it appears in literature.

Arturo B. Fallico, an exceptional professor of philosophy for a generation of students at San Jose State College, wrote that "man is a hunger for selfhood and for freedom," in "Existentialism and Education," in *Educational Theory* (April, 1954).

Herb Gardner's great play *A Thousand Clowns* (1961) presents a man who is himself and free—and magnificently maladjusted.

Ralph Ellison, *Invisible Man* (1952). The shocking "battle royal" of Chapter I is only a prelude to the battle for self-discovery with which this brilliant novel is concerned.

——————————GRAVEYARD REFLECTIONS

13

A *philosophy of death has two tasks: to portray life in terms of its mortality, and to speak of what might be contained in the darkness of the grave. The first of these functions has to do with what our present thoughts and feelings are about death; it contends with the question of the meaning of death for our lives now. We are all dying: we require an ethic of death. "To see life, and to value it," said Santayana, "from the point of view of death is to see and value it truly. . . . It is far better to live in the light of the tragic fact, rather than to forget or deny it, and build everything on a fundamental lie."[1]*

The second function of a philosophy of death is to resolve, at least to our own satisfaction, the question of human immortality. Does the grave mean the annihilation, the utter extinction of man, or is there something more? The hopes of men have clearly been for "something more." Hindu philosophers conceive of reincarnation and the possibility of a final "liberation"; for Buddhists there is nirvana. In the West the main tradition from Zoroastrianism to Christianity and Islam has held that there is eternal individual survival in a paradise or hell.

Perhaps foremost among our native feelings about death is sheer fright. Warren Beath, in the essay which follows, confesses candidly to a sometimes paralyzing fear—which is no more than that felt by most men. It is only more fashionable to conceal such emotions behind the façade of a brave indifference. At the same time Beath is drawn to and fascinated by the topic of death, and he almost fondly reveals a horde of memories of graveyards he has visited ("Every cemetery is Spoon River if you have the imagination"), of a death mask in a book, of a suicide, and of deaths that have touched his life.

In contrast, there is the cool reasonableness of Epicurus: the living, he argues, have no more reason to dwell on thoughts of death than the healthy have to preoccupy themselves with thoughts of illness. And because Epicurus was convinced that there was no conscious existence beyond the grave, he reasoned further that death most certainly meant nothing to the dead. John Donne, on the other hand, precisely because he thought that we are destined to "wake eternally" after death, saw nothing to dread. The emphasis among vast number of Christians like Donne on a future existence

[1] George Santayana, *Soliloquies in England* (Michigan: Ann Arbor Paperbacks, 1967), pp. 98–99.

> *What is life? It is a flash of a firefly in the night.*
> *It is a breath of a buffalo in the winter time. It is as*
> *the little shadow that runs across the grass and loses*
> *itself in the sunset.*

the last words of isapwo crowfoot, blackfoot chief

can hardly be overstated. Paul, in the New Testament, says, "If the dead are never raised to life, 'Let us eat and drink, for tomorrow we die.'"

There was often a radiant happiness in Edna St. Vincent Millay, but the other side of that coin was a capacity for an infinite sadness which is expressed here in "Dirge Without Music." Perhaps a love of life must entail a corresponding hatred for the indiscriminate destructiveness of death: those who are resigned to death may be equally resigned from life. To the "shutting away of loving hearts in the hard ground" Millay scorns resignation, and there is a quiet dignity in her firmly repeated "I do not approve." Resignation, nevertheless, is the advice of Buddhism. Here, as in Epicurus, there is the voice of reason: objections to death do not avail and tears are wasted. The wise man, the enlightened man, learns to accept and even welcome the inevitable.

The contention has been made many times that all philosophies and religions are no more than attempts to answer the problem of death. It is one of those exaggerations which is not entirely without merit, and there are moments when we wonder if it might not be true. In the Phaedo, Socrates lends support to the charge with his statement that the true philosopher "is always pursuing death and dying." He argues here for immortality, but the real point to his argument is that a man ought to seek in this world "the attainment of the highest virtue and wisdom."

Philosophers Corliss Lamont and C. J. Ducasse come down on opposite sides of the debate over human immortality. Lamont (though distressed by his own advancing age) finds it impossible to believe that any sort of consciousness survives the death of the body and brain. This conviction is an unhappy but prominent feature of his humanism: the finality of death is all the more reason to make sure that this one life is lived well.

Ducasse submits our ordinary thinking about death to a methodical and revealing analysis. The arguments against immortality, he points out, are formidable but not conclusive. There are lapses in the logic of the case against survival and there is, moreover, contrary evidence from the area of psychical research. There hangs over psychical phenomena, of course, a cloud of suspicion, but reputable investigators find no reason for writing off all the claims of psychical events as fraudulent. At the heart of all the arguments against immortality, Ducasse finds the epistemological and metaphysical assumption that only the empirically observable material world is real.

Warren Beath (1951–   ) was a sophomore in high school when his entry won in the short story division of the 1967 National Scholastic Creative Writing Awards Program. A precocious reader in childhood, he became an obsessive writer and has never considered any other career.

During his earlier years his family was nomadic; by the age of fourteen he had attended eleven different schools. Since then he has driven through much of the United States "seeking out lonely roads at night and dusty forgotten towns." Presently a student at the California State University at Fresno, California, he has worked variously as a truck loader, newspaperman, and musician. "Notes on Dying" is previously unpublished.

November 16, 1970. 7:00 P.M.

I considered doing a long essay on this topic, but I am temperamentally of such morbid bent that prolonged concentration on this subject could only have induced a depression wherein I would have accomplished little. Subjectively, I am very uncomfortable with this topic. Objectively, I am at ease, because everyone is equally unqualified to write on it. I am in a sense as much an authority as anyone. My credentials are a profound fear and the aforementioned absorption with the morbid.

I can trace this particular fear back to adolescence. There were times when I was perfectly happy, when all my temporal and prosaic problems were resolved and I would seem to have nothing to worry about. Then I would remember that I was going to die. I remember despairing between wanting to live forever and a resignation that wanted nothing better than to get the unpleasant over with.

Rachmaninoff always reminded me of death, for some reason. Maybe it was his sonorous minor chords, or the eerie, haunting resonance of his forte. There was a particularly melancholy work by him on a record my parents had. When the phonograph needle came to it, I would always change it.

Once I borrowed a book about Chopin from the library and in the frontispiece I found a photograph of that worthy's death mask. I could not sleep with that book in the room, and was uncomfortable with it in the house. I had never heard of a death mask before. Of course, I returned the book the next day, unread. It is only recently that I've been able to listen to Chopin without the music conjuring images of that mask.

In my fear, I turned to religion. I was never afraid of hell, but always afraid of dying. Hell would have been better than nothing.

I can remember almost believing in God and afterlife, though only for a few moments at a time, till some thought would disturb my security. If anyone was to live forever, by justice it should have been me, for I knew no one with my intensity of fear. The only Bible verses I remember from this pious time are such as "He that hath the Lord hath life" and "He that believeth in me. . . ."

I was obsessed with witchcraft, voodoo, premature burial, lycanthropy, black magic, and especially vampirism. By junior high school I had read *Dracula*, a difficult gothic novel of stilted style, four times. I had read all of Poe twice. Fantasy was my solace and passion, my refuge. As an escapist, I rivaled Houdini. Even today, I sometimes think that I must be California's leading authority on Jack the Ripper, vampirism, and all the Hollywood horror films produced from 1923 to 1958. I say this without pride. There is something wrong when someone of my ostensibly healthy disposition can flawlessly recite the entire cast list of *Bride of Frankenstein*.

After my grandfather died, I did not speak his name for four years. After John Kennedy's death, I did not say his name for four years. I mentioned him in a telephone conversation yesterday and tears came to my eyes. I cannot say Robert Kennedy's name. My father died in 1964 and I have not been able to speak his name.

I can objectify my fears much better today, except when the lights are out. I don't feel I'm revealing myself too much by these confessions, for I think these emotions are universal; certainly no one is exempted from them altogether. Keats wasn't:

> When I have fears that I may cease to be
> Before my pen has glean'd my teeming brain,
> Before high piled books in charactry,
> Hold like rich garners the full ripened grain;
> When I behold, upon the night's starr'd face,
> Huge cloudy symbols of high romance,
> And think that I may never live to trace
> Their shadows, with the magic hand of chance. . . .

Poe was bitter:

> Out!—Out all the lights, out all,
> And over each quivering form,
> The curtain, a funeral pall,
> Comes down with the rush of a storm,
> And the angels all pallid and wan,

Uprising, unveiling, affirm
The play is The Tragedy Man,
Its Hero—
The Conqueror Worm.

Shakespeare was philosophical and ironical:

Where be your gibes now? your gamols? your songs?
your flashes of merriment that were wont to set the table on a roar?
Not one now, to mock your own grinning—?
Imperious Caesar, dead and turned to clay,
Might stop a hole to keep the wind away.
O, that earth which kept the world in awe
Should patch a wall t' expel the winter's flaw!

Whenever I pick up a biography, I find myself turning to the back of the book to see how the subject died, for that is the most significant, revealing moment of a life, when a man is cornered in "the precincts of his last evasions," stranded on "the darkling plain." Whether one goes gentle into that good night is determined by the stuff of which he is made.

Suicides afford interesting fodder for reflection; my favorite case is Hemingway. "If I can't live life on my own terms, I refuse to live it." His is a very eloquent death. I think that when things are going well, when we have our health and are in a milieu in which we are secure and comfortable, we feel as though we could take anything life might throw at us. Hemingway was a physically courageous man, but possibly a spiritual coward. His grandstand courage was founded on a fundamental confidence in his own creative powers and his own physical indestructibility. When he felt these begin to wane, the cornerstone on which the impressive edifice was built crumbled. He became a paranoic, then a suicide.

To a person like me, who is cast into the deepest depression by a cold, Hemingway's rationale seems most sane and reasonable. It would appear possible for a person to arrive at a point after which life is not worth living. Perhaps we all arrive there.

On the other hand, there is the school of thought expressed by one of Dostoyevsky's characters when he says that he would rather spend all eternity stranded immobile on a rock in the middle of the ocean, then to be for a while free and happy only to die; that is to say, even the meanest, most abject existence is precious, and even the happiest life cannot recompense a person for one moment of existence lost.

We often feel both of these strains in conflict. We, the frightened.

Who builds stronger than a mason, a shipwright, or a carpenter?
A gravemaker! The houses he makes last till doomsday . . .

HAMLET

I love to spend an hour in an interesting cemetery. A good cemetery is like a book you can't put down. Every cemetery is Spoon River if you have the imagination.

I enjoy occasional communion with ghosts. There is nothing morbid or necrophilic about it. There is an elemental motive force in all men that draws them to the grave and the deathsite and their mysteries. Every generation visits the battlefields of the Civil War. Crowds still gather in Dealey Plaza. There have always been religious pilgrimages. Hitler at Napoleon's tomb. Napoleon at Alexander's. It is efficacious to the summoning of memories and it as close as we can get to the dead.

I never pass the intersection on Highway 41 where James Dean was killed, without stopping.

I've spent many hours resting under a tree above John Steinbeck in Salinas.

It was a college English instructor who taught me that these things are not unhealthy, but symptoms of a profound romanticism, the expressions of a poetic soul. I spent an hour with him in a wonderful cemetery on a hill above Cayucos, and I knew I had found a kindred spirit.

I have walked in many graveyards throughout California, Texas, Louisiana, Mississippi, and one in Indianapolis with 14,000 tenants. There is an interesting cemetery in Santa Cruz. There you can often find an open vault or grave. Looking up, lying on your back in a grave affords one a unique perspective offered by no other experience. It is a good exercise to acclimate and adjust oneself to the inevitable.

It is no accident that these notes are concerned with dying rather than death. We can talk only about dying, for only that is within our sphere of experience. That other "unknown land from whose bourne no traveller returns" is another matter altogether. That is, we can talk about death only insofar as it affects us, the living.

The deaths of members of our family are more important traumatic milestones in our lives than births or marriages. James Agee's A Death in the Family is to all of us a scrapbook in agony, all of his faded tintypes plucked from our own lives.

Only those who die suddenly are spared the personal embarrassment of this ultimate transition. It is most tragic when a person finds himself "the sole mourner at his own protracted funeral." That is, slow death is the worst, the most embarrassing. At best, it is never a decorous transition, from living to dead. I am depressed whenever I recall W. C. Field's demise, his violent trembling, the terrible hemorrhaging, the blood bubbling thickly from his lips. Think of the great men who have died on the floor of their bathroom.

Death is the ultimate humiliation, robbing one of all dignity, contorting one into all sorts of degrading postures and rigors. At the funeral, when through the nauseating perfume of the flowers we perceive the deceased calm and reposed, we cannot think that it is due to any grace of nature, but only to the embalmer's arts. I love Hemingway's remark on death: just another whore.

We are always especially outraged and frightened when someone young dies. Death is far more acceptable, even logical, when it consummates a long history of decline and decrepitude. In such cases, we sometimes call it a blessing, though, of course, it is a grace which we in our magnanimity would rather have bestowed on others.

When Rudolph Valentino's body was on display, 80,000 people rioted outside the New York funeral parlor. One year after James Dean died, he was receiving five times the fan mail of any other star in his studio. This, of course, is another story.

A boy with whom I shared a PE locker in high school was mashed under a truck while riding his motorcycle. I saw him, and so I believed he was dead and appreciated the extent to which he was dead.

Yesterday a teacher whom I had for four years in high school and of whom I was fond, died suddenly. It is under this pall and I am moved to write these notes on this subject and in this way. It is a sort of therapy, or at least an occupation, a distraction.

I can't imagine this man dead; I can't appreciate it emotionally. My mind keeps filling the hole which he leaves in life and in his family. The Rosary and funeral will, I am sure, bring it home to me. Always in these circumstances I am also sorry for myself, for it makes me aware of my own mortality —"It tolls for thee."

There is a belief held by some psychologists that none of us really believe we are going to die. It is a thing that happens to others, erasing them cleanly, antiseptically, thanks to modern mortuary science. This is the extent of our experience with death.

I am almost sure this is true. If we all believed that we are going to spend eternity in a casket, no matter how comfortable and cushioned—but the thought is insupportable.

Epicurus (see biographical note on p. 105) felt that freedom from fear was essential to the quiet tranquillity he held to be the greatest good in life. Of the various forms of fear, he was convinced that none was more shattering than the fear of death. Thus, in the following excerpt from his "Letter to Menoeceus," Epicurus attempts to assure us that this particular fear is groundless.

Become accustomed to the belief that death is nothing to us. For all good and evil consists in sensation, but death is deprivation of sensation. And therefore a right understanding that death is nothing to us makes the mortality of life enjoyable, not because it adds to it an infinite span of time, but because it takes away the craving for immortality. For there is nothing terrible in life for the man who has truly comprehended that there is nothing terrible in not living. So that man speaks but idly who says that he fears death not because it will be painful when it comes, but because it is painful in anticipation. For that which gives no trouble when it comes, is but an empty pain in anticipation. So death, the most terrifying of ills, is nothing to us, since so long as we exist death is not with us; but when death comes, then we do not exist. It does not then concern either the living or the dead, since for the former it is not, and the latter are no more.

But the many at one moment shun death as the greatest of evils, at another yearn for it as a respite from the evils of life. But the wise man neither seeks to escape life nor fears the cessation of life, for neither does life offend him nor does the absence of life seem to be any evil. And just as with food he does not seek simply the larger share and nothing else, but rather the most pleasant, so he seeks to enjoy not the longest period of time, but the most pleasant.

John Donne (1573–1631) took holy orders in the Anglican Church at the age of forty-three and ended his career as Dean of St. Paul's in London. His 160 extant sermons have been published in ten volumes. As a young man, Donne had been cynical, witty, and recklessly worldly. Educated at Oxford and Cambridge, Donne inherited wealth, traveled over Europe, was briefly a gentleman soldier, and wrote vividly sensual love poetry. He married secretly; when his influential father-in-law learned of the marriage he had Donne imprisoned. His inheritance dwindled away and he once had to pay his rent with one of his best poems. Twelve children (six of whom died) came of the marriage. Rediscovered in this century, Donne was Hemingway's source for these now well known lines: "No man is an island, entire of itself; every man is a piece of the continent, a part of the main. Never send to know for whom the bell tolls; it tolls for thee."

Death, be not proud, though some have called thee
Mighty and dreadful, for thou are not so;
For those whom thou think'st thou dost overthrow
Die not, poor Death; nor yet canst thou kill me.
From rest and sleep, which but thy picture be,
Much pleasure; then from thee much more must flow;
And soonest our best men with thee do go—
Rest of their bones and souls' delivery!
Thou'rt slave to fate, chance, kings, and desperate men,
And dost with poison, war, and sickness dwell;
And poppy or charms can make us sleep as well
And better than thy stroke. Why swell'st thou then?
One short sleep past, we wake eternally,
And Death shall be no more: Death, thou shalt die.

edna st. vincent millay   DIRGE WITHOUT MUSIC

Only nineteen when her poem "Renascence" won her immediate acclaim, Edna St. Vincent Millay (1892–1950) went on to become one of the heroines of the Jazz Age. Fresh, irreverent, and rebellious, she gave lyric voice to many of the same moods that F. Scott Fitzgerald captured in his fiction. A Vassar gradu-ate, she worked at her writing in Greenwich Village early in the 1920s, but she and her husband lived most of their years together on a farm in New York State. Her volumes of poetry include Renascence, A Few Figs from Thistles, Second April, *and* Wine from These Grapes. *"Dirge Without Music" is from* Collected Poems *(1928).*

I am not resigned to the shutting away of loving hearts in the hard
  ground.
So it is, and so it will be, for so it has been, time out of mind:
Into the darkness they go, the wise and the lovely. Crowned
With lilies and with laurel they go; but I am not resigned.

Lovers and thinkers, into the earth with you.
Be one with the dull, the indiscriminate dust.
A fragment of what you felt, of what you knew,
A formula, a phrase remains,—but the best is lost.

The answers quick and keen, the honest look, the laughter, the love,—
They are gone. They are gone to feed the roses. Elegant and curled
Is the blossom. Fragrant is the blossom. I know. But I do not approve.
More precious was the light in your eyes than all the roses of the world.

Down, down, down into the darkness of the grave
Gently they go, the beautiful, the tender, the kind;
Quietly they go, the intelligent, the witty, the brave.
I know. But I do not approve. And I am not resigned.

a buddhist parable THERE IS NO CURE FOR DEATH

The poignant story of Kisā Gotamī is one of the most famous in Buddhist literature. Numb with shock at the death of her baby, a young mother begs for medicine to cure him. Directed to the Buddha for help, she learns from him that death "is a law common to all mankind." It is, in fact, one of the fundamental premises of Buddhism that all things are impermanent: only through our acceptance of this truth can we escape futile grief.

Sometimes referred to as "The Parable of the Mustard-Seed," the story is from the Anguttara Commentary.

Gotamī was her family name, but because she tired easily, she was called Kisā Gotamī, or Frail Gotamī. She was reborn at Sāvatthi in a poverty-stricken house. When she grew up, she married, going to the house of her husband's family to live. There, because she was the daughter of a poverty-stricken house, they treated her with contempt. After a time she gave birth to a son. Then they accorded her respect.

But when that boy of hers was old enough to play and run hither and about, he died. Sorrow sprang up within her. Thought she: "Since the birth of my son, I, who was once denied honor and respect in this very house, have received respect. These folk may even seek to cast my son away." Taking her son on her hip, she went about from one house-door to another, saying: "Give me medicine for my son!"

Wherever people encountered her, they said: "Where did you ever meet with medicine for the dead?" So saying, they clapped their hands and laughed in derision. She had not the slightest idea what they meant.

Now a certain wise man saw her and thought: "This woman must have been driven out of her mind by sorrow for her son. But medicine for her, —no one else is likely to know,—the Possessor of the Ten Forces alone is likely to know." Said he: "Woman, as for medicine for your son,—there is no one else who knows,—the Possessor of the Ten Forces, the foremost individual in the world of men and the Worlds of the Gods, resides at a neighboring monastery. Go to him and ask."

"The man speaks the truth," thought she. Taking her son on her hip, when the Tathāgata sat down in the Seat of the Buddhas, she took her stand in the outer circle of the congregation and said: "O Exalted One, give me medicine for my son!"

The Teacher, seeing that she was ripe for conversion, said: "You did well, Gotamī, in coming hither for medicine. Go enter the city, make the rounds of the entire city, beginning at the beginning, and in whatever house no one has ever died, from that house fetch tiny grains of mustard-seed."

"Very well, Reverend Sir," said she. Delighted in heart, she entered within the city, and at the very first house said: "The Possessor of the Ten Forces bid me fetch tiny grains of mustard-seed for medicine for my son. Give me tiny grains of mustard-seed." "Alas! Gotamī," said they, and brought and gave to her.

"This particular seed I cannot take. In this house some one has died!"

"What say you, Gotamī! Here it is impossible to count the dead!"

"Well then, enough! I'll not take it. The Possessor of the Ten Forces did not tell me to take mustard-seed from a house where any one has ever died."

In this same way she went to the second house, and to the third. Thought she: "In the entire city this alone must be the way! This the Buddha, full of compassion for the welfare of mankind, must have seen!" Overcome with emotion, she went outside of the city, carried her son to the burning-ground, and holding him in her arms, said: "Dear little son, I thought that you alone had been overtaken by this thing which men call death. But you are not the only one death has overtaken. This is a law common to all mankind." So saying, she cast her son away in the burning-ground. Then she uttered the following stanza:

> No village-law, no law of market-town,
> No law of a single house is this,—
> Of all the world and all the Worlds of Gods
> This only is the law, that all things are impermanent.

Now when she had so said, she went to the Teacher. Said the Teacher to her: "Gotamī, did you get the tiny grains of mustard-seed?" "Done, Reverend Sir, is the business of the mustard-seed! Only give me a refuge!" Then the Teacher recited to her the following stanza in the Dhammapada:

> That man who delights in children and cattle,
> That man whose heart adheres thereto,
> Death takes that man and goes his way,
> As sweeps away a mighty flood a sleeping village. . . .

The Phaedo is the story of the last day in the life of Socrates. The scene is the prison where he has been confined. Plato (see biographical data on p. 90) was not present because of illness; hence it is Phaedo who relates the events of the day. Insofar as many of those who were present were still living when Plato's dialogue was circulated, it is usually assumed that this account of what happened must have been reasonably accurate.

At the beginning of the dialogue Socrates' wife and youngest child are taken away, leaving Socrates with his friends. They discuss immortality, appropriately enough, and its bearing upon our conduct of our lives. At the end of the day, Xanthippe and the children return for a final meeting with Socrates, and then the cup of hemlock is brought in.

Echecrates. Were you yourself, Phaedo, in the prison with Socrates on the day when he drank the poison?

Phaedo. Yes, Echecrates, I was.

Echecrates. I should so like to hear about his death. What did he say in his last hours? We were informed that he died by taking poison, but no one knew anything more; for no Phliasian ever goes to Athens now, and it is a long time since any stranger from Athens has found his way hither; so that we had no clear account. . . .

Phaedo. I had a singular feeling at being in his company. For I could hardly believe that I was present at the death of a friend, and therefore I did not pity him, Echecrates; he died so fearlessly, and his words and bearing were so noble and gracious, that to me he appeared blessed. I thought that in going to the other world he could not be without a divine call, and that he would be happy, if any man ever was, when he arrived there; and therefore I did not pity him as might have seemed natural at such an hour. But I had not the pleasure which I usually feel in philosophical discourse (for philosophy was the theme of which we spoke). I was pleased, but in the pleasure there was also a strange admixture of pain; for I reflected that he was soon to die, and this double feeling was shared by us all; we were laughing and weeping by turns, especially the excitable Apollodorus—you know the sort of man?

Echecrates. Yes.

Phaedo. He was quite beside himself; and I and all of us were greatly moved. . . .

Echecrates. Well, and what did you talk about?

Phaedo. I will begin at the beginning, and endeavour to repeat the entire conversation. On the previous days we had been in the habit of assembling early in the morning at the court in which the trial took place, and which is not far from the prison. There we used to wait talking with one another until the opening of the doors (for they were not opened very early); then we went in and generally passed the day with Socrates. On the last morning we assembled sooner than usual, having heard on the day before when we quitted the prison in the evening that the sacred ship had come from Delos; and so we arranged to meet very early at the accustomed place. On our arrival the jailer who answered the door, instead of admitting us, came out and told us to stay until he called us. "For the Eleven," he said, "are now with Socrates; they are taking off his chains, and giving orders that he is to die to-day." He soon returned and said that we might come in. On entering we found Socrates just released from chains, and Xanthippè, whom you know, sitting by him, and holding his child in her arms. When she saw us she uttered a cry and said, as women will: "O Socrates, this is the last time that either you will converse with your friends, or they with you." Socrates turned to Crito and said: "Crito, let some one take her home." Some of Crito's people accordingly led her away, crying out and beating herself. And when she was gone, Socrates, sitting up on the couch, bent and rubbed his leg, saying, as he was rubbing: How singular is the thing called pleasure, and how curiously related to pain, which might be thought to be the opposite of it; for they are never present to a man at the same instant, and yet he who pursues either is generally compelled to take the other; their bodies are two, but they are joined by a single head. . . .

[at this point Phaedo quotes Crito.]

. . . The attendant who is to give you the poison has been telling me, and he wants to tell you, that you are not to talk much; talking, he says, increases heat, and this is apt to interfere with the action of the poison; persons who excite themselves are sometimes obliged to take a second or even a third dose.

Then, said Socrates, let him mind his business and be prepared to give the poison twice or even thrice if necessary; that is all.

I knew quite well what you would say, replied Crito; but I was obliged to satisfy him.

Never mind him, he said.

And now, O my judges, I desire to prove to you that the real philosopher has reason to be of good cheer when he is about to die, and that after death he may hope to obtain the greatest good in the other world. And how this may be, Simmias and Cebes, I will endeavour to explain. For I deem that the true votary of philosophy is likely to be misunderstood by other men; they do not perceive that he is always pursuing death and

569

dying; and if this be so, and he has had the desire of death all his life long, why when his time comes should he repine at that which he has been always pursuing and desiring?

Simmias said laughingly: Though not in a laughing humour, you have made me laugh, Socrates; for I cannot help thinking that the many when they hear your words will say how truly you have described philosophers, and our people at home will likewise say that the life which philosophers desire is in reality death, and that they have found them out to be deserving of the death which they desire.

And they are right, Simmias, in thinking so, with the exception of the words 'they have found them out;' for they have not found out either what is the nature of that death which the true philosopher deserves, or how he deserves or desires death. But enough of them:—let us discuss the matter among ourselves. Do we believe that there is such a thing as death?

To be sure, replied Simmias.

Is it not the separation of soul and body? And to be dead is the completion of this; when the soul exists in herself, and is released from the body and the body is released from the soul, what is this but death?

Just so, he replied.

There is another question, which will probably throw light on our present enquiry if you and I can agree about it:—Ought the philosopher to care about the pleasures—if they are to be called pleasures—of eating and drinking?

Certainly not, answered Simmias.

And what about the pleasures of love—should he care for them?

By no means.

And will he think much of the other ways of indulging the body, for example, the acquisition of costly raiment, or sandals, or other adornments of the body? Instead of caring about them, does he not rather despise anything more than nature needs? What do you say?

I should say that the true philosopher would despise them.

Would you not say that he is entirely concerned with the soul and not with the body? He would like, as far as he can, to get away from the body and to turn to the soul.

Quite true.

In matters of this sort philosophers, above all other men, may be observed in every sort of way to dissever the soul from the communion of the body.

Very true.

Whereas, Simmias, the rest of the world are of opinion that to him who has no sense of pleasure and no part in bodily pleasure, life is not worth having; and that he who is indifferent about them is as good as dead.

570

That is also true.

What again shall we say of the actual acquirement of knowledge?—is the body, if invited to share in the enquiry, a hinderer or a helper? I mean to say, have sight and hearing any truth in them? Are they not, as the poets are always telling us, inaccurate witnesses? and yet, if even they are inaccurate and indistinct, what is to be said of the other senses?—for you will allow that they are the best of them?

Certainly, he replied.

Then when does the soul attain truth?—for in attempting to consider anything in company with the body she is obviously deceived.

True.

Then must not true existence be revealed to her in thought, if at all?

Yes.

And thought is best when the mind is gathered into herself and none of these things trouble her—neither sounds nor sights nor pain nor any pleasure,—when she takes leave of the body, and has as little as possible to do with it, when she has no bodily sense or desire, but is aspiring after true being?

Certainly.

And in this the philosopher dishonours the body; his soul runs away from his body and desires to be alone and by herself?

That is true.

Well, but there is another thing, Simmias: Is there or is there not an absolute justice?

Assuredly there is.

And an absolute beauty and absolute good?

Of course.

But did you ever behold any of them with your eyes?

Certainly not.

Or did you ever reach them with any other bodily sense?—and I speak not of these alone, but of absolute greatness, and health, and strength, and of the essence or true nature of everything. Has the reality of them ever been perceived by you through the bodily organs? or rather, is not the nearest approach to the knowledge of their several natures made by him who so orders his intellectual vision as to have the most exact conception of the essence of each thing which he considers?

Certainly.

And he attains to the purest knowledge of them who goes to each with the mind alone, not introducing or intruding in the act of thought sight or any other sense together with reason, but with the very light of the mind in her own clearness searches into the very truth of each; he who has got rid, as far as he can, of eyes and ears and, so to speak, of the whole body, these being in his opinion distracting elements which when they infect the soul hinder her from acquiring truth and knowledge—who, if not he, is likely to attain to the knowledge of true being?

What you say has a wonderful truth in it, Socrates, replied Simmias.

And when real philosophers consider all these things, will they not be led to make a reflection which they will express in words something like the following? 'Have we not found,' they will say, 'a path of thought which seems to bring us and our argument to the conclusion, that while we are in the body, and while the soul is infected with the evils of the body, our desire will not be satisfied? and our desire is of the truth. For the body is a source of endless trouble to us by reason of the mere requirement of food; and is liable also to diseases which overtake and impede us in the search after true being: it fills us full of loves, and lusts, and fears, and fancies of all kinds, and endless foolery, and in fact, as men say, takes away from us the power of thinking at all. Whence comes wars, and fightings, and factions? whence but from the body and the lusts of the body? Wars are occasioned by the love of money, and money has to be acquired for the sake and in the service of the body; and by reason of all these impediments we have no time to give to philosophy; and, last and worst of all, even if we are at leisure and betake ourselves to some speculation, the body is always breaking in upon us, causing turmoil and confusion in our enquiries, and so amazing us that we are prevented from seeing the truth. It has been proved to us by experience that if we would have pure knowledge of anything we must be quit of the body—the soul in herself must behold things in themselves: and then we shall attain the wisdom which we desire, and of which we say that we are lovers; not while we live, but after death; for if while in company with the body, the soul cannot have pure knowledge, one of two things follows —either knowledge is not to be attained at all, or, if at all, after death. For then, and not till then, the soul will be parted from the body and exist in herself alone. In this present life, I reckon that we make the nearest approach to knowledge when we have the least possible intercourse or communion with the body, and are not surfeited with the bodily nature, but keep ourselves pure until the hour when God himself is pleased to release us. And thus having got rid of the foolishness of the body we shall be pure and hold converse with the pure, and know of ourselves the clear light everywhere, which is no other than the light of truth.' For the impure are not permitted to approach the pure. These are the sort of words, Simmias, which the true lovers of knowledge cannot help saying to one another, and thinking. You would agree; would you not?

Undoubtedly, Socrates.

But, O my friend, if this be true, there is great reason to hope that, going whither I go, when I have come to the end of my journey, I shall at-

these things, and temperance, and justice, and courage, and wisdom herself are the purgation of them. . . .

[*The discussion continues at length: objections are raised and Socrates replies to them.*]

But then, O my friends, he said, if the soul is really immortal, what care should be taken of her, not only in respect of the portion of time which is called life, but of eternity! And the danger of neglecting her from this point of view does indeed appear to be awful. If death had only been the end of all, the wicked would have had a good bargain in dying, for they would have been happily quit not only of their body, but of their own evil together with their souls. But now, inasmuch as the soul is manifestly immortal, there is no release or salvation from evil except the attainment of the highest virtue and wisdom. For the soul when on her progress to the world below takes nothing with her but nurture and education; and these are said greatly to benefit or greatly to injure the departed, at the very beginning of his journey thither. . . .

When he had done speaking, Crito said: And have you any commands for us, Socrates—anything to say about your children, or any other matter in which we can serve you?

Nothing particular, Crito, he replied: only, as I have always told you, take care of yourselves; that is a service which you may be ever rendering to me and mine and to all of us, whether you promise to do so or not. But if you have no thought for yourselves, and care not to walk according to the rule which I have prescribed for you, not now for the first time, however much you may profess or promise at the moment, it will be of no avail.

We will do our best, said Crito: And in what way shall we bury you?

In any way that you like; but you must get hold of me, and take care that I do not run away from you. Then he turned to us, and added with a smile: —I cannot make Crito believe that I am the same Socrates who have been talking and conducting the argument; he fancies that I am the other Socrates whom he will soon see, a dead body—and he asks, How shall he bury me? And though I have spoken many words in the endeavour to show that when I have drunk the poison I shall leave you and go to the joys of the blessed,—these words of mine, with which I was comforting you and myself, have had, as I perceive, no effect upon Crito. And therefore I want you to be surety for me to him now, as at the trial he was surety to the judges for me: but let the promise be of another sort; for he was surety for me to the judges that I would remain, and you must be my surety to him that I shall not remain, but go away and depart; and then he will suffer less at my death, and not be grieved when he sees my body being burned or buried. I would not have him sorrow at my hard lot, or say at the burial, Thus we lay out Socrates, or, Thus we follow him to the grave or bury him; for false words are not only evil in themselves, but they infect the soul with evil. Be of good cheer then, my dear Crito, and say that you are burying my body only, and do with that whatever is usual, and what you think best.

When he had spoken these words, he arose and went into a chamber to bathe; Crito followed him and told us to wait. So we remained behind, talking and thinking of the subject of discourse, and also of the greatness of our sorrow; he was like a father of whom we were being bereaved, and we were about to pass the rest of our lives as orphans. When he had taken the bath his children were brought to him—(he had two young sons and an elder one); and the women of his family also came, and he talked to them and gave them a few directions in the presence of Crito; then he dismissed them and returned to us.

Now the hour of sunset was near, for a good deal of time had passed while he was within. When he came out, he sat down with us again after his bath, but not much was said. Soon the jailer, who was the servant of the Eleven, entered and stood by him, saying:—To you, Socrates, whom I know to be the noblest and gentlest and best of all who ever came to this place, I will not impute the angry feelings of other men, who rage and swear at me, when, in obedience to the authorities, I bid them drink the poison—indeed, I am sure that you will not be angry with me; for others, as you are aware, and not I, are to blame. And so fare you well, and try to bear lightly what must needs be—you know my errand. Then bursting into tears he turned away and went out.

Socrates looked at him and said: I return your good wishes, and will do as you bid. Then turning to us, he said, How charming the man is: since I have been in prison he has always been coming to see me, and at times he would talk to me, and was as good to me as could be, and now see how generously he sorrows on my account. We must do as he says, Crito; and therefore let the cup be brought, if the poison is prepared: if not, let the attendant prepare some.

Yet, said Crito, the sun is still upon the hill-tops, and I know that many a one has taken the draught late, and after the announcement has been made to him, he has eaten and drunk, and enjoyed the society of his beloved; do not hurry—there is time enough.

Socrates said: Yes, Crito, and they of whom you speak are right in so acting, for they think that they will be gainers by the delay; but I am right in not following their example, for I do not think that I should gain anything by drinking the poison a little later; I should only be ridiculous in my own eyes for sparing and saving a life which is already forfeit. Please then to do as I say, and not to refuse me.

Crito made a sign to the servant, who was standing by; and he went out, and having been absent for some time, returned with the jailer carrying the cup of poison. Socrates said: You, my good friend, who are experienced in these matters, shall give me directions how I am to proceed. The man answered: You have only to walk about until your legs are heavy, and then to lie down, and the poison will act. At the same time he handed the cup to Socrates, who in the easiest and gentlest manner, without the least fear or change of colour or feature, looking at the man with all his eyes, Echecrates, as his manner was, took the cup and said: What do you say about making a libation out of this cup to any god? May I, or not? The man answered: We only prepare, Socrates, just so much to deem enough. I understand, he said: but I may and must ask the gods to prosper my journey from this to the other world—even so—and so be it according to my prayer. Then raising the cup to his lips, quite readily and cheerfully he drank off the poison. And hitherto most of us had been able to control our sorrow; but now when we saw him drinking, and saw too that he had finished the draught, we could no longer forbear, and in spite of myself my own tears were flowing fast; so that I covered my face and wept, not for him, but at the thought of my own calamity in having to part from such a friend. Nor was I the first; for Crito, where he found himself unable to restrain his tears, had got up, and I followed; and at that moment, Apollodorus, who had been weeping all the time, broke out in a loud and passionate cry which made cowards of us all. Socrates alone retained his calmness: What is this strange outcry? he said. I sent away the women mainly in order that they might not misbehave in this way, for I have been told that a man should die in peace. Be quiet then, and have patience. When we heard his words we were ashamed, and refrained our tears; and he walked about until, as he said, his legs began to fail, and then he lay on his back, according to the directions, and the man who gave him the poison now and then looked at his feet and legs; and after a while he pressed his foot hard, and asked him if he could feel; and he said, No; and then his leg, and so upwards and upwards, and showed us that he was cold and stiff. And he felt them himself, and said: When the poison reaches the heart, that will be the end. He was beginning to grow cold about the groin, when he uncovered his face, for he had covered himself up, and said—they were his last words—he said: Crito, I owe a cock to Asclepius; will you remember to pay the debt? The debt shall be paid, said Crito; is there anything else? There was no answer to this question; but in a minute or two a movement was heard, and the attendants uncovered him; his eyes were set, and Crito closed his eyes and mouth.

Such was the end, Echecrates, of our friend; concerning whom I may truly say, that of all the men of his time whom I have known, he was the wisest and justest and best.

corliss lamont　　　THE CRISIS CALLED DEATH

Corliss Lamont (1902–　　) received his first degree from Harvard and his Ph.D. from Columbia University. He has taught at Columbia and has been a lecturer at the New School for Social Research, Cornell University, and the Harvard Graduate School of Education. A former Director of the American Humanist Association, he has long been a leading spokesman for humanistic philosophy and causes.

Among his writings are The Illusion of Immortality, The Philosophy of Humanism, Freedom Is as Freedom Does, Soviet Civilization, Civil Liberties Today, *and* Freedom of Choice Affirmed. *He edited* Man Answers Death: An Anthology of Poetry. *"The Crisis Called Death" is from* The Humanist *(Vol. XXVII, No. 1, 1967).*

No philosophy, religion, or overall way of life can be judged complete or adequate unless it includes a definite position on whether or not the human personality can surmount the crisis called death and continue its career in another and immortal realm of existence. Without being dogmatic about it, naturalistic humanism does give an answer on this issue.

Humanism, in line with its rejection of belief in any form of the supernatural, considers illusory the idea of personal immortality, or the conscious survival of the self beyond death for any period of time whatsoever. The basic reason for regarding a hereafter as out of the question is that since a human being is a living unity of body and personality, including the mind, it is impossible for the personality to continue when the body and the brain have ceased to function.

The sciences of biology, medicine, and psychology have accumulated an enormous amount of evidence pointing to the oneness and inseparability of personality and the physical organism. And it is inconceivable that the characteristic mental activities of thought, memory, and imagination could go on without the sustaining structure of the brain and cerebral cortex. The only possible way for a man to achieve immortality is to carry out its original meaning, "not-death," by keeping alive his natural body forever. Although such an outcome is extremely improbable, the average span of life, at least in the United States, has been increasingly extended during this twentieth century. I can imagine my own this-earthly "resurrection" taking place some twenty years hence at about the age of eighty-five, when I shall go for a week or so to the hospital and have my tiring natural heart replaced by an inexhaustible mechanical heart.

Paradoxically enough, traditional Christianity supports the humanist posi-

578

tion on the unity of body and personality by insisting that man can gain immortality only through the literal resurrection of the physical body. The promise of this resurrection was, according to the New Testament, the wonderful, world-shaking message that Jesus brought. Undoubtedly the best chance for personal survival after death is precisely through this resurrection route of old-time religion. The trouble here for humanists is that they cannot possibly accept the resurrection doctrine.

Since the humanist thinks that his one and only life is in the here and now, he aims to make the best of it in terms of attaining happiness for himself, his family, his countrymen, and all mankind. Accordingly, the humanist is a militant fighter for social justice, racial equality, higher living standards, and world peace. And he remembers that faith in immortality has often cut the nerve of effective action for improving the lot of humanity on this earth.

For example, during this crucial era when the folly, horror, and tragedy of international war continue to afflict mankind, we find the following gem of supernaturalist apologia in *The New York Times* of Sept. 11, 1950, at the height of the Korean War: "Sorrowing parents whose sons have been drafted for combat duty were told yesterday in St. Patrick's Cathedral that death in battle was part of God's plan for populating the kingdom of heaven." A Catholic prelate, Monsignor William T. Greene, offered this extraordinary form of consolation, but both Pope John XXIII and Pope Paul VI would surely have winced at it.

The humanist faces his own death and that of others with more equanimity than the average person, because he realizes that in the process of Nature death is a necessary corollary of life and has played an indispensable role in the evolution of the higher animals, including man. Death has rid the earth of unprogressive species and has given full meaning to the Darwinian doctrine of the survival of the fittest. Without our good friend death, the race of man would never have come into being at all.

Biologically speaking, Nature's method with the more complex forms of life is to discard the old and faltering organism at a certain stage to make way for newborn and lustier vitality. As the American novelist Anne Parrish says, each one of us "must die for the sake of life, for the flow of the stream too great to be dammed in any pool, for the growth of the seed too strong to stay in one shape. . . . Because these bodies must perish, we are greater than we know. The most selfish must be generous, letting his life pour out to others. The most cowardly must be brave enough to go." So it is that death gives the opportunity for the largest possible number of human beings, including our own descendants, to experience the joys of living. And in this sense, death acts as the firm ally of future and unborn generations, through the simple procedure of making room for them upon this planet.

To philosophize about man's mortality, as I have been doing, or to take seriously religious promises of an afterlife, may soften slightly the impact of death; but in my opinion nothing can really counteract its bitter sting. The humanist believes that death is a blow of such magnitude and finality that it is always a tragedy, either for the deceased or the survivors who were close to him, or for both. Even when dying puts an end to a painful and incurable illness, it remains tragic that extinction of the individual should be the only cure. Of course, the tragedy is greater when a person dies in youth or the prime of life.

But it is always too soon to die, even if you are three-score years and ten, even if you are four-score years and ten—indeed, no matter how young or old you may be. Hotspur's cry in *Henry IV* resounds down the ages, "O gentlemen! the time of life is short." I myself am almost sixty-five and have the familiar experience of looking back on my life and finding that it has all gone by with appalling swiftness. Days, years, decades have slipped by so quickly that now it seems I hardly knew what was happening. Have I been daydreaming all this time?

Today, more than ever, I feel the haunting sense of transiency. If only time would for a while come to a stop! If only each day would last 100 hours and each year 1,000 days! I sympathize with everyone who ever longed for immortality and I wish that the enchanting dream of eternal life could indeed come true. So it is that as a humanist I deeply regret that death is the end. Frankly, I would like to go on living indefinitely, providing that I could be assured of continued good health and economic security. And I would be most happy if anybody could prove to me that there actually is personal survival after death.

Humanists try to look death in the face—honestly, courageously, calmly. They recognize that it is one of the basic tragedies inherent in the great gift of life. We do not agonize over this fact, nor are we preoccupied with it. Our main antidote for death is *preoccupation with life*, with the manifold enjoyments that it brings and with creative work that contributes to the progress of our country and the welfare of humanity. We know there can be no individual immortality, but we have hopes that once global peace is permanently established, international cooperation and the steady advance of science will secure the immortality of the human race in this infinitely varied and beautiful world of Nature.

c. j. ducasse   IS LIFE AFTER DEATH POSSIBLE?

*Born in France, Curt John Ducasse (1881–1969) became a naturalized citizen
in 1910. He studied at the University of Washington and received his Ph.D.
from Harvard. He taught at Washington and at Brown University, lectured at
many other universities, and served as president of the American Philosophical
Association.*

Among his titles are The Philosophy of Art, Philosophy as a Science, A Philosophical Scrutiny of Religion, *and* A Critical Examination of the Belief in a
Life After Death. *The essay which follows was published in the* Newsletter of
the Parapsychology Foundation *(Jan.–Feb. 1956).*

The question whether human personality survives death is sometimes asserted to be one upon which reflection is futile. Only empirical evidence,
it is said, can be relevant, since the question is purely one of fact.

But no question is purely one of fact until it is clearly understood; and
this one is, on the contrary, ambiguous and replete with tacit assumptions.
Until the ambiguities have been removed and the assumptions critically
examined, we do not really know just what it is we want to know when we
ask whether a life after death is possible. Nor, therefore, can we tell until
then what bearing on this question various facts empirically known to us
may have.

To clarify its meaning is chiefly what I now propose to attempt. I shall
ask first why a future life is so generally desired and believed in. Then I shall
state, as convincingly as I can in the time available, the arguments commonly advanced to prove that such a life is impossible. After that, I shall
consider the logic of these arguments, and show that they quite fail to establish the impossibility. Next, the tacit but arbitrary assumption, which
makes them nevertheless appear convincing, will be pointed out. . . .

Let us turn to the first of these tasks.

WHY MAN DESIRES LIFE AFTER DEATH

To begin with, let us note that each of us here has been alive and conscious at all times in the past which he can remember. It is true that sometimes our bodies are in deep sleep, or made inert by anesthetics or injuries.
But even at such times we do not experience unconsciousness in ourselves
for to experience it would mean being conscious of being unconscious, and
this is a contradiction. The only experience of unconsciousness in ourselves
we ever have is, not experience of total unconsciousness, but of unconscious-

ness *of this or that*; as when we report: "I am not conscious of any pain," or "of any bell-sound," or "of any difference between those two colors," etc. Nor do we ever experience unconsciousness in another person, but only the fact that, sometimes, some or all of the ordinary activities of his body cease to occur. That consciousness itself is extinguished at such times is thus only a hypothesis which we construct to account for certain changes in the behavior of another person's body or to explain in him or in ourselves the eventual lack of memories relating to the given period.

Being alive and conscious is thus, with all men, a lifelong experience and habit; and conscious life is therefore something they naturally—even if tacitly—expect to continue. As J. B. Pratt has pointed out, the child takes the continuity of life for granted. It is the fact of death that has to be taught him. But when he has learned it, and the idea of a future life is then put explicitly before his mind, it seems to him the most natural thing in the world.

The witnessing of death, however, is a rare experience for most of us, and, because it breaks so sharply into our habits, it forces on us the question whether the mind, which until then was manifested by the body now dead, continues somehow to live on, or, on the contrary, has become totally extinct. This question is commonly phrased as concerning "the immortality of the soul," and immortality, strictly speaking, means survival forever. But assurance of survival for some considerable period—say a thousand, or even a hundred, years—would probably have almost as much present psychological value as would assurance of survival strictly forever. Most men would be troubled very little by the idea of extinction at so distant a time—even less troubled than is now a healthy and happy youth by the idea that he will die in fifty or sixty years. Therefore, it is survival for some time, rather than survival specifically forever, that I shall alone consider.

The craving for continued existence is very widespread. Even persons who believe that death means complete extinction of the individual's consciousness often find comfort in various substitute conceptions of survival. They may, for instance, dwell on the continuity of the individual's germ plasm in his descendants. Or they find solace in the thought that, the past being indestructible, their individual life remains eternally an intrinsic part of the history of the world. Also—and more satisfying to one's craving for personal importance—there is the fact that since the acts of one's life have effects, and these in turn further effects, and so on, therefore what one has done goes on forever influencing remotely, and sometimes greatly, the course of future events.

Gratifying to one's vanity, too, is the prospect that, if the achievements of one's life have been great or even only conspicuous, or one's benefactions or evil deeds have been notable, one's name may not only be remembered by acquaintances and relatives for a little while, but may live on in recorded history. But evidently survival in any of these senses is but a consolation prize—but a thin substitute for the continuation of conscious individual life, which may not be a fact, but which most men crave nonetheless.

The roots of this craving are certain desires which death appears to frustrate. For some, the chief of these is for reunion with persons dearly loved. For others, whose lives have been wretched, it is the desire for another chance at the happiness they have missed. For others yet, it is desire for further opportunity to grow in ability, knowledge or character. Often, there is also the desire, already mentioned, to go on counting for something in the affairs of men. And again, a future life for oneself and others is often desired in order that the redressing of the many injustices of this life shall be possible. But it goes without saying that, although desires such as these are often sufficient to cause belief in a future life, they constitute no evidence at all that it is a fact.

In this connection, it may be well to point out that, although both the belief in survival and the belief in the existence of a god or gods are found in most religions, nevertheless there is no necessary connection between the two beliefs. No contradiction would be involved in supposing either that there is a God but no life after death or that there is a life after death but no God. The belief that there is a life after death may be tied to a religion, but it is no more intrinsically religious than would be a belief that there is life on the planet Mars. The after-death world, if it exists, is just another region or dimension of the universe.

But although belief in survival of death is natural and easy and has always been held in one form or another by a large majority of mankind, critical reflection quickly brings forth a number of apparently strong reasons to regard that belief as quite illusory. Let us now review them.

THE ARGUMENTS AGAINST SURVIVAL

There are, first of all, a number of facts which definitely suggest that both the existence and the nature of consciousness wholly depend on the presence of a functioning nervous system. It is pointed out, for example, that wherever consciousness is observed, it is found associated with a living and functioning body. Further, when the body dies, or the head is struck a heavy blow, or some anesthetic is administered, the familiar outward evidences of consciousness terminate, permanently or temporarily. Again, we know well that drugs of various kinds—alcohol, caffein, opium, heroin, and many others—cause specific changes at the time in the nature of a person's mental states. Also, by stimulating in appropriate ways the body's sense organs, corresponding states of consciousness—namely, the various kinds of sensations—can be caused at will. On the other hand, cutting a sensory nerve immediately eliminates a whole range of sensations.

Again, the contents of consciousness, the mental powers, or even the personality, are modified in characteristic ways when certain regions of the brain are destroyed by disease or injury or are disconnected from the rest by such an operation as prefrontal lobotomy. And that the nervous system is the indispensable basis of mind is further suggested by the fact that, in the evolutionary scale, the degree of intelligence of various species of animals keeps pace closely with the degree of development of their brain.

That continued existence of mind after death is impossible has been argued also on the basis of theoretical considerations. It has been contended, for instance, that what we call states of consciousness—or more particularly, ideas, sensations, volitions, feelings, and the like—are really nothing but the minute physical or chemical events which take place in the tissues of the brain. For, it is urged, it would be absurd to suppose that an idea or a volition, if it is not itself a material thing or process, could cause material effects such as contractions of muscles.

Moreover, it is maintained that the possibility of causation of a material event by an immaterial, mental cause is ruled out *a priori* by the principle of the conservation of energy; for such causation would mean that an additional quantity of energy suddenly pops into the nervous system out of nowhere.

Another conception of consciousness, which is more often met with today than the one just mentioned, but which also implies that consciousness cannot survive death, is that "consciousness" is only the name we give to certain types of behavior, which differentiate the higher animals from all other things in nature. According to this view, to say, for example, that an animal is conscious of a difference between two stimuli means nothing more than that it responds to each by different behavior. That is, the difference of *behavior* is what consciousness of difference between the stimuli *consists in*; and is not, as is commonly assumed, only the behavioral *sign* of something mental and not public, called "consciousness that the stimuli are different."

Or again, consciousness, of the typically human sort called thought, is identified with the typically human sort of behavior called speech; and this, again not in the sense that speech *expresses* or *manifests* something different from itself, called "thought," but in the sense that speech—whether uttered or only whispered—*is* thought itself. And obviously, if thought, or any mental activity, is thus but some mode of behavior of the living body, the mind cannot possibly survive death. . . .

THE ARGUMENTS EXAMINED

Such, in brief, are the chief reasons commonly advanced for holding that suvival is impossible. Scrutiny of them, however, will, I think, reveal that they are not as strong as they first seem and far from strong enough to show that there can be no life after death.

Let us consider first the assertion that "thought," or "consciousness," is but another name for subvocal speech, or for some other form of behavior, or for molecular processes in the tissues of the brain. As Paulsen and others have pointed out; no evidence ever is or can be offered to support that assertion, because it is in fact but a disguised proposal to make the words "thought," "feeling," "sensation," "desire," and so on, denote facts quite different from those which these words are commonly employed to denote. To say that those words are but other names for certain chemical or behavioral events is as grossly arbitrary as it would be to say that "wood" is but another name for glass, or "potato" but another name for cabbage. What thought, desire, sensation, and other mental states are like, each of us can observe directly by introspection; and what introspection reveals is that they do not in the least resemble muscular contraction, or glandular secretion, or any other known bodily events. No tampering with language can alter the observable fact that thinking is one thing and muttering quite another; that the feeling called anger has no resemblance to the bodily behavior which usually goes with it; or that an act of will is not in the least like anything we find when we open the skull and examine the brain. Certain mental events are doubtless connected in some way with certain bodily events, but they are not those bodily events themselves. The connection is not identity.

This being clear, let us next consider the arguments offered to show that mental processes, although not identical with bodily processes, nevertheless depend on them. We are told, for instance, that some head injuries, or anesthetics, totally extinguish consciousness for the time being. As already pointed out, however, the strict fact is only that the usual bodily signs of consciousness are then absent. But they are also absent when a person is asleep; and yet, at the same time, dreams, which are states of consciousness, may be occurring.

It is true that when the person concerned awakens, he often remembers his dreams, whereas the person that has been anesthetized or injured has usually no memories relating to the period of apparent blankness. But this could mean that his consciousness was, for the first time, dissociated from its ordinary channels of manifestation, as was reported of the co-conscious personalities of some of the patients of Dr. Morton Prince. Moreover, it sometimes occurs that a person who has been in an accident reports lack of memories not only for the period during which his body was unresponsive but also for a period of several hours *before* the accident, during which he had given to his associates all the ordinary external signs of being conscious as usual.

But, more generally, if absence of memories relating to a given period proved unconsciousness for that period, this would force us to conclude that we were unconscious during the first few years of our lives, and indeed have been so most of the time since; for the fact is that we have no memories whatever of most of our days. That we were alive and conscious on any long past specific date is, with only a few exceptions, not something we actually remember, but only something which we infer must be true.

EVIDENCE FROM PSYCHICAL RESEARCH

Another argument advanced against survival was, it will be remembered, that death must extinguish the mind, since all manifestations of it then cease. But to assert that they invariably then cease is to ignore altogether the considerable amount of evidence to the contrary, gathered over many years and carefully checked by the Society for Psychical Research. This evidence, which is of a variety of kinds, has been reviewed by Professor Gardner Murphy in an article published in the Journal of the Society. He mentions first the numerous well-authenticated cases of apparition of a dead person to others as yet unaware that he had died or even been ill or in danger. The more strongly evidential cases of apparition are those in which the apparition conveys to the person who sees it specific facts until then secret. An example would be that of the apparition of a girl to her brother nine years after her death, with a conspicuous scratch on her cheek. Their mother then revealed to him that she herself had made that scratch accidentally while preparing her daughter's body for burial, but that she had then at once covered it with powder and never mentioned it to anyone.

Another famous case is that of a father whose apparition some time after death revealed to one of his sons the existence and location of an unsuspected second will, benefiting him, which was then found as indicated. Still another case would be the report by General Barter, then a subaltern in the British Army in India, of the apparition to him of a lieutenant he had not seen for two or three years. The lieutenant's apparition was riding a brown pony with black mane and tail. He was much stouter than at their last meeting, and, whereas formerly clean-shaven, he now wore a peculiar beard in the form of a fringe encircling his face. On inquiry the next day from a person who had known the lieutenant at the time he died, it turned out that he had indeed become very bloated before his death; that he had grown just such a beard while on the sick list; and that he had some time before bought and eventually ridden to death a pony of that very description.

Other striking instances are those of an apparition seen simultaneously by several persons. It is on record that an apparition of a child was perceived first by a dog, that the animal's rushing at it, loudly barking, interrupted the conversation of the seven persons present in the room, thus drawing their at-

586

tention to the apparition, and that the latter then moved through the room for some fifteen seconds, followed by the barking dog.

Another type of empirical evidence of survival consists of communications, purporting to come from the dead, made through the persons commonly called sensitives, mediums, or automatists. Some of the most remarkable of these communications were given by the celebrated American medium. Mrs. Piper, who for many years was studied by the Society for Psychical Research, London, with the most elaborate precautions against all possibility of fraud. Twice, particularly, the evidences of identity supplied by the dead persons who purportedly were thus communicating with the living were of the very kinds, and of the same precision and detail, which would ordinarily satisfy a living person of the identity of another living person with whom he was not able to communicate directly, but only through an intermediary, or by letter or telephone.

Again, sometimes the same mark of identity of a dead person, or the same message from him, or complementary parts of one message, are obtained independently from two mediums in different parts of the world.

Of course, when facts of these kinds are recounted, as I have just done, only in abstract summary, they make little if any impression upon us. And the very word "medium" at once brings to our minds the innumerable instances of demonstrated fraud perpetrated by charlatans to extract money from the credulous bereaved. But the modes of trickery and sources of error, which immediately suggest themselves to us as easy, natural explanations of the seemingly extraordinary facts, suggest themselves just as quickly to the members of the research committees of the Society for Psychical Research. Usually, these men have had a good deal more experience than the rest of us with the tricks of conjurers and fraudulent mediums, and take against them precautions far more strict and ingenious than would occur to the average sceptic.

But when, instead of stopping at summaries, one takes the trouble to study the detailed, original reports, it them becomes evident that they cannot all be just laughed off; for to accept the hypothesis of fraud or malobservation would often require more credulity than to accept the facts reported.

To *explain* those facts, however, is quite another thing. Only two hypotheses at all adequate to do so have yet been advanced. One is that the communications really come, as they purport to do, from persons who have died and have survived death. The other is the hypothesis of telepathy— that is, the supposition, itself startling enough, that the medium is able to gather information directly from the minds of others, and that this is the true source of the information communicated. To account for all the facts, however, this hypothesis has to be stretched very far, for some of them require us to suppose that the medium can tap the minds even of persons far away and quite unknown to him, and can tap even the subconscious part of their minds.

Diverse highly ingenious attempts have been made to devise conditions that would rule out telepathy as a possible explanation of the communications received; but some of the most critical and best-documented investigators still hold that it has not yet been absolutely excluded. Hence, although some of the facts recorded by psychical research constitute, prima facie, strong empirical evidence of survival, they cannot be said to establish it beyond question. But they do show that we need to revise rather radically in some respects our ordinary ideas of what is and is not possible in nature.

CAN MENTAL STATES CAUSE BODILY EVENTS?

Let us now turn to another of the arguments against survival. That states of consciousness entirely depend on bodily processes, and therefore cannot continue when the latter have ceased, is proved, it is argued, by the fact that various states of consciousness—in particular, the several kinds of sensations—can be caused at will by appropriately stimulating the body.

Now, it is very true that sensations and some other mental states can be so caused; but we have just as good and abundant evidence that mental states can cause various bodily events. John Laird mentions, among others, the fact that merely willing to raise one's arm normally suffices to cause it to rise; that a hungry person's mouth is caused to water by the idea of food; that feelings of rage, fear or excitement cause digestion to stop; that anxiety causes changes in the quantity and quality of the milk of a nursing mother; that certain thoughts cause tears, pallor, blushing or fainting; and so on. The evidence we have that the relation is one of cause and effect is exactly the same here as where bodily processes cause mental states.

It is said, of course, that to suppose something non-physical, such as thought, to be capable of causing motion of a physical object, such as the body, is absurd. But I submit that if the heterogeneity of mind and matter makes this absurd, then it makes equally absurd the causation of mental states by stimulation of the body. Yet no absurdity is commonly found in the assertion that cutting the skin causes a feeling of pain, or that alcohol, caffein, bromides, and other drugs, cause characteristic states of consciousness. As David Hume made clear long ago, no kind of causal connection is intrinsically absurd. Anything might cause anything; and only observation can tell us what in fact can cause what.

Somewhat similar remarks would apply to the allegation that the principle of the conservation of energy precludes the possibility of causation of a physical event by a mental event. For if it does, then it equally precludes causation in the converse direction, and this, of course, would leave us totally at a loss to explain the occurrence of sensations. But, as Keeton and others have pointed out, that energy is conserved is not something observation has revealed or could reveal, but only a postulate—a defining postulate for the notion of an "isolated physical system."

That is, conservation of energy is something one has to have if, but only if, one insists on conceiving the physical world as wholly self-contained, independent, isolated. And just because the metaphysics which the natural sciences tacitly assume does insist on so conceiving the physical world, this metaphysics compels them to save conservation by postulations *ad hoc* whenever dissipation of energy is what observation reveals. It postulates, for instance, that something else, which appears at such times but was not until then regarded as energy, is energy too, but it is then said, "in a different form."

Furthermore, as Broad has emphasized, all that the principle of conservation requires is that when a quantity Q of energy disappears at one place in the physical world an equal quantity of it should appear at some other place there. And the supposition that, in some cases, what causes it to disappear here and appear there is some mental event, such perhaps as a volition, does not violate at all the supposition that energy is conserved.

A word, next, on the parallelism between the degree of development of the nervous systems of various animals and the degree of their intelligence. This is alleged to prove that the latter is the product of the former. But the facts lend themselves equally well to the supposition that, on the contrary, an obscurely felt need for greater intelligence in the circumstances the animal faced was what brought about the variations which eventually resulted in a more adequate nervous organization.

In the development of the individual, at all events, it seems clear that the specific, highly complex nerve connections which become established in the brain and cerebellum of, for instance, a skilled pianist are the results of his will over many years to acquire the skill.

We must not forget in this context that there is a converse, equally consistent with the facts, for the theory, called epiphenomenalism, that mental states are related to the brain much as the halo is to the saint, that is, as effects but never themselves as causes. The converse theory, which might be called hypophenomenalism, and which is pretty well that of Schopenhauer, is that the instruments which the various mechanisms of the body constitute are the objective products of obscure cravings for the corresponding powers; and, in particular, that the organization of the nervous system is the effect and material isomorph of the variety of mental functions exercised at a given level of animal or human existence.

THE INITIAL ASSUMPTION BEHIND THE ARGUMENTS
AGAINST SURVIVAL

We have now scrutinized . . . the reasons mentioned earlier for rejecting the possibility of survival, and we have found them all logically weak. . . . It will be useful for us to pause a moment and inquire why so many of the persons who advance these reasons nevertheless think them convincing.

It is, I believe, because these persons approach the question of survival with a certain unconscious metaphysical bias. It derives from a particular initial assumption which they tacitly make. It is that *to be real is to be material*. And to be material, of course, is to be some process or part of the perceptually public world, that is, of the world we all perceive by means of our so-called five senses.

Now the assumption that to be real is to be material is a useful and appropriate one for the purpose of investigating the material world and of operating upon it; and this purpose is a legitimate and frequent one. But those persons, and most of us, do not realize that the validity of that assumption is strictly relative to that specific purpose. Hence they, and most of us, continue making the assumption, and it continues to rule judgment, even when, as now, the purpose in view is a different one, for which the assumption is no longer useful or even congruous.

The point is all-important here and therefore worth stressing. Its essence is that the conception of the nature of reality that proposes to define the real as the material is not the expression of an observable fact to which everyone would have to bow, but is the expression only of a certain direction of interest on the part of the persons who so define reality—of interest, namely, which they have chosen to center wholly in the material, perceptually public world. This specialized interest is of course as legitimate as any other, but it automatically ignores all the facts, commonly called facts of mind, which only introspection reveals. And that specialized interest is what alone compels persons in its grip to employ the word "mind" to denote, instead of what it commonly does denote, something else altogether, namely, the public behavior of bodies that have minds.

Only so long as one's judgment is swayed unawares by that special interest do the logically weak arguments against the possibility of survival, which we have examined, seem strong.

It is possible, however, and just as legitimate, as well as more conducive to a fair view of our question, to center one's interest at the start on the facts of mind as introspectively observable, ranking them as most real in the sense that they are the facts the intrinsic nature of which we most directly experience, the facts which we most certainly know to exist; and moreover, that they are the facts without the experiencing of which we should not know any other facts whatever—such, for instance, as those of the material world. . . .

FURTHER READING

"This may be an age of youth," writes Edwin S. Shneidman, "but it is also an age of *death*. . . . In the Western world we are probably more death-oriented today than we have been since the days of the Black Plague in the 14th Century." See his essay "The Enemy" in *Psychology Today* (August, 1970).

Michel de Montaigne quoted the ancient poets and philosophers with abandon in "That to Philosophize Is to Learn to Die." The best translation is by Donald M. Frame, *The Complete Essays of Montaigne* (1958).

Alan Harrington's *The Immortalist* (1969) is subtitled "An Approach to the Engineering of Man's Divinity." Harrington calls for a scientific end to death, but this volume is primarily a punishing critique of past thinking about death.

In separate essays both entitled "Death," Thomas Nagel considers whether death is an evil and Mary Mothersill disagrees with his conclusion. The essays are included in *Moral Problems* (1971), edited by James Rachels.

The Tragic Sense of Life (1913) was Miguel de Unamuno's greatest work, and it is concerned throughout with the question of man's immortality.

Herman Feifel (ed.), *The Meaning of Death* (1959). Twenty-one authors from a variety of fields confront the issue of death, which "has been relegated to the tabooed territory heretofore occupied by diseases like tuberculosis and cancer, and the topic of sex."

An outgrowth of lectures delivered at Oxford, *Man and His Destiny in the Great Religions* (1962), by S. G. F. Brandon, reviews a disheartening number of theories about what happens after death.

Simone de Beauvoir, *A Very Easy Death* (1966). Do not be misled by the title: this is a grim and factual account of the agonizingly slow death of the author's mother.

William Ernest Hocking, *The Meaning of Immortality in Human Experience* (1957). A revision of the author's *Thoughts on Death and Life* (1937), which is an indication of the Harvard idealist's long-term preoccupation with the topic.

epilogue

The theme of freedom, in one or the other of its many variations, is basic to a surprisingly large number of the preceding readings. Amiel held that philosophy itself means "the complete liberty of the mind"; Sartre said that man is freedom. Dewey explained that freedom is an assumption of morality, and Russell's essay is entitled "A Free Man's Worship." One chapter dealt explicitly with the question of the freedom of the will; another revolved around the related concepts of freedom and identity.

But do men really want to be free? Assuming for the moment that determinism is not the case, are we as interested in being free as our slogans and lavish lip service would have it? The free man creates himself and his life through his choices—at least in all those respects that matter most— and such choices entail heavy and frightening responsibilities. It is far easier to find leaders to follow and dogmas to swallow. Even the "true believers," of course, are choosing, but their choice is a kind of suicide.

Who would choose to relinquish their freedom? Perhaps the mass of men, said an extraordinary Russian named Fyodor Mikhailovitch Dostoyevsky.

fyodor dostoyevsky   THE GRAND INQUISITOR

Fyodor Dostoyevsky (1821–1881) lived a life of crises and chaos. His father was murdered, and a slight association with a politically liberal group led to his being sentenced to ten years in Siberia. His first marriage quickly became an unhappy one; it culminated in his wife's insanity and early death. He was for considerable periods of time a compulsive gambler, and the gambling compounded his always desperate need for money. There were turbulent and frustrating love affairs. He suffered from epileptic seizures, periods of depression, and there was the horror of the death of his first child. In spite of all this—or because of it— there came from his pen such works as Notes from the Underground, The House of the Dead, Crime and Punishment, The Idiot, *and* The Brothers Karamazov *(1880), from which the following selection is taken. In his final years, there was relative peace: there had been a happy second marriage, and his writing brought him fame in his own lifetime.*

"The Grand Inquisitor" is a story told by Ivan Karamazov to his younger brother Alyosha. Ivan is a doubt-ridden intellectual; Alyosha is "simple," and saintly, a Christian. Both speak for Dostoyevsky. Ivan's story contains the charge that men are not strong enough for the freedom offered them by Jesus. "Man is tormented by no greater anxiety than to find some one quickly to whom he can hand over that gift of freedom. . . ." All that man craves, Ivan continues, is "someone to worship, someone to keep his conscience, and some means of uniting all in one unanimous and harmonious ant-heap."

It was a story that D. H. Lawrence re-read periodically, but he said that it made his heart sink right through his shoes. "It is a deadly, devastating summing up, unanswerable because borne out by the long experience of humanity."

"My story is laid in Spain, in Seville, in the most terrible time of the Inquisition, when fires were lighted every day to the glory of God, and 'in the splendid *auto da fé* the wicked heretics were burnt.' Oh, of course, this was not the coming in which He will appear according to His promise at the end of time in all His heavenly glory, and which will be sudden 'as lightning flashing from east to west.' No, He visited His children only for a moment, and there where the flames were crackling round the heretics. In His infinite mercy He came once more among men in that human shape in which He walked among men for three years fifteen centuries ago. He came down to the 'hot pavement' of the southern town in which on the day before almost a hundred heretics had, *ad majorem gloriam Dei*,[1] been burnt by the cardinal, the Grand Inquisitor, in a magnificent *auto da fé*,[2]

[1] "for the greater glory of God"
[2] "act of faith"

in the presence of the king, the court, the knights, the cardinals, the most charming ladies of the court, and the whole population of Seville.

"He came softly, unobserved, and yet, strange to say, every one recognised Him. That might be one of the best passages in the poem. I mean, why they recognised Him. The people are irresistibly drawn to Him, they surround Him, they flock about Him, follow Him. He moves silently in their midst with a gentle smile of infinite compassion. The sun of love burns in His heart, light and power shine from His eyes, and their radiance, shed on the people, stirs their hearts with responsive love. He holds out His hands to them, blesses them, and a healing virtue comes from contact with Him, even with His garments. An old man in the crowd, blind from childhood, cries out, 'O Lord, heal me and I shall see Thee!' and, as it were, scales fall from his eyes and the blind man sees Him. The crowd weeps and kisses the earth under His feet. Children throw flowers before Him, sing, and cry hosannah. 'It is He—it is He!' all repeat. 'It must be He, it can be no one but Him!' He stops at the steps of the Seville cathedral at the moment when the weeping mourners are bringing in a little open white coffin. In it lies a child of seven, the only daughter of a prominent citizen. The dead child lies hidden in flowers. 'He will raise your child,' the crowd shouts to the weeping mother. The priest, coming to meet the coffin, looks perplexed, and frowns, but the mother of the dead child throws herself at His feet with a wail. 'If it is Thou, raise my child!' she cries, holding out her hands to Him. The procession halts, the coffin is laid on the steps at His feet. He looks with compassion, and His lips once more softly pronounce, 'Maiden, arise!' and the maiden arises. The little girl sits up in the coffin and looks round, smiling with wide-open wondering eyes, holding a bunch of white roses they had put in her hand.

"There are cries, sobs, confusion among the people, and at that moment the cardinal himself, the Grand Inquisitor, passes by the cathedral. He is an old man, almost ninety, tall and erect, with a withered face and sunken eyes, in which there is still a gleam of light. He is not dressed in his gorgeous cardinal's robes, as he was the day before, when he was burning the enemies of the Roman Church—at that moment he was wearing his coarse, old, monk's cassock. At a distance behind him come his gloomy assistants and slaves and the 'holy guard.' He stops at the sight of the crowd and watches it from a distance. He sees everything; he sees them set the coffin down at His feet, sees the child rise up, and his face darkens. He knits his thick grey brows and his eyes gleam with a sinister fire. He holds out his finger and bids the guards take Him. And such is his power, so completely are the people cowed into submission and trembling obedience to him, that the crowd immediately make way for the guards, and in the midst of deathlike silence they lay hands on Him and lead

Him away. The crowd instantly bows down to the earth, like one man, before the old inquisitor. He blesses the people in silence and passes on. The guards lead their prisoner to the close, gloomy vaulted prison in the ancient palace of the Holy Inquisition and shut Him in it. The day passes and is followed by the dark, burning 'breathless' night of Seville. The air is 'fragrant with laurel and lemon.' In the pitch darkness the iron door of the prison is suddenly opened and the Grand Inquisitor himself comes in with a light in his hand. He is alone; the door is closed at once behind him. He stands in the doorway and for a minute or two gazes into His face. At last he goes up slowly, sets the light on the table and speaks.

" 'Is it Thou? Thou?' but receiving no answer, he adds at once, 'Don't answer, be silent. What canst Thou say, indeed? I know too well what Thou wouldst say. And Thou hast no right to add anything to what Thou hadst said of old. Why, then, art Thou come to hinder us? For Thou hast come to hinder us, and Thou knowest that. But dost Thou know what will be to-morrow? I know not who Thou art and care not to know whether it is Thou or only a semblance of Him, but to-morrow I shall condemn Thee and burn Thee at the stake as the worst of heretics. And the very people who have to-day kissed Thy feet, to-morrow at the faintest sign from me will rush to heap up the embers of Thy fire. Knowest Thou that? Yes, maybe Thou knowest it,' he added with thoughtful penetration, never for a moment taking his eyes off the Prisoner."

"I don't quite understand, Ivan. What does it mean?" Alyosha, who had been listening in silence, said with a smile. "Is it simply a wild fantasy, or a mistake on the part of the old man—some impossible *quiproquo?*"

"Take it as the last," said Ivan, laughing, "if you are so corrupted by modern realism and can't stand anything fantastic. If you like it to be a case of mistaken identity, let it be so. It is true," he went on, laughing, "the old man was ninety, and he might well be crazy over his set idea. He might have been struck by the appearance of the Prisoner. It might, in fact, be simply his ravings, the delusion of an old man of ninety, over-excited by the *auto da fé* of a hundred heretics the day before. But does it matter to us after all whether it was a mistake of identity or a wild fantasy? All that matters is that the old man should speak out, should speak openly of what he has thought in silence for ninety years."

"And the Prisoner too is silent? Does He look at him and not say a word?"

"That's inevitable in any case," Ivan laughed again. "The old man has told Him He hasn't the right to add anything to what He has said of old. One may say it is the most fundamental feature of Roman Catholicism, in my opinion at least. 'All has been given by Thee to the Pope,' they say, 'and all, therefore, is still in the Pope's hands, and there is no need for

Thee to come now at all. Thou must not meddle for the time, at least.'
That's how they speak and write too—the Jesuits, at any rate. I have read
it myself in the works of their theologians. 'Hast Thou the right to reveal
to us one of the mysteries of that world from which Thou hast come?'
my old man asks Him, and answers the question for Him. 'No, Thou hast
not; that Thou mayest not add to what has been said of old, and mayest
not take from men the freedom which Thou didst exalt when Thou wast
on earth. Whatsoever Thou revealest anew will encroach on men's freedom
of faith; for it will be manifest as a miracle, and the freedom of their faith
was dearer to Thee than anything in those days fifteen hundred years ago.
Didst Thou not often say then, "I will make you free"? But now Thou
hast seen these "free" men,' the old man adds suddenly, with a pensive
smile. 'Yes, we've paid dearly for it,' he goes on, looking sternly at Him,
'but at last we have completed that work in Thy name. For fifteen centuries we have been wrestling with Thy freedom, but now it is ended and
over for good. Dost Thou not believe that it's over for good? Thou lookest
meekly at me and deignest not even to be wroth with me. But let me tell
Thee that now, to-day, people are more persuaded than ever that they
have perfect freedom, yet they have brought their freedom to us and laid
it humbly at our feet. But that has been our doing. Was this what Thou
didst? Was this Thy freedom?' "

"I don't understand again," Alyosha broke in. "Is he ironical, is he
jesting?"

"Not a bit of it! He claims it as a merit for himself and his Church
that at last they have vanquished freedom and have done so to make men
happy. 'For now' (he is speaking of the Inquisition, of course) 'for the
first time it has become possible to think of the happiness of men. Man
was created a rebel; and how can rebels be happy? Thou wast warned,' he
says to Him. 'Thou hast had no lack of admonitions and warnings, but
Thou didst not listen to those warnings; Thou didst reject the only way
by which men might be made happy. But, fortunately, departing Thou
didst hand on the work to us. Thou hast promised, Thou hast established
by Thy word, Thou hast given to us the right to bind and to unbind,
and now, of course, Thou canst not think of taking it away. Why, then,
hast Thou come to hinder us?' "

"And what's the meaning of 'no lack of admonitions and warnings?' "
asked Alyosha.

"Why, that's the chief part of what the old man must say."

" 'The wise and dread spirit, the spirit of self-destruction and non-
existence,' the old man goes on, 'the great spirit talked with Thee in the
wilderness, and we are told in the books that he "tempted" Thee. Is that
so? And could anything truer be said than what he revealed to Thee in

three questions and what Thou didst reject, and what in the books is called "the temptation?" And yet if there has ever been on earth a real stupendous miracle, it took place on that day, on the day of the three temptations. The statement of those three questions was itself the miracle. If it were possible to imagine simply for the sake of argument that those three questions of the dread spirit had perished utterly from the books, and that we had to restore them and to invent them anew, and to do so had gathered together all the wise men of the earth—rulers, chief priests, learned men, philosophers, poets—and had set them the task to invent three questions, such as would not only fit the occasion, but express in three words, three human phrases, the whole future history of the world and of humanity—dost Thou believe that all the wisdom of the earth united could have invented anything in depth and force equal to the three questions which were actually put to Thee then by the wise and mighty spirit in the wilderness? From those questions alone, from the miracle of their statement, we can see that we have here to do not with the fleeting human intelligence, but with the absolute and eternal. For in those three questions the whole subsequent history of mankind is, as it were, brought together into one whole, and foretold, and in them are united all the unsolved historical contradictions of human nature. At the time it could not be so clear, since the future was unknown; but now that fifteen hundred years have passed, we see that everything in those three questions was so justly divined and foretold, and has been so truly fulfilled, that nothing can be added to them or taken from them.

"'Judge Thyself who was right—Thou or he who questioned Thee then? Remember the first question; its meaning, in other words, was this: "Thou wouldst go into the world, and art going with empty hands, with some promise of freedom which men in their simplicity and their natural unruliness cannot even understand, which they fear and dread—for nothing has ever been more insupportable for a man and a human society than freedom. But seest Thou these stones in this parched and barren wilderness? Turn them into bread, and mankind will run after Thee like a flock of sheep, grateful and obedient, though for ever trembling, lest Thou withdraw Thy hand and deny them Thy bread." But Thou wouldst not deprive man of freedom and didst reject the offer, thinking, what is that freedom worth, if obedience is bought with bread? Thou didst reply that man lives not by bread alone. But dost Thou know that for the sake of that earthly bread the spirit of the earth will rise up against Thee and will strive with Thee and overcome Thee, and all will follow him, crying, "Who can compare with this beast? He has given us fire from heaven!" Dost Thou know that the ages will pass, and humanity will proclaim by the lips of their sages that there is no crime, and therefore no sin; there is only hunger?

"Feed men, and then ask of them virtue!" that's what they'll write on the banner, which they will raise against Thee, and with which they will destroy Thy temple. Where Thy temple stood will rise a new building; the terrible tower of Babel will be built again, and though, like the one of old, it will not be finished, yet Thou mightest have prevented that new tower and have cut short the sufferings of men for a thousand years; for they will come back to us after a thousand years of agony with their tower. They will seek us again, hidden underground in the catacombs, for we shall be agan persecuted and tortured. They will find us and cry to us, "Feed us, for those who have promised us fire from heaven haven't given it!" And then we shall finish building their tower, for he finishes the building who feeds them. And we alone shall feed them in Thy name, declaring falsely that it is in Thy name. Oh, never, never can they feed themselves without us! No science will give them bread so long as they remain free. In the end they will lay their freedom at our feet, and say to us, "Make us your slaves, but feed us." They will understand themselves, at last, that freedom and bread enough for all are inconceivable together, for never, never will they be able to share between them! They will be convinced, too, that they can never be free, for they are weak, vicious, worthless and rebellious. Thou didst promise them the bread of Heaven, but, I repeat again, can it compare with earthly bread in the eyes of the weak, ever sinful and ignoble race of man? And if for the sake of the bread of Heaven thousands and tens of thousands shall follow Thee, what is to become of the millions and tens of thousands of millions of creatures who will not have the strength to forego the earthly bread for the sake of the heavenly? Or dost Thou care only for the tens of thousands of the great and strong, while the millions, numerous as the sands of the sea, who are weak but love Thee, must exist only for the sake of the great and strong? No, we care for the weak too. They are sinful and rebellious, but in the end they too will become obedient. They will marvel at us and look on us as gods, because we are ready to endure the freedom which they have found so dreadful and to rule over them—so awful it will seem to them to be free. But we shall tell them that we are Thy servants and rule them in Thy name. We shall deceive them again, for we will not let Thee come to us again. That deception will be our suffering, for we shall be forced to lie.

" 'This is the significance of the first question in the wilderness, and this is what Thou hast rejected for the sake of that freedom which Thou hast exalted above everything. Yet in this question lies hid the great secret of this world. Choosing "bread," Thou wouldst have satisfied the universal and everlasting craving of humanity—to find some one to worship. So long as man remains free he strives for nothing so incessantly and so painfully as to find some one to worship. But man seeks to worship what is established beyond dispute, so that all men would agree at once to worship it. For these pitiful creatures are concerned not only to find what one or the other can worship, but to find something that all would believe in and worship; what is essential is that all may be *together* in it. This craving for *community* of worship is the chief misery of every man individually and of all humanity from the beginning of time. For the sake of common worship they've slain each other with the sword. They have set up gods and challenged one another, "Put away your gods and come and worship ours, or we will kill you and your gods!" And so it will be to the end of the world, even when gods disappear from the earth; they will fall down before idols just the same. Thou didst know, Thou couldst not but have known, this fundamental secret of human nature, but Thou didst reject the one infallible banner which was offered Thee to make all men bow down to Thee alone—the banner of earthly bread; and Thou hast rejected it for the sake of freedom and the bread of Heaven. Behold what Thou didst further. And all again in the name of freedom! I tell Thee that man is tormented by no greater anxiety than to find some one quickly to whom he can hand over that gift of freedom with which the ill-fated creature is born. But only one who can appease their conscience can take over their freedom. In bread there was offered Thee an invincible banner; give bread, and man will worship Thee, for nothing is more certain than bread. But if some one else gains possession of his conscience—oh! then he will cast away Thy bread and follow after him who has ensnared his conscience. In that Thou wast right. For the secret of man's being is not only to live but to have something to live for. Without a stable conception of the object of life, man would not consent to go on living, and would rather destroy himself than remain on earth, though he had bread in abundance. That is true. But what happened? Instead of taking men's freedom from them, Thou didst make it greater than ever! Didst Thou forget that man prefers peace, and even death, to freedom of choice in the knowledge of good and evil? Nothing is more seductive for man than his freedom of conscience, but nothing is a greater cause of suffering. And behold, instead of giving a firm foundation for setting the conscience of man at rest for ever, Thou didst choose all that is exceptional, vague and enigmatic; Thou didst choose what was utterly beyond the strength of men, acting as though Thou didst not love them at all—Thou who didst come to give Thy life for them! Instead of taking possession of men's freedom, Thou didst increase it, and burdened the spiritual kingdom of mankind with its sufferings for ever. Thou didst desire man's free love, that he should follow Thee freely, enticed and taken captive by Thee. In place of the rigid ancient law, man must hereafter with free heart decide for himself what is good and what is evil, having only Thy image before him as his guide. But didst Thou not know he would at last reject even Thy image and Thy truth, if he is weighed down with the fearful burden of free choice? They will cry aloud at last that the truth is not in Thee, for they could not have been left in greater confusion and suffering than Thou hast caused, laying upon them so many cares and unanswerable problems.

" 'So that, in truth, Thou didst Thyself lay the foundation for the destruction of Thy kingdom, and no one is more to blame for it. Yet what was offered Thee? There are three powers, three powers alone, able to conquer and to hold captive for ever the conscience of these impotent rebels for their happiness—those forces are miracle, mystery and authority. Thou hast rejected all three and hast set the example for doing so. When the wise and dread spirit set Thee on the pinnacle of the temple and said to Thee, "If Thou wouldst know whether Thou art the Son of God then cast Thyself down, for it is written: the angels shall hold him up lest he fall and bruise himself, and Thou shalt know then whether Thou art the Son of God and shalt prove then how great is Thy faith in Thy Father." But Thou didst refuse and wouldst not cast Thyself down. Oh! of course, Thou didst proudly and well, like God; but the weak, unruly race of men, are they gods? Oh, Thou didst know then that in taking one step, in making one movement to cast Thyself down, Thou wouldst be tempting God and have lost all Thy faith in Him, and wouldst have been dashed to pieces against that earth which Thou didst come to save. And the wise spirit that tempted Thee would have rejoiced. But I ask again, are there many like Thee? And couldst Thou believe for one moment that men, too, could face such a temptation? Is the nature of men such, that they can reject miracle, and at the great moments of their life, the moments of their deepest, most agonising spiritual difficulties, cling only to the free verdict of the heart? Oh, Thou didst know that Thy deed would be recorded in books, would be handed down to remote times and the utmost ends of the earth, and Thou didst hope that man, following Thee, would cling to God and not ask for a miracle. But Thou didst not know that when man rejects miracle he rejects God too; for man seeks not so much God as the miraculous. And as man cannot bear to be without the miraculous, he will create new miracles of his own for himself, and will worship deeds of sorcery and witchcraft, though he might be a hundred times over a rebel, heretic and infidel. Thou didst not come down from the Cross when they shouted to Thee, mocking and reviling Thee, "Come down from the cross and we will believe that Thou art He." Thou didst not come down, for again Thou wouldst not enslave man by a miracle, and didst crave faith given freely, not based on miracle. Thou didst crave for free love and not the base raptures of the slave before the might that has overawed him for ever. But Thou didst think too highly of men therein, for they are slaves, of course, though rebellious by nature. Look round and judge; fifteen centuries have passed, look upon them. Whom hast Thou raised up to Thyself? I swear, man is weaker and baser by nature than Thou hast believed him! Can he, can he do what Thou didst? By showing him so much respect, Thou didst, as it were, cease to feel for him, for Thou didst ask far too much from him—Thou who hast loved him more than Thyself! Respecting him less, Thou wouldst have asked less of him. That would have been more like love, for his burden would have been lighter. He is weak and vile. What though he is everywhere now rebelling against our power, and proud of his rebellion? It is the pride of a child and a schoolboy. They are little children rioting and barring out the teacher at school. But their childish delight will end; it will cost them dear. They will cast down temples and drench the earth with blood. But they will see at last, the foolish children, that, though they are rebels, they are impotent rebels, unable to keep up their own rebellion. Bathed in their foolish tears, they will recognise at last that He who created them rebels must have meant to mock at them. They will say this in despair, and their utterance will be a blasphemy which will make them more unhappy still, for man's nature cannot bear blasphemy, and in the end always avenges it on itself. And so unrest, confusion and unhappiness —that is the present lot of man after Thou didst bear so much for their freedom! Thy great prophet tells in vision and in image, that he saw all those who took part in the first resurrection and that there were of each tribe twelve thousand. But if there were so many of them, they must have been not men but gods. They had borne Thy cross, they had endured scores of years in the barren, hungry wilderness, living upon locusts and roots—and Thou mayest indeed point with pride at those children of freedom, of free love, of free and splendid sacrifice for Thy name. But remember that they were only some thousands; and what of the rest? And how are the other weak ones to blame, because they could not endure what the strong have endured? How is the weak soul to blame that it is unable to receive such terrible gifts? Canst Thou have simply come to the elect and for the elect? But if so, it is a mystery and we cannot understand it. And if it is a mystery, we too have a right to preach a mystery, and to teach them that it's not the free judgment of their hearts, not love that matters, but a mystery which they must follow blindly, even against their conscience. So we have done. We have corrected Thy work and have founded it upon *miracle, mystery* and *authority*. And men rejoiced that they were again led like sheep, and that the terrible gift that had brought them such suffering, was, at last, lifted from their hearts. Were we right teaching them this? Speak! Did we not love mankind, so meekly acknowledging their feebleness, lovingly lightening their burden, and permitting their weak nature even sin with our sanction? Why hast Thou come now to hinder us? And why dost Thou look silently and searchingly at me with Thy mild eyes? Be angry. I don't want Thy love, for I love Thee not. And what use is it for me to hide anything from Thee? Don't I know to Whom I am speaking? All that I can say is known to Thee already. And is it for me to conceal from Thee our mystery? Perhaps it is Thy will to hear it from my lips. Listen, then. We are not working with Thee, but with *him*—that is our mystery. It's long—eight centuries—since we have been on *his* side and not on Thine. Just eight centuries ago, we took from him what Thou didst reject with scorn, that last gift he offered Thee, showing Thee all the kingdoms of the earth. We took from him Rome and the sword of Cæsar, and proclaimed ourselves sole rulers of the earth, though hitherto we have not been able to complete our work. But whose fault is that? Oh, the work is only beginning, but it has begun. It has long to await completion and the earth has yet much to suffer, but we shall triumph and shall be Cæsars, and then we shall plan the universal happiness of man. But Thou mightest have, taken even the sword of Cæsar. Why didst Thou reject that last gift? Hadst Thou accepted that last counsel of the mighty spirit, Thou wouldst have accomplished all that man seeks on earth—that is, some one to worship, some one to keep his conscience, and some means of uniting all in one unanimous and harmonious ant-heap, for the craving for universal unity is the third and last anguish of men. Mankind as a whole has always striven to organise a universal state. There have been many great nations with great histories, but the more highly they were developed the more unhappy they were, for they felt more acutely than other people the craving for worldwide union. The great conquerors, Timours and Ghenghis-Khans, whirled like hurricanes over the face of the earth striving to subdue its people, and they too were but the unconscious expression of the same craving for universal unity. Hadst Thou taken the world and Cæsar's purple, Thou wouldst have founded the universal state and have given universal peace. For who can rule men if not he who holds their conscience and their bread in his hands? We have taken the sword of Cæsar, and in taking it, of course, have rejected Thee and followed *him*. Oh, ages are yet to come of the confusion of free thought, of their science and cannibalism. For having begun to build their tower of Babel without us, they will end, of course, with cannibalism. But then the beast will crawl to us and lick our feet and spatter them with tears of blood. And we shall sit upon the beast and raise the cup, and on it will be written, "Mystery." But then, and only then, the reign of peace and happiness will come for men. Thou art proud of Thine elect, but Thou hast only the elect, while we give rest to all. And besides, how many of those elect, those mighty ones who could become elect, have grown weary waiting for Thee, and have transferred and will transfer the powers of their spirit and the warmth of their heart to the other camp, and end by raising their *free* banner against Thee. Thou didst Thyself lift up that banner. But with us all will be happy and will no more rebel nor destroy one another as under Thy freedom. Oh, we shall persuade them that they will only become free when they renounce their freedom to us and submit to us. And shall we be right or shall we be lying? They will be convinced that we are right, for they will remember the horrors of slavery and confusion to which Thy freedom brought them. Freedom, free thought and science, will lead them into such straits and will bring them face to face with such marvels and insoluble mysteries, that some of them, the fierce and rebellious, will destroy themselves, others, rebellious but weak, will destroy one another, while the rest, weak and unhappy, will crawl fawning to our feet and whine to us: "Yes, you were right, you alone possess His mystery, and we come back to you, save us from ourselves!"

" 'Receiving bread from us, they will see clearly that we take the bread made by their hands from them, to give it to them, without any miracle. They will see that we do not change the stones to bread, but in truth they will be more thankful for taking it from our hands than for the bread itself! For they will remember only too well that in old days, without our help, even the bread they made turned to stones in their hands, while since they have come back to us, the very stones have turned to bread in their hands. Too, too well they know the value of complete submission! And until men know that, they will be unhappy. Who is most to blame for their not knowing it, speak? Who scattered the flock and sent it astray on unknown paths? But the flock will come together again and will submit once more, and then it will be once for all. Then we shall give them the quiet humble happiness of weak creatures such as they are by nature. Oh, we shall persuade them at last not to be proud, for Thou didst lift them up and thereby taught them to be proud. We shall show them that they are weak, that they are only pitiful children, but that childlike happiness is the sweetest of all. They will become timid and will look to us and huddle close to us in fear, as chicks to the hen. They will marvel at us and will be awestricken before us, and will be proud at our being so powerful and clever, that we have been able to subdue such a turbulent flock of thousands of millions. They will tremble impotently before our wrath, their minds will grow fearful, they will be quick to shed tears like women and children, but they will be just as ready at a sign from us to pass to laughter and rejoicing, to happy mirth and childish song. Yes, we shall set them to work, but in their leisure hours we shall make their life like a child's game, with children's songs and innocent dance. Oh, we shall allow them even sin, they are weak and helpless, and they will love us like children because we allow them to sin. We shall tell them that every sin will be expiated, if it is done with our permission, that we allow them to sin because we love them, and the punishment for these sins we take upon ourselves. And we shall take it upon ourselves, and they will adore us as their saviours who have taken on themselves their sins before God. And they will have no secrets from us. We shall allow or forbid them to live with their wives and mistresses, to have or not to have children—according to whether they have been obedient or disobedient—and they will submit to us gladly and cheerfully. The most painful secrets of their conscience, all, all they will bring to us, and we shall have an answer for all. And they will be glad to believe our answer, for it will save them from the great anxiety and terrible agony they endure at present in making a free decision for themselves. And all will be happy, all the millions of creatures except the hundred thousand who rule over them. For only we, we who guard the mystery, shall be unhappy. There will be thousands of millions of happy babes, and a hundred thousand sufferers who have taken upon themselves the curse of the knowledge of good and evil. Peacefully they will die, peacefully they will expire in Thy name, and beyond the grave they will find nothing but death. But we shall keep the secret, and for their happiness we shall allure them with the reward of heaven and eternity. Though if there were anything in the other world, it certainly would not be for such as they. It is prophesied that Thou will come again in victory, Thou wilt come with Thy chosen, the proud and strong, but we will say that they have only saved themselves, but we have saved all. We are told that the harlot who sits upon the beast, and holds in her hands the *mystery*, shall be put to shame, that the weak will rise up again, and will rend her royal purple and will strip naked her loathsome body. But then I will stand up and point out to Thee the thousand millions of happy children who have known no sin. And we who have taken their sins upon us for their happiness will stand up before Thee and say: "Judge us if Thou canst and darest." Know that I fear Thee not. Know that I too have been in the wilderness, I too have lived on roots and locusts, I too prized the freedom with which Thou hast blessed men, and I too was striving to stand among Thy elect, among the strong and powerful, thirsting "to make up the number." But I awakened and would not serve madness. I turned back and joined the ranks of those *who have corrected Thy work*. I left the proud and went back to the humble, for the happiness of the humble. What I say to Thee will come to pass, and our dominion will be built up. I repeat, to-morrow Thou shalt see the obedient flock who at a sign from me will hasten to heap up the hot cinders about the pile on which I shall burn Thee for coming to hinder us. For if any one has ever deserved our fires, it is Thou. To-morrow I shall burn Thee. Dixi.' " [3] . . .

[3] "I have spoken."

FURTHER READING

Modern man's freedom has made him feel isolated and anxious, says Erich Fromm. His alternatives are either to escape from freedom "into new dependencies and submission" or to realize his freedom in individuality. See Fromm's *Escape from Freedom* (1941).

Robert E. Dewey and James A. Gould's *Freedom: Its History, Nature, and Varieties* (1970) is a collection of forty-four readings ranging from one by Epictetus to an S.D.S. statement. Lengthy, annotated bibliographies are included.

Mortimer J. Adler, *The Idea of Freedom* (2 Vols., 1958–1961). A massive compilation of information compiled at the Institute for Philosophical Research.

Eric Hoffer's *The True Believer* (1951) is a study of the frustration and self-hate which drive "true believers" to attempt to forget themselves in *any* mass movement.

CHAPTER TWO

CHAPTER THREE

translated by Cyril Bailey, 1926. By permission of The Clarendon Press, Oxford. [Editor's title.]

Epictetus, "The Art of Living." From *The Discourses of Epictetus with the Encheiridion and Fragments*, A. L. Burt Company, Publishers, n.d. [Editor's title; notes have been omitted.]

C. D. Broad, "Critical Thought." From *Scientific Thought* by C. D. Broad. New York: Humanities Press, Inc., 1923. [Editor's title.]

José Ortega y Gasset, "What Is Philosophy?" Reprinted from *What Is Philosophy?* by José Ortega y Gasset, translated from the Spanish by Mildred Adams. By permission of W. W. Norton & Company, Inc. Copyright © 1960 by W. W. Norton & Company, Inc. [A note has been omitted.]

Henri-Frederic Amiel, "Philosophy Means Liberty." From *Amiel's Journal*, translated by Mrs. Humphry Ward, Macmillan, 1893. [Editor's title.]

CHAPTER FOUR

Franz Kafka, "The Bucket Rider." Reprinted by permission of Schocken Books Inc. from *The Penal Colony* by Franz Kafka. Copyright © 1948 by Schocken Books Inc.

Ernest Hemingway, "A Clean, Well-Lighted Place." Copyright 1933 Charles Scribner's Sons; renewal copyright © 1961 Ernest Hemingway. Reprinted by permission of Charles Scribner's Sons from *Winner Take Nothing* by Ernest Hemingway.

Rollo May, "The Hollow People." Reprinted from *Man's Search for Himself* by Rollo May. By permission of W. W. Norton & Company, Inc. Copyright 1953 by W. W. Norton & Company, Inc.

R. D. Laing, " 'Normal' Alienation." From *The Politics of Experience* by R. D. Laing. Copyright © R. D. Laing, 1967. Reprinted by permission of Penguin Books Ltd. [Editor's title; a note has been omitted.]

Karl Marx, "Alienated Labour." From *Karl Marx: Early Writings*, translated by T. B. Bottomore. © T. B. Bottomore, 1963. Used with permission of McGraw-Hill Book Company. [A note has been omitted.]

Jean-Paul Sartre, "Anguish, Forlornness, and Despair." From *Existentialism and the Human Emotions* by Jean-Paul Sartre, 1945. Reprinted by permission of Philosophical Library, Inc. [Editor's title.]

Michael Novak, "The Experience of Nothingness." "The Experience of America" and "In Europe: Nihilism" from *The Experience of Nothingness* by Michael Novak. Copyright © 1970 by Michael Novak. By permission of Harper & Row, Publishers, Inc. [Notes have been omitted.]

CHAPTER FIVE

Sinclair Lewis, "George F. Babbitt." From *Babbitt* by Sinclair Lewis, copyright, 1922, by Harcourt Brace Jovanovich, Inc.; renewed, 1950, by Sinclair Lewis. Reprinted by permission of the publisher.

The Foxfire Book, "Aunt Arie." From *The Foxfire Book* by Eliot Wigginton. Copyright © 1973 by Brooks Eliot Wigginton. Reprinted by permission of Doubleday & Company, Inc.

Carl R. Rogers, "The Valuing Process in the Mature Person." From "Toward a Modern Approach to Values" by Carl R. Rogers, *Journal of Abnormal and*

Social Psychology, Vol. 68, 1964, pp. 160–167. Copyright 1964 by the American Psychological Association, and reproduced by permission. [Editor's title; notes and references have been omitted.]

Aristotle. "The Ethics." From *The Ethics of Aristotle*, translated by James Alexander Kerr Thomson (Harper & Row, Publishers, Inc.; Barnes & Noble Books). [Notes have been omitted.]

Immanuel Kant, "The Good Will." From *Fundamental Principles of the Metaphysics of Morals* by Immanuel Kant, translated by Thomas K. Abbott, 1898. [Editor's title; notes have been omitted.]

John Stuart Mill, "Utilitarianism." Chapters I and II from *Utilitarianism* by John Stuart Mill, 1863.

CHAPTER SIX

Delmore Schwartz, "In Dreams Begin Responsibilities." From *The World Is a Wedding* by Delmore Schwartz. Copyright 1948 by Delmore Schwartz. Reprinted by permission of New Directions Publishing Corporation.

John Dewey, "The Nature of Moral Theory." From *Ethics*, revised edition, by John Dewey and James H. Tufts. Copyright 1908, 1932 by Holt, Rinehart and Winston, Inc. Copyright 1936 by John Dewey and James H. Tufts. Copyright © 1960 by Roberta L. Dewey. Reprinted by permission of Holt, Rinehart and Winston, Inc.

Kenneth Fearing, "Confession Overheard in a Subway." From *Afternoon of a Pawnbroker and Other Poems*, copyright, 1943, by Kenneth Fearing, renewed, 1970, by Bruce Fearing. Reprinted by permission of Harcourt Brace Jovanovich, Inc.

Don Marquis, "A Righteous Cockroach." Portions of the poem "Clarence the Ghost" from *Archy & Mehitabel* by Don Marquis. Copyright 1927. By permission of the publisher, Doubleday & Company, Inc. [Editor's title.]

W. T. Stace, "Ethical Relativity." Reprinted with permission of The Macmillan Company from *The Concept of Morals* by W. T. Stace. Copyright 1937 by The Macmillan Company. [A note has been omitted.]

Plato, "Gyges' Ring." From *The Dialogues of Plato*, translated by Benjamin Jowett, 3rd ed. 1892. By permission of The Clarendon Press, Oxford. [Editor's title; a note has been omitted.]

Kurt Baier, "Why Should We Be Moral?" From *The Moral Point of View* by Kurt Baier. Copyright © 1958 by Cornell University and © 1965 by Random House, Inc. Reprinted by permission of Cornell University Press and Random House, Inc. [Notes have been omitted.]

CHAPTER SEVEN

Mark Twain, "Letters from the Earth." Abridgment of "Satan's Letter," "Letter III, V, and VI" from "Letters from the Earth" in *Mark Twain Letters from the Earth*, edited by Bernard DeVoto. Copyright © 1962 by The Mark Twain Company. By permission of Harper & Row, Publishers, Inc.

Albert Camus, "A Plague Death." From *The Plague* by Albert Camus, translated by Stuart Gilbert. Copyright 1948 by Stuart Gilbert. Reprinted by permission of Alfred A. Knopf, Inc. [Editor's title.]

Gottfried Wilhelm Leibniz, "The Best of All Possible Worlds." Reprinted by permission of Charles Scribner's Sons from *Leibniz Selections*, edited by Philip

Wiener. Copyright © 1951 Charles Scribner's Sons. [Editor's title; parenthetical phrases in Latin have been omitted.]

J. L. Mackie, "Evil and Omnipotence." From *Mind*, 64:253, January 1955. By permission of Basil Blackwell, Publisher.

John Hick, "The Problem of Evil." From John Hick, *Philosophy of Religion*, © 1963. Reprinted by permission of Prentice-Hall, Inc., Englewood Cliffs, New Jersey. [Some notes have been omitted, and the remainder renumbered.]

CHAPTER EIGHT

Nicolas Berdyaev, "The Search for Truth." Reprinted with permission of The Macmillan Company from *Dream and Reality* by Nicolas Berdyaev. Copyright 1950 by Geoffrey Bles, Ltd. [Editor's title.]

Huston Smith, "Taoism." From *The Religions of Man* by Huston Smith. Copyright © 1958 by Huston Smith. By permission of Harper & Row, Publishers, Inc. [Some notes have been omitted, and the remainder renumbered.]

William James, "Mysticism." From *The Varieties of Religious Experience* by William James, 1902. By permission of Alexander R. James, Literary Executor. [Some notes have been omitted, and the remainder renumbered.]

Bertrand Russell, "A Free Man's Worship." From *Mysticism and Logic*. Reprinted by permission of Barnes & Noble Books, New York, and Allen & Unwin Ltd., London.

Paul Tillich, "The God Above God." "Theism Transcended" and "The God Above God and the Courage to Be" from *The Courage to Be* by Paul Tillich. Copyright © 1952 by Yale University Press.

CHAPTER NINE

Nels F. S. Ferré, "The Living God of Nowhere and Nothing." From *The Living God of Nowhere and Nothing* by Nels F. S. Ferré, The Westminster Press. © Nels F. S. Ferré, 1966. Used by permission.

Jacob Needleman, "Zen Center." From *The New Religions* by Jacob Needleman. Copyright © 1970 by Jacob Needleman. Reprinted by permission of Doubleday & Company, Inc. [Some notes have been omitted.]

Abraham H. Maslow, "Peak-Experiences." From *Religions, Values, and Peak-Experiences* by Abraham H. Maslow, The Kappa Delta Pi Lecture Series, copyright, 1964, by Kappa Delta Pi. By permission of Kappa Delta Pi, An Honor Society in Education, owners of the copyright. [Editor's title; notes have been omitted.]

Peter Marin, "Meditations on the Jesus Movement." From "Children of Yearning" by Peter Marin, *Saturday Review*, May 6, 1972. Reprinted by permission of International Famous Agency. Copyright © 1972 by Peter Marin.

Thomas Merton, "Rain and the Rhinoceros." From *Raids on the Unspeakable* by Thomas Merton. Copyright © 1965 by The Abbey of Gethsemani, Inc. Reprinted by permission of New Directions Publishing Corporation.

CHAPTER TEN

W. Somerset Maugham, "Appointment in Samarra." Reprinted by permission of the Literary Executor of W. Somerset Maugham and William Heinemann Ltd.

Richard Wilbur, "A Game of Catch." From *The New Yorker*, July 15, 1953. Reprinted by permission; copr. © 1953 The New Yorker Magazine, Inc.

CHAPTER ELEVEN

CHAPTER TWELVE